AF504912

STANO FILKO
A RETROSPECTIVE

HATJE CANTZ

HALLE FÜR KUNST Steiermark

Introduction

Sandro Droschl

With this retrospective of the work of Slovak artist Stano Filko, which has long been in preparation, the HALLE FÜR KUNST Steiermark takes a fresh look at a sustainably influential and utopian body of work. This publication is intended as a contribution to raising awareness of the significance of this outstanding artistic position and its progressive design for society for today's less visionary times. [01–03]

Filko was an important representative of the central European neo-avant-gardes, with an oeuvre that developed over many decades and remains remarkably contemporary. He had great success in the 1960s but then became a persona non grata after the Prague Spring was defeated, and after several years he fled the country in daredevil manner in a Škoda 120L, which he then painted white and presented at the center of his participation in documenta 7. Thereafter Filko emigrated to New York. Following the fall of the Iron Curtain he returned to Bratislava and established the studio building Snežienková in the style of a "total work of art" whose rooms and artworks all adhered in color and size to a prearranged structure called *System SF*.

This concept was on the one hand stringent and yet still flexible, enabling Filko not only to give structure to and question his expansive and originally conceptual work, but also to rethink ideas such as the transcendental in the sense of an overarching impulse, beyond any essentialist readings, which was evident in the media diversity and openness of this concept of art.

Filko's complex oeuvre refers to the Fluxus, Nouveau Réalisme, Dada, and Pop Art movements, while its independent multiperspectival development remains relevant today. In the early 1960s, Filko began to design installations, pneumatic sculptures, and utopian architectures that reflected his growing interest in cosmology and metaphysics. This was also seen in his happenings and actions. Always fascinated by anti-art, nihilism, and iconoclasm, Filko created several interactive environments based on his ideas of an open concept of media and interdisciplinarity.

To the last, Filko accompanied his artworks with texts, which he was always testing and rewriting. Notwithstanding all the creativity, this was a structured approach that made it possible for the artist to develop his projects simultaneously as production and reflection, as well as facilitating a better understanding of his originally conceptual approach. Thus Filko pursued a holistic way of working that places art and life together as one, so as to work toward an alternative view of reality by means of the unbounded work of art.

This publication illustrates selections of Filko's work from all periods, in order to draw attention from the systematic overview to individual works and their points of reference to each other. Alongside a focus on specific themes and periods, this book also aims to present works from different phases together in loose and yet intensive arrangements, so as to see the autonomy and dynamics of each single work within a process of free association. The distinctions between variously evaluated and studied different periods (the early phase that was recognized within a history of art, the neo-expressive "American" phase, and the self-reflective late phase) is here replaced by an overview and recognition of one entire artistic position.

Given the significance of Stano Filko's large oeuvre established over several decades, and his charismatic personality, comparisons with meta-artists such as Joseph Beuys, Dieter Roth, and Paul McCarthy seem evident, and yet these would take us in the wrong direction, as it is important to avoid any stylization of Filko as a mythical artist figure whose excessive production and own theoretical frameworks might seem to lead to an interplay between the total work of art and a defined system. Rather Filko was concerned to overcome barriers and enter into dialogue. His works are characterized by a highly developed dialogic element and are often intended as offers for involving viewers. Not least thanks to his curiosity, liking of experimentation, and self-criticism, Filko succeeded in keeping his works present, which is also due to his future-looking themes focusing on the cosmos and the body and spirit in reaction to experienced and projected realities.

Filko's work is telling in particular because individual works, which run counter to the wish for stringency that is sometimes projected onto them, often refute any kind of system. Unlike a classical monograph, this publication wishes not to present Filko's oeuvre as fit for a museum, but to show it in the form of a first attempt at an overview that also activates single works, so as to emphasize the topicality and visionary in Filko today.

Einführung

Sandro Droschl

Mit der lange vorbereiteten Retrospektive des slowakischen Künstlers Stano Filko wirft die HALLE FÜR KUNST Steiermark einen frischen Blick auf dieses nachhaltig wirksame, utopische Werk. Die vorliegende Publikation möchte einen Beitrag leisten um die Bedeutung dieser herausragenden künstlerischen Position und deren progressiven Gesellschaftsentwurf für die heutigen – weniger visionären – Zeiten wieder verstärkt in Erinnerung zu rufen. [01–03]

Filko war einer der wichtigsten Vertreter der mitteleuropäischen Neo-Avantgarden, dessen Werk sich über Jahrzehnte entwickelt und erstaunlich aktuell gehalten hat. Nach großen Erfolgen in den 1960er-Jahren wurde er infolge der Niederschlagung des Prager Frühlings zur Persona non grata, was nach schwierigen Jahren zu einer abenteuerlichen Flucht – mittels eines Škoda 120L, der weiß bemalt im Zentrum seiner Teilnahme an der documenta 7 stand – und schließlich zu seiner Emigration nach New York führte. Nach dem Fall des Eisernen Vorhangs kehrte Filko nach Bratislava zurück und baute das einem „Gesamtkunstwerk" ähnliche Atelierhaus Snežienková aus, dessen Räume und Kunstwerke einer nach Farben und Dimensionen geordneten Struktur folgten, dem *System SF*.

Diese bei aller Stringenz offene Konzeption hat es Filko gestattet nicht nur sein weitläufiges, ursächlich konzeptionelles Werk zu strukturieren und zu hinterfragen, sondern auch Begriffe wie das Transzendentale neu zu denken, im Sinne eines übergreifenden Impulses abseits einer essentialistischen Lesart, was sich auch in medialer Vielfalt und Offenheit des Kunstbegriffes zeigte.

Sein komplexes Œuvre verweist auf die Strömungen Fluxus, Nouveau Réalisme, Dada, Pop Art und strahlt in seiner eigenständigen, multiperspektivischen Entwicklung bis heute aus. Anfang der 1960er-Jahre begann Filko mit der Konzeption von Installationen, pneumatischen Skulpturen und utopischen Architekturen, die sein erstarkendes Interesse an Kosmologie und Metaphysik widerspiegeln, was sich auch in Happenings und Aktionen im öffentlichen Raum niederschlug. Daraufhin stellte Filko, der sich durchgängig von Anti-Kunst, Nihilismus und Bildersturm fasziniert zeigte, mehrere interaktive Environments her, die auf seiner Vorstellung von einem offenen Medienbegriff und Interdisziplinarität basierten.

Bis zuletzt begleitete Filko seine Arbeiten in Texten, die er in seiner Praxis überprüfte und fortlaufend überarbeitete. Diese bei aller Kreativität strukturierte Vorgangsweise erleichterte es Filko, seine Projekte parallel in ihrer Produktion und Reflexion zu entwickeln, auch dient es dem Verständnis seines ursächlich konzeptionellen Ansatzes. Insofern folgte Filko einem ganzheitlichen Ansatz, der Kunst und Leben in eines setzt, um in einem darin entgrenzten Werkbegriff an einer alternativen Fassung der Realität zu arbeiten.

In der vorliegenden Publikation wird sein Schaffen auszugsweise aus sämtlichen Perioden abgebildet, um den Blick von der Systematik hin zum einzelnen Werk und dessen Verbindungen zu weiteren Arbeiten zu lenken. Neben thematisch und periodisch orientierten Bereichen soll der Versuch unternommen werden, Werke aus unterschiedlichen Phasen in loser, verdichteter Präsentation zu zeigen, um den Arbeiten in freier Assoziation ihre Eigenständigkeit und Dynamik zuzugestehen. Auch die Gegenüberstellung in bislang unterschiedlich bewertete und untersuchte Perioden – in eine frühe, kunsthistorisch anerkannte, in eine neo-expressive „amerikanische" und eine selbstreflexive späte Phase – soll im Sinne eines Überblicks und in Anerkennung der gesamten künstlerischen Position überwunden werden.

Angesichts des über Jahrzehnte aufgebauten, bedeutungsvollen Gesamtwerkes und der charismatischen Persönlichkeit von Stano Filko liegen Vergleiche mit Meta-Künstlern wie Joseph Beuys, Dieter Roth oder Paul McCarthy nahe, und doch führt dies hier auf eine falsche Fährte, soll doch die Stilisierung von Filko zu einer mythischen Künstlerfigur vermieden werden, die durch exzessive Produktion und theoretische Einbettung an einem Zusammenspiel aus Gesamtkunstwerk und Systematik zu arbeiten schien. Vielmehr lag Filko viel daran, Schranken zu überwinden und ins Gespräch zu kommen. Seine Arbeiten zeichnen sich durch ein ausgeprägtes dialogisches Element aus und verstehen sich oftmals als ein Angebot, die Betrachter*innen mit ins Bild zu nehmen. Nicht zuletzt durch seine Neugier, Experimentierfreude und Selbstkritik hat es Filko vollbracht, dass seine Arbeiten gegenwärtig bleiben, was auch an seinen zukunftsorientierten Themensetzungen um Kosmos, Körper, Geist in Reaktion auf die – erlebte und projizierte – Wirklichkeit liegt.

Filkos Arbeit besticht gerade in den einzelnen Kunstwerken, die entgegen des teilweise projiziert wirkenden Wunsches nach Stringenz mitunter jegliche Systematik zurückweisen.

With the participation of Lucia Gregorová Stach, Patricia Grzonka, Christian Höller, Mira Keratová, Boris Ondreička, and Jan Verwoert it has been possible to include a number of high-quality essays. The publication opens with an edited conversation between Hans Ulrich Obrist and Stano Filko that allows the artist himself to be heard.

On a tour of his legendary Sneženková studio and its rooms ordered according to dimensions, chakras, and colors, Filko talks with Obrist about his motivation and methods in art, while a desire for order and system becomes ever clearer amidst a plethora of artworks and their diverse forms, and the reader almost gains the impression that this desire emanates from the objects themselves so that each of them can then be better seen and appreciated. This building in a former area of allotment gardens underwent continuous reconstruction and expansion. Its appeal was due to its location on the Kamzík hill with a wide-ranging view of Bratislava, while the proximity of the impressive radio tower seems to be no mere coincidence, since from the very beginning of his career Filko took an interest in the relationship between his own everyday environment and its extra-territorial expansion, and in his key concept of *HAPPSOC* he developed the idea of a "happy society" or a "happy socialism" that declared the city with all its objects and living creatures and the cosmos of which it was part to be art. Due to his sensitivity for complex personalities, the curator Obrist was able to tease very specific answers about his work out of Filko, who was visibly relieved to have the assistance of his artist friend Roman Ondák as a translator.

The curator and artist Boris Ondreička can probably be seen as the one man who knows Filko and his work the best, as he spent much time with him and the two of them also collaborated as artists, leading to their shared presentation at the Slovak (and alternating Czech) Pavilion at the 51st Biennale di Venezia (2005, with Ján Mančuška and Marek Pokorný). Together with Vit Havránek, Ondreička often visited Filko and conducted numerous conversations with him for the platform transit.sk. The photo documentation by Martin Marenčin included in this book derives from this context. At almost the same time as the Graz exhibition, Ondreička curated the remarkable show *Registration of Stano Filko / Registrace Stana Filka* at Fait Gallery (Brno, 2021/2022), which had a different structure to our exhibition in that it used a design based on the form of an archive but nonetheless pursued a similar interest in re-evaluating the artist in terms of a unifying view of his entire oeuvre independent of different phases or periods. To do this, Ondreička developed an interpretative scale for Filko's system and its recurring concepts that transpired to be so convincing for the complex context that it is included in this publication as an illustrative meta-quotation. In his sensitive text "Filko's Snowdrops," Ondreička manages to delineate Filko's expansive artistic production in terms of a reaction to his studio. With his "House-Studio-Object-Cenotaph" at the street named "Snowdrop Street" he designed a fascinating phantasmagorical place that permitted art and life to meld into one. Everything could become art, and often enough it really did.

In her essay "System of Systems," Lucia Gregorová Stach, chief curator at the Slovak National Gallery, which holds the largest public collection of works by the artist, writes about Filko's system and his *Archive SF*. In the exhibition, Stach, editor (with Aurel Hrabušizký) of the only monograph on Filko to date, created a room dedicated to biographical and archive materials, using more than 6,000 scanned pages of images and text in this large archive of the artist's work as an introduction to his always developing theoretical construct known as *System SF*. After his return from the USA in 1990, Filko's *System SF* became increasingly more of a complex meta-system that he used to reorder and further develop his work. This was then a dynamic under the influence of which Filko sometimes reworked and redated earlier pieces in order to relate them to his current production. This continuous process led to the *Archive SF*, a journal-like magazine and comprehensive system of cross-references made of texts, concepts, text-art, drawings, photographs, and exhibition documentation, which Filko collected in probably a total of 82 files and used as his personal medium of reflection. We here see the artist's attempts to create connections between text and image material that would coherently depict his view of the world, and then to see these materials as what amounted to a total work of art. This attempt to grasp reality in a single concept also leads to Filko's specific way of writing that uses rich imagery to mirror the objects addressed in language, combining fragments from different languages and traditions of thought into a significant form. Ultimately, the *Archive SF* is a kind of self-museum that can in future be researched and exhibited as such.

In "Signs and Rockets: On Stano Filko's Anti-Art," Jan Verwoert, who has been writing about Filko for some time and also presented an exhibition focusing on the artist's "American" phase and its expressive painting simultaneously to our exhibition in 2022 at Layr (Vienna, with Søren Grammel), explores the influence of Filko's rural origins that were to shape his production significantly. Normally, it is the large cities that are celebrated as the birthplaces of modern art. Filko's life and work, however, overcome the divide between the city and the country. He was born in the country, went to the city, died twice along the way, and produced a body of art that speaks of technological production, destruction, and travelling, but that also never lost contact to what it means to spend a lifetime struggling for the means of survival and taking objects by the hand. This hands-on access to available materials and the reaction to socially virulent issues very clearly influence Filko's production. This direct and down-to-earth approach makes for the tangible presence and aura of many of Filko's works that draw on his rural roots and their spiritual traditions, to then drive these into unprecedented heights with an intuitively constructed theoretical superstructure, as if he wanted to move heaven and earth and then have them become one.

Swiss art and architecture theorist Patricia Grzonka published a brief introduction to Filko already in 2005, and was thus one of the first international critics to take a renewed interest in the artist's work. She based her study on personal conversations with the artist and her own long-standing interest in his work. In her text, "Blue Ladders in the Universe: Space and Cosmos as Sensual Topoi" she looks at key elements of Filko's development and offers an analysis of them in terms of their present-day relevance. Grzonka traces an artistic logic in this late avant-garde work that positioned itself between East, West, and the universes. Notwithstanding

  Sandro Droschl

Entgegen einer klassischen Monografie versucht die Publikation das Œuvre nicht zu musealisieren, sondern es in einem ersten Versuch einer Zusammenschau hin zu einzelnen Werken zu aktivieren, um die Aktualität und das visionäre Element von Filko zu betonen.

Unter Mitwirkung von Lucia Gregorová Stach, Patricia Grzonka, Christian Höller, Mira Keratová, Boris Ondreička und Jan Verwoert konnte eine Reihe an hochwertigen Texten erarbeitet werden. Die Publikation wird von einem redigierten Gespräch von Hans Ulrich Obrist mit Stano Filko eingeleitet und lässt so den Künstler noch einmal zu Wort kommen.

Im Rundgang durch sein legendäres Studio Snežienková und seine nach Dimensionen, Chakren und Farben geordneten Atelierräume spricht Filko mit Obrist nicht nur über seine Motivation und Vorgangsweise, vielmehr wird inmitten der Überfülle von Kunstwerken und ihrer vielfältigen Ausführung nicht nur der Drang hin zu einer Ordnung und Systematik klar, sondern man gewinnt fast den Eindruck, dass dieser auch von den Objekten eingefordert wird, um schließlich jedes einzelne besser sehen und würdigen zu können. Das fortlaufend umgebaute und erweiterte Gebäude einer ehemaligen Kleingartensiedlung besticht nicht nur durch seine Hügellage am Kamzík und den weitläufigen Blick auf Bratislava, vielmehr wirkt auch die Nähe des imposanten Funkturms nicht ganz zufällig, hat sich Filko doch von Anfang an mit dem Verhältnis seines erlebten Umfelds bis hin zu extraterritorialen Erweiterungen beschäftigt und im zentralen Werkbegriff *HAPPSOC* eine „happy society" bzw. einen „happy socialism" entworfen, der die Stadt mit all ihren Gegenständen und Lebewesen bis hin zum Kosmos zu Kunst erklärte. Dank seines Gespürs für komplexe Persönlichkeiten gelingt es dem weitgereisten Kurator, Filko zu recht konkreten Antworten über seine Arbeit zu bewegen, spürbar erleichtert durch die übersetzende Mithilfe des ihm nahestehenden Künstlers Roman Ondák.

Der Kurator und Künstler Boris Ondreička kann wohl als bester Kenner von Filko gesehen werden, da er mit ihm viel Zeit verbracht hat und auch künstlerisch zusammenarbeitete, was bis zu einer gemeinsamen Bespielung des slowakischen (und alternierend tschechischen) Pavillons auf der 51. Biennale di Venezia (2005, mit Ján Mančuška und Marek Pokorný) führte. Gemeinsam mit Vit Havránek hat er Filko oft besucht und nicht zuletzt für die Plattform transit.sk diverse Gespräche geführt, in diesem Kontext ist auch die hier abgebildete Foto-Dokumentation von Martin Marenčin entstanden. Nahezu zeitgleich zur Grazer Ausstellung kuratierte Ondreička die bemerkenswerte Show *Registration of Stano Filko / Registrace Stana Filka* bei Fait Gallery (Brno, 2021/2022), die trotz gegensätzlicher Aufbereitung – einer archivarisch orientierten Architektur – ein ähnliches Interesse an einer Neubewertung des Künstlers hin zu einer periodenunabhängigen, verbindenden Sicht auf das Œuvre antrieb. Dafür erarbeitete Ondreička eine interpretative Skala der Systematik und ihrer wiederkehrenden Begriffe, die sich als derart überzeugend für den komplexen Kontext herausstellte, dass sie in dieser Publikation illustrierend als Meta-Zitat abgebildet wird. In seinem feinfühligen Text „Filkos Schneeglöckchen" gelingt es ihm, Filkos ausufernde künstlerische Produktion in Reaktion auf sein Atelier zu umreißen. Mit seinem „Haus-Studio-Objekt-Kenotaph" an der Schneeglöckchenstraße entwarf er einen schillernd-phantasmagorischen Ort um Kunst und Leben in eines fallen zu lassen. Alles konnte Kunst werden, und wurde es oft genug.

In ihrem Beitrag „System der Systeme" schreibt Lucia Gregorová Stach, Chefkuratorin der Slovak National Gallery und damit der Institution mit der größten öffentlichen Sammlung des Künstlers, über die Systematik von Stano Filko und sein *Archív SF*. Bereits in der Ausstellung gestaltete die Herausgeberin (mit Aurel Hrabušický) der bislang einzigen Monografie einen eigenen Raum mit biografischen und archivarischen Materialien, um in über 6.000 eigens gescannten Bild- und Textseiten des umfangreichen Künstler-Archivs in sein fortlaufend entwickeltes theoretisches Konzept einzuführen, das *System SF*. Nach seiner Rückkehr aus den USA im Jahr 1990 entwickelte sich Filkos *System SF* zunehmend zu einem komplexen Metasystem, anhand dessen er sein Werk neu ordnete und weiter vorantrieb. Es kam eine Dynamik auf, unter deren Einfluss Filko frühere Arbeiten mitunter neu überarbeitete und datierte, um sie in Bezug zu seiner aktuellen Produktion zu stellen. In diesem kontinuierlichen Prozess entstand das *Archív SF*, ein tagebuchartiges Magazin und umfassender Verweiszusammenhang aus Schriften, Konzepten, Text-Kunst, Zeichnungen, Fotografien und Ausstellungsdokumentationen, das Filko in vermutlich insgesamt 82 Ordnern sammelte und als persönliches Reflexionsmedium nutzte. Zutage tritt der Versuch des Künstlers, eine Verbindung von Text- und Bildmaterial zu entwickeln, die in sich schlüssig seine Sicht auf die Welt abbildet, um diese als Materialien hin zu einem (vermeintlichen) Gesamtkunstwerk zu denken. Dieser Versuch einer Fassung von Realität in einer eigenen Konzeption lässt auch eine spezifische Art des Schreibens entstehen, die bildhaft die besprochenen Gegenstände in der Sprache spiegeln und dabei Versatzstücke aus diversen Sprachen und Denktraditionen in eine signifikante Form einbinden. Schließlich ist das *Archív SF* auch eine Art „Selbstmuseum", das als solches auch zukünftig erforscht und ausgestellt werden kann.

In „Zeichen und Raketen: Zu Stano Filkos Antikunst" geht Jan Verwoert, der sich als Autor schon seit geraumer Zeit mit Filko auseinandersetzt und 2022 zeitgleich bei Layr (Wien, mit Søren Grammel) eine Ausstellung mit Schwerpunkt auf die „amerikanische" Phase und ihre expressive Malerei präsentierte, auf Filkos prägende ländliche Herkunft ein, die seine Produktion nachhaltig beeinflussen sollte. Normalerweise wird die Großstadt als Geburtsort der modernen Kunst gefeiert. Filkos Leben und Werk jedoch überschreiten die Kluft zwischen Stadt und Land. Er wurde auf dem Land geboren, ging in die Stadt, starb zweimal auf dem Weg und brachte eine Kunst hervor, die zwar von Technoproduktion, Zerstörung und Reisen spricht, aber nie den Kontakt zu dem verliert, was es bedeutet, sich zeitlebens unter Verwendung der verfügbaren Mittel zu bemühen und die Dinge selbst in die Hand zu nehmen. Dieser hemdsärmlige Zugriff auf verfügbare Materialien und die Reaktion auf gesellschaftlich virulente Fragestellungen beeinflusste spürbar seine Produktion. Auch erklärt sich in dieser direkten, bodenständigen Machart die spürbare Präsenz und Ausstrahlung vieler von Filkos Arbeiten, die auf seine ländlichen Wurzeln und ihre spirituellen Traditionen zurückgehen, um diese mit einem intuitiv zusammengestellten Theorieüberbau in ungeahnte Höhen zu treiben, als ginge es ihm darum Himmel und Hölle in Bewegung zu versetzen und schließlich in eines fallen zu lassen.

all its independence, Filko's work developed under a socialist system was also accessible to the Western avant-gardes and neo-avant-gardes, with references back to the cosmism of the early twentieth century. This utopian approach met with deep resonance particularly in a biotope like Bratislava, at the long-standing geopolitical zone border between East and West, and in direct proximity to the city's neutral "sister city" of Vienna; overcoming the miserable challenges of the everyday by moving in the direction of the seemingly liberating and unlimited opportunities of the cosmos seemed all the more attractive and urgent here.

Art historian and curator Mira Keratová explores divergent perspectives of the work and position of the artist from East and West. The artistic work of Stano Filko begins in Czechoslovakia (today Slovakia) in the 1960s, a time when artistic freedom was becoming more and more restricted. While the real-socialist regime was establishing its one-sided worldview, Filko was known for his attempts in his art to depict the entire world as an outer and inner reality. In 1981 Filko emigrated, living first in Düsseldorf and from 1982 in New York, to return to Bratislava in 1990. These biographical stages are also roughly equivalent to the different work phases, in which the specific conditions pertaining to the biography can also be seen. Particularly in the early phase, when the *System SF* had only three colors, Filko played with a national identification with his home country, opening it up to an international and multicolor position. A further focus of Keratová's essay looks at the artist's sometimes very problematic view of gender. Filko's self-mythology operates using male clichés and advocates an image of the artist that is strongly defined by the male gender. From today's perspective, this certainly requires a critical gaze. In her essay "Genealogy of Modernist Essentialism," Keratová asks as to identity and gender in an impressive tour de force of Filko's diverse oeuvre.

Christian Höller's interest in Stano Filko first focused on the *White Space in White Space* project, which Filko had developed over several years together with Miloš Laky and Ján Zavarský. This key conceptual work was realized as an installation in several different forms. The first and legendary version took place on February 18, 1974, for the duration of a few hours far away from the public eye at Dům umění (House of Arts) in Brno, and consisted mainly of an attempt to transform the exhibition space into a transcendental white. Höller, who also co-edited a publication of the same name on the project (with Daniel Grúň and Kathrin Rhomberg), addresses the central concept of *Transcendencja* in his text "Ciphers of Transcendency," which registers the artist's metaphysical interest in extrasensory versions of reality or realities and constructs of the subject. Across his broad use of different media in his art production, Filko worked with the idea of transcendency on nearly all the aspects of his work. Thus, different arguments may be found as to why a reading of nearly the entire oeuvre can be based on this charged term, which for Filko has a liberating force that counters any essentialisms.

For making this comprehensive publication possible, I am deeply grateful to the authors and to the Slovak National Gallery (Bratislava), the Linea Collection (Bratislava), and Layr (Vienna) for their generous support in assisting us with numerous loans, photographs, and valuable information. In particular I would like to thank Lucia Gregorová Stach, Roman Zubaľ, Michal Zubaľ, Emanuel Layr, Alexandra Kuša, Štefan Cebo, and Richard Filko for their personal support. The production of this book would not have been possible without the intensive work of Helga Droschl, Alexander Nussbaumer & Leonard Siegwardt, Manuel Carreon Lopez, Tobias Ihl, Greg Bond, Thomas Raab, Kevin Slavin, and Sonja Altmeppen. This large project will long remain vivid in my memory thanks to the many conversations with all the participants and visits to and remarkable hospitality in Bratislava, making an intensive exploration of the work of Stano Filko all the more pleasurable and facilitating significant exchange across borders. It remains to hope that reading this publication will inspire further adventures with Stano Filko.

Bereits 2005 veröffentlichte die schweizer Kunst- und Architekturtheoretikerin Patricia Grzonka eine kursorische Einführung in das Werk von Filko und war damit eine der Ersten, die sich damals international wieder für die Arbeit des Künstlers zu interessieren begannen. Dabei baut sie auf einigen persönlichen Gesprächen mit dem Künstler und ihrem langjährigen inhaltlichen Interesse an seiner Arbeit auf. In ihrem Text „Blaue Leitern im Universum: Raum und Kosmos als sinnliche Topoi" blickt sie auf zentrale Elemente seiner Entwicklung und versucht sie auf ihre Gegenwärtigkeit zu untersuchen. Grzonka spürt damit einer künstlerischen Logik dieses eindrucksvollen Spät-Avantgardisten nach, der sich selbst zwischen Ost, West und dem Universum positionierte. Bei aller Eigenständigkeit ist sein im sozialistischen Staatssystem entwickeltes Werk auch für die westlichen Avantgarden und Neo-Avantgarden anschlussfähig, wobei Bezüge bis auf den Kosmismus des frühen 20. Jahrhunderts zurückgehen. Diese utopistische Haltung fand gerade in einem Biotop wie Bratislava einen reichhaltigen Resonanzraum, wo an der lange Jahre existierenden geopolitischen Zonengrenze zwischen Ost und West – und in unmittelbarer Nähe zu ihrer „neutralen Schwesternstadt" Wien – die Überwindung der leidvoll erlebten Zumutungen des Alltags hin zu den vermeintlich befreienden, unbegrenzten Möglichkeiten des Kosmos umso verlockender wie drängender erschienen.

Die Kunsthistorikerin und Kuratorin Mira Keratová untersucht divergierende Sichtweisen von Ost und West auf Werk und Position des Künstlers. Das künstlerische Schaffen von Stano Filko beginnt in der Tschechoslowakei (heute Slowakei) der 1960er-Jahre, einer Zeit, in der die künstlerische Freiheit zunehmend eine Begrenzung erfuhr. Während das realsozialistische Regime eine einseitige Weltsicht errichtete, ist Filko für den Versuch bekannt, in seiner Kunst den Gesamtzusammenhang der Welt als äußere und innere Realität abzubilden. 1981 emigrierte Filko, lebte zuerst in Düsseldorf und ab 1982 in New York, um 1990 nach Bratislava zurückzukehren. Diese biografischen Stationen gliedern ebenfalls grob die verschiedenen Werkphasen, in denen sich die jeweiligen Rahmenbedingungen ablesen lassen. Gerade in der frühen Phase, als das *System SF* nur drei Farben umfasste, spielte Filko mit einer nationalen Identifikation seines Heimatlandes, was er hin zu einer internationalen, mehrfarbigen Position erweiterte. Ein weiterer Fokus ihrer Betrachtungen geht dem teils sehr problematischen Genderbegriff des Künstlers nach. Die Selbstmythologie von Filko hantiert mit männlichen Klischees und propagiert ein Künstlerbild, welches stark über männliche Geschlechtlichkeit definiert ist. Aus heutiger Sicht bedarf es hier mindestens einer kritischen Betrachtung. In ihrem Essay „Genealogie eines modernistischen Essentialismus" geht Keratová den Fragestellungen nach Identität und Gender entlang einer eindrucksvollen Tour de Force durch sein weitläufiges Schaffen nach.

Christian Höllers Interesse für Stano Filko entwickelte sich in Beschäftigung mit dem Projekt *White Space in White Space*, welches er über mehrere Jahre gemeinsam mit Miloš Laky und Ján Zavarský entwickelt hat. Diese wesentliche konzeptuelle Arbeit wurde in unterschiedlichen Ausführungen als Installation realisiert. Die erste, legendäre Realisation fand am 18. Februar 1974 für die Dauer von ein paar Stunden abseits der Öffentlichkeit im Dům umění (House of Arts), Brno statt und bestand im Wesentlichen in dem Versuch, den Ausstellungort zu einem transzendentalen Weiß hin aufzulösen. Höller, der auch als Herausgeber (mit Daniel Grúň, Kathrin Rhomberg) an einer gleichnamigen Publikation zu dem Projekt mitwirkte, widmet sich in seinem Text „Chiffren von Transzendenz" dem zentralen Begriff *Transcendencja*, der ein metaphysisches Interesse des Künstlers an übersinnlichen Fassungen von Realität/en und Subjektkonstruktionen erkennen lässt. Dabei hat Filko in seinem breiten medialen Zugang auf Seiten der Kunstproduktion in fast allen Facetten seines Werks mit der Idee von Transzendenz gearbeitet. Somit lassen sich verschiedene Argumente finden, warum sich eine Lesart fast der gesamten Arbeit anhand dieses aufgeladenen Begriffs entwickeln lässt, der bei Filko entgegen möglicher Essentialismen einen befreienden Charakter hat.

Für die Realisierung der umfangreichen Publikation gilt mein großer Dank den Autor*innen und der umfangreichen Unterstützung der Slovak National Gallery (Bratislava), der Linea Collection (Bratislava) und Layr (Wien), die uns mit zahlreichen Leihgaben, Fotografien und wertvollen Informationen versorgt haben. Im Besonderen möchte ich mich bei Lucia Gregorová Stach, Roman Zubaľ, Michal Zubaľ, Emanuel Layr, Alexandra Kuša, Štefan Cebo und bei Richard Filko für ihre persönliche Unterstützung bedanken. Die Produktion der Publikation wäre ohne die intensive Mitarbeit von Helga Droschl, Alexander Nussbaumer & Leonard Siegwardt, Manuel Carreon Lopez, Tobias Ihl, Greg Bond, Thomas Raab, Kevin Slavin, und Sonja Altmeppen nicht möglich gewesen. Das umfangreiche Projekt bleibt durch die zahlreichen Gespräche mit allen Beteiligten und den von großer Gastfreundlichkeit begleiteten Besuchen in Bratislava in nachhaltiger Erinnerung, was die intensive Auseinandersetzung mit Stano Filko noch erfreulicher gemacht hat und einen echten Austausch über letzte Grenzen hinweg ermöglicht hat. Nun bleibt zu hoffen, dass die Lektüre der Publikation Anregungen für weitere Abenteuer mit Stano Filko gibt.

   Sandro Droschl   Einführung

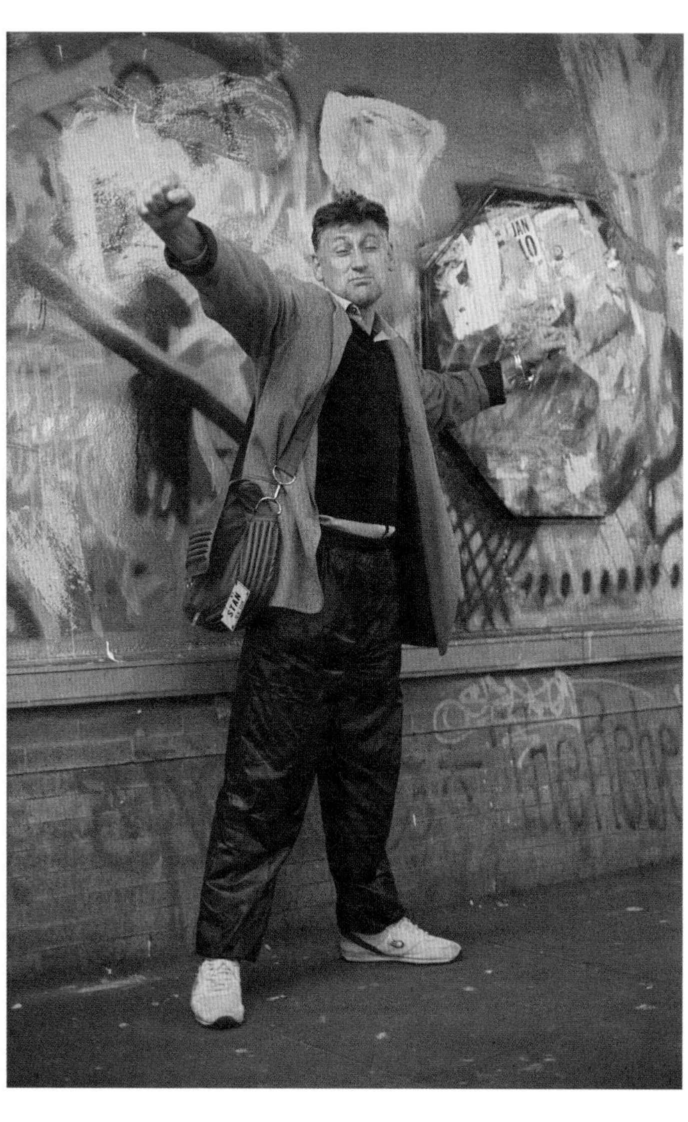

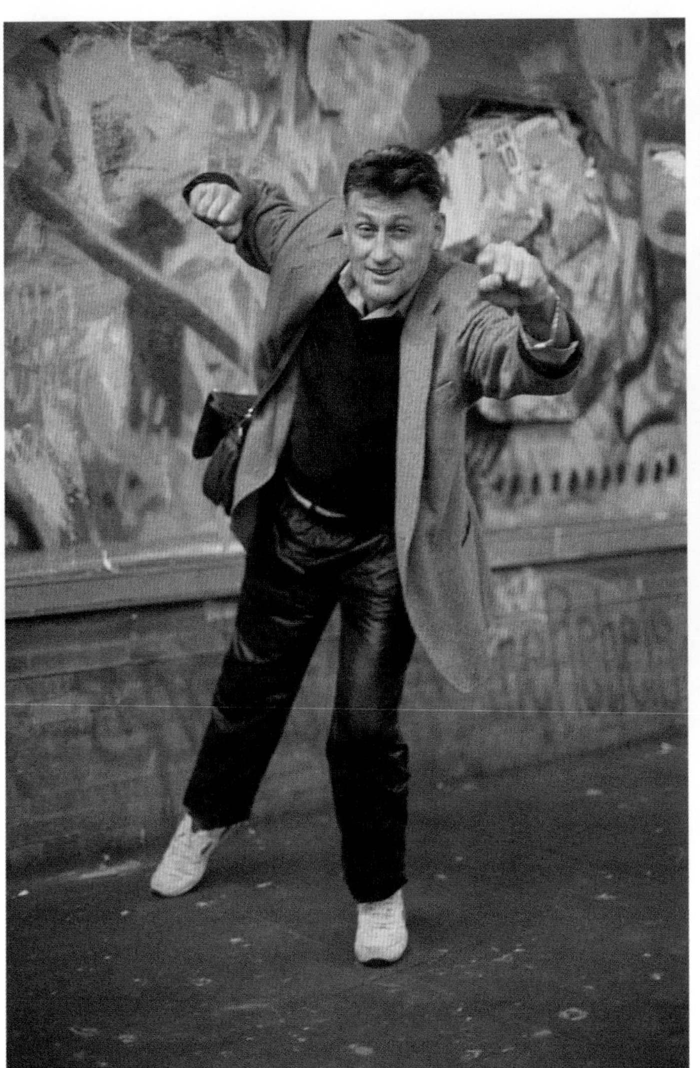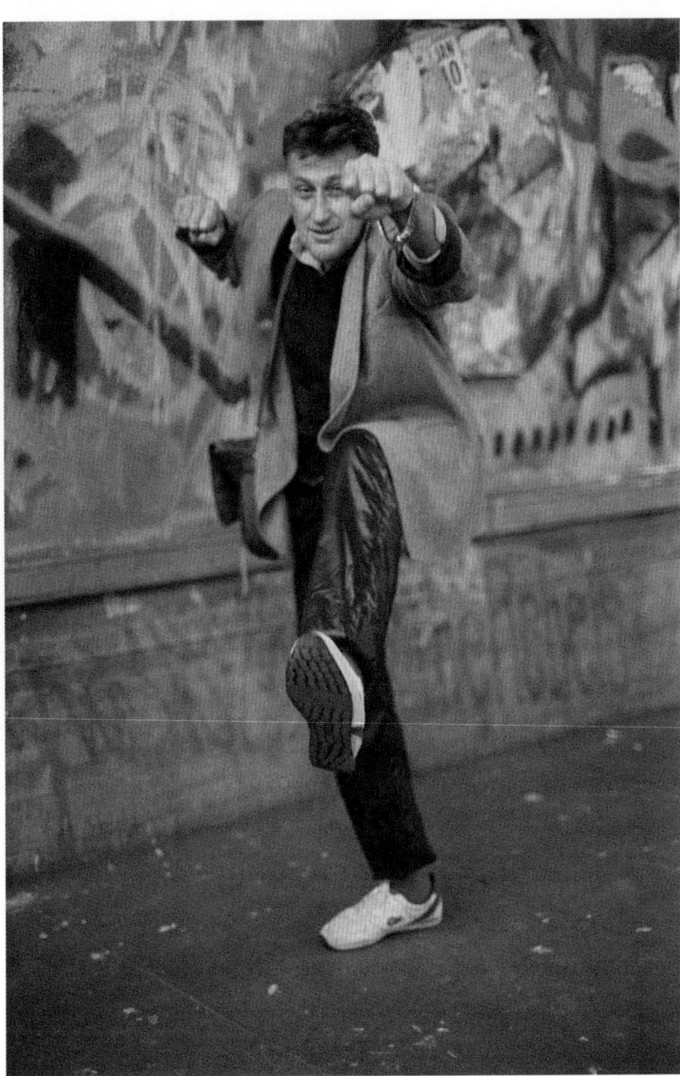

System SF: System Stano Filko

The Slovak universalist und utopian Stano Filko strongly identified with the cosmos and took therein his own "transcendent" perspective on the world, free of conventional ways of seeing. The Greek concept of the *kósmos* stands for an order of the world including the whole universe. The artist developed his own intellectual and ordering system in order to symbolize and express his view of the world. Colors and dimensions are central to this system. Over several decades Filko enriched his system on the conceptual level with further levels of meaning and ascription, leading to a multi-dimensional system that he called *System SF*.

In his *System SF* Filko connects colors with different dimensions, points of the compass, elements and chakras. In Hinduism, the latter are understood to be the energy centers of the human body and spirit. The color red, for example, stands for the third dimension, the realm of the material world and life. This color is frequently seen in connection with the body or flesh. Filko laid the ground for his actual *System SF* in the 1970s, beginning with the three colors red (third dimension: biology/material), blue (fourth dimension: cosmos), and white (fifth dimension: ontology/spirituality), and then further colors were gradually added. The chakra system came later, during Filko's time in New York (1982–90). Up to the late 1990s the chakra system comprised seven colors, and was expanded to a total of twelve from the year 2000.

The multi-dimensional *System SF* subdivides the twelve colors into chakras with a clearly defined order. The drawing *VACUUMDREAM-SEXISTENCEDSAOOQ* (2000–10) [01] reproduced here illustrates the series using vertical rods from left to right: red (first, chakra, earth/east), orange (second, fire/south), yellow (third, air/west), green (fourth, water/north), blue (fifth, cosmos), and black/indigo (sixth, ego). Filko places the first six chakras in the realm of the third dimension, that of the material world and living organisms. The first four chakras also indicate points of the compass. There follow violet (seventh, altruism), pink (eighth, faith), and silver (ninth, transcendence) as components of the fourth dimension, that of the universe and cosmic consciousness. The fifth dimension is the highest level and comprises the colors gold (tenth, singularity), white (eleventh, essence), and transparent (twelfth, entity). Each higher dimension contains all those beneath it.

Behind the lines denoting the order of the chakras this drawing also refers to Filko's famous Snežienková studio on Kamzík hill in the northern outskirts of Bratislava. Even the rooms there were ordered according to his *System SF*, with works in a certain color predominant in each room. Filko used the studio as his personal archive and showed how inseparable art and life were in his work.

The *System SF* seems at first sight to categorize artistic creation and thus also to serve a meta-function for Filko's entire oeuvre. The artist's use of this system can be seen in countless of his works. Seeing the artworks in dialog with each other, however, makes it very clear that the individual works, just as the artist in his lifetime, often resist any kind of ordering structures and instead provoke the imagination and critical faculties of the beholders. This permits a contemporary reading of this historical body of work that enacts utopia.

Der slowakische Universalist und Utopist Stano Filko identifizierte sich stark mit dem Kosmos und nimmt darin eine von üblichen Sichtweisen befreite, „transzendente" Perspektive auf die Welt ein. Der griechische Begriff *Kósmos* steht für eine Weltordnung und bezeichnet das Universum und das gesamte Weltall. Der Künstler entwickelte ein eigenes Gedanken- und Ordnungssystem, mit dem er seine Weltsicht symbolisch zum Ausdruck bringt und in dessen Zentrum Farben und Dimensionen stehen. Über Jahrzehnte hinweg reichert Filko diese auf konzeptueller Ebene mit weiteren Bedeutungsebenen und Zuschreibungen an, woraufhin ein multidimensionales System, das sogenannte *System SF*, entsteht.

Im *System SF* verknüpft Filko die Farben mit verschiedenen Dimensionen, Himmelsrichtungen, Elementen und Chakren, letztere werden im Hinduismus gemeinhin als Energiezentren des menschlichen Körpers und des Geistes begriffen. So steht beispielsweise die Farbe Rot für die 3. Dimension, die für die Materie und das Lebendige steht. Wie sich zeigen wird, taucht diese dann immer in körperlichen oder fleischlichen Zusammenhängen auf. Die Anfänge zum genuinen *System SF* setzt Filko in den 1970er-Jahren, ausgehend von den drei Farben Rot (3. Dimension: Biologie/Materie), Blau (4. Dimension: Kosmos) und Weiß (5. Dimension: Ontologie/Spiritualität), sukzessive kamen weitere Farben hinzu. Das damit verbundene Chakrensystem entstand allerdings erst später, während Filkos Zeit in New York (1982–1990). Bis Ende der 1990er-Jahre umfasste das Chakrensystem sieben und erweiterte sich ab 2000 zu insgesamt zwölf Farben.

Das mehrdimensionale *System SF* untergliedert die zwölf Farben in jeweils ein Chakra mit einer festgelegten Rangfolge. Die hier abgedruckte Zeichnung *VACUUMDREAMSEXISTENCEDSAOOQ* (2000–2010) [01] verdeutlicht die Abfolge mittels einer stabartigen Vertikalstruktur von links nach rechts: Rot (1. Chakra, Erde/Osten), Orange (2., Feuer/Süden), Gelb (3., Luft/Westen), Grün (4., Wasser/Norden), Blau (5., Kosmos) und Schwarz/Indigo (6., Ego). Den ersten sechs Chakren weist Filko den Bereich der 3. Dimension zu, der Dimension der materiellen Welt und der lebenden Organismen. Die ersten vier Chakren verweisen außerdem auf Himmelsrichtungen. Darauf folgen Violett (7., Altruismus), Pink (8., Glaube) und Silber (9., Transzendenz) als Bestandteil der 4. Dimension, der des Universums und des kosmischen Bewusstseins. Die 5. Dimension bildet die höchste Stufe und umfasst die Farben Gold (10., Singularität), Weiß (11., Essenz) sowie Transparent (12., Entität). Jede höhere Dimension beinhaltet alle niedrigeren.

Hinter der Säulenfolge der Chakren wird auf der Zeichnung außerdem auf Filkos berühmtes Studio Snežienková verwiesen, welches sich auf dem Hügel Kamzík in der nördlichen Peripherie von Bratislava befindet. Sogar die dortigen Räume wurden nach seinem *System SF* untergliedert: In jedem Raum dominierten jeweils Werke einer bestimmten Farbe. Das Studio diente Filko als sein persönliches Archiv und zeigt wie untrennbar Kunst und Leben in seinem Œuvre verbunden sind.

Das *System SF* scheint auf den ersten Blick das künstlerische Schaffen zu kategorisieren und somit auch eine Metafunktion für das gesamte Werk einzunehmen. Die Beschäftigung des Künstlers damit lässt sich in zahlreichen Arbeiten nachverfolgen. Im Dialog der Werke wird jedoch verdeutlicht, dass einzelne Arbeiten, wie zeitlebens auch der Künstler selbst, sich wiederholt jeglicher Ordnungsstruktur entziehen und vielmehr einen phantasievollen und kritischen Umgang der Betrachter*innen provozieren. Somit wird eine zeitgenössische Lesart des historischen Werks aufgemacht, das Utopie in Szene setzt.

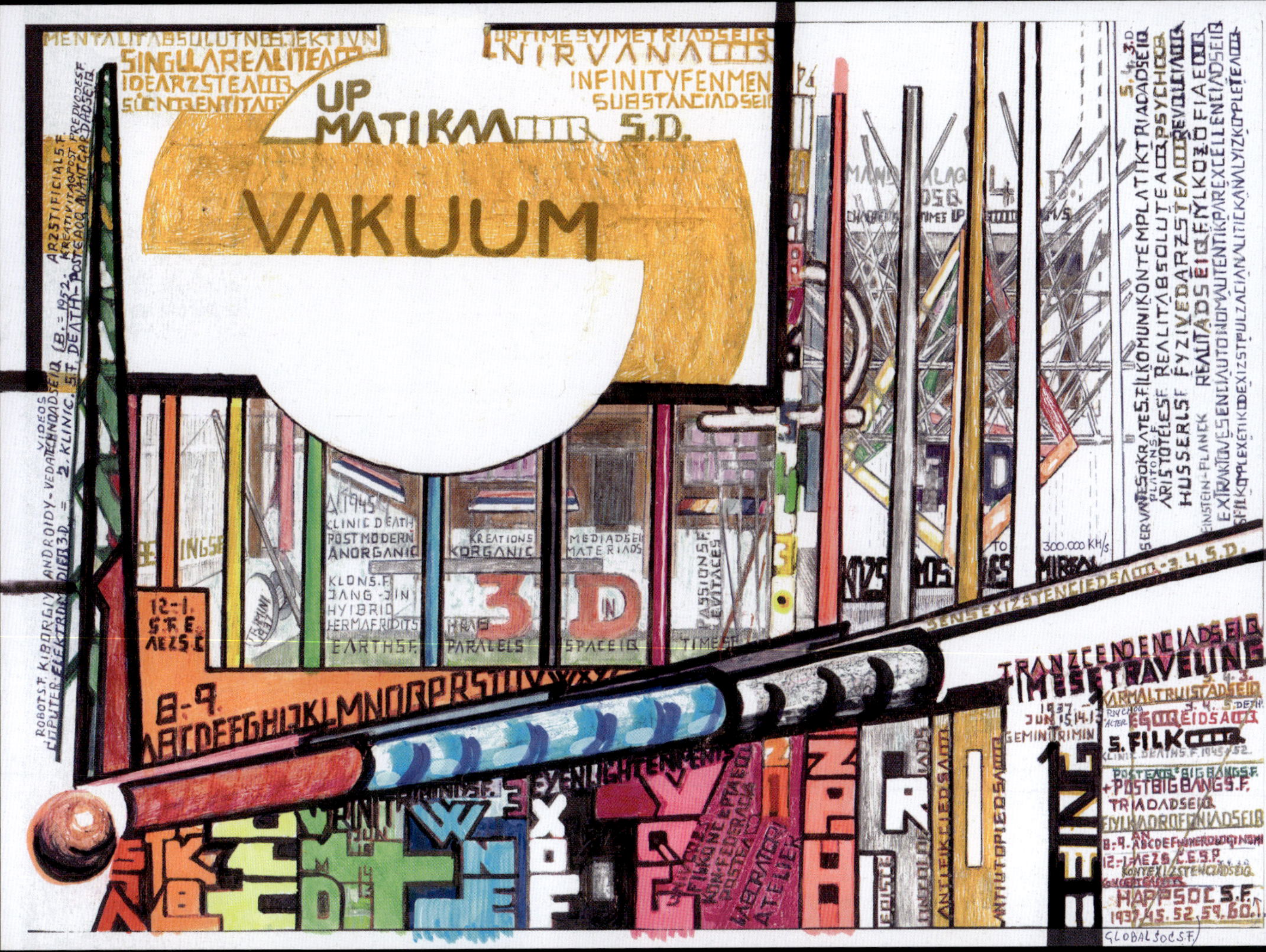

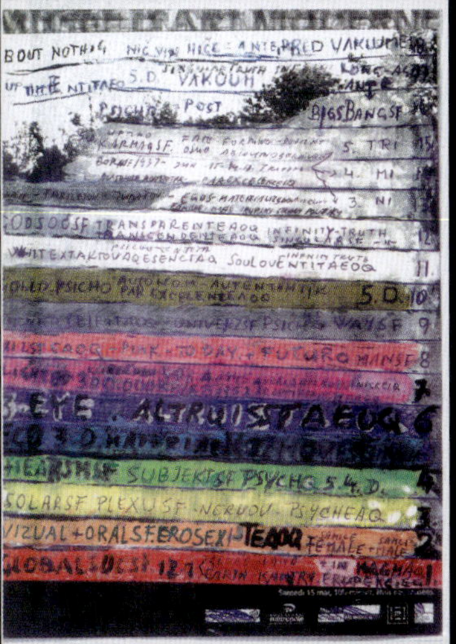

[02] Untitled (subtitled PSYCHOAQ 5.4.D. - PHYSICS 3.D. - FEMALES - FEMALESF - FEMINISF - VAGINES - PUSSIES / PSICHOAQ 5.4.D. - FYZIKA 3.D. - SAMIČKY - FEMALESF - FEMINISF - VAGINKY - PIČKY), 2000s

[01] *VACUUMDREAMSEXISTENCEDSAOOQ*, 2000-10

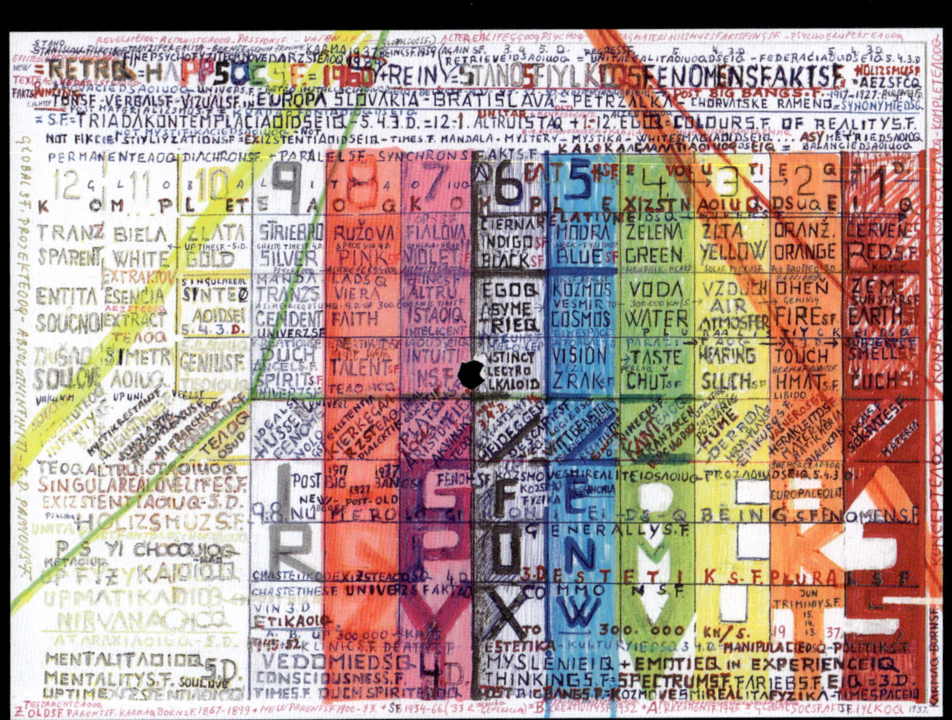

[03] *RETROQ System SF*, 1995-2005

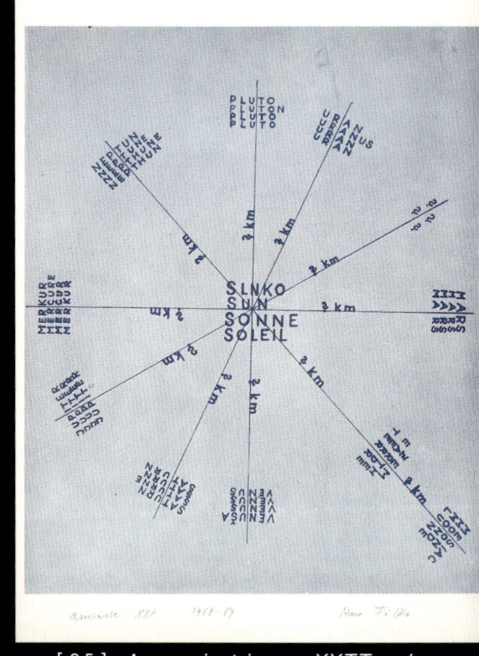

[04] *Cosmos. Associations XVII. /
Cosmos. Asociácie XVII.*, 1970

[05] *Associations XXII. /
Asociácie XXII.*, 1968–69

[06] *Associations XIX. /
Asociácie XIX.*, 1968–69

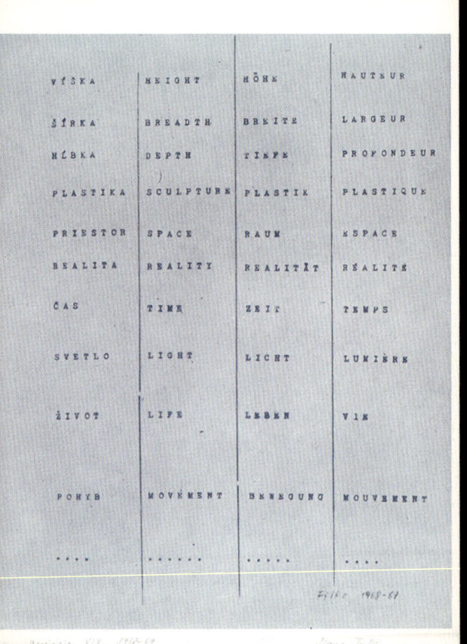

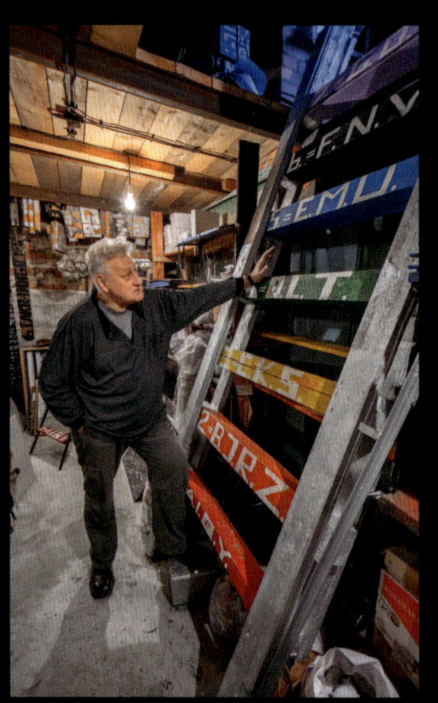

[07] Artist's studio
Snežienková / Umelcov
ateliér Snežienková, 2007

[08] *7 Chakra Colors
Ladder / Rebrík vo farbách 7
čakier*, c. 2000

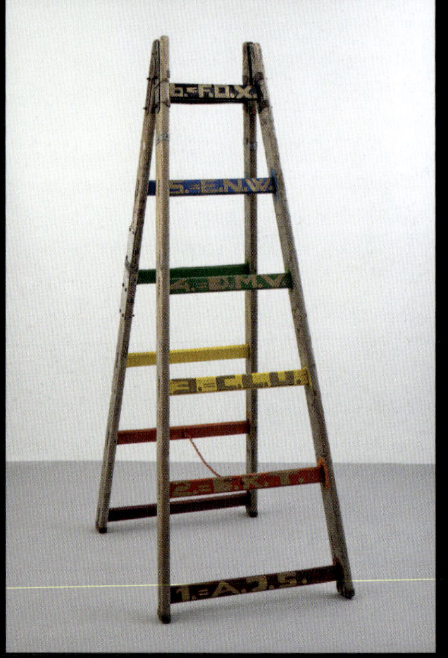

#	Color				
1	RED	EARTH	SMELL	EXPERIENCE	
2	ORANGE	FIRE	TOUCH		
3	YELLOW	AIR	HEARING	SENSATION	3-D.
4	GREEN	WATER	TASTE		
5	BLUE	COSMOS	SIGHT	THINKING	
6	BLACK (INDIGO)	EGO	INSTINCT		
7	VIOLET	ALTRUISM	INTUITION		4-D.
8	PINK	FAITH	TALENT	CONSCIOUSNESS	
9	SILVER	TRANSCENDENCE	SOUL		
10	GOLD	SYNTHESIS	GENIUS	MENTALITY	5-D.
11	WHITE	(EXTRACT) ESSENCE	SYMMETRY	SINGULAR	
12	TRANSPARENT	ENTITY (BEING)	SPIRIT		

RED	COCCYX	EAST	EARTH	EROS / CREATIVITY	
ORANGE	UNDERBELLY – SEX	SOUTH	FIRE	IQ / EQ	
YELLOW	ABOVE THE BELLYBUTTON	WEST	AIR	LOVE	
GREEN	HEART	NORTH	WATER		
BLUE	HEAD				

#	Barva				
1	ČERVENÁ	ZEMĚ	ČICH	ZKUŠENOST	
2	ORANŽOVÁ	OHEŇ	HMAT	ZÁŽITEK	
3	ŽLUTÁ	VZDUCH	SLUCH	CIT	3-D.
4	ZELENÁ	VODA	CHUŤ		
5	MODRÁ	KOSMOS	ZRAK		
6	ČERNÁ (INDIGO)	EGO	INSTINKT		
7	FIALOVÁ	ALTRUISMUS	INTUICE		4-D.
8	RŮŽOVÁ	VÍRA	TALENT	VĚDOMÍ	
9	STŘÍBRNÁ	TRANSCENDENCE	DUŠE		
10	ZLATÁ	SYNTÉZA	GÉNIUS	MENTALITA	5-D.
11	BÍLÁ	(EXTRAKTOVÁ) ESENCE	SYMETRIE	SINGULÁR	
12	PRŮSVITNÁ	ENTITA (BYTÍ)	DUCH		

ČERVENÁ	KOSTRČ	VÝCHOD	ZEM	EROS / KREATIVITA	
ORANŽOVÁ	POD BŘICHEM – SEX	JIH	OHEŇ	IQ / EQ	
ŽLUTÁ	NAD PUPKEM	ZÁPAD	VZDUCH	LÁSKA	
ZELENÁ	SRDCE	SEVER	VODA		
MODRÁ	HLAVA				

Boris Ondreička, *Registration of Stano Filko / Registrace Stano Filko*, exh-cat. Fait Gallery (Brno 2022), np.

    I. *System SF*: System Stano Filko

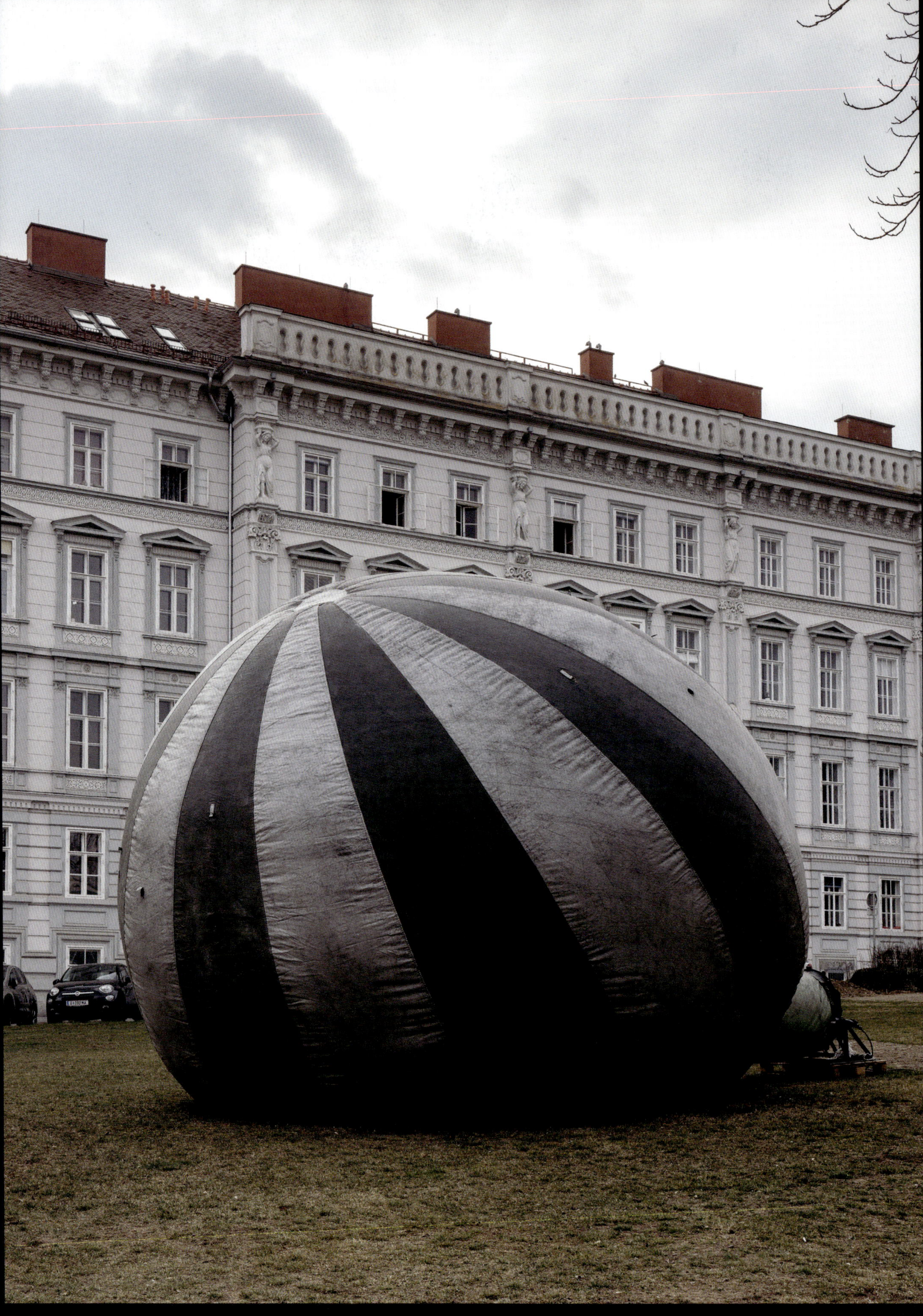

II

Interventions in Public Space / Interventionen im öffentlichen Raum

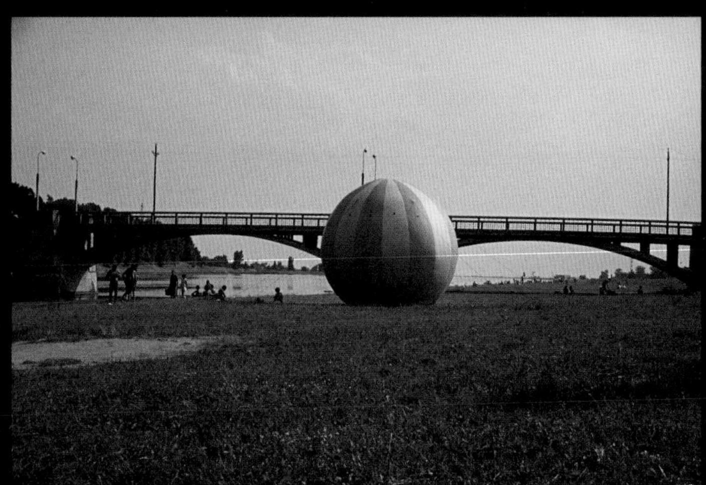

[02] *Breathing - The Celebration of Air / Dýchanie - oslava vzduchu*, 1970

The year 1970 marked an important turning point in the history of the neo-avant-gardes. In Czechoslovakia artists began to increasingly undertake actions, multimedia installations, and interventions in public space. Stano Filko is also known for his installations in public spaces, by means of which he resisted the monumental representations of the socialist regime and opened up a more far-reaching reality.

In his public installations Filko uses a (retro-)futurist formal language and turns to the cosmic space. The dynamic environment *Breathing – The Celebration of Air / Dýchanie – oslava vzduchu* (1970) [01-02] can be understood as a key early work in Filko's cosmic consciousness. With the spherical form of this installation that looks like a giant balloon Filko draws on a trend toward geodetic structures that had been particularly popular in the progressive architecture of the 1960s. The monumental object is reminiscent of a spacecraft or a mechanical organ. In the interior, the air is made to circulate, so that the round shape continually expands and deflates. With this dynamic movement, Filko is referring to breathing and connecting this basic function of the human body with the pulsations of the universe.

Das Jahr 1970 ist ein wichtiger Wendepunkt in der Geschichte der Neo-Avantgarden. In der Tschechoslowakei beginnen Künstler*innen vermehrt Aktionen, multimediale Installationen, sowie Interventionen im öffentlichen Raum vorzunehmen. Auch Stano Filko ist für seine Installationen im öffentlichen Raum bekannt, durch die er sich der monumentalen Repräsentanz des sozialistischen Regimes widersetzt und eine weitreichendere Realität aufspannt.

Filko verwendet in seinen öffentlichen Installationen eine (retro-)futuristische Formensprache und wendet sich dem kosmischen Raum zu. Das dynamische Environment *Breathing – The Celebration of Air / Dýchanie – oslava vzduchu* (1970) [01-02] kann als ein frühes Schlüsselwerk von Filkos kosmischem Bewusstsein verstanden werden. Mit der Kugelform der Installation, die einem riesenhaften Ballon ähnelt, greift Filko einen Trend um geodätische Strukturen auf, die sich vor allem in der progressiven Architektur der 1960er-Jahre großer Beliebtheit erfreuten. Das monumentale Objekt erinnert an ein Raumschiff oder ein mechanisches Organ. Im Inneren wird Luft zur Zirkulation gebracht, wobei sich die runde Form immer wieder ausdehnt und zusammenzieht. Filko greift mit dieser Dynamik das Konzept des Atems auf und verbindet diese grundlegende Funktionsweise des menschlichen Körpers mit dem Pulsieren des Universums.

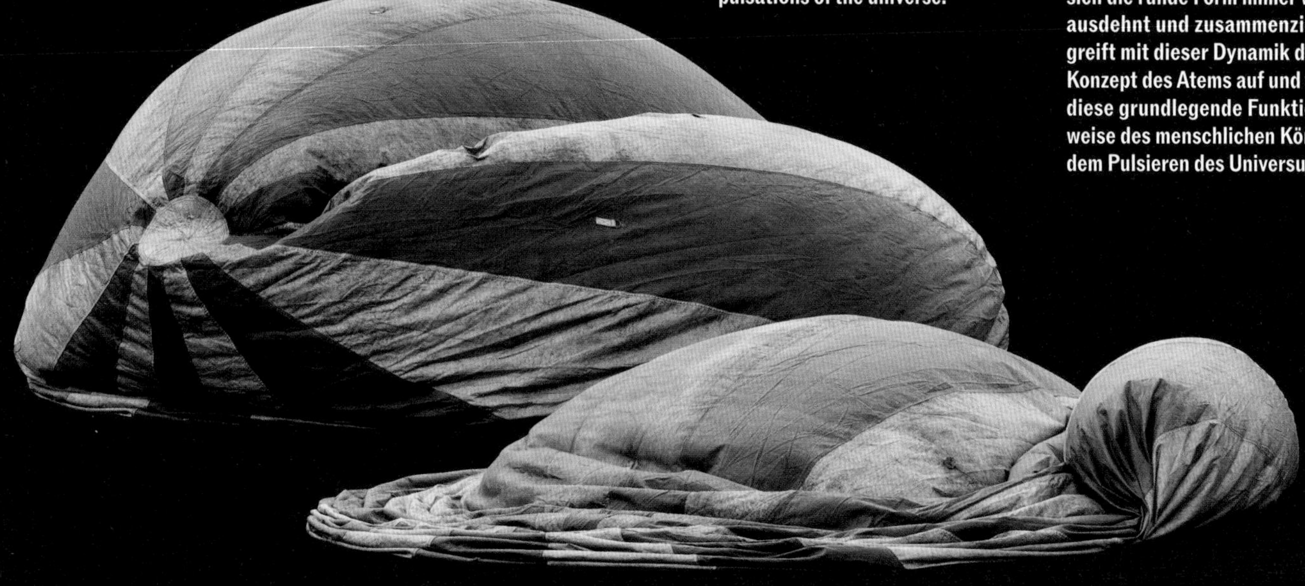

←[01A] ↑[01B-C] *Breathing - The Celebration of Air / Dýchanie - oslava vzduchu*, 1970, HALLE FÜR KUNST Steiermark, Graz, 2022

Twelve outsized balloon objects, *12 Colors of Reality (Balloons) / 12 farieb reality (Balóny)* (1978–2011) [03], are presented in public space. They represent the artist's color system, which began with the three colors red, blue, and white but that Filko then developed into his *System SF* with a total of twelve colors, each of which has a symbolic meaning determined by the artist as well as embodying specific dimensions and chakras. Via these twelve monumental balloon objects Filko's system is extended into the public space, which thus becomes a part of his cosmic visions.

In einer Aktion im öffentlichen Raum sind zwölf überdimensionale Ballonobjekte *12 Colors of Reality (Balloons) / 12 farieb reality (Balóny)* (1978–2011) [03] zu sehen, die das Farbsystem des Künstlers repräsentieren. Während Filko anfangs von den drei Farben Rot, Blau und Weiß ausgegangen ist, hat sich im Laufe seines Schaffens das sogenannte *System SF* entwickelt. Dieses umfasst insgesamt zwölf Farben, wobei jede Farbe eine von Filko festgelegte symbolische Bedeutung aufweist und spezifische Dimensionen und Chakren verkörpert. Durch die zwölf monumentalen Ballonobjekte erweitert sich Filkos System auf den öffentlichen Raum, der ein Teil seiner kosmischen Visionen wird.

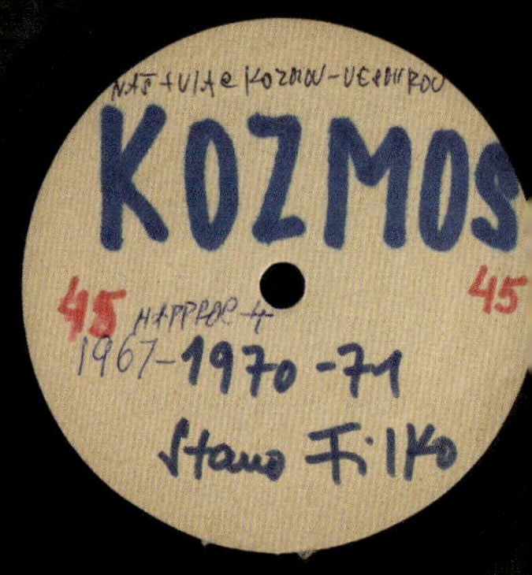

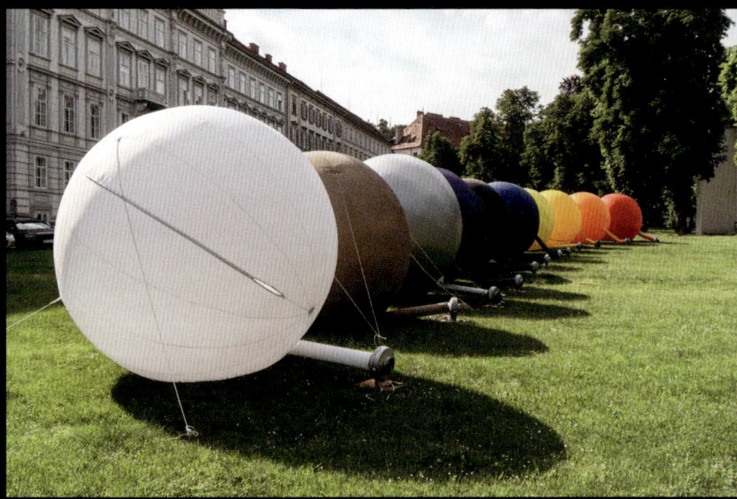

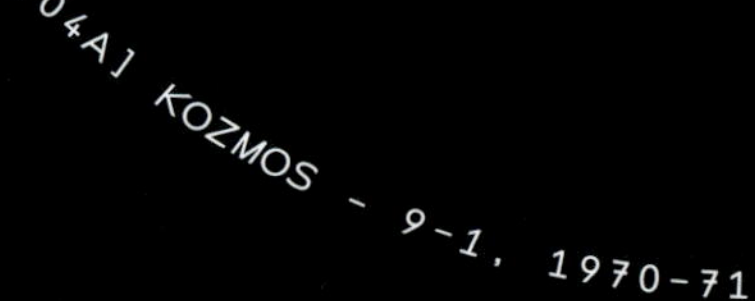

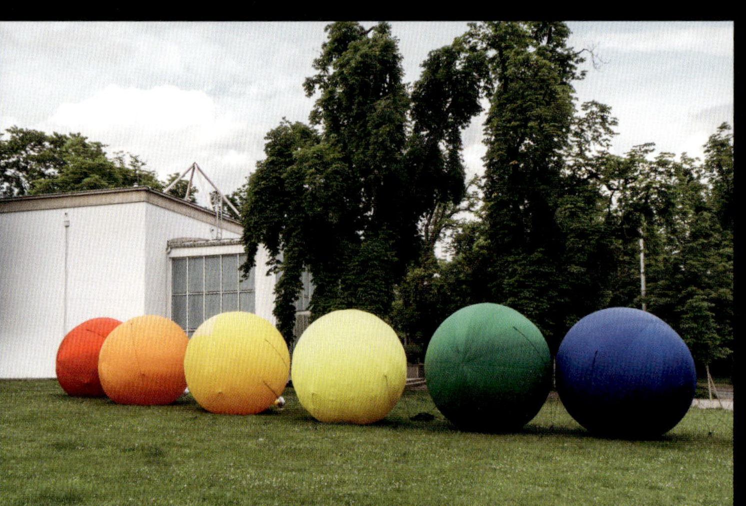

↑[03A-B] *12 Colors of Reality (Balloons) / 12 farieb reality (Balóny)*, 1978–2011, HALLE FÜR KUNST Steiermark, Graz, 2022

Especially after the defeat of the Prague Spring in 1968 artistic freedom was severely restricted in Czechoslovakia. With his sound works Filko further pursues the idea of the open work of art and also creates an alternative form of publicity. In 1971/72 Filko added his own voice to his artistic cosmos by recording it for vinyl. Based on this, there is the sound installation *SP Record / SP gramoplatňa KOZMOS – 9–1; FUTÚR – COSMOS FUTÚR; ATOM – REÁL; COSMOS – COSMOS ESPACE UNIVERSE* (1970–71) [04] in the exterior, in which Filko's voice is heard projecting into the four directions of the compass and speaking as on his own record: "kozmos," "futúr," "atom," and "real."

Vor allem nach der Niederschlagung des Prager Frühling im Jahr 1968 wurde die künstlerische Freiheit in der Tschechoslowakei stark begrenzt. Mit seinen Soundarbeiten verfolgt Filko die Idee des offenen Kunstwerkes weiter und kreiert eine alternative Form der Öffentlichkeit. 1971/72 hat Filko die eigene Stimme seinem künstlerischen Kosmos hinzugefügt, indem er sie auf Vinyl aufgenommen hat. Daraus entsteht die Soundinstallation *SP Record / SP gramoplatňa KOZMOS – 9–1; FUTÚR – COSMOS FUTÚR; ATOM – REÁL; COSMOS – COSMOS ESPACE UNIVERSE* (1970/71) [04] im Außenbereich, bei der in vier verschiedenen Himmelsrichtungen die Stimme Filkos wie auf den gleichnamigen Schallplatten zu hören ist: „kozmos", „futúr", „atom" und „real".

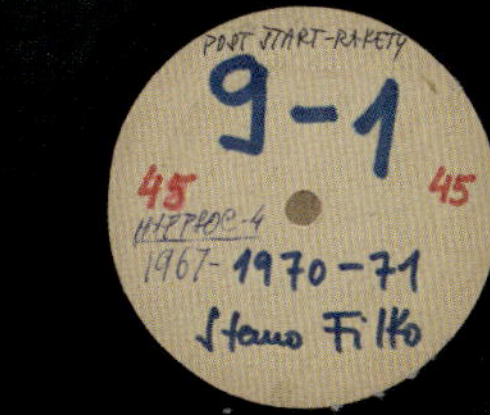

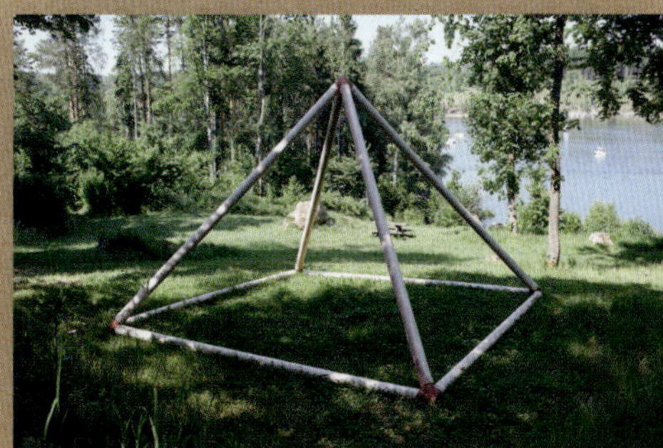

[05A] *Pyramid / Pyramída,*
c. 1995, Lichtenfels
Sculpture, 2021

The large installation *Pyramid / Pyramída* (c. 1995) [05], presented on the roof of HALLE FÜR KUNST Steiermark, has a comparable place on the legendary artist's studio Snežienková, which stands on a hill on the northern margin of Bratislava and offers a wide-ranging view of the city and its environs. According to Filko's understanding, both the pyramid and the associated figure of the triangle are obvious shapes for embodying the cosmos. The artist strongly identifies with the universe and thus it is no surprise that he sees these shapes as symbols by means of which his own self is projected into a transcendental and more comprehensive form, whereby this can also be seen as conceptual self-portrait.

Die großformatige Installation *Pyramid / Pyramída* (ca. 1995) [05] am Dach der HALLE FÜR KUNST Steiermark hat einen vergleichbaren Platz auf dem legendären Künstleratelier Snežienková, die mit ihrer Hügellage am nördlichen Stadtrand einen weitläufigen Blick über Bratislava und seine Umgebung anbietet, eingenommen. Nach Filkos Verständnis ist sowohl die Pyramide als auch die assoziierte Figur des Dreiecks die naheliegende Form, um den Kosmos zu verkörpern. Der Künstler identifiziert sich stark mit dem Universum und so ist es auch nicht verwunderlich, diese Formen als Symbol zu begreifen, mit dem sein Selbst in eine transzendente und umfassendere Form projiziert wird, was auch als konzeptuelles Selbstporträt aufgefasst werden kann.

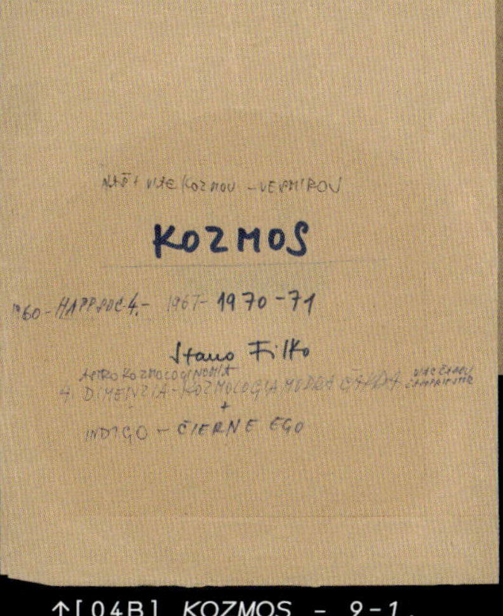

↑[04B] KOZMOS - 9-1,
1970-71

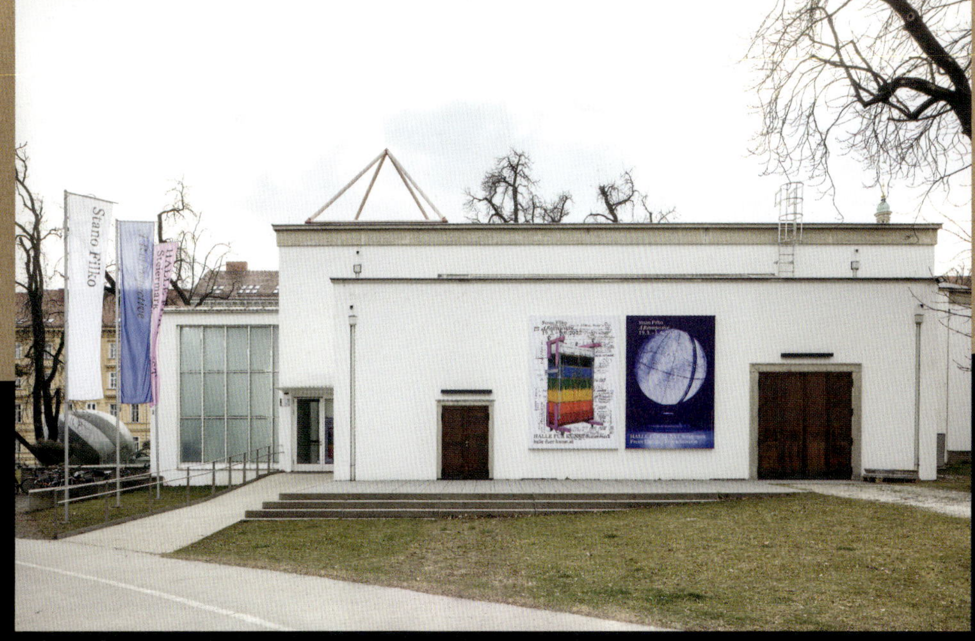

[05B] *Pyramid / Pyramída,* c. 1995,
HALLE FÜR KUNST Steiermark, Graz, 2022

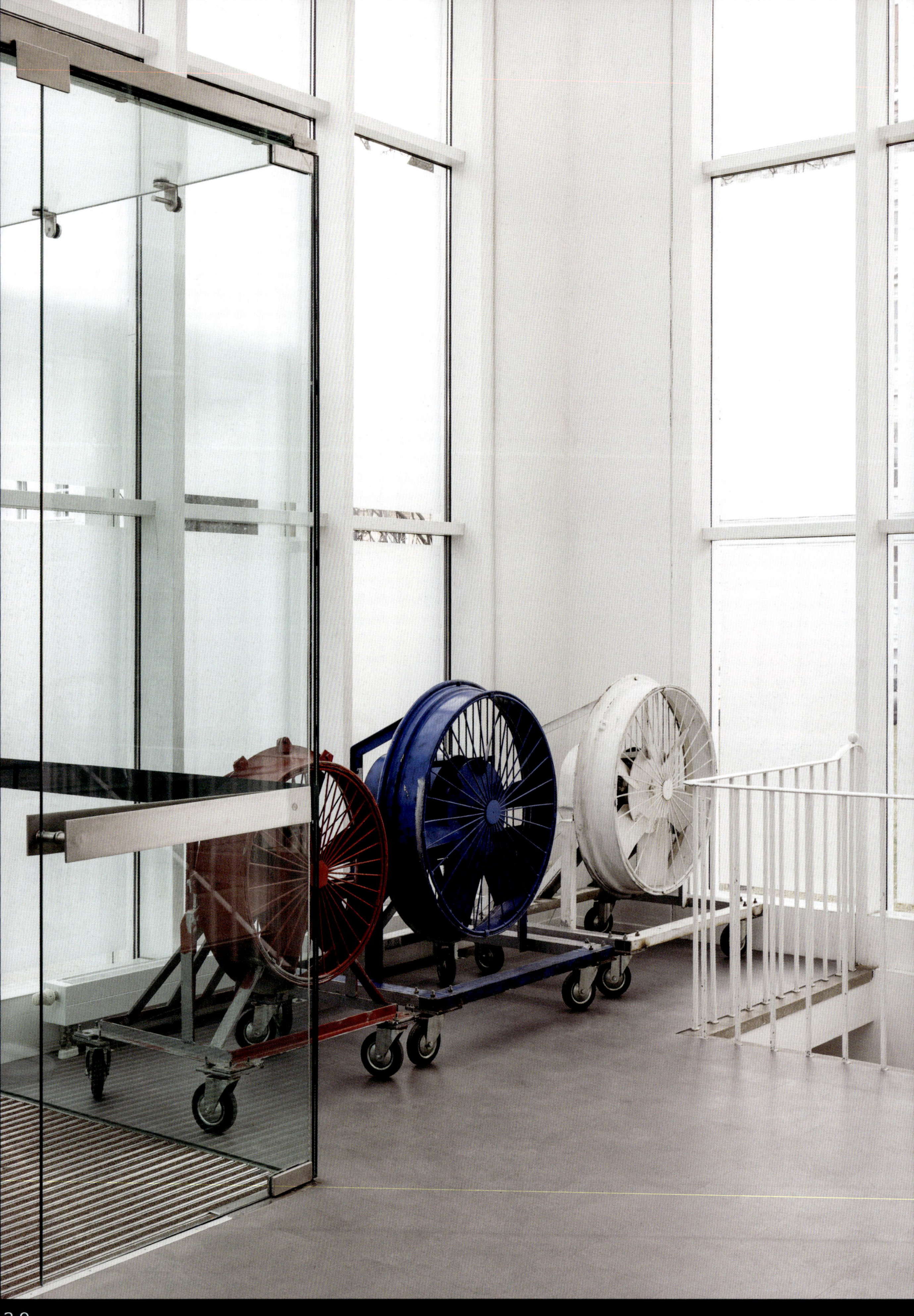

III

First Insight / Erste Annäherung

Towards the late 1960s the *System SF* consisted in its first development phase of three main axes, based on the colors red, blue, and white.

The artist's decisive colors flank the visitors upon entering in the form of the installation *Wind / Vietor* (1967/c. 1995), [01] consisting of three painted fans. In Filko's interpretation each of the three colors symbolizes a different field of being and is the expression of a certain dimension. Red is the color of the third dimension and includes the material world and biology. Blue represents the forth dimension, the cosmos that contains on the one hand space and time and on the other artistic consciousness. Finally, white is this highest fifth dimension, embodying spirituality, the void or vacuum and death. By connecting these turbine-like objects and using this color sequence, *Wind / Vietor* presents these dimensions as the central energy sources of the system. At the same time this work raises questions as to the consistency and yet also inherent openness and irony in Filko's systemic thinking.

Gegen Ende der 1960er-Jahre umfasste das *System SF* in seiner ersten Entstehungsphase drei Hauptachsen, ausgehend von den Farben Rot, Blau und Weiß.

Diese als für den Künstler grundlegend entscheidenden Farben treten auch bei drei eingangs am Boden gruppierten Objekten auf, die aus bemalten Ventilatoren bestehende Installation *Wind / Vietor* (1967/ca. 1995) [01]. Nach Filkos Vorstellung symbolisiert jede der drei Farben einen unterschiedlichen Daseinsbereich und ist Ausdruck einer bestimmten Dimension. Rot ist die Farbe der 3. Dimension und umfasst den Bereich der Materie und der Biologie. Die Farbe Blau stellt die 4. Dimension dar, den Bereich des Kosmos, der zum einen Raum und Zeit, zum anderen das künstlerische Bewusstsein beinhaltet. Schließlich stellt Weiß die höchste, die 5. Dimension dar und verkörpert Spiritualität, Leere/Vakuum und Tod. Durch die Verbindung zwischen den turbinenartigen Objekten und der farblichen Abfolge treten in *Wind / Vietor* die Dimensionen als zentrale Energiequellen des Systems in Erscheinung. Gleichzeitig wirft die Arbeit Fragen nach der durchgängigen Beständigkeit wie einer darin zugleich angelegten Offenheit und Ironie von Filkos systemischem Denken auf.

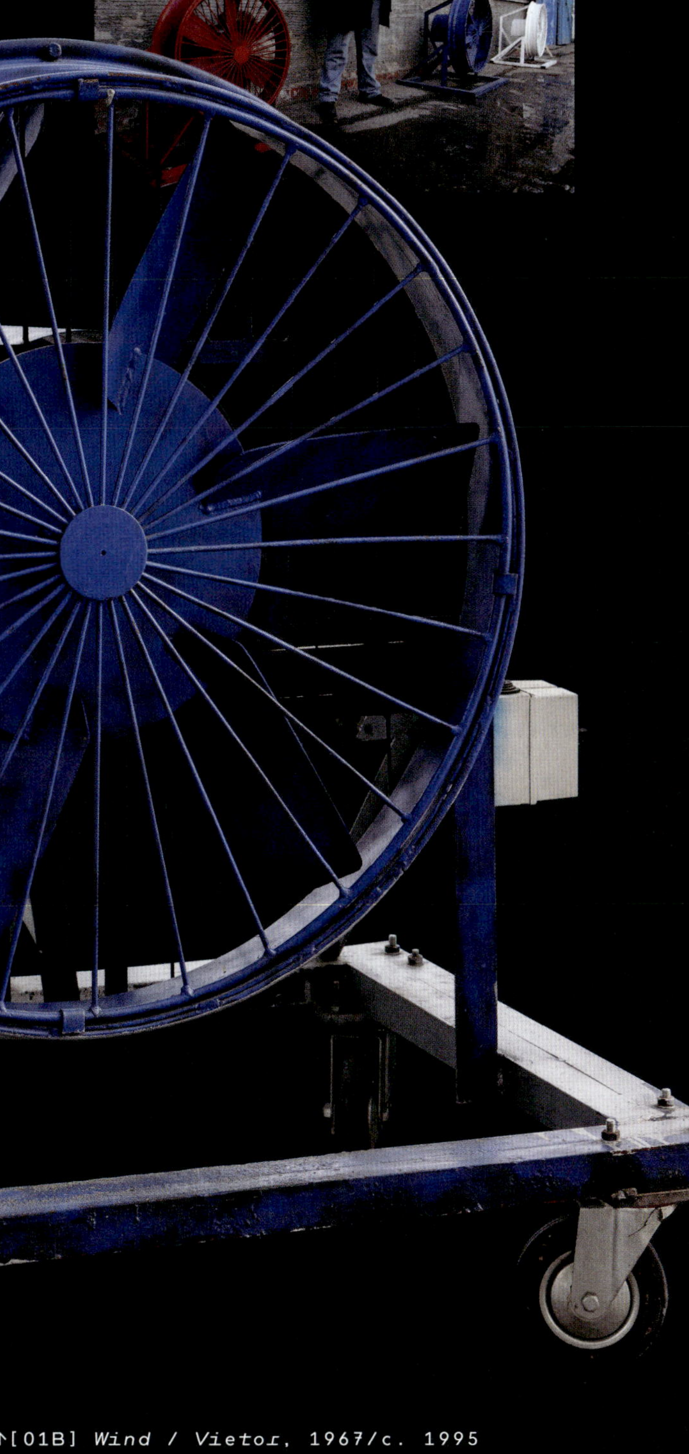

[02] *Wind / Vietor*, 1967/c. 1995, tranzit.sk, Bratislava, 2005

↑[01B] *Wind / Vietor*, 1967/c. 1995

←[01A] *Wind / Vietor*, 1967/c. 1995, HALLE FÜR KUNST Steiermark, Graz, 2022

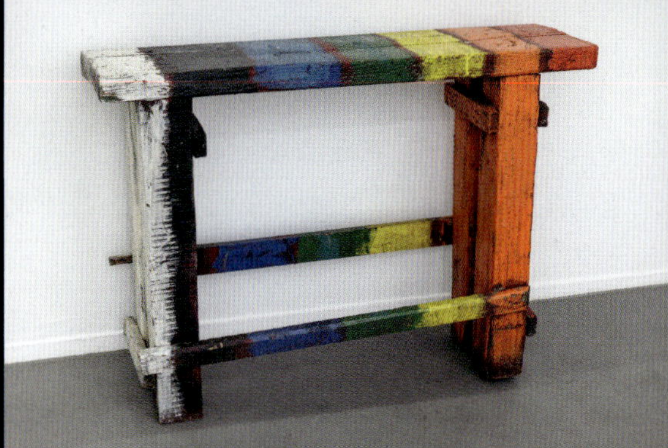

[03] *7 Chakra Colors Bench /
Lavička vo farbách 7 čakier*, c. 2000

On the surface of the object *7 Chakra Colors Bench / Lavička vo farbách 7 čakier* (c. 2000) [03] Filko repeats the fixed color sequence of the seven chakras. The object shows Filko's affinity for everyday objects, which he frequently integrated into his works as found ready-mades declared art or as rearranged and partially reworked assemblages. As a painted-over bench this object illustrates the proximity of art and life by means of a harmony of functionality and aesthetics.

Auf der Fläche des Objekts *7 Chakra Colors Bench / Lavička vo farbách 7 čakier* (ca. 2000) [03] wiederholt Filko die festgelegte Farbabfolge der sieben Chakren. Das Objekt weist auf die Affinität Filkos zu Gegenständen des Alltags hin, die er oftmals wie gefundene und zu Kunstwerken erklärte Readymades oder neu angeordnete und teils überarbeitete Assemblagen in sein Œuvre integriert. Als übermalte Sitzbank verdeutlicht das Objekt die Nähe von Kunst und Leben durch den Gleichklang von Funktionalität und Ästhetik.

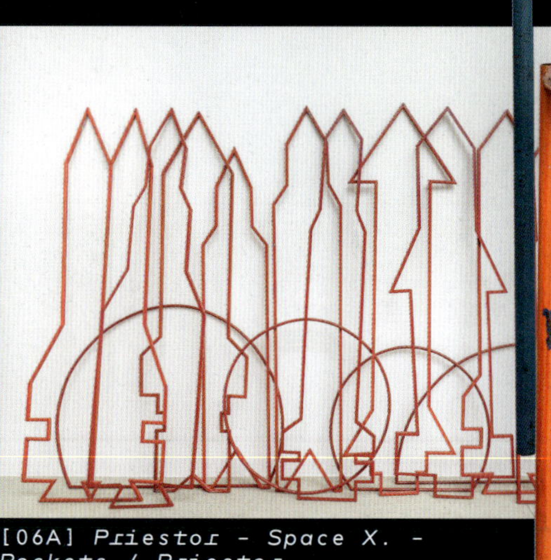

[06A] *Priestor - Space X. - Rockets / Priestor - Space X. - Rakety*, 1967

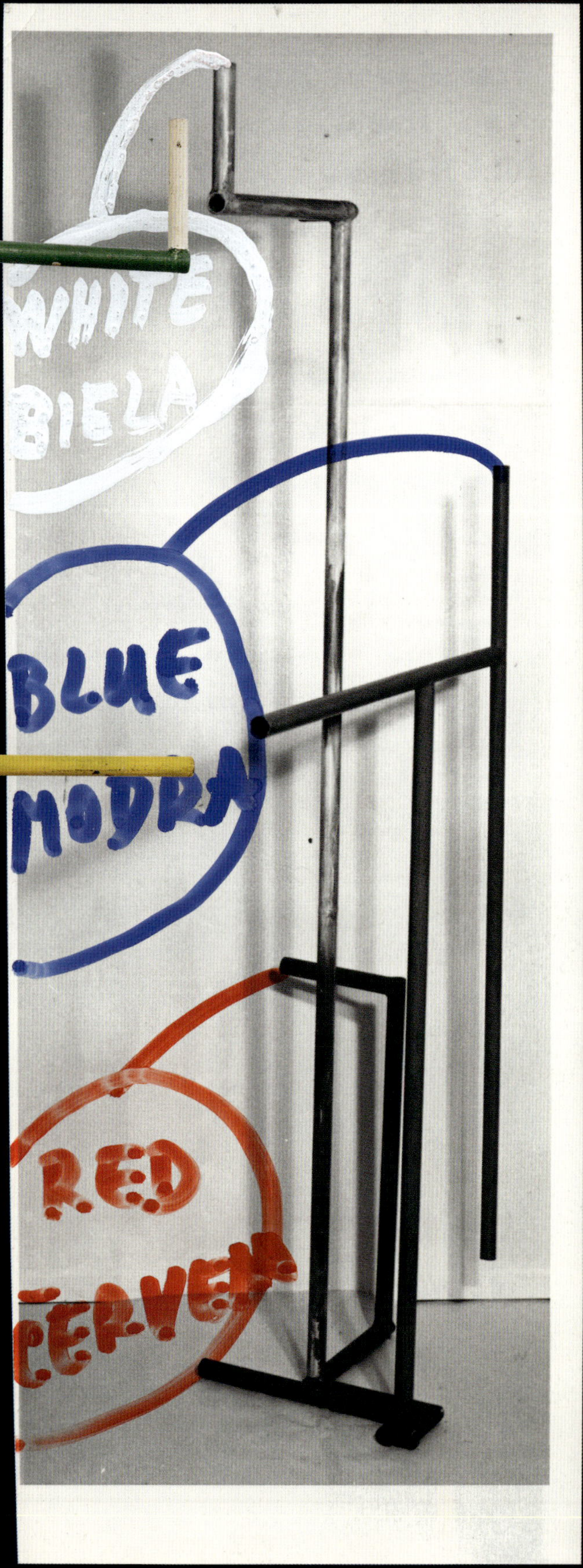

←[04A] ↑[05] *Monument - Czechoslovak Flag / Pomník - zástava Československa*, 1968/93

A colorfully painted frame of iron pipes that looks like a clothes rack is the basis of *Monument – Czechoslovak Flag / Pomník – zástava Československa* (1968/1993) [04–05]. Originally this sculpture was painted red, blue, and white, but decades later Filko overpainted it with the seven-part color system. Filko refers here to the colors of the flag of Czechoslovakia, which at the time of the Prague Spring and the "empire" of the Soviet Union had gained a new meaning, full of hope for (relative) freedom and then bitter disappointment. Filko here reinterprets it within his own system and creates a kind of "anti-monument" that follows his own ideas and "laws" outside the scope of the national and totalitarian context.

The rocket motif is recurring in Filko's oeuvre. The artist's use of rocket shapes goes back to as early as the mid-1960s, as seen in the fifteen-part work in red, *Priestor – Space X. – Rockets / Priestor – Space X. – Rakety* (1967) [06], in which the outlines of rockets and other planetary shapes are traced.

Ein bunt bemaltes Gestell aus Eisenrohren, das an einen Kleiderständer erinnert, bildet das Grundgerüst für die Arbeit *Monument – Czechoslovak Flag / Pomník – zástava Československa* (1968/1993) [04–05]. Ursprünglich war die Skulptur in Rot, Blau und Weiss bemalt, nach Jahrzehnten übermalte Filko diese mit dem siebenteilige Farbsystem. Filko spielt auf die Farben der tschechoslowakischen Nationalflagge an, die zu Zeiten des Prager Frühlings und des unionistischen Sowjetreiches eine andere, mit erhofften und schließlich bitter enttäuschten relativen Freiheiten verbundene Bedeutung hat, und schafft mit der Umdeutung durch sein eigenes System eine Art „Anti-Monument", das seinen eigenen Vorstellungen und „Gesetzen" abseits eines nationalen und totalitären Zusammenhangs folgt.

Das Raketenmotiv ist in Filko's Œuvre wiederkehrend. Ihren Ausgang nahm die Raketenform bereits Mitte der 1960er-Jahre, wie beispielsweise in der 15-teiligen in Rot gehaltenen Arbeit *Priestor – Space X. – Rockets / Priestor – Space X. – Rakety* (1967) [06], die jeweils schablonenhaft die Umrisse von Raketen und anderen planetarischen Formen andeutet.

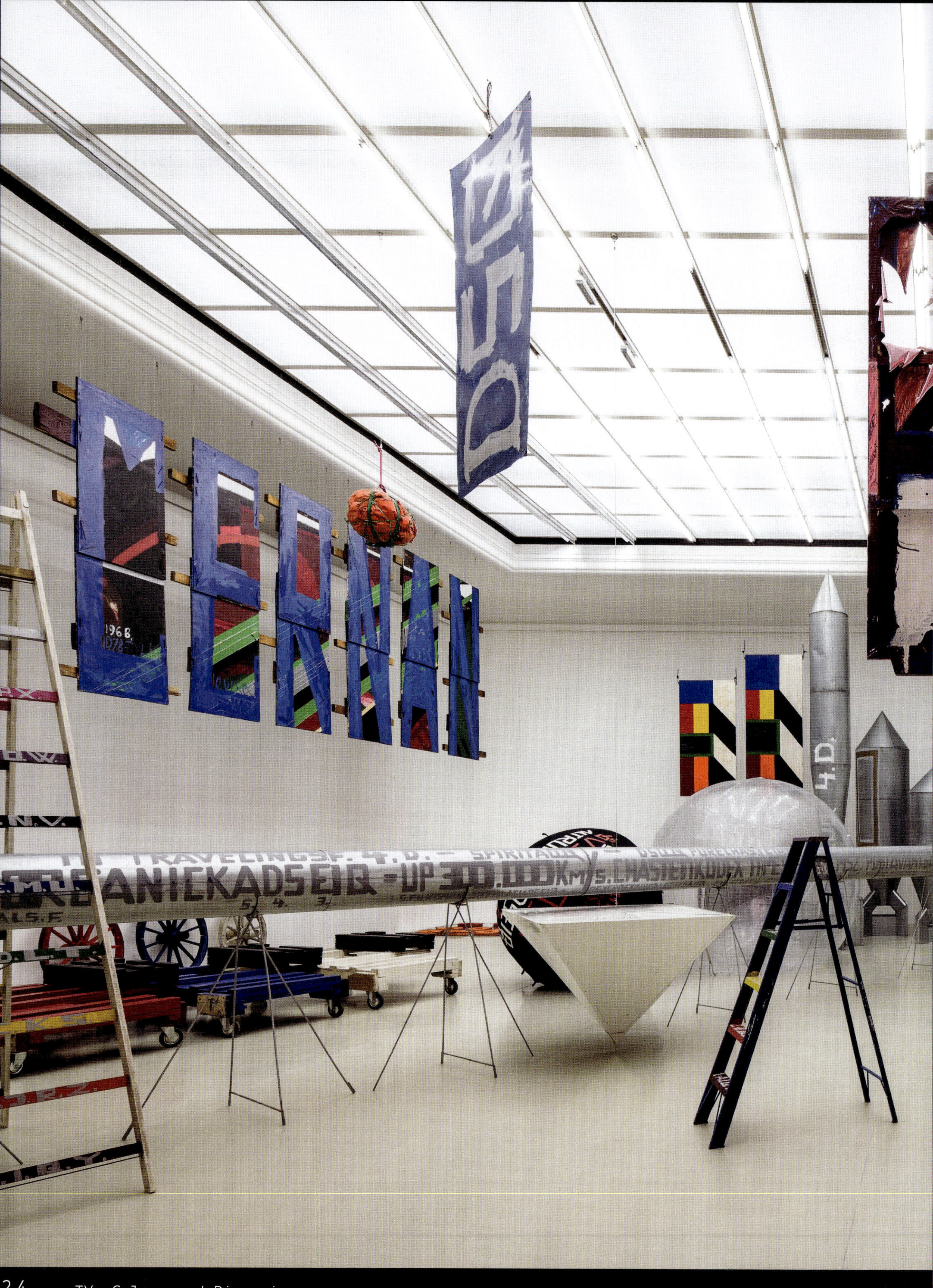

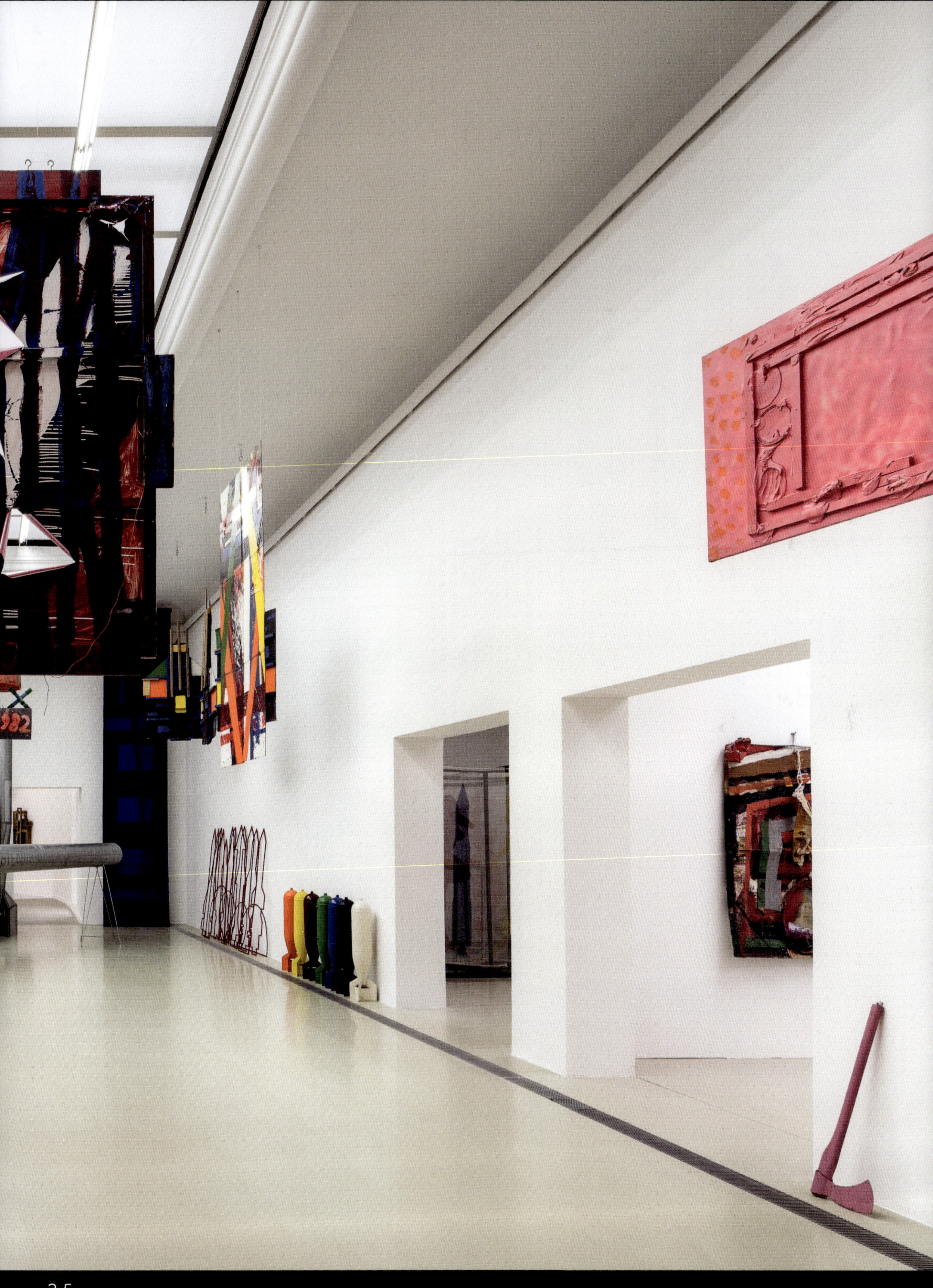

    IV. Farbe und Dimensionen

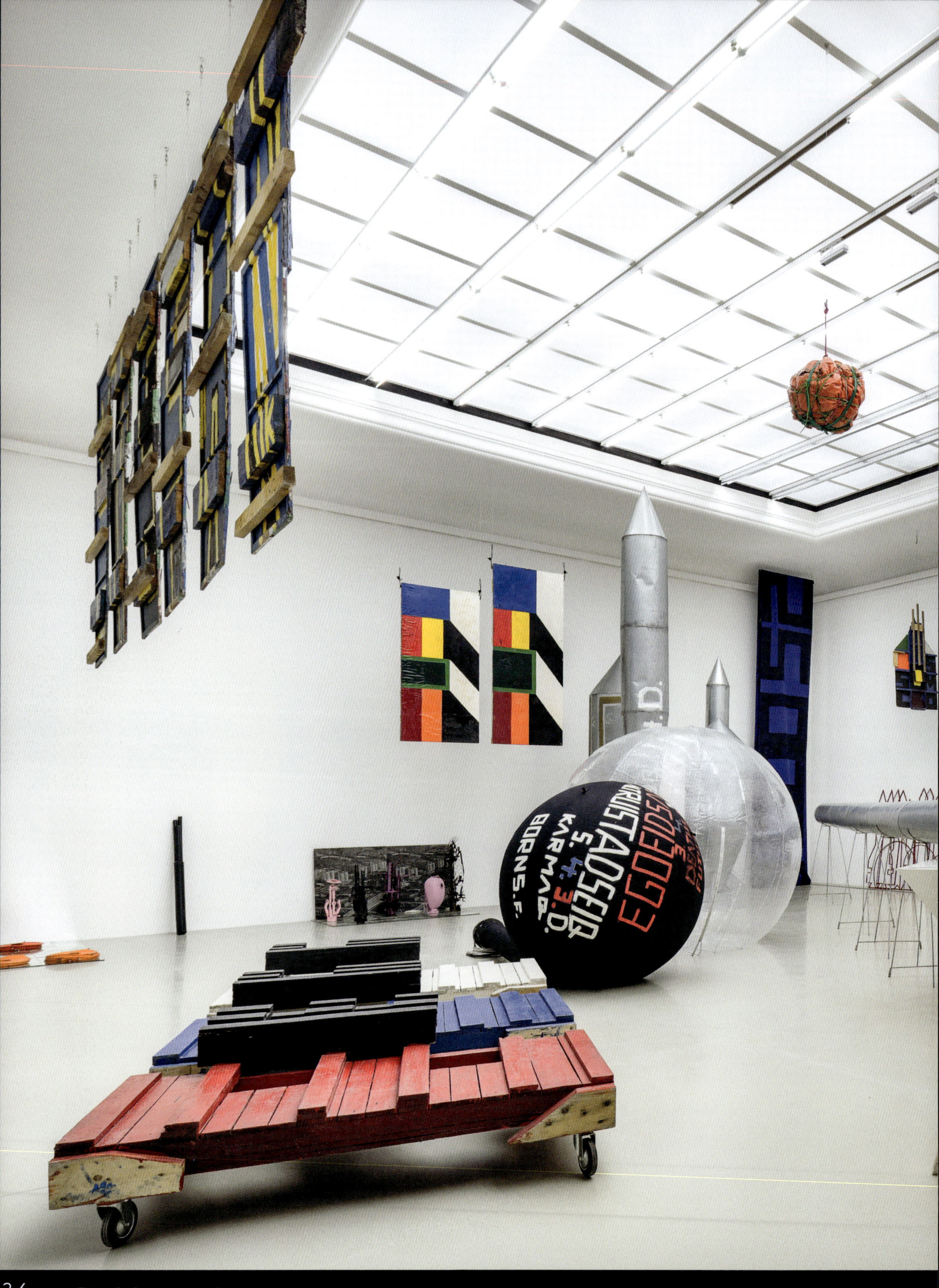

EGGDISG
KARUISTADT
KARMAD
5. 4. 3. D.
BORNS.F.

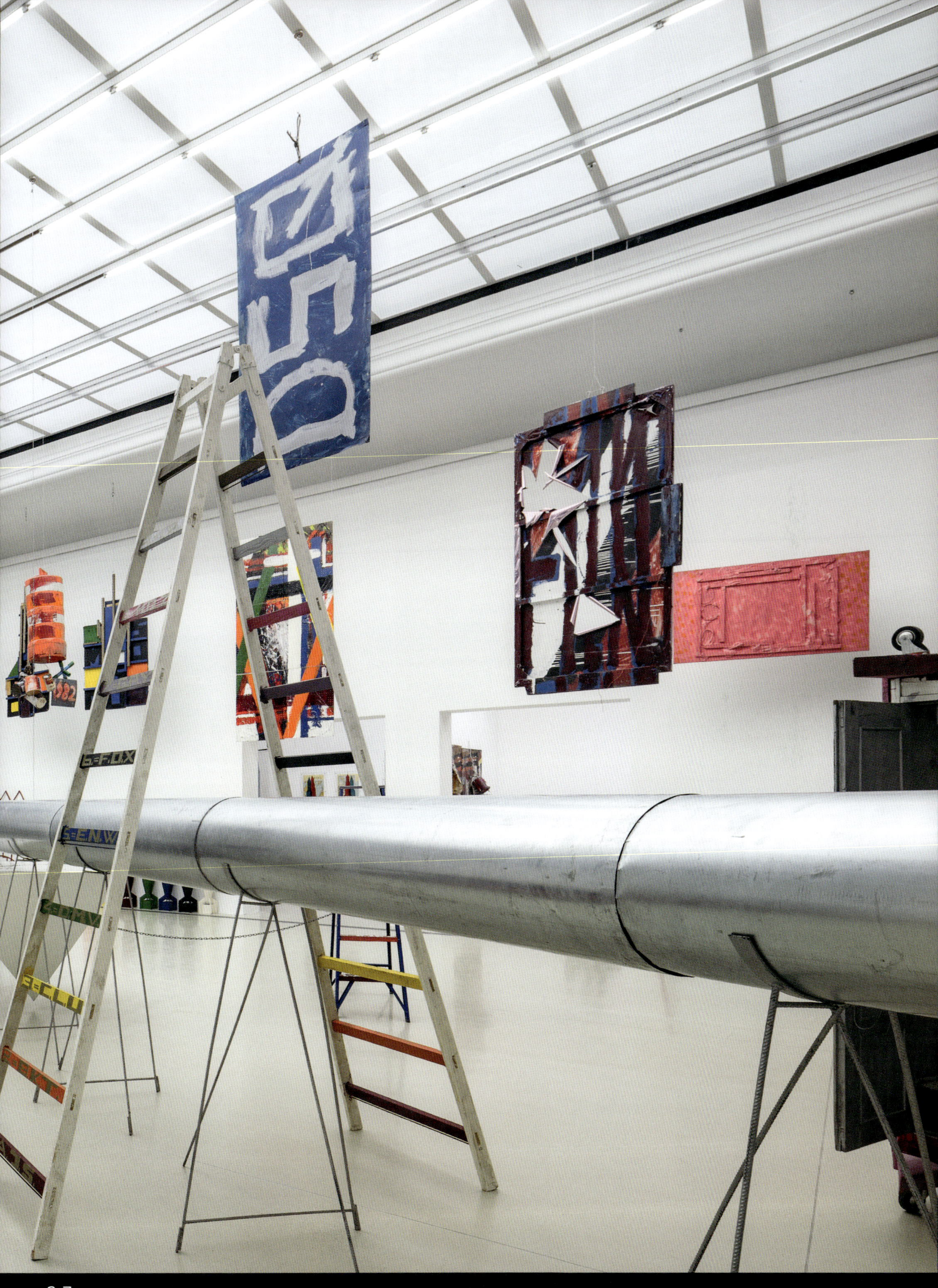

    IV. Farbe und Dimensionen

Colors and Dimensions / Farbe und Dimensionen

Throughout his life Stano Filko took an intensive interest in different areas of knowledge such as far-eastern philosophy, religion, astronomy, and metaphysics, but also with texts from the Western philosophy of Plato, Hume, Kant, Hegel, and Wittgenstein. Filko was particularly interested in holistic connections between phenomena, which is something we can also see in his art. With his *System SF* Filko developed an overarching order that gave the colors he used in his works different meanings and attributed them to chakras and dimensions.

System SF is an artistic cosmos that came over the years to include all the areas of Filko's life. He untiringly produced works in his studio, whereby the logic of his system led to new spatial and symbolic connections between everyday objects. Filko began this system with three colors, and then from the mid-1980s to the late 1990s it had seven, and thereafter the number increased to twelve, finally to twenty.

Stano Filko hat sich Zeit seines Lebens intensiv mit ganz unterschiedlichen Wissensbereichen wie fern-östlicher Philosophie, Religion, Astronomie und Metaphysik auseinandergesetzt, aber auch mit Texten aus der westlichen Philosophie von Platon, über Hume, Kant, Hegel bis hin zu Wittgenstein. Was Filko daran interessiert hat, ist der ganzheitliche Zusammenhang zwischen den Dingen, ein Interesse, das sich auch in seiner Kunst ausdrückt. Mit dem sogenannten *System SF* entwickelt Filko ein übergreifendes System, welches die Farben seiner Werke mit verschiedenen Bedeutungen wie Chakren und Dimensionen auflädt.

Das *System SF* ist ein künstlerischer Kosmos, der zunehmend alle Bereiche von Filkos Lebens umfasste. Unermüdlich produzierte Filko Werke in seinem Atelier, wobei sich durch die Logik seines Systems neue räumliche wie auch symbolische Verbindungen zwischen alltäglichen Gegenständen erschließen lassen. Die Anfänge machte Filko mit drei Farben, von Mitte der 1980er- bis Ende der 1990er-Jahre bestand das System schließlich aus sieben Farben bzw. Chakren, worauf er es in weiterer Folge auf insgesamt zwölf, schließlich sogar zwanzig Farben erweiterte.

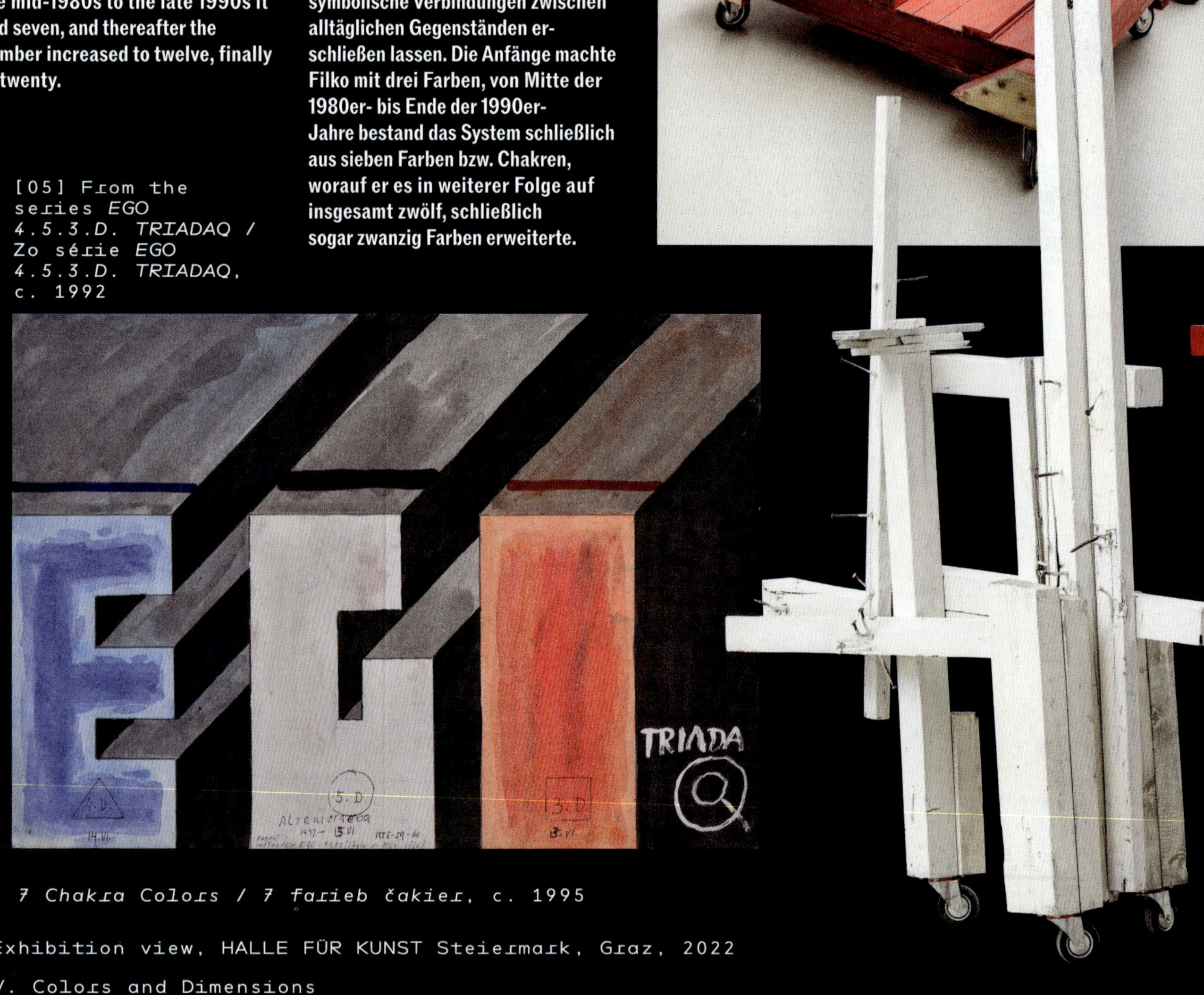

[04] *EGO – Gemini – Reincarnation (5.4.3.D.) / EGO – Blíženci – Reinkarnácia (5.4.3.D.)*, c. 1995

[05] From the series *EGO 4.5.3.D. TRIADAQ / Zo série EGO 4.5.3.D. TRIADAQ*, c. 1992

[03] *7 Chakra Colors / 7 farieb čakier*, c. 1995

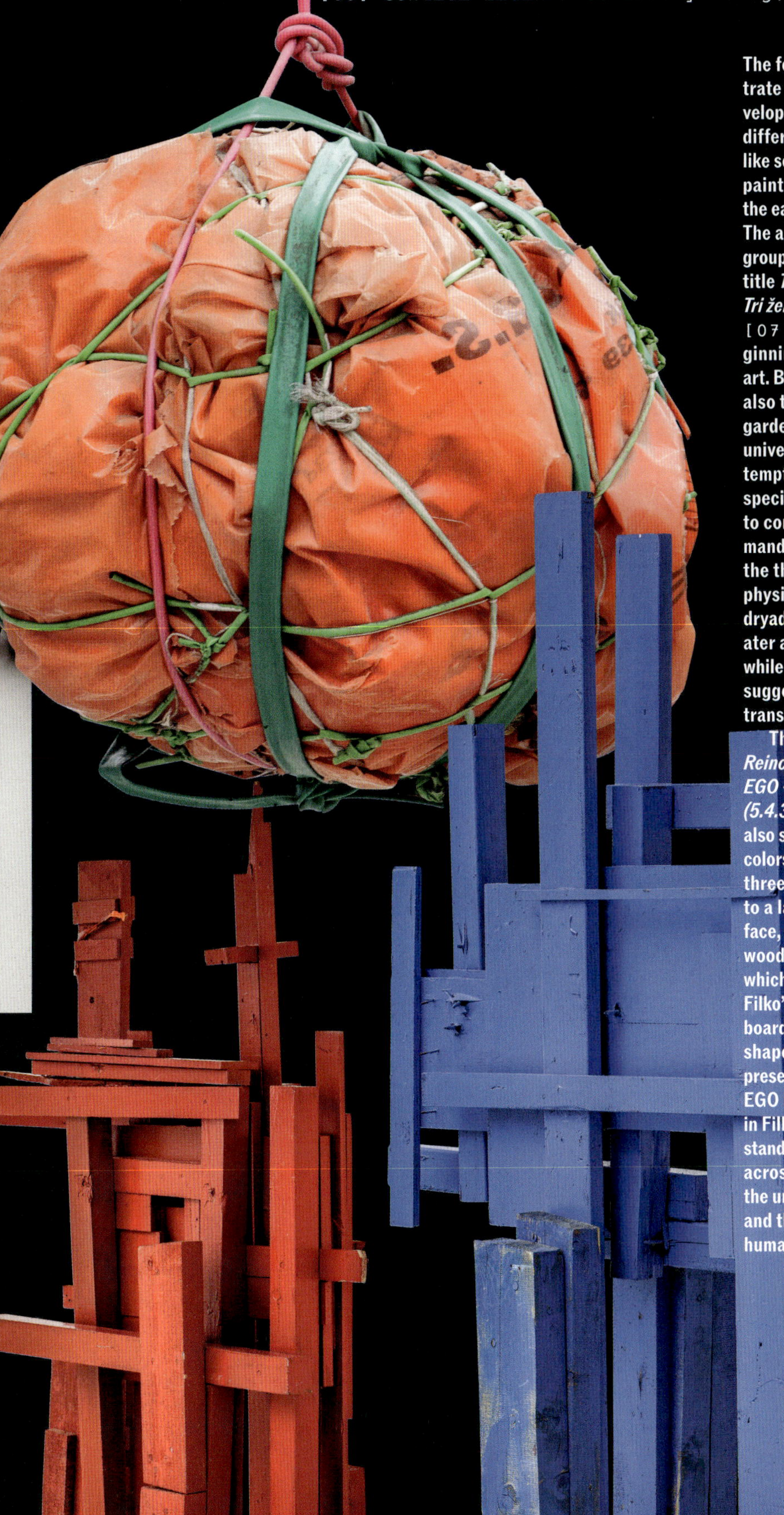

The following artworks illustrate the progress in developing the *System SF* and its differentiations. Three grid-like sculptures made of painted wooden planks recall the early three-color system. The abstract expression of this group with the figurative title *Three Women (3.4.5.D.) / Tri ženy (3.4.5.D.)* (c. 1995) [07] recalls the cubist beginnings of abstract art. Both Filko's *System SF* and also the modernist avant-gardes have claims to universality, and here Filko attempts to make these very specific spatially and to connect them with the demands of reality. Finally the three women's abstract physical nature like a dryadic ballet also recalls theater and performance, while the ground-level rollers suggest movements and transformation.

The work *EGO – Gemini – Reincarnation (5.4.3.D.) / EGO – Blíženci – Reinkarnácia (5.4.3.D.)* (c. 1995) [04] also shows the three original colors of the system. The three colors are each applied to a large wooden surface, with intermediate smaller wooden boards in black, which is the color of the ego in Filko's system. These painted boards include cut out shapes that form a rough representation of the letters EGO in reverse order. The ego in Filko's artistic system stands as a backdrop or pattern across the dimensions, as the unfolding of the self and the basis of the world of human experience.

An den folgenden Kunstwerken lassen sich die voranschreitende Entwicklung des *System SF* und seine Ausdifferenzierung beobachten. Dabei knüpfen drei rasterartige Skulpturen aus farbigen Holzbalken an das anfänglich dreifarbige System an. Der abstrakte Ausdruck der Gruppe wird mit dem figurativen Titel *Three Women (3.4.5.D.) / Tri ženy (3.4.5.D.)* (ca. 1995) [07] verbunden und erinnert dadurch an die kubistischen Anfänge der Abstraktion. Sowohl Filkos *System SF* als auch die modernistischen Avantgarden treten mit einem universellen Anspruch auf, den Filko hier versucht, räumlich zu konkretisieren und mit den Ansprüchen der Realität in Verbindung zu bringen. Schließlich lassen die drei Damen in ihrer abstrahierten Körperlichkeit ähnlich einem driadischen Ballett an Theatralität und Performativität denken, auch durch die bodennahen Lenkrollen wird Bewegung und Veränderbarkeit betont.

Die Arbeit *EGO – Gemini – Reincarnation (5.4.3.D.) / EGO – Blíženci – Reinkarnácia (5.4.3.D.)* (ca. 1995) [04] zeigt ebenfalls die drei ursprünglichen Farben des Systems. Die drei Farben sind auf jeweils einer größeren Holzfläche aufgebracht, dazwischen kleinere Holzplatten in schwarz, in Filkos System die Farbe des Egos. Die bemalten Platten sind mit Durchlässen versehen und bilden eine grobe Buchstabenfolge: EGO in verkehrter Leserichtung. Das Ego liegt in Filkos künstlerischem System als Hintergrundfolie bzw. Raster quer zu den Dimensionen, als Ausfaltung des Selbst und Grundlage der menschlichen Erfahrungswelt.

←[07A–C] *Three Women (3.4.5.D.) / Tri ženy (3.4.5.D.)*, c. 1995

There are also several objects from the seven-chakra phase of this system. The sculpture *Wardrobe in the 7 Chakra Colors / Skriňa vo farbách 7 čakier* (c. 1995) [09] appears as a highly concentrated block. The object is painted in rough stripes in the seven colors, with the upside-down drips giving it a dynamic quality that is further emphasized by the rollers on the bottom and top. The original function of the wardrobe as a piece of furniture for storing clothes and everyday objects also indicates the archiving function of *System SF*, which Filko used to categorize his work. The colors also structure the rooms of his studio, which he himself often referred to as a store.

Hier sind einige Objekte aus der Phase des siebenstufigen Chakrensystems zu sehen. Die Skulptur *Wardrobe in the 7 Chakra Colors / Skriňa vo farbách 7 čakier* (ca. 1995) [09] wirkt durch ihre Blockstruktur stark konzentriert. In den sieben Farben überziehen grob gemalte Streifen das Objekt und dynamisieren es gleichzeitig durch den umgekehrten Farbspurenverlauf, was sich durch die Lenkrollen an Unter- und Oberseite weiter verstärkt. Die ursprüngliche Funktion des Schrankes als Möbel zur Aufbewahrung von Kleidung und alltäglichen Dingen verweist auf die Archivfunktion des *System SF*. Das System wurde von Filko zur Kategorisierung seines Werkes herangezogen, wobei die Farben auch die Räume seines Studios untergliedern, welches er selbst gerne als Lager bezeichnete.

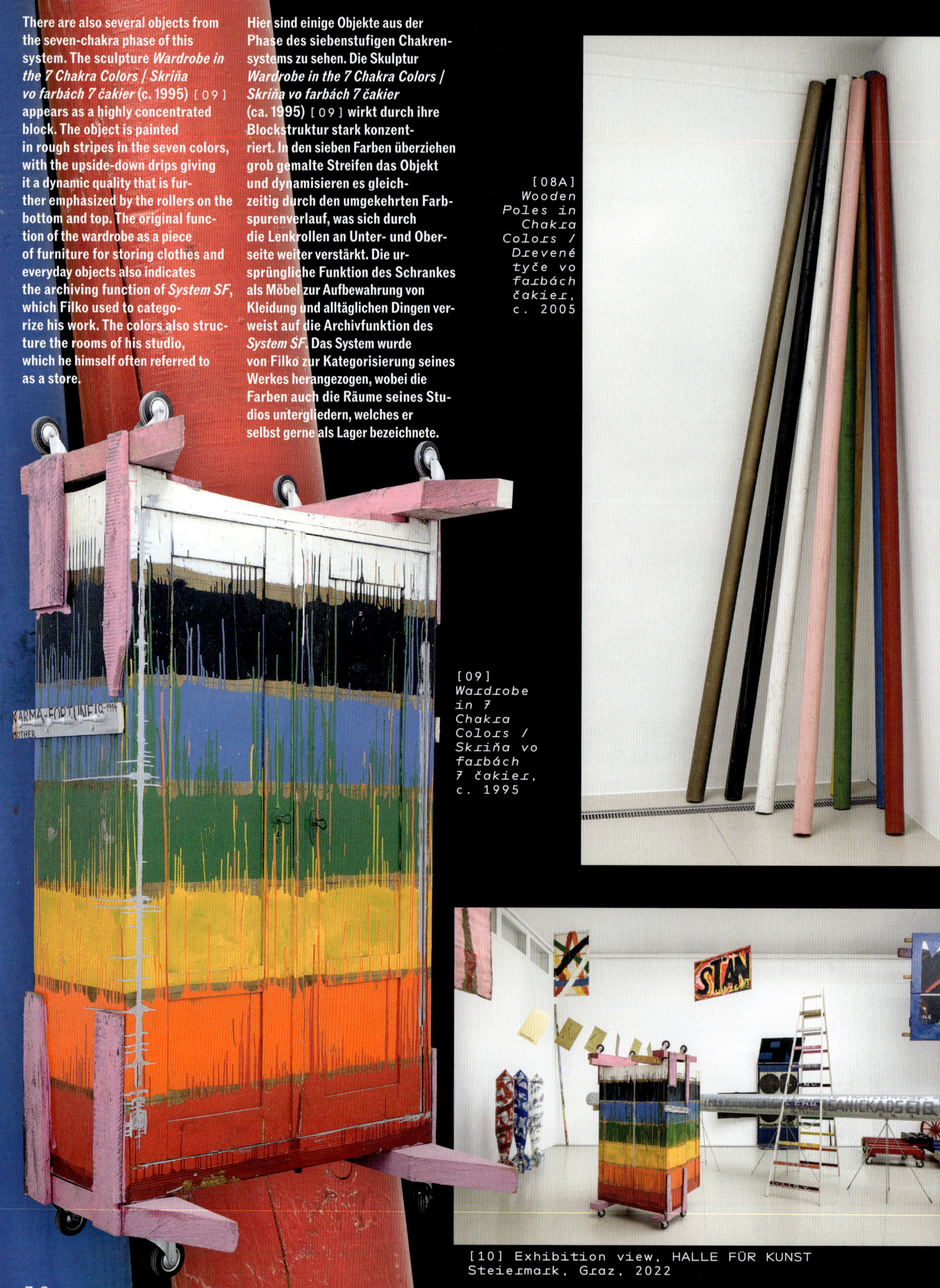

[08A]
Wooden Poles in Chakra Colors / Drevené tyče vo farbách čakier, c. 2005

[09]
Wardrobe in 7 Chakra Colors / Skriňa vo farbách 7 čakier, c. 1995

[10] Exhibition view, HALLE FÜR KUNST Steiermark, Graz, 2022

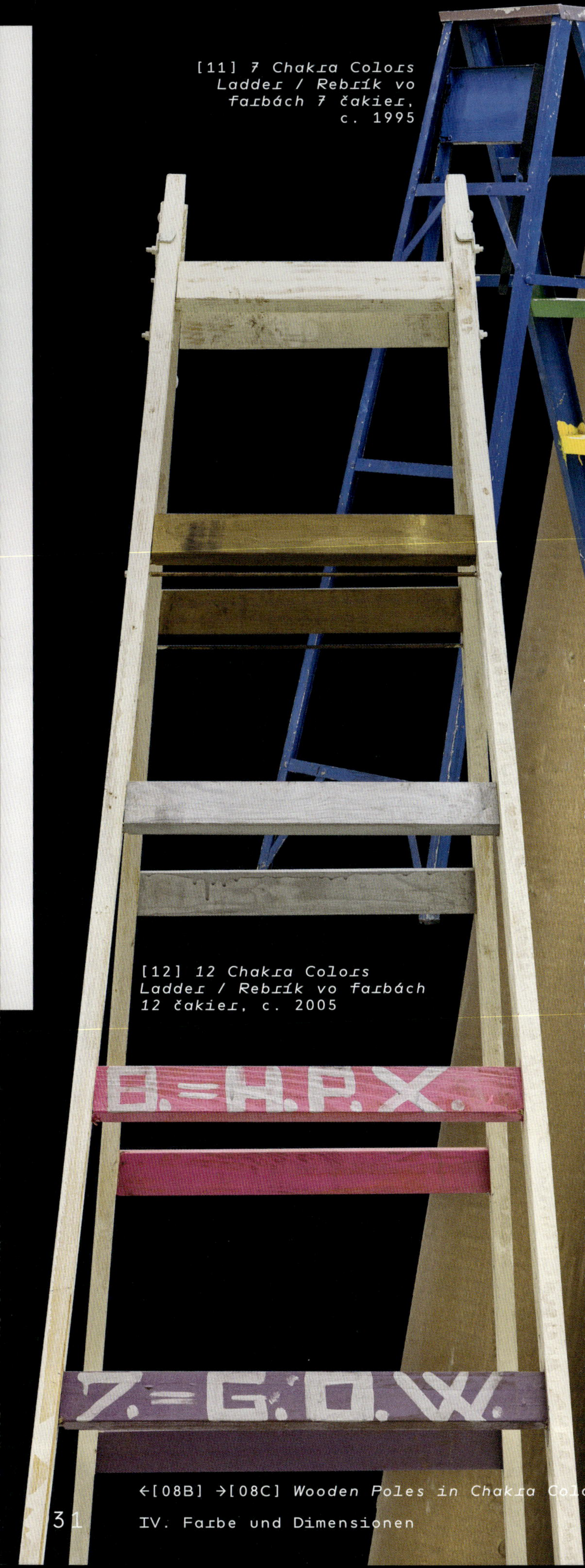

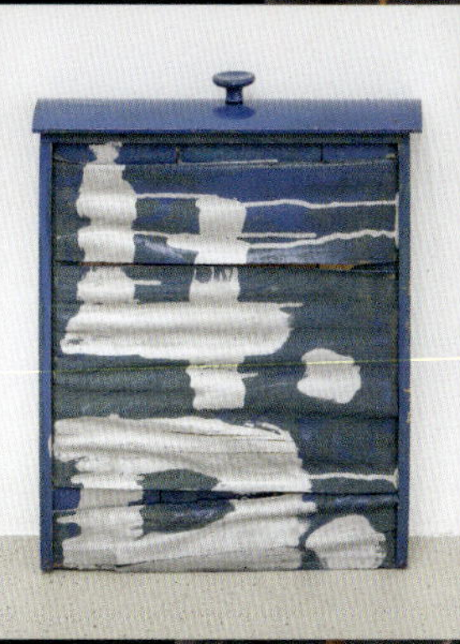

This storage and orientation function of the system is also continued with several drawers and boxes painted with colorful characters, spread around the room and demonstrating the system's basic colors and dimensions. [13]

The two sculptural ladders *7 Chakra Colors Ladder / Rebrík vo farbách 7 čakier* (c. 1995) [11] and *12 Chakra Ladders / 12 Chakra Colors Ladder / Rebrík vo farbách 12 čakier* (c. 2005) [12] were originally part of Filko's studio. By linking rungs of the ladders with colors, Filko accorded each color's chakra a firm place in the system. At the same time the symbol of the triangle or the pyramid associated with the ladders represents an idealized form of the universe in Filko's cosmic worldview. The colored rungs integrate invisible space by means of the spaces between them and they also raise *System SF* onto a cosmic and conceptual level.

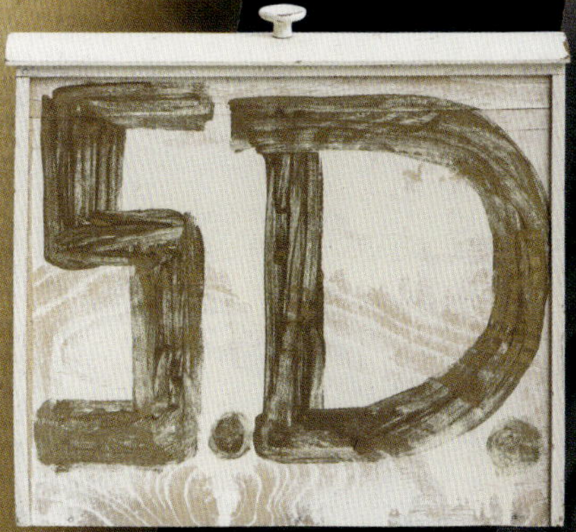

The color axes of the system spread horizontally through the rooms, in the form of painted wooden sticks leaning on the walls, transforming the whole space into a field of different forces. [08]

Die Lager- und Orientierungsfunktion des Systems wird außerdem durch mehrere mit farbigen Schriftzeichen bemalte Schubladen und Kisten weitergeführt, die sich durch den Raum verteilen und die Grundfarben und Dimensionen zeigen. [13]

Die zwei skulpturalen Leitern *7 Chakra Colors Ladder / Rebrík vo farbách 7 čakier* (ca. 1995) [11] und *12 Chakra Ladders / 12 Chakra Colors Ladder / Rebrík vo farbách 12 čakier* (ca. 2005) [12] waren ursprünglich Teil von Filkos Studio. Indem Filko die Farben mit den Sprossen der Leitern verbindet, weist er jeder Farbe bzw. dessen Chakra einen festen Platz im System zu. Gleichzeitig stellt das mit den Leitern verbundene Symbol des Dreiecks bzw. der Pyramide in Filkos kosmischer Weltsicht eine idealisierte Form des Universums dar. Die farblichen Sprossen integrieren durch die Lücken zwischen den Ebenen den unsichtbaren Raum und heben das *System SF* gleichzeitig in einen kosmischen, konzeptuellen Zusammenhang.

Die farblichen Achsen des Systems breiten sich zudem quer durch die Räume aus, in der Form von bemalten Holzstäben, die an den Wänden lehnen und diese in ein Feld aus verschiedenen Kräften verwandeln. [08]

Stano Filko – An Interview

Hans Ulrich Obrist

Hans Ulrich Obrist (HUO) together with the artists Roman Ondák (RO) and Koo Jeong A visited Stano Filko (SF) in his studio Snežienková in Bratislava in June 2005.[1]

HUO Stano, is this your studio? [01–24]
SF This is my deposit! It contains works from the 1950s, 60s, 70s, 80s and 90s, and current works. My work is *HAPPSOC*, it is an Anti-happening, Anti-Fluxus and Anti-performance. It is a place for contemplating the action, a Proto-*HAPPSOC* in five editions. *HAPPSOC I.* (1965) is a genius loci and my birthplace. *HAPPSOC I.* is Bratislava and Trenčín, a city in Slovakia, in Czechoslovakia, in Europe. *HAPPSOC II.* (1965) is a contemplation action on women and anorganic organics, on being and revolutionary evolution—like transplantation and clones.
HUO We were talking about Schwitters and the *Merzbau* earlier. Would you describe this place as a "Gesamtkunstwerk?"
SF Yes, since the *HAPPSOC* (1965–67) spreads through five parts. Each part deals with a different subject, but these problems deal simultaneously throughout all of them: Hybrids, chimeras and hydras, sphinxes from the historical times until now.
HUO Why are you calling it a depository and not a studio?
SF Because there are more old artworks than contemporary ones here. The contemporary things are here as well, but they are in minority. There are several rooms that are divided into separate areas. I have been producing for 50 years. It's the whole of history until now. When I come here, it's about going into the past.
HUO And do you have another studio for the present?
SF I spend a minority of my time in the present, and a majority in the past.
HUO Can you please give us a tour of these zones?
SF Yes, of course, just follow me. My work is based on an alphabetical and numerical order. There are seven colors for the codes, as you can see on this ladder: red, orange, yellow, green, blue, black and white. The rooms as well as all *HAPPSOC*s are distinguished by these colors. It also works in absolute dimensions, everything takes place in the third, fourth and fifth dimension.

   I'll show you this sound sculpture to demonstrate how to cross these dimensions. This is like when a human rein-carnates. One goes from the fifth dimension (absolute, intelligence, soul, love, total) through EGO—black, then one continues through the fourth dimension (universe or more like cosmo-universes), and arrives to the third dimension (symbol, sign, quotation), to end up as a born person on the earth.
HUO Please tell me more about the colors. Are they multidimensional?
SF Yes, it starts with red for the East, orange for the South, yellow for the West and green is the North. All these are symbols, like the Egyptians had. When you sit in the one place, it all comes together at that point. That's why there is a pyramid on the cover of my catalog.[2] This next one uses symbols from Leonardo's last supper.
HUO As far as I can see the whole place is a multi-dimensional construction of many dimensions. The whole life, you have been working on assemblages!
SF Yes. I have been working on these kinds of assemblages since the 1950s, and I have regularly remade some of them. Sit down here! My work comes from a pyramid which has been calculated for this region. It is of slightly different measures than the Egyptian one because we are in a different country. When you are sitting here, you are receiving the energy from the universe.
HUO So, I should ask for a permission to sit down there as well, I suppose.
SF Yes. I have a big pyramid as well. It is as big as this yard, even bigger, it is of four meters.
HUO Incredible, I am very impressed.
SF I made this as a television set. It is from times when the TV emerged and became widely available on the market. This is my geometric work referring to seven chakras. I have a work called *Introvert* (1957/1987), and one called *Extrovert* (1957/1987). This is the *Extrovert*. This work is both extroverted as well as introverted. That one is about my reincarnation, though also about my biography.
HUO So you also have multi-identities?
SF Yes. This one is for 2037. I'll be hundred years out of then. I'll carry on until then and then I am going to die. I will be finished with art, not with life.

   I have changed my identity several times and call it clones. I have not made a multiple out of myself, only cloned/altered it. I have cloned my name four times, now I'm "Phys."

Stano Filko – Ein Interview

Hans Ulrich Obrist

Gemeinsam mit den Künstlern Roman Ondák (RO) und Koo Jeong A besuchte Hans Ulrich Obrist (HUO) im Juni 2005 Stano Filko (SF) in seinem Atelier Snežienková in Bratislava.[1]

HUO Stano, ist das dein Atelier? [0 1 – 2 4]

SF Das ist mein Depot! Es enthält Werke aus den 1950er-, 60er-, 70er-, 80er- und 90er-Jahren, sowie aktuelle Arbeiten. Meine Arbeit nenne ich *HAPPSOC*, das steht für Anti-Happening, Anti-Fluxus und Anti-Performance. Es ist ein Ort der Kontemplation, der Aktion, ein Proto-*HAPPSOC* in fünf Ausgaben. *HAPPSOC I.* (1965) ist ein Genius Loci und mein Geburtsort. *HAPPSOC I.* ist Bratislava und Trenčín, eine Stadt in der Slowakei, in der Tschechoslowakei, in Europa. *HAPPSOC II.* (1965) ist eine Reflexionsübung über Frauen und anorganische Organik, über das Sein und die revolutionäre Evolution, wie Transplantation und Klone.

HUO Wir haben vorhin über Schwitters und den *Merzbau* gesprochen. Würdest Du diesen Ort als ein „Gesamtkunstwerk" bezeichnen?

SF Ja, denn *HAPPSOC* (1965–1967) erstreckt sich über fünf Teile. Jeder Teil befasst sich mit einem anderen Thema, aber Fragestellungen nach Hybriden, Chimären und Hydras, Sphinxen aus vergangenen Zeiten bis ins Heute ziehen sich gleichzeitig durch alle Teile.

HUO Warum nennst du es Depot und nicht Atelier?

SF Weil es hier mehr historische als zeitgenössische Kunstwerke gibt. Die zeitgenössischen Werke lagern zwar auch hier, aber sie sind in der Minderheit. Es gibt mehrere Räume, die in verschiedene Bereiche unterteilt sind. Ich produziere nun schon seit 50 Jahren. Hier liegt mein gesamtes historisches Werk bis heute. Wenn ich hierher komme, dann um zurück in die Vergangenheit zu schauen.

HUO Hast du auch ein anderes Studio für die Gegenwart?

SF Ich verbringe einen kleinen Teil meiner Zeit in der Gegenwart, und den Großteil in der Vergangenheit.

HUO Kannst du uns bitte einen Rundgang durch die Räume geben?

SF Ja natürlich, folgt mir einfach. Meine Arbeit basiert auf einer alphabetischen und numerischen Ordnung. Es gibt sieben Farben für die Codes, wie man auf dieser Leiter sehen kann: Rot, Orange, Gelb, Grün, Blau, Schwarz und Weiß. Sowohl die Räume als auch alle Teile von *HAPPSOC* sind durch diese Farben gekennzeichnet. Das funktioniert auch in absoluten Dimensionen, alles spielt sich in der 3., 4. und 5. Dimension ab.

Ich werde euch diese Klangskulptur zeigen, um zu demonstrieren wie man die Dimensionen durchquert. Das ist so, wie wenn ein Mensch reinkarniert. Man geht von der 5. Dimension (Absolutheit, Intelligenz, Seele, Liebe, Totalität) durch EGO-Schwarz, dann geht man weiter durch die 4. Dimension (Universum oder eher Kosmo-Universen) und kommt in der 3. Dimension an (Symbol, Zeichen, Zitat), um als wiedergeborener Mensch auf der Erde zu landen.

HUO Bitte erzähle mir mehr über die Farben. Sind sie multidimensional?

SF Ja, es beginnt mit Rot für den Osten, dann Orange für den Süden, Gelb für den Westen und Grün für den Norden. All dies sind Symbole, wie sie schon die Ägypter hatten. Wenn man an dem einen Ort sitzt, kommt alles an diesem Punkt zusammen. Deshalb ist auf dem Cover meines Katalogs[2] eine Pyramide abgebildet. Das nächste Bild verwendet Symbole aus Leonardos letztem Abendmahl.

HUO Soweit ich es sehen kann ist der ganze Ort eine multidimensionale Konstruktion mit vielen Dimensionen. Du hast dein ganzes Leben lang an Assemblagen gearbeitet!

SF Ja, ich arbeite seit den 1950er-Jahren an dieser Art von Assemblagen und habe einige von ihnen immer wieder neu gestaltet. Setz dich hierher! Meine Arbeiten verweisen auf eine Pyramide, die für diese Region geplant wurde. Sie hat etwas andere Maße als die ägyptische, weil wir uns in einem anderen Land befinden. Wenn du hier sitzt, empfängst du die Energie des Universums.

HUO Ich sollte also um Erlaubnis bitten, mich auch da hinsetzen zu können, nehme ich an.

SF Ja. Ich habe auch eine große Pyramide produziert. Sie ist so geräumig wie dieser Hof, sogar noch breiter, sie ist vier Meter hoch.

HUO Unglaublich, ich bin sehr beeindruckt.

SF Das hier habe ich als Fernsehgerät konzipiert. Es stammt aus der Zeit, als das Fernsehen aufkam und sich auf dem Markt durchsetzte. Und dies ist eine geometrische Arbeit, die sich auf die sieben Chakren bezieht. Ich habe eine Arbeit, die *Introvert* (1957/1987) heißt, und eine, die *Extrovert* (1957/1987) heißt. Das hier ist *Extrovert*, die Arbeit ist sowohl extrovertiert als

HUO Let's go into the second zone. Do you consider these as separate works or as part of the whole environment?

SF This is the second room on women, *HAPPSOC II*. Any piece could be separated from the rest. You can also create new combinations from these things. These ones have been here for over fifty years. I have been producing environments and installations since I was five years old. These are my earliest pieces, my beginnings in 1953.

HUO What is your relationship with science? Do you actually not distinguish science and art?

SF I see the artist as a scientific researcher. I interconnect art and science. Artists and scientists are both researchers for me. My relationship to science is fantastic.

HUO The link goes through the research. The scientist produces knowledge. So, what is your product? Does this extend to the production of knowledge?

SF It's about searching for light in the dark.

HUO And have you had dialogs with scientists?

SF I used to collaborate with scientists—with mathematicians and physicists. We used to discuss a lot, and my work was very much inspired by this at that time. That was during the 1960s.

I was born in 1937 and in 1945 I experienced my first clinical death. I fell into an open stone pit five meters deep. At that moment, I had my first post-modern thought—from somewhere in between my subconscious and my conscious I realized that it was very much about the ironic identification of mystification.

HUO At the age of eight?

SF Even before, because I was working with my grandfather. He was a philosopher, and he translated Thomas Aquinas. I used to talk and work with him. My Post-Modernism, after the first clinical death, is the creativity, it's my nature. And then in 1952, I experienced another clinical death. I touched a life wire on a crane. I was 15 at the time. The second clinical death initiated a sort of "B Creativity"—Post-Avant-garde—, which is something like a science-technical intelligence.

HUO And where do you see the role of the artist in this complex interdisciplinary approach?

SF An artist is a being in the third, fourth and fifth dimension.

HUO That is the definition of the artist?

SF It is a structure. I have to have a structure. I work intuitively as well as intellectually because I am born under the Gemini star sign, a complexity of philosophical approaches.

HUO You started out with drawings and paintings, but language also featured from a very early stage. Could you tell me about this?

SF I started as a graphic artist, but my interest was psycho-philosophical. I introduced the "psycho" into visual and I was inputting the philosophy by words, through texts. I titled it "verbal Text-art." I work simultaneously in both media. I produce visual works as well as Text-arts. I have more than a 1,000 pages of these texts.

HUO I'm interested in this idea of the accumulation of everything. It's not unlike Steven Wolfram who recently published an encyclopedic book *A New Kind of Science*.[3] Could you tell me about your early performance in which you declared that everything was happening between one day and seven days later?

SF It was a collective work by Zita Kostrová, Alex Mlynárčik and me, called *HAPPSOC*. It was a week-long piece between the first and ninth of May, 1965, referring to the celebration of the working day (May 1) and the military parade to remember the end of World War II (May 9). I persuaded them to use "seven days" referring to seven days of creation, seven chakras, seven days of a week. But it might also exist in different time and space.

HUO Do you know approximately how many works you have made in your encyclopaedic career?

SF Perhaps ten thousand.

HUO So you produce several works every day?

SF Yes, I make several pieces every day, and during the 1960s I was even doing this in a factory. Particularly those in the catalog,[4] they were produced in such way. Those pieces represent the moment when the post-modern turns into the post-avant-garde. When the *natural* turns into the *techno-intelligence*.

HUO I am interested in unrealized projects. Can you point out one of your favorite ones?

SF I have very many of those. They are in the catalog[5] as well. For instance, one project was *Way, Flight of Cosmonauts to the Moon in Stages and their Return to the Earth I. – XV. – Prospectart (+ 5 loudspeakers)* (1968–69).

HUO Was it conceived before the voyage actually happened?

SF The work was done before, and was quite utopian. Then I remade it with real photos from the moon landing. The work was buried in the ground, under the pavement and loud-speakers were placed around, from which information about what had happened was broadcasted. Another related project was about men living on Mars and women living on Venus, and about them meeting. Men came from Mars to Venus on a rocket billions of years ago. Prior to those men cloned themselves on Mars and women on Venus. They were lesbians and gays. When they met, they started to copulate and to reproduce. To avoid a dispute over the territory they moved to the earth.

HUO How do you feel about the notion of utopia? Do you think it's a useful term for considering your work?

SF Utopia is a psycho-philosophical reality for me.

HUO Is it a concrete utopia?

SF Yes, it is a vision as well as a utopia. The visions are more concrete, and those I realize.

HUO I noticed that there is one more room with a bed in. Is that your bedroom?

SF Come and have a look at it, it is a sort of a library. This is a book about *HAPPSOC II.*, including fragments of the project. Every book has a picture within, which you can hang or store. It was done within the next, the later post-modern period of mine from 1979 to 1983. Here are other fragments.

HUO Do you know John Latham?

SF No. Why?

HUO He also worked a lot on the fourth and fifth dimension.

SF This part is an extension, all about *The Old and New Testament* (c. 1995). Not as a synthesis but an extract, an essential of *The Old and New Testament*.

HUO We have spoken about philosophy and science, but religion also clearly plays a role in your work and life. This room is almost like a chapel!

SF I extract the essence from various religious doctrines. And here we can see such an extract of the essence in these

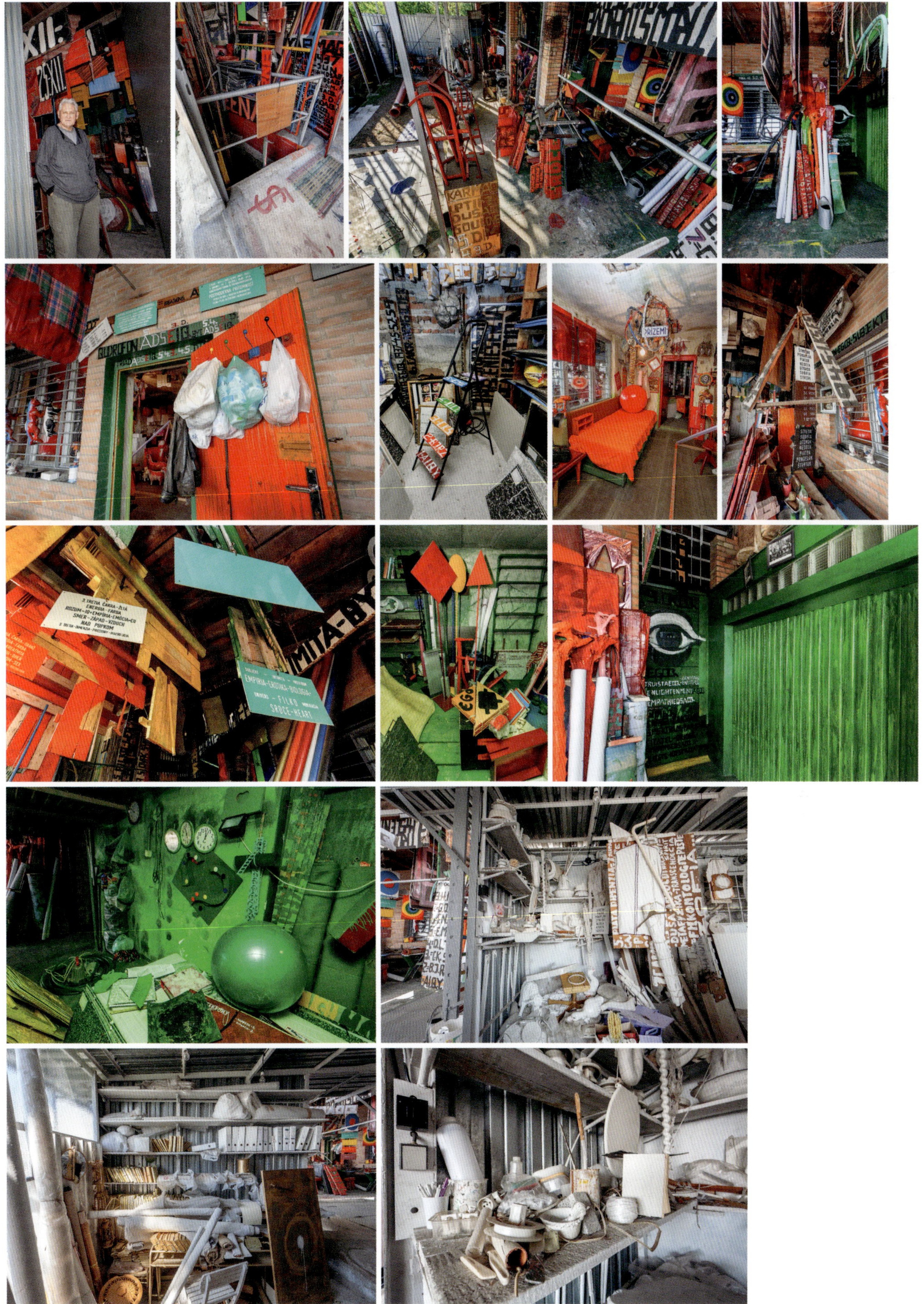

[01-15] Artist's studio Snežienková / Umelcov ateliér Snežienková, 2007,
photographed by Pato Safko

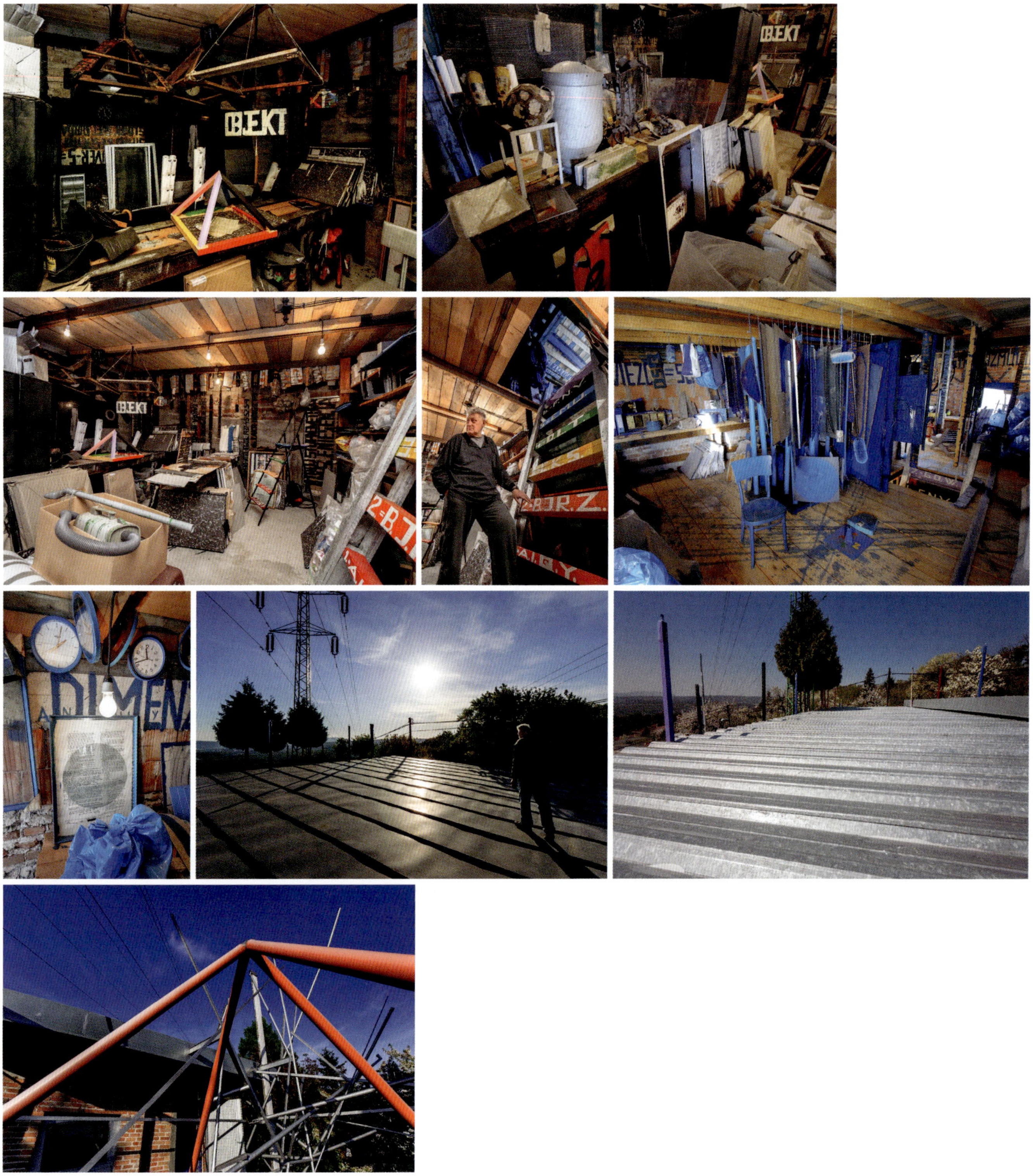

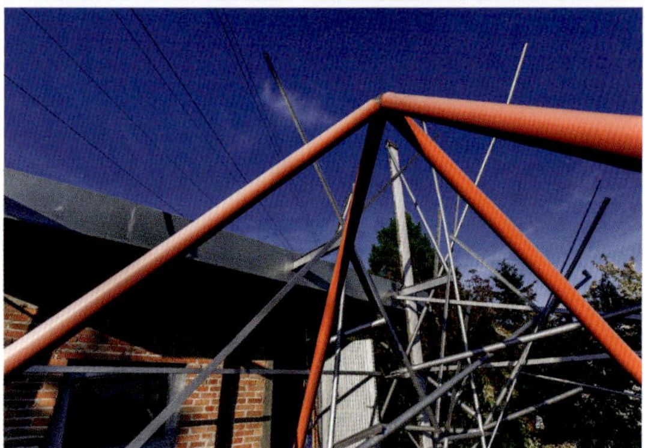

[16–24] Artist's studio Snežienková / Umelcov ateliér Snežienková, 2007,
photographed by Pato Safko

auch introvertiert. In dieser anderen Arbeit geht es um meine Reinkarnation, zugleich aber auch um meine Biografie.

HUO   Du hast also auch mehrere Identitäten?

SF   Ja. Diese hier steht für das Jahr 2037, ich werde dann hundert Jahre alt sein. Ich werde bis dahin weitermachen, und dann werde ich sterben. Dann werde ich mit der Kunst fertig sein, nicht mit dem Leben.

Auch habe ich mehrmals meine Identität gewechselt und nenne diese Klone. Ich habe kein Multiple aus mir gemacht, mich nur geklont, also verändert. Bislang habe ich meinen Namen viermal geklont, aktuell heiße ich „Phys".

HUO   Lass uns in den zweiten Raum gehen. Betrachtest du diese Werke hier als eigenständig oder als Teil der gesamten Anordnung?

SF   Das ist der zweite Raum über Frauen, *HAPPSOC II*. Jedes Stück könnte von den anderen getrennt gezeigt werden, es lassen sich auch neue Kombinationen aus diesen Objekten zusammenstellen. Einige dieser Arbeiten sind schon seit über fünfzig Jahren hier. Ich produziere Environments und Installationen, seit ich fünf Jahre alt bin. Das sind meine frühesten Arbeiten, meine Anfänge gehen auf das Jahr 1953 zurück.

HUO   Wie ist dein Verhältnis zur Wissenschaft? Unterscheidest du eigentlich zwischen Wissenschaft und Kunst?

SF   Ich sehe die Künstler*innen als wissenschaftliche Forscher*innen. Insofern verbinde ich Kunst und Wissenschaft miteinander. Künstler*innen und Wissenschaftler*innen sind für mich beides Forscher*innen. Meine Beziehung zur Wissenschaft ist eine fantastische.

HUO   Die Verbindung zwischen Wissenschaft und Kunst geht über die Forschung. Die Wissenschaftler*innen produzieren Wissen. Was ist dein Produkt? Beziehst du dich auch auf die Produktion von Wissen?

SF   Es geht darum, Licht in der Dunkelheit zu suchen.

HUO   Und hast du Dialoge mit Wissenschaftler*innen geführt?

SF   Ich habe früher mit Wissenschaftler*innen zusammengearbeitet – mit Mathematiker*innen und Physiker*innen. Wir haben viel diskutiert, und meine Arbeit wurde damals sehr stark davon inspiriert, das war in den 1960er-Jahren.

Ich wurde 1937 geboren und erlebte 1945 meinen ersten klinischen Tod. Ich stürzte in eine fünf Meter tiefe, offene Steingrube. In diesem Moment hatte ich meinen ersten postmodernen Gedanken: Irgendwo zwischen meinem Unterbewusstsein und meinem Bewusstsein erkannte ich, dass es dabei um ein ironisches Erkennen von Verwirrspielen ging.

HUO   Im Alter von acht Jahren?

SF   Sogar noch früher, denn ich habe viel von meinem Großvater gelernt. Er war ein Philosoph und übersetzte Thomas von Aquin. Ich habe oft mit ihm gesprochen und wir haben zusammengearbeitet. Nach meinem ersten klinischen Tod beginnt für mich die Postmoderne, die damit verbundene Kreativität ist meine Natur. Und dann, 1952, erlebte ich einen weiteren klinischen Tod. Ich berührte ein Starkstromkabel an einem Kran, damals war ich 15 Jahre alt. Der zweite klinische Tod löste eine Art „B Kreativität" aus, eine Post-Avantgarde, die so etwas wie eine wissenschaftlich-technische Intelligenz ist.

HUO   Und wo siehst du die Rolle der Künstler*innen in diesem komplexen interdisziplinären Ansatz?

SF   Künstler*innen sind Wesen der 3., 4. und 5. Dimension.

HUO   Das ist die Definition von Künstler*innen?

SF   Es geht um eine Struktur. Ich muss einer Struktur folgen. Ich arbeite sowohl intuitiv als auch intellektuell, weil ich im Sternzeichen Zwilling („Gemini") geboren bin und es mit einer komplexen Konstellation von philosophischen Ansätzen zu tun habe.

HUO   Du hast mit Zeichnung und Malerei begonnen, aber auch die Sprache spielte schon sehr früh eine wesentliche Rolle. Kannst du mir mehr davon erzählen?

SF   Ich habe als Grafiker angefangen, wobei mein Interesse ein psycho-philosophisches war. Ich führte das Psychische ins Visuelle ein und brachte die Philosophie durch Worte und Texte ein. Ich nenne es „verbale Text-Kunst". Ich arbeite gleichzeitig in beiden Medien, und produziere sowohl visuelle Werke als auch Text-Kunst. Ich habe mehr als 1.000 Seiten an Text-Kunst produziert.

HUO   Ich interessiere mich für die Idee der alles umfassenden Akkumulation. Das ist nicht unähnlich zu Steven Wolfram, der kürzlich ein enzyklopädisches Buch *A New Kind of Science*[3] veröffentlicht hat. Kannst du mir von deiner frühen Performance erzählen, in der du erklärt hast, was alles im Zeitraum von einem und sieben Tagen passiert ist?

SF   Es war eine kollektive Arbeit von Zita Kostrová, Alex Mlynárčik und mir, genannt *HAPPSOC*. Es war ein einwöchiges Werk zwischen dem 1. und 9. Mai 1965 und bezog sich auf die Feier des Tages der Arbeit am 1. Mai und die Militärparade zur Erinnerung an das Ende des Zweiten Weltkriegs am 9. Mai. Ich habe meine Kolleg*innen überredet, die Bezeichnung „sieben Tage" zu verwenden, was sich auf die sieben Tage der Schöpfung, die sieben Chakren, die sieben Tage einer Woche bezieht. Aber die Arbeit könnte auch zu einer anderen Zeit und an einem anderen Ort existieren.

HUO   Weißt du ungefähr, wie viele Werke du in deiner enzyklopädischen Karriere gemacht hast?

SF   Vielleicht zehntausend Arbeiten.

HUO   Also produzierst du jeden Tag mehrere Werke?

SF   Ja, ich realisiere jeden Tag mehrere Werke, und in den 1960er-Jahren habe ich das sogar in einer Fabrik gemacht. Vor allem die im Katalog[4] abgebildeten Werke wurden auf diese Weise hergestellt. Diese Arbeiten repräsentieren den Moment, in dem die Postmoderne in die Postavantgarde übergeht: Wenn das *Natürliche* sich in *Techno-Intelligenz* verwandelt.

HUO   Ich interessiere mich für nicht realisierte Projekte. Kannst du mir eines deiner Lieblingsprojekte nennen?

SF   Ich habe sehr viele unrealisierte Arbeiten, sie befinden sich teils auch in diesem Katalog[5]. Ein Projekt war zum Beispiel *Way, Flight of Cosmonauts to the Moon in Stages and their Return to the Earth I. – XV. – Prospectart (+ 5 loudspeakers)* (1968–1969).

HUO   Wurde das Projekt geplant, bevor die Reise tatsächlich stattfand?

SF   Die Arbeit wurde vorher konzipiert und war ziemlich utopisch. Später habe ich sie mit echten Fotos von der Mondlandung neu gestaltet. Die Arbeit wurde im Boden unter dem Pflaster vergraben und es wurden Lautsprecher aufgestellt, über die Informationen über die Geschehnisse ausgestrahlt wurden. In einem anderen Projekt ging es um auf dem Mars lebende Männer und auf der Venus lebende Frauen, und darum, wie sie sich schließlich trafen. Die Männer kamen vor Milliarden von Jahren mit einer Rakete vom Mars zur Venus. Davor klonten sich Männer auf dem Mars und Frauen auf

altars. These are fragments from the installation *Altars of Contemporaneity* (1963–66). There were mirrors on the floor, which one could walk on and in which the spectators can see themselves. It is all connected to the present. I have been collecting images referring to it for several years.

HUO Do you have an assistant? How do you find time to organize all of this material?

SF I have never had an assistant, I could not afford one. Here are binders containing works from the 1950s and 1960s. Here are projects and drawings.

RO Do you also sleep here?

SF I don't live here but I take a nap here occasionally. Or someone else can. Here and there.

HUO Could you tell me about the role of drawing in your practice?

SF My drawings are also my projects. I don't do regular drawing. Even when I was doing figural drawings, I meant it as a project. All the projects start out as drawings with the hope that they will be realized. One piece is called *Map of the World (Women)* (1967), so here are some drawings of women. That piece was from the end of the 1950s and the beginning of the 1960s.

HUO It's an amazing display. The density reminds me of the Sir John Soane's Museum in London.

SF Some of the drawings and final pieces are in museum collections. The Slovak National Gallery has some of them as well as other collectors.

HUO This section here seems to be a kind of retrospective based on the EGO.

SF Yes. These works are about the EGO—the third eye. And this Ego gives a structure to my whole life. Here are works from the 1950s, 60s, 70s, 80s, 90s. It all comes together here.
   Come on upstairs, to the fourth dimension.

HUO So the fourth dimension is blue!

SF It is the fourth dimension and more cosmo-universe. Here is also a chronology from the 1950s to the 1990s.

HUO A retrospective again.

SF The total blue…

HUO This piece includes the view on Bratislava. We have a different view than this morning.

SF This is the third, fourth, fifth dimension (pointing at the power line structure outside).

HUO This is energy and it runs right the way through!

SF It is the energy.
   Here are those seven trees. This is a project which you can find in the catalog.[6] I conceived it in the 1960s and realized it here. This is a typical post avant-garde work. Not post-modern, but post avant-garde. It is a sort of a gate, you see, this is the psycho-techno intelligence.

HUO So now we are in the heartland of the psycho-techno intelligence?

SF Yes. And it incorporates the whole universe. It is the "B creativity," post-modern, creation. This blue room is only the universe, the fourth dimension. The fifth dimension is above the universe.

to the *System SF*. The system was based on dimensions and a seven color structure by then and was extended to twelve, finally to twenty, in the last years of Filko's life.
   This extented version follows the structure of the first printed text in *Spike* 07/2006. It is based on a literal transcript of the interview by Štefan Cebo and Lucia Gregorová Stach, Slovak National Gallery, and a direct transcript by Miroslava Urbanová and Tobias Ihl, HALLE FÜR KUNST Steiermark. Further help by Jan Tappe and Helga Droschl. Final version by Sandro Droschl, with a feedback by Hans Ulrich Obrist.

2   *Stano FILKO II. 1965–69. Tvorba / Works – Creation / Werk – Schaffung / Ouvrages*, ed. Stano Filko (Bratislava, 1970).
3   Steven Wolfram, *A New Kind of Science*, Champaign / Illinois, 2002/2022.
4   Ibid.
5   Ibid.
6   Ibid.

1   The present interview is a transcript of an original video of 52:31 min. lenght, documenting the following conversation situation: Hans Ulrich Obrist, artists Roman Ondák and Koo Jeong A visited Stano Filko in his studio in Bratislava in 2005. Obrist and Koo Jeong A filmed this visit with a handheld camera. While talking about Filko's work, they walk through the estate, which bears the name Snežienková (Street of Snowdrops). At this point, most of the works were still gathered in this place and to a large extent sorted and arranged according

der Venus. Sie waren lesbisch und schwul. Als sie sich trafen, begannen sie sich zu paaren und zu vermehren. Um einen Streit um das Territorium zu vermeiden, zogen sie auf die Erde.

HUO Was hältst du von dem Begriff der Utopie? Hältst du ihn für einen nützlichen Begriff, um deine Arbeit zu betrachten?

SF Für mich ist Utopie eine psycho-philosophische Realität.

HUO Ist es eine konkrete Utopie?

SF Ja, es ist sowohl eine Vision als auch eine Utopie. Die Visionen sind konkreter, und die realisiere ich.

HUO Mir ist aufgefallen, dass es noch ein weiteres Zimmer mit einem Bett gibt. Ist das dein Schlafzimmer?

SF Komm und sieh es dir an, es ist eine Art Bibliothek. Hier siehst du ein Buch über *HAPPSOC II.*, das Fragmente des Projekts enthält. In jedem Buch findet sich ein Bild, das man aufhängen oder aufbewahren kann. Es ist in der nächsten, meiner späteren postmodernen Periode von 1979 bis 1983 entstanden. Hier befinden sich weitere Fragmente.

HUO Kennst du John Latham?

SF Nein. Warum?

HUO Er hat auch viel über die 4. und 5. Dimension gearbeitet.

SF Dieser Bereich ist eine Erweiterung, hier findet sich vieles über meine Arbeit *The Old and New Testament* (ca. 1995), nicht als eine Synthese, sondern als eine Essenz.

HUO Wir haben über Philosophie und Wissenschaft gesprochen, aber auch die Religion spielt eindeutig eine Rolle in deiner Arbeit und deinem Leben. Dieser Raum ist ja fast wie eine Kapelle!

SF Ich extrahiere das Wesentliche aus verschiedenen religiösen Lehren. Hier in diesen Altären können wir einen Auszug des Essentiellen sehen. Das sind Fragmente aus der Installation *Altars of Contemporaneity* (1963–1966). Auf dem Boden befanden sich Spiegel, über die man gehen konnte und in denen die Betrachtenden sich selbst sehen konnten. Das ist alles mit der Gegenwart verbunden. Ich sammle schon seit einigen Jahren Bilder, die sich darauf beziehen.

HUO Hast du eine Assistenz? Wie findest du die Zeit, all dieses Material zu ordnen?

SF Ich hatte nie eine Assistent*in, ich konnte mir keine leisten. Hier sind Ordner mit Arbeiten aus den 1950er- und 1960er-Jahren, da sind Projekte und Zeichnungen.

RO Schläfst du auch hier?

SF Ich wohne hier nicht, aber ich mache da gelegentlich ein Nickerchen. Oder jemand anderes könnte es, hier oder dort.

HUO Kannst du mir etwas über die Rolle der Zeichnung in deiner Praxis erzählen?

SF Meine Zeichnungen sind zugleich auch meine Projekte. Ich mache keine herkömmlichen Zeichnungen. Selbst wenn ich figurative Zeichnungen mache, verstehe ich sie als ein Projekt. Alle Projekte beginnen als Zeichnungen in der Hoffnung, dass sie verwirklicht werden. Eine Arbeit heißt *Map of the World (Women)* (1967), hier sind also einige Zeichnungen von Frauen. Dieses Werk stammt aus dem Ende der 1950er- und dem Anfang der 1960er-Jahre.

HUO Das ist eine erstaunliche Präsentation. Die Dichte erinnert mich an das Sir John Soane's Museum in London.

SF Einige der Zeichnungen und letzten Arbeiten befinden sich in Museumssammlungen. Die Slowakische Nationalgalerie hat einige davon, aber auch andere Sammlungen.

HUO Dieser Bereich hier scheint eine Art Retrospektive zu sein, die auf dem EGO basiert.

SF Ja, in diesen Werken geht es um das EGO – das dritte Auge. Dieses Ego gibt meinem ganzen Leben eine Struktur. Hier sind Werke aus den 1950er-, 60er-, 70er-, 80er- und 90er-Jahren, das alles kommt hier zusammen.
Komm mit nach oben, in die 4. Dimension.

HUO Die 4. Dimension ist also blau!

SF Es ist die 4. Dimension, diese steht für ein Kosmo-Universum. Hier findet sich auch eine Chronologie von den 1950er- bis zu den 1990er-Jahren.

HUO Nochmals eine Retrospektive.

SF Das totale Blau…

HUO Dieses Werk beinhaltet den Blick auf Bratislava. Wir haben einen anderen Blick als heute morgen.

SF Das ist die 3., 4., 5. Dimension (deutet auf die Stromleitungsstruktur im Außenraum).

HUO Das ist Energie, und sie fließt durch das ganze Gebiet!

SF Es ist die Energie.
Hier sind diese sieben Bäume. Das ist ein Projekt, das du im Katalog[6] finden kannst. Ich habe es mir in den 1960er-Jahren ausgedacht und es hier realisiert. Das ist ein typisches post-avantgardistisches Werk. Nicht postmodern, aber post-avantgardistisch. Es ist eine Art Tor, siehst du, das ist die psycho-technische Intelligenz.

HUO Wir befinden uns also im Kernland der Psycho-Techno-Intelligenz?

SF Ja, und sie umfasst das gesamte Universum. Es ist die „B Kreativität", die postmoderne Schöpfung. Dieser blaue Raum ist nur das Universum, die 4. Dimension. Die 5. Dimension befindet sich oberhalb des Universums.

1   Das vorliegende Interview ist ein Transkript eines 52:31-minütigen Originalvideos, das die folgende Gesprächssituation dokumentiert: Hans Ulrich Obrist, die Künstler Roman Ondák und Koo Jeong A haben Stano Filko im Jahr 2005 in seinem Atelier in Bratislava besucht. Obrist und Koo Jeong A haben den Besuch mit einer Handkamera gefilmt. Während sie über Filkos Arbeit sprechen, gehen sie durch das Anwesen, das den Namen Snežienková (Schneeglöckchenstraße) trägt. Zu diesem Zeitpunkt waren die meisten Werke noch an diesem Ort versammelt und größtenteils nach dem *System SF* sortiert und angeordnet. Das System basierte damals auf Dimensionen und einer Sieben-Farben-Struktur und wurde in den letzten Lebensjahren von Filko auf zwölf, schließlich auf zwanzig erweitert.
     Die vorliegende Fassung folgt der Struktur des ersten gedruckten Textes in *Spike* 07/2006. Sie basiert auf einer wörtlichen Abschrift des Interviews von Štefan Cebo und Lucia Gregorová Stach, Slowakische Nationalgalerie, und einer direkten Abschrift von Miroslava Urbanová und Tobias Ihl, HALLE FÜR KUNST Steiermark. Weitere Hilfe von Jan Tappe und Helga Droschl. Endgültige Fassung von Sandro Droschl, mit einem Feedback von Hans Ulrich Obrist.
2   *Stano FILKO II. 1965–69. Tvorba / Works – Creation / Werk – Schaffung / Ouvrages*, hrsg. von Stano Filko, Bratislava 1970.
3   Steven Wolfram, *A New Kind of Science*, Champaign / Illinois, 2002/2022.
4   Ebd.
5   Ebd.
6   Ebd.

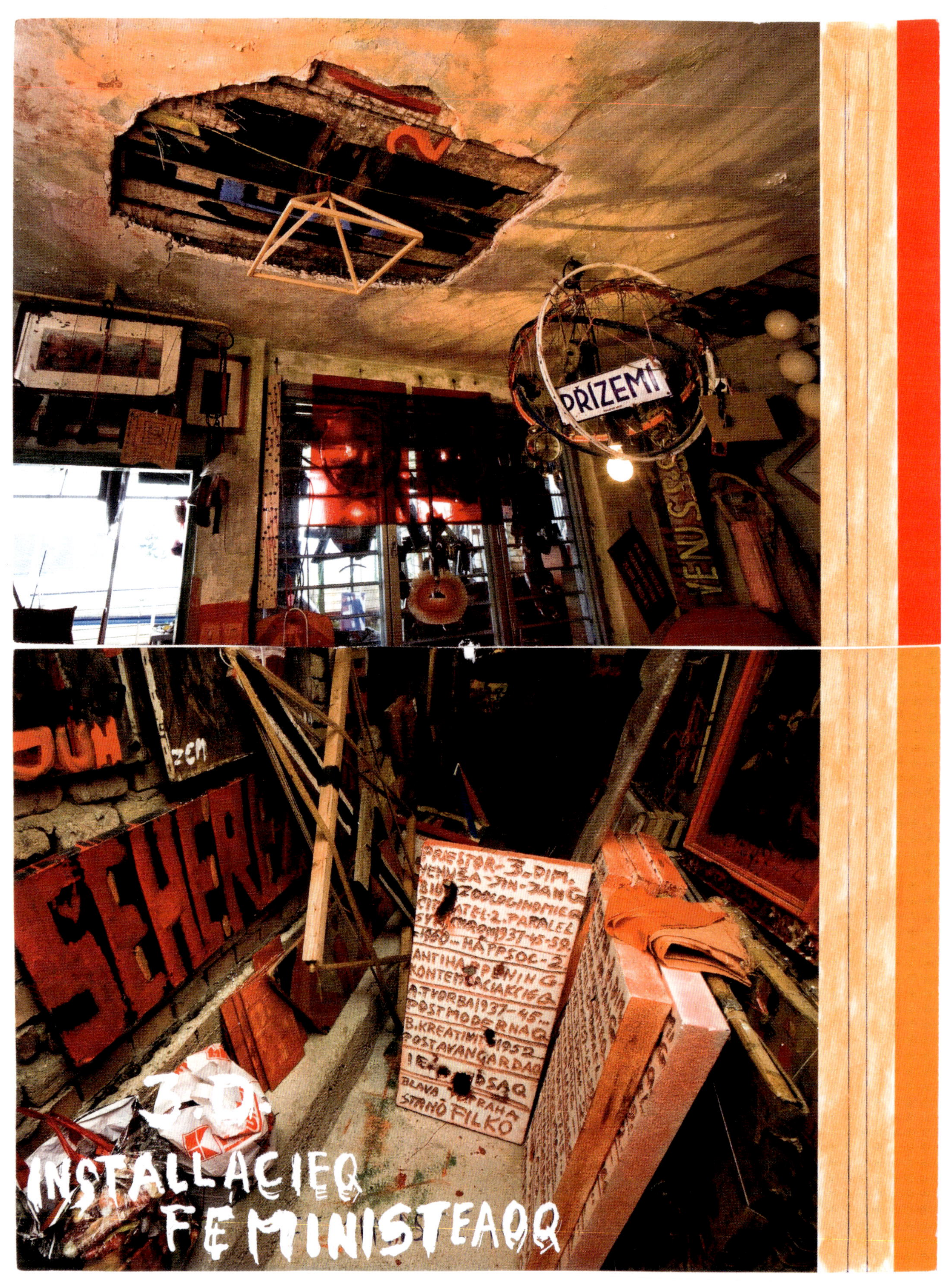

[25] From the cycle *Sketches from Snežienková* / *Z cyklu Skice zo Snežienkovej*, c. 2005

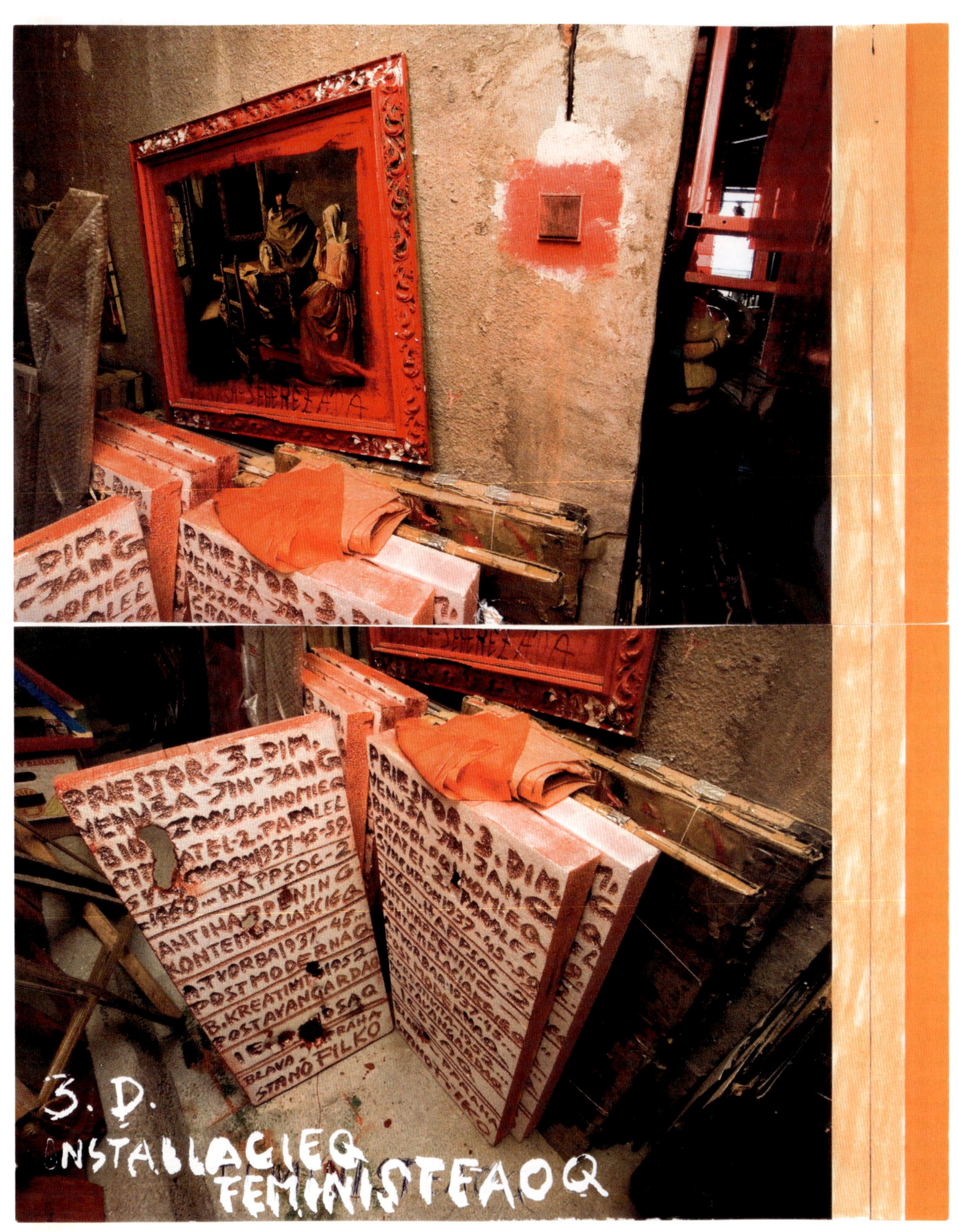
PRIESTOR-3.DIM.
MENULSA-JIN-JANG
ZOOLOGINOMIEG
BIO
CIT ATEL-2.PARALEL
SV ROND37-47-59
1960 HAPPSOC-2
ANTIHAPENING
KONTEMPLACIAKCIG
TVORBA1937-45
POSTMODERNAG
B.KREATIM 1952
POSTAVANGARDAG
1E SAG
BLAVA STANO FILKO
3.D.
NSTALLACIEG
FEMINISTFAOQ

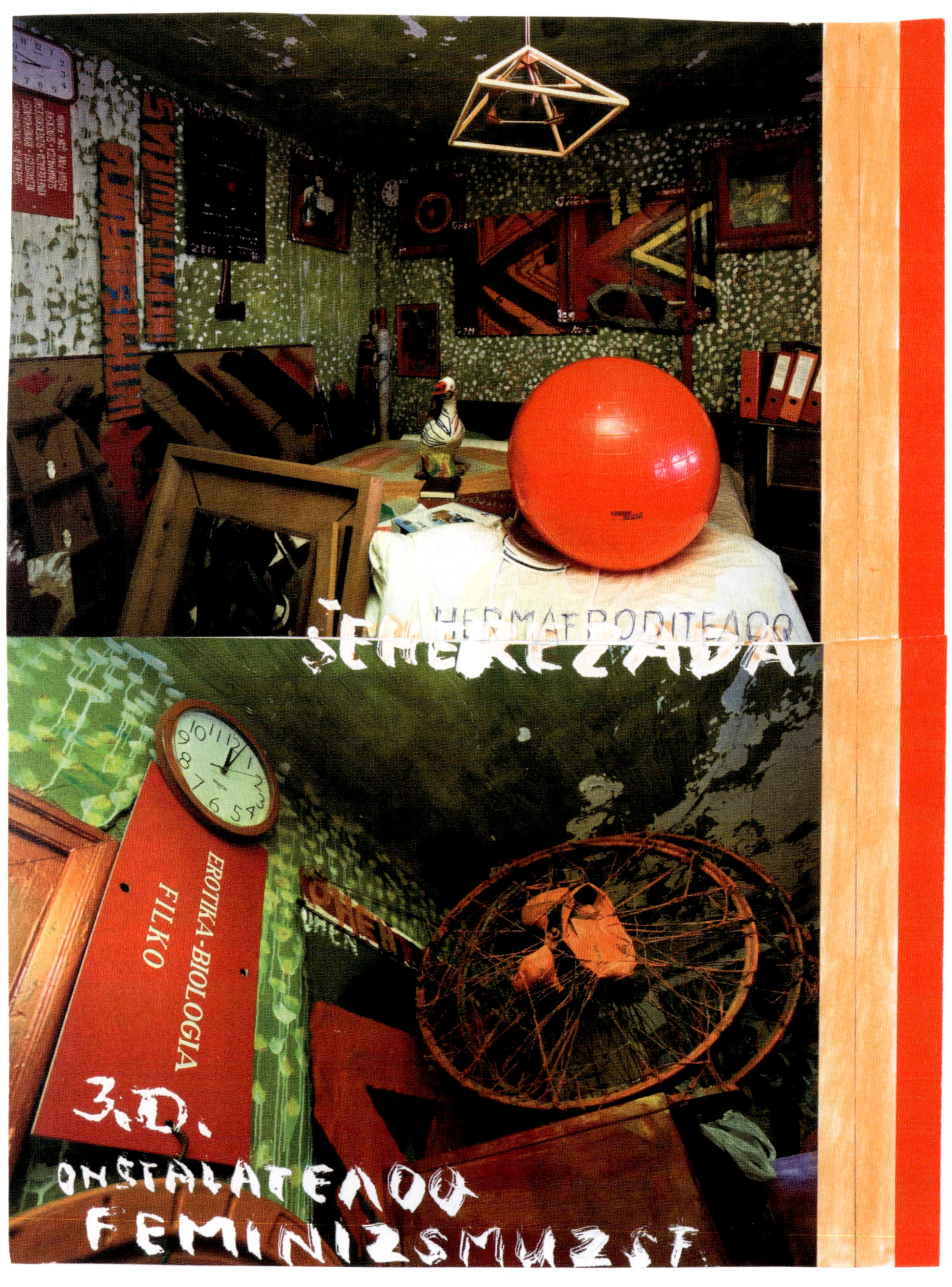

[27] From the cycle Sketches from Snežienková / Z cyklu Skice zo Snežienkovej, c. 2005

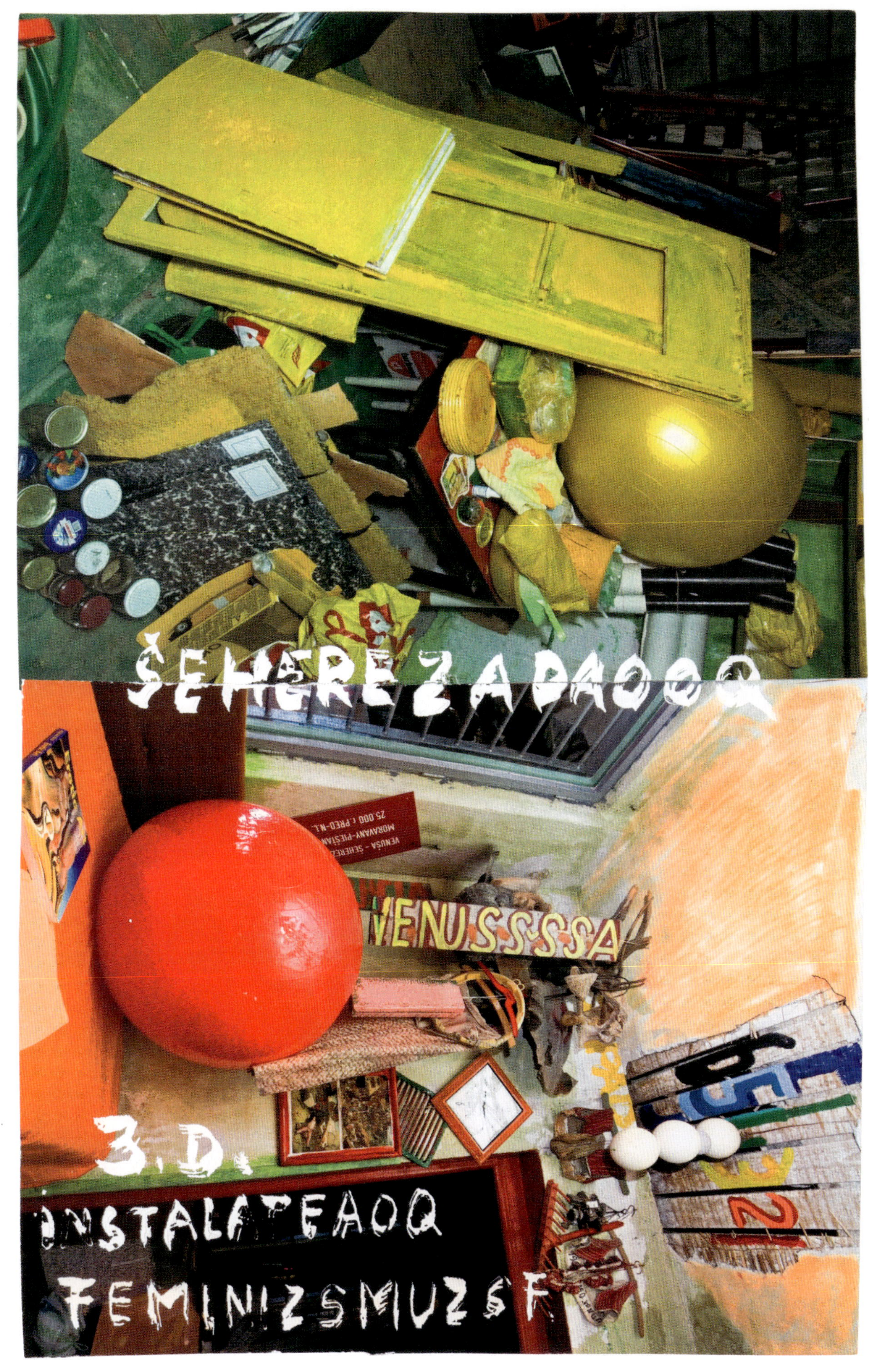

[28] From the cycle *Sketches from Snežienková / Z cyklu Skice zo Snežienkovej*, c. 2005

     Hans Ulrich Obrist   Stano Filko – Ein Interview

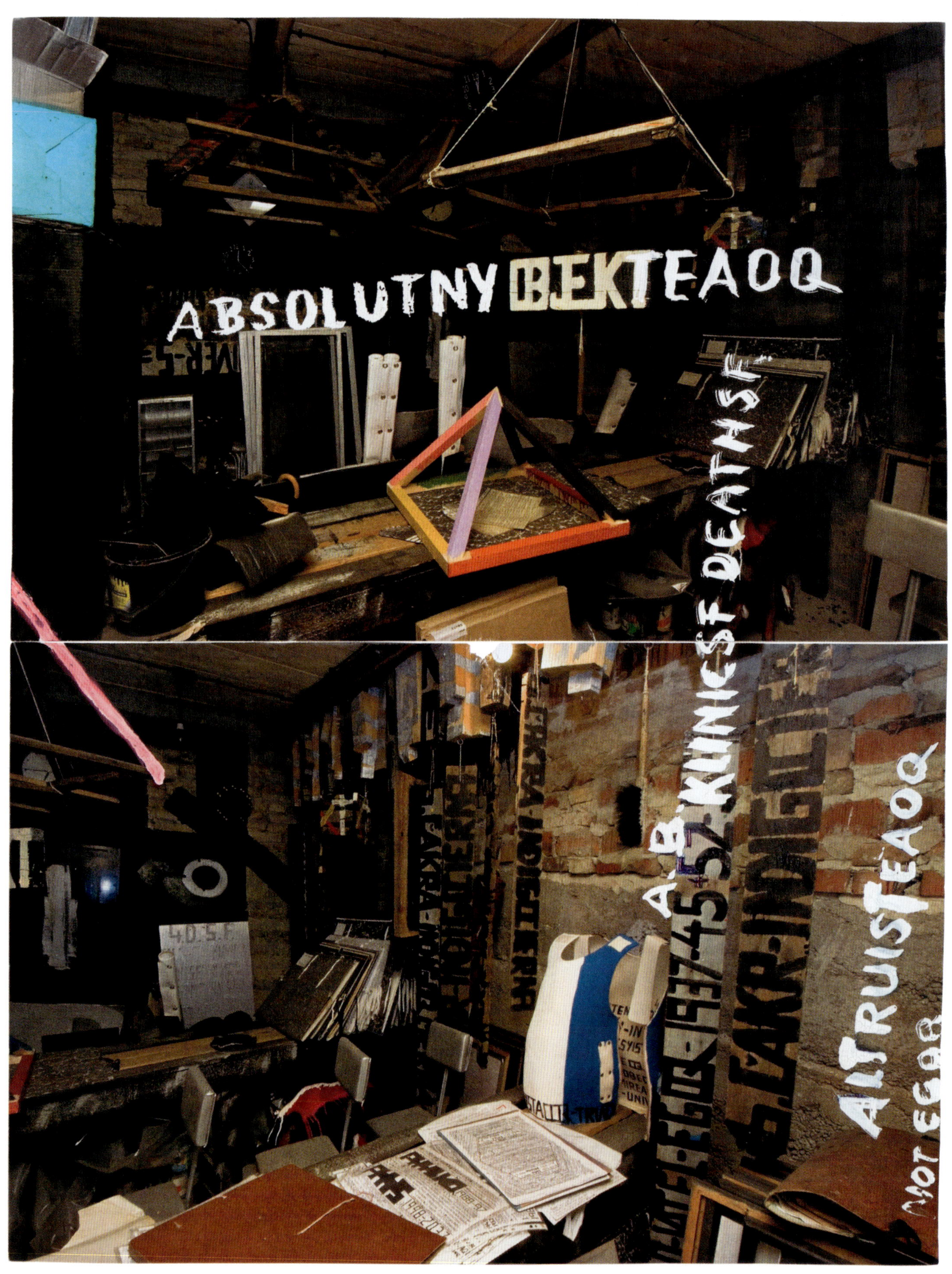

[29] From the cycle *Sketches from Snežienková* / *Z cyklu Skice zo Snežienkovej*, c. 2005

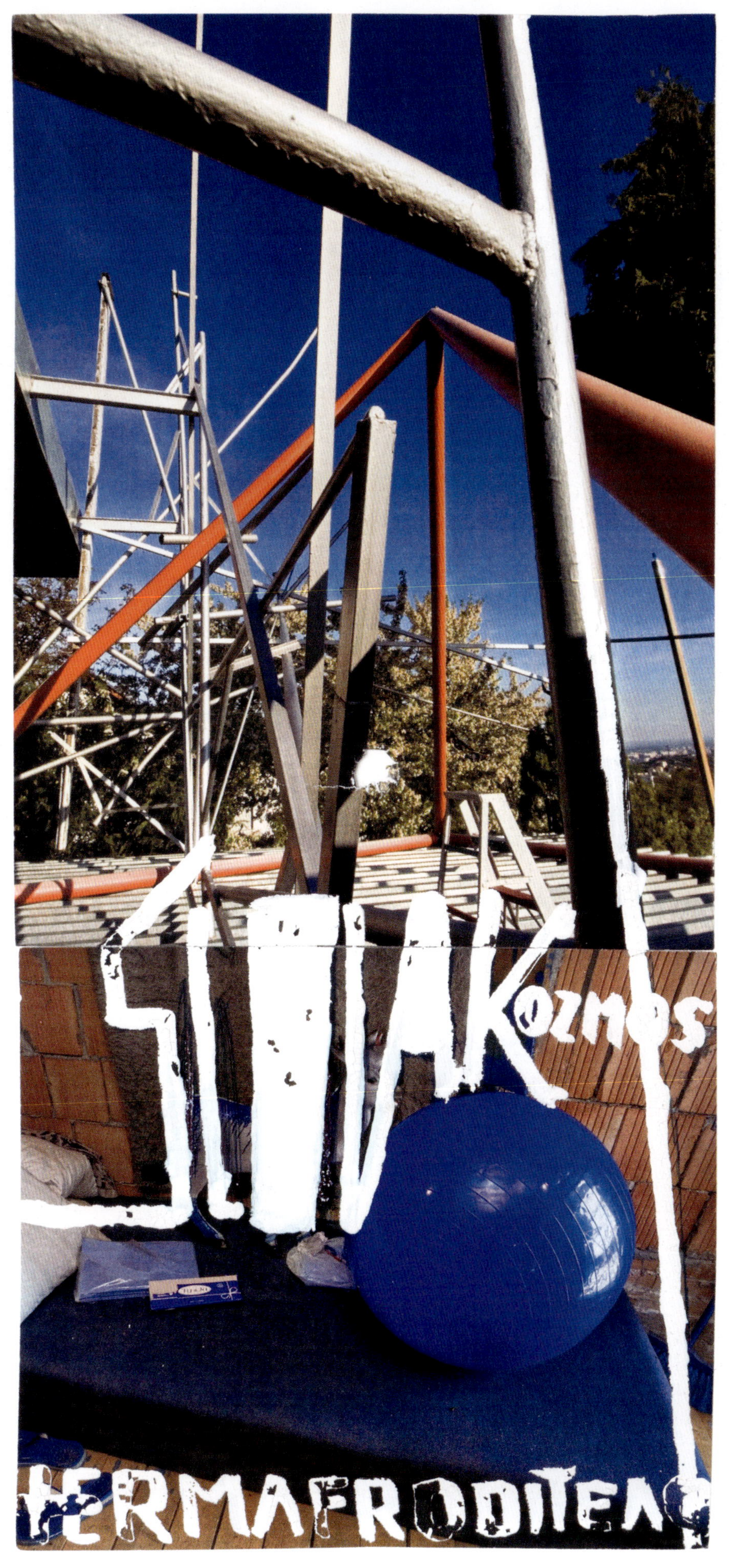

[30] From the cycle *Sketches from Snežienková / Z cyklu Skice zo Snežienkovej*, c. 2005

Filko's Snowdrops

Boris Ondreička

Stano Filko acquired a tiny house at the beginning of the 1970s in Bratislava (at that time ČSSR, Czechoslovak Socialist Republic, and back then part of a gardeners' colony). Even abandoned in large part, it is still located and exclusively accessible at Snežienková (Snowdrop) street on the downhill of Koliba (Shepherd's Hut) district. It is located just below the television tower (a phallic relic of late modernity, related to rockets and towers of churches appearing on numerous projects of the artist) on Kamzík (Chamois) hill, which dominates the horizon of Bratislava (meaning "Brotherglory," even of different etymological background). It is a spot at the most south-western foot of the Little Carpathians. It is a south-oriented garden of about 300 square meters in size.

One has an enormous view across the borders of Slovakia, Hungary, Austria and now the Czech Republic (or Moravia) from up there. One can observe the junction of the rivers Morava and Danube and the peaks of the Alps from there. During pseudo-socialist times (1955–91) there was that ambivalent and painful momentum to look beyond the iron curtain, one could not cross legally.

I had visited the house frequently since 1999. Together with Vít Havránek, we initiated a very detailed photo documentation (by Martin Marenčin) over a timespan of 4 years for the tranzit network in 2003. [01–11] In the same period (until 2011), there was an intense research, reading and consequent scanning of works on paper (drawings, collages, diagrams, essays of Filko etc.) happening from there. There were numerous really comprehensive interviews recorded and transcribed. It all to date expects huge editorial engagement and potential publishing.

Snowdrops (genus: *galanthus*, Fr. *violette de la chandeleur*, Ger. *Schneeglöckchen*) are one of the first flowers after winter. They are signs of life reborn, and symbols of purity and spirituality. Just remember the emancipatory slogan *Ver sacrum* (sacred spring) on the façade of Vienna Secession—symbolizing a free, new, contemporary and young movement of division from mainstream. It all connotes perfectly with Filko's robust still very romantic avant-garde (or, as he used to characterize it, "modern after postmodern") nature. In the sense of his vehement demand for universality, he was a rigorous puritan. It also associates with Filko's syncretism of Slavic pagan and Judeo-Christian traditions frequently discussed in his iconography. Filko was a true believer (in transfiguration, reincarnation, etc.) who was partially raised on rudimental Catholic education. Filko felt like he was a shepherd of thought and transmitter of knowledge. For Pierre Restany he was an architect of information. To him every element of any moment and place played more than a symbolical role in the overwhelming holistic mosaic. Snowdrops and their white color relate to the transcendence of one of the most fabled projects of Stano Filko (with Miloš Laky and Ján Zavarský) *White Space in White Space / Biely priestor v bielom priestore* (1973–82) as well.

That house had just electricity. Filko had to bring water always with him. He did not throw anything into the garbage. Somehow he was specifically ecological. He collected empty plastic bottles in large cluster-sculptures. Anything what surrounded him was a possible surface, material of an object of arts—of appropriation and postproduction and performativity. He did not differentiate between art and industrial materials. For Filko there was no difference between an aesthetic, functional, refunctioned or dysfunctioned quality. A sculpture was a table and a table was a sculpture. Even the latrine was understood as a vital model of a black-hole there. The house originally served as a simple storage and studio. Therein, an object was a subject and a subject was an object. Many artworks were *produced* by simple verbal declaration. Yes, the production (*poiesis*) of spoken words was considered equal to making objects. Anything could become art and became art.

After his return from the decade-long immigration to Germany and the United States at the very beginning of the 1990s, simultaneously to his *self-musealization* process in other media, he started to turn the house in some kind of deconstructivist-like installation according to Vladimir Tatlin's legacy (described by Dan Graham as main influence for Minimalists amongst others), an accessible object, and spontaneous continuity of his 1960s multimedia universal polyphonic environments and cathedrals, to a habitable maquette, a prototype or monument and finally a tomb/columbarium of the absolute/himself, as planned. It remains just as the ruin of a cenotaph unfortunately. Scaffolding tubes as one of the main creative prefabricates were versatile elements he did not stop using for the whole of his life.

Filkos Schneeglöckchen

Boris Ondreička

Anfang der 1970er-Jahre erwarb Stano Filko ein kleines Häuschen in einer Kleingartenanlage in Bratislava (damals noch Teil der Tschechoslowakischen Sozialistischen Republik, ČSSR). Mittlerweile verlassen, lässt sich das Haus noch immer und ausschließlich über die Snežienková-Straße (Schneeglöckchenstraße) am Rande des Koliba-Viertels (Strohhütten-Viertel) erreichen. Es befindet sich direkt unterhalb des Fernsehturms (einem phallischen Relikt aus der Spätmoderne, das an die Raketen und Kirchtürme erinnert, wie sie in zahlreichen von Filkos Projekten zu sehen sind) auf dem Kamzík-Hügel (Gams-Hügel), der den Horizont von Bratislava (Bruderehre; der etymologische Hintergrund ist allerdings ein anderer) beherrscht. Das Grundstück mit Garten liegt am südwestlichsten Ausläufer der Kleinen Karpaten. Es ist nach Süden ausgerichtet und hat eine Fläche von 300 Quadratmetern.

Von dort oben bietet sich einem eine grandiose Aussicht auf die Grenzen der Slowakei zu Ungarn, Österreich und der heutigen Tschechischen Republik (bzw. Mähren). Man sieht den Zusammenfluss von March und Donau und einige Alpengipfel. In pseudo-sozialistischen Zeiten (1955–1991) ergriff einen das ambivalente und schmerzhafte Gefühl, durch den Eisernen Vorhang schauen zu können, ohne diesen durchqueren zu dürfen.

Seit 1999 war ich regelmäßig vor Ort. Zusammen mit Vít Havránek habe ich dazu 2003 eine sehr ausführliche, sich über vier Jahre erstreckende Fotodokumentation (von Martin Marenčin) für das tranzit-Netzwerk initiiert. [01–11] Zugleich gab es dort (bis 2011) intensive Recherchen, das Material wurde gesichtet und alle Arbeiten auf Papier (Zeichnungen, Collagen, Schaubilder, Essays von Filko) wurden komplett eingescannt. Zahlreiche wirklich ausführliche Interviews wurden aufgezeichnet und transkribiert. All das wartet noch darauf, für eine mögliche Veröffentlichung umfassend redigiert zu werden.

Schneeglöckchen (Gattung: *Galanthus*, Frz. *violette de la chandeleur*, Engl. *snowdrops*) gehören zu den ersten Blumen nach dem Winter. Sie sind Zeichen für die Wiedergeburt des Lebens und Symbole der Reinheit und Spiritualität. Man denke nur an den emanzipatorischen Wahlspruch *Ver Sacrum* (Heiliger Frühling) an der Fassade der Wiener Secession — freie, neue, aktuelle und junge Bewegungen der Abspaltung von der vorherrschenden Kunstrichtung. All das passt perfekt zu Filkos zwar robusten, aber dennoch sehr romantischen Avantgarde (oder, wie er es zu nennen pflegte, der „Moderne nach der Postmoderne"). Was seine vehemente Forderung nach Universalität anbetrifft, so war er ein strenger Puritaner. Dies zeigt sich auch in Filkos Synkretismus aus heidnischen slawischen und jüdisch-christlichen Traditionen, die in seiner Ikonografie häufig behandelt werden. Filko war wirklich gläubig (er glaubte unter anderem an Verklärung und Reinkarnation) und hatte eine rudimentäre katholische Erziehung erhalten. Er fühlte sich als Hüter des Denkens und Vermittler von Wissen. Für Pierre Restany war er ein Informationsarchitekt. Für Filko spielte jedes einzelne Element, egal aus welcher Zeit oder von welchem Ort, in dem überwältigenden ganzheitlichen Mosaik eine Rolle, die über das rein Symbolische hinausging. Die Schneeglöckchen mit ihrer weißen Farbe schaffen auch eine Verbindung zur Transzendenz eines der legendärsten Projekte von Stano Filko (mit Miloš Laky und Ján Zavarský), *White Space in White Space / Biely priestor v bielom priestore* (1973–1982).

Das Haus hatte lediglich Strom. Wasser musste Filko stets mitbringen. Er warf nichts in den Müll. Auf seine eigene Weise war er sehr umweltbewusst. Er sammelte leere Plastikflaschen in großen Gebindeskulpturen. Alles, was ihn umgab, war eine mögliche Oberfläche, Material für ein Kunstobjekt – ein Objekt der Aneignung, der Postproduktion und der Performativität. Dabei machte er keinen Unterschied zwischen Kunst- und industriellen Materialien. Für Filko gab es keinen Unterschied zwischen ästhetisch oder funktional, umfunktioniert oder dysfunktional. Eine Skulptur war ein Tisch und ein Tisch war eine Skulptur. Sogar die Latrine wurde dort als grundlegendes Modell eines schwarzen Lochs verstanden. Das Haus diente ursprünglich als einfaches Lager und Atelier. Dort war ein Objekt ein Subjekt und ein Subjekt ein Objekt. Viele Kunstwerke wurden mit einfachen verbalen Erklärungen *produziert*. Ja, die Produktion (*poiesis*) von gesprochenen Worten wurde mit der Herstellung von Objekten gleichgesetzt. Alles konnte Kunst werden und wurde Kunst.

Anfang der 1990er-Jahre kehrte Filko, der ein Jahrzehnt zuvor nach Deutschland und in die Vereinigten Staaten emigriert war, zurück und begann parallel zu seinem Prozess der *Selbstmusealisierung* in anderen Medien, das Haus nach Plan umzuwandeln in eine Art dekonstruktivistischer Installation

Self-musealization included making dense physical quasi-explanatory commentaries to/inside of his works, and space of their placement. Quasi-explanatory means that he did it in edgy personal neological vocabulary, acronyms, attributes, qualifiers, modifiers and signs one has to learn to understand before reading the whole. It reminds us of codes of hermetical writing, which are dedicated to chosen ones only. He regrouped his works to new organizations/organisms, ecotopes, families of meaning in the entire civilization of his art. This is the result of deep diagrammatic reasoning or, as Dana H. Ballard might call it, "hierarchical abstraction." Items were interlinked by virtual (as Filko called it) "strings."

Any activity there was at the same time ordinary as well as a mythopoetic form of happening, event, performance, ritual of arts. Filko was a true (even if unconscious) follower of Kenneth Burke's "Life is not like a drama. Life is a drama." or François Truffaut's "mise-en-scène" or Richard Sennet's "Theatrum mundi." For him art made sense only if it was total—in his words "par excellence" (synesthetic and holistic). In this sense his house means a radical ontological and spiritual way of living art and not (just) doing, making it (close to manifestations of Allan Kaprow). Art is living and living is art was a legacy of his *HAPPSOC* series from the 1960s as well. The house might remind one to the *Merzbau* (1920–36) of Kurt Schwitters, too. In Filko's case, *Merz* means a disregard for anything profane, carnal, etc. (the "third dimension," in his words). He even called pieces of his art "Post-Dada." Actually, his personal belief-system was (intuitively) more than similar to the gnostic division into the lowest hylics (*hyle*—matter, "third dimension"), medium psychics (*psyché*—personal soul, "fourth dimension") and highest pneumatics (*pneuma*—superpersonal spirit, "fifth dimension"). The Snowdrop street house is the realization or spontaneous next step of his previous models of utopic architecture (gazebos, watch-towers, prospects evolving to projects) as well. Since then, he spent most of his time there. He (his genius or *Geist*) was extremely productive. In the house one is literary inside of an artwork, being part of an artwork.

He painted single rooms in hierarchical spectra according to his *System SF* of colors, which is correspondent to neuro-vegetative plexes (bundles, knots) or in other (his) words "chakras," analogical to the genealogical tree of Kabbalah and more. According to that he distributed related artworks in it. The main interiors of the ground floor were dedicated to a yellow, orange, red (color of the most zoic, obviously furnished as a sleeping room). The former garage was reserved for a green, and a kind of workshop for silver, gold, white and transparent. There he allocated the spot for his ashes (to be placed under the simple glass cover of an industrial lamp). The third room (a former stall) was packed with a black. From there over the rainbow- and Ramon Llull-like ladder (still there) one can climb up to the blue (cosmic) room and finally the zinc and very shiny roof-tops. Under the house there is a reservoir for keeping rain-water, and in the garden, amongst many objects installed, is a fireplace (grill) in the shape of a mandala. Everything was kinetic and permutable. Shelves and cupboards were full of administrative folders filled with documentation and works on paper side by side with food and other trivial things.

Filko's heroic process of ptolemo-egocentric cosmological systematization, ecumenical diagrammatical dogma of the whole body of his work (literary rewriting, repainting each piece of art of the past and its surroundings of present, semantics and syntax) was concentrated to the desire for preservation of his memory and legacy. It was made to frame, to prospectively control the future reading of his rather strict order/mission. His method is not complicated, only complex. We have received an exhaustive sum of guidelines from him to lead our reading in a correct direction. He considered that "delivery" (verbatim) as an act of pure *altruism* (gifting oneself to others). Egocentricity does not mean selfishness here, only that a self is the point of departure, the screen, the stage of the figuration of the universe/watch-tower (receiver) or television-tower (transmitter).

In the sense of all of this he started to call his house *Ark* (from argosy to spaceship). So it was meant to be also the *Ark of the Covenant* to keep his laws, testaments, etc. safe. He wanted to transform it into a large museum (the temple of muses) for himself, built at his birthplace—the village Veľká Hradná (Big Castle Village, a two hours' drive north of Bratislava). He even laid a massive concrete foundation of it and erected several iron pillars. It was meant to be the *ars magna* of his synthetizing endeavor. His energetic ambition was to embrace complexity in completion. Obviously, he did not manage to do so in his lifetime. His magnum opus remains open.

Filko was a hierarchical archivist and an eschatological architect at the same time. His interest in *archē* ("big-bang" in his words, even quite anarchistically) was always simultaneously connected to his hedonistic engagement with the future and keeping himself permanently abreast of the *Zeitgeist*. One can find the whole spectrum of artistic tendencies of the last 80 years in his art. To call him conceptualist is simply a misinterpreting reduction. But his inner goal was timelessness (one can see it for example also in terms of his way of re- or un-dating his own works, where the date of idea was many times exposed), rigorous immateriality, (buddhist-like) holy nothingness. That's why the final color (?) of his scale of notation is the transparent one and the non-dimensionality of a hole (and an act of perforation, penetration) is worshipped. That is completely legitimate, because the so-called "dark matter" which fills approximately 85% of the universe is truly transparent.

We can understand the house-studio-depository-shrine (I limit myself to calling it registry) of Stano Filko as a *khôra*—the innocent but fertile place of figurative becoming and not yet transfigured being. In his hierarchical system real being begins just after the physical life is over.

Cosmos is the source of everything. Cosmos is the home (*oikos* = eco) of all (*holos*).

   Filko's Snowdrops

in der Tradition von Wladimir Tatlin (wie sie zum Beispiel von Dan Graham als Haupteinfluss für den Minimalismus beschrieben wurde), in ein begehbares Objekt, die spontane Fortsetzung seiner multimedialen universellen polyphonen Environments und Kathedralen aus den 1960er-Jahren, eine bewohnbare Maquette, einen Prototypen oder ein Monument und schließlich in ein Grabmal bzw. Kolumbarium des Absoluten bzw. seiner selbst. Davon sind leider nur die Reste eines Kenotaphs geblieben. Gerüstrohre gehörten als vielseitige Elemente zu den wichtigsten Fertigprodukten, die er Zeit seines Lebens in seinem kreativen Schaffen verwendete.

Zur *Selbstmusealisierung* gehörte auch die Herstellung physisch dichter quasi-erläuternder Kommentare in bzw. zu seinen Arbeiten und dem Ort, an dem diese platziert wurden. Mit *quasi-erläuternd* meine ich, dass er diese in einem exzentrischen persönlichen, neologischen Vokabular verfasste, mit Akronymen, Attributen, Qualifikatoren, Modifizierern und Zeichen, die man vor dem Lesen lernen muss, um das Ganze verstehen zu können. Dies erinnert an die Kodizes hermetischer, nur für Auserwählte bestimmte Schriften. Er gruppierte seine Werke zu neuen Strukturen/Organismen, Ökotopen und Bedeutungsfamilien in der Gesamtzivilisation seiner Kunst. Dies ist das Ergebnis gründlicher diagrammatischer Überlegungen oder, wie Dana H. Ballard es nennen würde, einer „hierarchischen Abstraktion". Die Elemente waren durch virtuelle „Fäden" (wie Filko sie nannte) miteinander verbunden.

Alle vor Ort stattfindenden Aktivitäten waren alltäglich und zugleich auch eine mythopoetische Form von Happening, Event, Performance oder Kunstritual. Filko war, wenn auch ohne sich dessen bewusst zu sein, ein echter Anhänger von Kenneth Burkes „Betrachtung des Lebens als Drama", von Francois Truffauts „mise-en-scène" oder Richard Sennets „Theatrum mundi". Kunst machte für ihn nur Sinn, wenn sie absolut war – in seinen Worten „par excellence" (synästhetisch und ganzheitlich). In dieser Hinsicht steht sein Haus für eine radikale ontologische und spirituelle Weise, Kunst zu leben und sie nicht (nur) zu tun, zu machen (ähnlich wie die Manifestationen von Allan Kaprow). Kunst ist Leben und Leben ist Kunst, so lautete auch das Vermächtnis seiner *HAPPSOC*-Reihe aus den 1960er-Jahren. Das Haus erinnert vielleicht auch an den *Merzbau* von Kurt Schwitters. In Filkos Fall bedeutet *Merz* eine Verachtung für alles Weltliche, Fleischliche (die „3. Dimension", wie er es nannte). Er bezeichnete einige seiner Kunstwerke sogar als „Post-Dada". Im Grunde war sein persönliches Glaubenssystem (intuitiv) der gnostischen Einteilung der Menschen in die niedrigste Klasse der Hyliker*innen (*hyle* – die Materie, „3. Dimension"), die mittlere Klasse der Psychiker*innen (*psyché* – die persönliche Seele, „4. Dimension") und die höchste Klasse der Pneumatiker*innen (*pneuma* – der Geist jenseits des Persönlichen, „5. Dimension") mehr als ähnlich. Das Haus in der Schneeglöckchenstraße ist auch die Verwirklichung bzw. der spontane nächste Schritt seiner vorherigen Modelle einer utopischen Architektur (Pavillons, Wachtürme, von Perspektiven zu Projekten). Seither hat er die meiste Zeit dort verbracht. Er (sein Genie oder Geist) war äußerst produktiv. In dem Haus befindet man sich buchstäblich im Inneren eines Kunstwerks, man ist Teil eines Kunstwerks.

Er strich einzelne Räume in hierarchischen Spektren nach seinem *System SF*, bei dem die Farben neurovegetativen Plexus (Geflechten, Knoten) oder, in anderen (seinen) Worten, „Chakren" entsprachen, analog zum Lebensbaum der Kabbala und Ähnlichem. Nach diesem Prinzip verteilte er entsprechende Kunstwerke in den Räumen. Das Hauptinterieur im Erdgeschoss war gelb, orange und rot (der Farbe des zoischsten Raums, der offensichtlich als Schlafzimmer eingerichtet war). Die ehemalige Garage war grün und ein werkstattartiger Raum silber, gold, weiß und transparent gestaltet. Dort war auch der Ort, an dem seine Asche aufbewahrt werden sollte (unter dem einfachen Glasschirm einer Industrielampe). Der dritte Raum (ein ehemaliger Stall) war ganz in Schwarz gehalten. Von dort konnte man über die (noch heute vorhandene) regenbogenfarbene, an Ramon Llull erinnernde Leiter in den blauen (kosmischen) Raum und schließlich auf das intensiv schimmernde Zinkdach klettern. Unter dem Haus befand sich ein Regenwassertank und im Garten, neben zahlreichen Objektinstallationen, eine Feuerstelle (ein Grill) in der Form eines Mandalas. Alles war kinetisch und wandelbar. Regale und Schränke waren voller Aktenordner mit Dokumentationen und Arbeiten auf Papier, direkt neben Lebensmitteln und anderen alltäglichen Dingen.

Im Zentrum von Filkos heroischem Prozess der ptolemäisch-egozentrischen kosmologischen Systematisierung, des ökumenischen diagrammatischen Dogmas seines Gesamtwerkes (die buchstäbliche Neuschreibung bzw. Übermalung aller Kunstwerke aus der Vergangenheit und ihrer Umgebung aus Gegenwart, Semantik und Syntax) stand der Wunsch, seine Erinnerung und sein Erbe zu bewahren. Der Prozess war dazu gedacht, die zukünftige Lesart seiner ziemlich strikten Anweisungen/Mission nach Möglichkeit zu gestalten, zu kontrollieren. Seine Methode ist nicht kompliziert, nur komplex. Wir haben von ihm eine umfassende Reihe an Richtlinien erhalten, die unsere Deutung in die richtige Richtung lenken sollen. Er betrachtete diese „Übergabe" (wortwörtlich) als Akt reinen *Altruismus* im Sinne von *sich selbst an andere verschenken*. Egozentrik bedeutet hier nicht Egoismus, sondern nur, dass das Selbst der Ausgangspunkt, die Leinwand, die Bühne der Figuration des Universums bzw. Wachturms (Empfänger) oder Fernsehturms (Sender) ist.

Getreu dieser Logik begann er, sein Haus *Ark* (Arche) zu nennen (in der Bedeutung von Argosy bis Raumschiff). Es war auch als Bundeslade (engl. Ark of the Covenant) gedacht, die der sicheren Unterbringung seiner Gesetze, Testamente etc. dienen sollte. Er wollte es in ein großes Museum (einen Musentempel) überführen, das für ihn an seinem Geburtsort, dem Dorf Veľká Hradná (großes Burgdorf, zwei Autostunden nördlich von Bratislava) errichtet werden sollte. Filko legte sogar ein massives Betonfundament an und errichtete mehrere Eisenstützen. Es sollte die *Ars magna* seines Bestrebens nach Synthese sein. Sein entschiedener Ehrgeiz galt der Erfassung der Komplexität in der Vollendung. Offensichtlich ist ihm das zu Lebzeiten nicht gelungen. Sein Opus Magnum bleibt unvollendet.

Filko war gleichzeitig hierarchischer Archivar und eschatologischer Architekt. Sein Interesse an *archē* (er nannte es, eigentlich ziemlich anarchistisch, „Big Bang") war stets auch verbunden mit seiner hedonistischen Auseinandersetzung mit der Zukunft und dem Bemühen, auf der Höhe des Zeitgeistes zu bleiben. In seiner Kunst lässt sich das gesamte Spektrum künstlerischer Tendenzen der letzten 80 Jahre wiederfinden. Ihn als Konzeptkünstler zu bezeichnen, ist schlicht eine

   Boris Ondreička   Filkos Schneeglöckchen

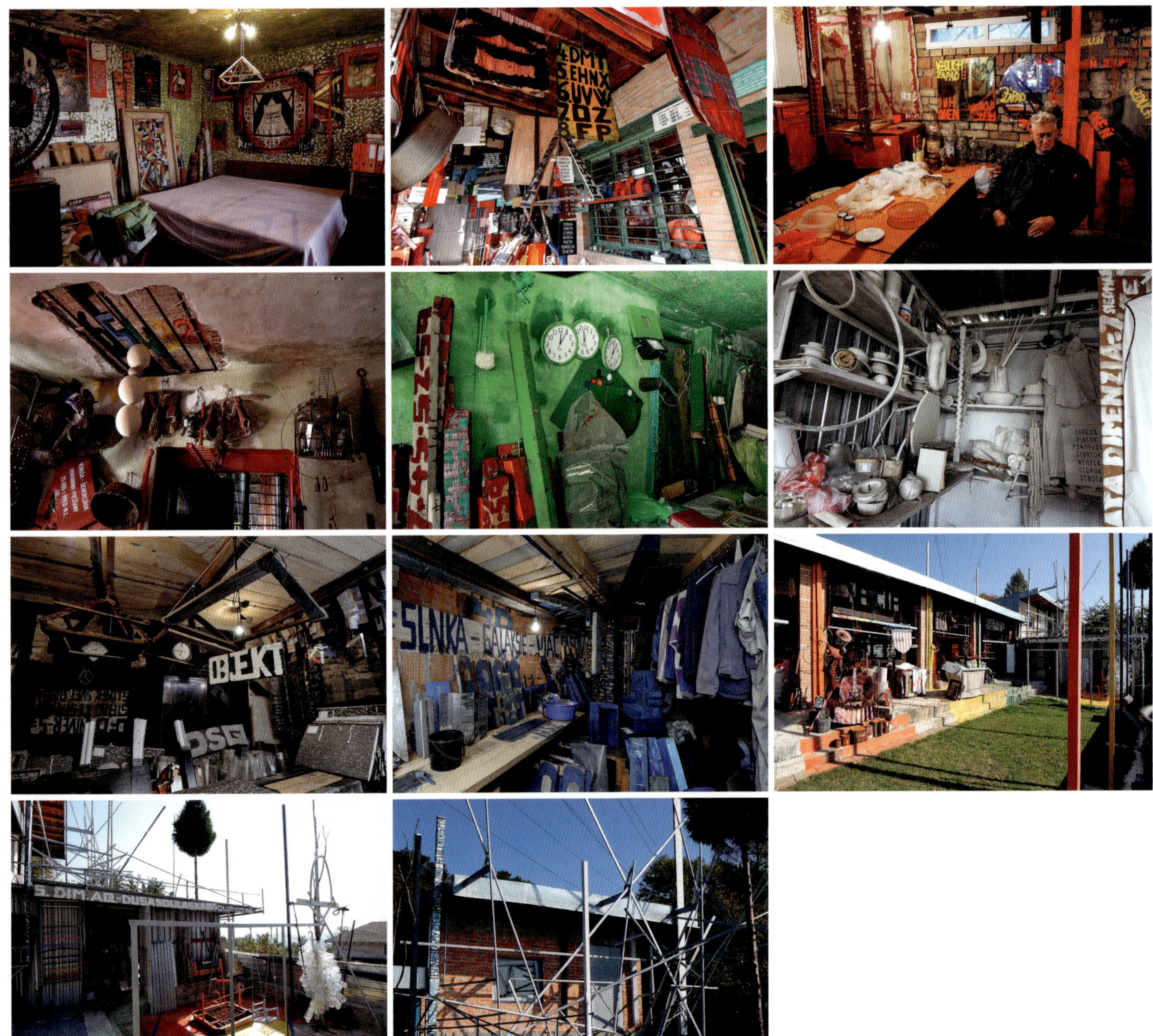

[01–11] Artist's studio Snežienková / Umelcov ateliér Snežienková, 2003, photographed by Martin Marenčin

verkürzende Fehlinterpretation. Sein innerstes Ziel war je-
doch die Zeitlosigkeit (erkennbar auch an seiner Praxis, seine
Werke, auf denen häufig das Datum zu sehen war, an dem die
Idee entstand, umzudatieren oder das Datum ganz zu ent-
fernen), eine rigorose Immaterialität, eine Art buddhistisches
heiliges Nichts. Daher rührt auch die Transparenz als letzte
Farbe (?) in seiner Farbskala und die Verehrung der Nicht-
Dimensionalität von Löchern (als Akt der Perforation, der
Durchdringung). Das ist völlig legitim, ist die so genannte
„dunkle Materie", aus der etwa 85% des Universums besteht,
doch tatsächlich transparent.

Man kann das Haus/Atelier/Depot/den Schrein (ich
beschränke mich darauf, es als Registratur zu bezeichnen)
von Stano Filko als *chora* verstehen – einen unschuldigen,
aber fruchtbaren Ort des figurativen Werdens und noch nicht
des verklärten Seins. In seinem hierarchischen System beginnt das wirkliche Sein gleich nach dem Ende des physischen
Lebens.

Aus dem Kosmos geht alles hervor. Der Kosmos ist das
Zuhause (*oikos* = öko) von allem (*holos*).

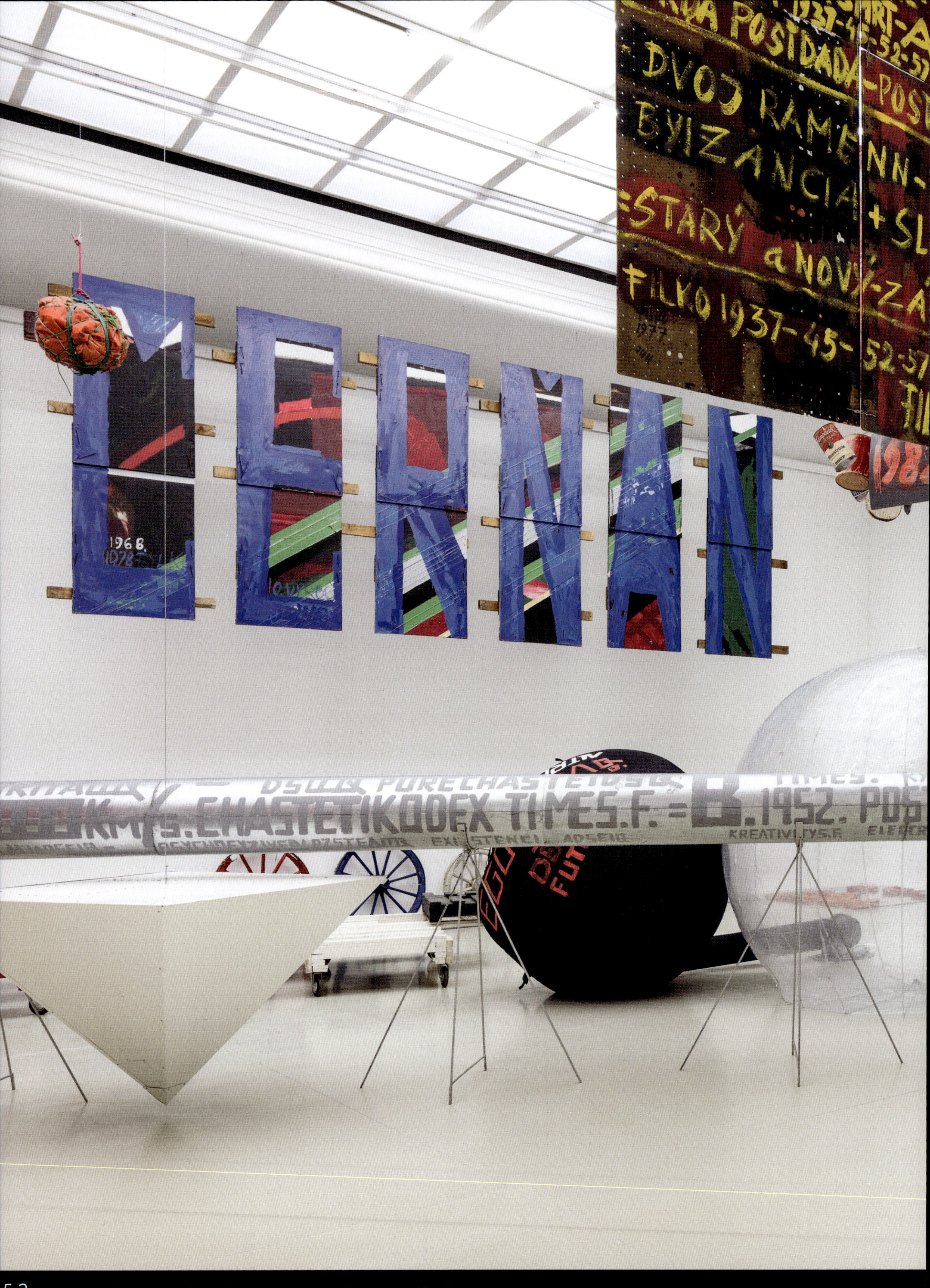
TERNAN
POSTDADA-POS
DVOJ. RAME NN-
BYZANCIA +SL
=STARÝ a NOVÝ-ZA
FILKO 1937-45- 52-57

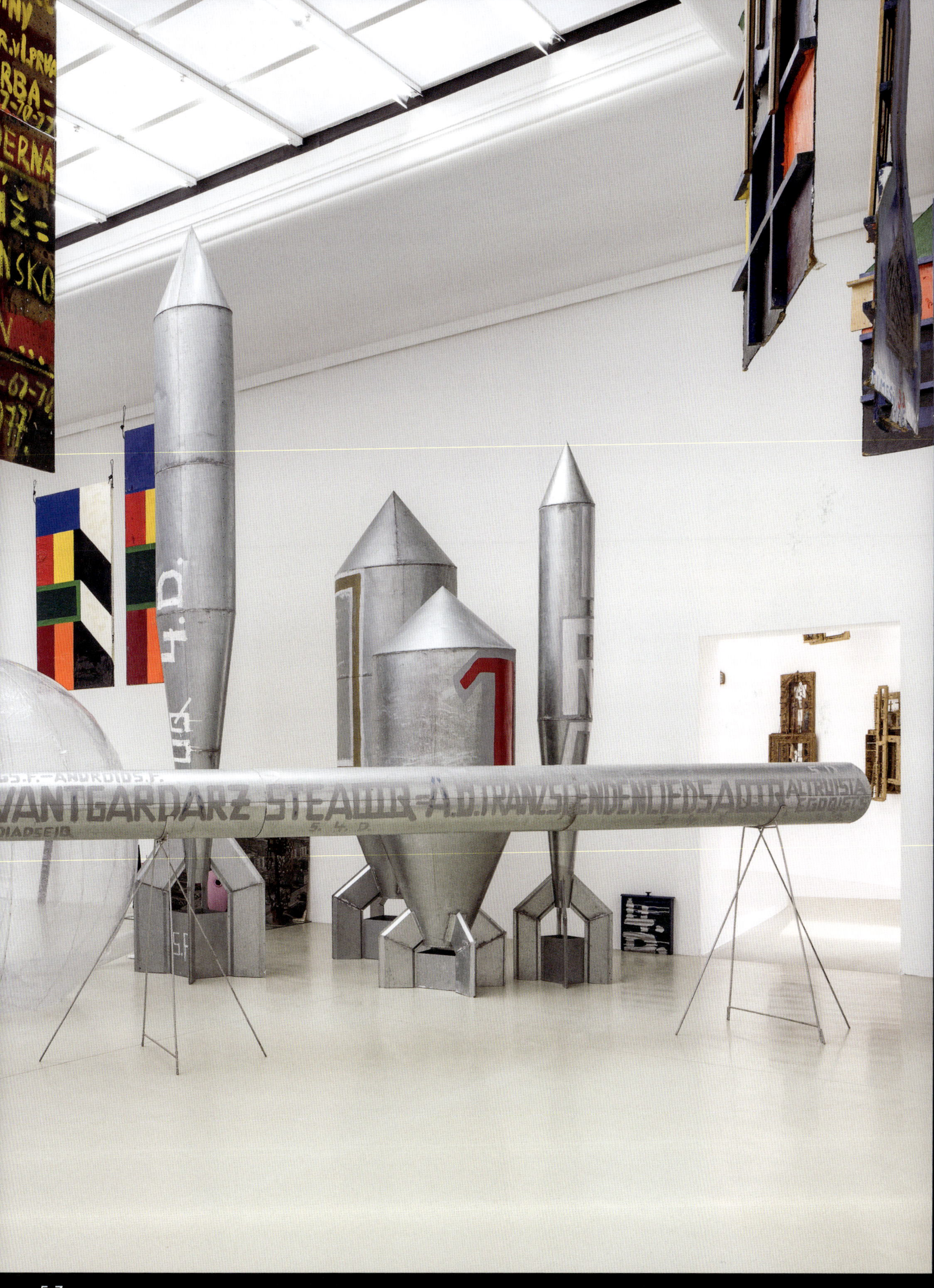

AVANTGARDARE STEAUA=A.D.TRANZSENDENDIEDSADOR ALTRUISTA EGOISTA

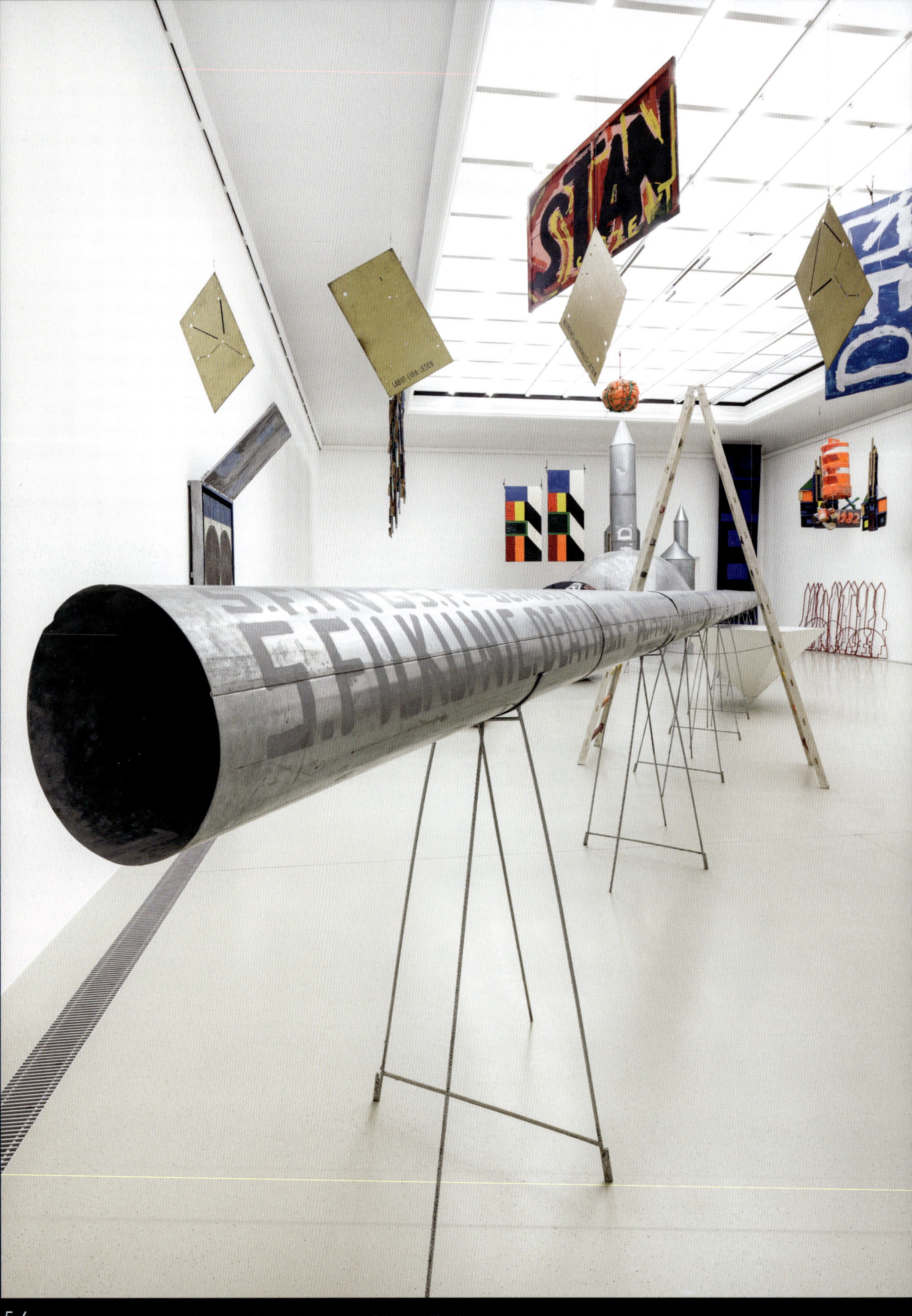

    V. Clinical Death Tunnel and Balloon Works

klinickej smrti (c. 2010) [04], an extended silver tube, is placed in a central position. This hosepipe-like structure seems to be floating in space and to create its own field of gravity. The installation is unusually long and adds a dynamic to the room by drawing attention to its horizontal level. At the same time, it also has the function of a barrier. *Clinical Death Tunnel* thrusts forward into the empty space beneath the larger ladder-shaped work, and it is also linked up with a pointing-down pyramid [05].

sich anhand einer silberfarbenen Röhre das Werk *Clinical Death Tunnel / Tunel klinickej smrti* (ca. 2010) [04]. Diese schlauchartige Architektur scheint im Raum zu schweben und ihr eigenes Gravitationsfeld zu erzeugen. Die Installation ist ungewöhnlich lang und dynamisiert den Raum, indem sie die Horizontalebene ins Bewusstsein bringt. Gleichzeitig nimmt sie auch die Funktion einer Blockade ein. *Clinical Death Tunnel* dringt in den Leerraum unter der größeren Leiterarbeit vor und ist zusätzlich mit einer nach unten gerichteten Pyramide verbunden [05].

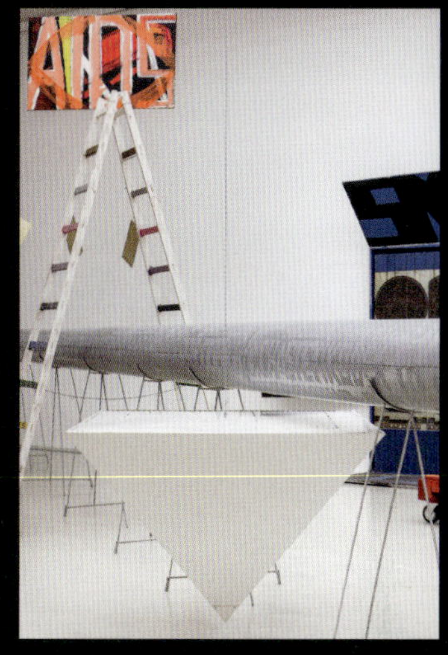

[03] Exhibition view, HALLE FÜR KUNST Steiermark, Graz, 2022

[04A] *Clinical Death Tunnel / Tunel klinickej smrti*, c. 2010

The form of the tunnel is often used in order to depict intergalactic travel, and *Clinical Death Tunnel* thus also suggests an unusual level of time. Filko saw tubes and tunnels as the visualization of the fifth dimension, with the pyramid as a portal into this dimension. The colors silver and white also facilitate the further unfolding of the fifth dimension. It is something absolute, as it comprises all the other dimensions and contains unfathomable themes like emptiness, nothingness, and death. With this ensemble of works Filko explores existential themes that are situated within the force fields of the spiritual world.

Die Form des Tunnels wird oft verwendet um intergalaktische Reisen darzustellen und so erinnert auch *Clinical Death Tunnel* an eine ungewöhnliche Zeitebene. Nach Filkos Vorstellung sind Röhren und Tunnel die Visualisierung der 5. Dimension, wobei die Pyramide das Portal zur Dimension bildet. Durch die Farben Silber, sowie Weiß kann sich die 5. Dimension weiter entfalten. Sie ist etwas Absolutes, weil sie alle anderen Dimensionen umfasst und unergründliche Themen wie Leere, das Nichts und den Tod beinhaltet. Mit dem Werkensemble bearbeitet Filko existenzielle Themen, die sich im Kräftefeld des Spirituellen bewegen.

↑[05] *Rotated Pyramid – Woman / Otočená pyramída – Žena*, 2000–06

←[01–02] Exhibition view, HALLE FÜR KUNST Steiermark, Graz, 2022

The tunnel can also symbolize restriction and death, while life is often seen as light and expansion. Restriction and expansion can be seen as one cosmic principle—one which is key in the two balloon works here. Air pumps create a cycle of movement within the balloons, so that these continually expand and contract. The symbolism of the color black on the balloon with the text *ALTRUISTADSEIQ 5.4.3.D. (EGO Balloon)* / *ALTRUISTADSEIQ 5.4.3.D. (EGO Balón)* (c. 2005) [07] also denotes that here the ego as a human principle is involved. It stands for a tense state in which on the one hand the ego can be strongly reduced and become nothing, while on the other hand humankind expands and takes effect by means of the ego, including to the point of altruism.

Der Tunnel kann auch Verengung und Tod symbolisieren, wohingegen das Leben oft als Licht bzw. als Ausbreitung aufgefasst wird. Verengung und Ausbreitung lassen sich als ein kosmisches Prinzip verstehen, das auch für die beiden Ballonarbeiten ausschlaggebend ist. Durch Luftzirkulationsmaschinen entsteht ein Kreislauf innerhalb der Ballons, worauf sich diese ausbreiten und immer wieder zusammenziehen. In Verbindung mit der Symbolik der schwarzen Farbe auf der beschriebenen Ballonarbeit *ALTRUISTADSEIQ 5.4.3.D. (EGO Balloon)* / *ALTRUISTADSEIQ 5.4.3.D. (EGO Balón)* (ca. 2005) [07] geht es außerdem um das Ego als menschliches Prinzip. Es steht für ein Spannungsverhältnis, welches das Ich zum einen stark reduzieren kann und zum Nichts werden lässt, zum anderen breitet sich der Mensch durch das Ego aus, bis hin zum Altruismus.

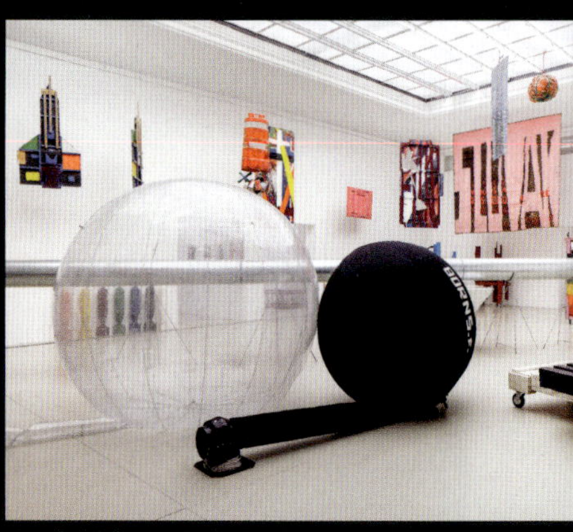

[06] Exhibition view, HALLE FÜR KUNST Steiermark, Graz, 2022

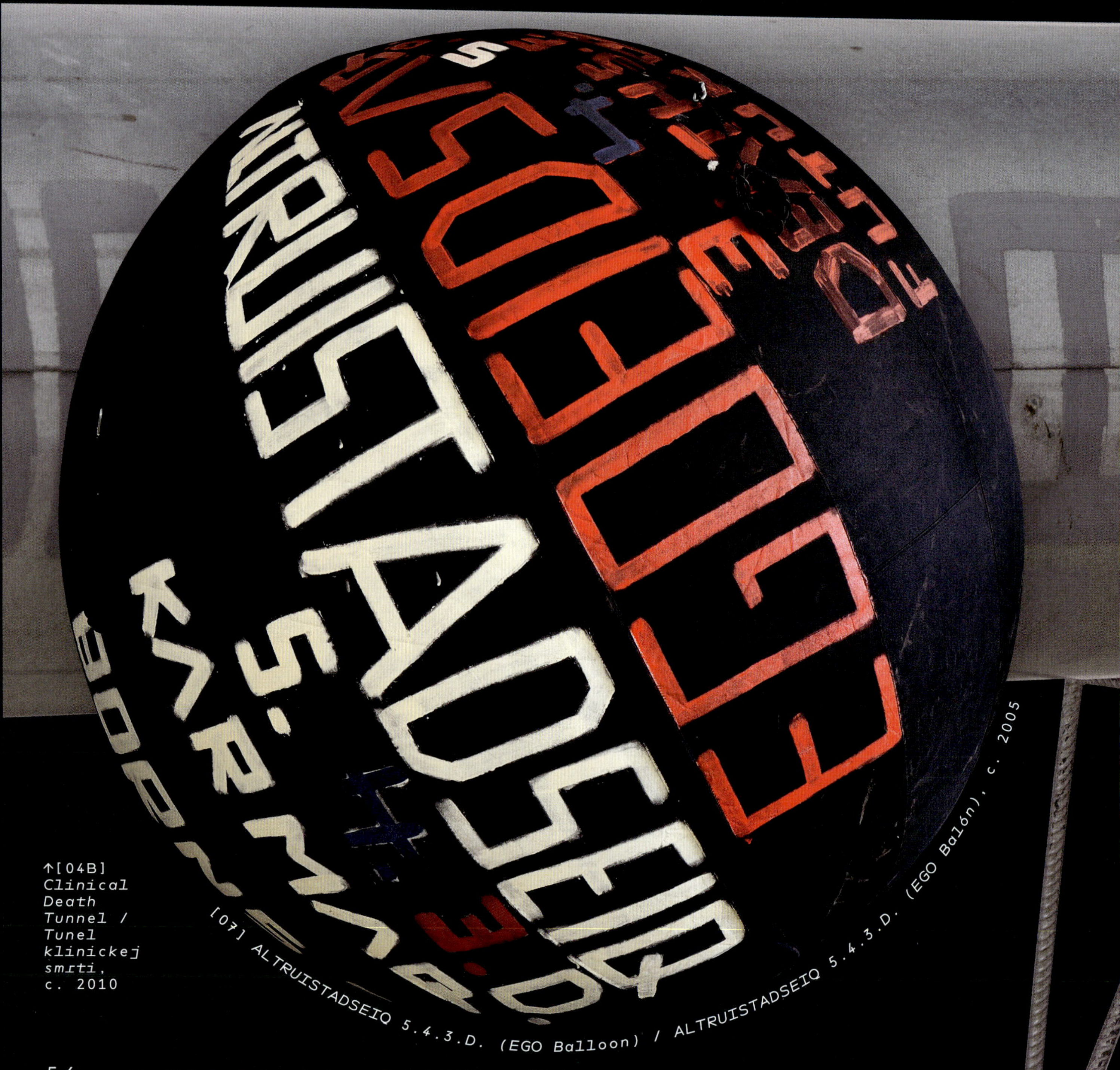

↑[04B] Clinical Death Tunnel / Tunel klinickej smrti, c. 2010

[07] ALTRUISTADSEIQ 5.4.3.D. (EGO Balloon) / ALTRUISTADSEIQ 5.4.3.D. (EGO Balón), c. 2005

Among the words that the text-images on the black balloon present are the words "Altruista," an unselfish altruism, and also "Borns" and "Deaths." This indicated a further dimension of the ego that Filko generated in a story he told about himself. He spoke of several "clinical deaths" he had experienced in serious accidents in 1945, 1952, and 1977. This also leads back to the *Clinical Death Tunnel*. Filko's birth was also complicated, lasting three days, as surviving documentation witnesses. Birth and death do not seem to be contradictions, and Filko uses both in the plural, probably in order to further subdivide his own identity and artistic creation. In this way, Filko as a person becomes a part of his own reflective system, and art and life become one.

Schriftbilder auf dem schwarzen Ballon lassen neben „Altruista", einem uneigennützigen Altruismus, auch noch Wörter wie „Borns" oder „Deaths" erkennen. Dies verweist auf eine weitere Dimension des Egos, die Filko anhand der Erzählung um die eigene Person generiert. Im Verlauf seines Lebens spricht Filko von mehreren „klinischen Toden" (clinical deaths), die er durch schwere Unfälle in den Jahren 1945, 1952 und 1977 erlebt hat. Dies führt wieder zurück zum *Clinical Death Tunnel*. Auch seine Geburt verlief kompliziert und schrittweise über drei Tage, was durch Unterlagen belegt ist. Geburt und Tod scheinen keine Widersprüche darzustellen und Filko verwendet beide im Plural, wohl um seine Identität und sein Schaffen weiter zu untergliedern. Filkos eigene Person wird so zum Teil seines reflexiven Systems, Kunst und Leben werden zu einer Einheit.

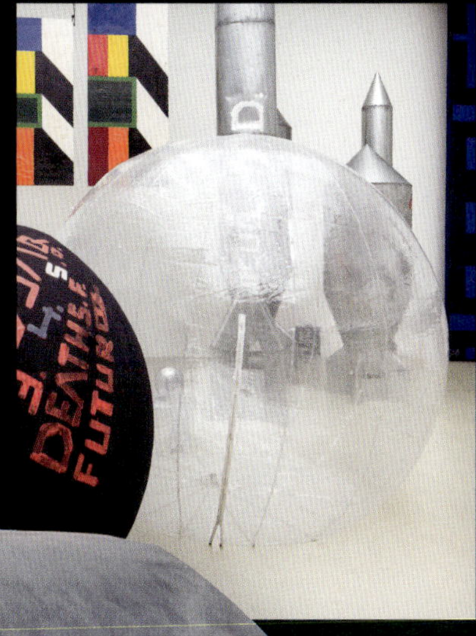

[08] *Globe in the Transparent Color Chakra / Guľa vo farbe transparentnej čakry,* c. 2005

A contrast to the expansion of the ego is presented in the transparent balloon *Globe in the Transparent Color Chakra / Guľa vo farbe transparentnej čakry* (c. 2005) [08]. For this work Filko used the highest chakra of the fifth dimension: transparency. Several levels higher than white, transparency represents a force that is closest to the void without however become an ultimate nothingness. Transparent emptiness is (active and passive) nothingness and death, but at the same time also the endless space in which life unfolds. Here Filko draws on an element of the cyclical logic of far-eastern and transcendental philosophy. Nothingness had a high status for the intelligentsia of the late 1960s, as the ultimate negative form and attitude of refusal, and Filko and his circle identified with this idea.

Der Ausbreitung des Egos steht die durchsichtige Ballonkugel *Globe in the Transparent Color Chakra / Guľa vo farbe transparentnej čakry* (ca. 2005) [08] gegenüber. Für die Arbeit verwendet Filko das höchste Chakra der höherwertigsten, 5. Dimension: Die Transparenz. Noch mehrere Ebenen höher als das Weiß, stellt das Transparente die Kraft dar, die der Leere am nächsten ist, ohne jedoch zum finalen Nichts zu werden. Die transparente Leere ist das (aktive und passive) Nichts und der Tod, gleichzeitig aber auch der unendliche Raum, in dem sich das Leben abspielt. Damit greift Filko ein Element aus der zyklischen Logik fern-östlicher und transzendentaler Philosophie auf. Das Nichts hatte als ultimative Negativ-Form und Verweigerungshaltung einen hohen Stellenwert innerhalb der Intelligenzia der späten 1960er-Jahre, dem sich auch der Kreis um Filko anschloss.

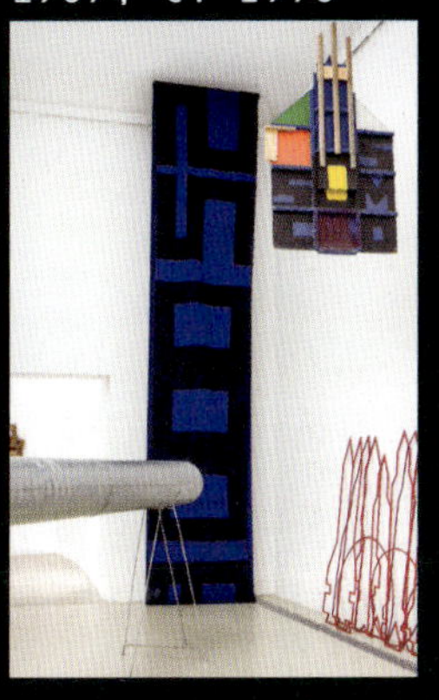

[09] *25,000 BC–1937,* c. 1995

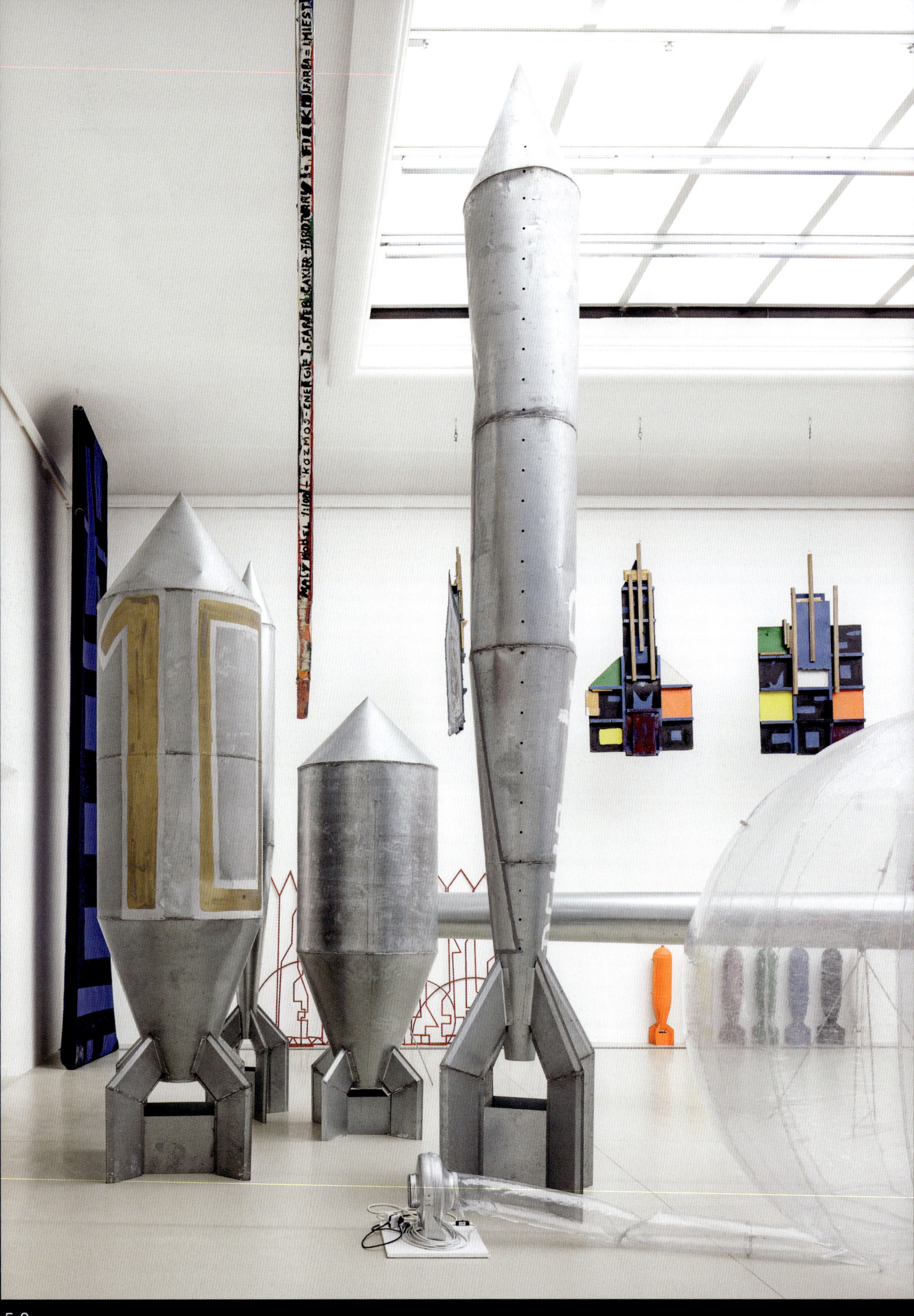

VI

Rockets and Space / Raketen und Weltraum

Rockets are a recurring motif that Filko used in different media and phases of his work. The artist's use of rocket shapes goes back to as early as the mid-1960s, as seen in the fifteen-part work in red, *Priestor – Space X. – Rockets / Priestor – Space X. – Rakety* (1967) [05], in which the outlines of rockets and other planetary shapes are traced. *Rockets 5.4.3.D. / Rakety 5.4.3.D.* (2000) [02] is presented, with its three objects in the three basic dimensions of Filko's ordering system he called *System SF*. The silver rocket shape is made more dynamic—and also gains a certain banality and irony—through quickly undertaken gestural painting in each of the three colors red (third dimension), blue (forth dimension), and white (fifth dimension).

Raketen sind ein wiederkehrendes Motiv, welches Filko in verschiedenen Medien und Werkphasen verwendet. Ihren Ausgang nahm die Raketenform bereits Mitte der 1960er-Jahre, wie beispielsweise in der fünfzehnteiligen in rot gehaltenen Arbeit, *Priestor – Space X. – Rockets / Priestor – Space X. – Rakety* (1967) [05], die jeweils schablonenhaft die Umrisse von Raketen und anderen planetarischen Formen andeutet. Die Arbeit *Rockets 5.4.3.D. / Rakety 5.4.3.D.* (2000) [02] spielt mit den drei grundlegenden Dimensionen von Filkos Ordnungssystem *System SF*. Die silberfarbene Raketenform wird durch schnell ausgeführte, gestische Malerei in jeweils einer der drei Hauptfarben Rot (3.D.), Blau (4.D.) und Weiß (5.D.) dynamisiert, aber auch ironisch trivialisiert.

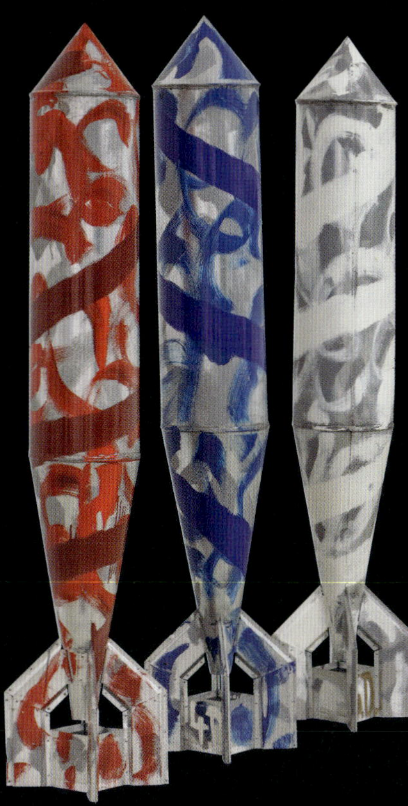

[02] Rockets 5.4.3.D. /
Rakety 5.4.3.D., 2000

Opposite them is the installation *Chakra Colors Rockets – Bombs / Rakety – bomby vo farbách čakier* (1985) [03], a row of seven bomb-like rocket objects. The dimensions have now expanded and the later *System SF* here manifests itself in a series of seven colors or chakras. The shapes here lead to associations of space travel and military weapon, so that on the one hand we note the historical context with military armament and attempts to take possession of space. On the other hand, Filko here expresses his inexorable will to artistic expression, a determination that transcends all borders between nations and political systems and that does not shy away from occasionally violent gestures.

Demgegenüber ist die Installation *Chakra Colors Rockets – Bombs / Rakety – bomby vo farbách čakier* (1985) [03] zu sehen, eine Reihe von sieben bombenartigen Raketenobjekten. Die Dimensionen haben sich geöffnet und das spätere *System SF* materialisiert sich in seiner Abfolge an sieben Farben bzw. Chakren. Die Form der Arbeit wie damit verknüpfte Assoziationen changieren zwischen Raumfahrt und Kriegswaffe. Zum einen rückt dadurch der historische Kontext rund um die militärische Aufrüstung und Eroberung des Weltraums in den Blick. Zum anderen bringt Filko seinen unbeugsamen Willen zur künstlerischen Expansion zum Ausdruck, ein Wille, der sich über jegliche Grenzen zwischen Nationen und politischen Systemen hinwegsetzt, und mitunter auch nicht vor gewaltvollen Gesten zurückschreckt.

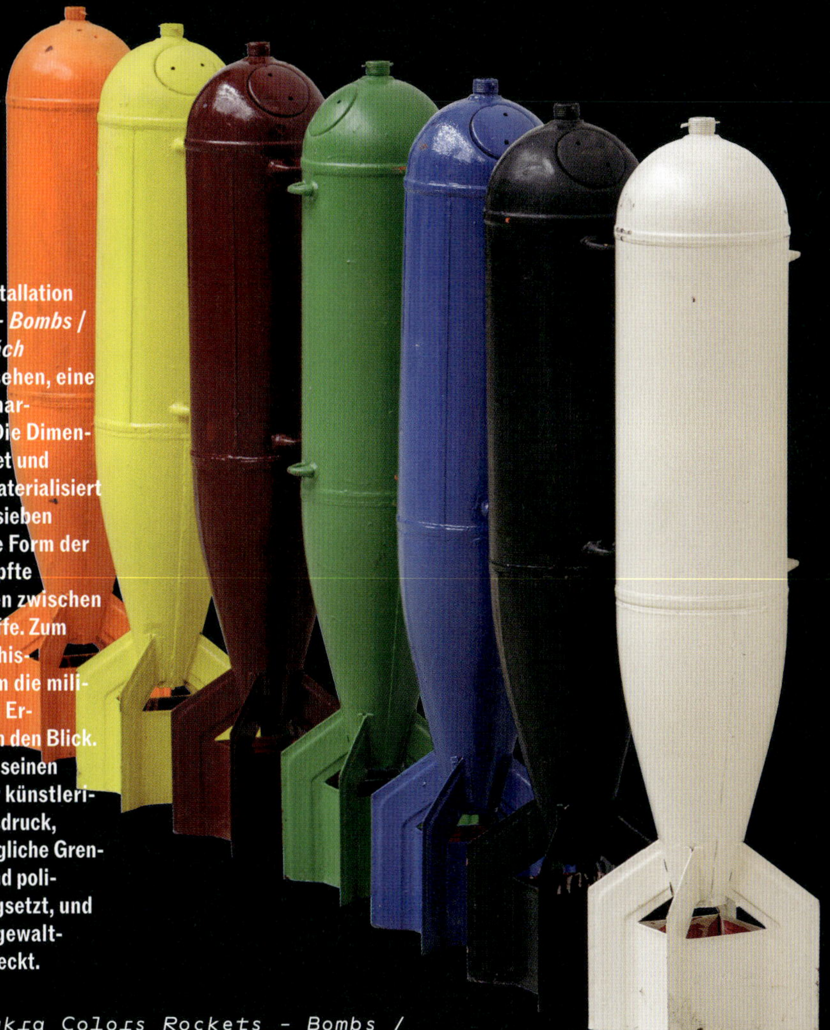

↗[03] Chakra Colors Rockets - Bombs /
Rakety - bomby vo farbách čakier, c. 1985

The rocket motif is particularly powerful in the six-meter high sculpture *DSUQ 4.D. Rocket / DSUQ 4.D. Raketa* (2000) [07]. This work is an enactment of the ninth chakra in Filko's system, as denoted by the silver color and the lettering "IR 9." While Filko's early rockets addressed (geo-)political and ideological contexts, the reference here to his *System SF* stresses the significance of this work within his artistic worldview. The silver chakra belongs to the highest dimensions and stands for transcendence.

An installation in three parts hangs from the ceiling. Here Filko also takes a sculptural approach to the rocket motif in terms of the relationship between its outlines and physical body, but he also resolves this tension through painting. The elements of the work *TIMESPACE – 4.3.D. (Rockets) / TIMESPACE – 4.3.D. (Rakety)* (1968/1993) [08] are each different on each side, with the rockets seen on the one side as broad and flat spaceships in blue and black. On the other side there are various color fields that are given spatial depth by means of flanking wooden bars, so that they are also reminiscent of an easel. This installation derives its energy from the tension between spatial object and painterly sign.

In beeindruckender Singularität kommt das Raketenmotiv in der sechs Meter hohen Skulptur *DSUQ 4.D. Rocket / DSUQ 4.D. Raketa* (2000) [07] zur Geltung. Das Werk setzt mit silberner Farbe und der Aufschrift „IR 9" das neunte Chakra von Filkos System in Szene. Während Filkos frühe Raketen-Arbeiten um (geo-)politische und ideologische Zusammenhänge kreisen, hebt die Weiterführung zum *System SF* die Bedeutung innerhalb seiner künstlerischen Weltanschauung hervor. Das silberne Chakra ist den höchsten Stufen der Dimensionen zugehörig und steht für den Bereich der Transzendenz.

Von der Decke hängt eine Installation aus drei Teilen, in der Filko das Raketenmotiv auch in einem plastischen Verhältnis zwischen Umriss und Räumlichkeit bearbeitet, das malerisch aufgelöst wird. Die verschiedenen Teile der Arbeit *TIMESPACE – 4.3.D. (Rockets) / TIMESPACE – 4.3.D. (Rakety)* (1968/1993) [08] sind beidseitig ausgeführt, auf der einen Seite haben sich die Raketen in die Breite gezogen und werden zu flachen Raumschiffen aus blauer und schwarzer Farbe. Auf der anderen Seite werden verschiedene Farbfelder verräumlicht, indem sie von Holzstreben flankiert sind, die an eine Staffelei erinnern. Die Installation lebt von ihrer Spannung zwischen räumlichem Objekt und malerischem Zeichen.

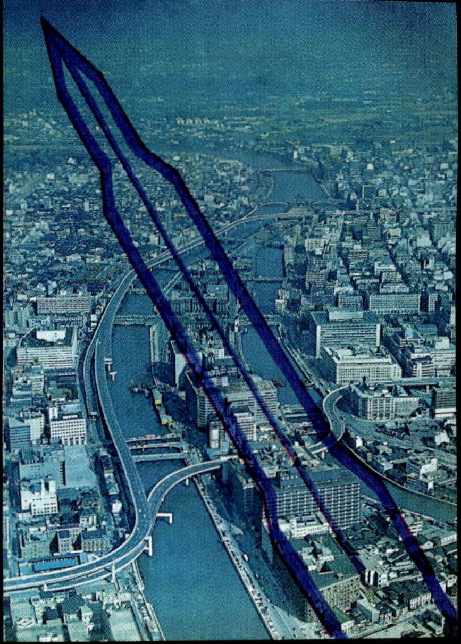

[04] From the series *Sculptures of the Twentieth century IV. / Zo série Sochy XX. storočia IV.*, 1968–69

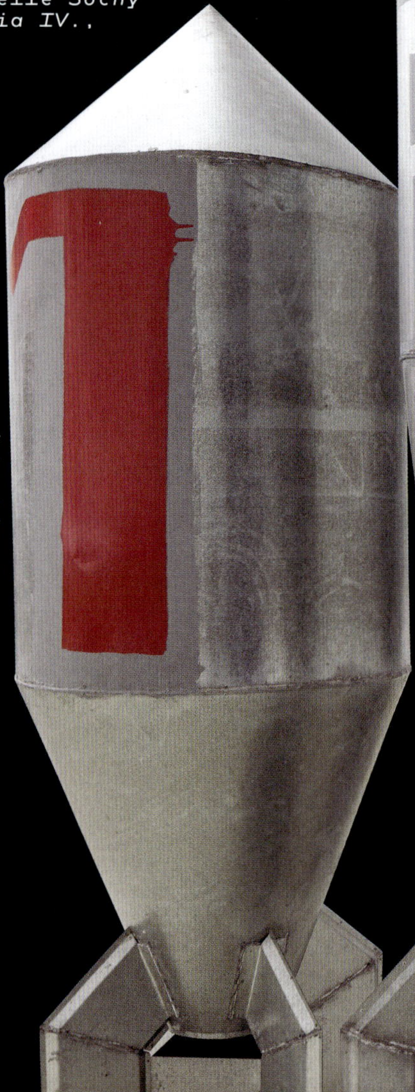

[06] First Chakra Rocket / Raketa prvej čakry, c. 2005

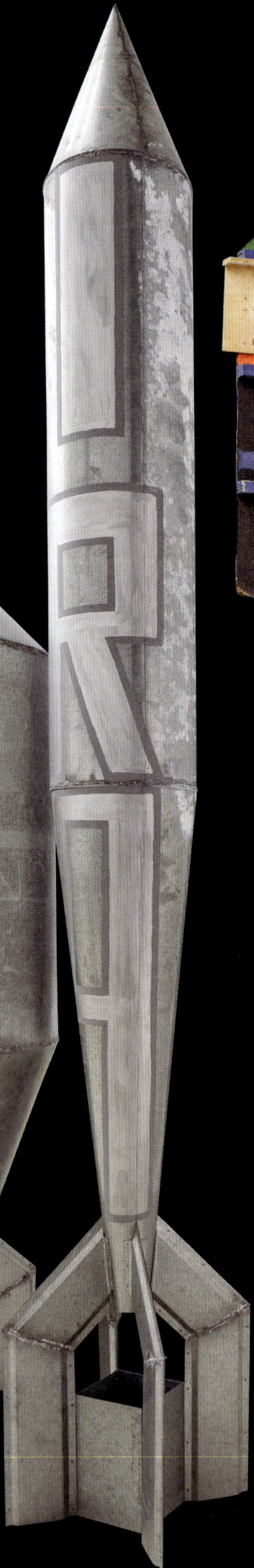

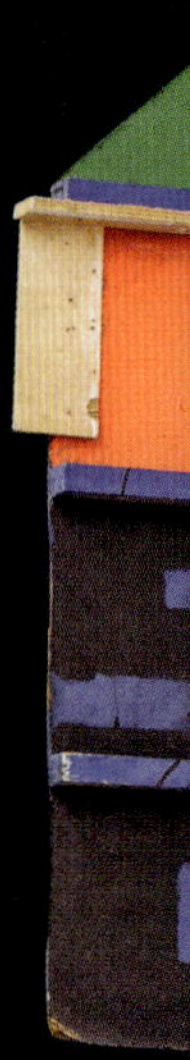

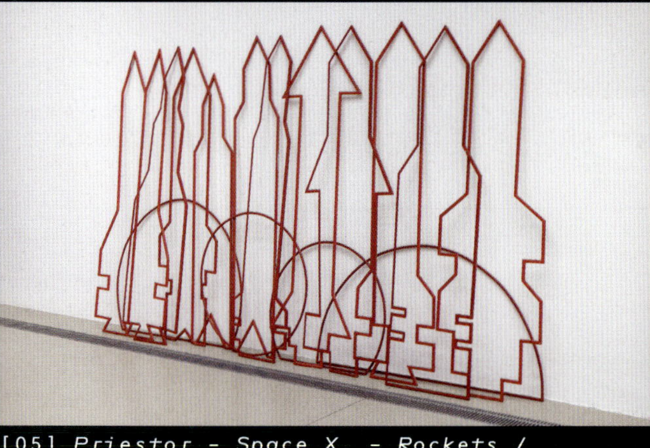

[05] *Priestor – Space X. – Rockets / Priestor – Space X. – Rakety*, 1967

[07] *DSUQ 4.D. Rocket / DSUQ 4.D. Raketa*, 2000

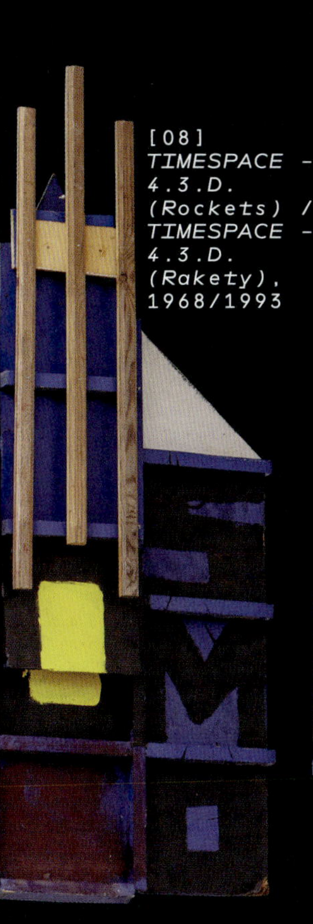

[08] *TIMESPACE - 4.3.D. (Rockets) / TIMESPACE - 4.3.D. (Rakety)*, 1968/1993

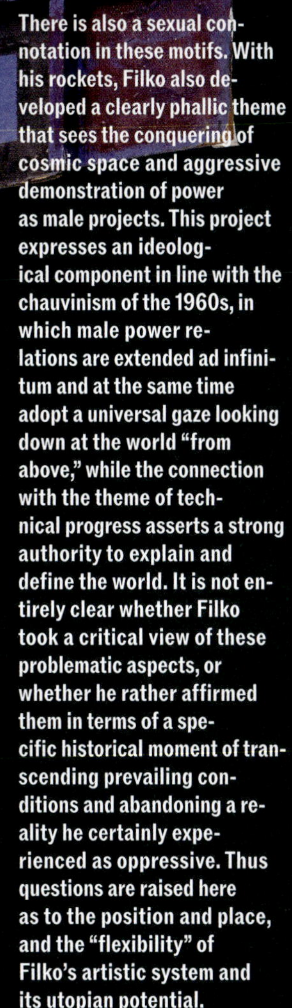

[09] *DSQ 4.D. Bomb / DSQ 4.D. Bomba*, 1985–95

Spectators encounter the rocket shape again with the installation *Universal Environment / Univerzálne prostredie* (1966–67). Here the motifs are on transparent banners that have great presence in the physical space of the gallery but are nonetheless flat surfaces. Here too, these rockets reflect the geopolitical relations between Russia and America and address global themes such as armament and the conquering of outer space. In the series *Map of the World (Rockets) / Mapa sveta (Rakety)* (1967) [10] the colored outlines of rockets are drawn on world maps and cover up various countries and continents. This motif is also seen as an outline drawn onto photographs from the series *Sculptures of the Twentieth Century / Sochy XX. storočia* (1968–69) [04].

Die Raketenform zeigt sich auch in der Installation *Universal Environment / Univerzálne prostredie* (1966–1967). Hier wird das Motiv auf transparente Banner gesetzt und dringt damit zwar in den Ausstellungsraum vor, bleibt aber gleichzeitig flächig. Die Raketen reflektieren hier auch die geopolitischen Verhältnisse zwischen Russland und Amerika und thematisieren weltumspannende Logiken wie Aufrüstung und die Eroberung des Weltraums. In der Serie *Map of the World (Rockets) / Mapa sveta (Rakety)* (1967) [10] bedecken Raketen als farbliche Umrisse auf Weltkarten verschiedene Länder und Kontinente. Das Motiv taucht auch als Umriss vor fotografischen Arbeiten in der Serie *Sculptures of the Twentieth Century / Sochy XX. storočia* (1968–1969) [04] auf.

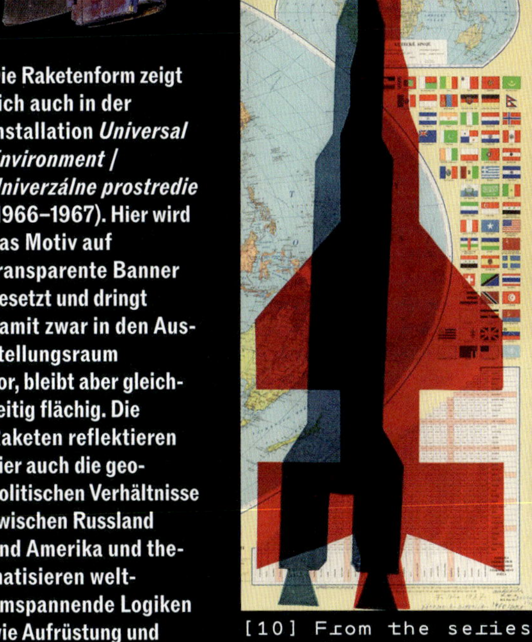

[10] From the series *Map of the World (Rockets) / Zo série Mapa sveta (Rakety)*, 1967

There is also a sexual connotation in these motifs. With his rockets, Filko also developed a clearly phallic theme that sees the conquering of cosmic space and aggressive demonstration of power as male projects. This project expresses an ideological component in line with the chauvinism of the 1960s, in which male power relations are extended ad infinitum and at the same time adopt a universal gaze looking down at the world "from above," while the connection with the theme of technical progress asserts a strong authority to explain and define the world. It is not entirely clear whether Filko took a critical view of these problematic aspects, or whether he rather affirmed them in terms of a specific historical moment of transcending prevailing conditions and abandoning a reality he certainly experienced as oppressive. Thus questions are raised here as to the position and place, and the "flexibility" of Filko's artistic system and its utopian potential.

Offensichtlich schwingt bei dieser Sujetwahl auch eine geschlechtliche Konnotation mit. Mit den Raketen bildet Filko nicht zuletzt ein dezidiert phallisches Motiv aus, welches die Eroberung des kosmischen Raumes und kriegerische Machtgebärden als maskuline Projekte ausweist. In diesem Projekt äußert sich analog zum Chauvinismus der 1960er-Jahre eine ideologische Komponente, in der sich männliche Machtverhältnisse bis ins Unendliche ausdehnen und gleichsam einen universalen Blick „von oben" auf die Welt einnehmen, was in Verbindung mit dem rasanten technischen Fortschritt eine starke Definitionsmacht beinhaltet. Fraglich ist, ob Filko diesen problematischen Verhältnissen kritisch gegenüberstand oder ob er diese nicht vielmehr aus der spezifischen historischen Position eines Aufbruchs aus den Verhältnissen heraus und dem potentiellen Zurücklassen der teils bedrückend erlebten Wirklichkeit affirmierte. Insofern stellen sich in diesem Kontext Fragen nach der Positionierung, Verortung und „Beweglichkeit" von Filkos künstlerischem System, wie nach seinem utopischen Potential.

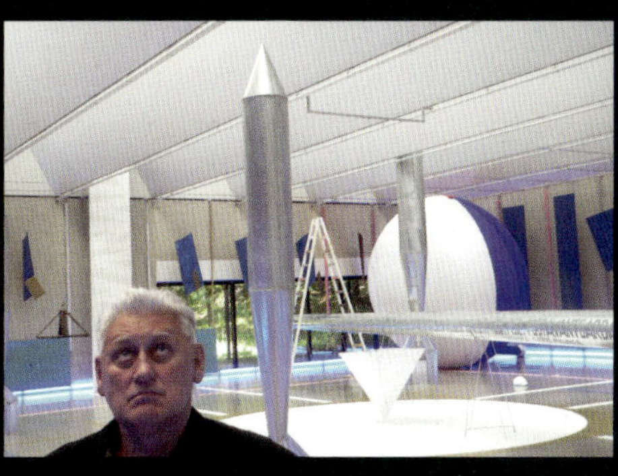

[11] *Living Art - On the Edge of Europe*, Kröller-Müller Museum, Otterlo, 2006

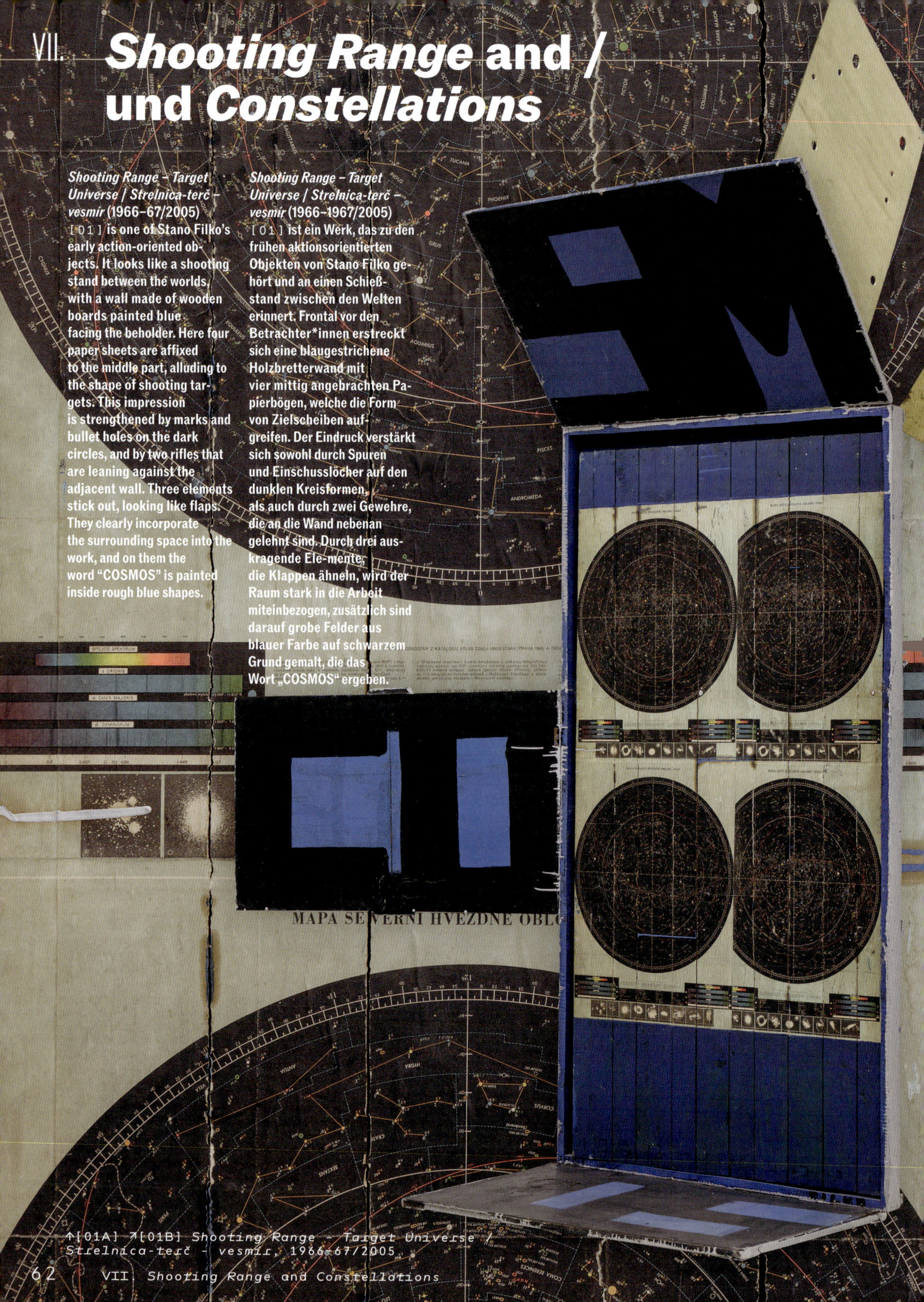

VII

Shooting Range and / und *Constellations*

Shooting Range – Target Universe / Strelnica-terč – vesmír (1966–67/2005)
[01] is one of Stano Filko's early action-oriented objects. It looks like a shooting stand between the worlds, with a wall made of wooden boards painted blue facing the beholder. Here four paper sheets are affixed to the middle part, alluding to the shape of shooting targets. This impression is strengthened by marks and bullet holes on the dark circles, and by two rifles that are leaning against the adjacent wall. Three elements stick out, looking like flaps. They clearly incorporate the surrounding space into the work, and on them the word "COSMOS" is painted inside rough blue shapes.

Shooting Range – Target Universe / Strelnica-terč – vesmír (1966–1967/2005)
[01] ist ein Werk, das zu den frühen aktionsorientierten Objekten von Stano Filko gehört und an einen Schießstand zwischen den Welten erinnert. Frontal vor den Betrachter*innen erstreckt sich eine blaugestrichene Holzbretterwand mit vier mittig angebrachten Papierbögen, welche die Form von Zielscheiben aufgreifen. Der Eindruck verstärkt sich sowohl durch Spuren und Einschusslöcher auf den dunklen Kreisformen, als auch durch zwei Gewehre, die an die Wand nebenan gelehnt sind. Durch drei auskragende Ele-mente, die Klappen ähneln, wird der Raum stark in die Arbeit miteinbezogen, zusätzlich sind darauf grobe Felder aus blauer Farbe auf schwarzem Grund gemalt, die das Wort „COSMOS" ergeben.

↑[01A] ↗[01B] *Shooting Range – Target Universe / Strelnica-terč – vesmír, 1966–67/2005*

This arrangement conceives of real and cosmic space together. Filko's blue symbolizes the cosmos, appearing together with the targets, which can also be seen to be starlit skies. The cosmic space is also expressed by various diagrams and images of stars. The object itself bears marks that indicate action art. The cosmic targets imply a struggle while also adding connotations of rockets and spacecraft. In this way Filko enacts humanity's forays into space and reflects on the dissonance between political and artistic appropriation of the cosmos. As in many of his works, his ideas ultimately take the position of the recipients including it as part of the work.

Durch dieses Arrangement werden realer Raum und kosmischer Raum zusammengedacht: Filkos blaue Farbe symbolisiert den Kosmos, der zusammen mit den Zielscheiben in Erscheinung tritt, die auch als Sternenhimmel erkennbar sind. Den kosmischen Raum bringen außerdem verschiedene Messdiagramme und Sternaufnahmen zum Ausdruck. Auf dem Objekt selbst befinden sich Spuren, die auf Aktionskunst hinweisen. Die kosmischen Zielscheiben implizieren Wettkampf und stellen gleichzeitig eine gedankliche Verbindung zwischen Projektilen und Raumschiffen her. Auf diese Weise setzt Filko das menschliche Vordringen in den Weltraum in Szene und reflektiert Verwerfungen zwischen realpolitischer und künstlerischer Aneignung des Kosmos. Wie bei vielen seiner Arbeiten beziehen seine Überlegungen letztlich die Position der Rezipient*innen mit ein und setzt sie ins Werk.

↑[02A] ←[02B]
Constellations / Súhvezdia,
1968–69

Floating in space there are seven works from Filko's series *Constellations / Súhvezdia* (1968–69) [02], which also address the theme of the appropriation of the cosmic space by humankind. The perforated copper sheets look like a machine-made cartographic system, while also displaying elements of the fantastic. On the one side the perforations are linked by straight lines that create star signs. On the other side the holes are presented without any links, but linguistic categories have been written on the sheets. Some of these words name star signs or seasons of the year like spring and fall.

The *Constellations* raise the question as to our perspective on cosmic space. From the human viewpoint, the stars are collated into pictures, even though they are celestial objects that are millions of kilometers apart. Filko explores the question of the insights and new realities the stars and their constellations might provide. At the same time he rejects the idea of individual artistic expression by using a machine aesthetics that negates artisanship, and that tends to asserts the objectivity of these *scientific* insights and the subjective artistic practice.

Im Raum schwebend sind sieben Werke aus Filkos Serie der *Constellations / Súhvezdia* (1968–1969) [02] zu sehen, die ebenfalls die Aneignung des kosmischen Raumes durch den Menschen thematisieren. Die perforierten Kupferblätter wirken wie ein maschinell gefertigtes kartografisches System, lassen aber gleichzeitig eine gewisse Fantastik nicht vermissen. Auf der einen Seite sind die Perforierungen durch Geraden verbunden und zeigen Sternbilder. Auf der anderen Seite werden die Löcher unverbunden dargestellt, aber die Platte mit sprachlichen Kategorisierungen versehen. Teilweise bezeichnen die Wörter verschiedene Sternbilder und Jahreszeiten wie Frühling oder Herbst.

Durch die *Constellations* stellt sich die Frage der Perspektive auf den kosmischen Raum: Aus dem menschlichen Blickwinkel werden die Sterne zu Bildern zusammengefasst – Himmelskörper, die aber teilweise Millionen von Kilometern voneinander entfernt sind. Filko beschäftigt sich mit der Frage, welche Erkenntnisse und neuen Realitäten aus den Sternen und ihren Konstellationen gewonnen werden können. Gleichzeitig verneint er durch eine dem Handwerk widerstrebende, maschinelle Ästhetik den individuellen, künstlerischen Ausdruck und spielt mit einem Anspruch auf die Objektivität dieser *wissenschaftlichen* Erkenntnisse und der subjektiven künstlerischen Praxis.

[01C] *Shooting Range – Target Universe / Strelnica-terč – vesmír,* 1966–67/2005

VIII

(Model) Architecture as Artistic Utopia / (Modell-)Architektur als künstlerische Utopie

During his early creative period in the 1960s Stano Filko also worked on a series of designs for monumental sculptures for public space. He planned many of these so that they could never be implemented—they have utopian associations as models that express the tension between an idea and its capacity for realization. Here Filko also makes ironic reference to the architecture and sculpture of realist Soviet monumentalism.

The several-part installation with four works from the series *Models of Observation Towers / Modely pozorovacich veží* (1966–67/c. 1990) [01–03] is an interesting example of Filko's exploration of the structure of public space. The so-called "observation towers" are placed on a floor with mirrors, and they are bizarre pieces of mechanical equipment standing before a three-part photograph of the urban space of Bratislava. The colors seem strange, giving these objects a partly animal-like appearance, whereby Filko probably only added the colors in the 1990s.

Während seiner frühen Schaffensphase in den 1960er-Jahren hat sich Stano Filko auch mit einer Reihe an Entwürfen für monumentale Skulpturen für den öffentlichen Raum beschäftigt. Viele dieser Ideen von Filko sind so konzipiert, dass sie gar nicht realisierbar gewesen wären. Sie weisen utopische Anklänge auf und werden zu modellartigen Werken, die das Spannungsverhältnis zwischen Idee und Realisierbarkeit zum Ausdruck bringen. Filko stellt dabei unter anderem einen ironischen Bezug zur Architektur und Skulptur der sowjet-realistischen Monumentalität her.

Die mehrteilige Installation aus vier Arbeiten der Werkserie *Models of Observation Towers / Modely pozorovacich veží* (1966–1967/ca. 1990) [01–03] stellt ein besonderes Beispiel von Filkos Auseinandersetzung mit der Struktur des öffentlichen Raumes dar. Auf verspiegelten Bodenplatten sind die sogenannten *Observation Towers* zu sehen, bizarre, mechanische Geräte, die vor einer dreiteiligen Fotografie des städtischen Raumes von Bratislava stehen. Seltsam wirken die Farben, welche den Objekten ein teilweise kreaturhaftes Aussehen verleihen, wobei Filko die Farblichkeit wahrscheinlich erst nachträglich in den 1990er-Jahren angebracht hat.

These sculptural observation towers are linked up with a photographic view of the city of Bratislava in the late 1960s, showing a marginal area of the city where monumental real-socialist apartment blocks contrast with the surrounding countryside. The latter looks like an enormous gap in the building project, a gaping hole between city and country and also between the neighboring sister cities of Bratislava and Vienna. The forms of buildings can be understood as expressions of different worldviews and traditions. While Soviet architecture attempted to appropriate the utopia of aesthetic modernism, we can also ask whether Vienna is modern at all, given its manifold connections to history and the shared experience and suffering during the long years of the monarchy. Filko also enacts failed utopias, raising the question as to at which point universalism shifts to standardization and individuals are sacrificed to an art inadequate to their needs.

Die skulpturalen Aussichts- oder Überwachungstürme sind mit einer fotografischen Ansicht des Stadtgebiets von Bratislava aus den späten 1960er-Jahren räumlich verbunden. Man sieht ein Randgebiet der Stadt, in dem monumentale, real-sozialistisch geprägte Wohnblockbauten auf das Umland treffen. Das Umland erinnert an die enorme bauliche Lücke, die zwischen Stadt und Land, aber auch den benachbarten Schwesterstädten Bratislava und Wien klafft. Baustrukturen können auch als Ausdruck unterschiedlicher Weltbilder und Traditionen verstanden werden. Während die sowjetische Architektur versucht hat, sich die Utopie der ästhetischen Moderne anzueignen, lässt sich der Frage nachgehen, ob Wien mit seinen vielfältigen Verbindungen zur Historie und der gemeinsam erlebt und erlittenen Periode der Monarchie je modern gewesen ist. Filko setzt darüber hinaus auch gescheiterte Utopien in Szene, wobei sich die Frage stellt, ab welchem Punkt Universalismus in Standardisierung übergeht und das Individuum auch durch seine nicht adäquate Kunst auf der Strecke bleibt.

→[02] *Model of Observation Tower / Model pozorovacej veže, 1967*

A further fascinating aspect of these works is Filko's artistic incorporation of found objects. For the *Observation Towers* he uses parts of various machines, but does not deploy these in isolation, instead transferring their functions into new contexts by means of his own adjustments and combinations. A more radical use of found objects is seen in the installation *Pneumatic Circles I. – XXXX. / Pneumatické kolesá I. – XXXX.* (1968) [04-05]. Filko's artistic interventions here consist only of a reordering of the inflatable rubber tires that are piled up on mirrors. In the work of Stano Filko there is a continuous and complex approach to the theme of authorship. With turning against artisanal artistic practices and the search for a form of art that is free of any personal signature, changes in the authorial position evolve in the environments and assemblages. These ways of searching are typical for different trends of the period ranging from Proto-Pop to Concept Art. On the other hand, he at the same time pursued his ongoing inclusion of his art into his own *System SF* over several decades, placing his works in a specific context and desubjectifying them from within his own conceptual and metaphysical understanding.

Ein weiterer, spannender Aspekt der Werke liegt in Filkos künstlerischer Einbindung von gefundenen Objekten. Für die *Observation Towers* zieht Filko Teile von verschiedenen Maschinen heran, verwendet diese aber nicht allein, sondern überführt deren Funktionalität durch eigene Bearbeitungen und Kombinationen in neue Zusammenhänge. Eine radikalere Verwendung von gefundenen Objekten wird in der Installation *Pneumatic Circles I. – XXXX. / Pneumatické kolesá I. – XXXX.* (1968) [04-05] deutlich. Filkos künstlerische Eingriffe bestehen hier lediglich in einer Neuanordnung von aufblasbaren Gummireifen, die auf Spiegelplatten übereinandergeschichtet werden. Im Œuvre von Stano Filko lässt sich so ein komplexer Bezug zum Thema Autorenschaft erkennen. Mit dem Rückzug aus handwerklichen künstlerischen Praktiken und der Suche nach einer Kunst, die von persönlicher Handschrift befreit ist, ergeben sich in den Environments und Assemblagen auch Veränderungen in der auktorialen Position. Diese Suchbewegungen sind typisch für verschiedene Strömungen der Zeit, von Proto-Pop bis Konzeptkunst. Zum anderen setzt er gleichzeitig über Jahrzehnte die laufende Einschreibung seiner Kunst in das *System SF* fort, indem er diese dadurch kontextualisiert und aus seinem konzeptionellen und metaphysischem Verständnis heraus entsubjektiviert.

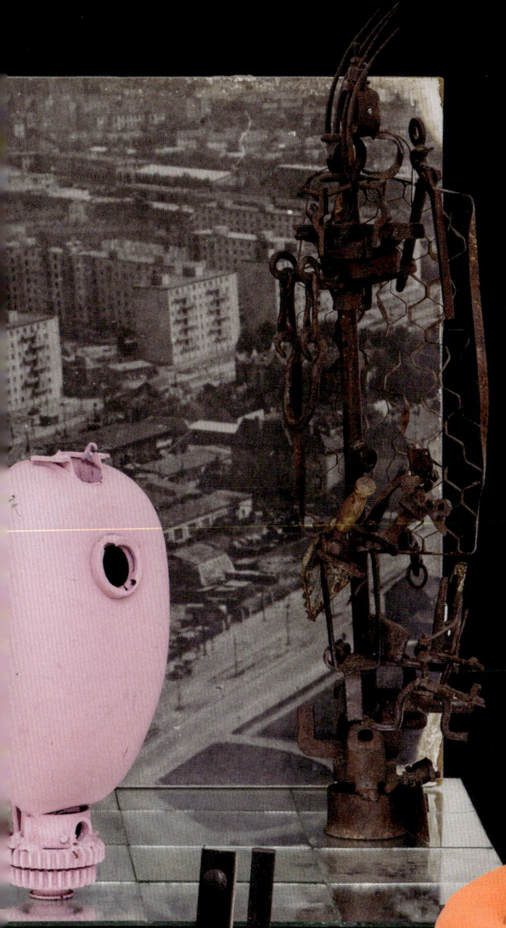

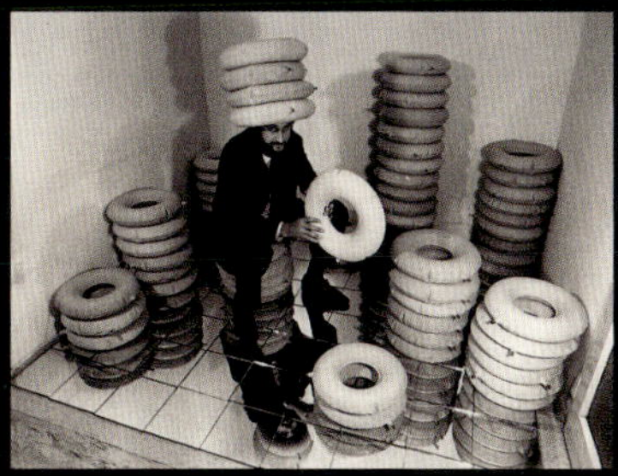

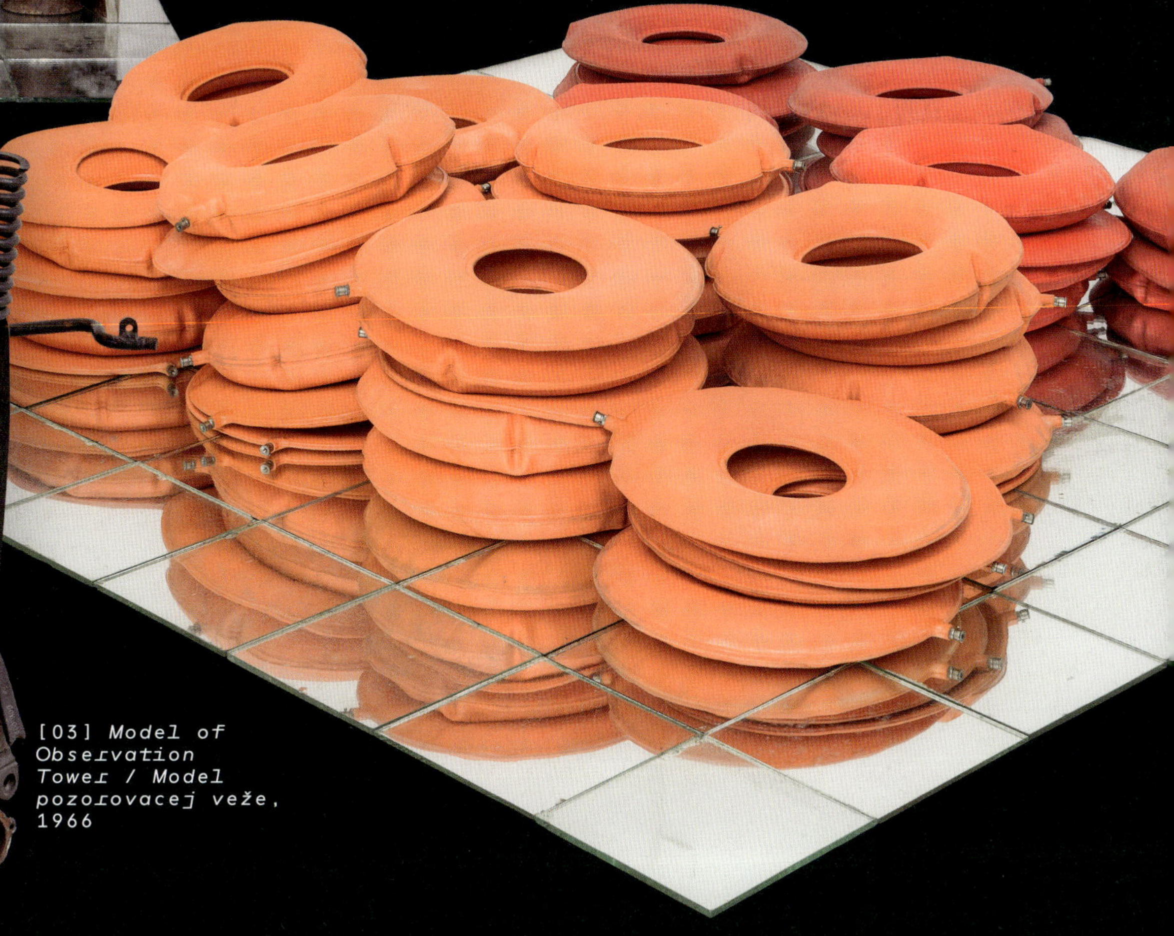

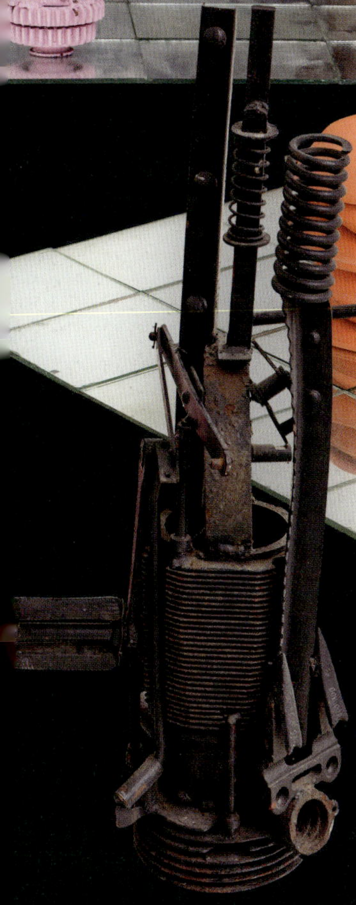

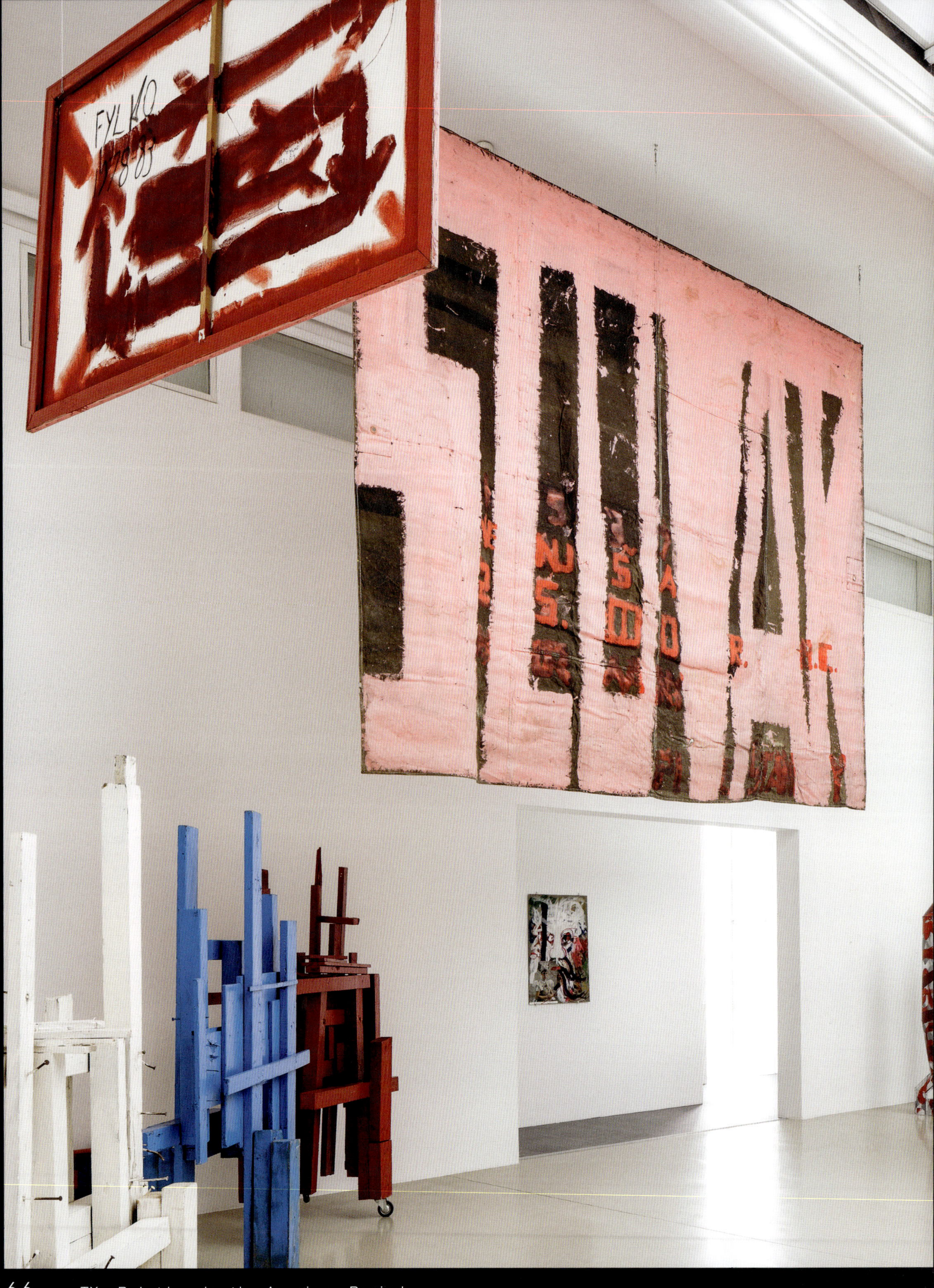
FYLKO

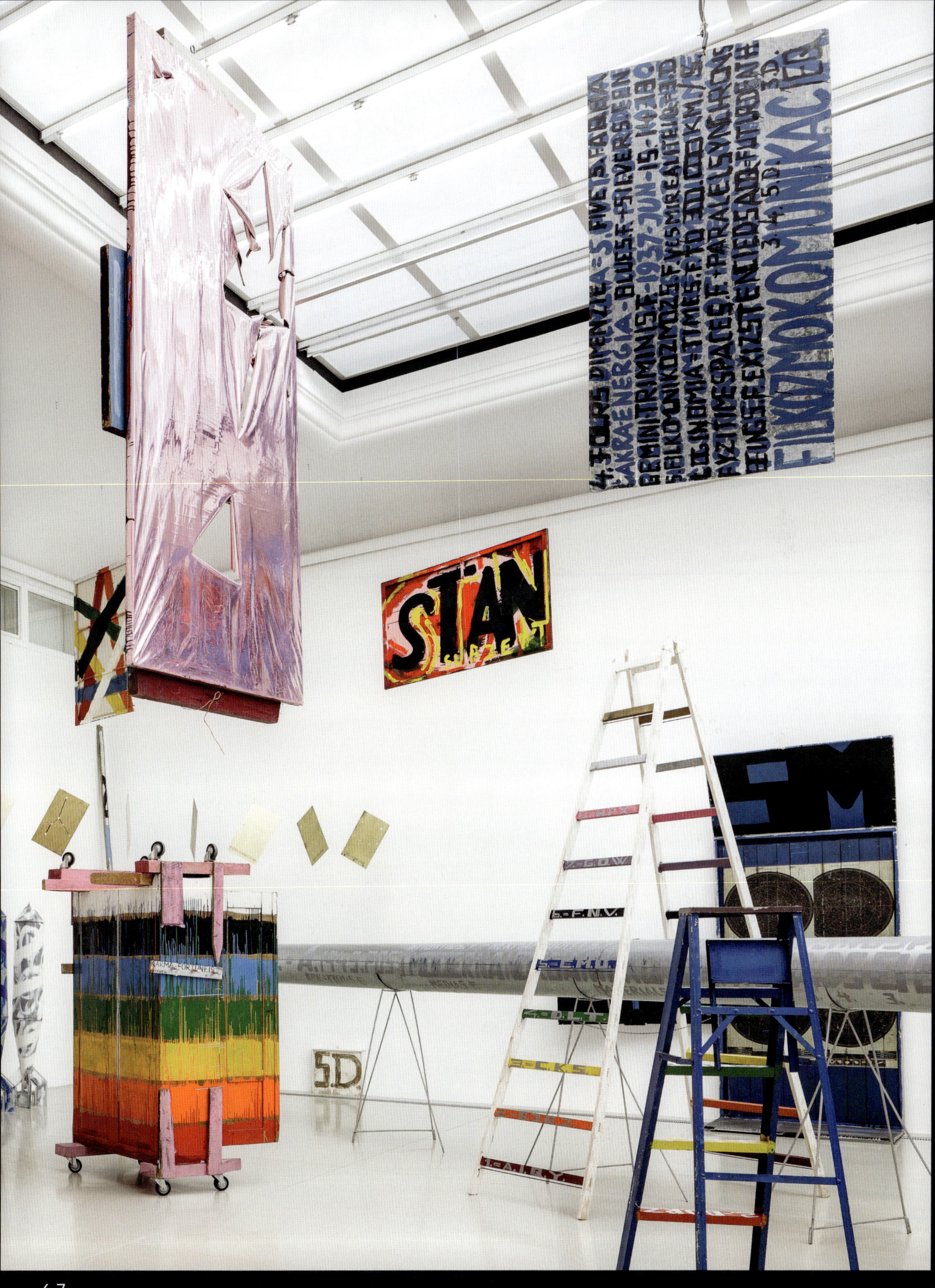

STAN
SUBJECT
5.D.

Painting in the American Period / Malerei in der amerikanischen Periode

Painting presents another facet of Filko's multidimensional work. Whereas the color white was dominant in the artist's works in the mid-1970s, and subjective expression became less and less significant, many of his paintings from the 1980s are highly expressive, and they often use the color red. Filko's participation in documenta 7 (1982) and his subsequent emigration to New York marked a change in his work, and there was a new energy to his American phase (1982–90).

These works give us an idea how emotional it must have been for Filko to find himself in the very heart of capitalist America. The excessive nature of these paintings matches this mood. For some of them, Filko used unusual media such as cardboard, and he also sometimes painted them on both sides, as in *SLOVAK* (1985) [02] and *AIDS – STAN* (1983) [03]. While the reverse of *SLOVAK* (1985) explored the potential and limits of the pictorial space with painterly stripes in Filko's chakra colors, in *AIDS – STAN* (1983) he seems to be expressing a new identity by using the American form of his own name and also placing himself in relationship with the AIDS crisis of the time.

Malerei eröffnet eine weitere Facette von Filkos mehrdimensionalem Werk. Während in Filkos Œuvre zu Mitte der 1970er-Jahre die Farbe Weiß dominierte und der subjektive Ausdruck immer weiter zurückging, sind viele der Malereien aus den 1980er-Jahren äußerst ausdrucksstark und mit der Farbe Rot verbunden. Einen starken Einschnitt im Werk von Filko bilden vor allem seine Teilnahme an der documenta 7 (1982) und die anschließende Emigration nach New York. Eine neue Energie wird in seiner amerikanischen Schaffensphase (1982–1990) freigesetzt.

Es lässt sich eine ungefähre Ahnung davon erlangen, wie aufwühlend es für Filko gewesen sein muss, sich im Herzen des kapitalistischen Amerika wiederzufinden. Dazu passt der ausschweifende Charakter der Malerei: Sie wird von Filko teilweise mit ungewöhnlichen Trägermaterialien wie Pappkarton verbunden und bedeckt zudem oft die Hinterseite der Arbeiten. So sind auch *SLOVAK* (1985) [02] und *AIDS – STAN* (1983) [03] auf beiden Seiten der Leinwand mit Farbe versehen. Während auf der Rückseite von *SLOVAK* (1985) durch malerische Bahnen in den Chakrenfarben die Möglichkeiten und Grenzen des Bildraumes ausgelotet werden, scheint Filko in *AIDS – STAN* (1983) durch die Amerikanisierung seines Namens eine neue Identität auszudrücken und sich mit der damaligen AIDS-Krise in Beziehung zu setzen.

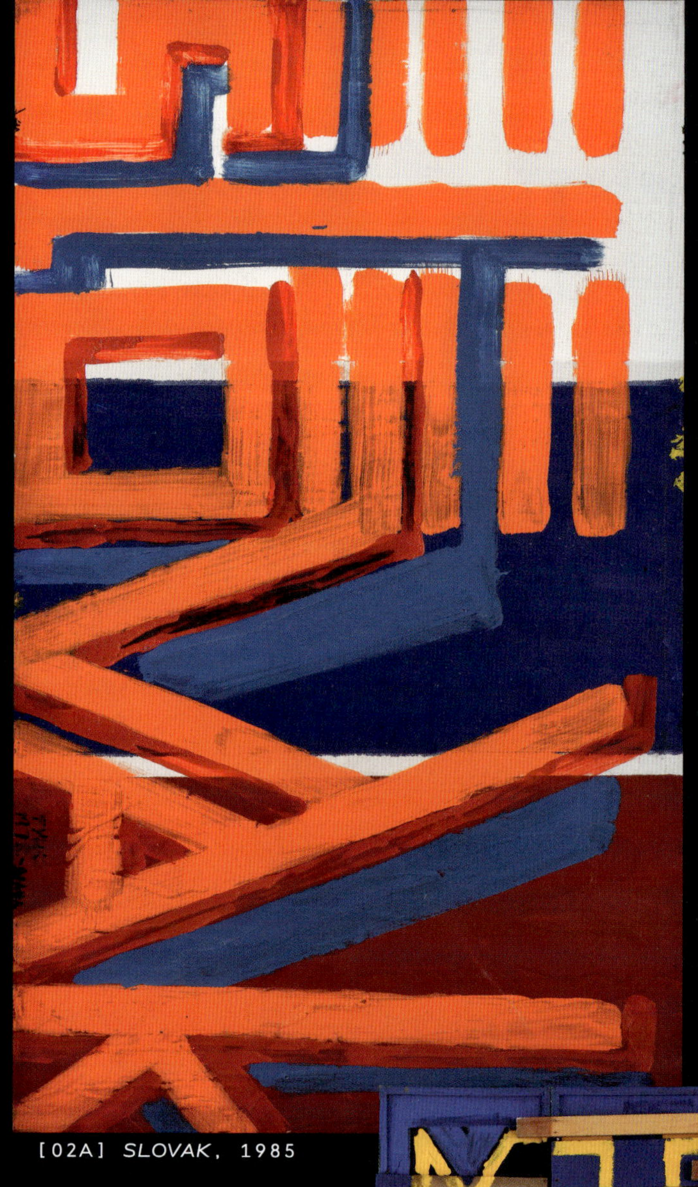
[02A] SLOVAK, 1985

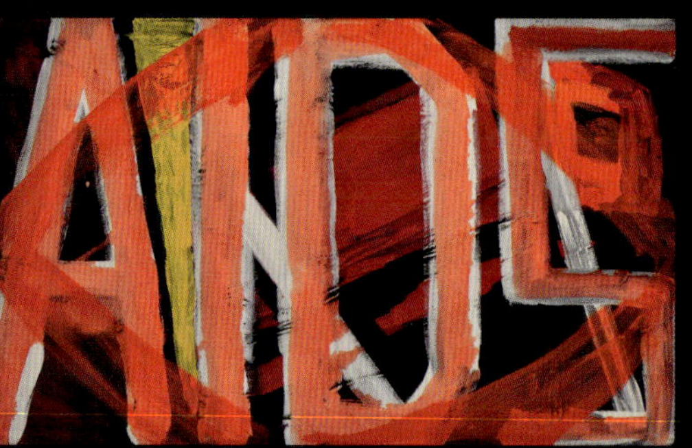
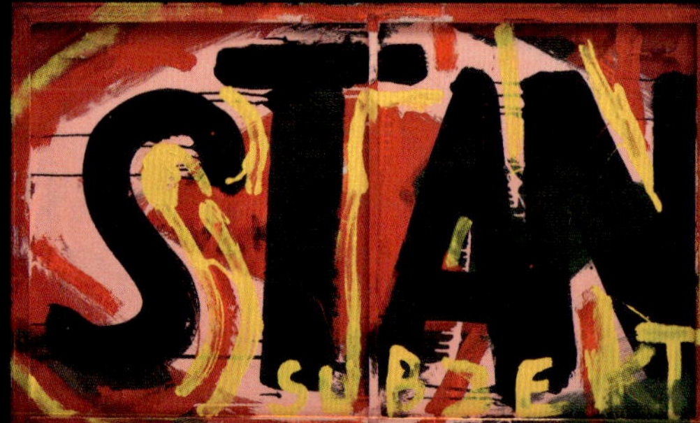
[03A–B] AIDS - STAN, 1983

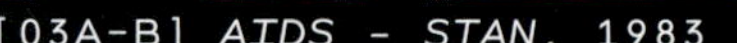

←[01] Exhibition view, HALLE FÜR KUNST Steiermark, Graz, 2022

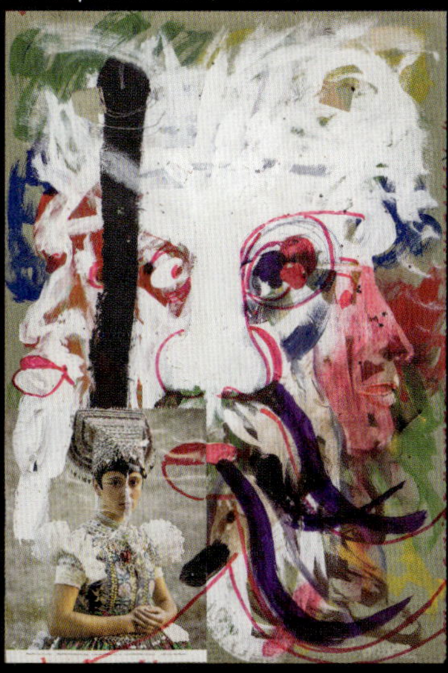

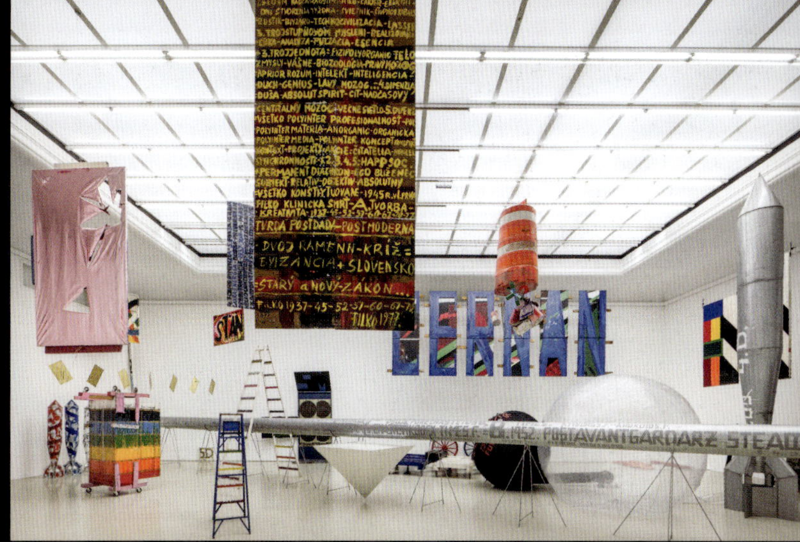

[05] Exhibition view, HALLE FÜR KUNST Steiermark, Graz, 2022

Works such as *SLOVAK* (1985) show that Filko's painting was often paintings of texts. These works on the one hand revolve around Filko's artistic principle of the ego, as a form of expression when they depict his own name, and on the other hand the texts also denote broader matters in politics and society. Alongside the figurative *Self-Portrait / Autoportrét* (1982) [04] the almost monumental acrylic painting *Filko – Name Pink – Eight Chakra / Filko – Meno Ružová – Ôsma Čakra* (1983–86) [07] can also be seen as a conceptual self-portrait, with the word "SLOVAK" in large letters on the back. This work shows Filko's name in the sign of the pink chakra, a symbol of the spirit and of his trust in being able to become established and make his way in a completely new environment. In New York in the 1980s with its art scene strongly focused again on painting, this turned out to be difficult, however. Filko was confident and had the artistic wherewithal, but different understandings of culture, insufficient knowledge of English, and financial difficulties all stood in the way.

Werke wie *SLOVAK* (1985) zeigen, dass zu Filkos Malerei gerade Schriftbilder gehören. Die Arbeiten kreisen zum einen um Filkos künstlerisches Prinzip des Egos, als eine Form des Ausdrucks wenn sie seinen Namen abbilden, zum anderen umfasst die Schriftform aber auch weite Bereiche wie Politik und Gesellschaft. Neben dem figurativen Selbstbildnis *Self-Portrait / Autoportrét* (1982) [04] kann die nahezu monumentale Acrylmalerei *Filko – Name Pink – Eight Chakra / Filko – Meno Ružová – Ôsma Čakra* (1983–1986) [07] als Selbsportrait in konzeptueller Hinsicht aufgefasst werden, wobei rückseitig wiederum das Wort „SLOVAK" in ähnlich großen Lettern aufgeführt wird. Es zeigt Filkos Namen im Zeichen des pinken Chakras, Sinnbild für Spirit und Glaube, auch in einer komplett neuen Umgebung Fuß fassen und reüssieren zu können. Im New York der 1980er-Jahre samt Kunstszene mit wiedererstarkender Orientierung an der Malerei sollte sich dies bei allem Selbstbewusstsein und künstlerisch guten Voraussetzungen, jedoch erschwert durch ein gegenläufiges Kunstverständnis, bescheidene Englischkenntnisse und materielle Unzulänglichkeiten, als schwierig herausstellen.

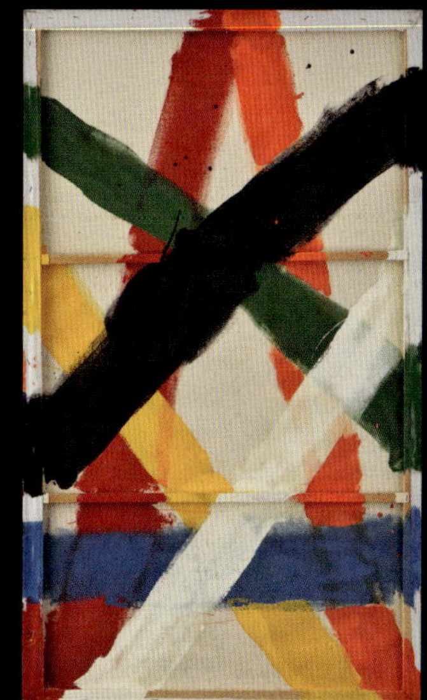

[02B] *SLOVAK*, 1985

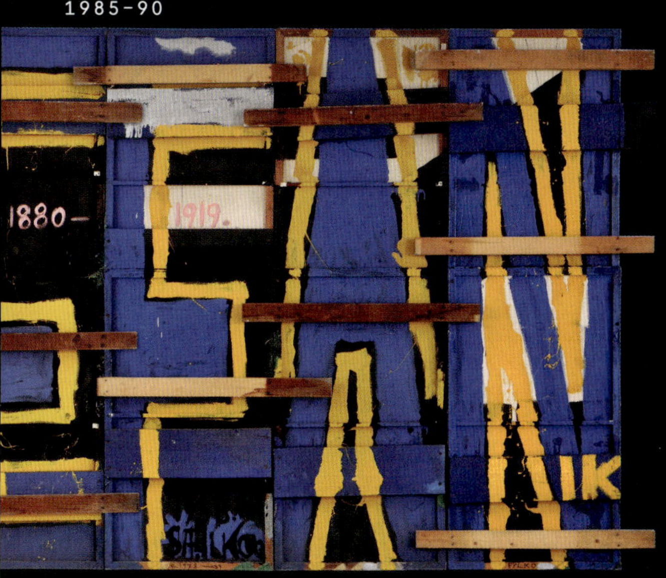

[07] *Filko - Name Pink - Eight Chakra / Filko - Meno Ružová - Ôsma Čakra*, 1983–86

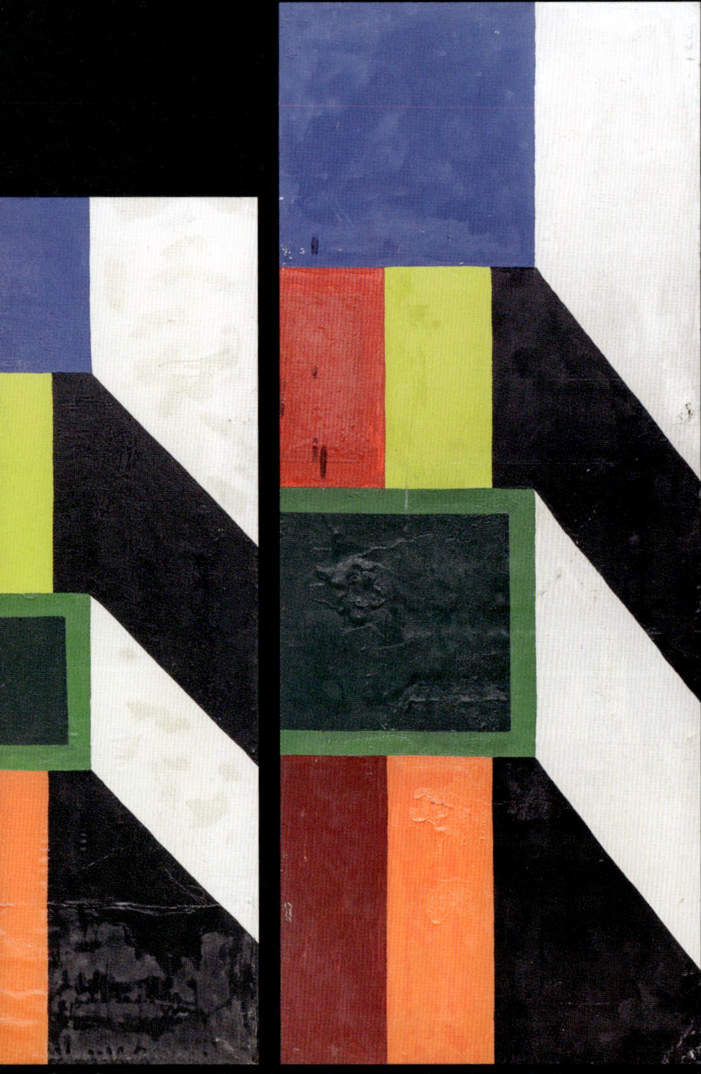

In contrast to the red paintings, the color blue dominates the work *Štefánik/Černan* (1985–90) [06], symbolizing the broad cosmic context in Filko's work. References are made here to historical figures, to which Filko attributes symbolic capital as role models and precursors of his own self. Eugene Andrew Cernan was a US-American astronaut with Czech and Slovak ancestors. As a member of the risky Apollo 17 mission, he was the last man to date to leave the moon's surface, on December 12, 1972. The reverse of the work remembers the Slovak politician, officer, and astronomer Milan Rastislav Štefánik, who is seen alongside Masaryk and Beneš as one of the three founding fathers of Czechoslovakia. As a diplomat and as the founder of the Czechoslovak Legions in the French Foreign Legion, he fought successfully for secession from Austria-Hungary. The cosmos and astronomy seem to be a principle for communication between the nations, even if here and in other places Filko adds his pride in the Czech and especially the Slovak causes to his own internationalism.

Im Gegensatz zu den roten Malereien steht die Farbe Blau, die im Werk *Štefánik/Černan* (1985–1990) [06] dominiert und den weiten, kosmischen Zusammenhang in Filkos Œuvre symbolisiert. Referenzen werden hier auch hinsichtlich historischer Persönlichkeiten eingelöst, die Filko wie Vorbilder, aber auch Vorläufer seiner selbst, ähnlich symbolischem Kapital einbringt. Eugene Andrew Cernan war ein US-amerikanischer Astronaut mit tschechischen und slowakischen Vorfahren, der als Teil der abenteuerlichen Apollo 17-Mission am 12. Dezember 1972 als vorerst letzter Mensch die Mondoberfläche verließ. Auf der zweiten Seite der Arbeit wird an den slowakischen Politiker, Offizier und Astronomen Milan Rastislav Štefánik erinnert, der neben Masaryk und Beneš als einer der drei Gründerväter der Tschechoslowakei gilt, indem er als Diplomat und Begründer der tschechoslowakischen Legionen in französischen Diensten erfolgreich für eine Abspaltung von Österreich-Ungarn kämpfte. Der Weltraum und die Astronomie scheinen da ein kommunizierendes Prinzip zwischen den Nationen zu sein, wiewohl Filko abseits seiner internationalen Haltung hier wie an anderer Stelle seinen Stolz für die tschechische und vor allem slowakische Sache erkennen lässt.

[08] *Contemplation in the Chakra Color Spectrum / Kontemplácia vo farbách čakier-spektier, c. 1993–95*

↖[06B] ↓[06C] *Štefánik/Černan, 1985–90*

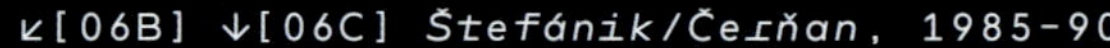

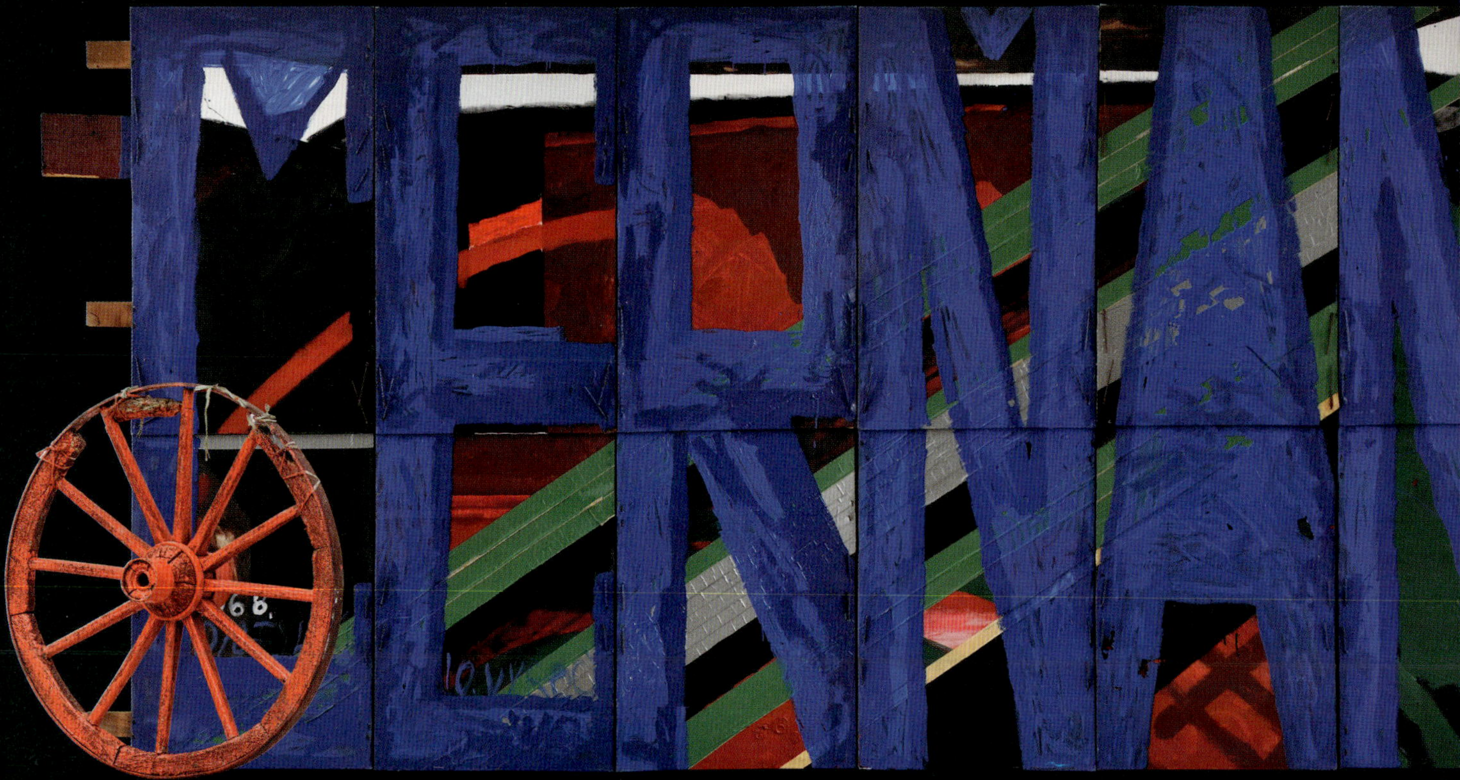

[09A] *The Old and New Testament / Starý a Nový Zákon,* c. 1995

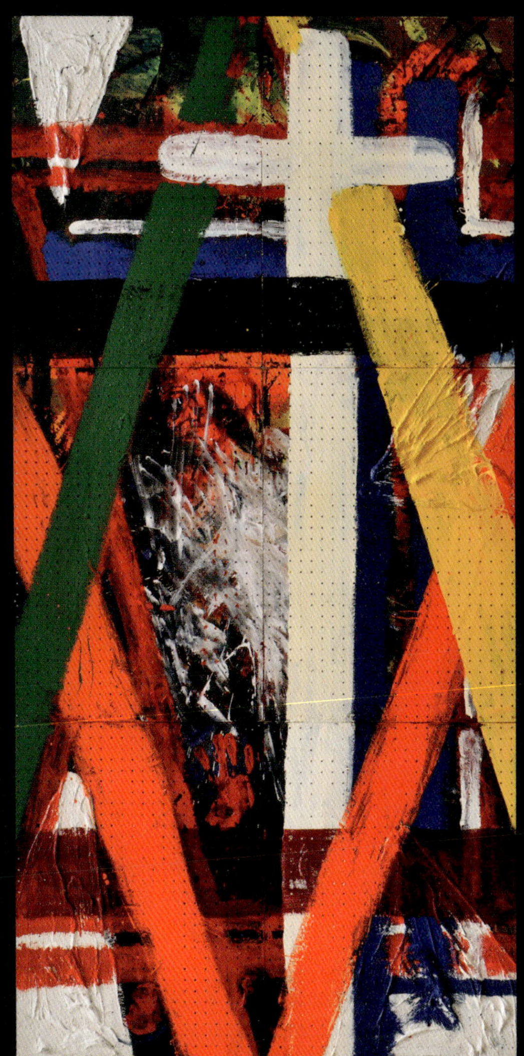

[09B] *The Old and New Testament / Starý a Nový Zákon,* c. 1995

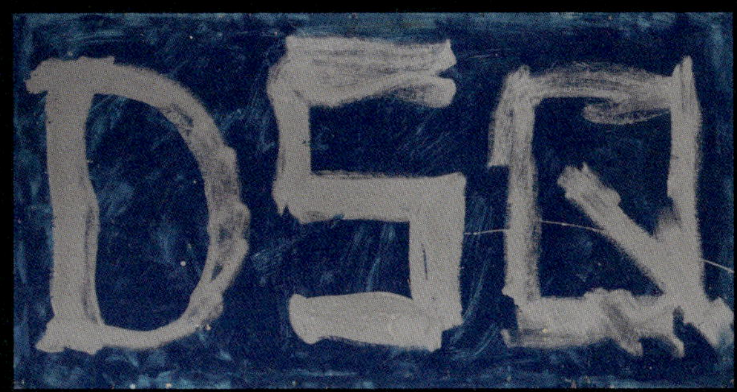

[10] *DSQ,* c. 2000

The paintings *Contemplation in the Chakra Color Spectrum / Kontemplácia vo farbách čakier-spektier* (c. 1993–95) [08] and *The Old and New Testament / Starý a Nový Zákon* (c. 1995) [09] refer to the formal idioms of gestural geometric abstraction. The former piece expands the three colors with the seven colors of the chakra system and operates on the basis of a paradoxical composition. The arrangement of the work faciliates the beholder's own body entering into contact with it, and the form of some of the color fields forces them out of the image into the exterior, as the construction of lines and colors creates spatial levels that move away from each other.

Die Malereien *Contemplation in the Chakra Color Spectrum / Kontemplácia vo farbách čakier-spektier* (ca. 1993–1995) [08] wie auch *The Old and New Testament / Starý a Nový Zákon* (ca. 1995) [09] greifen die Formensprache einer gestischen geometrischen Abstraktion auf. Erstere Arbeit erweitert die drei Farben um das siebenfarbige Chakrensystem und entfaltet sich mittels einer paradoxen Komposition. Durch das Arrangement der Arbeit lässt sich der eigene Körper in Bezug dazu setzen, auch der Duktus mancher Farbfelder strebt aus dem Bild nach außen, denn aufgrund der Konstruktion der Linien und Farben werden auseinanderstrebende räumliche Ebenen konstruiert.

System of Systems
On the *Archive SF*

Lucia Gregorová Stach

Archives of artists and art groups in the totalitarian regimes of Central and Eastern Europe performed the role of memory pseudo-institutions, and in many cases, they also had a particular function as essential communication nodes of the network in the alternative scene. Archives often housed samizdat printed matter and small artworks from art actions and private exhibitions. Archives also supported the mail-art circulation of messages and art concepts and they were bases through which underground exhibitions and actions could be carried out and documented; often they helped to found parallel collections of small artefacts through exchanges among the artists and intellectuals, making up for the void of an institutional landscape. Archives as "systems of statements (whether events or things)"[1] according to Michel Foucault, have become a very frequent and emphasized term after the year 2000, especially due to their performative qualities in the artistic and institutional practice in relation to the changed attitudes of artists and institutions to production of meanings and interpretations.

In many cases, art archives grew out of the need for an *internal* emigration of their creators. Under the oppressive Socialist regime (1948–89), which lacked real cultural institutions and a free public space for the public presentation and evaluation of art, most artists' archives had become repositories of both historical artefacts and important records of the past. While they were repositories of the ideas and concepts of the archiving artists, they were also structured and shaped subjectively according to the nature of each individual artist's work and strategies. Moreover, the archives demonstrate individual creative ways of overcoming constraints during the era of unfreedom in one's own country. On the Slovak neo-avant-garde scene, this feature was particularly represented by the now internationally well-known work and archive of Július Koller (1938–2007).[2]

However, in contrast to the extensive archive of Filko's generationally and artistically close compatriot, which had been built up throughout the course of his life in Czechoslovakia since the 1960s, Filko's archive [01–21] was born at the time of his exile in the USA and only acquired its unique structure after he returned to his native country in 1991. The archive in its final form was established out of its need for a new kind of radical *internal* emigration after the fall of the undemocratic socialist regime during the Velvet Revolution in 1989. One cannot lose sight of the fact that Filko had never stopped referring to his origins in his work and in his communication with people. It was as if he carried with him everywhere the history, stories and personalities of his homeland, which he used to connect in his emerging holistic "psycho-philosophical," spiritual and cosmological system (hereafter referred to as the *System SF*) with the people he met abroad and the new information he learned. He processed those connections as new impulses in his postmodern intermedia neo-expressive artwork. Within this, he could become the central figure of a grand narrative, and this was most clearly reflected in his archive. It is the archive which reveals Filko's messianic approach to art as a means of transforming humanity. On the basis of text-art, clippings and photo-documentation, which he had carefully made, Filko began to systematically create his archive (hereafter referred to as the *Archive SF*) after his return from American emigration in 1990. He placed the dynamically evolving meta-work according to the *System SF* in the relevant parts of the studio house on Snežienková street. The *Archive SF* was changed and supplemented in conjunction with the changes and ramifications of the *System SF* until approximately 2010. By applying the principle of ordering topics and events according to the *System SF* at all levels, thus denying above all the usual logic of organizing them according to the time linear progression within it, Filko provided a complex guide to reading his heterogeneous art program. Since the 1970s and even more so during his emigration in the 1980s, "verbal painting," i.e., text-art as a conceptual work complementary to his objects and installations, allowed him, among other things, to record his own existence in a world that was alien to him. Conceptualizing time as a theme, he repeatedly returned to his roots in older works and documents, layering,

System der Systeme
Über das *Archív SF*

Lucia Gregorová Stach

Archive von Künstler*innen und Künstlergruppen übernahmen in den totalitären Staaten Mittel- und Osteuropas die Rolle von Pseudo-Institutionen für Erinnerung und dienten insbesondere auch häufig als wichtige Kommunikationsknoten im Netzwerk der alternativen Szene. Oft beherbergten die Archive inoffizielle, im Selbstverlag publizierte Schriften (Samisdat) und kleine Kunstwerke aus Kunstaktionen und privaten Ausstellungen. Sie unterstützten außerdem die *Mail-Art*-Zirkulation von Mitteilungen und Kunstkonzepten und waren Stützpunkte, über die Underground-Ausstellungen und -Aktionen durchgeführt und dokumentiert werden konnten. Oftmals halfen sie, durch den Austausch unter Künstler*innen und Intellektuellen Sammlungen kleiner Artefakte zu gründen, die eine Leerstelle in der institutionellen Landschaft füllten. Der Begriff des Archivs im Foucaultschen Sinne, mit Archiven als „Aussagensysteme (Ereignisse einerseits und Dinge andererseits)"[1], trat nach 2000 sehr häufig und prononciert in Erscheinung, insbesondere wegen ihrer performativen Eigenschaften in der künstlerischen und institutionellen Praxis vor dem Hintergrund der geänderten Haltung von Künstler*innen und Institutionen zur Produktion von Bedeutungen und Interpretationen.

Häufig entstanden Kunstarchive, weil ihre Schöpfer*innen sich gezwungen sahen, sich in die *innere* Emigration zu begeben. Während des repressiven sozialistischen Regimes (1948–1989), unter dem es keine echten Kulturinstitutionen und keinen freien öffentlichen Raum für die öffentliche Präsentation und Evaluierung von Kunst gab, waren die Künstlerarchive zu Aufbewahrungsorten für historische Artefakte und für wichtige Aufzeichnungen der Vergangenheit geworden. Sie waren nicht nur Aufbewahrungsorte für die Ideen und Konzepte der archivierenden Künstler*innen, sondern angesichts ihrer unterschiedlichen Arbeitsweisen und Strategien auch subjektiv organisiert und geformt. Darüber hinaus zeigen die Archive individuelle kreative Wege, die in der Ära der Unfreiheit im eigenen Land geltenden Beschränkungen zu überwinden. Bezeichnend hierfür war in der slowakischen Neo-Avantgarde-Szene das inzwischen international bekannte Werk und Archiv von Július Koller (1938–2007).[2]

Doch während sein ihm altersmäßig und künstlerisch nahestehender Landsmann sein Archiv ab den 1960er-Jahren über die gesamte Dauer seines Lebens in der Tschechoslowakei aufgebaut hatte, entstand Filkos Archiv [01-21] in der Zeit seines Exils in den USA und sollte seine einzigartige Struktur erst nach seiner Rückkehr in die Heimat 1990 erhalten. Seine endgültige Form verdankte das Archiv der Notwendigkeit einer neuen Art der radikalen *inneren* Emigration nach dem Sturz des undemokratischen sozialistischen Regimes während der Samtenen Revolution 1989. Es sollte nicht vergessen werden, dass Filko in seiner Arbeit und seiner Kommunikation mit anderen nie aufgehört hatte, sich auf seine Herkunft zu beziehen. Es war, als trüge er die Geschichte, die Geschichten und die Persönlichkeiten seiner Heimat überall mit sich, um diese in seinem im Entstehen begriffenen, ganzheitlichen „psychophilosophischen", spirituellen und kosmologischen System (im Folgenden *System SF* genannt) in Verbindung zu bringen mit den Menschen, die er im Ausland traf, und den neuen Dingen, die er dort erfuhr. Diese Verbindungen verarbeitete er als neue Impulse in seinen postmodernen intermedialen neo-expressiven Werken. Dabei konnte er zur zentralen Figur einer großen Erzählung werden, was sich am deutlichsten in seinem Archiv zeigte. Darin offenbart sich Filkos messianische Herangehensweise an Kunst als Mittel zur Transformation der Menschheit. Auf der Grundlage von Textkunst, Ausschnitten und Fotodokumentationen, die er sorgfältig angefertigt hatte, begann Filko nach seiner Rückkehr aus der amerikanischen Emigration im Jahr 1990 mit dem systematischen Aufbau seines Archivs (im Folgenden *Archív SF* genannt). Das sich dynamisch entwickelnde Meta-Werk platzierte er nach dem *System SF* in den entsprechenden Teilen des Atelierhauses in der Snežienková-Straße. Das *Archív SF* wurde in Verbindung mit den Veränderungen und Verzweigungen des *System SF* bis etwa 2010 verändert und ergänzt. Mit der Anwendung des Prinzips, Themen und Ereignisse auf allen Ebenen nach dem

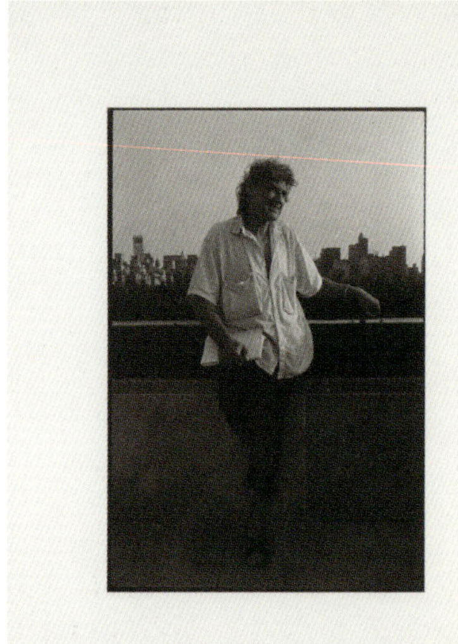

[01] *N. Y. C. -*
ROOF - METROPOLITAN
MUSEUM - FYLKO - 1978 -
80 - 82 - 83 - 84 /
N. Y. C. - STRECHA -
METROPOLITAN MUZEUM -
FYLKO - 1978 - 80 - 82 -
83 - 84, 1989

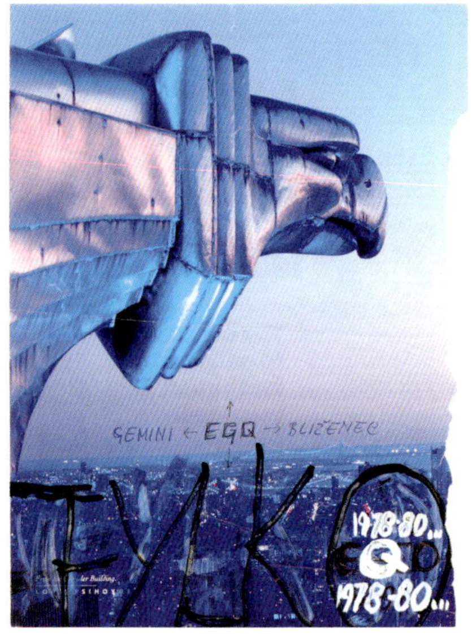

[02] *FYLKO GEMINI + EGQ*
1978-80, c. 1985/c. 1990

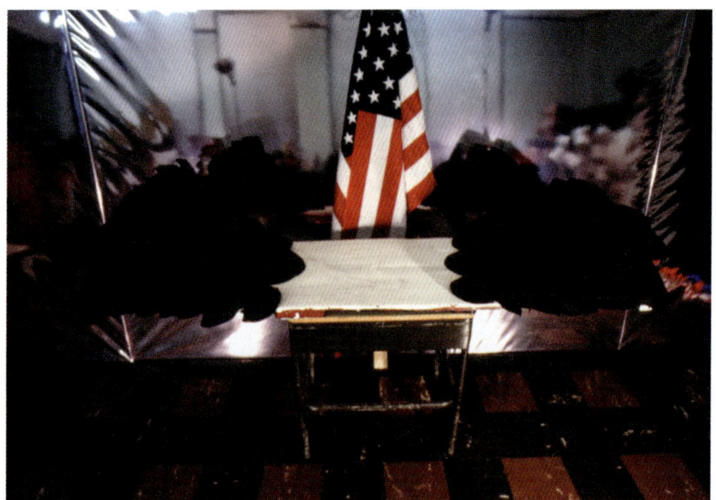

[03A] *Self Installation - Idealism, 1984*

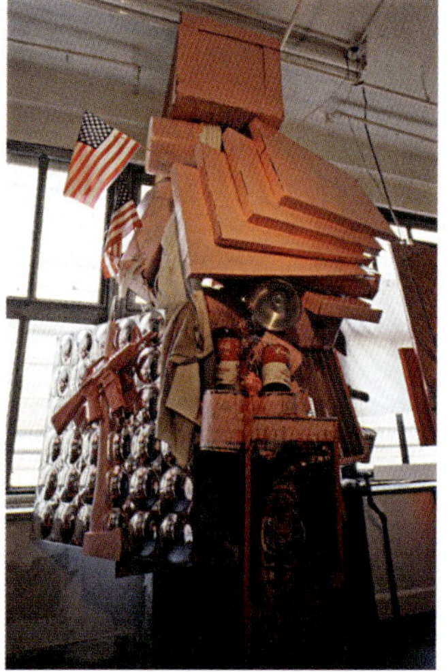

[04A] *Spirit of the*
Artist, 1983

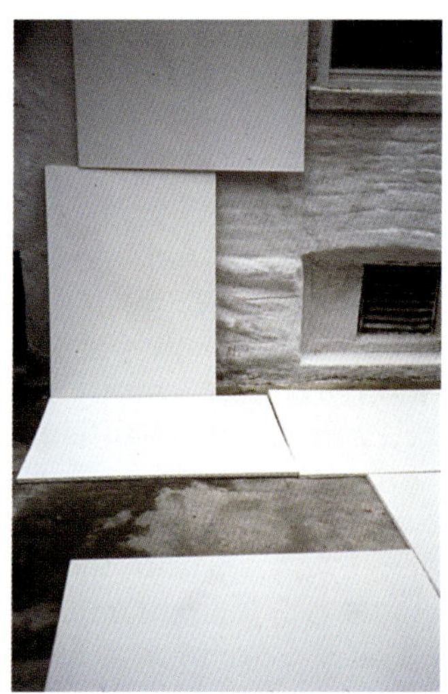

[05A] *White S.*
Slovak, c. 1987

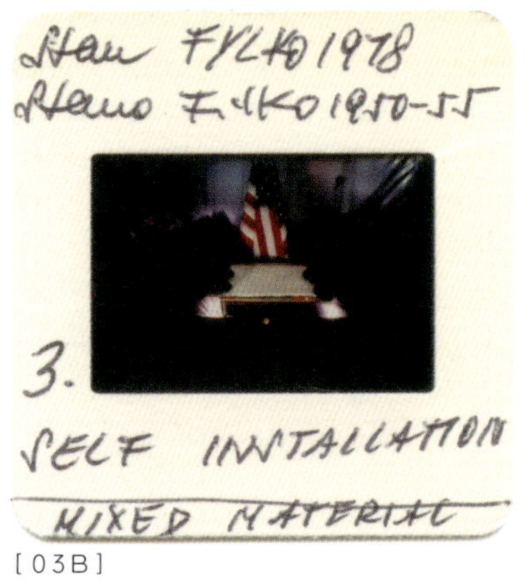

[03B]

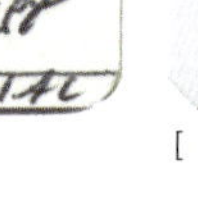

[04B]

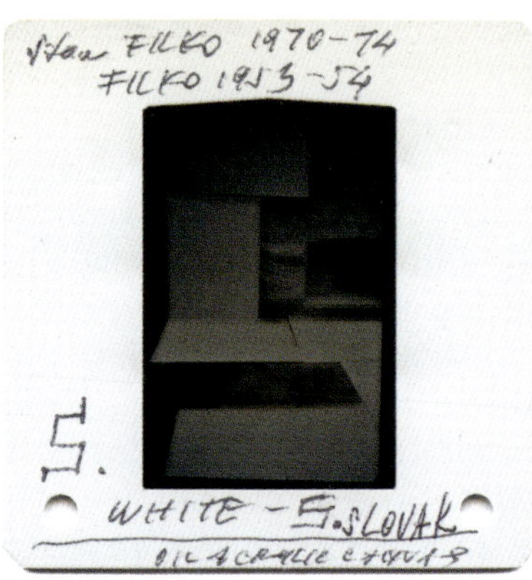

[05B]

System SF zu ordnen und so insbesondere die übliche Logik einer inneren chronologischen Ordnung zurückzuweisen, lieferte Filko eine komplexe Anleitung für das Verständnis seines heterogenen Kunstprogramms. Ab den 1979ern und mehr noch während seiner Emigration in den 1980er-Jahren verschaffte ihm die „verbale Malerei" – Textkunst als konzeptuelles, seine Objekte und Installationen ergänzendes Werk – unter anderem die Möglichkeit, seine eigene Existenz in einer Welt aufzuzeichnen, die ihm fremd war. Die Zeit als Thema aufgreifend, kehrte er wiederholt zu seinen Wurzeln in älteren Arbeiten und Dokumenten zurück, indem er diese transkribierte und mit unterschiedlichen Datumsangaben versah. Mit dem Verlassen der Tschechoslowakei hatte er begonnen, die Datierung seiner Arbeiten an wichtigen Daten in seinem Leben auszurichten. In seiner Auseinandersetzung mit der Zeit und der Bedeutung von Zahlen und Farben floss auch sein Interesse an alternativen Denkweisen und Systemen ein, das ihn schon als Kind inspiriert hatte – wie etwa die Kabbala, Zahlenkunde, Astrologie, später Theosophie und esoterisches Wissen. Das *Archiv SF* entwickelte sich auf diese Weise nach und nach zu einem einzigartigen Verwahrungsort für Filkos Konzepte und künstlerische Lösungen und ermöglicht zugleich eine rückblickende Interpretation und Neubewertung seines Werkes. Es spiegelt umfassend die Entwicklung des *System SF* wider, an dem Filko bis zu seinem Tod im Jahr 2015, vor allem aber in der Zeit zwischen 2000 und 2010 gearbeitet hat. Das Ergebnis ist ein gewaltiges autonomes Kunstwerk bestehend aus verschiedenen *Cut-outs*, Texten, Fotos, Dias, Arbeiten auf Papier und Objekten. Der Künstler hat alle in einer dynamischen Struktur arrangiert, die er „PSYCHO-PHYSISCIENCEFIYLCOSMONTOLOEPISTESOPHY" nannte, als Teil seines kosmologischen *System SF*. Filko vollendete darin sein „Post-Selbst – seine alten Ideen – Skizzen, Projekte […] in einer anderen Zeit, überarbeitet, erneuert, etc. […] in der Überzeitlichkeit", wie er es formulierte.[3] Als wunderbarer und sehr komplizierter Leitfaden für die Deutung des *System SF* wurde das *Archiv SF* letztlich vielleicht zur Synthese von Filkos gesamter Selbstprojektion ins Universum sowie zu seiner ultimativen Selbstverwirklichung, entstanden aus seinem Wunsch nach absoluter künstlerischer und persönlicher Freiheit. In dem noch erhaltenen Teil seiner 38 Archivmappen kann man Filkos „Künstlerlegende" studieren, und zwar nicht durch das Nachzeichnen seiner Biografie und der Chronologie seines Œuvres, sondern in der seltenen Form einer komplexen und authentischen individuellen Mythologie, die entscheidend ist für das Verständnis eines außergewöhnlich umfassenden und vielseitigen Gesamtwerkes. Diese beruhte auf seinem Bedürfnis nach einer neuen Spiritualität als kosmologisches System. Wie das *Archiv SF* zeigt, hat er sein gesamtes Werk und Wissen aufgenommen, von ersten Texten und Mitschriften aus dem Gymnasium und der Akademie über verschiedene Zeitschriftenartikel, Broschüren, Karten und verschiedene Bilder und Informationen über neue Entdeckungen oder spirituelle Praktiken bis hin zur Dokumentation seiner eigenen Gemälde, Installationen, Objekte und neuen Kunstwerke, die im Mappenformat entstanden, wie Zeichnungen, Collagen und Montagen. Filkos Kosmologie entsprang in der Tat seiner Besessenheit von der Zeit, die sein Leben und sein Werk bestimmen sollte, und seiner Leidenschaft für das Entdecken von Beziehungen zwischen Ideen und Objekten. Da Filko bekanntlich danach

strebte, bei den aktuellen Trends in der Kunstwelt stets auf dem Laufenden und nie außen vor zu sein, lässt sich diese Besessenheit auf seinen lebenslangen Wunsch zurückführen, ein wahrer zeitgenössischer Künstler zu sein und zu bleiben. Zu diesem Zweck musste er alle neuen Ideen in Kultur und Kunst und in Wissenschaft und Religion verfolgen. Das ist auch der Grund, warum er die lineare chronologische Abfolge der Ereignisse in seinem Leben und seine eigenen sich nach und nach entfaltenden ikonografischen Motive in eine Struktur verwandelte, die sich als dreidimensionales Modell all der Wechselbeziehungen zwischen Konzepten und Formen visualisieren lässt: das *System SF* als Transmutation der eigenen individuellen Mythologie in ein Paradigma universellen Wissens über die Welt und das Universum. Das *Archiv SF* lässt sich somit nicht nur als dokumentarische Quelle für das Verständnis des Künstlers betrachten, sondern auch als *opera aperta* mit proteischem Charakter. Jozef Cseres bemerkte 1997, dass Filkos Œuvre zwar als „lückenhaft" gelten könne, seine Gedankenwelt jedoch nicht chaotisch sei, sondern sich im Gegenteil in ein Schema fassen lasse. „Hier können wir von ‚pyknoleptischen' Aussetzern sprechen, um einen der Lieblingsbegriffe von Paul Virilio zu verwenden, der das Nichtvorhandensein eines kontinuierlichen und das Vorhandensein eines aus verschiedenen Komponenten bestehenden Bewusstseins verkündet. Sie erscheinen als unmittelbare Folge von Filkos einzigartiger Herangehensweise an die konzeptionelle künstlerische Arbeit – einer Art intellektueller *bricolage*, die sich praktisch alles zunutze macht, was zur Hand ist, unabhängig von dessen ursprünglichem Kontext und Zweck. Diese Art der Montage hinterlässt Lücken in ehemals konsistenten Gedankensystemen."[4] Durch sein Archiv betrachtete Filko, um es mit den Worten Italo Calvinos zu sagen, die Welt als ein „System der Systeme", in dem jedes einzelne System die anderen bedingt und von ihnen bedingt wird.[5]

Das *Archiv SF* entstand 1990 in Filkos Atelierhaus in der Snežienková-Straße. Die einzelnen Mappen wurden auf die jeweiligen Räume verteilt, die einer der drei vorhandenen Dimensionen und einem der sieben, später zwölf und schließlich zwanzig Chakren entsprachen. Die Mappen selbst wurden nach Farbe ausgewählt, beschriftet und wie bereits erwähnt mit einer Vielzahl an Materialien von Textkunst, Zeichnungen, Dias, Fotos, Collagen, Montagen, bearbeiteten und umfunktionierten Zeitschriften- und Zeitungsausschnitten bis zu kleinen Objekten in transparenten Plastikverpackungen gefüllt. Viele der Werke arbeiten, sei es in Entwürfen oder im Original, auf eindrucksvolle Weise mit Text, dessen visuelle Darstellung den zentralen Inhalt ausmacht. Die Textkunst entsteht nach der ideologischen Struktur des Autors, der dann mittels Assoziation weitere Wörter und Ideen hinzugefügt werden. „Filkos Textkunst, manchmal auch verbale Malerei genannt, entstand als lückenhafte Montage von Wörtern, die oft nur durch eine lose Syntax verbunden waren; es handelte sich eher um eine assoziative Aneinanderreihung von Schlüsselbegriffen – Schlüsselwörtern – seines Denkens, die nach einem bestimmten, sich im Laufe der Zeit verändernden Rahmensystem zusammengesetzt wurden."[6] In gewisser Weise erinnert seine Methode an eine postmoderne Version des berühmten *Bilderatlas Mnemosyne* (1926–1929), bei dem symbolische, symptomatische Bilder auf dreiundsechzig großen, mit schwarzem Stoff bespannten Holztafeln metonymisch an- und umgeordnet wurden, um diese dann

transcribing and multi-dating them. He had based the dating of his works on important dates in his life since he left Czechoslovakia. In his operations with time and with the meanings of numbers and colors, he also applied his interest in alternative ways of thinking and systems that had inspired him since his childhood—let us think of Kabbalah, numerology, astrology, later theosophy and esoteric learning. The *Archive SF* has thus gradually emerged as a unique vault of Filko's concepts and artistic solutions, which at the same time provides a reverse interpretation and a new evaluation of his work. It comprehensively mirrors the development of the *System SF*, which Filko was working on until his death in 2015, but most significantly in the period between 2000 and 2010. The outcome is a huge autonomous work of art composed of various cut-outs, texts, photographs, slides, works on paper and objects. The artist has arranged them all within a vivid dynamic structure, which he called "PSYCHO-PHYSISCIENCEFIYLCOSMONTOLOEPISTESOPHY," being part of his cosmological *System SF*. In his own words, Filko thus accomplishes in it his "post-self—his old ideas—sketches, projects… in another time, revises, innovates, etc.… in supertemporality."[3] As a wonderful and very complicated guide to reading the *System SF*, perhaps the *Archive SF* ultimately became the synthesis of Filko's entire self-projection into the universe, as well as his ultimate self-realization, born of his desire for absolute artistic and personal freedom. In the surviving part of the thirty-eight archival folders, Filko's "legend of the artist" can be studied, which can be traced not in terms of his biography and the chronology of his oeuvre, but as a rare example of a complex and authentic individual mythology, crucial for understanding his extraordinarily vast and diverse oeuvre. This was based on his need for a new spirituality as a cosmological system. As the *Archive SF* shows, he included his entire body of work and knowledge, from his early writings and lecture notes from the high school and the academy, various magazine articles, pamphlets, maps, and assorted images and information about new discoveries or spiritual practices, to documentation of his own paintings, installations, objects and new art works created within the format of the binders, such as drawings, collages, and montages. Filko's cosmology was indeed born out of his obsession with time, which framed his life and work, and from his passion for finding relationships between ideas and objects. Knowing Filko's eagerness to keep up to date with the current trends in the art world and to never stand on the sidelines, this obsession was sprouting from his life-time desire to be and to stay a genuine contemporary artist. Therefore, he had to track all the new ideas in culture and art, as well as in science and religion. This is also why he transformed the linear chronological sequence of events in his life and his own gradually unfolding iconographic motifs into a structure that can be visualized as a three-dimensional model with all the interrelationships of concepts and forms, which is the *System SF* as a transmutation of one's own individual mythology into a paradigm of universal wisdom about the world and universe. The *Archive SF* can therefore be seen not only as a documentary resource for understanding the artist, but also as an *opera aperta*, protean in character. As Jozef Cseres claimed in 1997, Filko's intellectual world, even though his oeuvre can be considered as "gappy," is not chaos, just the contrary,

it can be rendered by a scheme. "Here we may talk of 'picnoleptic' interruptions, using one of the favourite terms of Paul Virilio, who proclaims the non-existence of continual and the existence of component consciousness. They appear as the immediate consequence of Filko's unique approach to conceptual artistic work—a kind of *intellectual bricolage*, which makes use of virtually anything at hand, regardless of the initial context and purpose. Such way of montage leaves gaps in formerly consistent systems of thoughts."[4] We can also borrow Italo Calvino's expression for the statement that in his archive Filko "sees the world as a 'system of systems' in which each individual system conditions the others and is conditioned by them."[5]

The *Archive SF* was created in 1990 in Filko's studio house on Snežienková street. The individual folders were placed in the respective rooms, which corresponded to one of the three dimensions and one of the seven, later twelve, up to final twenty chakras. The binders themselves were selected according to color, described and filled as previously mentioned with a variety of material ranging from text-art, drawings, slides, photographs, collages, montages, edited and repurposed magazine and newspaper clippings, to small objects based in transparent plastic packages. Many of the works, in documentation or in originals on paper, work impressively with text, the visual representation of which forms the point of its content. The text-art works are created according to the author's ideological structure and then additional words and ideas are added to them by a method of association. "Filko's text-art, sometimes called verbal painting, was created as a jagged montage of words, often connected only by loose syntax; rather, it was an associative string of key terms—keywords—of his thought, assembled according to a certain framework system that changed over time."[6] In a way, his method is reminiscent of a postmodern version of the famous *Mnemosyne Atlas* (1926−29), where the atlas of images metonymically arranged and rearranged symbolic, symptomatic images on sixty-three large wooden panels covered with black cloth, which were then placed in loose historical and thematic sequences.[7] However, Filko's version might be more akin to a deliberate forgetting of the original content, and thus more like something we could rather call *Lethe Atlas*. As previously claimed, Filko's obsession with time grew out of his desire to be contemporary forever, which may also be interpreted as a desire to achieve immortality through the denial of *chronos*, the personification of time in Greek mythology. His obsession with systems is therefore fully under the reign of *cairos*, the time of the occasion personified in Greek mythology by a god. Again, we can borrow words from Italo Calvino referring to the "open encyclopedia" of the great novels of the twentieth century to describe the feature of a complex ideological structure fully based on the knowledge and life of an individual. The *Archive SF*, which has unfortunately survived only fragmentarily complete, then presents Filko's elaborate guide to life, the universe, and the understanding of art in general, and is also an attempt to provide a constant proof of the contemporaneity and eternal validity of his own oeuvre in the Western art canon.

Filko's obsession with systems can also be traced back to American Conceptual Art, which became his inspiration even before he arrived in the New World, where a variety of Conceptual artists, such as Bruce Nauman, Bruce Conner,

in freier historischer und thematischer Folge zu platzieren.[7] Filkos Version könnte jedoch eher einem absichtlichen Vergessen des ursprünglichen Inhalts gleichkommen und somit eher als *Atlas Lethe* bezeichnet werden. Wie bereits erwähnt, entsprang Filkos Besessenheit von der Zeit seinem Verlangen, auf ewig zeitgenössisch zu sein, was sich auch als Wunsch nach Unsterblichkeit durch die Verleugnung von *chronos*, der Personifizierung der Zeit in der griechischen Mythologie, interpretieren ließe. Seine große Leidenschaft für Systeme steht also ganz unter der Herrschaft von *kairos*, dem günstigen Zeitpunkt für eine Entscheidung, der in der griechischen Mythologie durch einen Gott verkörpert wird. Auch hier können wir uns auf Italo Calvino beziehen, der auf die „offene Enzyklopädie" der großen Romane des 20. Jahrhunderts verweist, um die Besonderheit einer komplexen ideologischen Struktur zu beschreiben, die vollständig auf dem Wissen und dem Leben eines Individuums basiert. Das *Archív SF*, von dem leider nur Fragmente erhalten sind, stellt somit Filkos ausführlichen Leitfaden zum Leben, zum Universum und zum Kunstverständnis im Allgemeinen dar und ist zugleich der Versuch, einen beständigen Beweis für die Zeitgenossenschaft und die ewige Gültigkeit seines eigenen Werks im westlichen Kunstkanon zu erbringen.

Filkos Systembesessenheit lässt sich auch zur amerikanischen Konzeptkunst zurückverfolgen. Diese diente ihm bereits als Inspirationsquelle, bevor er in die Neue Welt kam, wo eine Reihe von Konzeptkünstler*innen wie Bruce Nauman, Bruce Conner, George Brecht, Joseph Kossuth, John Baldessari oder Robert Smithson Konzepte entwickelt hatten, mit denen sie ihre künstlerischen Bestrebungen in einer definierten philosophischen Ordnung systematisieren und organisieren wollten. Bereits Ende der 1960er-Jahre machten sich selbst amerikanische Künstler*innen über diese Tendenz lustig, darunter auch Robert Smithson: „Ich treffe Leute, ich treffe jemanden, der einen Graben aushebt, und frage: ‚Wie geht's?' Und er sagt: ‚Sieh dir den Himmel an.' Und ich schaue in den Himmel und sage: ‚Wunderschön, Mann.' Und was sagst du dann? Du sagst: ‚Mach ein System draus.'"[8] Schon die Begegnung mit Japan und seiner Kultur während eines dreimonatigen Aufenthalts in Osaka und Umgebung 1970 bedeutete für Filko eine entscheidende Erweiterung seiner bis dahin vor allem mit der jüdisch-christlichen Tradition verknüpften Geisteswelt. Hinsichtlich des spirituellen Charakters von Filkos künstlerischem Programm, das sich im späteren *System SF* widerspiegeln sollte, war sein Aufenthalt in den Vereinigten Staaten wichtig, um neue Impulse für diese Verbindung aus Kunst, Wissenschaft und neuen religiösen Doktrinen und verschiedenen anderen spirituellen Lehren und Praktiken zu erhalten. Das Projekt *White Space in White Space / Biely priestor v bielom priestore* (1973–1976) des Trios Stano Filko, Ján Zavarský und Miloš Laky ist unter anderem stark von Filkos Begegnung mit ganz unterschiedlichen spirituellen Traditionen in Japan und einer internationalen zeitgenössischen Kunst geprägt, die zwischen Materialismus und sich an Metaphysik und Transzendenz orientierenden Tendenzen schwankt.

Das Projekt mit den beiden jüngeren Künstlern war für Filko der Beginn eines neuen Lebens und eines neuen Stadiums in seinem kreativen Schaffen. Es begann als Fortsetzung ihres gemeinsamen konzeptuellen Projekts *Time I. – III. / Čas I. – III.* (1973), in dem es noch um die Zukunft und eine mögliche Reise in den Weltraum und die Kommunikation der Menschen mit dessen Bewohner*innen ging. Das Projekt wurde jedoch maßgeblich von seinen Umständen beeinflusst – vor allem für Filko war die Krankheit von Miloš Laky und dessen langsames Sterben eine einschneidende Erfahrung, die das gesamte Konzept und den Prozess gemeinschaftlicher Produktion auf entscheidende Weise beeinflussen sollte. Während Laky das gesamte Konzept des Projekts authentisch auf der Grundlage seines eigenen Lebens aufbaute, bezog sich Ján Zavarský auf Ludwig Wittgenstein und die Phänomenologie. Die Philosophie der Leere als offener Raum für den Eintritt in etwas Neues, eine Bedingung der Transformation, kannte Filko möglicherweise bereits aus dem Zen-Buddhismus, der japanischen Kunst und von der deutschen Künstlergruppe Zero, da er auch mit den Werken von Otto Piene vertraut war, sowie durch Robert Rauschenbergs Arbeiten. Voll zum Ausdruck kam dies in seiner alleinigen Fortführung des Projekts *White Space in White Space / Biely priestor v bielom priestore* nach Miloš Lakys Tod 1975, in den Zyklen *Emotion / Emócia* (1976), *Transcendency / Transcendencia* (1977–1978) und *Meditation Transcendental / Transcendetálna meditácia* (1980). Sie markieren den Anfang von Filkos fünfter Dimension und dem gesamten System der drei bereits vorhandenen Dimensionen – Rot für Biologie, Blau für Kosmologie und Weiß für Ontologie (später 3.D., 4.D., 5.D.). Andererseits manifestierte sich diese Art der völligen Leere, die die Möglichkeit zur Transformation und Einführung des Neuen und Anderen bot, bereits in Filkos Arbeiten wie *Breathing – The Celebration of Air / Dýchanie – Oslava vzduchu* (1969–1970) oder *Pneumatic Heart / Pneumatické srdce* (1970) und *Pumping of Water / Prečerpávanie vody* (1970) anlässlich des Projekts *Polymuse Space / Polymúzický priestor* (1970) in Piešťany.

Mitte der 1970er-Jahre, unter dem zunehmenden politischen Druck durch die Doktrin der so genannten „Normalisierung" der sozialistischen Gesellschaft in der Tschechoslowakei und nach dem Scheitern seiner ersten Ehe, plante Filko bereits intensiv seine Emigration aus der Tschechoslowakei, die er 1981 in die Tat umsetzen konnte. 1982 stellte er dank der Unterstützung von Joseph Beuys, den er über Tomáš Štrauss und László Beke kennengelernt hatte, seinen weißen (und weiß übermalten) Škoda in der mittlerweile berühmt gewordenen Installation *Liebe zur Ontologie / Love of Ontology* (1982) auf der documenta 7 in Kassel aus. Nach seinen eigenen Worten war das, was er dort präsentierte, ein furioser Gegenentwurf zu der „Bauchkunst", die die gesamte Ausstellung beherrschte. Aurel Hrabušický drückte es in diesem Zusammenhang so aus: „In gewisser Weise erweiterten Filkos neue Bilder lediglich eine mit malerischen Mitteln manipulierte Fotoserie, die ebenfalls Teil der Installation in Kassel war und zuvor in Polen unter dem Titel *Transcendency* mehrfach ausgestellt worden war."[9] Der Künstler nutzte diese früheren Arbeiten, um die Umgebung mit einer Assemblage aus großen, frisch bemalten Papierbögen und Leinwänden auszustatten, die in ihrer Mitte auch die Reifenabdrücke seines Autos trugen. Sie waren „fast ganz geweißt, übermalt mit wirbelnden weißen Kreismustern und anderen weißen Interventionen mit Pinselstrichen, Farbspritzern, Handabdrücken und manchmal durch das Hineinrollen von Reifen in den Kreis."[10] Hrabušický zufolge wurden diese und andere expressive Werke, in denen die Möglichkeiten der Farbe Weiß erkundet wurden und die 1981 und 1982 in Deutschland

George Brecht, Joseph Kossuth, John Baldessari or Robert Smithson had developed concepts that sought to systematize and organize their artistic endeavors into defined philosophical orders. As early as the late 1960s, this tendency was even parodied by American artists themselves, such as Robert Smithson, when he stated: "I meet people, I meet a ditch digger and I say, 'How are you doing today?' And they say, 'Look at the sky.' And I look at the sky and I say, 'Beautiful, man.' And what do you say? You say, 'Make a system out of it'."[8] Already the encounter with Japan and its culture in 1970, during a three-month stay in Osaka and its surroundings in 1970, brought to Filko a crucial broadening of his spiritual world, until then primarily bound to Judeo-Christian tradition. From the perspective of the spiritual nature of Filko's artistic program, which would be reflected in the future *System SF*, his residency in the United States was important for receiving new stimuli for this combination of art, science, and new religious doctrines and various other spiritual teachings and practices. The project *White Space in White Space / Biely priestor v bielom priestore* (1973–76) by the trio of Stano Filko, Ján Zavarský and Miloš Laky was drawn heavily, among other things, from Filko's Japanese experience of an encounter with completely different spiritual traditions and international contemporary art, vibrating between materialism and tendencies directed towards metaphysics and transcendence.

This project with two younger artists was the dawn of a new life and creative stage for Filko. It began as a continuation of their collaborative conceptual project *Time I. – III. / Čas I. – III.* (1973), still focused on the future and a potential journey into space and humanity's communication with its inhabitants. However, the project was significantly influenced by circumstances—especially for Filko, the experience of Miloš Laky's illness and gradual dying from it was essential, and it shaped the whole concept and process of collaborative production in an instrumental way. Laky created the whole concept of the project authentically on the basis of his own life, Ján Zavarský made reference to Ludwig Wittgenstein and to phenomenology. Filko could have known the philosophy of emptiness as a space open for entering (into) the new, which is a condition of transformation already from Zen Buddhism, Japanese art and the German art group Zero, being also informed about the works by Otto Piene and Robert Rauschenberg. It was fully expressed in his solo continuation of the project *White Space in White Space / Biely priestor v bielom priestore* after Miloš Laky's death in 1975, in his cycles *Emotion / Emócia* (1976), *Transcendency / Transcendencia* (1977–78) and *Meditation Transcendental / Transcendetálna meditácia* (1980). This was the beginning of Filko's fifth dimension and the whole system of three dimensions—red for biology, blue for cosmology and white for ontology (later 3.D., 4.D., 5.D.). On the other hand, this kind of full emptiness, ripe for transformation and introduction of the new and the other, was already manifested in Filko's works such as *Breathing – The Celebration of Air / Dýchanie – Oslava vzduchu* (1969–70) or *Pneumatic Heart / Pneumatické srdce* (1970) and *Pumping of Water / Prečerpávanie vody* (1970) at the project *Polymuse Space / Polymúzický priestor* (1970) in Piešťany.

In the mid-1970s, during the increased political pressure of the doctrine of the so-called *normalization* of the socialist society in Czechoslovakia and after the collapse of his first marriage, Filko was already intensively planning his emigration from Czechoslovakia, which he succeeded in putting to practice in 1981. In 1982, thanks to the support of Joseph Beuys whom he met through Tomáš Štrauss and László Beke, he exhibited his white Škoda car (also painted white) in the now famous installation *Love of Ontology / Liebe zur Ontologie* (1982) at the documenta 7 in Kassel. By his own words, what he presented was a furious antithesis to the "abdominal art" that dominated the entire exhibition. As Aurel Hrabušický put it in this context: "In a sense, Filko's new paintings merely expanded a painterly manipulated series of photographs that was also part of the installation in Kassel and had previously been exhibited repeatedly in Poland under the title *Transcendency*."[9] The artist used these earlier works of his to complement the environment with an assemblage of large freshly painted papers and canvases, which also bore the tire tracks of his own car, displayed in the middle. They "…were almost whitewashed, repainted by swirling white circular patterns and other white interventions with brushstrokes, splashes of paint, handprints, and sometimes by pushing tires into the circle."[10] According to Hrabušický, these and other expressive works exploring the possibilities of the color white, created in Germany in 1981 and 1982, were later in New York regarded by Filko as "spirits," such as *BIG POPULAR SPIRIT* (after 1980) or *ABSOLUTE POPULAR SPIRIT* (after 1980).[11] While still in Germany, also due to the influence of the new generation of Expressionist painters of the Neue Wilde movement, bright, vivid tones of color gradually began to emerge in his paintings, as if from beneath the transcendent surface of the white-painted and plain natural canvases and linens. We can understand Filko's German phase as a transitional period before the full eruption of artistic energy in the USA, where he was able to unleash both his imagination and his art in quite unexpected ways.

For the further formation of the *System SF*, Filko's explorations of hitherto unfamiliar societal and cultural phenomena in the subsequent "American period" (1983–90) were essential. His work reflected dynamically on themes concerning the discovery of the HIV virus and the AIDS disease, as well as on fashion trends and popular New Age spiritual doctrines. He was also strongly driven by his up-close examination of the mesmerizing metropolis as well as the New York art scene in general. At first he lived in Buffalo, where he was acquainted, for example, with the Czech composer and conductor Petr Kotík and his wife, Charlotta Kotík, who worked as a curator at the Brooklyn Museum. However, he also thematized and even mystified his arrival in the America of his dreams, using, for instance, a photograph of the Manhattan skyline with an image of an inflatable rubber mattress from his earlier artworks of the 1960s, suggesting that he had sailed to New York on it. In several of the works and text-art pieces that are part of his *Archive SF*, he refers to this very day: "13 December 1982: the first day in the USA—NYC in America." Filko's "American period" is thus key for his approach and methodology to the *Archive SF*. Documents from a private archive from New York[12] illustrate that as early as 1985 Filko began to seriously consider the system of the radiant energetic centers within multidimensional time-space—the seven chakras in

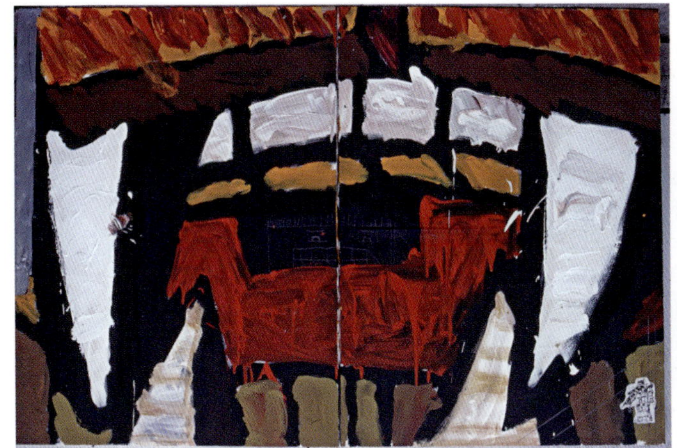

[06A] *Mobil*, 1983

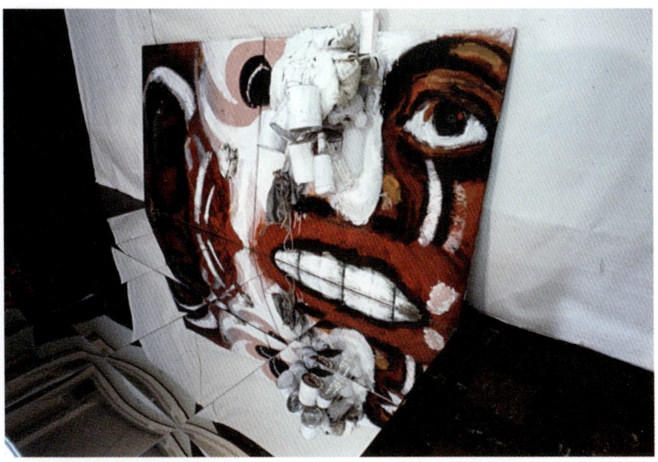

[07A] *Slovak Baby in America*, 1983

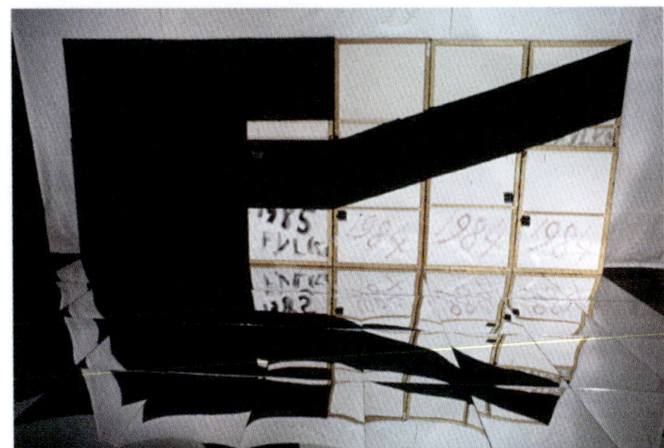

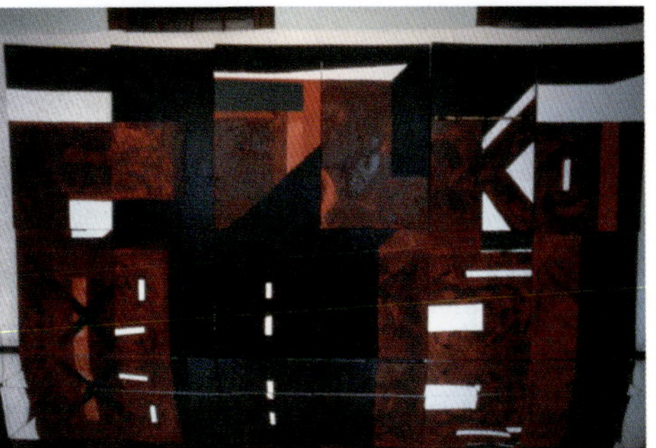

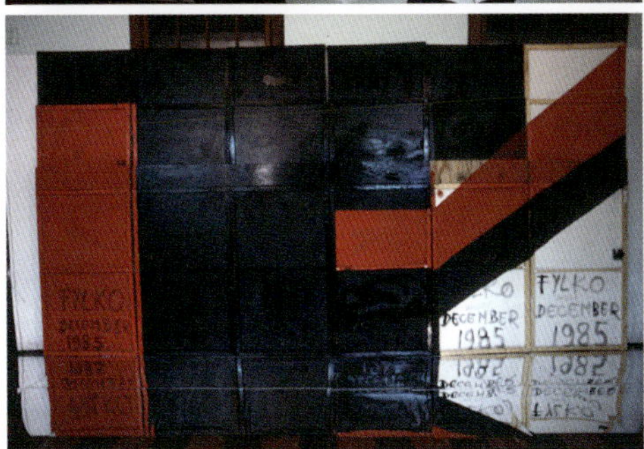

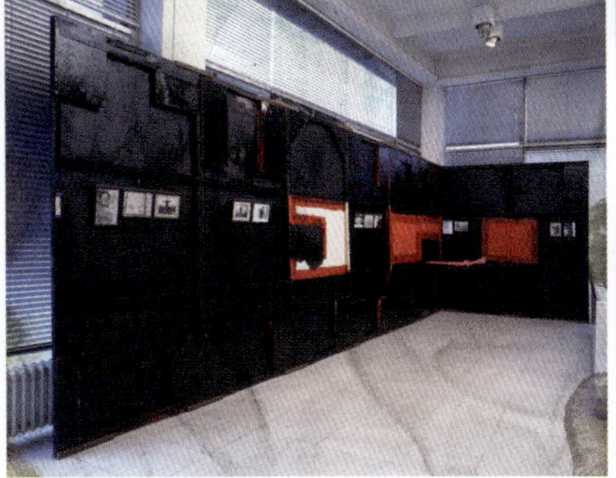

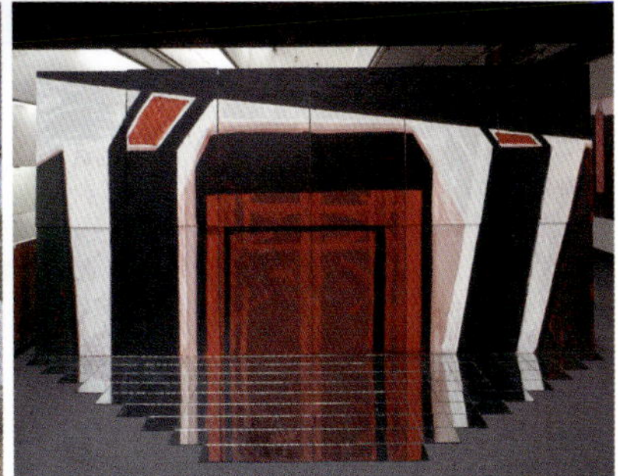

[08–12] From the series *CURTAINS* / Zo série *CURTAINS*, 1985–88

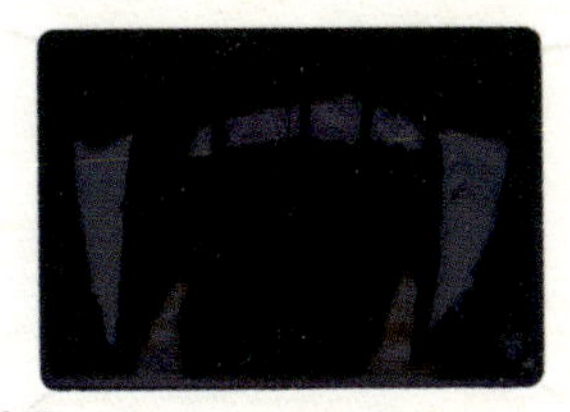

[06B]

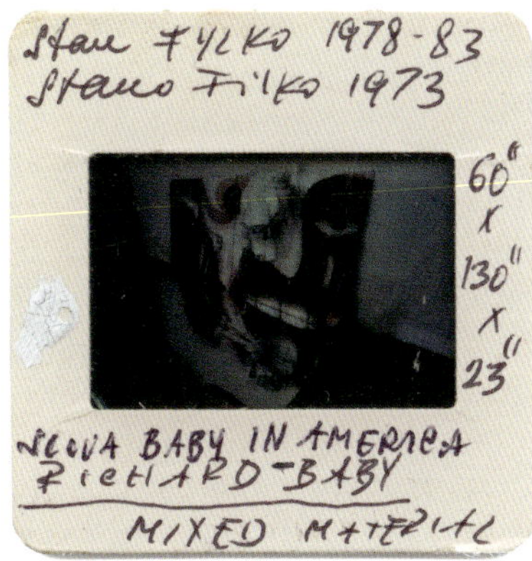

[07B]

the already existing three-dimensional scale—with the intentions of restructuring his entire existing oeuvre and positioning his future art strategies.[13] Several separate reflections on Filko's work from 1984 point to the artist's independence, his uncompromising and his non-commercial stance. At the same time, curators and critics have also noted how the social and cultural themes of his new home milieu in the United States authentically informed and permeated the new phase of his work. Critic John Russell wrote in a *New York Times* review of a three-artist 1984 show at the Jack Tilton Gallery in New York, that Filko "gets the authentic energy of Expressionism into his images of Superman and Superwoman." This reflection was ultimately decisive in the selection of Filko to participate in the group show *Special Projects* (Spring 1986) at MoMA PS1. Charlotta Kotík included Filko in the group show *Working in Brooklyn: Painting* at the Brooklyn Museum in 1987 that was one of a series showcasing both the local and international art scene currently "dominated by individual sensibilities exploring various neo-isms."[14] In his artist's statement for the catalog, Filko presented his legend as an "underground" artist from Czechoslovakia, currently working in the most recent of his four creative periods (with the year 1970 missing): "1st Period, 1960–65: Gnoseological; 2nd Period, 1965–69: Cosmological; 3rd Period, 1971–77: Theosophical-Total… 4th Period, 1978–87: Empirical, Present, the Transformers, Garbage, Abstract…" Following is a series of terms that the artist associates with this fourth period of his as defining, including, for example, in the context of the age of the Moravian Venus at about 25,000 years BC. In one of the archive's black EGO folders was Charlotta Kotík's letter from this period, a recommendation for Filko to the Pollock-Krasner Foundation: "Filko calls his current creative period (1978–present) an 'empirical' one. Among his present themes one finds motives from the American Indian Art, Punk Rock and people living in the contemporary jungle. He is also commenting to his previous creative periods and criticizes the present materialism and decadence in a non-figurative fashion. Stano Filko appears to be a sensitive and imaginative artist, who sticks to his rather unique principles. His life suggests that he doesn't mind sacrificing his personal comfort and material well-being to his ideals."[15]

It is worth mentioning that Thomas M. Messer, then director of the Guggenheim Museum, whose parents came from Slovakia, also wrote a letter in support of Filko for the Pollock Krasner Foundation: "I personally react strongly to his uncompromising work that, despite the heavy pressures that are presently upon him, has never conceded anything to public taste, dealer's pressure and other lures, that, under the circumstances might be easily expected. A strong abstract expressionism in the main tradition of modern post-war painting, modified of course, through the years that have transformed the style, marks Filko's achievement. I was happy to acquire a prime example of his most recent production for the permanent collection of the Guggenheim Museum, and have had no difficulty persuading collector friends that they should do likewise."[16] Both of them refer to Filko's living conditions, which threatened not only his work but also his life: "I feel strongly that there is a human tragedy to be avoided here."[17] This difficult life period has entered the *System SF* in the shape of the number 1984, that

appears on many of Filko's works from the (black) EGO series. In 2018, the Kunstmuseum Basel acquired a larger selection of Filko's objects and concepts with the theme of the black EGO, which stands above the three dimensions in the *System SF*. It can be found several times mentioned (rather cryptically) as his third clinical death in the "text-arts" in the *Archive SF*: "1984 POSTINSTALLATION – POSTENVIRONMENT – POST DADA – POST SURREAL – POSTPAINTING – POST RESEARCH FINE ART."[18] According to the testimony of his acquaintances in New York at the time, that year had brought a borderline near-death experience, giving evidence that the number refers to the year in question, not to George Orwell's famous novel *1984*, as also has been assumed. The year 1984 was in many ways a breakthrough in his work. As Charlotta Kotík described it in 1987: "Filko has moved from violent figurative imagery … toward non-referential compositions that investigate basic geometric shapes and color combinations."[19] It was in 1984 that EGO as a concept was introduced for the first time into the *System SF*, which Filko began to elaborate and layer in detail at that time.

"A – CREATION – POST MODERN – POST PRESENT – 1937 – 45 – 53 – 54 – 60 – 70 – 80 – 84

B – CREATIVITY – POST AVANT-GARDE – POST VANGUARD – 1952 – 59 – 60 – 65 – 70 – 75 – 80 – 84

N.Y.C. – ROOF – METROPOLITAN MUSEUM – FYLKO – 1978 – 80 – 82 – 83 – 84"[20]

As Filko immigrated to the USA in the 1980s Reagan era, which was full of contrasts and paradoxes, he was able to see the absurdity of the Cold War from a whole new perspective. The harshness of American politics and the consequences of his own disillusionment with the end of the dream of humanity's conquest of space, and the aftermath of the failed revolutions of the 1960s that failed in their attempt to bring balance and justice to the world, influenced his thinking and his work in a substantial way. He turned against such a world with his playground machismo, which was beneath the surface of his destructive expressionism, and the disillusionment manifested itself in his work with an even more rugged relationship to the opposite sex, regressing into a bad-boy identity. His American works, however, thereby acquired a tremendous expressive power coming of him, a fiercely untamed and angry man, reminiscent to some aspects of the distinctive masculine thrusts of artists such as Willem de Kooning and Jean-Michel Basquiat. Many of the *Archive SF*'s red binders mention women in the biological third dimension in connection with the elements and as phenomena that are mysterious and at the same time dangerous to men: "3rd DIMENSION – ZOO – BIOLOGY, EMPIRICISM, GNOSEOLOGY, NOETICS, EPICUREANISM, EROS (EARTH, WATER, FIRE, AIR) … MATTER VENUS SCHEHERAZADE – ALSO THE SUBJECT OF AIDS – 1983."[21]

This period has been described as the American "misplaced faith in technology" that could "coexist with a revival of ancient superstitions, a belief in reincarnation, a growing fascination with the occult, and the bizarre forms of spirituality associated with the New Age movement."[22] These impulses of a new hybrid spirituality in a society dominated by the myth of the dream of success and self-fulfillment were very important for Filko. They combined with his former inspiration with the myth of humankind's future conquest

entstanden, später in New York von Filko als „Geister" betrachtet, so auch *BIG POPULAR SPIRIT* (nach 1980) oder *ABSOLUTE POPULAR SPIRIT* (nach 1980).[11] Noch während seiner Zeit in Deutschland tauchten in seinen Gemälden, auch bedingt durch den Einfluss einer neuen Generation expressionistischer Maler*innen aus der Bewegung der Neuen Wilden, nach und nach bunte, leuchtende Farben auf, so, als seien sie unter der durchscheinenden Oberfläche der weiß bemalten oder naturbelassenen Leinwände und Leinenstoffe verborgen gewesen. Filkos deutsche Phase lässt sich als Übergangszeit betrachten, bevor seine künstlerische Energie in den USA ihre volle Wirkung entfaltete, wo er sowohl seiner Vorstellungskraft als auch seiner Kunst auf unerwartete Weise freien Lauf lassen konnte.

Für die weitere Entstehung des *System SF* waren Filkos Erkundungen bis dahin unbekannter gesellschaftlicher und kultureller Phänomene in der anschließenden „amerikanischen Periode" (1983–1990) von entscheidender Bedeutung. In seiner Arbeit befasste er sich auf dynamische Weise mit Themen wie der Entdeckung des HIV-Virus und der AIDS-Krankheit sowie Modetrends und populären spirituellen New-Age-Lehren. Ein weiterer starker Antrieb war die intensive Auseinandersetzung mit der faszinierenden Metropole und der New Yorker Kunstszene im Allgemeinen. Zunächst lebte er in Buffalo, wo er unter anderem den tschechischen Komponisten und Dirigenten Petr Kotík und dessen Frau Charlotta Kotík kennenlernte, die als Kuratorin am Brooklyn Museum arbeitete. Er thematisierte und mystifizierte aber auch seine Ankunft im Amerika seiner Träume, indem er beispielsweise ein Foto der Skyline von Manhattan mit dem Bild einer aufblasbaren Gummimatratze aus seinen früheren Arbeiten der 1960er-Jahre kombinierte, um zu suggerieren, er sei auf dieser nach New York gesegelt. In verschiedenen Arbeiten und Textkunstwerken seines *Archív SF* verweist er auf genau diesen Tag: „13. Dezember 1982: der erste Tag in den USA – NYC in Amerika." Filkos „amerikanische Periode" ist somit der Schlüssel für seine Herangehensweise an das *Archív SF* und dessen Methodik. Dokumente aus einem privaten New Yorker Archiv[12] zeigen, dass Filko bereits 1985 begann, sich ernsthaft mit dem System der strahlenden energetischen Zentren im mehrdimensionalen Zeit-Raum – den sieben Chakren in den bereits vorhandenen drei Dimensionen – auseinanderzusetzen, um sein gesamtes bisheriges Werk neu zu strukturieren und seine zukünftigen Kunststrategien zu positionieren.[13] In verschiedenen Betrachtungen von Filkos Werk ab 1984 wird auf die Unabhängigkeit des Künstlers verwiesen, auf seine kompromisslose, nichtkommerzielle Haltung. Gleichzeitig bemerkten Kurator*innen und Kritiker*innen auch, dass die sozialen und kulturellen Themen seiner neuen Heimat in den Vereinigten Staaten die neue Phase seiner Arbeit unmittelbar beeinflussten und durchdrangen. Der Kritiker John Russell schrieb in einer Rezension in der *New York Times* über eine Ausstellung von drei Künstlern 1984 in der Jack Tilton Gallery in New York, Filko bringe die „authentische Energie des Expressionismus in seine Bilder von Superman und Superwoman". Diese Betrachtung gab letztendlich den Ausschlag dafür, dass Filko zur Teilnahme an der Gruppenausstellung *Special Projects* (Frühjahr 1986) im MoMA PS1 eingeladen wurde. Charlotta Kotík nahm Filko in die Gruppenausstellung *Working in Brooklyn: Painting 1987* im Brooklyn Museum auf. Sie war Teil einer Reihe, in der die lokale und die

internationale Kunstszene vorgestellt wurde, die aktuell „von individuellen Sensibilitäten dominiert wird, die verschiedene Neo-Ismen erforschen".[14] In seiner Künstlererklärung für den Katalog präsentierte Filko seine Legende als „Untergrundkünstler" aus der Tschechoslowakei, der aktuell in seiner vierten Schaffensphase tätig sei (wobei das Jahr 1970 fehlte): „1. Phase, 1960–1965: gnoseologisch, 2. Phase, 1965–1969: kosmologisch, 3. Phase, 1971–1977: theosophisch-total …, 4. Phase, 1978–1987: empirisch, gegenwärtig, die Transformatoren, Abfall, abstrakt …" Es folgt eine Reihe von Themen, die der Künstler als prägend für seine vierte Periode erachtet, darunter beispielsweise seine Datierung des Alters der Venus von Mähren (Moravia) auf etwa 25000 Jahre. In einer der schwarzen EGO-Mappen des Archivs befand sich Charlotta Kotíks Brief aus dieser Periode, als Empfehlung für Filko bei der Pollock-Krasner Foundation: „Filko bezeichnet seine derzeitige Schaffensphase (1978–heute) als ‚empirisch'. Unter seinen gegenwärtigen Themen finden sich Motive aus indigener Kunst, Punkrock und von Menschen aus dem Dschungel unserer Zeit. Darüber hinaus nimmt er auch Bezug auf seine früheren Schaffensphasen und kritisiert den gegenwärtigen Materialismus und die Dekadenz auf nichtgegenständliche Weise. Bei Stano Filko scheint es sich um einen sensiblen, fantasievollen Künstler zu handeln, der seinen ziemlich einzigartigen Prinzipien treu bleibt. Sein Leben lässt darauf schließen, dass es ihm nichts ausmacht, persönlichen Komfort und materielles Wohlergehen seinen Idealen zu opfern."[15]

Interessant ist, dass auch Thomas M. Messer, der damalige Direktor des Guggenheim-Museums, dessen Eltern aus der Slowakei stammten, ein Empfehlungsschreiben für Stano Filko bei der Pollock-Krasner Foundation verfasste: „Mich persönlich spricht sein kompromissloses Werk sehr an, das trotz des starken Drucks, der derzeit auf ihm lastet, nie dem öffentlichen Geschmack, dem Druck des Kunsthandels und anderen Verlockungen nachgegeben hat, wie man es unter den gegebenen Umständen leicht erwarten könnte. Filkos Werk zeichnet sich aus durch einen starken abstrakten Expressionismus in der Haupttradition der modernen Nachkriegsmalerei, natürlich beeinflusst durch stilistische Änderungen im Laufe der Jahre. Ich hatte das Glück, ein hervorragendes Beispiel seines neuesten Schaffens für die permanente Sammlung des Guggenheim Museums erwerben zu können und konnte Sammlerfreunde mühelos davon überzeugen, es mir gleichzutun."[16] Beide nehmen Bezug auf Filkos Lebensumstände, die nicht nur seine Arbeit, sondern auch sein Leben gefährdeten: „Ich bin überzeugt, dass es hier eine menschliche Tragödie zu vermeiden gilt."[17] Diese schwierige Lebensphase hat in Form der Zahl 1984 Einzug in das *System SF* gehalten. Sie erscheint auf zahlreichen Werken Filkos aus der Reihe des (schwarzen) EGO. 2018 erwarb das Kunstmuseum Basel eine größere Auswahl von Filkos Objekten und Konzepten mit dem Thema des schwarzen EGO, das im *System SF* über den drei Dimensionen steht. Mehrfach wird in der „Textart" seines *Archív SF* (ziemlich kryptisch) darauf verwiesen: „1984 POSTINSTALLATION – POSTENVIRONMENT – POST DADA – POST SURREAL – POSTPAINTING – POST RESEARCH FINE ART."[18] Nach Aussage seiner damaligen Bekannten in New York hatte er in jenem Jahr eine grenzwertige Nahtoderfahrung, was darauf hindeutet, dass sich die Zahl auf das betreffende Jahr bezieht und nicht auf George Orwells berühmten Roman *1984*, wie ebenfalls angenommen wurde.

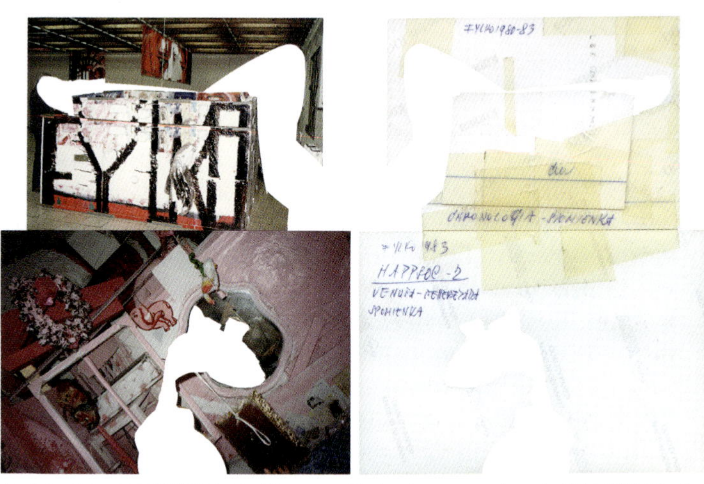

[13A-B] *HAPPSOC 2 Venus Scheherazade / HAPPSOC 2 Venuša Šeherezáda*, 1983

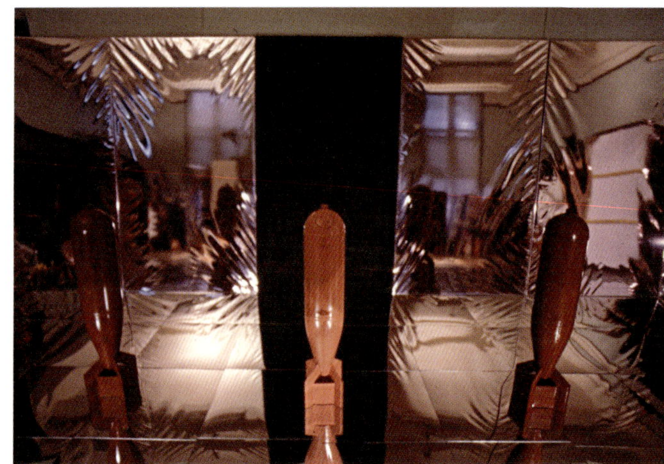

[14A] *Bombs Altar - Foil Installation*, 1986

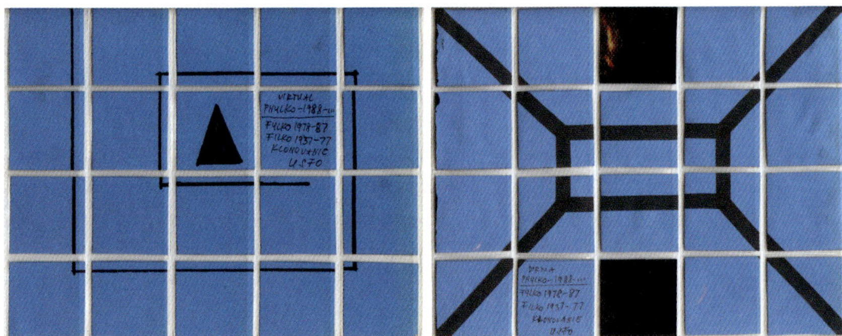

[16A-B] From the series *Cloning USFO / Zo série Klonovanie USFO*, c. 1990

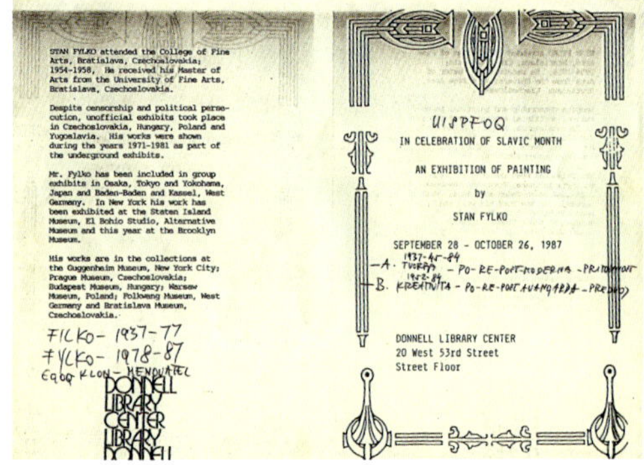

[17] *An Exhibition of Painting by Stano Filko*, invitation card, Donnel Library Center, New York, 1987

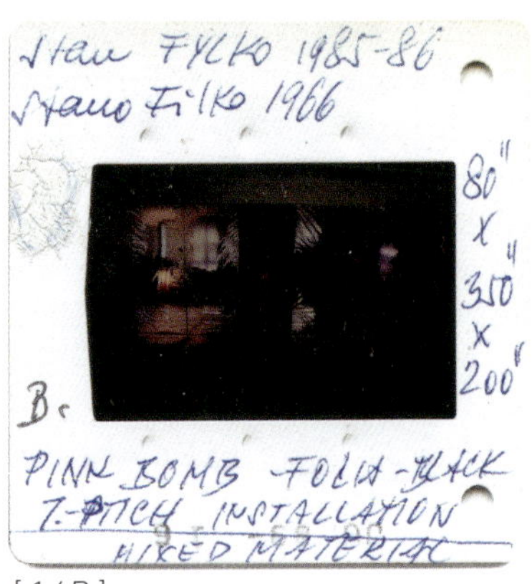

[14B]

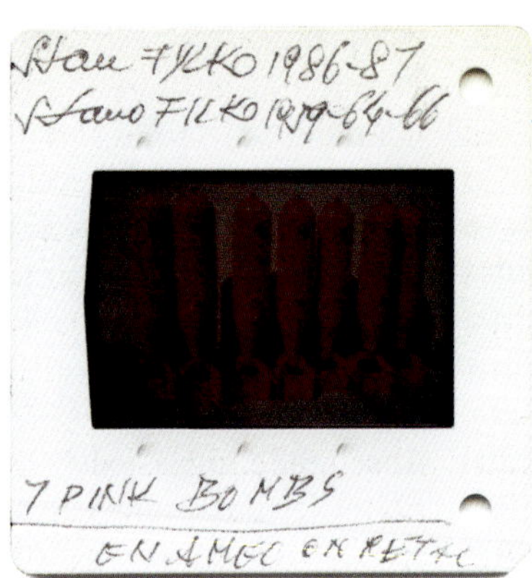

[15] *7 Pink Bombs / 7 ružových bômb*, 1987

Das Jahr 1984 stellte in vielerlei Hinsicht einen Durchbruch in seinem Werk dar. Charlotta Kotík beschrieb es 1987 so: „Filko hat sich von gewalttätigen gegenständlichen Bildern […] zu nichtreferenziellen Kompositionen hinbewegt, die geometrische Grundformen und Farbkombinationen erforschen."[19] 1984 hielt EGO als Konzept zum ersten Mal Einzug in das *System SF*, dessen Ebenen von Filko damals im Detail ausgearbeitet wurden.

„A – CREATION – POST MODERN – POST PRESENT – 1937 – 45 – 53 – 54 – 60 – 70 – 80 – 84
B – CREATIVITY – POST AVANT-GARDE – POST VANGUARD – 1952 – 59 – 60 – 65 – 70 – 75 – 80 – 84
N.Y.C. – ROOF – METROPOLITAN MUSEUM – FYLKO – 1978 – 80 – 82 – 83 – 84"[20]

Als Filko in der Reagan-Ära der 1980er-Jahre in die durch Kontraste und Paradoxe geprägte USA emigrierte, konnte er die Absurdität des Kalten Krieges aus einer ganz neuen Perspektive betrachten. Die Härte der amerikanischen Politik und seine eigene Enttäuschung über das Ende des Traums von der Eroberung des Weltraums durch die Menschheit sowie die Nachwirkungen der gescheiterten Revolutionen der 1960er-Jahre, denen es nicht gelungen war, der Welt Gleichgewicht und Gerechtigkeit zu bringen, hatten maßgeblichen Einfluss auf sein Denken und sein Werk. Gegen diese Welt wandte er sich mit einem Macho-Gehabe, das unter der Oberfläche seines destruktiven Expressionismus verborgen war; die Desillusionierung manifestierte sich in seinem Werk mit einem noch schrofferen Verhältnis zum anderen Geschlecht, mit einer Regression zum Selbstbild eines *bad boy*. Seinen amerikanischen Arbeiten verlieh dies jedoch eine enorme Ausdruckskraft. Sie entsprang einem wilden, ungezähmten, wütenden Mann und erinnert in gewisser Weise an die ausgeprägt maskuline Energie von Künstlern wie Willem de Kooning und Jean-Michel Basquiat. In zahlreichen roten Mappen des *Archív SF* werden Frauen in der biologischen 3. Dimension in Verbindung mit den Elementen und als zugleich mysteriöses und für Männer gefährliches Phänomen erwähnt: „3rd DIMENSION – ZOO – BIOLOGY, EMPIRICISM, GNOSEOLOGY, NOETICS, EPICUREANISM, EROS (EARTH, WATER, FIRE, AIR) … MATTER VENUS SCHEHERAZADE – ALSO THE SUBJECT OF AIDS – 1983."[21]

Diese Zeit wurde als Ära des „Irrglaubens an die Technologie" beschrieben, der „neben einem Wiederaufleben alten Aberglaubens, dem Glauben an die Reinkarnation, einer zunehmenden Faszination für das Okkulte und die bizarren Formen der Spiritualität, wie sie mit der New-Age-Bewegung verbunden sind, bestehen konnte".[22] Für Filko waren diese Impulse einer neuen hybriden Spiritualität in einer Gesellschaft, die von dem Mythos des Traums von Erfolg und Selbsterfüllung beherrscht wurde, äußerst wichtig. Sie passten zu seiner früheren Inspiration durch den Mythos der zukünftigen Eroberung des Weltraums durch die Menschheit, die in den 1960ern bereits eine ganze Generation junger Künstler*innen beeinflusst hatte.

Im Sowjetblock stand der Weltraum darüber hinaus auch für einen Raum der individuellen Projektion von Freiheit und einer utopischen Zukunft, in der Vadim Zakharov zufolge jeder Autor aktiv „eine Utopie seiner eigenen Persönlichkeit gestaltete und sich selbst in dieser Utopie verwirklichte, indem er ihre Grenzen in alle möglichen unterschiedlichen Räume ausdehnte, einschließlich des Kosmos, der letztlich das primäre Ziel seiner Ambitionen ist. Wobei sich die Vorstellung vom ‚Kosmos' häufig ändert."[23] In dieser Hinsicht finden sich bei Stano Filko in der internationalen Szene Parallelen zur Geschichte und zum Werk von Ilya Kabakov, der 1987 über Österreich aus Russland emigrierte und sich schließlich in den Vereinigten Staaten niederließ. Kabakov hat diesen Traum von einer kosmischen Zukunft „entmythologisiert", insbesondere in seiner Installation *The Man Who Flew Into Space From His Apartment* (Der Mensch, der aus seiner Wohnung in den Kosmos flog) (1985). In einer ergreifenden und zugleich ironischen Szene aus einem Zimmer in einer Moskauer Gemeinschaftswohnung katapultiert sich ein Mann, eine fiktionale Figur, die gewisse Züge des Künstlers selbst aufweist, nach jahrelanger Vorbereitung mit einem selbstgebauten Apparat in den Weltraum. Kabakov schrieb später treffend über die Bedingungen in der Moskauer Kunstszene, die denen in anderen osteuropäischen Ländern entsprach: „Fast dreißig Jahre lang fand das Leben inoffizieller Künstler*innen in einer abgesperrten, versiegelten Welt statt. In dieser ganzen Zeit wurden inoffizielle Künstler*innen durch eine strikte politische, ideologische und ästhetische Zensur daran gehindert, ihr Werk auszustellen oder zu veröffentlichen. Gefangen in dieser nahezu ‚kosmischen' Isolation waren die Künstler*innen in diesen Kreisen ganz auf sich allein gestellt und mussten sich aufeinander verlassen, um die Aufgaben zu übernehmen, die eigentlich andere hätten übernehmen sollen: Publikum, Kritiker*innen, Expert*innen, Historiker*innen und sogar Sammler*innen."[24] Ähnlich wie Kabakov hatte auch Filko eine starke Neigung zur Selbstinstitutionalisierung und damit zur Musealisierung seiner Kunst. Kabakov nutzte dazu fiktive Figuren, die Künstler*innen darstellten, während seine Installationen eine Metapher für das Museum und die Kunstwelt waren. Filko hingegen entwickelte sein komplexes *System SF* mit zahlreichen seiner eigenen fiktiven *Personas*. Am bedeutendsten ist jedoch die Einführung seiner vier Klone, von denen die ersten drei bereits 1988 in den Vereinigten Staaten konzipiert wurden: „Stanislav Filko (1937–1977)", „Stan Fylko (1978–1987)", „Stan Phylko (1988–1997)" und „Phys (1998–2037)". Die ersten drei sind auf dem Flyer für seine Einzelausstellung 1987 im Donnell Library Center zu sehen [17], in dem Jozef Staško arbeitete: unter einem Foto der Arbeit *Mobile Installation* – einem kryptischen dreidimensionalen Selbstporträt als gemalte Installation mit weichen, reflektierenden Oberflächen, in denen sich eine pinkfarbene Rakete in der Mitte spiegelte, mit folgendem rätselhaften Titel: „1958 – 60 – 78 Filko – Fylko." Auf der Rückseite des gedruckten Flyers befindet sich die Trikolore. Im Entwurf fügte Filko eine grundlegende Erklärung seiner Kunst hinzu, die wahrscheinlich für seine Landsleute bestimmt war: „Meine Kunst gehört zur konzeptuellen Bewegung; sie hat drei verschiedene Dimensionen oder drei Wege gleicher Energie, wie die slowakische Flagge: Biologie – Rot; Kosmologie – Blau; Ontologie – Weiß."[25]

Abschließend lässt sich sagen, dass das *System SF* für seinen Schöpfer zu einem gigantischen konzeptuellen Werkzeug wurde, mit dem er seine extreme Lebenserfahrungen und die Enttäuschungen, die ihm die Welt bereitete, überwinden konnte. Es entstand nicht allein aus dem größenwahnsinnigen Wunsch seines Schöpfers, seinen Namen und sein Land fest im Kanon der westlichen Kunst zu verankern, sondern auch

of the cosmos, which had already influenced an entire generation of young artists in the 1960s.

In the Soviet bloc, moreover, space meant also a space of individual projection of freedom and a utopian future, where according to Vadim Zakharov, every author actively structured "utopia of his own individual personality and realized himself in this utopia expanding its boundaries in all manner of diverse spaces, including the cosmos which, in the final analysis, is the goal towards which his primary ambitions are directed. Of course, the very concept 'cosmos' often changes."[23] In this sense, in the international scene Stano Filko can be thought of in comparison with the story and work of Ilya Kabakov, who emigrated from Russia in 1987 via Austria to finally settle in the United States. Kabakov "demythologized" this dream of a cosmic future, particularly in his installation *The Man Who Flew Into Space From His Apartment* (1985), a poignant yet ironic scene from a room in a Moscow communal apartment, where, after years of preparation, a fictional character of man, representing certain parts of the artist himself, catapulted himself into space with a homemade device. Later, Kabakov aptly wrote about the conditions in the Moscow art scene, similar in all the Eastern European countries: "For almost thirty years the life of an unofficial artist was spent inside a locked and sealed world. All this time unofficial artists and authors were barred by strict political, ideological and aesthetic censorship from exhibiting or publishing their work. Caught in this virtually 'cosmic' isolation, artists in these circles had to be entirely self-reliant and depend on one another to perform the roles that others should have played: viewers, critics, experts, historians and even collectors."[24] Like Kabakov, Filko also had a strong vocation for self-institutionalization, and thus for the musealization of his art. Kabakov realized it through fictional characters who were artists, his installations being a metaphor for the museum and the art world. Filko on the contrary developed his complex *System SF* with many of his own fictional personas. Most significant, though, is the introduction of his four clones, the first three of which were already conceived in the United States in 1988: *Stanislav Filko 1937–1977, Stan Fylko 1978–1987, Stan Phylko 1988–1997* and *Phys 1998–2037*. The first three appear on the flyer for his 1987 solo exhibition at the Donnell Library Center [17], where Jozef Staško worked: under a photograph of the work *Mobile Installation*—a cryptic spatial self-portrait as a painterly installation with soft reflective surfaces mirroring a pink rocket in the middle with an enigmatic caption: "1958 – 60 – 78 Filko – Fylko." The reverse side of the printed matter consists of the tricolor. In the manuscript entry Filko added a basic statement explaining his art, which was probably intended for his compatriots: "My art belongs to the conceptual movement; it has three distinct dimensions, or three paths of equal energy, like the Slovak flag: biology – red; cosmology – blue; ontology – white."[25]

It can be concluded that the *System SF* became a gigantic conceptual tool for its author, through which he could overcome his strong life experiences and disappointments with the world. It emerged not only from its author's megalomaniacal desire to plant his name and his country firmly in the canon of Western art, but also from the wound left by the loss of his home. It was also his attempt to understand a complicated world and the utopia of an idea that transcends time and space and offers solutions for the future. Filko's work and the story of the artist in a way symbolize the crossroad between East and West. Beyond the context of Eastern European and American art, it is also interesting to consider Filko in relation to other European artists such as Joseph Beuys who is of particular interest in relation to Filko in the light of his concept of self-institutionalization and the messianism and of shamanism of the German artist in general, which certainly also influenced him to a great extent, especially during his 1960s stay and later exile in Düsseldorf. Beuys was also important as an inspirational source for Filko's "legend of the artist," his *Gesamtkunstwerk* as a medium and also for his self-institutionalization, because he was the first to bring the artist's life and work together in such a unique and instrumental way to the art world. Some aspects of Beuys's work were particularly inspiring to Filko, such as the complicated relationship between his life and his art. According to Gene Ray, his "objects are relics of his utopian program—of the public persona, the unceasing pronouncements and provocations, the lectures and actions, the challenging exhortations to create a new social order," in his conception of art, "the whole of society and the whole world is regarded as the material of a vast collaborative *Gesamtkunstwerk*."[26] For Filko, the focus on self-institution was set after his return from the United States, first at his studio Snežienková, then, from 2005 onwards, in the concept of the museum—the so called Filko Foundation in Veľká Hradná. As Marek Pokorný observed in 2015, Filko belonged among "artists with a strong personal history, with a semiotic morphological system of their own and an ability to incorporate it in their work with particularities having a value derived from designating gesture and structure in which it is materially fixed."[27] During his lifetime though, Filko was mostly misunderstood, and at home in his homeland he remained forever a stranger, an alien element who fitted in nowhere—as an emigrant, he became homeless a second time. His art as a "system of systems," described on many pages of his text-arts, was thus his only real home. Text-art as a samizdat practice provided a working method of *self-publishing* that was inherent in his artistic practice from the 1960s onwards, which was fully developed in the *Archive SF*. Filko paid great attention to the graphic form and editing of his manuscripts, text-art and concepts, although he did not archive them in the classical chronological method but as a work of art per se. He worked continuously on the structure and arrangement of the *Archive SF* and on the architecture of the individual folders in relation to the space of the house on Snežienková, and thus the *System SF*, was obviously significant for him. The spatial organization, visual arrangement and subdivision, as well as the topographical relationships of the various themes are manifested in the artistic solutions of the *Archive SF*, starting with the careful and dynamically complemented chained titles of the folders as thematic units. The preserved part of the *Archive SF* thus constitutes a work comprehensively representing the thinking of its author. In the way he worked with images and concepts, Filko fully exploited the possibilities of visual art in the "epoch of mechanical reproduction" announced by Walter Benjamin as early as 1935. *Archive SF* has qualities that reveal an inspiration from the age of cybernetics and

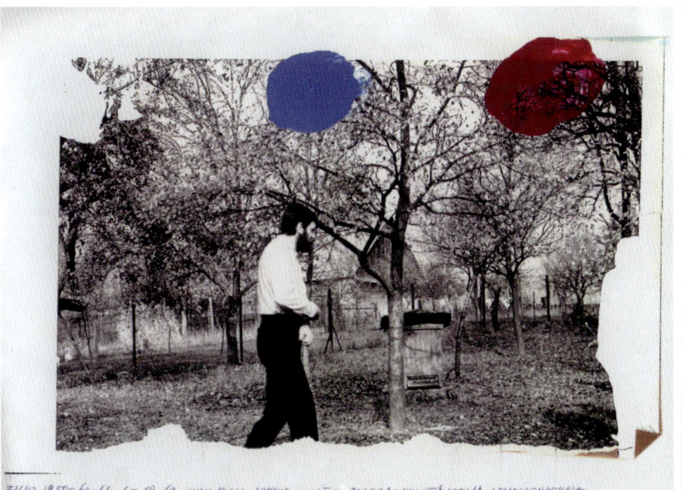
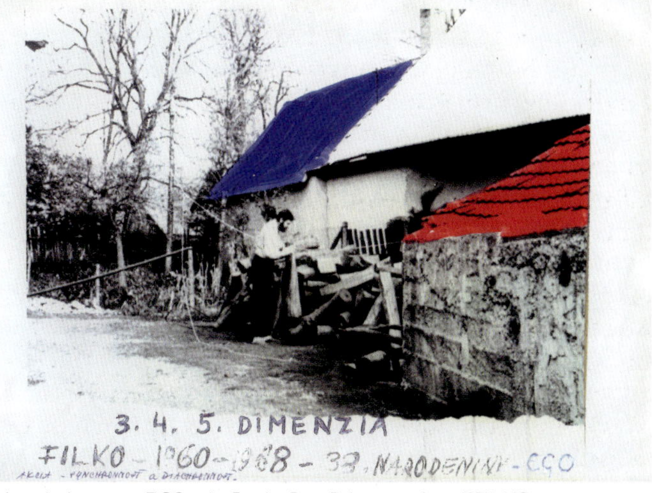

[18A–B] 3.4.5. Dimension FILKO 1960–1968 to 33. Birthday = EGO / 3.4.5. Dimenzia FILKO 1960–1968 k 33. narodeninám = EGO, 1970/ c. 1990

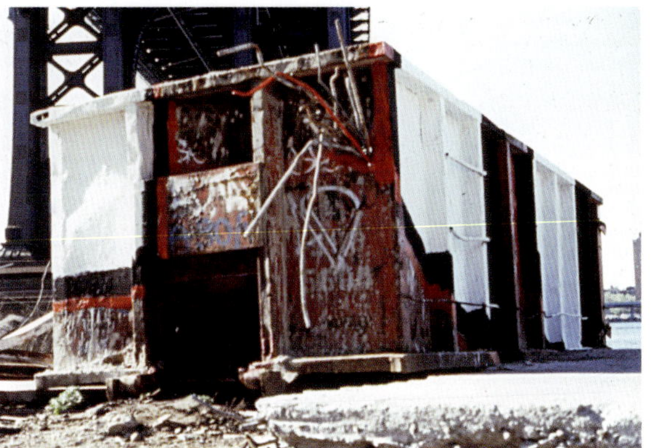

[19A] Cannibal, c. 1985

[20A] ABSOLUTE ONTOLOGIA, 1988

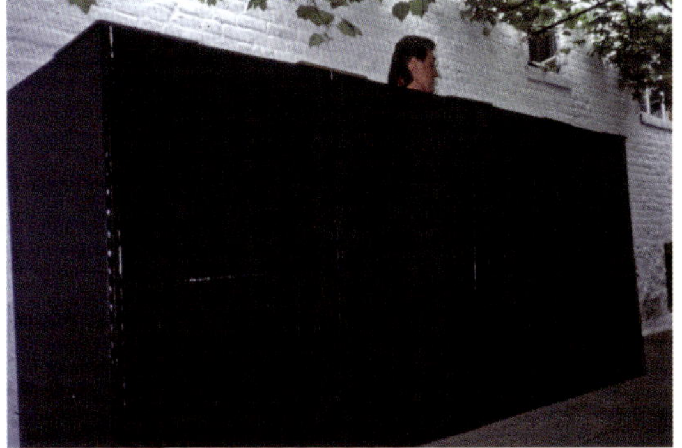

[21A] Black Space Installation, 1984

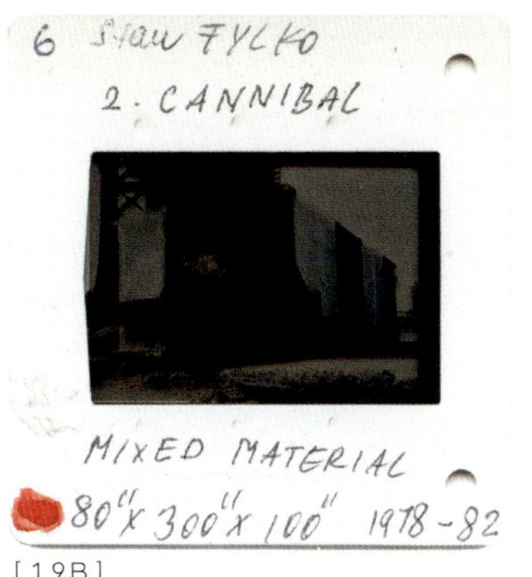

[19B]

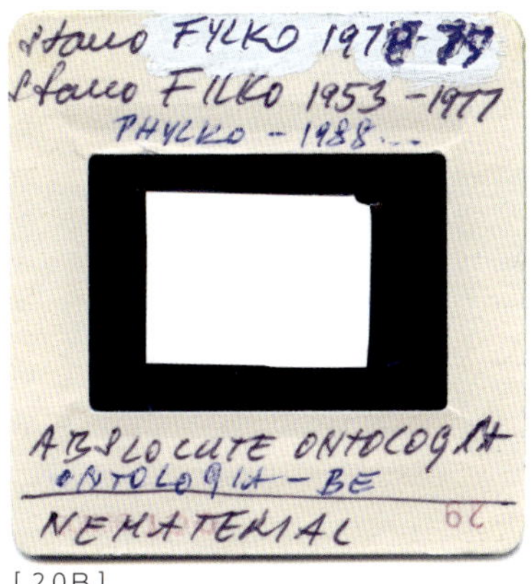

[20B]

[21B]

information. Archival items are points in a web of meanings, so that the overall significance and of this vast meta-work derives from the authenticity of its structure, not from the "aura" of the original and style. *Archive SF* is closely related to Filko's concept for his *self-museum* and was born to ensure nothing less than the project of his immortality. For Filko, his own individualized archive as a fully-blown post-modern and post-conceptual meta-work also deprives things, visual or textual information of their utilitarian value and assigns them a value (i.e., meaning) of his own discretion. The *Archive SF* is then for Filko both his own universe and also his eternal case and as such is a challenge to research and exhibit in detail in the future.

1   Michel Foucault, *The Archaeology of Knowledge* (London, 1972), p. 129.

2   The Július Koller Archive achieved international acclaim, especially after the retrospective exhibition *Július Koller. One Man Anti Show* at the mumok – Museum moderner Kunst Stiftung Ludwig, in Vienna in 2016/17 (curators Daniel Grúň, Kathrin Rhomberg, Georg Schöllhammer). The exhibition grew out of a long-term research project dedicated to the artist's work and to his vast archive.

3   Stano Filko, "Poézia = Próza z klinickej smrti" (Poetry = Prose from the Clinical Death), Text-art, typewritten, undated, 6 pages. Courtesy the *Archive of Visual Art* (AVU), The Slovak National Gallery (Bratislava).

4   Jozef Cseres, "Filko Problem," in *60/90: 4. Výročná výstava SCCA Slovensko / 60/90: 4th Annual exhibition of SCCA Slovakia* (Bratislava, 1997), p. 45.

5   Italo Calvino, "On Multiplicity," in *Six Memos for the Next Millenium* (London, 2016), p. 129.

6   Aurel Hrabušický, "Filkova novosvetská. 1982–1990," in *STANO FILKO. 80s in N.Y.C. Paintings & Objects*, exh. cat. Art Capital (Bratislava, 2014), n. p.

7   Christopher D. Johnson, *Memory, Metaphor and Aby Warburg's Atlas of Mnemosyne* (Ithaca, New York, 2012), p. 11.

8   Robert Smithson quoted from the play "East Coast/West Coast," (1969) by Eve Meltzer in *Systems We Have Loved: Conceptual Art, Affect, and the Antihumanist Turn* (Chicago, 2013), p. 140.

9   Aurel Hrabušický, "Filkova novosvetská. 1982–1990," in *STANO FILKO. 80s in N.Y.C. Paintings & Objects*, exh. cat. Art Capital (Bratislava, 2014), n. p.

10   Ibid.

11   Ibid.

12   The information was obtained from Ema Staško, who kept the documents of her husband Jozef Staško (1917–99), a former Czechoslovak and Slovak diplomat. In 1961 he left with his family for exile and later became an important figure in the Slovak immigration circles in the USA. He worked, amongst others, for the *Voice of America*, through which in 1985 he conducted a broadcast on the work of Stano Filko in cooperation with the artist himself. Staško was helping him to find jobs and make contacts in New York.

13   Ema Staško, interview recorded by Lucia Gregorová Stach, New York, October 29, 2018.

14   Charlotta Kotík, *Working in Brooklyn/Painting*, exh. cat. Brooklyn Museum (New York, 1987), p. 10.

15   Rewritten from the *Archive SF*, ed. Slovak National Gallery, DSF bc 2 (Bratislava), p. 10.

16   Ibid., p. 11.

17   Ibid., p. 12.

18   Ibid., p. 1.

19   Charlotta Kotík, *Working in Brooklyn/Painting*, exh. cat. Brooklyn Museum (New York, 1987), p. 13.

20   Rewritten from the *Archive SF*, ed. Slovak National Gallery, DSF bc 2 (Bratislava), p. 1.

21   Ibid., p. 1.

22   Christopher Lasch, "Afterword: The Culture of Narcissism Revisited," in *The Culture of Narcissism, American Life in an Age of Diminishing Expectations* (London/New York, 1991), p. 244.

23   Vadim Zakharov, "Author, cosmos, archive," in *Cosmic Shift: Russian Contemporary Art Writing* (London, 2017), p. 248.

24   Ilya Kabakov quoted in Boris Groys "Re-Inventing Authorship," in *Not Everyone will be Taken to the Future*, exh. cat. Tate Gallery (London, 2017), p. 37.

25   Rewritten from the *Archive SF*, ed. Slovak National Gallery, DSF bc 2 (Bratislava), p. 40.

26   Gene Ray, "Joseph Beuys and the After Auschwitz Sublime," in *Joseph Beuys. Mapping the Legacy* (New York, 2001), p. 56.

27   Marek Pokorný, "Generative Grammar of the World, or Tentative Propedeutics to the Work of Stano Filko," in *Stano Filko 5.D.*, exh. cat. PLATO platform (for contemporary art) (Ostrava, 2015), p. 18.

aus der Wunde, die der Verlust seiner Heimat hinterlassen hatte. Zugleich war es sein Versuch, eine komplexe Welt und die Utopie einer Idee, die Raum und Zeit überwindet und Lösungen für die Zukunft bietet, zu verstehen. Filkos Werk und die Geschichte des Künstlers symbolisieren in gewisser Weise die Schnittstelle zwischen Ost und West. Jenseits des Kontexts osteuropäischer und amerikanischer Kunst lohnt es sich, Filko im Verhältnis zu anderen europäischen Künstler*innen zu betrachten, insbesondere im Vergleich zu Joseph Beuys sowie dessen Konzept der Selbstinstitutionalisierung und dem Messianismus und Schamanismus des deutschen Künstlers im Allgemeinen, die ihn sicherlich auch in hohem Maße beeinflusst haben, insbesondere während seines Aufenthalts in Düsseldorf in den 1960er-Jahren und seines späteren dortigen Exils. Ebenso wichtig war Beuys als Inspirationsquelle für Filkos „Künstlerlegende", sein Gesamtkunstwerk als Medium sowie auch für seine Selbstinstitutionalisierung, denn er war der Erste, der Leben und Werk als Künstler auf solch einzigartige und instrumentelle Weise in der Kunstwelt verband. Einige Aspekte von Beuys' Werk waren für Filko besonders inspirierend, darunter beispielsweise das komplizierte Verhältnis zwischen seinem Leben und seiner Kunst. Gene Ray zufolge sind „seine Objekte Relikte seines utopischen Programms – der öffentlichen Persona, den endlosen Ankündigungen und Provokationen, den Vorlesungen und Aktionen, den fordernden Mahnungen zur Schaffung einer neuen gesellschaftlichen Ordnung", in seinem Kunstverständnis „werden die Gesellschaft und die Welt als Ganzes als Material eines gewaltigen gemeinschaftlichen Gesamtkunstwerks betrachtet".[26] Bei Filko rückte die Selbstinstitutionalisierung nach seiner Rückkehr aus den Vereinigten Staaten in den Mittelpunkt, zunächst in seinem Atelier in der Snežienková, ab 2005 dann im Konzept des Museums – der sogenannten Filko Foundation in Veľká Hradná. Wie Marek Pokorný 2015 feststellte, gehörte Filko zu den „Künstler*innen mit einer starken persönlichen Geschichte, mit einem eigenen semiotischen morphologischen System und der Fähigkeit, dieses in ihr Werk zu integrieren, mit Eigenheiten, die einen Wert haben, der sich aus der Bezeichnung der Geste und der Struktur ergibt, in der dieses materiell fixiert wird".[27] Zu seinen Lebzeiten wurde Filko jedoch meistens missverstanden, und in seiner Heimat blieb er stets ein Fremder, ein fremdes Element, das nirgendwo hineinpasste – als Emigrant wurde er ein zweites Mal heimatlos. Seine Kunst als „System der Systeme", auf vielen Seiten seiner Textkunst beschrieben, war somit seine einzige wahre Heimat. Die Textkunst als Samisdat-Praxis bot eine Arbeitsmethode zur *Selbstveröffentlichung*, die ab den 1960er-Jahren Teil seiner künstlerischen Praxis wurde und im *Archív SF* zur vollen Entfaltung fand. Filko legte großen Wert auf die grafische Form und Bearbeitung seiner Manuskripte, Textkunst und Konzepte, die er jedoch nicht in der klassischen chronologischen Weise, sondern als Kunstwerk an sich archivierte. Er arbeitete fortlaufend an der Struktur und Anordnung des *Archív SF* und an der Aufteilung der einzelnen Mappen in den verschiedenen Räumen des Hauses in der Snežienková-Straße; das *System SF* war für ihn offensichtlich von Bedeutung. Die räumliche Organisation, die visuelle Anordnung und Unterteilung sowie die topografischen Beziehungen der verschiedenen Themen zeigen sich in den künstlerischen Lösungen des *Archív SF*, angefangen bei der sorgfältig und dynamisch ergänzten Verkettung der Mappentitel zu thematischen Einheiten. Der erhaltene Teil des

Archív SF stellt somit ein Werk dar, das die Denkweise seines Schöpfers umfassend repräsentiert. In der Art und Weise, wie er mit Bildern und Konzepten arbeitete, nutzte Filko alle Möglichkeiten der visuellen Kunst im „Zeitalter der mechanischen Reproduktion", wie es Walter Benjamin bereits 1935 angekündigt hatte. Einige Merkmale des *Archív SF* deuten auf eine Inspiration aus dem Kybernetik- und Informationszeitalter hin. Die Archivstücke sind Punkte in einem Netz aus Bedeutungen, sodass die Gesamtbedeutung dieses umfangreichen Meta-Werks von der Authentizität seiner Struktur und nicht von der „Aura" des Originals und dessen Stil herrührt. Das *Archív SF* ist eng verknüpft mit Filkos Konzept für sein *Selbstmuseum* und entstanden, um nichts Geringeres als das Projekt seiner Unsterblichkeit zu gewährleisten. Sein eigenes individualisiertes Archiv als vollendetes postmodernes und postkonzeptionelles Meta-Werk raubt Dingen, visuellen oder textbasierten Informationen ihren Gebrauchswert und weist ihnen nach eigenem Ermessen einen Wert (also eine Bedeutung) zu. Das *Archív SF* ist für Filko also sowohl sein eigenes Universum als auch ein Fall für die Ewigkeit und bereit, in Zukunft im Detail erforscht und ausgestellt zu werden.

1   Michel Foucault, *Archäologie des Wissens*, Frankfurt/Main 1981, S. 186–187.
2   Internationale Anerkennung erlangte das Július-Koller-Archiv insbesondere nach der Retrospektive *Július Koller. One Man Anti Show* im mumok – Museum moderner Kunst Stiftung Ludwig, in Wien 2016/17 (kuratiert von Daniel Grúň, Kathrin Rhomberg und Georg Schöllhammer). Die Ausstellung ging aus einem langfristigen Forschungsprojekt hervor, das dem Werk des Künstlers und seinem umfangreichen Archiv gewidmet war.
3   Stano Filko, „Poézia = Próza z klinickej smrti" (Poesie = Prosa vom klinischen Tod), Textkunst, mit Schreibmaschine geschrieben, undatiert, 6 Seiten. Freundlicherweise zur Verfügung gestellt vom *Archive of Visual Art* (AVU), Slovak National Gallery (Bratislava).
4   Jozef Cseres, „Filko Problem", in: *60/90: 4. Výročná výstava SCCA Slovensko / 60/90: 4th Annual exhibition of SCCA Slovakia*, Bratislava 1997, S. 45.
5   Italo Calvino, „On Multiplicity", in: *Six Memos for the Next Millenium*, London 2016, S. 129.
6   Aurel Hrabušický, „Filkova novosvetská. 1982–1990", in: *STANO FILKO. 80s in N.Y.C. Paintings & Objects*, Ausst.-Kat. Art Capital, Bratislava 2014, o. S.
7   Christopher D. Johnson, *Memory, Metaphor and Aby Warburg's Atlas of Mnemosyne*, Ithaca, New York 2012, S. 11.
8   Robert Smithson, zitiert aus dem Video „East Coast/West Coast" (1969) von Eve Meltzer, in: *Systems We Have Loved: Conceptual Art, Affect, and the Antihumanist Turn*, Chicago 2013, S. 140.
9   Aurel Hrabušický, „Filkova novosvetská. 1982–1990", in: *STANO FILKO. 80s in N.Y.C. Paintings & Objects*, Ausst.-Kat. Art Capital, Bratislava 2014, o. S.
10   Ebd.
11   Ebd.
12   Diese Information stammt von Ema Staško, die die Dokumente ihres Mannes Jozef Staško (1917–1999), einem ehemaligen tschechoslowakischen und slowakischen Diplomaten, verwahrt hatte. Jozef Staško war 1961 mit seiner Familie ins Exil gegangen und wurde später in slowakischen Immigrantenkreisen in den USA zu einer wichtigen Persönlichkeit. Staško war unter anderem für den Sender *Voice of America* tätig, über den er 1985 eine Sendung über das Werk von Stano Filko machte, in Zusammenarbeit mit dem Künstler selbst. Staško war ihm dabei behilflich, in New York Arbeit zu finden und Kontakte zu knüpfen.
13   Ema Staško im Interview mit Lucia Gregorová Stach, New York, 29. Oktober 2018.
14   Charlotta Kotík, *Working in Brooklyn: Painting*, Ausst.-Kat. Brooklyn Museum, New York 1987, S. 10.
15   Nach einem Auszug aus dem *Archív SF*, hrsg. von Slovak National Gallery, DSF bc 2, Bratislava, S. 10.
16   Ebd., S. 11.
17   Ebd., S. 12.
18   Ebd., S. 1.
19   Charlotta Kotík, *Working in Brooklyn/Painting*, Ausst.-Kat. Brooklyn Museum, New York 1987, S. 13.
20   Nach einem Auszug aus dem *Archív SF*, hrsg. von Slovak National Gallery, DSF bc 2, Bratislava, S. 1.
21   Ebd., S. 1.
22   Christopher Lasch, „Afterword: The Culture of Narcissism Revisited", in: *The Culture of Narcissism, American Life in an Age of Diminishing Expectations*, London/New York 1991, S. 244.
23   Vadim Zakharov, „Author, cosmos, archive", in: *Cosmic Shift: Russian Contemporary Art Writing*, London 2017, S. 248.
24   Ilja Kabakow zitiert in Boris Groys, „Re-Inventing Authorship", in: *Not Everyone will be Taken to the Future*, Ausst.-Kat. Tate Gallery, London 2017, S. 37.
25   Nach einem Auszug aus dem *Archív SF*, hrsg. von Slovak National Gallery, DSF bc 2, Bratislava, S. 40.
26   Gene Ray, „Joseph Beuys and the After Auschwitz Sublime", in: *Joseph Beuys. Mapping the Legacy*, New York 2001, S. 56.
27   Marek Pokorný, „Generative Grammar of the World, or Tentative Propedeutics to the Work of Stano Filko", in: *Stano Filko 5.D.*, Ausst.-Kat. PLATO platform (for contemporary art), Ostrava 2015, S. 18.

P.S. NUMERATOR 1-2-3-4-5 HAPPSOC
RESEARCHER REBEL - DENOMINATOR - CONDUCTOR-SCREENWRITER

1937 - 45 - 52 - 60 - 70 - 80 - 84

PRECISION - EXACT - SCIENCE

MEDIUM - FINE ART

- EXTROVERT - EQ - IQ + INTROVERT - DSQ - AQ

TEXT ART

6. CHAKRA - INDIGO-BLACK - SATURDAY

NAME STANO FILKO

3. EYE - LENS - OQ - PERSONALITY

P.S. NUMERATOR 1-2-3-4-5 HAPPSOC
RESEARCHER REBEL - DENOMINATOR - CONDUCTOR-SCREENWRITER

1937 - 45 - 52 - 60 - 70 - 80 - 84

PRECISION - EXACT - SCIENCE

MEDIUM - FINE ART

- EXTROVERT - EQ - IQ + INTROVERT - DSQ - AQ

[22A] Untitled (*Rebel*), 1984–2015

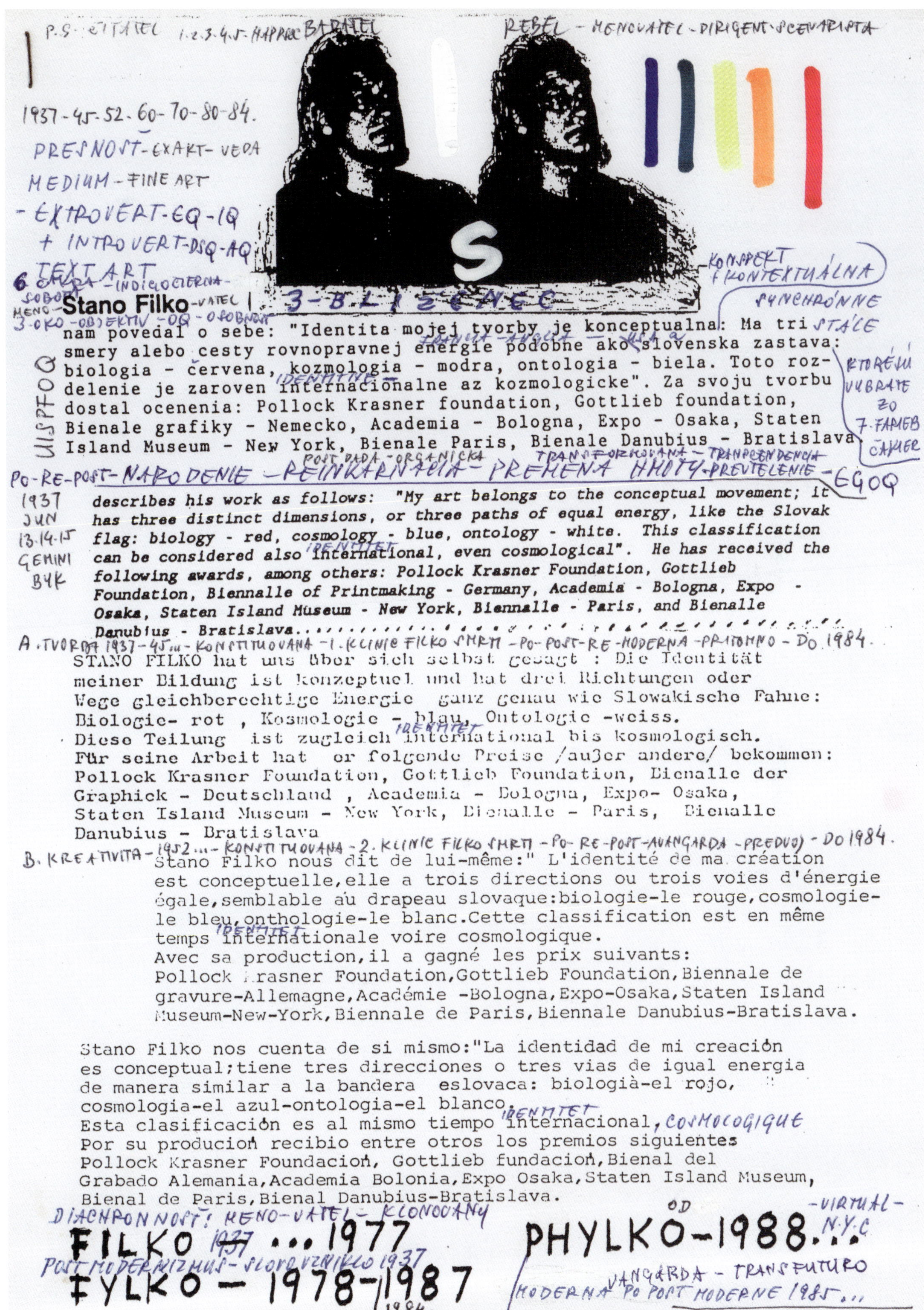

Stano Filko
nam povedal o sebe: "Identita mojej tvorby je konceptuálna: Ma tri smery alebo cesty rovnoprávnej energie podobné ako slovenská zastava: biologia - červena, kozmologia - modra, ontologia - biela. Toto rozdelenie je zaroveň internacionalne az kozmologicke". Za svoju tvorbu dostal ocenenia: Pollock Krasner foundation, Gottlieb foundation, Bienale grafiky - Nemecko, Academia - Bologna, Expo - Osaka, Staten Island Museum - New York, Bienale Paris, Bienale Danubius - Bratislava

describes his work as follows: "My art belongs to the conceptual movement; it has three distinct dimensions, or three paths of equal energy, like the Slovak flag: biology - red, cosmology - blue, ontology - white. This classification can be considered also international, even cosmological". He has received the following awards, among others: Pollock Krasner Foundation, Gottlieb Foundation, Biennalle of Printmaking - Germany, Academia - Bologna, Expo - Osaka, Staten Island Museum - New York, Biennalle - Paris, and Biennalle Danubius - Bratislava.........

STANO FILKO hat uns über sich selbst gesagt : Die Identität meiner Bildung ist konzeptuel und hat drei Richtungen oder Wege gleichberechtige Energie ganz genau wie Slowakische Fahne: Biologie- rot , Kosmologie - blau, Ontologie -weiss. Diese Teilung ist zugleich international bis kosmologisch. Für seine Arbeit hat er folgende Preise /außer andere/ bekommen: Pollock Krasner Foundation, Gottlieb Foundation, Bienalle der Graphick - Deutschland , Academia - Bologna, Expo- Osaka, Staten Island Museum - New York, Bienalle - Paris, Bienalle Danubius - Bratislava

Stano Filko nous dit de lui-même:" L'identité de ma création est conceptuelle,elle a trois directions ou trois voies d'énergie égale,semblable au drapeau slovaque:biologie-le rouge,cosmologie- le bleu, onthologie-le blanc.Cette classification est en même temps internationale voire cosmologique. Avec sa production,il a gagné les prix suivants: Pollock Krasner Foundation,Gottlieb Foundation,Biennale de gravure-Allemagne,Académie -Bologna,Expo-Osaka,Staten Island Museum-New-York,Biennale de Paris,Biennale Danubius-Bratislava.

Stano Filko nos cuenta de si mismo:"La identidad de mi creación es conceptual;tiene tres direcciones o tres vias de igual energia de manera similar a la bandera eslovaca: biologià-el rojo, cosmologia-el azul-ontologia-el blanco. Esta clasificación es al mismo tiempo internacional, COSMOLOGIQUE Por su produción recibio entre otros los premios siguientes Pollock Krasner Foundación, Gottlieb fundación,Bienal del Grabado Alemania,Academia Bolonia,Expo Osaka,Staten Island Museum, Bienal de Paris,Bienal Danubius-Bratislava.

FILKO ... 1977
FYLKO - 1978-1987
PHYLKO - 1988.

GENIUS LOCI 1937-1988 VO FINE ARTE — 1988 — N.Y.C. — PHYLKO — ZÁMERNÁ CELOŽIVOTNÁ (VO VŠETKÝCH FILKOVÝCH)
ĎALŠÍ — TEXT ART — 1988 — N.Y.C. — PHYLKO + VIAC KOLAJNOSŤ PROFÉCIÍ...

POST MODERNÁ — AŽ KOMPUTROVÁ UŽ VŠEOBECNÁ — 1988 R.
SLOVENSKÁ — SVETOVÁ — VIRTUÁLNA REALITA — MODERNA PO POST MODERNE OD 1985.
IDENTITNÝ ECOM I VLASTNECKY A ZÁROVEŇ SVETOVÝ — ESENCIOVÝ CELOŽIVOTNE
AKO SYNCHRÓNNY a DIACHRÓNNY BLÍŽENEC — BIELOČIERNY, ROZUMOVÝ — CITOVÝ, SLOBODNE
VOĽNÝ — LIBERALISTICKY — PORUŠOVANIE NORIEM — KÁNONOV AŽ V MATEMATICKOM — NUMERICKOM — CABALOVOM
VEDOMÍ — PODVEDOMÍ + VIAC EXPOZIČNÝ — VIAC PULZAČNÝ... V CELEJ HĹBKE A ŠÍRKE.
V ETIKE + NEKOMPROMISNOSTI — NEKOMERČNOSŤ — IDEALIZMU — KONTRASTOV + BIOLÓGIA — VEDA — FILOZOFIE
V ICH TOTOŽ. — NETOTOŽNOSTIACH + OVPLIV. — NEOVPLIVNOVANIACH :: NEAKADEMICKY FINE ART...
DIACHRÓNNOSŤ FILKO 1937-77 = POST MODERNOSŤ — VZNIKLO 1937 KUNICKA SPJAT 1945 —
VEĽKÁ HRADNÁ @ 1952 — TRENČÍN, AKO PODVEDOMÉ KREATIVITY +) 40 VÝROČIE FILKA 1977.
FYLKO 1978-87 = ĎALŠÍ POST MODERN + POST REINKARNÁCIA + I SÁM SEBA +
MODERNA PO POST MODERNE OD R. 1985 — N.Y.C. +) 50 VÝROČIE FILKA 1987.
PHYLKO — 1988... N.Y.C. — VIRTUÁLNA REALITA — MODERNA PO POST MODERNE.

SYNCHRÓNNOSŤ = VO ZNAKOCH — SIMBOLOCH — ENERGIACH —
VO FARBÁCH 7. ČAKIER — 7. DNI STVORENIA SVETA...
a EGO — OSOBITÝ VÝBER 3. FARIEB = BIELA, MODRÁ, ČERVENÁ,
AKO TROJJEDNOTA — FEDERÁCIA — TROJOSOBNOSŤ,
ZÁROVEŇ — ZVLÁŠŤ KONFEDERÁCIA + TRIPTYCH...

○ BIELA = 5. DIMENZIA = EPISTEMOLOGICKÁ ONTOLÓGIA — METAFYZIKA — ABSOLÚTNE
NADČASOVÝ SPIRIT + VEČNE SVETLO — BIELA ČAKRA — TRANSCENDENCIA —
REINKARNÁCIA...

△ MODRÁ = 4. DIMENZIA = KOZMOLÓGIA — KOZMOS — HELIOCENTRIZMUS —
OBJEKTIVITA — MODRÁ ČAKRA — TRANSCENDENCIA...

▢ ČERVENÁ = 3. DIMENZIA = BIOLÓGIA — EMPÍRIA — GNOZEOLÓGIA —
(ZEM — VODA — OHEŇ — VZDUCH) EPIKUREY — EROS — RELATIVITA —
ČERVENÁ ČAKRA — TRANSCENDENCIA...

TOTO VŠETKO PULZUJE Z REINKARNÁCIE 5 DIMENZIE CEZ 4. DIMEN.
DO 3 DIMEN. a ZNOVA NA SPÄŤ a ZNOVA DO 3 DIMENZIE, A.T.D.
TOTO VŠETKO JE SVOJOU POVAHOU POCHOPITEĽNE a VYSVETLITEĽNE.
TOTO VŠETKO JE I APRIÓRNE + JE TO CELÁ HISTÓRIA + PALEOLIT,
NA CELOM SVETE — TEDA I SLOVENSKU — KDE SA NAŠLA R. 1937 PRVÁ
PALEOLITNÁ SOCHA ŠEHEREZÁDA — VEIXUŠA — MORAVANY — PIEŠŤANY
25. 000 B.C. — AKO DOKAZ 3. DIMENZIE — FINE ARTY NA SVETE.
JE TO BIOLÓGIA CELÉHO ČLVEKA — ZVIERAT a RASTLÍN — CELÁ PRÍRODA — ZEM, CELÉ BYTIE
V TEJTO SYNCHRÓNNEJ a DIACHRÓNNEJ DANOSTI FILKO VEČNE + I ŠPIRÁLOVITE
TVORÍ — OD ZAČ. 50 ROKOV AŽ PO DNEŠOK — KDE STÁLE INOVUJE TVORBU.
FINE ART: JE DEMOKRACIA — KOMPROMISOV EGA INDIVIDUALIZMOV — SLOBODA — NEZÁVISLOSŤ
NIČOMU (SERVISNOSŤ JE KULTÚRA) — ORIGINÁLNOSŤ — PRÍTOMNOSŤ — ESENCIA IDENTITY a SVETA...
KVALITA FINE ARTU: JE ABSOLÚTNE NEKOMPROMISNÁ — NEDEMOKRATICKÁ... ETICKÁ KVALITA.

GENIUS LOCI 1937-1988

NEXT TEXT ART VO FINE ARTE - 1988 - N.Y.C. - PHYLKO (DELIBERATE LIFELONG MULTI-TRACKEDNESS
IN ALL OF FILKO'S PROFESSIONS)

POST MODERNA - SLOVAK WORLD (UNTIL THE COMPUTER IN THE 60S) VIRTUAL REALITY - 1988 POST
MODERN - POST MODERN FROM 1985

AS SYNCHRONIC AND DIACHRONIC TWIN (IDENTITY EGO PATRIOTIC AND AT THE SAME TIME WORLD-ESSENTIAL
LIFELONG) WHITE-BLACK, RATIONAL-CYNICAL, FREELY FREE - LIBERAL - BREAKING NORMS - CANONS
DOWN TO MATHEMATICAL - NUMERICAL - CABAL - CONSCIOUS UNCONSCIOUS + MULTI-EXPOSITORY - MORE
PULSATORY IN ALL DEPTH AND BREADTH IN ETHICS + UNCOMPROMISING - NON-COMMERCIAL - IDEALISM -
CONTRASTS + BIOLOGY - SCIENCE - PHILOSOPHIES IN THEIR IDENTITIES. - NON-IDENTITY + INFLUENCES +
INFLUENCES - NON-INFLUENCES::: NON-ACADEMIC
FINE ART…

DIACHRONICITY = FILKO 1937-77 (VEĽKÁ HRADNÁ - BRATISLAVA) = POST MODERNITY (THIS WORD
ORIGINATED 1937 AS AN IRONIC IDENTIFICATION - MYSTIFICATION) + CLINICAL DEATH 1945 -
VEĽKÁ HRADNÁ + 1952 - TRENČÍN, AS SUBCONSCIOUS CREATIVITY + 40. ANNIVERSARY OF FILKO 1977
(10TH ANNIVERSARY OF THE OCCUPATION OF THE CZECHOSLOVAK REPUBLIC)

FYLKO 1978-87 = ANOTHER POSTMODERN + POSTREINCARNATION + I MYSELF + MODERNITY AFTER
POSTMODERNITY SINCE 1985 N.Y.C. + 50. ANNIVERSARY OF FILKO 1987 (20. ANNIVERSARY OF THE
OCCUPATION OF THE CZECHOSLOVAK REPUBLIC - USSR w)

PHYLKO - 1988… N.Y.C. - VIRTUAL REALITY - MODERNITY AFTER POSTMODERNITY

SYNCHRONICITY = IN THE COLORS OF THE 7 CHAKRAS (IN SIGNS - SYMBOLS = ENERGIES) - 7 DAYS OF THE
CREATION OF THE WORLD…

and EGO - PERSONAL SELECTION OF 3 COLORS - ENERGIES = O WHITE, △ BLUE, □ RED (+ FILKO EGO
BLACK - AS THE INTELLECT OF THE STRUCTURALITY OF EVERYTHING) AS (SIGN - SYMBOLIC - COLOR)
TRINITY - FEDERATION - TRINITY - PERSONALITY, AT THE SAME TIME - SEPARATELY (SIGN - SYMBOLIC -
COLOR TO MONOCHROME) CONFEDERATION + TRIPTYCH…

O   WHITE = 5. DIMENSION = EPISTEMOLOGICAL ONTOLOGY = METAPHYSICS - ABSOLUTELY TIMELESS
     SPIRIT + ETERNAL LIGHT - WHITE CHAKRA - TRANSCENDENCE - REINCARNATION…

△   BLUE = 4. DIMENSION = (UNIVERSE UNIVERSE) COSMOLOGY - COSMOS - HELIOCENTRISM -
     OBJECTIVITY - BLUE CHAKRA - TRANSCENDENCE…

□   RED = 3. DIMENSION = BIOLOGY - EMPIRICISM - GNOSIS - (EARTH - WATER - FIRE - AIR)
     EPICUREANISM - EROS - RELATIVITY - RED CHAKRA - TRANSCENDENCE…

(WE CONSCIOUSLY REPEAT) ALL THIS (ABSOLUTELY) PULSATES FROM REINCARNATION 5. DIMENSION, THROUGH
THE 4. DIMENSION TO 3. DIMENSION and BACK (FORWARD) to the 5. DIMENSION and BACK (BACK FORWARD)
to the 3. DIMENSION and BACK (BACK FORWARD) to the 3. DIMENSION. DIMENSION, THEN.

THESE THINGS ARE IN THEIR OWN WAY UNDERSTANDABLE, EXPLICIT (and UNEXPLICIT).

ALL THIS IS A PRIORI + IT IS THE WHOLE (PREHISTORY) HISTORY + PALEOLITHIC ALL OVER THE WORLD -
SO ALSO IN SLOVAKIA - WHERE THE FIRST PALEOLITHIC STATUE OF SCHEHERAZADE WAS FOUND IN 1937 -
VENUS - MORAVANY - PIEŠŤANY 25.000 B.C. - AS A (STRONG FACT) PROOF 3. DIMENSIONS - FINE ART IN
THE WORLD (and in SLOVAKIA)

IT IS THE (WHOLE) BIOLOGY OF THE WHOLE MAN - ANIMALS + PLANTS - THE WHOLE NATURE - THE EARTH,
THE WHOLE BEING

IN THIS SYNCHRONIC AND DIACHRONIC GIVENNESS FILKO (CIRCULARLY) ETERNALLY + SPIRALLY FORMS
(CONSCIOUSLY) FROM 50. FROM THE TWENTIETH CENTURY TO TODAY (AND TOMORROW) - WHERE IT CONSTANTLY
INNOVATES ITS CREATION.

FINE ART: IS DEMOCRACY - COMPROMISES + EGASES OF INDIVIDUALISM - FREEDOM - SERVILITY
TO NOBODY (SERVILITY IS CULTURE) - ORIGINALITY - PRESENCE - ESSENCE OF IDENTITY AND THE WORLD…

THE QUALITY OF FINE ART: IT IS ABSOLUTELY UNCOMPROMISING - UNDEMOCRATIC… ETHICAL QUALITY

[22B] Untitled (*Rebel*), 1984-2015

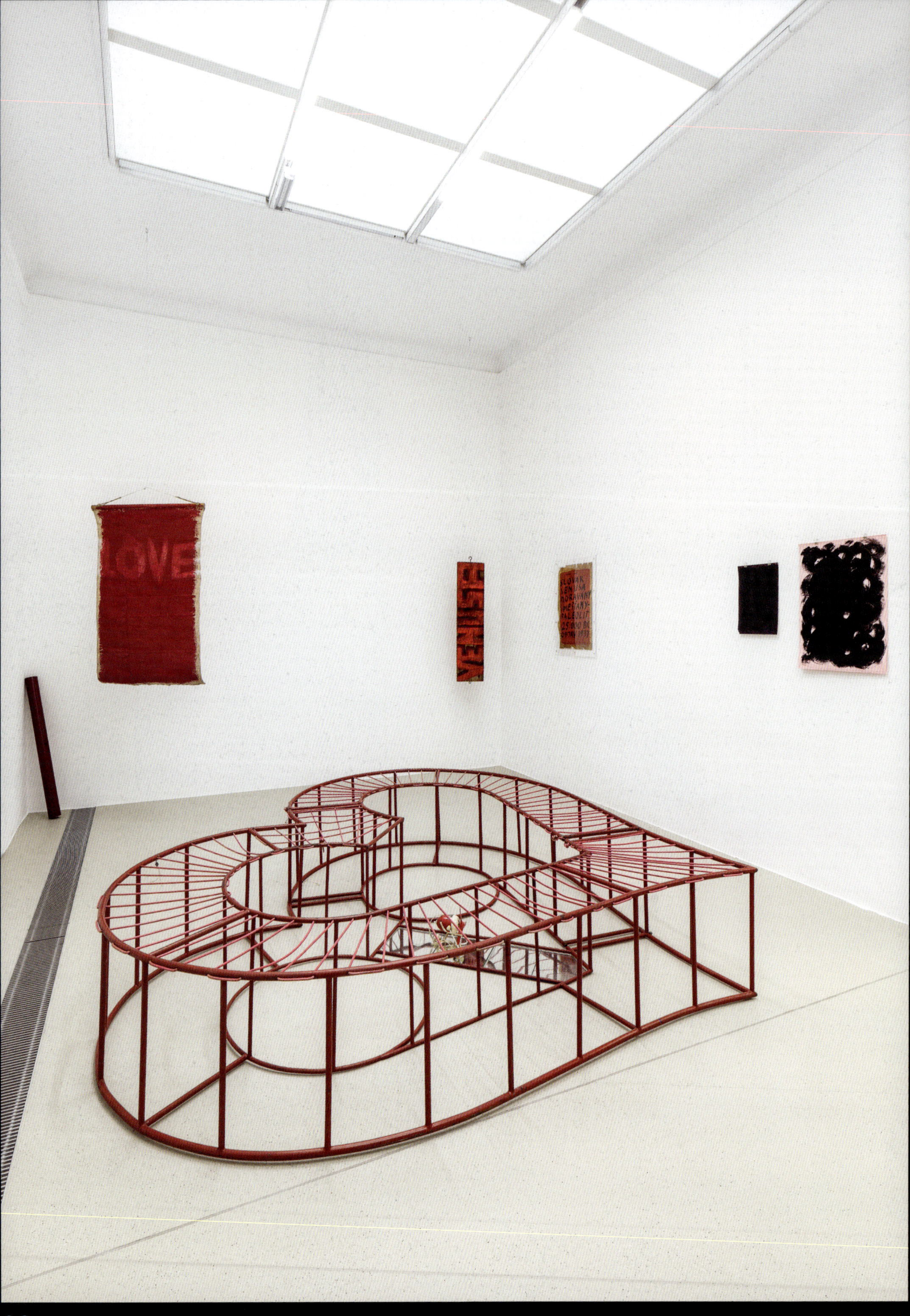

X

Heart of Love: Romance and Eroticism / Liebe und Erotik

Love and eroticism are recurring themes in Filko's oeuvre, playing a particularly important role in all creative phases of the artist. This can be seen in numerous pieces. In Filko's symbolic system, red, the color of love, stands for the physical realm (biology) and life energy.

In the center stands the sculpture *Heart of Love / Srdce lásky* (1966) [04], a construction of iron bars painted bright red that looks like a heart. The theme of love is seen pragmatically here, and in earlier arrangements this object also served as a kind of seat. Love appears as a personal phenomenon between intimacy and openness, as something quotidian whose diverse forms are denoted in this sculpture through a recognizable but very open shape. In the interior of *Heart of Love* different shapes can be discerned, perhaps suggesting a face, a phallic symbol, or a playground piece for children. In a straight and simple manner, and yet also full of premonition, the object entitled *LOVE / LÁSKA* (1966) also seems to be raising a banner for love.

Liebe und Erotik sind wiederkehrende Themen in Filkos Œuvre und spielen in allen Schaffensperioden eine zentrale Rolle. Dies lässt sich anhand verschiedenster Arbeiten ablesen und nachverfolgen. Rot als die Farbe der Liebe steht in Filkos symbolischem System für den Bereich des Körperlichen (Biologie) und der Lebensenergie.

Zentral befindet sich die Skulptur *Heart of Love / Srdce lásky* (1966) [04], ein plastisches Konstrukt, das aus hellrot bemalten Eisenstreben besteht und an ein Herz erinnert. Das Thema Liebe wird hier pragmatisch behandelt, das Objekt diente in früheren Arrangements auch als Sitzgelegenheit. Liebe tritt als ein persönliches Phänomen zwischen Intimität und Öffentlichkeit auf, als etwas Alltägliches, dessen vielfältige Ausprägungen die Skulptur in einer erkennbaren Form mit großer Durchlässigkeit aufnimmt. *Heart of Love* changiert in der inneren Begrenzung der Installation zwischen Formen, die ein Gesicht andeuten, an ein phallisches Symbol erinnern oder an ein Spielgerät für Kinder denken lassen. Lapidar und darin voller Vorahnungen scheint auch das Objekt *LOVE / LÁSKA* (1966) die Flagge für die Liebe hoch zu halten.

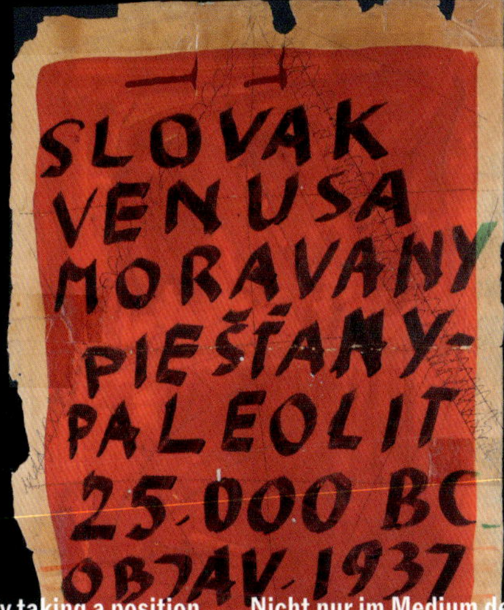
[03] From the Series *Slovak Venus / Zo série Slovenská Venuša*, 1958/c. 1995

[02] *Venus / Venuša*, c. 1995

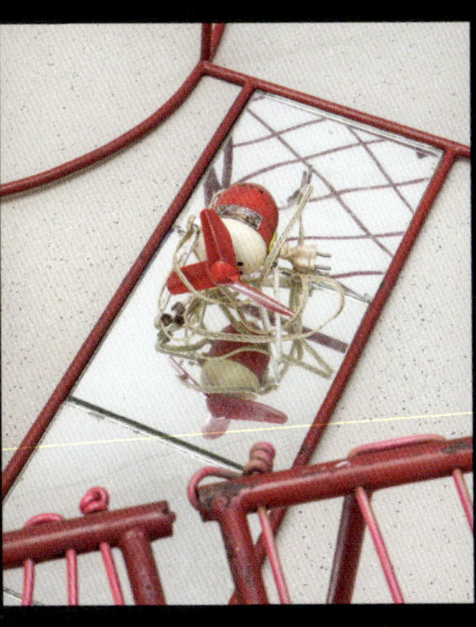
[04A] *Heart of Love / Srdce lásky*, 1966

Not merely taking a position on the medium of the installation, Filko here also negotiates different aspects of the treatment of love and eroticism in painting, as well as in object and text art. Filko began to fictionalize his person in connection with the Venus of Moravany, as seen in his work from the series *Slovak Venus / Slovenská Venuša* (1958) [03]. This ancient Venus figurine was discovered some time before 1930 near Veľká Hradná, Filko's Slovak place of birth, and it was estimated to stem from around 22,800 BC. Filko used it to create a myth out of his own birth, which took more than three days in 1937, and of his own artistic impact. His *Slovak Venus* includes "25,000 BC" as a text-image, a generously rounded number that Filko sees in relation to his own lifetime and his effects on posterity. The color red is used here in connection with traditional symbols of fertility, blood, and birth. The wooden object *Venus / Venuša* (1995) [02] hangs from the ceiling like a faded symbolic marker, denoting a place.

Nicht nur im Medium der Installation verhandelt Filko die unterschiedlichen Aspekte des Themenbereichs Liebe und Erotik sondern ebenfalls in der Malerei, sowie in Objekt- und Textkunst. Am Beginn seiner Selbstfiktionalisierung steht die sogenannte Venus von Moravany, wie in der Arbeit aus der Serie *Slovak Venus / Slovenská Venuša* (1958) [03] ersichtlich wird. Das Auffinden der auf ein Alter von rund 22.800 Jahre geschätzten Venusfigur im Jahr 1930 in der Nähe seines slowakischen Geburtsortes Veľká Hradná nutzt Filko später, um seine eigene, sich über drei Tage hinziehende Geburt im Jahr 1937 und sein künstlerisches Erbe zu mythologisieren. Als Schriftbild ist auf der Arbeit 25.000 BC zu erkennen, eine großzügig aufgerundete Bezugnahme dieses Zeitverlaufs, die Filko in Bezug zu seiner Lebensdauer und seinem Nachwirken stellt. Die Farbe Rot zeigt sich hier in Verbindung mit einem traditionellen Symbolismus und wird mit Fruchtbarkeit, Blut und Geburt assoziiert. Wie ein verblichener symbolischer und darin einen Ort anzeigender Marker hängt das Holzobjekt *Venus / Venuša* (1995) [02] von der Decke.

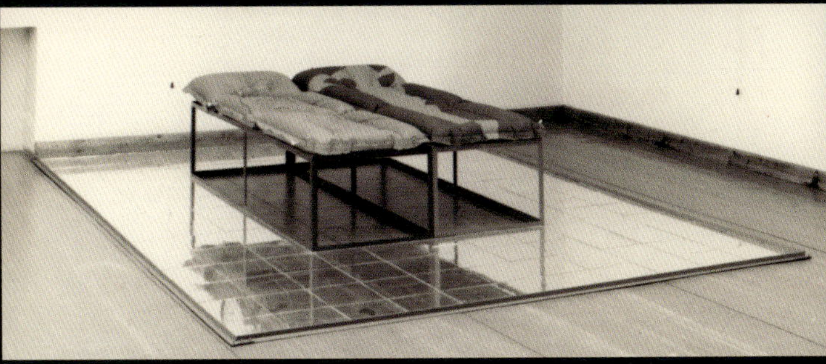
[05] *Room of Love – Environment / Izba lásky – environment*, 1966

←[01] Exhibition view, HALLE FÜR KUNST Steiermark, Graz, 2022

In the two works from the series of Plexiglas multiples, *Female Breast I. – X. (Blue/Red) | Ženský prsník I. – X. (Modrý/Červený)* (1966) [10], here floating in the space, Filko takes a rather playful approach to the aesthetics of Minimal Art, but he heightens the emotional content through a strong use of different colors that can be seen as representing the opposing principles of life and cosmos, activity and passivity, and also tension and relaxation.

In Filko's New York period (1982–90), the themes of love and eroticism play an important role. There, in the social and economic heart of America, Filko was confronted with new images of gender and with the capitalist pervasion of all fields of life.

Fast spielerisch orientiert an der Ästhetik der Minimal Art verwendet Filko in den beiden im Raum schwebenden Arbeiten aus der Multiple-Serie *Female Breast I. – X. (Blue/Red) | Ženský prsník I. – X. (Modrý/Červený)* (1966) [10] Plexiglas, steigert den emotionalen Gehalt jedoch durch die starke Farbigkeit, die als gegensätzliche Prinzipien von Leben und Kosmos, Aktivität und Passivität oder auch Anspannung und Entspannung verstanden werden könnten.

In Filkos New Yorker Zeit (1982–1990) nehmen die Themen um Liebe und Erotik einen wichtigen Stellenwert ein. Im gesellschaftlichen und wirtschaftlichen Herzen Amerikas sieht sich Filko mit neuen Geschlechterbildern und der kapitalistischen Durchdringung aller Lebensbereiche konfrontiert.

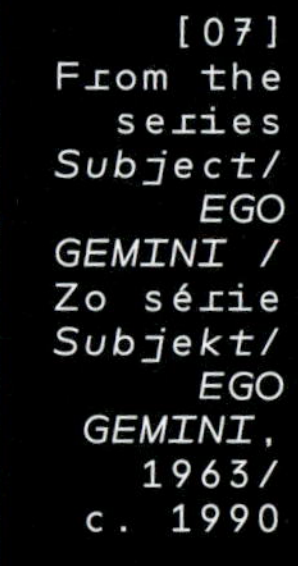

[07] From the series *Subject/ EGO GEMINI* / Zo série *Subjekt/ EGO GEMINI*, 1963/ c. 1990

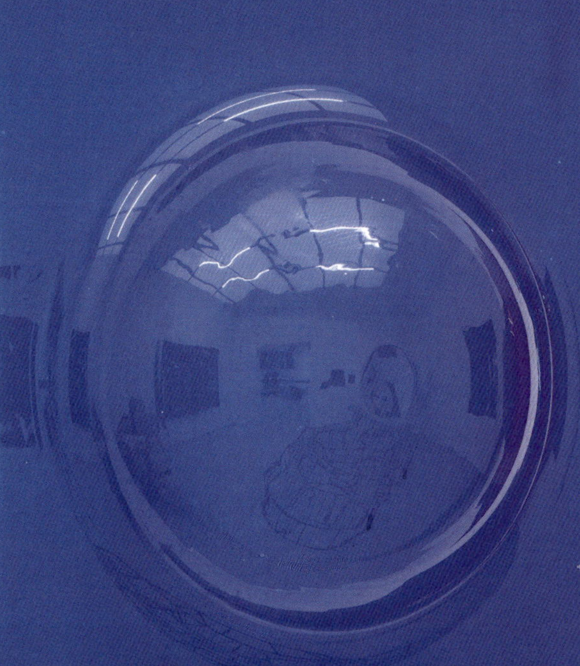

[06] From the series *EGO – ON – IN – RED* / Zo série *EGO – ON – IN – RED*, c. 1990

[08] *Heart of Love I. – II.* / *Srdce lásky I. – II.*, 1966

[09] Exhibition view, HALLE FÜR KUNST Steiermark, Graz, 2022

Two painterly works from the two series *Subject/EGO GEMINI | Subjekt/EGO GEMINI* (1963/1990) [07] and *EGO – ON – IN – RED* (1990) [06], both dark with bright red interruptions, address Filko's complex relationship to the notion of the ego, which he saw as a central entity like a super-ego that he separated from his own self and then correspondingly heightened and generalized in social terms. He possibly also reflected on his own relationship to sexuality in these works. From the starting point of the black power of the ego, the spectrum includes feelings of both admiration and fear, and also a desire for control, and the tension between fulfillment and desperation is notable here.

Zwei malerische, dunkel angelegte und hellrot durchbrochene Arbeiten aus den Serien *Subject/EGO GEMINI | Subjekt/EGO GEMINI* (1963/1990) [07] und *EGO – ON – IN – RED* (1990) [06] verhandeln Filkos komplexe Beziehung zu der für ihn zentralen Entität des Egos, die er als eine Art Über-Ich von seinem Selbst ablöst und entsprechend überhöht und gesellschaftlich verallgemeinert. Möglicherweise reflektiert er in diesen Arbeiten auch seine eigene Beziehung zur Sexualität. Von der schwarzen Kraft des Egos ausgehend sind sowohl Gefühle der Bewunderung, als auch Angst und das Verlangen nach Kontrolle Teil des Spektrums, daneben sind Spannungen zwischen Erfüllung und Verzweiflung spürbar.

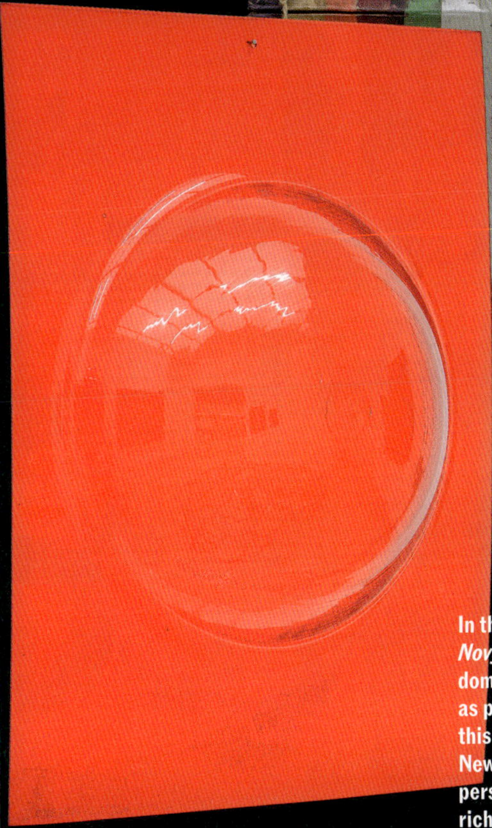

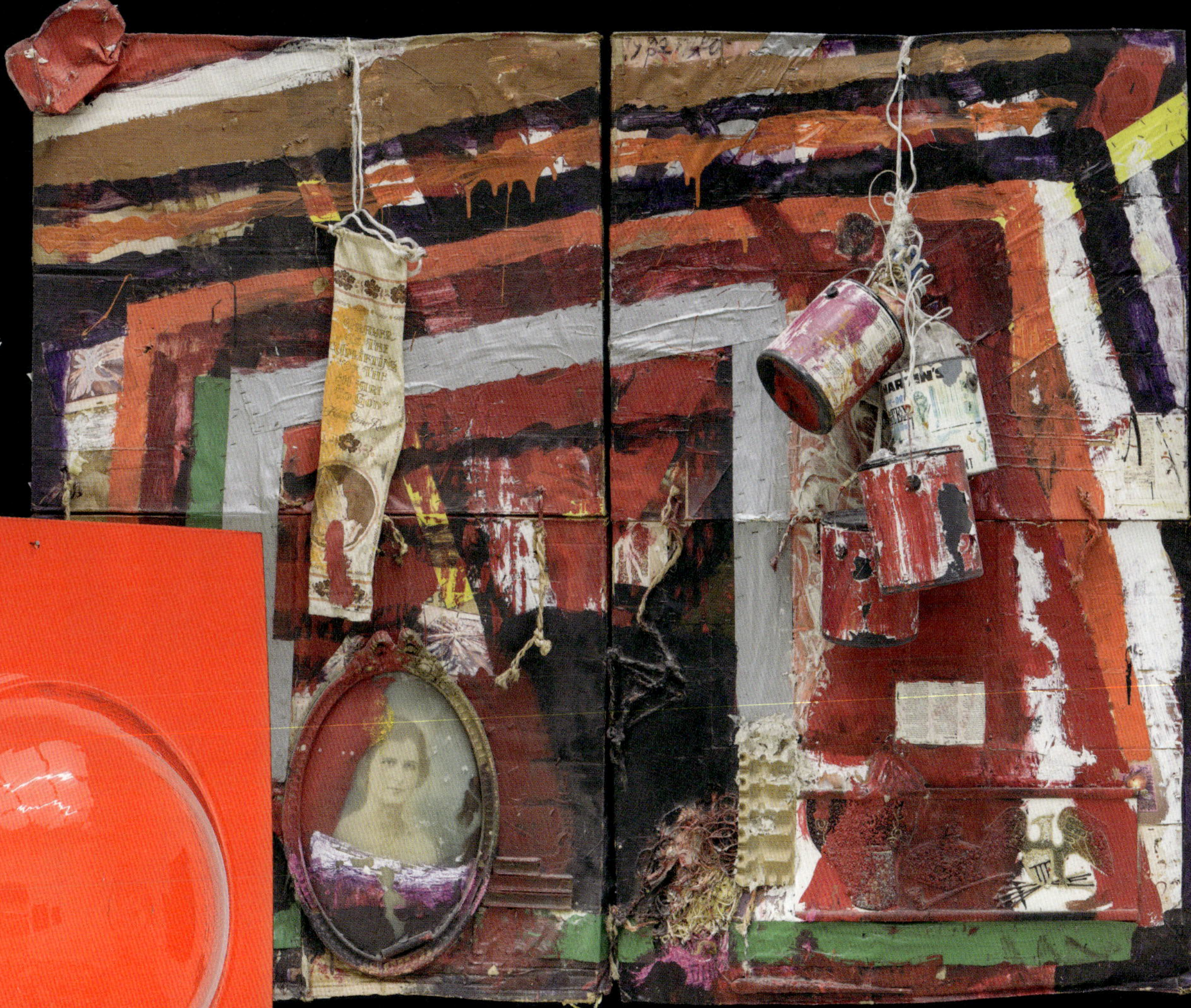

[11A] *The Old and New Testament / Starý a Nový Zákon*, 1983

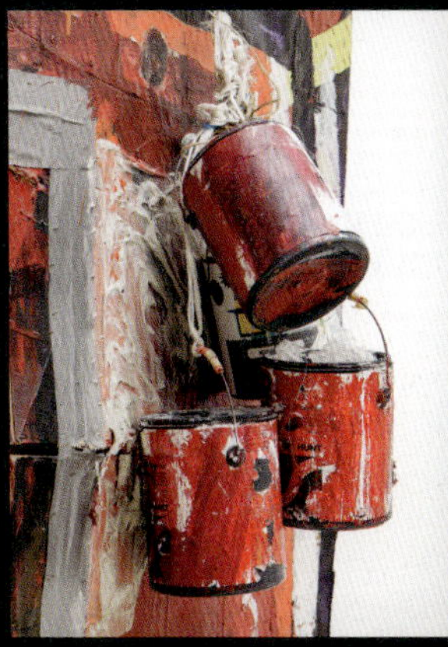

In the work *The Old and New Testament / Starý a Nový Zákon* (1983) [11] it is again red that dominates. Filko included many found objects such as pieces of string, paint cans, and a broach in this diptych. The reference to the Old and New Testaments seems to amount to incorporating personal history within a historical framework rich with mythological narratives and sexualized events. The strikingly sculptural quality of what remains a painterly process as well as the psychoanalytical investigation of introspective and sexual elements of the self, aimed towards depicting society—not for the first time in Filko's oeuvre—are reminiscent of the work of artists like Paul McCarthy and Mike Kelley. Filko thus also makes use of an activist, neo-expressive, and early post-media shift in painting that spilled over from the Californian West Coast, with its counterculture and spirituality, to take effect in Filko's New York domicile, where it also recalled Vienna Actionism.

In der Arbeit *The Old and New Testament / Starý a Nový Zákon* (1983) [11] dominiert hingegen wieder das Rot. Filko versah das Diptychon mit gefundenen Objekten wie Seilstücken, Farbdosen und einer Brosche. Der Bezug zum Alten und Neuen Testament scheint auf das Einarbeiten der persönlichen Geschichte in einen an mythologischen Geschichten und sexualisierten Ereignissen überreichen historischen Rahmen hinauszulaufen. Der forciert plastische, aber ursächlich malerische Prozess sowie die psychoanalytische Verarbeitung introspektiver sexueller Momente des Selbst hin zu einem gesellschaftlichen Bild lässt hier nicht zum ersten Mal an Künstler wie Paul McCarthy oder Mike Kelley denken. Damit bedient sich Filko auch an einem aktivistischen, neo-expressiven und frühen post-medialen Aufbruch in der Malerei, der von der kalifornischen, gegenkulturell und mitunter spiritistisch geprägten West Coast aus auf Filkos Domizil in New York einwirkt, aber dabei auch an den Wiener Aktionismus denken lässt.

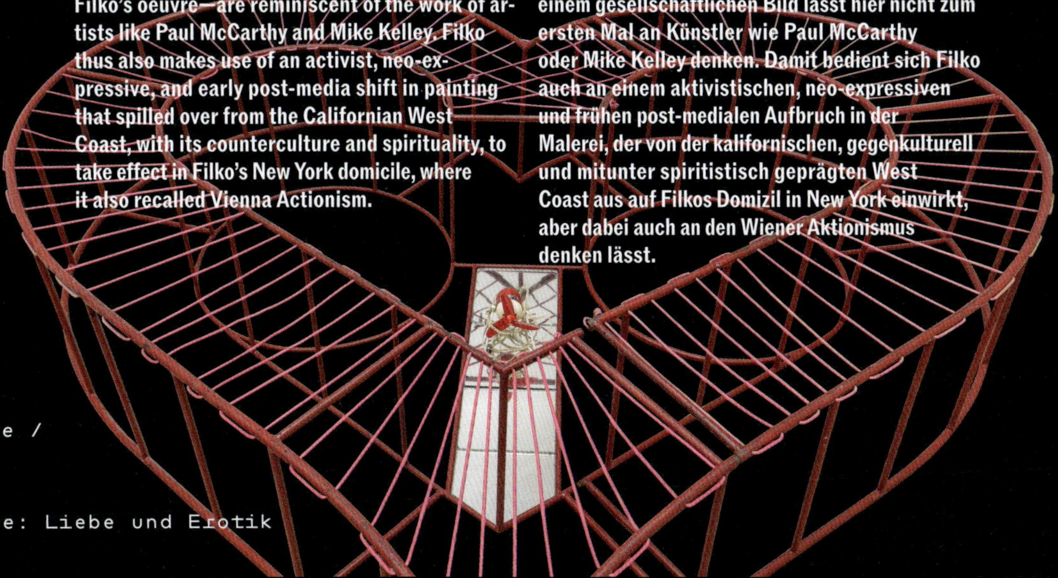

     X. Heart of Love: Liebe und Erotik

Filko attempts to integrate the full scope of reality into his artistic creations. This is very clearly the case particularly in the painting and sculpture of the American phase, for which the artist used a wide range of found objects. A notable example of this is the sculpture *SPIRIT – Shadow Super Head Baby* (1985) [13], in which Filko addresses the difficulties he experienced and the longing he felt from his New York emigration for his family and friends back in Czechoslovakia. It is remarkable to see here how Filko succeeds in bringing together such a diverse and apparently arbitrary selection of materials into a single memorable form. The body of the figure is made of soft drinks bottles, soup and paint cans, partly overpainted and with added old items of clothing, all stuck into each other to rise up before the beholder.

Filko versucht den vollen Umfang der Realität in sein künstlerisches Schaffen zu integrieren. Dies wird auch und vor allem anhand von Malerei und Plastik aus der amerikanischen Phase ersichtlich, für die der Künstler eine Fülle an vorgefundenen Gegenständen verwendet. Ein besonderes Beispiel dieser Verwendung von gefundenen Objekten bildet die Plastik *SPIRIT – Shadow Super Head Baby* (1985) [13], mit der Filko aus der New Yorker Emigration auf die schwierige, sehnsuchtsvolle Beziehung zu seinen in der Tschechoslowakei zurückgebliebenen Nächsten anspricht. Beachtlich ist, wie es Filko trotz der Vielfalt und scheinbaren Beliebigkeit des Materials gelingt, zu einer einprägsamen Formfindung zu kommen. Der Körper der Figur türmt sich durch teils bemalte und ineinander gesteckte Softdrinkflaschen, Suppen- und Lackdosen, sowie alte Kleidung vor den Betrachter*innen auf.

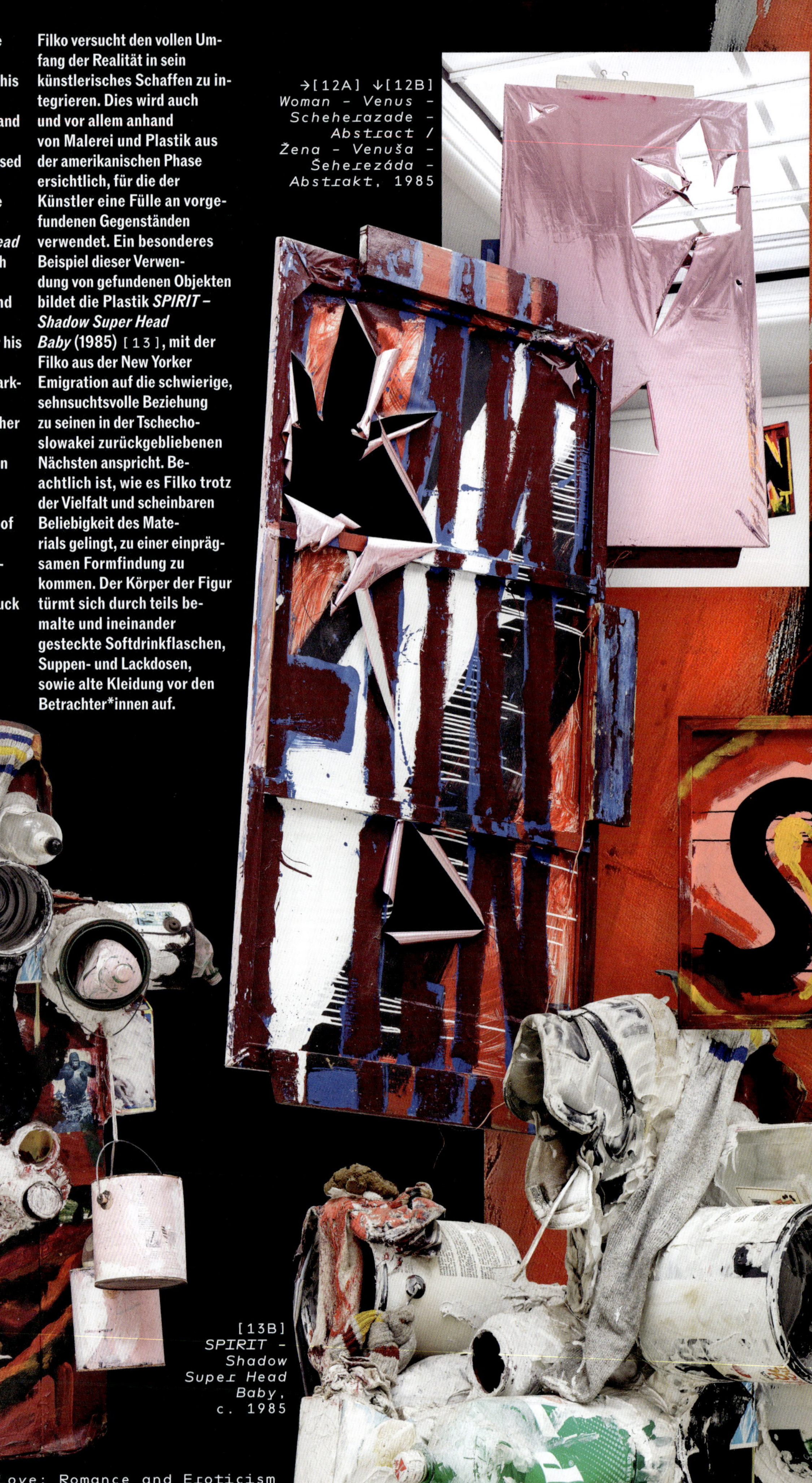

[12A] ↓[12B]
Woman – Venus – Scheherazade – Abstract / Žena – Venuša – Šeherezáda – Abstrakt, 1985

[13A]
SPIRIT – Shadow Super Head Baby, c. 1985

[13B]
SPIRIT – Shadow Super Head Baby, c. 1985

There is a work that is formally untypical of Filko and thus all the more interesting, consisting of a stretcher frame to which a reflecting pink foil has been attached. With the title *Woman – Venus – Scheherazade – Abstract / Žena – Venuša – Šeherezáda – Abstrakt* (1985) [12] Filko names various typological roles for women, from the loving mother to the dominant and powerful Scheherazade, a seductive and cunning character from the Persian tales in *One Thousand and One Nights*. Here the idea of the feminine as a threat to male decisiveness plays a role, while the tears and openings on the foil and the added *Axe in Pink / Ružová sekera* (1990) [16] probably stand for an attempt to somehow manage these tensions.

Above this work hangs the double-sided work *AIDS – STAN* (1983) [14], painted in large reddish letters. In New York in the 1980s, Filko was concerned about the rampant AIDS crisis, in which this new and initially uncurable immune deficiency caused great worry and fear particularly in the liberal art milieu. Filko addressed this theme in a series of installation paintings, as if he wanted to posit an inviting and warning counterpart with the bold simplistic letters standing for this ominous disease and the accompanying media hysteria.

Eine formal eher untypische, aber umso interessantere Arbeit besteht aus einem Keilrahmen, auf dem eine pinke, reflektierende Folie aufgespannt ist. Mit dem Titel *Woman – Venus – Scheherazade – Abstract / Žena – Venuša – Šeherezáda – Abstrakt* (1985) [12] spricht Filko verschiedene typologische Frauenrollen an, die von der Rolle der liebenden Mutter bis hin zum dominanten und machtvollen Typus der Scheherazade, einer auf Verführung und List aufbauenden Figur aus der persischen Geschichte von *Tausendundeiner Nacht*, reichen. Das Weibliche als Bedrohung der männlichen Entschlossenheit fließt hier mit ein, wobei die Risse und Öffnungen an der Oberfläche und die beigefügte Axt *Axe in Pink / Ružová sekera* (1990) [16] wohl einen Versuch darstellen, mit diesen Spannungen umzugehen.

Darüber hängt die zweiseitig in großen, rötlich geprägten Lettern bemalte Arbeit *AIDS – STAN* (1983) [14]. Im New York der 1980er-Jahre wurde Filko mit der grassierenden AIDS-Krise befasst, einer damals neuen und anfangs als unheilbar geltenden Immunerkrankung, die im liberalen Kunstmilieu für Bestürzung und große Ängste sorgte. In einer Serie von installativen Malereien hat sich Filko mit dem Thema auseinandergesetzt, als wollte er in den plakativ wirkenden Schriftbildern der verhängnisvollen Krankheit und der damit einhergehenden Medienhysterie eine appellative, warnende Gegenstimme entgegensetzen.

[15] SPIRIT BABY, 1985

[14B] AIDS STAN, 1983

[16] Axe in Pink / Ružová sekera, c. 1990

[17] Pink / Ružová, 1984

The cursorily painted sculpture *SPIRIT BABY* (1985) [15] hanging freely from the ceiling, is a work that accompanies *SPIRIT – Shadow Super Head Baby* of the same year. A dynamic fluid sculpture is developed from several orange tubs, from which paint and soup cans are suspended, while a sign indicates the eventful year of 1982. In different creative periods always anew, works which topicalize death or illness are realized more or less simultaneously to pieces which in a similar way strive to mythologize the beginning of live.

Frei im Raum hängt die flüchtig bemalte Skulptur *SPIRIT BABY* (1985) [15], eine im selben Jahr entstandene Schwesternarbeit von *SPIRIT – Shadow Super Head Baby*. Aus mehreren orangefarbigen Tonnen entwickelt sich eine kraftvolle, fluide Plastik, an deren Ende wiederum Farb- und Suppendosen hängen, und ein Schild, welches das ereignisreiche Jahr 1982 anzeigt. Immer wieder entstehen in verschiedenen Schaffensphasen mehr oder weniger gleichzeitig Arbeiten, die Tod oder Krankheit thematisieren, neben solchen, die den Beginn des Lebens auf eine ähnliche Weise zu mythologisieren suchen.

↑[14A] AIDS – STAN, 1983

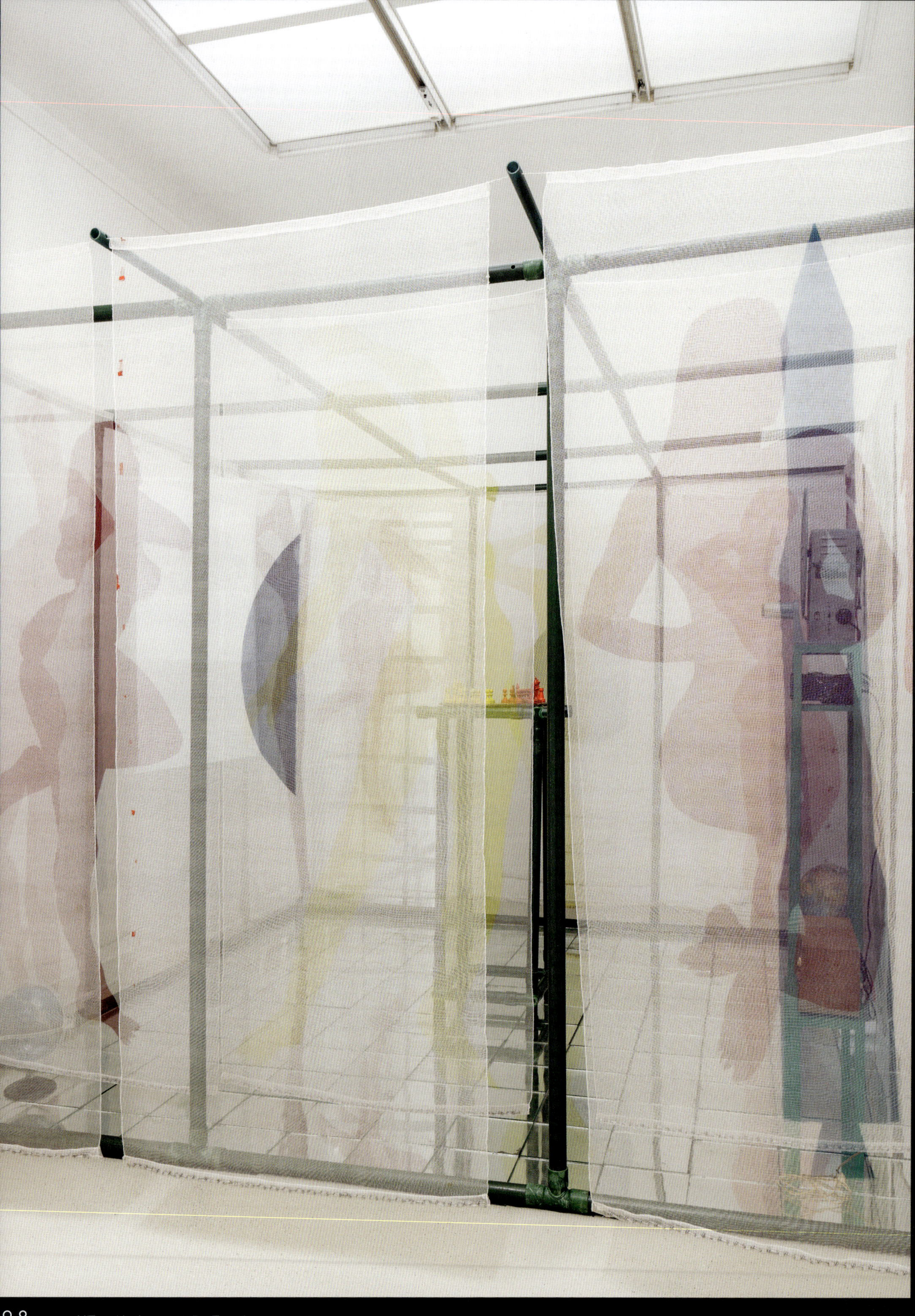

XI

Universal Environment

Filko's first attempts to open art up to its viewers are already in evidence in the early series *Altars of Contemporaneity / Oltáre súčasnosti* (1964–65). In his first large installation *Universal Environment / Univerzálne prostredie* (1966–67) [01-03] he then took a next big step toward a concept of the open work of art.

Filko first planned this environment as a walk-in installation. With its scaffold-like see-through cubist structure this installation recalls the formal idioms of modernist architecture. The frame divides the interior space into two vertical fields each accessible by walking through transparent banners, and each with mirrors on the floors. There are various objects with symbolic connotations placed in the interior of the environments. A globe represents the world and another the universe, a chess set stands for strategy and conflict.

Erste Bestrebungen Filkos, die Kunst in Richtung der Betrachter*innen zu öffnen, wurden bereits in der frühen Serie *Altars of Contemporaneity / Oltáre súčasnosti* (1964–1965) ersichtlich. Ein nächster großer Schritt hin zu einem offenen Werkbegriff gelingt ihm mit seiner ersten großformatigen Rauminstallation, *Universal Environment / Univerzálne prostredie* (1966–1967) [01-03].

Das Environment ist ursprünglich von Filko als eine begehbare Rauminstallation konzipiert worden. Mit seinem gerüstartigen, kubischen Aufbau und der visuellen Durchlässigkeit erinnert die Installation an die Formensprache modernistischer Architektur. Das Gerüst unterteilt den Innenraum in zwei vertikale Felder, Spiegel begegnen den Betrachter*innen hier als Grundfläche am Boden, der Raum selbst wird durch transparente Banner zugänglich. Im Innenraum des Environments befinden sich verschiedene Objekte, die symbolisch aufgeladen sind: Ein Globus repräsentiert die Welt, ein weiterer das Universum, ein Schachspiel Strategie und Konflikt.

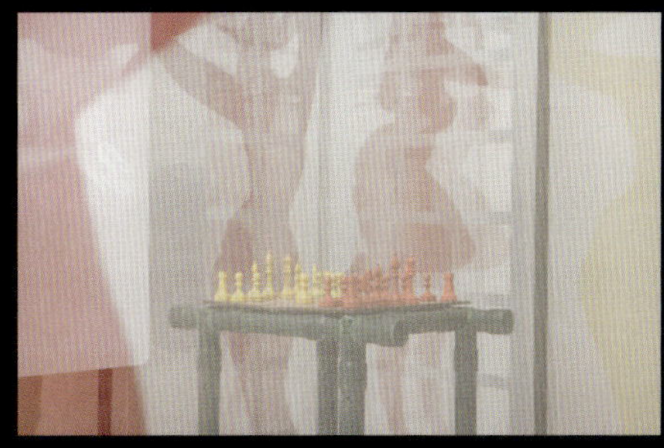

[03] Exhibition view, HALLE FÜR KUNST Steiermark, Graz, 2022

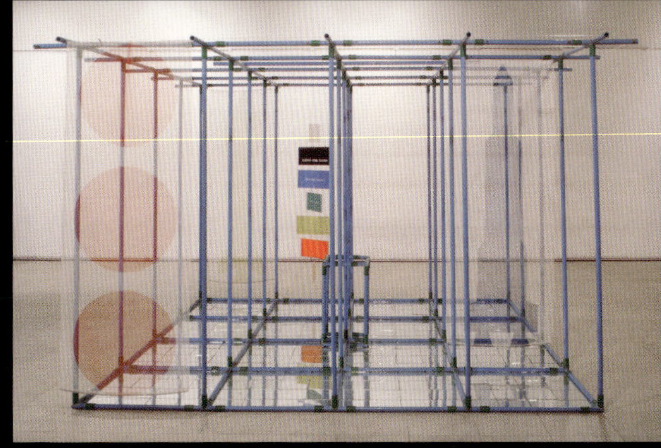

[04] *Meditation of 7 Chakras. Red – Blue – White 3.4.5.D. / Meditácia 7 čakier. Červená – modrá – biela 3.4.5.D.*, c. 1985

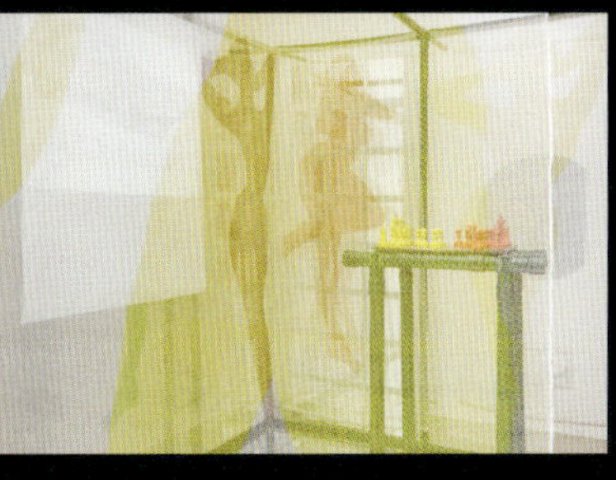

[02] Exhibition view, HALLE FÜR KUNST Steiermark, Graz, 2022

In *Universal Environment* a slide projector presents different images, including expensive cars and women in pin-up poses—here Filko shows a world based on consumerism and chauvinism. In this installation, the beholder is offered a space of enticing and promising symbols in a theatrical presentation of the alternative values and ideas of Western capitalism and Soviet communism. Filko asks questions as to the temptations and promises behind these political systems and seems in this way to be contrasting the two different ideologies while at the same time showing them from one universal standpoint. The mirrors integrate the beholders into the work and make them also part of a global and inexorable economy of desire.

In *Universal Environment* zeigt ein Diaprojektor verschiedene Bilder, unter anderem von teuren Autos und Frauen in Pin-up-Pose, mit deren Hilfe Filko eine am Konsum orientierte, chauvinistische Weltordnung in Szene setzt. Ein Raum verheißungsvoller Symbole eröffnet sich den Betrachter*innen, ähnlich eines theatralen Wechselspieles um Werte und Vorstellungen über den westlichen Kapitalismus und den sowjetischen Kommunismus. Filko stellt Fragen nach den Verlockungen und Versprechen, die hinter den politischen Systemen liegen und scheint auf diese Weise die verschiedenen Ideologien hin zu einer universellen Sichtweise auszuspielen. Durch die Spiegelelemente werden die Betrachter*innen ins Werk integriert und gleichzeitig Teil einer global umspannenden, ausweglosen Ökonomie des Begehrens.

[05] *Space X. – Rockets / Priestor X. – Rakety*, 1967

←[01] *Universal Environment / Univerzálne prostredie*, 1966–67

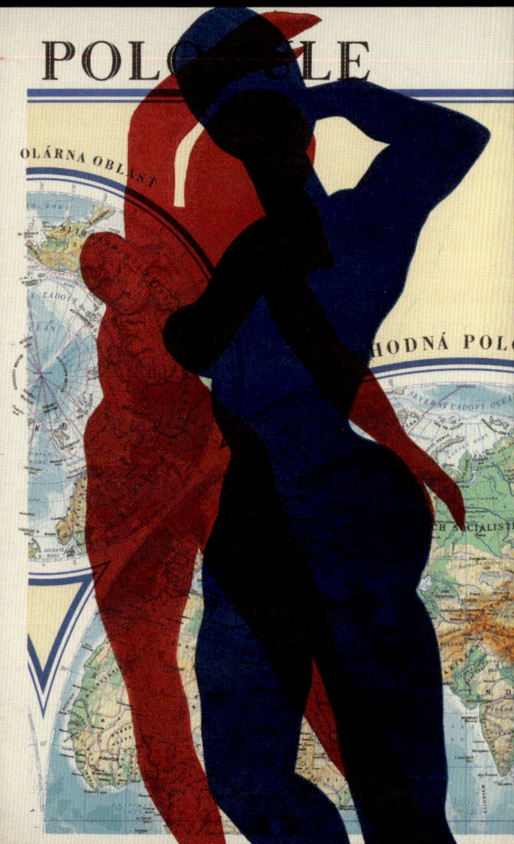

[06] From the series *Hemispheres of Earth* / Zo série *Zemské pologule*, 1967

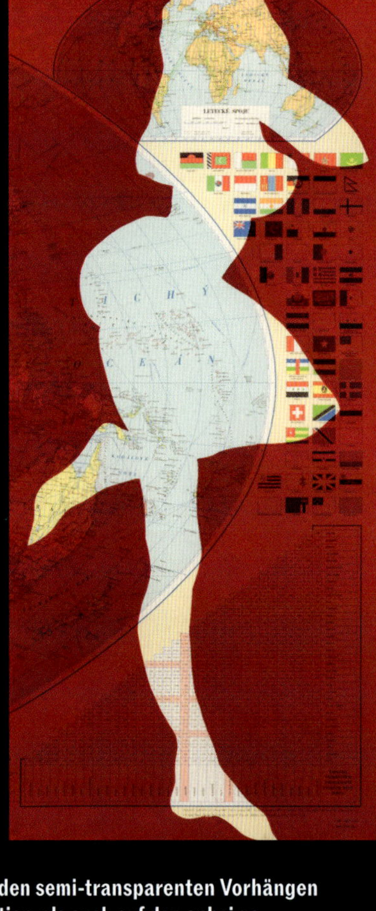

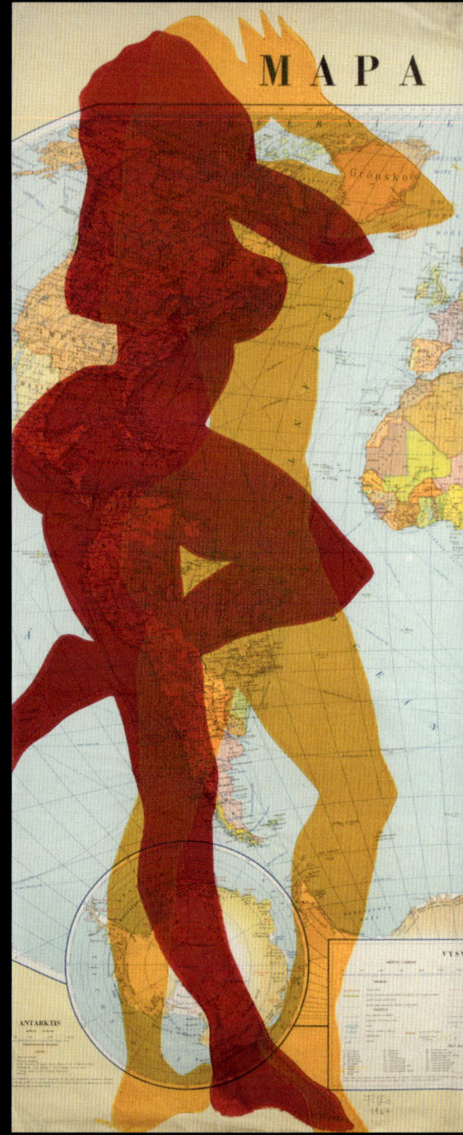

Monochrome emblematic images are placed both on the semi-transparent curtains and on the works from the two series *Map of the World (Rockets)* / Zo série *Mapa sveta (Rakety)* (1967) [14] and *Map of the World (Women)* / Zo série *Mapa sveta (Ženy)* (1966–67) [07-08] that are attached to the installation. These show rockets and female figures, but highly stylized so as to make them universal signs that inscribe themselves into the order of the world.

Sowohl an den semi-transparenten Vorhängen der Installation, als auch auf den anbei gehängten Arbeiten aus den Serien *Map of the World (Rockets)* / Zo série *Mapa sveta (Rakety)* (1967) [14] und *Map of the World (Women)* / Zo série *Mapa sveta (Ženy)* (1966–67) [07-08] sind einfarbige, emblematische Bilder zu sehen. Auffällig sind vor allem Raketen und weibliche Figuren, die durch den hohen Grad an Stilisierung zu universalen Zeichen werden, welche sich in die Weltordnung einschreiben.

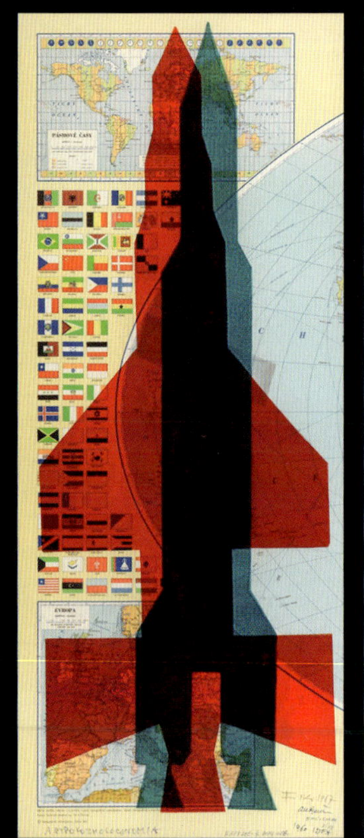

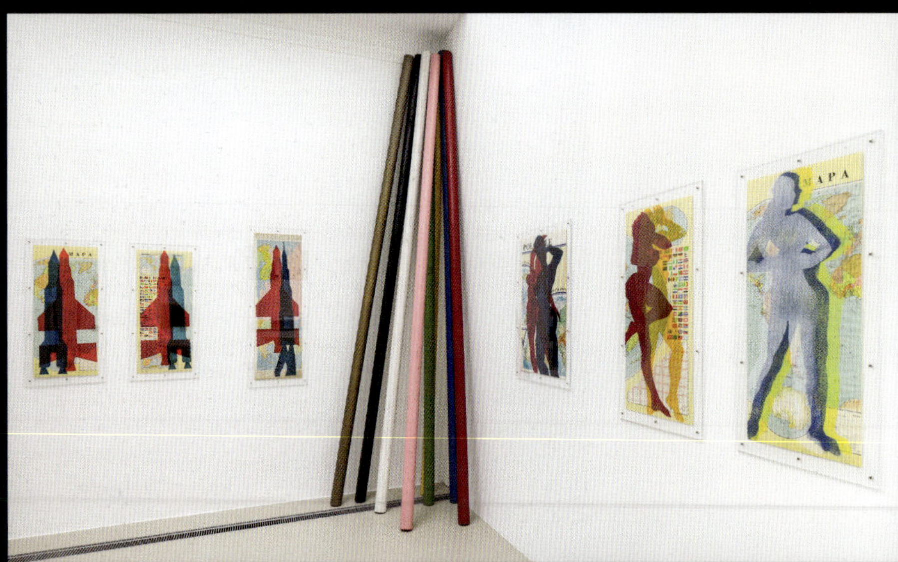

[09] Exhibition view, HALLE FÜR KUNST Steiermark, Graz, 2022

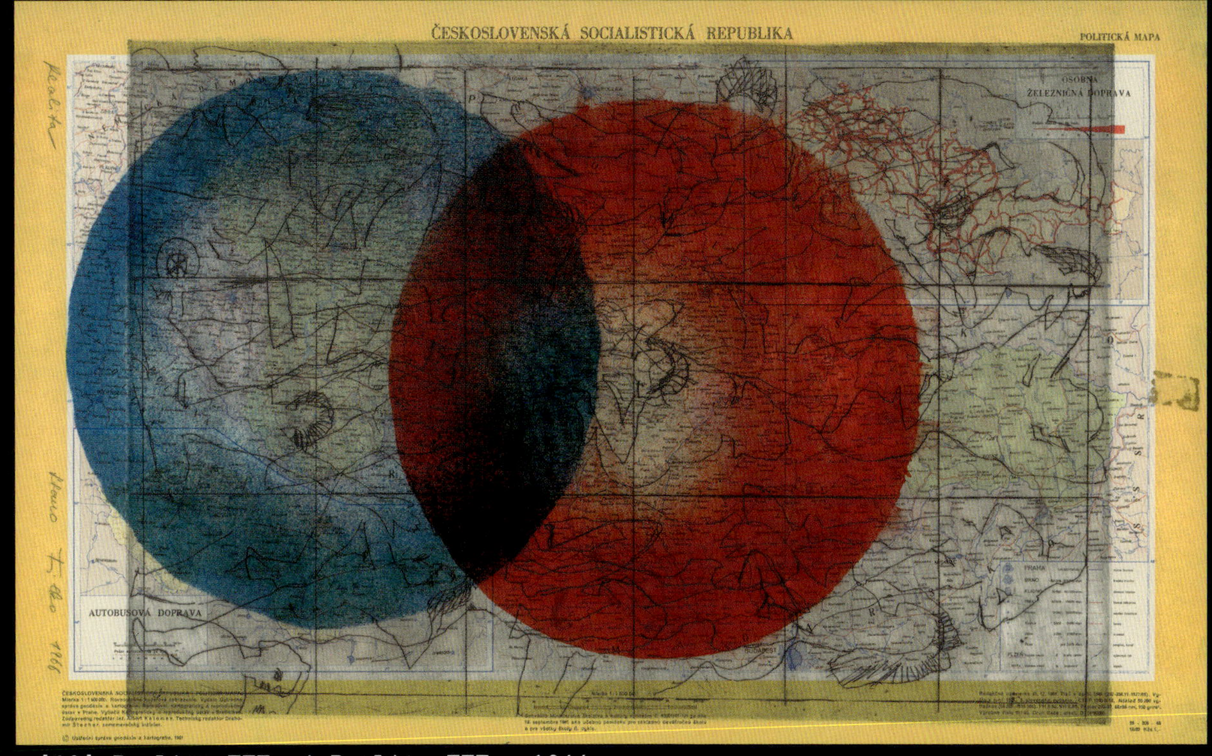

[10] *Reality III. / Realita III.*, 1966

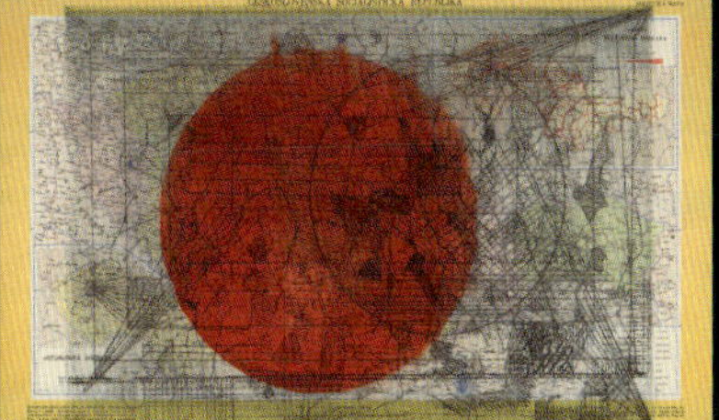

[11] *Reality I. / Realita I.*, 1966

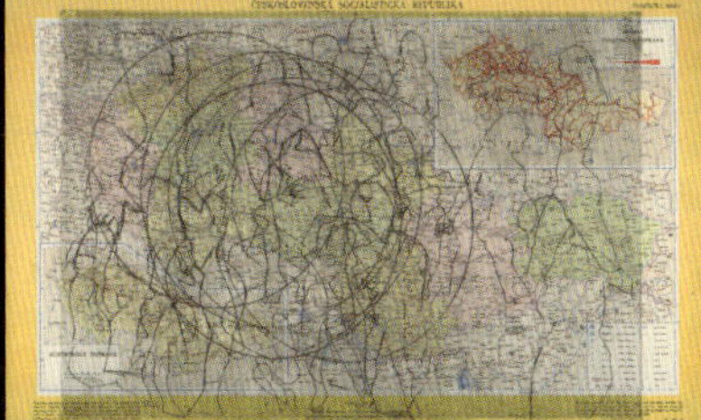

[12] *Reality II. / Realita II.*, 1966

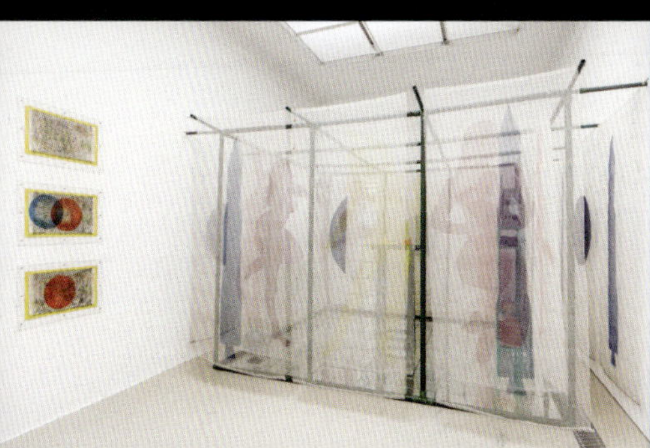

[13] Exhibition view, HALLE FÜR KUNST Steiermark, Graz, 2022

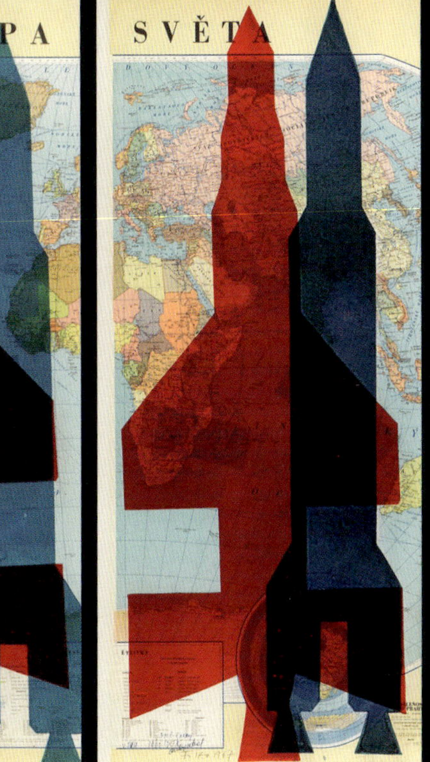

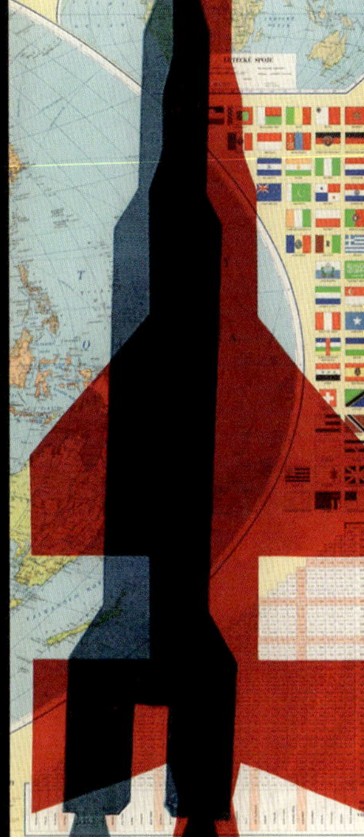

These conflicts of power, economics, and sexuality are also evident in the series *Reality I. – III. / Realita I. – III.* (1966) [10-12], with its reworked maps of the former Czechoslovakia. In this context Filko talked of the viewers as living sculptures, referring to aspects of an action art that aims to undermine physical or intellectual interpretations in the interaction between the beholders and the installation.

Diese Konflikte um Macht, Ökonomie, Sexualität und Territorium zeigen sich auch in der Serie *Reality I. – III. / Realita I. – III.* (1966) [10-12], ausgeführt auf überarbeiteten Karten der ehemaligen Tschechoslowakei. Filko spricht in diesem Zusammenhang auch von Betrachter*innen als lebende Skulpturen, womit er Aspekte einer Aktionskunst anspricht, die darauf abzielt, physische oder intellektuelle Leerstellen zwischen Besucher*innen und Installation zu unterwandern.

[14] From the series *Map of the World (Rockets) / Zo série Mapa sveta (Rakety)*, 1967

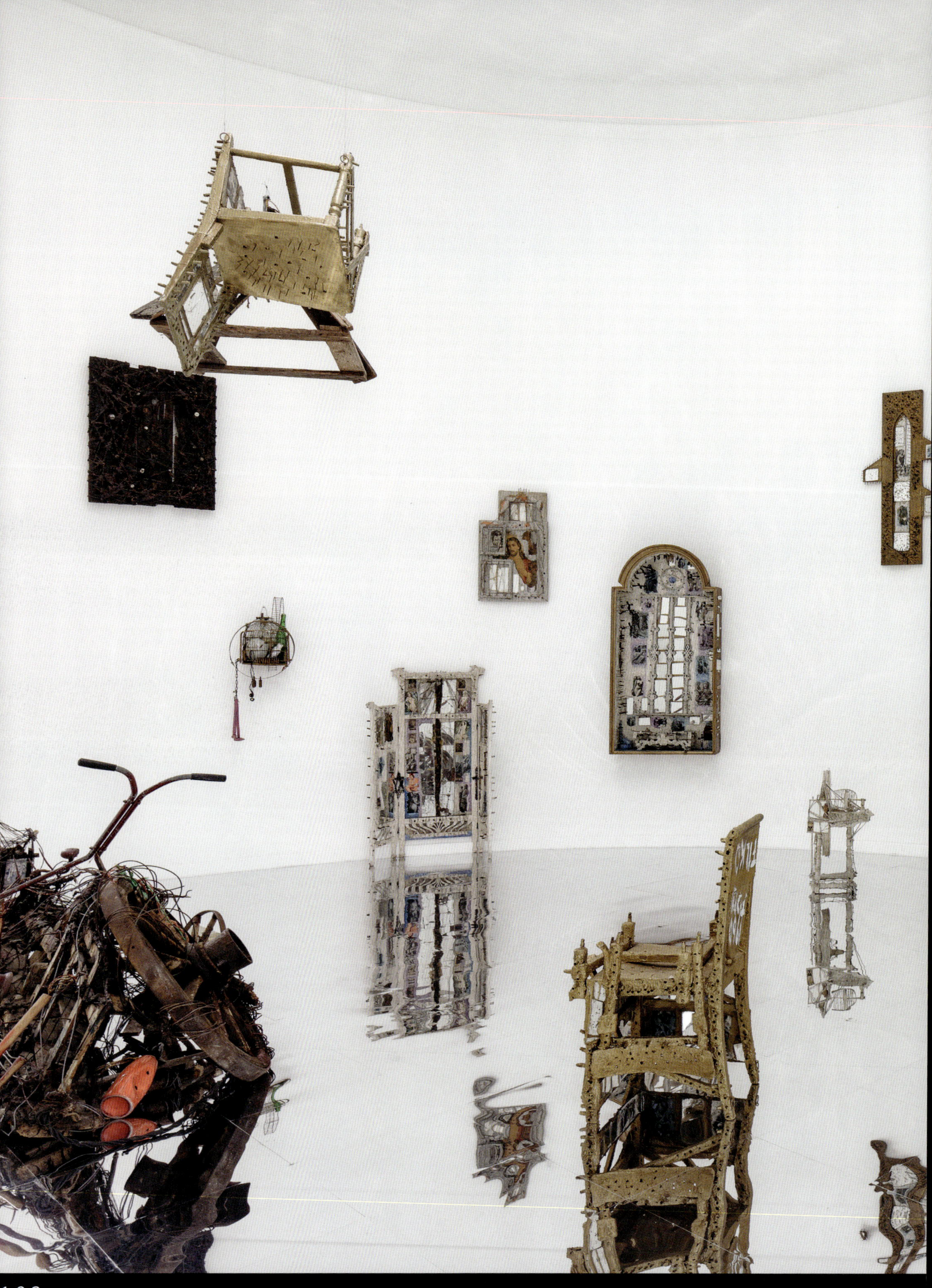

   XII. Altars and *Grandpa - Grandma Are Listening to the Radio*

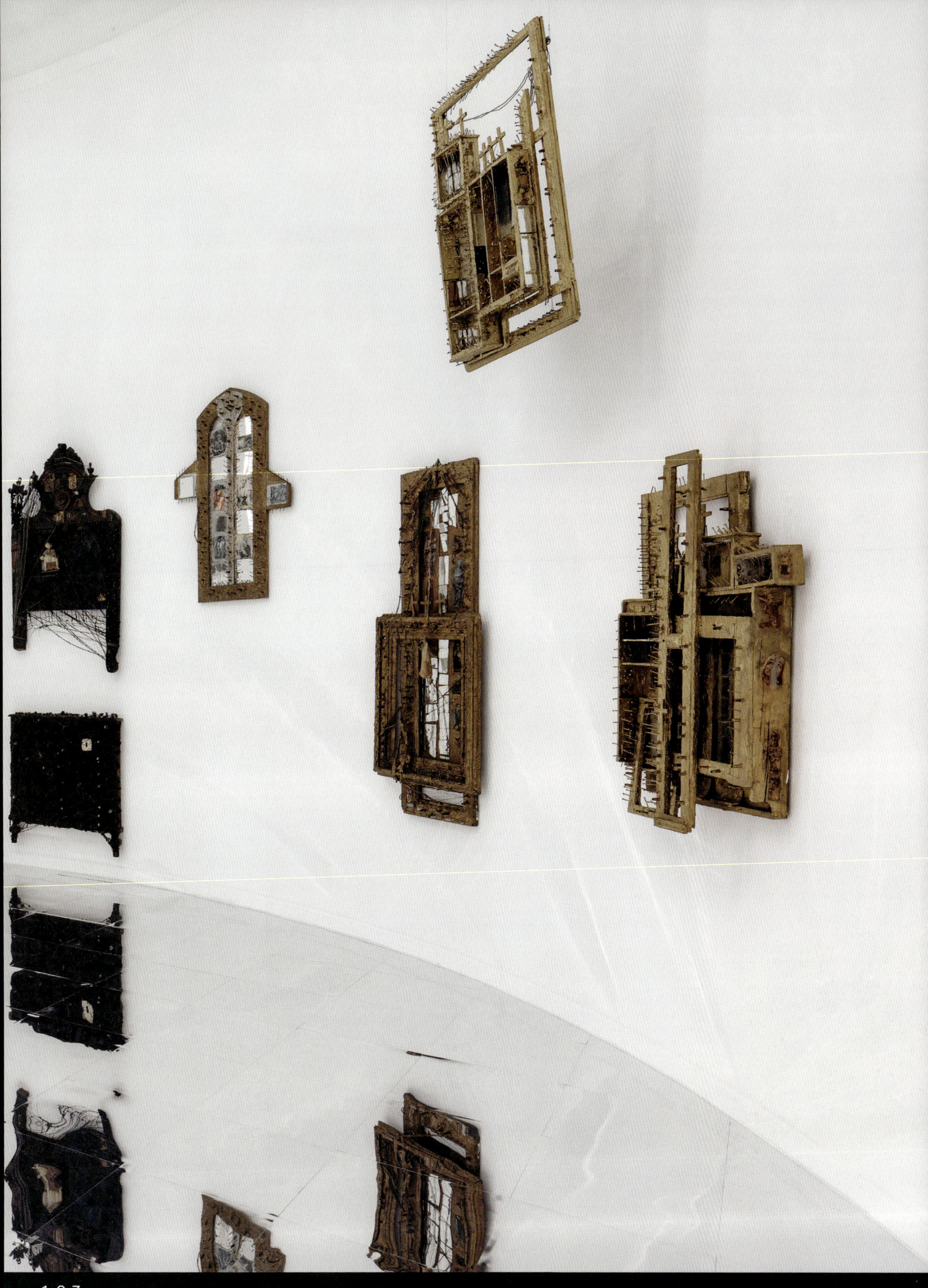

XII

Altars and / Altäre und *Grandpa – Grandma Are Listening to the Radio*

Filko always also asks as to the relationship of the beholder to the object. This leads to questions concerning the nature of art itself and of the author, and also the origin and production of the work, which both as an object and as a symbol is, like in a religion, directed to an emotional content. Filko's work is characterized by this reflective approach right from his early days, as referred to in this room recalling an apse and decorated with mirror foil, in which a series of altars and the work *Grandpa – Grandma Are Listening to the Radio / Dedko – babka počúvajú rádio* (1965) [05] are presented.

Filko befragt immer auch das Verhältnis von Betrachter*in hin zum Objekt. Dabei kommen Fragestellungen nach Kunst an sich auf. Diese zielen auf den Autor, aber auch auf dessen Herkunft sowie Produktionsweisen, die ähnlich einer Religion symbolisch wie objektbezogen auf eine emotionale inhaltliche Ebene gelenkt werden. Diese reflektierte Haltung kennzeichnet die künstlerische Praxis von Filko bereits zu Beginn seiner Karriere und lässt sich in diesem an eine Apsis erinnernden und mit Spiegelfolie ausgelegten Raum durch eine Serie von Altären und der Arbeit *Grandpa – Grandma Are Listening to the Radio / Dedko – babka počúvajú rádio* (1965) [05] ablesen.

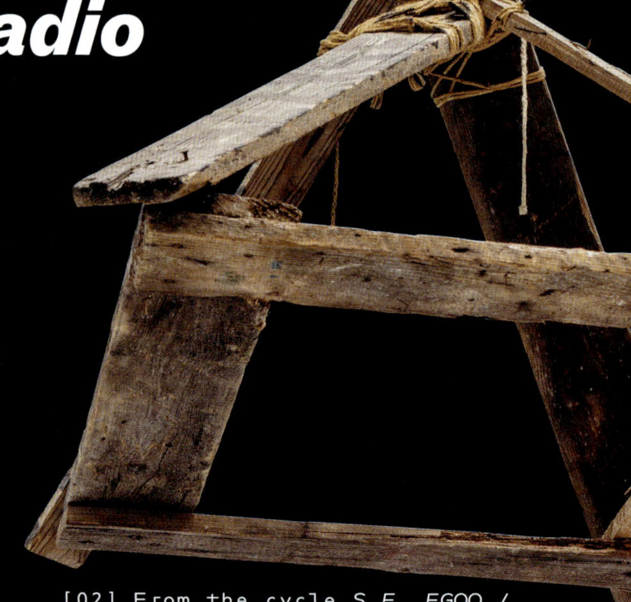

[02] From the cycle *S.F. EGOQ* / Z cyklu *S.F. EGOQ*, c. 1995

[04] From the series *Altars of Contemporaneity (Chair)* / Zo série *Oltáre súčasnosti (Stolička)*, 1965

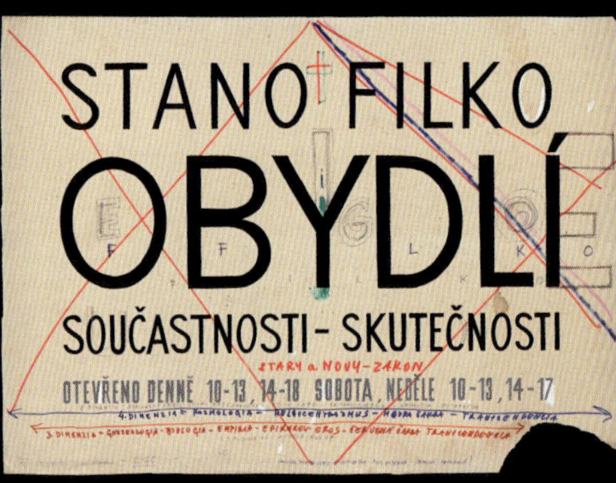

[03] Dwelling 1966 of Contemporaneity - Reality / Obydlie 1966 súčasnosti - skutočnosti, Poster / Plagát, 1967/c. 2000

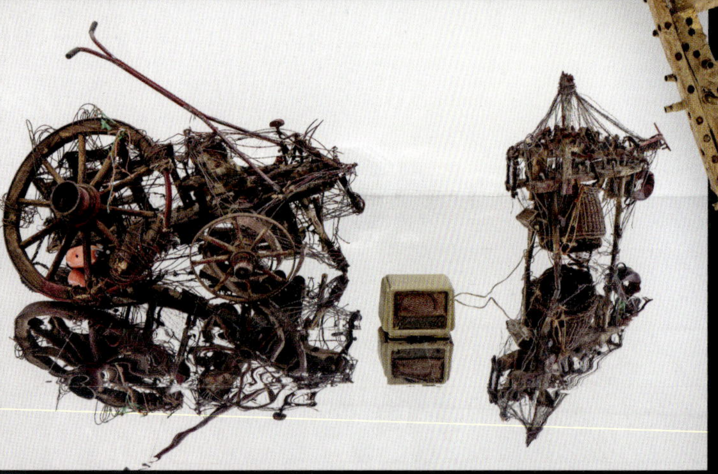

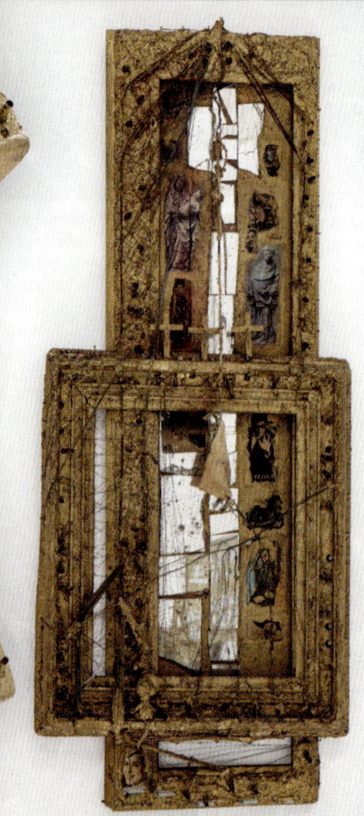

[06] From the series *Altars of Contemporaneity* / Zo série *Oltáre súčasnosti*, 1965–66

[05A] *Grandpa - Grandma Are Listening to the Radio / Dedko - babka počúvajú rádio*, 1965

←[01] Exhibition view, HALLE FÜR KUNST Steiermark, Graz, 2022

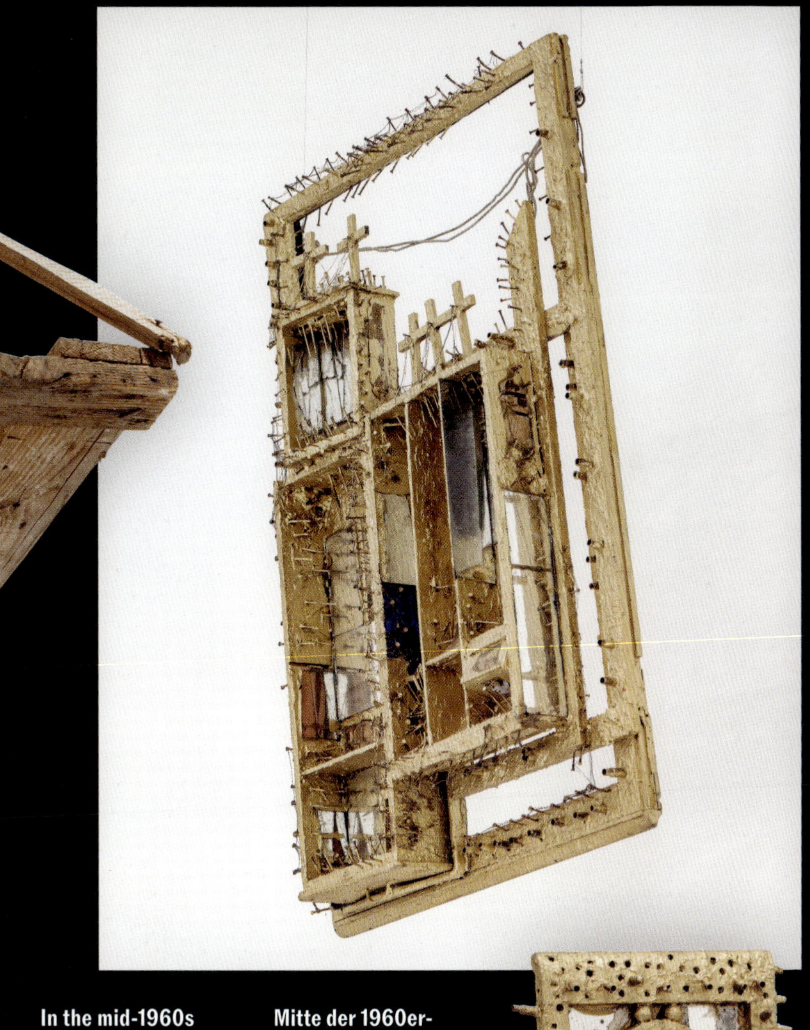

[08] From the series Altars of Contemporaneity (Chair) / Zo série Oltáre súčasnosti (Stolička), 1965

A large early series of works presented is titled *Altars of Contemporaneity / Oltáre súčasnosti* (1963–66), which was included as part of Filko's first important solo exhibition in 1967 in Prague. Many of these assemblages begin as wooden paneling to which the artist adds fragments of mirrors, nails, ropes, and various images. There is a striking juxtaposition of erotic images of women and reproductions of gothic artworks, including several madonnas. While these works are today seen as rather conservative, in the context of Czechoslovakia in the 1960s they were clearly provocative. Both religion and eroticism were seen by the socialist regime as aspects of an unacceptable Western ideology. Both offer an alternative form of faith, a different kind of salvation beyond the spaces of desire permitted in the socialist system. Filko here contrasts the different worldviews and at the same time attempts to involve the beholder by adding mirrors. He spoke of overcoming the distinction between beholder and artwork and making art "inhabitable." As well as using reflecting mirrors he also added specific objects such as a gas mask [09] and painted garments [20] [22] to this purpose, as these could be activated in actions.

Eine umfangreiche frühe Werkreihe ist die Serie *Altars of Contemporaneity / Oltáre súčasnosti* (1963–1966). Sie war zentraler Teil von Filkos erster wichtiger Einzelausstellung 1967 in Prag. Viele dieser Assemblagen nehmen Ihren Ausgang in Holzverkleidungen, an die der Künstler Spiegelfragmente, Nägel, Seile und verschiedene Bilder anbringt. Markant ist vor allem das Aufeinandertreffen erotischer Frauenbilder mit Reproduktionen gotischer Kunstwerke, darunter auch einige Madonnen. Heute eher konservativ erscheinend, entfalteten Werke dieser Art in der Tschechoslowakei der 1960er-Jahre eine provokative Wirkung. Sowohl Religion als auch Erotik wurden vom sozialistischen Regime als Teil einer abzulehnenden, westlichen Ideologie betrachtet. Beide bieten einen gegenläufigen Glauben an, eine alternative Art der Erlösung, die sich den Begehrensräumen der sozialistischen Herrschaft entzieht. Filko spielt die verschiedenen Weltanschauungen gegeneinander aus und versucht gleichzeitig durch die Verwendung von Spiegeln die Betrachter*innen zu involvieren. Filko sprach davon, den Gegensatz von Betrachter*in und Kunstwerk zu überwinden und die Kunst „bewohnbar" zu machen. Neben der Verwendung von reflektierenden Spiegeln fügte er zu diesem Zweck Objekte wie eine Gasmaske [09] und bemalte Gewänder hinzu [20] [22], die durch Aktionen dahingehend aktiviert wurden.

In the mid-1960s Filko's artistic career begins with a series of hybrid pieces for which he uses found objects. He utilizes the technique of assemblage in order to liberate the objects he finds from their own contexts and he adds objects to them that he makes himself, thereby altering them. Filko's avant-garde approach is here already linking up with international developments in art at the time, and can be seen as evidence of his own capacity to innovate. These objects open up an unusual view of things and themes that seem to have fallen into a realm beyond time. This room is characterized by a nostalgic and archaic atmosphere.

Mitte der 1960er-Jahre beginnt Filkos künstlerische Karriere mit einer Reihe hybrider Objekte, für die er vorgefundene Gegenstände verwendet. Er nutzt die Technik der Assemblage um die Gegenstände aus ihrem Kontext zu befreien und durch die Zugabe selbstgefertigter Objekte zu verändern. Damit knüpft Filko bereits früh in avantgardistischer Haltung an das damalige internationale Kunstgeschehen an und stellt seine Innovationsfähigkeit unter Beweis. Die ausgestellten Objekte eröffnen einen ungewöhnlichen Blick auf Dinge und Themen, die wie aus der Zeit gefallen wirken. Eine nostalgisch-archaische Atmosphäre bestimmt den Raum.

[09] Gas mask from the exhibition *Dwelling 1966 of Contemporaneity – Reality / Plynová maska z výstavy Obydlie 1966 súčasnosti – skutočnosti*, 1967

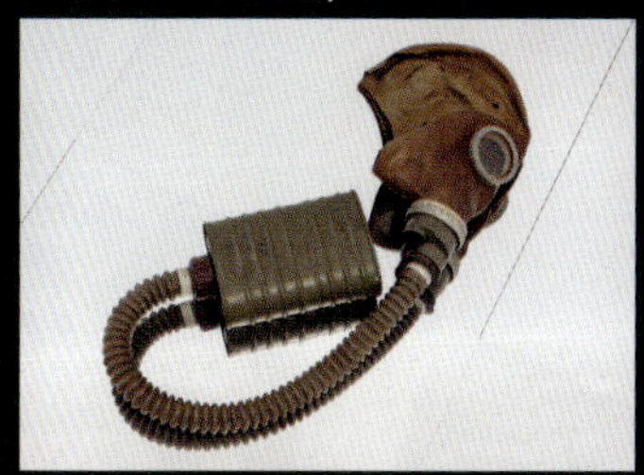

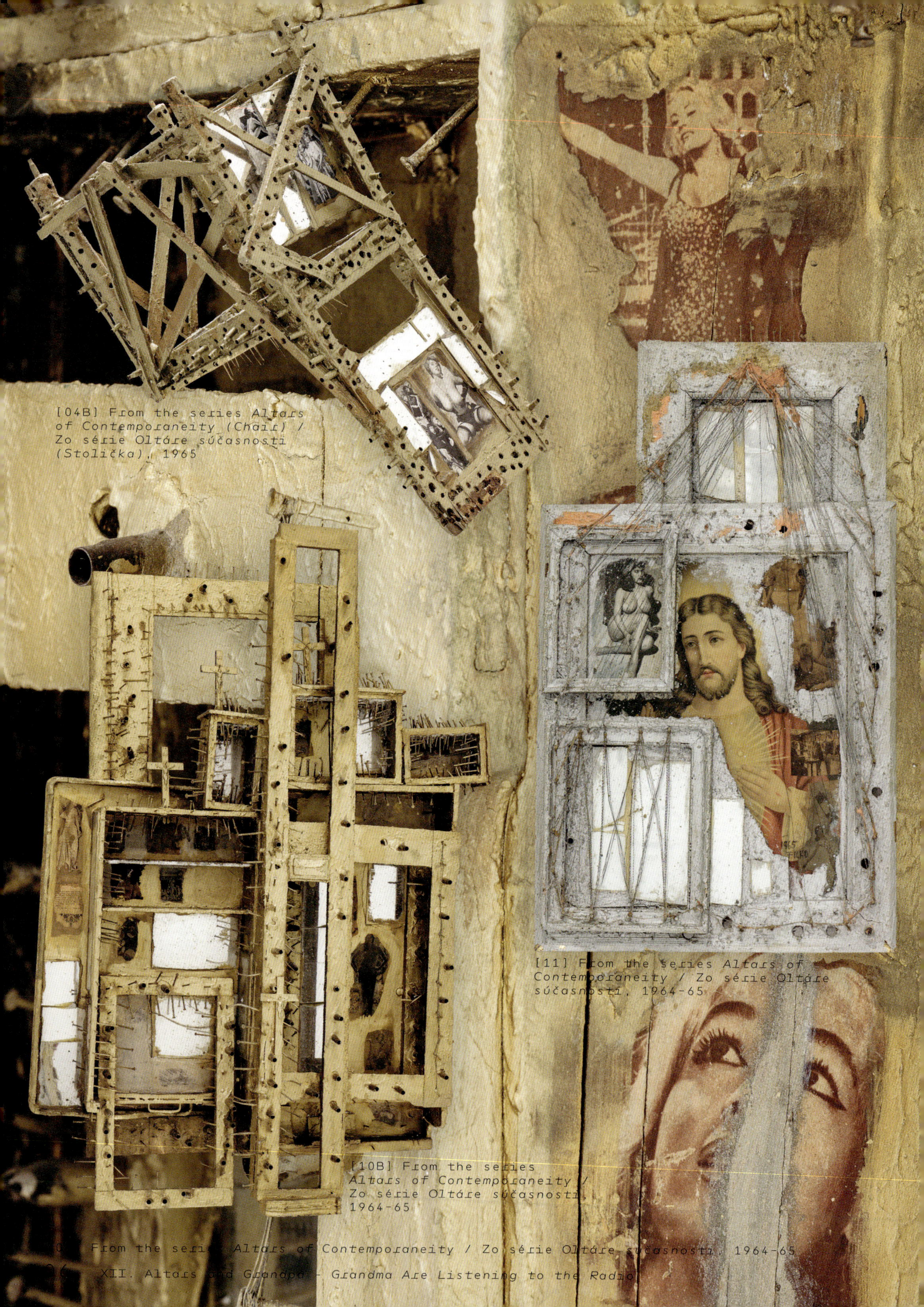

[04B] From the series *Altars of Contemporaneity (Chair)* / Zo série *Oltáre súčasnosti (Stolička)*, 1965

[11] From the series *Altars of Contemporaneity* / Zo série *Oltáre súčasnosti*, 1964–65

[10B] From the series *Altars of Contemporaneity* / Zo série *Oltáre súčasnosti*, 1964–65

From the series *Altars of Contemporaneity* / Zo série *Oltáre súčasnosti*, 1964–65

XII. Altars and *Grandpa – Grandma Are Listening to the Radio*

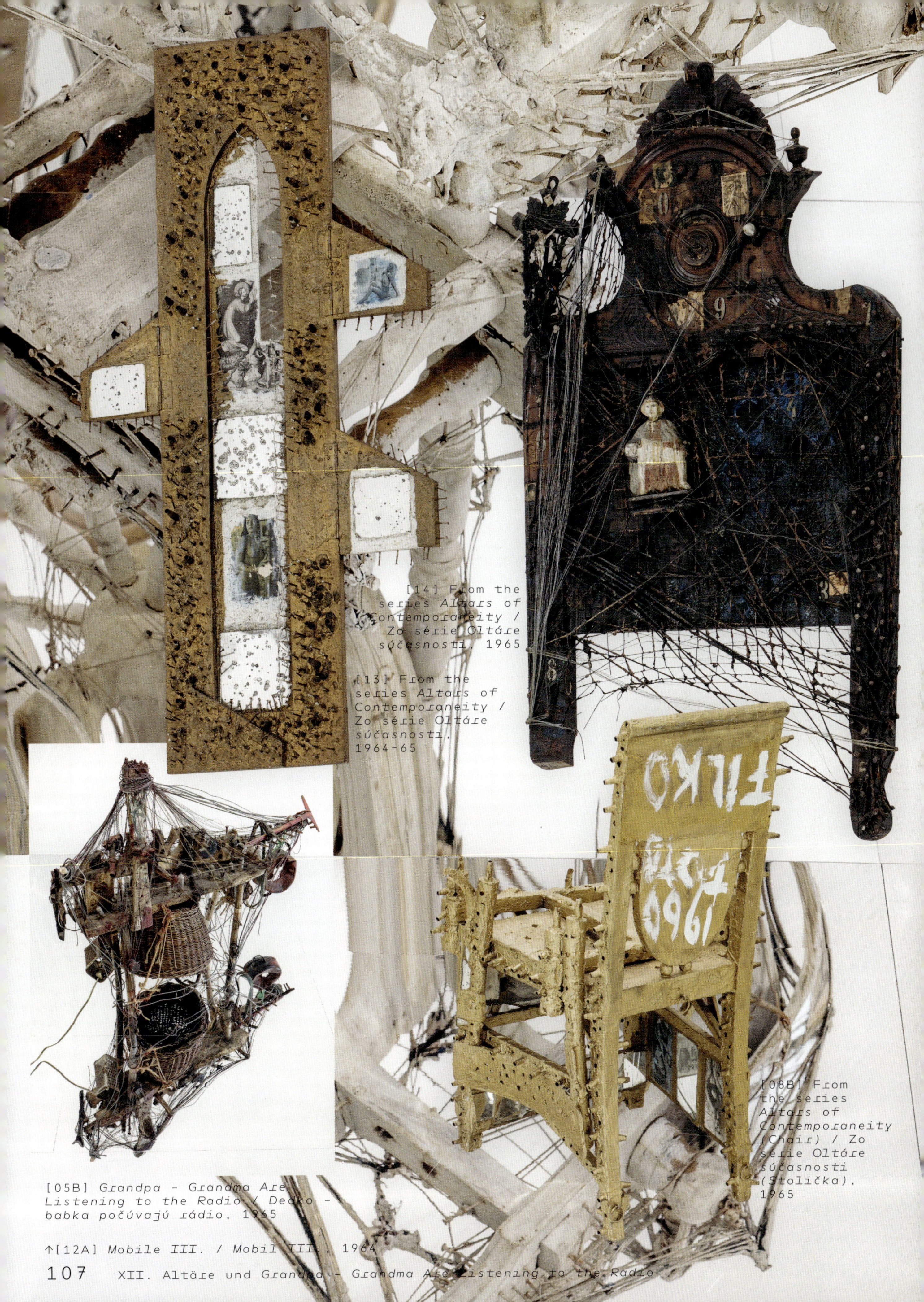

[14] From the series *Altars of Contemporaneity / Zo série Oltáre súčasnosti*, 1965

[13] From the series *Altars of Contemporaneity / Zo série Oltáre súčasnosti*, 1964–65

[08B] From the series *Altars of Contemporaneity (Chair) / Zo série Oltáre súčasnosti (Stolička)*, 1965

[05B] *Grandpa – Grandma Are Listening to the Radio / Dedko – babka počúvajú rádio*, 1965

↑[12A] *Mobile III. / Mobil III.*, 1964

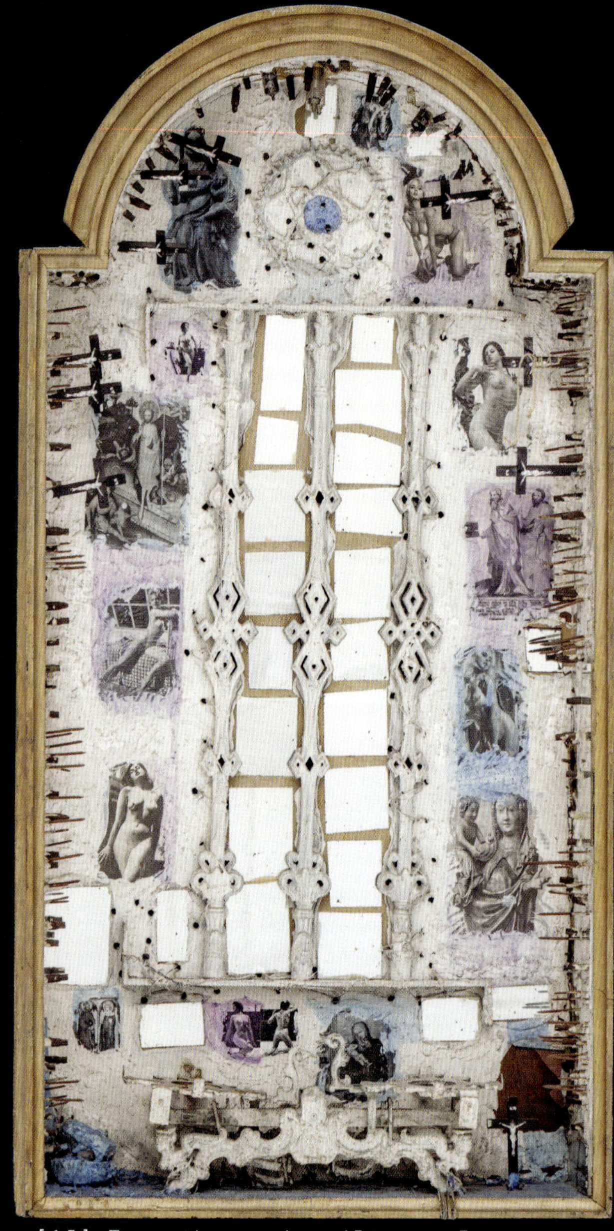

[15] From the series Altars of Contemporaneity / Zo série Oltáre súčasnosti, 1965

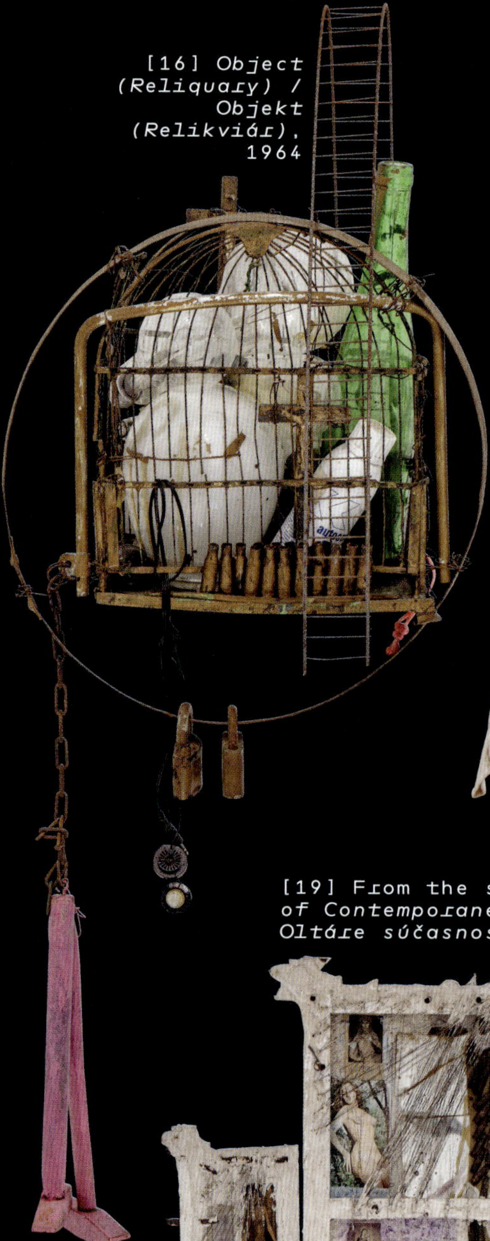

[16] Object (Reliquary) / Objekt (Relikviár), 1964

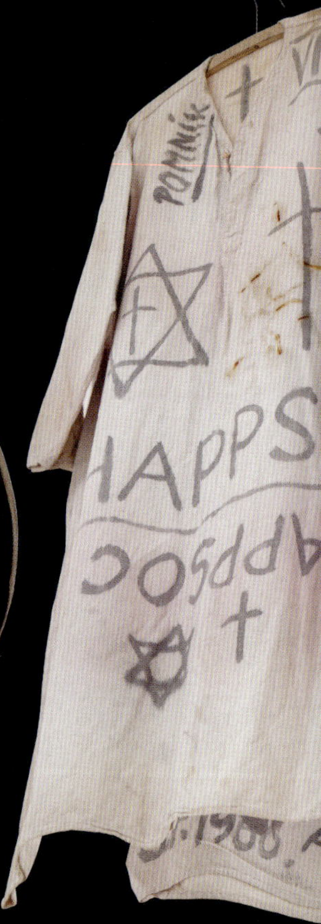

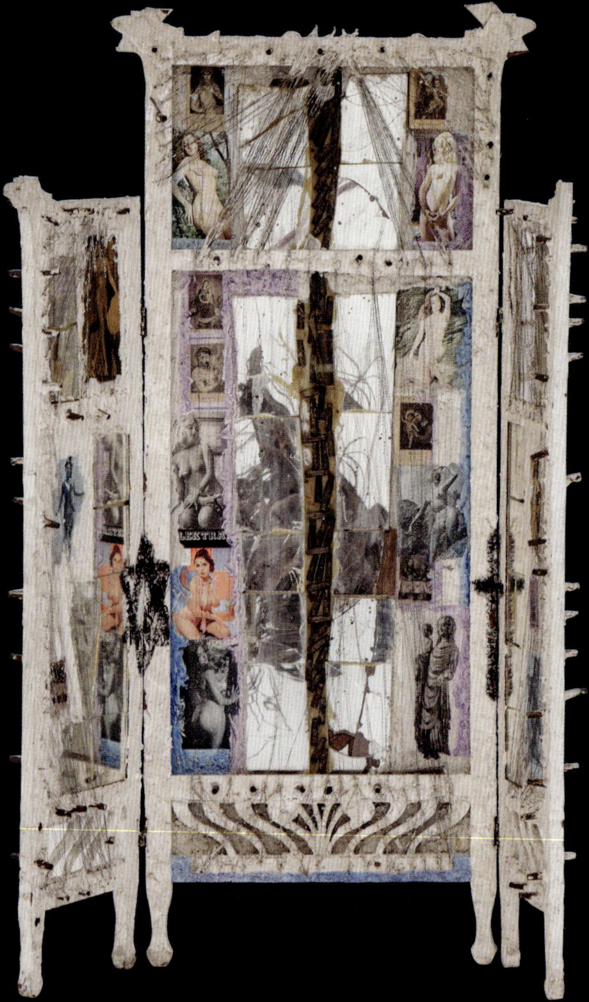

[19] From the series Altars of Contemporaneity / Zo série Oltáre súčasnosti, 1965

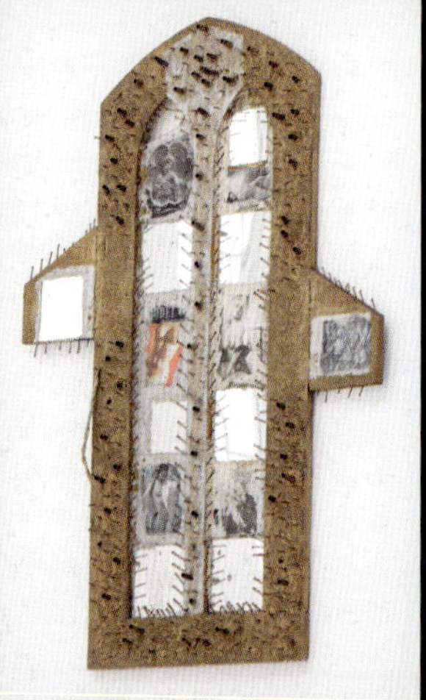

[17] From the series Altars of Contemporaneity / Zo série Oltáre súčasnosti, 1964–65

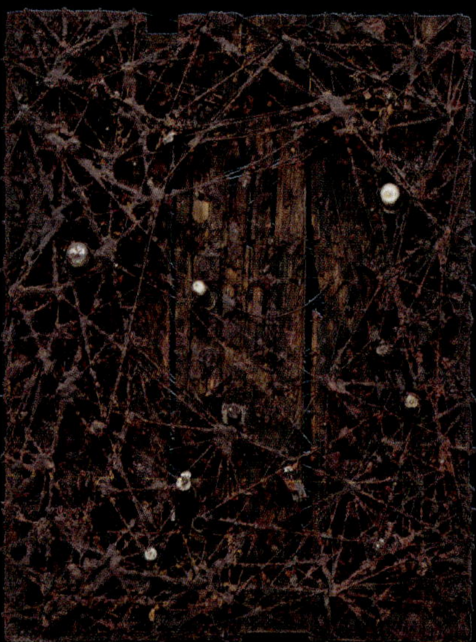

[18] Shattered Reality / Rozbitá skutočnosť, 1960–65

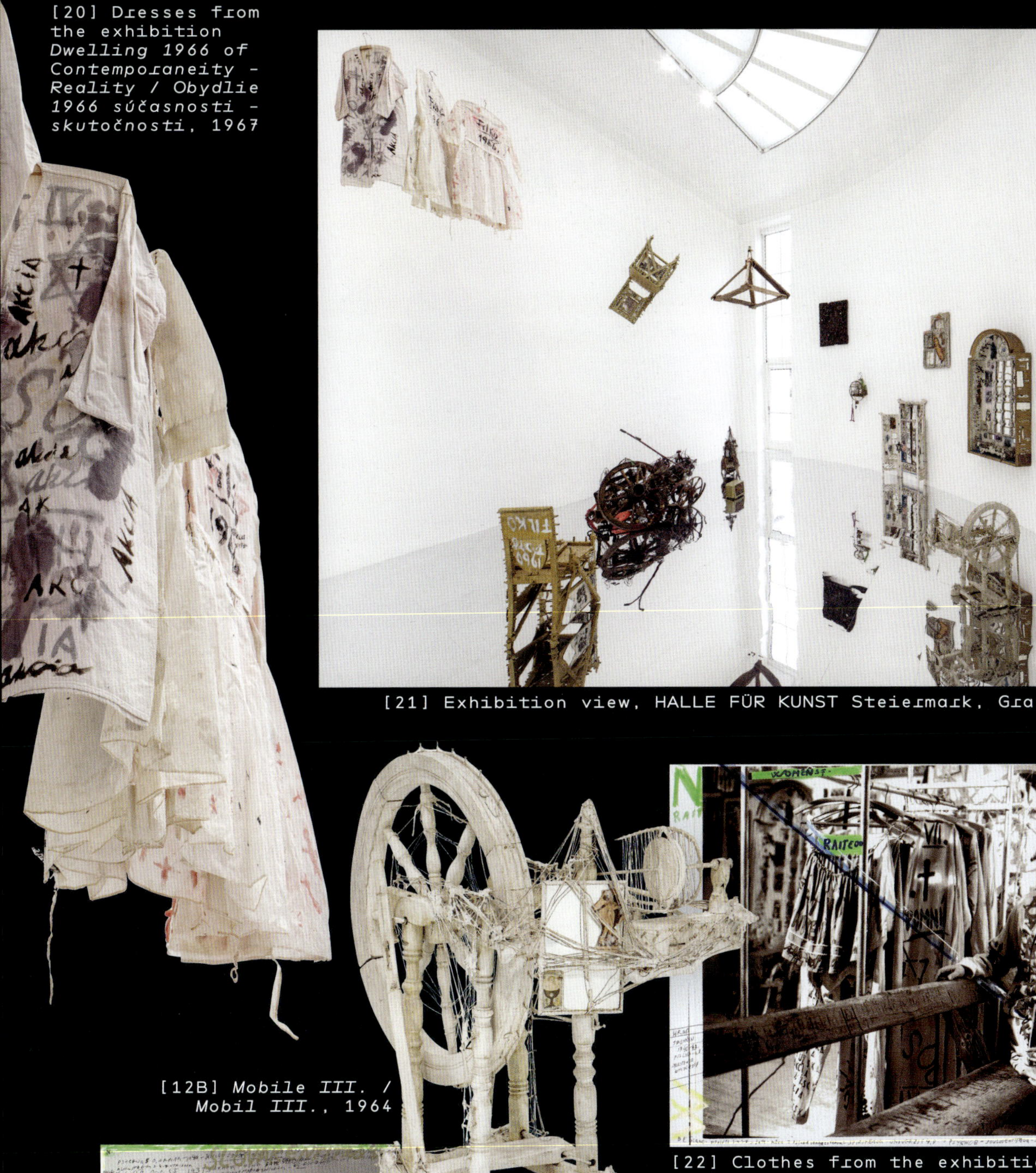

[20] Dresses from the exhibition *Dwelling 1966 of Contemporaneity - Reality / Obydlie 1966 súčasnosti - skutočnosti*, 1967

[21] Exhibition view, HALLE FÜR KUNST Steiermark, Graz, 2022

[12B] *Mobile III. / Mobil III.*, 1964

[22] Clothes from the exhibition *Dwelling 1966 of Contemporaneity - Reality / Obydlie 1966 súčasnosti - skutočnosti*, 1967

[23] *SLOVAK ENTITAQ 4.D. Mobil III.*, 1964/c. 2010

A further series of objects cites wooden tools such as old farming carts and spinning wheels [12]. Wheels are conspicuous elements in the structure of these works, on the one hand indicating movement and productivity and yet on the other they are blocked by meshing and strings, which are sometimes reminiscent of spiders' webs. The aspects of ageing and a loss of functionality suggested here are particularly emphasized in the most striking work in the series, *Grandpa – Grandma Are Listening to the Radio / Dedko – babka počúvajú rádio* (1965). In these works there is always an element of opposition politics that negates the totalitarian socialist doctrine of the time, with its vision of an ideal social order and a blessed future based on a stateprescribed optimism.

Eine weitere Objektreihe zitiert hölzerne Geräte wie alte Landwirtschaftskarren und Spinnräder [12]. Auffällig in der Struktur der Werke sind Räder, die zum einen Bewegung und Produktivität andeuten, zum anderen aber durch Ge-flechte von Seilen blockiert werden. Das Geflecht erinnert teilweise auch an Spinnweben. Diese Aspekte des Alterns und des Funktionsverlusts werden auch anhand des auffälligsten Werks aus der Serie hervorgehoben: *Grandpa – Grandma Are Listening to the Radio / Dedko – babka počúvajú rádio* (1965). Dabei schwingt immer auch ein oppositionelles politisches Moment mit: sich über die damals gültige real-sozialistische totalitäre Doktrin einer vergesellschafteten, idealisierten Vorstellung einer erfreulichen Zukunft und eines staatlich verordneten Optimismus hinwegzusetzen.

Signs and Rockets
On Stano Filko's Anti-Art

Jan Verwoert

Stano Filko creates worlds and systems in his work. His approach is holistic in two ways. Building worlds and designing systems are both means to articulate totality. Both seek to grasp reality as a whole. But they go very different ways to achieve this: world building is a very old operation and uses the means of sympathetic magic to engender a cosmic and elementary confluence of all the forces in the world. In contrast, *system design*, a principle of modernist thinking through and through, wishes to have nothing more to do with sorcery and instead to dominate the world with technical means. This distinction seems necessary in order to be able to name the tension at the very heart of Filko's work, which marks how he does what he does. He indeed always goes for the whole. In his view and presentation of himself, he does this however in two different capacities—on the one hand as an *artist*, the boy from the country, born near the place where the Venus of Moravany was found and therefore imbued with her primeval powers and destined to give the cosmos a voice in his art. On the other hand as a systems thinker and engineer, more precisely as a *semiotician* and *constructor of rockets*, who, with the authority of his modernist mandate, sweepingly reinterprets and aggressively attacks the state of reality. Taking this tension seriously means to accept that you cannot do justice to Filko by seeing him purely as an artist and his work solely as *art*. The aggressivity with which he asserts the modernity of his person as a constructor of signs/bombs and his actions as *anti-art* must also be appreciated. [01-02]

The contradiction between anti-art and art is a motor of the avant-gardes, and, historically, the intimate interplay between the impulses to destroy and to create art has been a driving force in the discussion and production of key modernist works. In his pivotal essay *The Total Art of Stalinism*,[1] Boris Groys shows how this interplay unfolded in the endeavors and disputes within the Russian avant-garde after the October Revolution. In terms of the dual role of destroyer (technical) and creator of worlds (cosmic) there are strong affinities between Filko and Malevich. The latter also saw modern technology as a means to radically transform social conditions. Whereas art had hitherto only depicted the nature of things in various ways, what mattered now was to use technology to change the world. Becoming an advocate of this change meant agreeing with the death of God, nature, and art, and using anti-art to attack the bastions of the old belief and value systems in people's minds. According to Groys, Malevich, however, sees the ultimate aim of this work of destruction as the creation of a cosmically expanded consciousness emancipated from all mundane content. Art was to play a spiritual role in the creation of this state, end its relations with bourgeois aesthetics and realize its ties to religious folk art (icons are the traffic signs for the transportation of the soul).

Malevich formulated his ideas in the late 1910s, and since then much happened. Stalin came and went, a zero point of total destruction was passed, Moscow organized industrial development, the avant-garde fell out of grace, and the advent of the future was now proclaimed by "social realist" art. One should therefore not assume that the ideas of the Malevich generation were easily accessible to the Filko generation. Rather than just a reenactment of history, their new experience of the tensions at the core of the avant-garde aggression and aspiration, just under fifty years after their first manifestation, is perhaps even the first time that their potential and contradictions became so baldly apparent. If the generation of Rosalind Krauss and Bob Morris in New York had not brought Marcel Duchamp (a long-term resident of the city) out of obscurity, declaring him the model for what they thought doing art and being an artist was about, he would today most likely be no big story. Probably, *mutatis mutandis*, something similar can be said about how the ideas of the early Soviet avant-gardes may have gained currency for the postwar universe thanks to their appropriation and translation by the Filko generation.

A very clear example for the practical appropriation of Malevich's principles in the name of art and anti-art is the clandestine intervention *White Space in White Space /*

Zeichen und Raketen
Zu Stano Filkos Antikunst

Jan Verwoert

In seinem Werk schafft Stano Filko Welten und Systeme. Sein Vorgehen ist in zweierlei Hinsicht ganzheitlich. Weltenbau und Systementwurf sind beides Mittel zum Darstellen von Totalität. Beide wollen die Wirklichkeit als Ganze erfassen. Sie gehen dabei aber auf höchst unterschiedliche Weise zu Werke: *Weltenbau* ist ein sehr altes Geschäft und vollzieht mit Mitteln sympathischer Magie das Zusammenwirken aller Kräfte in der Welt kosmisch-elementar nach. Im Gegensatz dazu will der *Systementwurf*, als modernes Denkprinzip schlechthin, mit Zauberei nichts mehr zu tun haben und stattdessen mit technischem Wissen die Welt beherrschen. Diese Unterscheidung erscheint nötig, um die Spannung im Herzen von Filkos Werk zu benennen, die sein Tun prägt. Zwar geht er stets aufs Ganze. In seiner Selbstauffassung und -darstellung tut er dies aber in zwei verschiedenen Kapazitäten: Zum einen als *Künstler*, Kind vom Land, geboren nahe des Fundorts der Venus von Moravany und deshalb beseelt von ihren Urkräften und berufen dazu, in seiner Kunst dem Kosmos eine Stimme zu geben. Zum anderen als Systematiker und Ingenieur, genauer gesagt als *Semiotiker* und *Raketenbauer*, der, kraft seines modernen Amtes, gründlich und aggressiv die Verhältnisse erklärt und angreift. Diese Spannung ernst zu nehmen, heißt einzusehen, dass man Filko nicht entgegenkommt, wenn man ihn rein als Künstler und sein Tun allein als *Kunst* begreift. Die Aggressivität, mit der er die Modernität seiner Person als Konstrukteur von Zeichen/Bomben und seines Handelns als *Antikunst* behauptet, gilt es ebenso anzuerkennen. [01-02]

Der Widerspruch zwischen Antikunst und Kunst ist – so wie das Ringen damit, beide Kräfte, das Zerstören und das Produzieren von Kunst, im Herzen zu tragen und im eigenen Tun am Werk zu sehen – ein Motor moderner Avantgarden. Also hat er Geschichte. In seinem einschlägigen Essay *Gesamtkunstwerk Stalin*[1] zeigt Boris Groys, wie sich dieser Widerspruch im Streben und Streiten der russischen Avantgarde nach der Oktoberrevolution entfaltet. Mit Blick auf die Doppelrolle von Zerstörer (technisch) und Weltschöpfer (kosmisch) ergeben sich starke Bezüge zwischen Filko und Malewitsch: Auch letzterer sieht in moderner Technik ein Mittel zur radikalen Umwälzung der Verhältnisse. Wenn Kunst bisher die Natur der Dinge nur verschieden abgebildet hat, gilt es jetzt, die Welt durch Technologie zu verändern. Sich auf die Seite dieser Veränderung zu schlagen, heißt, dem Tod von Gott, Natur und Kunst zuzustimmen und mit Antikunst die Bastionen alten Werteglaubens im Denken der Leute anzugreifen. Ziel des Zerstörungswerks ist für Malewitsch, so Groys, jedoch letztlich die Erreichung des kosmisch erweiterten Bewusstseins einer von aller Gegenständlichkeit befreiten Wahrnehmung. Bei deren Erzeugung spielt Kunst nun wieder eine Rolle, und zwar eine spirituelle. Sie kündigt ihr Verhältnis zur bürgerlichen Ästhetik auf und wird sich ihrer Verwandtschaft zu religiöser Volkskunst gewahr (Ikonen sind Verkehrszeichen für den Transport der Seele).

Malewitsch formuliert seine Ideen Ende der 1910er-Jahre. Seitdem ist viel passiert. Stalin ist gekommen und gegangen, der Nullpunkt totaler Zerstörung ist durchschritten, Moskau steuert den industriellen Aufbau, die Avantgarde ist in Ungnade gefallen, die Ankunft der Zukunft verkündet nun „sozial realistische" Kunst. Man darf also nicht davon ausgehen, dass das Wissen um die Ideen der Generation Malewitsch der Generation Filko einfach zugänglich gewesen wären. Mehr als nur Nachvollzug der Geschichte, ist das erneute Durchleben der Spannungen im Kern der avantgardistischen Aggression und Hoffnung, knapp 50 Jahre nach ihrer Aufkommen vielleicht sogar das erste Mal, dass deren Potenziale und Widersprüche ungeschminkt hervortreten. Ohne dass die Generation von Rosalind Krauss und Bob Morris im New York der 1960er-Jahre (den dort ansässigen) Marcel Duchamp aus der Versenkung gezogen, und zum Vorbild ihres Tuns und Denkens erklärt hätten, wäre er heute wohl kaum Geschichte. Vermutlich ließe sich *mutatis mutandis* ähnliches über das Wissen um die Ideen des sowjetischen Avantgardismus sagen, die in ihrer Aneignung und Übersetzung durch die Generation Filko Geltung für das Universum der Nachkriegszeit erhalten.

Ein unmittelbares Beispiel für die praktische Anverwandlung von Malewitschs Prinzipien im Zeichen von Kunst und Antikunst liefert die Intervention *White Space in White Space /*

Biely priestor v bielom priestore, which Filko, Miloš Laky, and Ján Zavarský undertook at the House of Art (Dům umění, Brno) in 1974, with the consent of director Greta Pospíšilová and curator Jiří Valoch. While the museum was closed on a Monday, the conspirators installed a series of canvas strips painted only in white industrial paint for one day and one night in the empty galleries. Some of them were hung from the ceilings like banners, others rolled out like scrolls on the floors or along the walls. The action was accompanied by a paper with twelve theses that was clandestinely distributed. Here Filko, Laky, and Zavarský claimed that they had successfully produced a condition of total void, and thus helped to bring into the world an art of pure sensibility. As Daniel Grúň explains in his essay on this work,[2] the three artists had read Malevich's book *The Non-Objective World* (1927) under the influence of the Slovak literature scholar Oskár Čepan. The latter read Malevich's work in the light of new science *semiotically* as the production of iconic signs. So Filko, Laky, and Zavarský proceeded to produce consequently cosmic anti-art. They monotonously colored metres of canvases with industrial paint, with a blunt anti-art attitude, as if they were painting traffic signs. They used these signs, however, to then dress up the museum like a universal temple devoted to the spirit of pure sensibility. Like many of the avant-garde's actions, this intervention has the nature of an act of proof. The crude making of the whitewashed canvases corresponds to their status as demonstrative objects. Anti-art provides arguments to underpin and signs to signify the potential of a new art.

One realm where anti-art comes into its own therefore is the theory of its inner necessity. At the same time it is a material practice, existentially so. In this latter sense, *White Space in White Space / Biely priestor v bielom priestore* equally testifies to a joint attempt of organizing intellectual survival after the optimism of the 1960s (that the arrival of new technologies would now really make socialism come true) had been defeated by the crushing of the Prague Spring in 1968. Together with his wife Anna Lakyová, Laky had decorated their living room completely in white before the intervention, so as to provide a space to talk together about what to do after the disaster of 1968. In a sense this also shows that there is no permanently designated place for the construction and destruction of the meaning, freedom, function, and history of art. Neither the disciplines at universities nor ideological programs offer this security and continuity. It requires places like the living room of Lakyová/Laky in order to vent despair and ask if there is any future for art. In retrospect, even such moments of radical insecurity can of course be reinscribed into a history of art, as one moment in its seemingly continuous evolution. Given the traumatic rupture, in the wake of which the meetings in the home of Lakyová/Laky were held, however, it seems vital to grasp how deeply the caesura of 1968 inscribed itself into people's souls, how much of the subsequent disillusionment and violence hence finds its expression in the anti-artistically aggressive qualities of Filko's work, and how the manifestations of this aggression are no longer contained by ideological programs (à la Malevich) but instead become more and more anarchic.

It is not easy to retroactively filter out the anti-artistic drive from all of Filko's actions and thinking. This is largely due to the fact that toward the end of his life Filko prioritized the cosmic artistic dimension of his work and thought, extending the systematic color codes of his earlier work groups (red for the body, green for society, blue for flying into space, white for nothing and limitless perception) into a spiritual constellation of twelve color chakras, and also painted his studio building on the periphery of Bratislava according to these colors. While the colors in the late 1960s still operate with the function of a code denoting fields of action, as if they were part of a state-military semiotics (body brigade, social division, space commando, department of nothing), they seem in the course of the 1990s to clearly represent the integral aspects of a total work of art. The system designs that Filko made by arranging grouped concepts on graph paper during these years are colored with all the chakra colors, and their dynamic colorfulness gives them the character of mandalas. Does this make for a mild and conciliatory tone? Was it in fact all art in the end? A post-Soviet take on Wagner's *Gesamtkunstwerk*? Clearly not. When visiting Filko's studio building it's apparent right away that this is not the lineage the work stands in. It's far too unceremonious and rustic how Filko painted rooms and objects in the chakra colors (and wrote words from his vocabulary everywhere and on everything) for anything to aspire to the status of *fine* art or *high culture*. This is *applied* art, Filko folk art. Rooms and furniture are only deemed ready to move into and use when they have been completely painted. Granted, the giant steel rockets stored in the inner yard could be seen to qualify as sculpture and therefore art. But contemplating them in this light only would mean denying their most prominent characteristic, namely their blatantly obscene material feature: They first and foremost remain dummies of mega-ton bombs with coded blue inscriptions.

But what is the reason for this proximity of bombs and color codes, rocket building and semiotics? And why would it historically be seen in the context of anti-art? Filko is a child of his own time. In the postwar period the victory march of the hard sciences radically alters the understanding of the conditions of human action and speech. *Rocket building* and *semiotics* are the epitome of anti-art in this context. [03–04] Rocket building (including its icon Wernher von Braun) stands for the knowledge of the capacity to systematically destroy everything and everyone—the end of all action. Semiotics (including its icon Roman Jakobson) stands for the knowledge of the capacity to systematically construct any utterance—the beginning of all speech. Why do we still need art? As a *techne* to imitate nature, it withers before the modern *technologies* for the systematic destruction and construction of the world. Ruthlessly, Filko thus undertakes a farewell to art and turns to the sciences of the end of all action and the beginning of all speech. He uses the silhouettes of rockets in drawings, sculptures, and environments. At first they emanate something hopeful. Presumably in the spirit of Alexander Bogdanov's novel *Red Star* of 1907, which describes the establishment of the perfect communist society on Mars, Filko's rockets around 1967 still seem like the means of transportation to a better future, and are produced under the project title *Priestor* (space) side by side with designs and models for irrigation plants. But after the crushing of the Prague Spring the rockets increasingly look like cruise missiles, and at the latest after Filko's flight to the USA

Biely priestor v bielom priestore, die Filko zusammen mit Miloš Laky und Ján Zavarský 1974 im Haus der Kunst (Dům umění, Brno) in Absprache mit Direktorin Greta Pospíšilová und Kurator Jiří Valoch klandestin durchführten. Während das Museum montags geschlossen war, installierten die drei Konspiratoren für die Dauer eines Tages und einer Nacht in den, zu dieser Zeit leeren, Ausstellungsräumen eine Serie von Leinwandbahnen, die schlicht mit weißer Industriefarbe bestrichen waren. Manche von ihnen waren wie Banner von der Decke gehängt, andere wie Schriftrollen auf dem Boden oder an den Wänden entrollt. Zu der Aktion erschien ein ebenfalls nur unter der Hand verbreitetes Papier mit zwölf Thesen. Hier stellten Filko, Laky und Zavarský die Behauptung auf, sie hätten erfolgreich den Zustand totaler Leere hergestellt und damit einer Kunst der reinen Sensibilität zur Geburt verholfen. Wie Daniel Grúň in einem Essay zur Arbeit ausführt,[2] hatten die drei Künstler Malewitschs Buch *Die Gegenstandslose Welt* (1927) unter dem Einfluss des slowakischen Literaturwissenschaftler Oskár Čepan gelesen. Dieser deutete Malewitschs Tun im Licht der neuen Wissenschaft *semiotisch* als Produktion ikonischer Zeichen. Konsequent machten Filko, Laky und Zavarský daraufhin kosmische Antikunst. Sie strichen Leinwand antikünstlerisch stumpf wie Verkehrszeichen mit Industriefarbe, richteten das Museum mithilfe dieser Zeichen aber her wie einen, dem Geist reiner Sensibilität geweihten Universaltempel. Wie viele Aktionen der Avantgarde wirkt die Intervention wie ein Akt der Beweisführung. Die krude Machart der geweißelten Leinwände entspricht ihrem Status als Demonstrationsobjekte. Antikunst liefert Zeichen für die thesenhafte Darlegung der Potenziale neuer Kunst.

Ein Ansatz, der Antikunst zu ihrem Recht kommen lässt ist die Theorie ihrer inneren Notwendigkeit. Gleichzeitig ist Antikunst eine materielle und darin existenzielle Praxis. In diesem Sinne ist *White Space in White Space / Biely priestor v bielom priestore* wohl eher Ausdruck des Versuchs, geistiges Überleben zu organisieren, nachdem 1968 der Prager Frühling niedergeschlagen und der Optimismus der 1960er-Jahre, das Versprechen des Sozialismus mit den neuen Technologien nun echt wahr werden zu lassen, zerstört worden war. Zusammen mit seiner Ehefrau Anna Lakyová hatte Laky das gemeinsame Wohnzimmer vor der Intervention bereits komplett weiß eingerichtet, um den gemeinsamen Gesprächen darüber, wie es nach dem Desaster von 1968 weiter gehen könnte, einen Ort zu geben. Auf eine Art zeigt das: Für die Konstruktion und Destruktion der Bedeutung, Freiheit, Funktion und Geschichte von Kunst gibt es keinen dauerhaft festgelegten Platz. Weder universitäre Disziplinen noch ideologische Programme stellen diese Sicherheit und Kontinuität her. Es braucht Orte wie das Wohnzimmer Lakyová/Laky, um Wut und Widersprüchen Luft zu machen – bis hin zur Frage, ob Kunst noch irgend eine Zukunft hätte. Rückblickend betrachtet können natürlich auch derart radikal verunsichernde Episoden als kontinuierliche Entwicklung in die Kunstgeschichte eingeschrieben werden. Im Sinne der Kunstgeschichte kann man sich sicherlich darauf einigen, dass Filko am Ende doch Kunst produziert hat. Im Geist der Gespräche bei Lakyová/ Laky und ihres traumatischen Umfeldes wäre aber auch zu fragen: Wie viel der Desillusionierung und Aggression, die der Einschnitt von 1968 in die Seelen der Leute einschrieb, steckt nicht nur tief in Filkos Arbeit, sondern macht sich auf eine völlig anarchische, von ideologischen Programmen (à la

Malewitsch) nie gänzlich erfassbare Art in einer Praxis Luft, die durchweg starke Züge von Antikunst hat?

Den antikünstlerischen Zug im Rückblick neu aus Filkos Tun und Denken herauszuschälen, ist nicht einfach. Das liegt wohl auch daran, dass Filko zum Ende seines Lebens selbst der kosmisch künstlerischen Dimension seines Handelns und Denkens eine übergeordnete Stellung gab, indem er die systematische Farbcodierung seiner früheren Werkgruppen (Rot für Leib, Grün für Gesellschaft, Blau für Flug ins All, Weiß für das Nichts und entgrenzte Wahrnehmung) zu einer spirituellen Konstellation von 12 Farbchakras ausbaut und sein Atelierhaus am Stadtrand von Bratislava entsprechend ausmalt. Wirken die Farben Ende der 1960er-Jahre in ihrer Funktion als Code zur Bezeichnung von Handlungsfeldern noch, als wären sie Teil einer staatlich-militärischen Semiotik (Brigade Körper, Division Soziales, Kommando Weltraum, Abteilung Nichts), dann scheinen sie im Laufe der 1990er-Jahre eindeutig eher die integralen Aspekte eines Gesamtkunstwerks zu vergegenwärtigen. In allen Chakrafarben koloriert erhalten auch die Systementwürfe, die Filko in diesen Jahren anfertigt, indem er Begriffsgruppen auf Millimeterpapier arrangiert, in ihrer lebendigen Vielfarbigkeit geradezu den Charakter von Mandalas. Stimmt einen das milde und versöhnlich? War am Ende doch alles Kunst? Und Filko ein postsowjetischer Wagner? Der Eindruck verliert sich schnell, wenn man Filkos Atelierhaus besucht. Die Ausmalung der Räume, Bemalung zahlloser Objekte in Chakrafarben und Beschriftung von Wänden und Dingen mit Begriffen aus Filkos Wortschatz is viel zu ruppig und rustikal, um nur *freie* Kunst oder gar *Hochkultur* sein zu wollen. Es ist *angewandte* Kunst, Filko-Folk-Art. Hütten und Möbel gelten erst als bezugs- oder gebrauchsfertig, wenn sie ganz be- und ausgemalt sind. Stößt man im Innenhof auf die dort gelagerten riesigen Stahlraketen, könnte man noch behaupten: Das ist Bildhauerei, also Kunst. Die Obszönität dieser Objekte beschreibt man damit aber nicht. Sie sind zuallererst und immer noch Attrappen von Megatonnen-Bomben mit blau kodierten Markierungen.

Was ist nun mit der Nähe zwischen Bomben und Farbcodes, Raketenbau und Semiotik? Und warum würde man sie historisch mit Antikunst in Verbindung bringen? Filko ist Kind seiner Zeit. In der Zeit nach dem zweiten Weltkrieg wälzt der Siegeszug der harten Wissenschaften das Verständnis von den Bedingungen menschlichen Handelns und Sprechens radikal um. *Raketenbau* und *Semiotik* sind in dieser Hinsicht die Antikünste schlechthin. [03-04] Raketenbau (inklusive seiner Ikone Wernher von Braun) steht für das Wissen von den Möglichkeiten einer systematischen Zerstörung von allem und jedem, vom Ende alles Handelns also. Semiotik (inklusive ihrer Ikone Roman Jakobson) steht für das Wissen von den Möglichkeiten der systematischen Konstruktion jedweder Aussage, vom Anfang alles Sprechens also. Wozu noch Kunst? Als *Techne* zur Nachahmung von Natur verblasst sie vor den modernen *Technologien* zur systematischen Destruktion und Konstruktion von Welt. Mit ganzer Härte vollzieht Filko also die Abkehr von Kunst und Hinwendung zu den Wissenschaften vom Ende alles Handelns und Anfang jeden Sprechens. Er verwendet die Silhouetten von Raketen in Zeichnungen, Skulpturen und Environments. Zunächst geht von ihnen noch etwas Hoffnungsvolles aus. Vermutlich im Geist von Alexander Bogdanovs Roman *Roter Stern* von 1907, der die Verwirklichung der perfekten kommunistischen

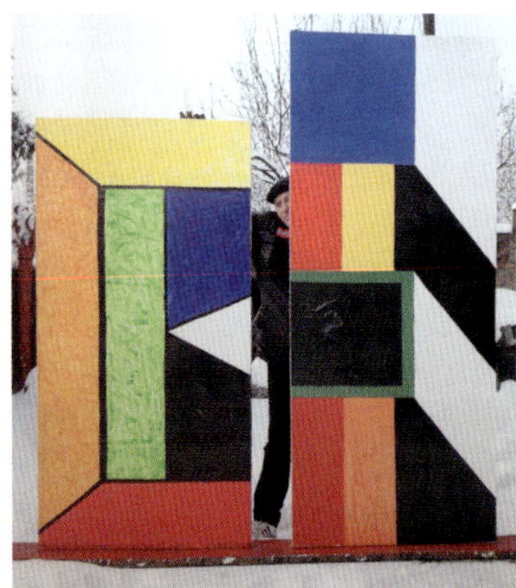

[01] *Contemplation in the Chakra Color Spectrum / Kontemplácia vo farbách čakier-spektier*, c. 1993-95

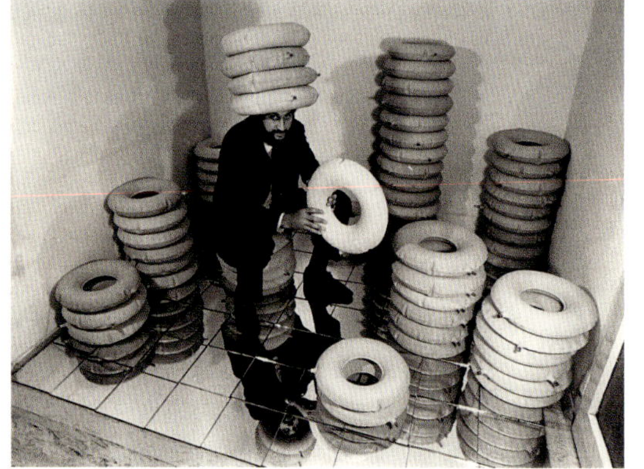

[02] *Pneumatic Circles I. - XXXX. / Pneumatické kolesá I. - XXXX.*, 1968

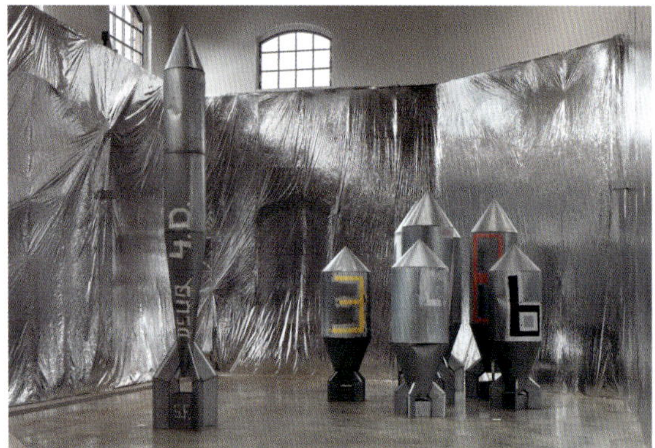

[03] *Registration of Stano Filko / Registrace Stana Filka*, 2022

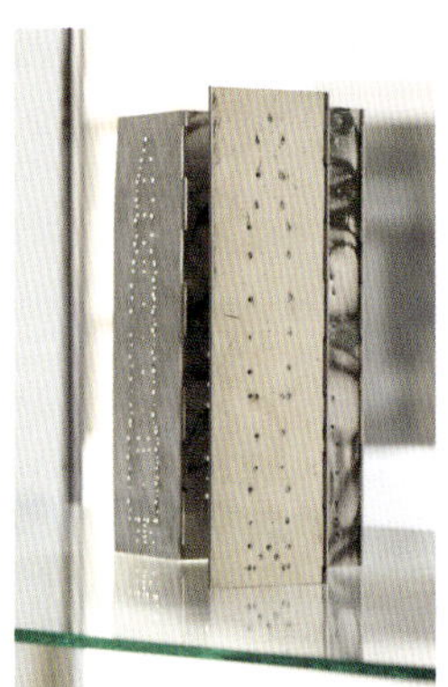

[04] *Cathedral of Rockets* (model), 1967

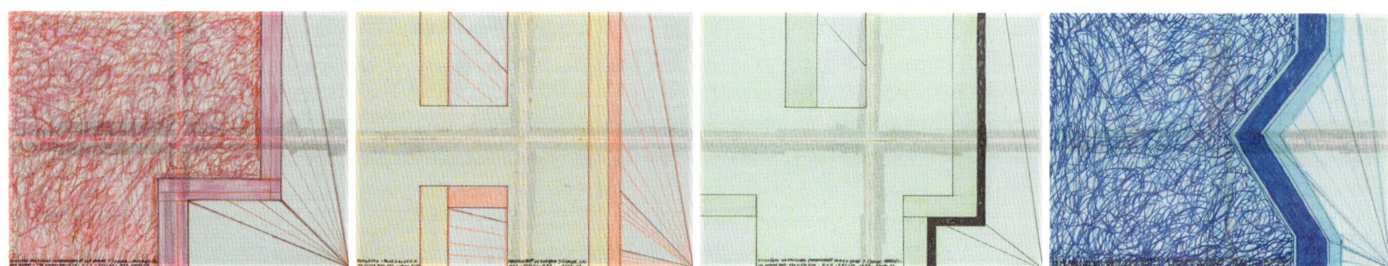

[05-08] From the series *PHYS / Zo série PHYS*, after 1995

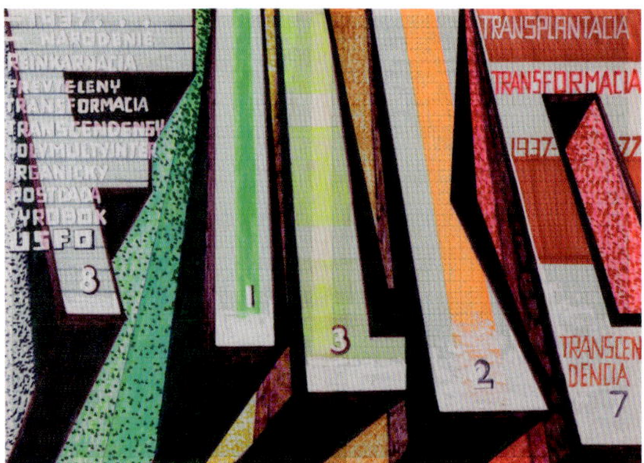

[09] From the series *Klony / Zo série Klony*, c. 2000

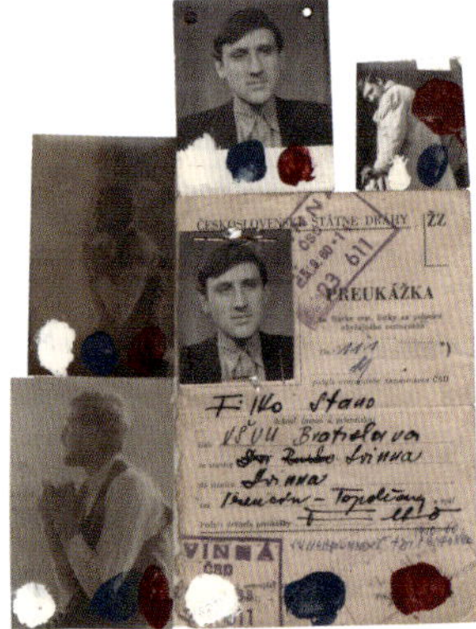

[10] *SF Railway Customer Card / SF Železničná preukážka*, 1964

Gesellschaft auf dem Mars beschreibt, wirken die Raketen um 1967 noch wie Transportmittel in eine bessere Zukunft und entstehen, unter dem Projektitel *Priestor* (Raum), Seite an Seite mit Entwürfen und Modellen für Bewässerungsanlagen. Nach der Niederschlagung des Prager Frühlings aber wächst die Ähnlichkeit der Raketen zu Marschflugkörpern und spätestens nach Filkos Flucht in die USA in den 1980er-Jahren sind die Raketen Riesenbomben aus Metall. Das sind aggressive Bekenntnisse gegen eine sympathische Kunst des Weltbauens und zu einer unsympathischen Technologie des Weltbeendens.[3]

Filkos Umgang mit Semiose hat zunächst einen klar konstruktiven Charakter. Er misst systematisch das Feld aller möglichen Bedeutungen seiner Praxis aus und findet besondere Bezeichnungen für alle Bereiche seines Tuns, Denkens und Lebens. Zu diesem Zweck verfasst er einerseits Dokumente, die überblicksartig sein gesamtes Bezeichnungs-System vor Augen führen. Nicht selten benutzt er für diese Systementwürfe dasselbe Millimeterpapier wie für Konstruktionszeichnungen. Andererseits bezeichnet, beschreibt und bemalt er seine Arbeiten tatsächlich. Er kritzelt, schreibt und malt Bezeichnungen aus seinem System auf die Artefakte, schnell und ruppig, wie Graffiti. Von der Energie und Haltung her ist das spürbar Antikunst: Das Beschriften hat ikonoklastische Züge. Filko nimmt den Kunstobjekten ihren eigenständigen Wert (als autonome Werke) und erniedrigt sie zu Zeichenträgern in seinem Zeichensystem. Alle Dinge werden der Logik einer totalen Ordnung unterworfen, als deren Chefingenieur er selbst auftritt.

Studiert man die Systementwürfe auf Millimeterpapier, stellt man aber fest, dass Filko die Unterwerfung der Welt unter seine Semiotik mit der eigenen Biografie beginnt. [05-09] Alle Teile seines Werdegangs sind begrifflich erfasst, unterschieden und systematisiert. Die Beschreibung des eigenen Lebens ist das erste Beispiel für die Unterwerfung von allem und jedem unter die Herrschaft der Zeichen. Da Filkos Name nun über allem und überall auf den System-Entwurfs-Papieren steht und er – wie zum Beispiel in *Ego Diachron Synchron* (ca. 1990–1999) – dem Text zuweilen ein Passfoto hinzufügt und das Textblatt rahmt, erhalten solche Blätter durchaus den Charakter von *Urkunden*: von Diplomen etwa, die Leute in ihre Praxis oder ihr Büro hängen, um zu zeigen, dass sie die Lizenz zur Ausübung ihres Berufs besitzen. [10] Antikunst geht bei Filko also soweit, dass er sich (nicht als schöpferischer Mensch, sondern) als semiotischer Apparatchik – diplomierter Meister von Raketen und Zeichen – portraitiert. Sichtlich treibt ihn dabei eine gewisse Lust an unsympathischer Überzeichnung. Seine Totalsemiotik entspringt in dieser Hinsicht wohl also einem ähnlichen Geist wie das groteske Spiel mit den Insignien totalitärer Macht, das später Laibach und NSK in ihrer Selbstinszenierung betreiben werden.

Insofern Filko Raketenbau und Zeichentheorie als Wissenschaften des totalen Staats (von den absoluten Enden des Handelns und Anfängen des Sprechens) ausweist, kehrt er die Aggressivität dieser Disziplinen hervor. Woraus speist sich dieses Aggressionspotenzial und gegen wen oder was richtet sich seine Kraft? Wie Boris Groys in *Gesamtkunstwerk Stalin*[4] schreibt, war die Brutalität riesig, mit der die Sowjetunion Schwerindustrie als Motor der Zukunftsgesellschaft einführte. Von traditionell stark durch Landwirtschaft geprägten Kulturen wie der Slowakei musste die abrupte

Zwangsmodernisierung einen extrem gewaltsamen Eingriff darstellen. [11] Filko lädt Teile seiner Arbeit mit dem Potenzial dieser Gewalt auf, indem er sie nachahmt und sich so anverwandelt, dass er selbst, als Zeicheningenieur und Bombenburschi, die Gewalt gegen das alte Land symbolisch ausübt. Er tut dies allerdings meist auf derart grotesk überspitzte Weise, die offen lässt, ob er die Brutalität der Modernität feiert oder verhöhnt. Schlüsselarbeiten in dieser Hinsicht sind wahrscheinlich die Dioramen *Models of Observation Towers / Modely pozorovacích veží* (1966/1967) [12]. Sie bestehen je aus drei Komponenten: einem schwarz-weißen Panoramafoto des Bratislaver Stadtteils Petržalka, der im Zuge der Radikalmodernisierung zu einer Planstadt aus Stahlbeton ausgebaut wurde. Den Boden vor den Fotos bedeckt eine Fläche von Spiegelfliesen. Sie eröffnen einen virtuellen Raum, alles ist doppelt: das Foto, aber auch die drei Skulpturen, die vor dem Foto auf den Fliesen stehen. Sie sind aus Altmetallteilen – Zahnrädern, Kurbelwellen und Motorrad-Tanks – zusammengeschweißt und je einfarbig silber, orange und blau bemalt. Laut Titel sind sie Architektur. Sie könnten auch Raumfähren sein. So oder so sind sie ganz und gar Motor und versprechen die totale Modernität. Gemacht sind sie aus Schrott. Auf Spiegelfliesen platziert, schweben sie im luftleeren Raum ihrer eigenen Reflektionen.

In die Lust an Science Fiction mischt sich das Bewusstsein um den Charakter totaler Macht. Planstadtgebäude sind wie Spielzeuge des von Moskau gelenkten Superstaats. Dessen Macht kehrt sich ein Jahr später in der Niederschlagung des Prager Frühlings gegen die Menschen. Filko bezeugt diesen Moment unter anderem in einer Serie von unbetitelten, undatierten Arbeiten, in denen er, auf Fotos von russischen Panzern in Prag 1968, diese Panzer rosa aus- und übermalt [13]. Filko identifiziert die Waffen der Diktatur als Breschnews Spielzeuge, vielleicht sogar als Werkzeuge zur Neuauflage von Stalins Auslegung totaler Staatsgewalt als Ausübung einer totalen Kunst. Boris Groys hat in *Gesamtkunstwerk Stalin*[5] aufgeschlüsselt, wie der avantgardistische Wille zur ebenso aggressiven Abkehr vom Alten wie radikalen Schaffung des Neuen, kunstnahe Revolutionäre wie Trotzki in dem Vorhaben der vollständigen Umwälzung der Verhältnisse (der zaristischen Feudal- und Agrargesellschaft) bestärkten, die Stalin dann mit eiserner Hand (und den Mitteln industrieller Produktion und Zerstörung) erzwang. Wenn das so stimmt, wäre es auch wahr, dass Panzer als Mittel der Zurschaustellung staatsmilitärindustrieller Tötungsmacht Medien einer Staatskunst sind, mittels derer Moskau dem Tod der Freiheit ein Monument setzt. Indem er die Panzer rosa ausmalt, demonstriert Filko sarkastisch: wenn Breschnews Panzer pinkes Spielgut brutaler Staatskunst sind, haben Kunst und Pink jede Unschuld verloren. Ein Grund mehr im Widerspruch dazu Antikunst zu betreiben und (statt Protestsongs zu komponieren) die eigene Reaktion auf die betont unkünstlerische Handlung des stumpfen Ausweißelns (Auspinkens) genau der Machtmittel zu reduzieren, die freies Handeln und Sprechen ohnehin von Grund auf unmöglich machen.

Mit dieser Erfahrung im Hintergrund ist das antikünstlerische Aggressionspotenzial in Filkos Tun und Denken deutlich unverhohlener und unversöhnlicher als das in der Arbeit vieler seiner Kolleg*innen aus dem damaligen Westen. [14] Was nicht heißt, dass Antikunst dort im Ansatz nicht genauso relevant gewesen wäre. Zeichen und Raketen

in the 1980s the rockets have become giant metal bombs. These are aggressive statements against a sympathetic art of world-building and for an unsympathetic technology of world-ending.[3]

Filko's approach to semiosis initially has a clearly constructive character. He systematically takes stock of the field of all possible meanings of his practice and finds particular terms for all the areas of his action, thought, and life. For this purpose he on the one hand writes documents that give overviews of his entire system of relationships, and often he uses the same graph paper for these system designs as he does for his construction drawings. On the other hand, he also literally names, describes, and paints his work. He scribbles, writes, and paints terms from his system on the artifacts, quickly and roughly, like graffiti. In terms of the energy and attitude, this is tangible anti-art—the labeling has iconoclastic features. Filko deprives the art objects of their independent value (as autonomous works) and scales them down as the bearers of signs from his own sign system. All objects are subjected to the logic of a total order, as whose engineer-in-chief he presents himself.

Studying the system designs on graph paper shows that Filko begins his subjecting of the world to his own semiotics with his own biography. [05–09] All the elements in his own development are denoted by terms, distinguished from each other, and systemized. The description of his own life is the first example of subjecting everything and everyone to the rule of signs. As Filko's name now stands above everything and everywhere on his system design papers, and he, as for example in *Ego Diachron Synchron* (c. 1990–99), sometimes adds a passport photograph to the text and frames the piece of paper, these papers look very much like *certificates*, of diplomas for example, such as people hang up in their practices or offices in order to show that they have a license to carry out their professions. [10] For Filko, anti-art thus goes so far that he depicts himself as a semiotic apparatchik, a diploma-bearing master of rockets and signs (and not a creative individual). He is visibly motivated by a certain pleasure in unsympathetic exaggeration. In this sense, his total semiotics convey a spirit similar to the grotesque game with the insignia of totalitarian power that Laibach and NSK would later play in their own self-enactments.

Insofar as Filko identifies rocket-building and sign theory as sciences of the total state (of the absolute end of action and the beginnings of language), he emphasizes the aggressivity of these disciplines. What does this potential for aggression feed upon, and against whom or what is its force directed? As Boris Groys writes in *The Total Art of Stalinism*,[4] the brutality with which the Soviet Union intended heavy industry to be the engine of a future society was truly massive. For cultures that were traditionally strongly shaped by farming, such as Slovakia, this abrupt and forced modernization must have produced an extremely violent incision. [11] Filko charges elements of his work with the potential of this violence, by imitating it and appropriating it in such a way that he himself, as an engineer of signs and rocket boy, symbolically uses this violence against the old country. But he mostly does this in a so very exaggerated and grotesque manner that it is provocatively rendered unclear whether he is celebrating or mocking this brutality of modernity. Key works here are probably the dioramas

Models of Observation Towers / Modely pozorovacích veží (1966/67) [12]. They consist of three components: a black-and-white panorama photograph of the Bratislava suburb Petržalka, which was expanded in the course of radical modernization into a planned town of reinforced concrete. The floor in front of the photos is covered in mirror tiling that opens up a virtual space. Everything is double—the photo and also the three sculptures that are placed on the tiles in front of the photo. They are made of scrap metal, with cogs, crankshafts, and motorcycle fuel tanks, welded together and painted in monotone silver, orange, and blue. The title states that they are entirely engines and promise total modernity. But they are made of trash. Placed on mirrors, they stand suspended in the airless space of their own reflections.

The pleasure taken in science fiction is amalgamated with an awareness of the character of total power. Buildings for a satellite city are like the toys of a Moscow-controlled super state. And a year later, the power of the latter turns against the people in putting down the Prague Spring. One of the ways in which Filko bears witness to this moment is a series of untitled and undated works in which he paints in and overpaints tanks in pink depicted on photographs of Russian tanks in Prague in 1968 [13]. Filko identifies the weapons of the dictatorship as Brezhnev's playthings, perhaps even as the tools to revive Stalin's version of total state violence as the practice of total art. In *The Total Art of Stalinism*,[5] Boris Groys showed how the self-fashioning of avant-gardist as radical destroyers of the old and creators of the new provided a character template to embolden revolutionaries with an affinity for art, like Trotsky, in their aim to utterly transform social conditions (the Tsarist feudal and agricultural society), which Stalin then forced with an iron hand (and the means of industrial production and destruction). If this was the case, then it would also be true that tanks as a means of the illustration of a state-military-industrial power to kill are the media of an art of the state that Moscow used to erect a monument to the death of freedom. By painting the tanks pink, Filko sarcastically demonstrates that if Brezhnev's tanks are the pink playthings of brutal state art, then art and pink have lost all innocence. This is one further reason to engage in anti-art, as a counterpoint, and (instead of composing protest songs) reducing your own reaction to the markedly unartistic act of a simple whitening (pinking out) of precisely those tools of power that have anyway made free action and speech fundamentally impossible.

In the light of this experience, the anti-artistic potential for aggression in Filko's actions and thinking is significantly less covert and less conciliatory then in the work of many of his colleagues from the West at the time. [14] This does not mean that the approach of anti-art was not equally relevant there. Signs and rockets determined the reality on both sides of the Iron Curtain. It was no coincidence that the 1970 MoMA group exhibition that contributed to the genre-making of US-American conceptualism was entitled *Information*. In programmatically provocative and unsubtle fashion, the artists represented here used means of communication and new information technologies—machine-written text, news tickers, press photography—instead of the classical artistic media like painting or sculpture. Benjamin Buchloh correctly described this turn as the imitation of the

bestimmten immerhin die Wirklichkeit auf beiden Seiten des Eisernen Vorhangs. Die für den US-amerikanischen Konzeptualismus genrebildende Gruppenausstellung *Information* am MoMA trug 1970 nicht umsonst ihren Titel. So programmatisch provokativ wie plakativ setzten die Künstler*innen hier Kommunikationsmittel neuer Informationstechnologien – maschinengeschriebenen Text, Nachrichtenticker, Pressefotografie – statt klassischer künstlerischer Medien wie Malerei oder Bildhauerei ein. Benjamin Buchloh beschrieb diese Wendung korrekt als Nachahmung der Ästhetik des bürokratischen Apparats[6], übersah aber die dieser Anverwandlung innewohnende Provokation: Die USA glich der UdSSR wohl darin fast völlig, dass sie Herrschaft während der Anfänge des kalten Krieges noch zentral und disziplinarisch organisierte, nach dem Vorbild von Militär und Industrie, aber eben mit den Mitteln der Verwaltung (das heißt imperialer Bürokratie). Man könnte also durchaus sagen, dass der Konzeptualismus im damaligen Westen dem bürokratischen Apparat des Staats ein Spiegelbild der Semiotik seiner Macht vorhielt, indem er Museumswände mit Schreibmaschinentexten und Nachrichtenfotografie voll hing. Der Affront wird sich im selben Zug gegen die wohlhabenden Schichten gerichtet haben, die in New York Kunst finanzieren und konsumieren, deren Machtstellung durch den bürokratisch-militärisch-industriellen Apparat gesichert wird, die in einem Museum aber durch Kunst von der kruden Wirklichkeit dieses Apparats erlöst werden wollen und die man also vor den Kopf stößt, indem man ihnen diese Erlösung verwehrt und statt Kunst eine Antikunst vorhält, die die Macht des Verwaltungsapparats kopiert.

Die Brutalität der Verhältnisse mit Mitteln provokativer Antikunst nachzuempfinden wird deshalb im ehemaligen Westen wie im ehemaligen Osten ein vergleichbarer Beweggrund zur Arbeit mit der Semiotik der Macht gewesen sein. Da der heutige Westen die Ähnlichkeit zwischen USA und UdSSR, was die Schlüsselrolle imperialer Bürokratie zur Organisation des Herrschaftsapparats betrifft, bis heute leugnet, bleibt die perverse Anverwandlung von entfremdenden Machtmitteln durch Antikunst ein Moment, das in Bezug auf Künstler*innen aus dem ehemaligen Osten, wie Filko, (als „kafkaesk") diskutiert wird, aber nicht in Bezug auf die des West-Konzeptualismus. Deren Arbeit wurde schnell wieder regulär als Kunst gehandelt und als neuster Zugang zum Stammbaum moderner Ismen gedeutet.

Die widerspruchslose Eingemeindung der antikünstlerischen Kräfte des Konzeptualismus in die Kunst hat besonders in der universitären Kunstausbildung fatale Folgen. Wer Kunststudierenden Konzeptualismus nicht als Antikunst sondern Kunst vermittelt, drückt ihnen eine geladene Waffe in die Hand, ohne zu erwähnen, dass diese Waffe *gegen* ihre künstlerische Praxis als künstlerische Praxis gerichtet ist. Das ist gerade dann der Fall, wenn konzeptuelle Antikunst, durchaus aus strategisch gerechtfertigten Gründen, die Semiotik der Universität als bürokratischer Machtapparat (der industriell Formulare, Dissertationen, BFAs, MFAs, PPPs und PhDs produziert) nachahmt. Es macht einen riesigen Unterschied, ob man das Gewaltpotenzial, das in der antikünstlerischen Anverwandlung von Machtsemiotik liegt, noch als solches wahrnimmt – und sich die von Machtapparaten im täglichen Leben erzeugte Entfremdung bewusst aneignet, um sie als Verfremdungseffekt und Zuspitzungsmoment einzusetzen – oder man es für ausgemacht hält, dass sich

Kunst beim Kontakt mit dem Apparat aggressiv entfremdend verzerrt und diesen Weg als institutionell vorgezeichneten wahrnimmt und geht.

Nehmen wir ein plakatives Beispiel. Joseph Kosuths Installation *One and Three Chairs* (1965) und sein Traktat *Art after Philosophy* (1969) gilt allen Ernstes bis jetzt als einschlägiges Beispiel dafür, wie Konzeptkunst einem Werk den Status eines diskursiven Arguments geben und dieses dann durch Nachlegen eines Textes theoretisch begründen kann. Dabei kommt der antikünstlerische Charakter von Arbeit und Text nicht zur Sprache. Die Installation besteht aus einem einfachen Stuhl, der zwischen einem lebensgroßen Foto seiner selbst und einer, auf dieselbe Größe vergrößerten Kopie des Wörterbuch-Eintrags „Stuhl" ausgestellt wird. Der Text ist eine bis an die Grenzen der Unlesbarkeit akademisch entstellte (inhaltlich haltlose aber rhetorisch einschüchternde) Abhandlung über Analytik nach Kant. Effektiv handelt es sich also um die stumpfe Vorführung der Macht von semiotischen Apparaten, Unterschiede einzuebnen: den Unterschied zwischen Ding, Definition und Abbildung zum einen, den zwischen Sinn und Unsinn zum anderen. Als antikünstlerische Groteske hätte das seinen Zweck. Als Vorbild für intellektuelle Kunst dagegen liefert es eine Folie für das Machtgebaren von Uni-Apparatschiks oder die unfreiwillige Komik von gestreamlinten PowerPoint-Präsentationen, die praktisch nur noch die abgrundtiefe Gleichgültigkeit von Gegenstand, Wort und Bild in universitären Deutungsroutinen vorführen. Das passiert, wenn Antikunst – aus jedem Zusammenhang gerissen, indem ihr Antagonismus noch als solcher wahrnehmbar gewesen wäre – zum Industriestandard für Institutionskunst erklärt wird. [15-16]

Wieder sichtbar werden Antagonismus und Provokationslust von Antikunst vielleicht eher durch ihre Nähe zu Antimusik, zum Beispiel zu Punk. Auf einem inszenierten Porträtfoto, das Filko nach seiner Flucht aus der Tschechoslowakei in die USA im Jahr 1982 zeigt, übersetzt er sein Image des Ingenieurs von Zeichen und Raketen so in die Stilistik des New Yorker Punk der Zeit. Im durchlöcherten schwarzen T-Shirt präsentiert er sich mit gewinnendem Gaunerblick. Er trägt dabei eine Fliegerbombe (vermutlich eine seiner Skulpturen, aber wer weiß) so leger auf der Schulter wie ein Matrose den Seesack. Nachträglich schreibt er in den Farben der slowakischen Nationalfahne, Rot, Weiß und Blau, dreimal das Wort „Bomba" so auf das Foto, dass es aussieht, als trage der Sprengkörper selbst diese Beschriftung. [17] Diese Selbstdarstellung als slowakischer Bombenburschi spricht in vieler Hinsicht eine ähnliche Sprache wie die der Ramones. Mit dem Titel ihres 1977 erschienen Albums *Rocket to Russia* hatte die Band ihrerseits die Kraft ihres Punksounds (Songs so kompakt abgefeuert wie Projektile) mit der Raketentechnik des kalten Kriegs auf einen Nenner gebracht. Die Liebesbekundung zur Bombe beinhaltet für die Ramones wie für Filko potenziell das Bekenntnis zum antikünstlerischen Moment totaler Entwertung: So wie Bomben faktisch alles *platt* machen, *nivellieren* die Ramones durch hartes, schnelles, gezielt emotionslos maschinelles, stumpf gleichförmiges Spielen die Motive (aus der Rock'n'Roll Tradition der USA), aus denen sie ihre Songs zusammenhauen. Antikunst und Antimusik treffen sich hier, unter dem Stern des kalten Kriegs, im Zeichen der provokativen Bejahung einer Nivellierung aller Werte, im Angesicht der allzeit möglichen industriellen Zerstörung der Welt. [18]

aesthetics of the bureaucratic apparatus,[6] but he ostracized this development as an unwitting cooption of art by the apparatus rather than recognizing its mimicry as a deliberate (anti-)artistic provocation. Arguably, the USA almost completely resembled the USSR during the early years of the Cold War, in that the disciplinary organization of power was centralized around the military-industrial complex and bolstered by administration (i.e. imperial bureaucracy). One can thus conceivably say that also artists of the West were holding a semiotic mirror up to the apparatus of state power when they filled museum walls with typewritten documents and forms. Apart from this, this affront no doubt was equally aimed at the wealthy elites that financed and consumed art in New York, and whose positions of power were secured by the bureaucratic-military-industrial apparatus, and who wished to be redeemed via art in a museum from the crude reality of this apparatus. Instead they were shown a cold shoulder, as this redemption was refused and they were presented not with art but with anti-art that copied the power of the administrative apparatus.

Imitating the brutality of real conditions with the means of provocative anti-art will thus have been a comparable motivation for working with the semiotics of power in both the former West and the former East. Unfortunately, the West today still denies any similarity between the USA and the USSR. The key role of imperial bureaucracy to organize the apparatus of power on either side of the iron curtain is rarely recognized. Therefore the perverse appropriation of alienating means of bureaucratic power in anti-art remains something that is discussed when referring to art from the former East (as "Kafkaesque"), and less so in relation to art from the former West, including conceptualism. The latter was rapidly traded in the usual ways as art, and validated as the newest addition to the family tree of modernist isms.

This contradictive incorporation into art of the anti-art forces in conceptualism has fatal consequences in particular in the teaching of art at universities. If you teach conceptualism as art rather than anti-art, then you are handing a loaded gun to your students, without mentioning that this gun is pointed *against* their artistic practice as artistic practice. This is especially then the case when conceptual anti-art, certainly for strategically justified reasons, imitates the semiotics of the university as a bureaucratic apparatus of power (which industrially produces forms, dissertations, BFAs, MFAs, PPPs, and PhDs). It makes an enormous difference whether you still perceive the potential for violence that lies in the anti-artistic appropriation of power semiotics as such—and deliberately appropriate the everyday alienation that the power apparatuses create in order to deploy it as a defamiliarization effect and moment of pointed emphasis, or whether you consider it a done deal that art becomes aggressively alienated and distorted when it comes into contact with the apparatus, and then perceive this as an institutionally prescribed path that is to be taken.

Let's take a striking example. Joseph Kosuth's installation *One and Three Chairs* (1965) and his treatise *Art after Philosophy* (1969) have in all seriousness been seen to this day as a telling example of how conceptual art can bestow the status of a discursive argument onto an artwork, and then can theoretically underpin this by providing an accompanying piece of writing. The anti-artistic character of such work

and writing, however, is at no point taken into consideration. *One and Three Chairs*, for instance, consists of a simple chair placed between a life-size photograph of itself and a copy of a dictionary entry on the word "chair" enlarged to the same size. *Art after Philosophy* in turn is a barely readable academically distorted treatment of analytics after Kant (the contents are groundless but the rhetoric is intimidating). In effect, this is thus a blunt demonstration of the power of semiotic apparatuses to level out differences—the difference between thing, definition, and depiction on the one hand, and between sense and nonsense on the other. As a grotesque piece of anti-art this would all have a purpose, but as a role model for intellectual art it offers us a foil for the power games of university apparatchiks or the involuntary humor of streamlined PowerPoint presentations that practically do no more than illustrate the deep and disturbing indifference of object, word, and image in the interpretative regimes of the universities. This all happens when anti-art, taken out of all context in which its antagonism might still be seen as such, is declared to be the industrial standard for institutional art. [15-16]

The antagonism and provocative drive of anti-art perhaps better become visible in its proximity to anti-music, such as punk. On a staged portrait photograph that shows Filko after his flight from Czechoslovakia to the USA in 1982, he transfers his image as the engineer of signs and rockets into the stylistic idioms of the New York punk of the time. In a black T-shirt with holes he presents himself with the endearing look of a rascal. He has an aerial bomb (probably one of his own sculptures, but who knows) so nonchalantly on his shoulder like a sailor might carry his kit bag. He added the word "bomba" to this photograph in the colors of the Slovak national flag, red, white, and blue, so that it looked like the bomb itself was labelled in this way. [17] This self-enactment as a Slovak rocket boy in many ways speaks the same language as the Ramones. With the title of their 1977 album *Rocket to Russia* the band had already pointedly equated the force of their punk sound (songs fired out as compactly as projectiles) with the rocket technology of the Cold War. This declaration of love for the bomb by Filko and the Ramones voices the appetite for annihilation at the heart of anti-art provocations. Just as modern bombing indiscriminately razes cities to the ground, the hard, fast, and deliberately emotionless bluntly monotone music of the Ramones mechanically flattens out all motifs (from the rock'n'roll tradition of the USA) with which they bash all their songs together. Anti-art and anti-music here converge, under the star of the Cold War, in the sign of the provocative embrace of a leveling of all values, in the face of the industrial destruction of the world that is possible any time. [18]

Even though after his return to Slovakia in the 1990s, Filko again turned to the cosmic sympathetic artistic construction of worlds in the sign of a popular art to his own taste, punk still remains present. [19] Filko's worlds will never be completely safe worlds and they retain raw elements. The birth of artistic worlds takes place from the spirit of a proximity to anti-artistic destructive power. [20] On the one hand Filko now invokes the Venus of Moravany as the cosmic source of the power of indigenous primeval artistic creation magic, and casts himself in the role of her medium. On the other hand he gives his invocations of the power of Venus the

    Signs and Rockets

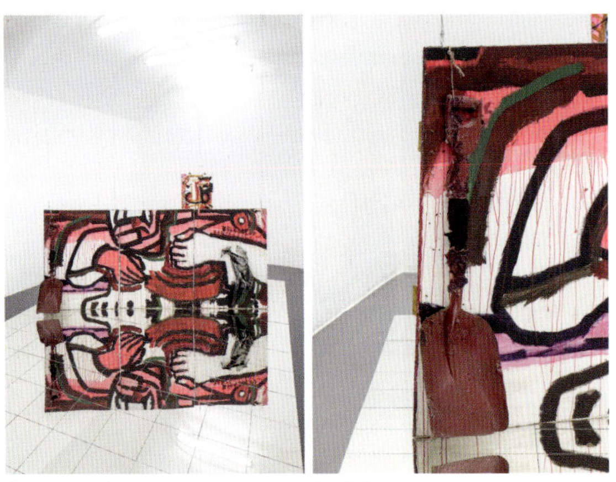

[11A-B] *Boy Angel*, 1983

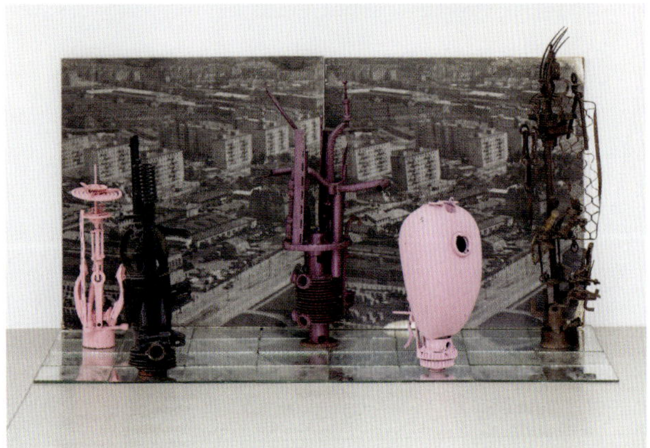

[12] *Models of Observation Towers / Modely pozorovacích veží*, 1966–67

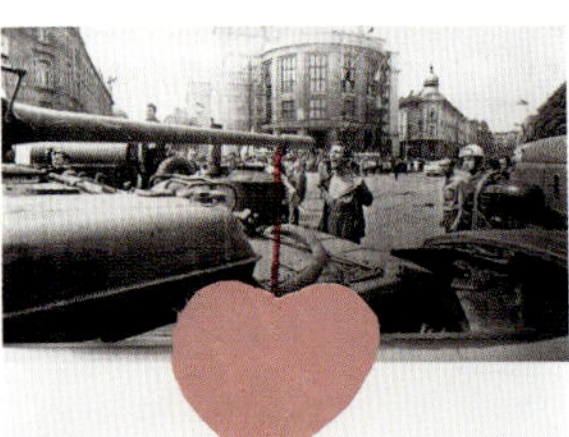

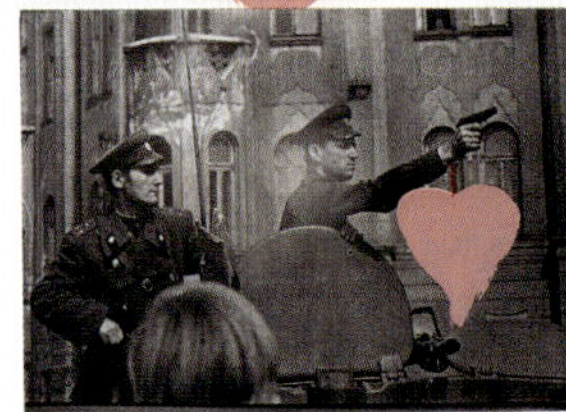

[13] *Occupation of the Czechoslovak Socialist Republic – Pink Heart / Okupácia ČSSR – Ružové srdce*, 1968/1978

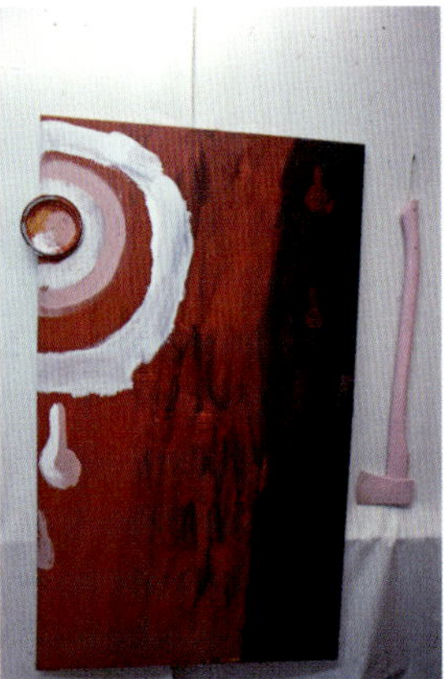

[14] *Mobile Germ*, 1987

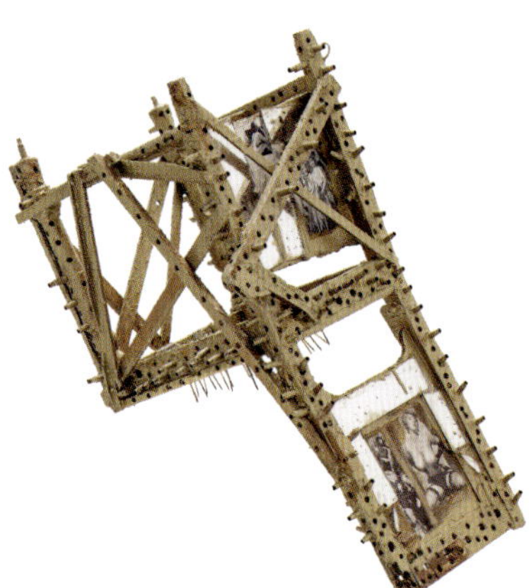

[15] *From the series Altars of Contemporaneity (Chair) / Zo série Oltáre súčasnosti (Stolička)*, 1965

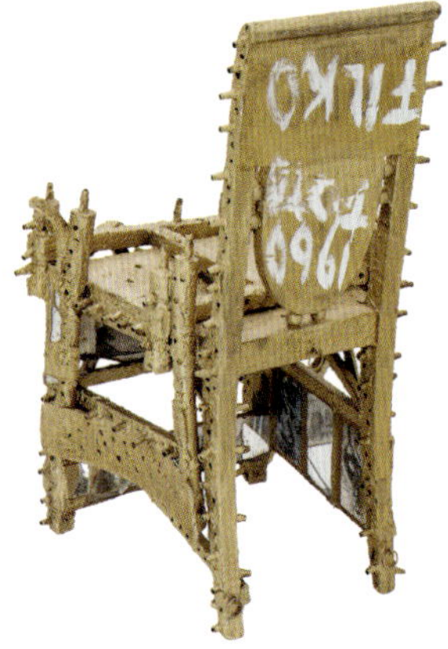

[16] *From the series Altars of Contemporaneity (Chair) / Zo série Oltáre súčasnosti (Stolička)*, 1965

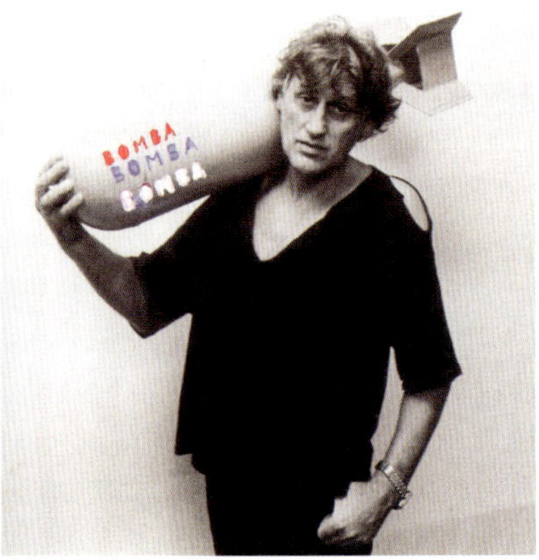

[17] *White Bomb in Action. N.Y.C. / Biela Bomba v akcii. N.Y.C.*, 1989

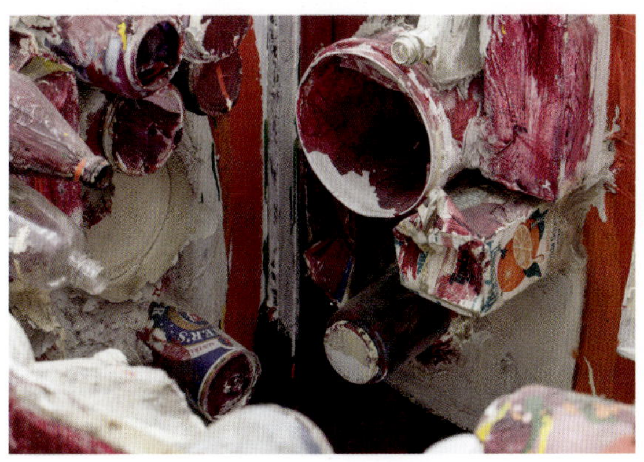

[18] *AIDS (Barbecue)*, 1983

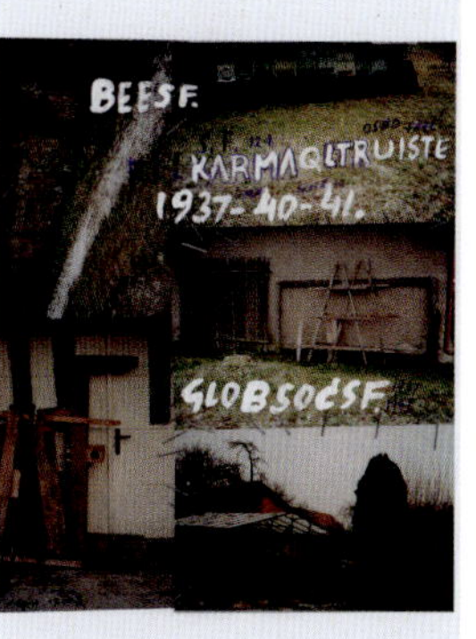

[19] *OLD + NEW TESTAMENT / Dwelling 1966 of Contemporaneity - Reality / OLD + NEW TESTAMENT / Obydlie 1966 súčasnosti - skutočnosti, 1985-95*

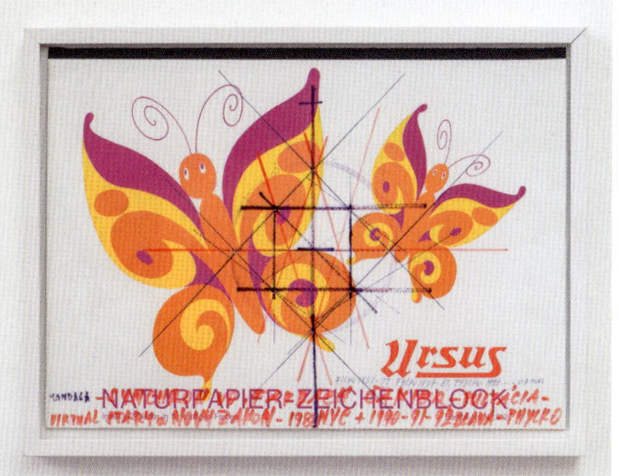

[20] *Virtual Old and New Testament*, 1992

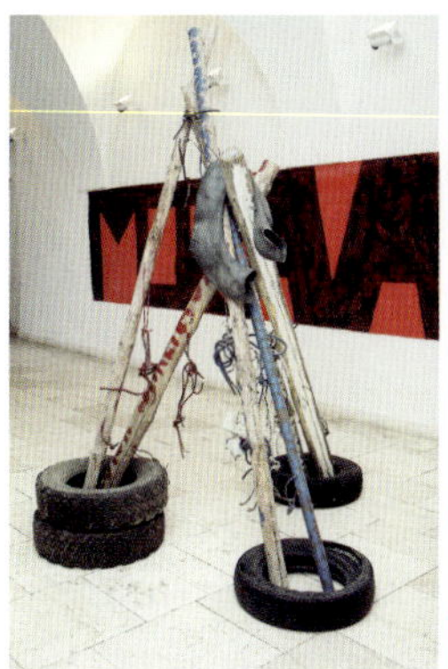

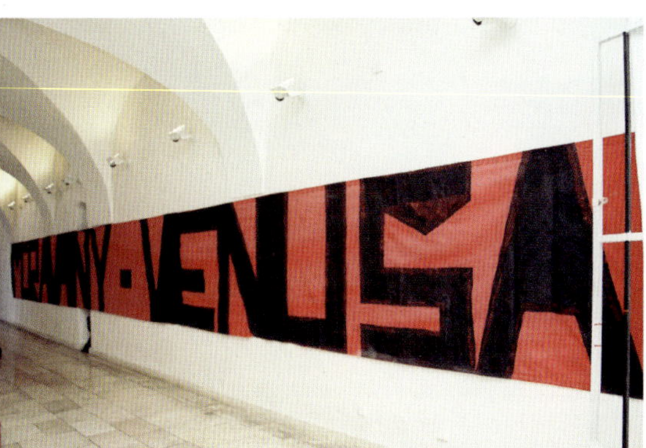

[21-22] *Stano Filko, FIYLKONTEMPLACIAKCIEQ, State Gallery (today's Central Slovakian Gallery), Banská Bystrica*, 2003

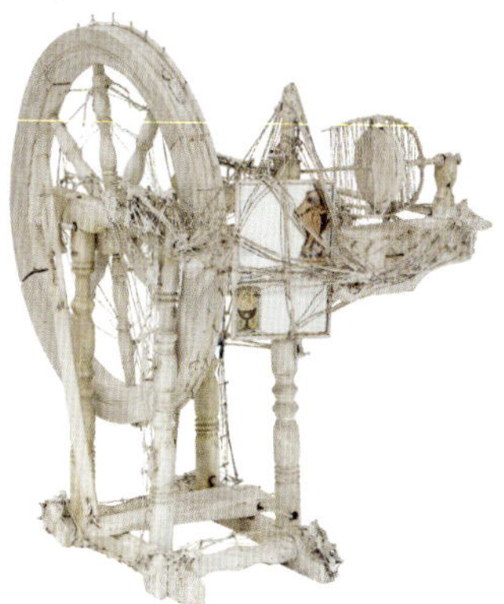

[23] *Mobile III. / Mobil III.*, 1964

Auch wenn sich Filko nach seiner Rückkehr in die Slowakei in den 1990er-Jahren erneut dem kosmisch sympathischen, künstlerischen Aufbau von Welten im Zeichen einer Volkskunst nach seinem Geschmack zuwendet, bleibt der Punk präsent. [19] Filkos Welten werden nie *heile* Welten sein. Etwas Rohes wohnt ihnen weiterhin inne. Die Geburt künstlerischer Welten geschieht aus dem Geist einer Nähe zu antikünstlerischer Zerstörungskraft. [20] Zum einen bezieht er sich nun auf die Venus von Moravany als kosmische Kraftquelle indigen urkünstlerischer Gestaltungsmagie, als deren Medium er sich begreift. Zum anderen gibt er seinen Anrufungen der Venuskraft die Form von Skulpturen, die grob aus Überbleibseln bäuerlicher Arbeit collagiert sind: Zaunpfähle, eine Stahlstange und alte Reifen taut er mit dicken Drähten zu einer trotzig aufragenden Pyramide zusammen und deklariert sie durch Beschriftung mit Graffiti zum Venusheiligtum. Auf einem, hinter der Arbeit an der Wand aufgespannten, geradezu endlos breiten roten Banner, sind mit riesigen schwarzen Blockbuchstaben die Worte MORAVANY – VENUSA gepinselt. [21-22] Auch seine Hommage an die Magie vorindustrieller Handwerklichkeit fällt punkig (übersetzt ruppig, dreckig) aus: Er zurrt mit Seilen alte Nähmaschinen mit Schwungrädern zu Assemblagen zusammen. Es wirkt so, als hätten Riesenspinnen die Relikte einer verlorenen Zeit aus dem hintersten Winkel einer Scheune in einen kompakten Kokon eingesponnen. Im Volksmund heißen die Spinnräder *Babka* [23], Großmutter. Filko feiert die Wiedergeburt der Omawelt vom Land als kosmische Venuskunst. Insofern er als Material dazu kaputtes Zeug vom Hof verwendet, erklärt er aber restaurativer Nostalgie (die das Alte als Heile verklärt) genauso wie technologischer Zukunftsgläubigkeit (die wahren Powertools hatte Oma) eine Absage. Der Kunstsammler und Weggefährte Roman Zubaľ erwähnte ihm Gespräch, dass Filko während seines Studiums an der Kunstakademie Bratislava regelmäßig wegen seiner ländlichen Herkunft verspottet wurde. Nicht zuletzt vor diesem Hintergrund haben seine Bekenntnisse zur Urkunst im Zeichen von Venuszaunpfählen und Omaspinnrädern weiterhin den aggressiven Charakter einer Absage an das, was snobistische Städter so für Kunst halten mögen.

Die intime Nähe von Negation und Wiedergeburt unterstreicht schließlich die Legende zweier klinischer Tode, die Filko als Leitmotiv in seine Systementwürfe aufnimmt.[7] Nach eigenen Aussagen ist er zu Lebzeiten zweimal zu Tode gekommen und wieder geboren worden: Zum ersten Mal 1945, als er mit acht Jahren beim Viehhüten mit dem Kopf auf einen Stein fiel und zum zweiten Mal 1952, als er bei der Fabrikarbeit einen Stromschlag von einer Starkstromleitung bekam. Der erste Tod machte ihn, schreibt er, postmodern, der zweite postavantgardistisch. Darüber hinaus wirkt bezeichnend, dass der erste ein Tod in bäuerlicher, der zweite einer in industrieller Umgebung, einem Metallwerk, ist. Wenn man der Todeskraft des Industriellen neben der totaler Wissenschaften von Zeichen und Raketen hier also Metall und Starkstrom zuordnen kann, bleibt das Ländliche kein Ort der Unschuld und Heilung. Seit jeher kostet Landarbeit Unzählige das Leben. Beide Tode sind fast beifällig und auf banale Art brutal beziehungsweise brutale Art banal. Sie sind Signaturen der traditionell feudalen und modern industriellen Ordnung. Vor und nach dem Einschnitt der Industrialisierung bringt nichtsdestotrotz Arbeit potenziell den Tod.

Und die Neugeburt. [24-27] Was zerstört und was gebiert, Antikunst und Kunst sind Seiten derselben Münze. Das war seit Nietzsche klar. Was Filko dem Entscheidendes hinzufügt, sind die Welten, die er über sein Leben hinweg in seine Antikunstkunst aufsaugt und aus ihr auswirft: die aggressive Welt der Semiotik und Raketen neben der nicht minder rauhen Welt der Urvenusheiligtümer und Omaspinnräder.

1 Boris Groys, *Gesamtkunstwerk Stalin: Die gespaltene Kultur in der Sowjetunion*, München 1988.

2 Daniel Grúň, „Notes of a Belated Viewer. Revisiting White Space in White Space", in: *White Space in White Space. Biely priestor v bielom priestore, 1973–1982. Stano Filko, Miloš Laky, Ján Zavarský*, hrsg. von Daniel Grúň, Christian Höller und Kathrin Rhomberg für Kontakt Collection, Wien 2021.

3 Modernes Denken ist unsympathisch, traditionelles sympathisch. Das liegt daran, dass moderne Wissenschaften dem *Konzept des Systems* all die Macht (Welt zu schaffen und zu deuten) zusprechen, das zuvor der *Kraft der Sympathie* zuerkannt wurde. Das traditionelle, in vielen Kulturen global verbreitete Wissen begreift das Weltgeschehen als Ausdruck des qualitativen Zusammenwirkens elementarer Kräfte: *Sympathie* ist das Prinzip des *Zusammen*wirkens, sie ist die allen Dingen innewohnende Ausrichtung, die beeinflusst, was wie mit welchen anderen Kräften, Stoffen und Charakteren zusammenwirkt, aneinander gerät, anzieht, abstößt, heilt oder kränkt. Während traditionelles Wissen sich so als Einsicht in ein Weltgefüge begreift, an dem es teilhat, koppelt sich moderne Wissenschaft aus diesem Gefüge aus und beschreibt es mit Abstand, wie von außen. Insofern es sich methodisch aus der Gemengelage *sympathisch* reagierender Kräfte und verwobener Schicksale auskoppelt, um die Dinge der Welt aus der Distanz heraus *systematisch* zu analysieren und manipulieren, ist moderne Wissenschaft gezielt unsympathisch. *Sympathien* sind traditionell das *kompositorische Medium und Milieu der Künste*. Im graeco-romanischen Kanon versuchen die sieben freien Künste Musik, Astronomie, Arithmetik, Geometrie, Grammatik, Rhetorik und Logik Einblicke in das Zusammenwirken kosmischer Kräfte zu gewinnen, um in deren Konstellationen eingreifen zu können. Sie begreifen alles Sprechen und Handeln aber von Grund auf als elementar planetarischen Kräften unterworfen und nicht über sie triumphierend, wie Technik und Wissen der Moderne.

Sympathische Künste und unsympathische Systeme unterscheiden sich am Ende auch und vor allem in Bezug auf den Status, dem sie ihrem Medium, den Zeichen, zusprechen. Systemdenken begreift Zeichen als Instrumente, die die Dinge der Welt genau deshalb präzise abbilden, weil sie es aus der Distanz heraus tun, also nicht an der Dingwelt teilhaben, sondern, ganz wie die Operatoren kybernetischer Systeme, funktionale Bestandteile in sich abgeschlossener Strukturen (Sprachen) sind. Sympathische Künste und traditionelle Wissenschaften verstehen die Gestalt und Konstellation der Dinge selbst zeichenhaft. Sternzeichen sind planetarisch ebenso gegeben wie die Prägung, die die unterschiedliche Teilhabe an den Elementen Feuer, Wasser, Erde und Luft verschiedenen Stoffen und Charakteren gibt. Was sie darin als Planet, Mineral, Pflanze oder Kreatur unterscheidet sind die unterschiedlichen Proportionen und verschobenen Bedeutungen, die sich im Verhältnis zu den darin kommunizierenden Elementen ergeben. Diese Prägungen geben den Dingen ihre *Signatur*. Eine bestimmte Konstellation von Tönen zu spielen oder aus Mineralien, Erden oder anderen Stoffen bestimmte Farben anzumischen, aktiviert das Kräftepotenzial dieser Signaturen. Sympathische Künste sprechen nie *über* die Welt, sondern *durch* die der Welt innewohnenden Signaturen. Systematische Semiotik zerschneidet mit dem Skalpell struktureller Analyse den Stoff der intimsten Verwobenheit zwischen Zeichen und Welt, den sympathische Künste als ihr Element und Milieu begreifen. Der Punkt ist, dass sich Filko die Gewaltsamkeit dieses Schnitts genauso zum Markenzeichen macht, wie die Magie von Farben und Chakren als seine Signaturen. Um die Doppelbödigkeit seines Tuns und Sprechens nachzuvollziehen – und einer Deutung entgegenzuwirken, die sein Werk im Rückblick vor allem unter kosmisch künstlerischen Vorzeichen wahrnimmt – stellt dieser Essay den unsympathischen, aggressiv antikünstlerischen Aspekt seiner Praxis in den Vordergrund.

4 Groys 2008 (wie Anm. 1).

5 Ebd.

6 Benjamin H. D. Buchloh, „Conceptual Art 1962–1969: From the Aesthetic of Administration to the Critique of Institutions", in: *October*, 55, Winter 1990, S. 105–143.

7 Das System-Entwurfs-Textblatt *Projekt myslenia* (ca. 2000) zum Beispiel datiert die genannten zwei Tode auf 1945 und 1952 und deklariert ihren Status als „KLINIC". Ohne dieses Attribut listet Filko danach als drittes Todesjahr, 1985, aber nur in Verbindung mit dem Kürzel N.Y.C., vermutlich in Bezug auf den Moment seiner Zeit in New York, als er den Boden unter den Füßen verlor und Erzählungen zufolge, sich eine Weile als Obdachloser durchschlug. Diesem sozialen Tod sind im System-Entwurf Begriffe zugeordnet, die geradezu eine kämpferische Rückkehr zum Avantgardismus sind (nach dessen einstweiliger Überwindung in der, dem zweiten Tod zugeordneten POSTAVANTGARDA-Phase B): Mit dem Leben Phase C nach dem sozialen Tod assoziiert Filko die Qualitäten TRANSFUTURO und MODERNAVANGARDA, ganz so, als wollte er der US-Kunstszene signalisieren: Wenn mein Avantgardismus für Euch unverdaulich ist, dann werde ich, in dieser Zeit nach der Ankunft der Zukunft, erst recht an ihm festhalten!

form of sculptures that are very roughly collaged from the remains of agricultural labor: fenceposts, old steel bars, and old tires tied together with thick wires to form a pyramid that defies the odds, and declaring this through labelling to be a holy Venus relic. On a seemingly endlessly long banner hung on the wall behind this work, the words MORAVANY — VENUSA are painted in enormous black block capitals. [21–22] Filko's homage to the magic of pre-industrial artisanship is thus also punky (rough, ready, and dirty); using ropes he binds together old sewing machines with flywheels together as assemblages. It looks as if giant spiders had spun the relics of a lost age found in the hithermost corner of a barn into a compact cocoon. In the vernacular, these flywheels are called *babka* [23], grandmother. Filko celebrates the rebirth of the world of the granny from the countryside as cosmic Venus art. By using broken stuff from the yard as his materials, he rejects both restorative nostalgia (that idealizes the old as the unbroken) and a technological faith in the future (granny had the true power tools). Roman Zubaľ, art collector and companion, noted in conversation that, during his studies at the art academy in Bratislava, Filko was regularly mocked for his rural origins. Not least in the light of this, his advocacy of primeval art in the sign of Venus fenceposts and granny spinning wheels retain the aggressive character of the rejection of whatever snobby city people take to be art.

The intimate proximity of negation and rebirth is, finally, underscored by the legend of the two clinical deaths that Filko incorporates into his system designs as a leitmotif.[7] He claimed that he had died and been reborn twice during his life, the first time in 1945 when as an eight-year old he fell and banged his head against a stone while watching the cattle, and the second time in 1952 when he suffered an electric shock from a power line when working in a factory. The first death made him postmodern, he wrote, and the second post-avant-garde. In addition to this it seems vital to note that, while the first death took place in a rural and the second an industrial environment, a metal works, both deaths are named in the same vain. So while it is understood that, alongside the total sciences of signs and rockets, heavy industry is identified as a force of death and destruction, Filko does not pit the rural against the modern as a site of innocence and redemption. Instead he testifies to the fact that work on the land has also always cost countless lives. What further puts both deaths on a par is their arbitrary character: they are brutal in a banal way, or banal in a brutal way. They are signatures of the traditional feudal and the modern industrial orders. What remains the same, before and after the incision of industrialization is that work may bring death. And rebirth. [24–27] What destroys and what gives birth, anti-art and art are sides of one coin. Nietzsche may have said it. But the point is how Filko did it: Throughout his life, he sucked in whole worlds and spewed them out as anti-art: the aggressive world of semiotics and rockets alongside the no less rough world of rural Venus deities and granny spinning wheels.

1   Boris Groys, *The Total Art of Stalinism: Avant-Garde, Aesthetic Dictatorship, and Beyond*, (Princeton, New Jersey, 1992).
2   Daniel Grún, "Notes of a Belated Viewer. Revisiting White Space in White Space," in *White Space in White Space. Biely priestor v bielom priestore, 1973–1982, Stano Filko, Miloš Laky, Ján Zavarský,* eds. Daniel Grún, Christian Höller, Kathrin Rhomberg for Kontakt Collection (Vienna, 2021).

3   Modernist thought is unsympathetic, traditional sympathetic. This is because modernist sciences accord all the power (to create and interpret the world) to the concept of the system that was previously accorded to the power of sympathy. Traditional knowledge in many cultures around the world understood the way of the world as an expression of the qualitative interplay of elementary forces: sympathy is the key in which this interplay occurs, in accordance with the elementary disposition of certain forces, materials, and characters to attract, repel, heal, or harm each other. While traditional knowledge sees itself as insight into the essence of the world in which it participates, modern science dissociates itself from this essence and describes it from a distance, as if from the outside. Insofar as it decouples methodologically from the interplay of sympathetically reacting forces and interlinked fates, in order to systematically analyze and manipulate things in the world from a distance, modernist science is intentionally unsympathetic. Sympathies are traditionally the compositional medium and milieu of the arts. In the Greek-Roman canon the seven free arts music, astronomy, arithmetic, geometry, grammar, rhetoric, and logic endeavor to gain insight into the interplay of cosmic forces in order to be able to intervene in their constellations. But they understand speech and action as subject to elementary planetary forces and not as triumphing over these, unlike the technology and knowledge of modernity.

Sympathetic arts and unsympathetic systems ultimately differ from one another also and primarily in reference to the status that they accord their medium, the signs. Systems thinking sees signs as instruments that so well depict the things of the world precisely because they do this from a distance and do not participate in the world of things, but, just as the operators of cybernetic systems, are rather functional components of inherently closed systems (languages). Sympathetic arts and traditional sciences understand the shape and constellation of things themselves as signs inscribed in creation. So, zodiac signs are a planetary fact in much the same way that the particular way a mineral, plant or creature signifies is a direct manifestation of its material composition: the different proportions to which the planet, mineral, plant or creature partakes in the elementary forces of fire, water, earth, and air disposes it towards entering into relation with other parts of creation in a certain manner, and thereby acquire its particular meaning (relative to the constellation entered). This disposition to relate and signify in characteristic ways was known as the "signature" engraved in each little particle of the world. Playing a certain constellation of notes, or mixing certain colors from minerals, earths, or other materials activates the potential force of these signatures. Sympathetic arts never speak *about* the world but *through* the signatures inherent to it. Systematic semiotics uses the scalpel of structural analysis to cut the stuff of the most intimate interlinkage between sign and world that the sympathetic arts understand to be their element and milieu. The point is that Filko embraces *both* the violence of the analytic incision *and* the magic of color chakras and cosmic signatures. In order to show the ambivalence in what he does and says about it—and in order to counter an interpretation that sees his work in retrospect primarily under cosmic artistic auspices—this essay focuses on the unsympathetic, aggressive anti-artistic aspect of his practice.

4   Boris Groys, *The Total Art of Stalinism: Avant-Garde, Aesthetic Dictatorship, and Beyond* (see note 1).
5   Ibid.
6   Benjamin H. D. Buchloh, "Conceptual Art 1962–1969: From the Aesthetic of Administration to the Critique of Institutions," *October* 55 (winter 1990), pp. 105–43.
7   The system design text sheet *Projekt myslenia* (c. 2000), for example, dates the two deaths in 1945 and 1952 and declares their status as "KLINIC." Without this attribute, Filko thereafter lists 1985 as the third year of death, but only in connection with the abbreviation N.Y.C., presumably referring here to the moment during his time in New York when he lost the ground under his feet and, so the story, spent some time somehow surviving homeless. In the system design this social death is associated with concepts that very much stand for a belligerent return to avant-gardism (after it had already been overcome in the POSTAVANTGARDA-Phase B associated with the second death). With life in phase C after the social death, Filko associates the qualities TRANSFUTURO and MODERNAVANGARDA, pretty much as if he wished to signal to the US art scene that if his avant-gardism was not digestible for them, then he would most definitely stick with it, in this time after the arrival of the future!

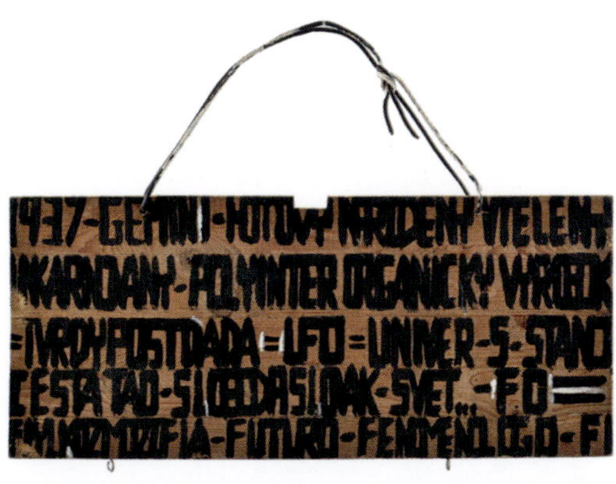

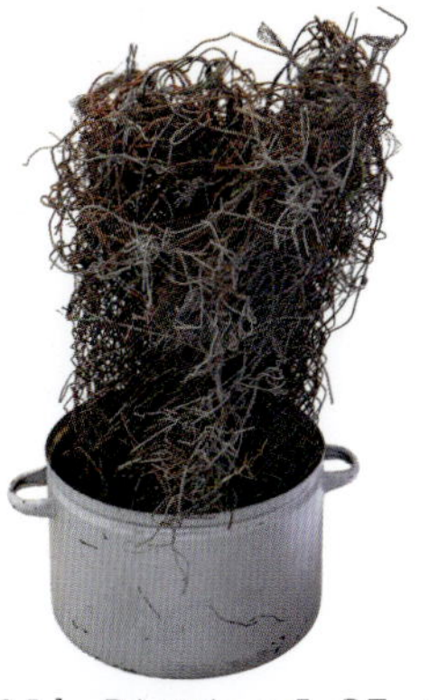

[24] Retro SF (Birth and Clinical
Deaths) / Retro SF (narodenie a
klinické smrte), 2000

[25] Birth of SF /
Narodenie SF,
c. 1960

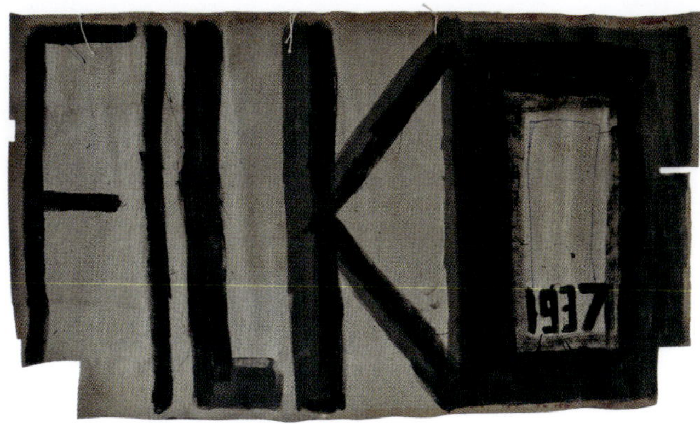

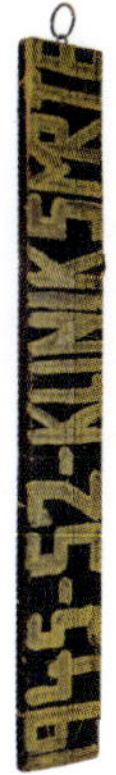

[26] FILKO CLINICAL DEATHS 1945 and 1952 /
FILKO KLINICKÉ SMRTE 1945 a 1952, 1995

[27] SF Clinical
Deaths / SF
Klinické smrte,
1995

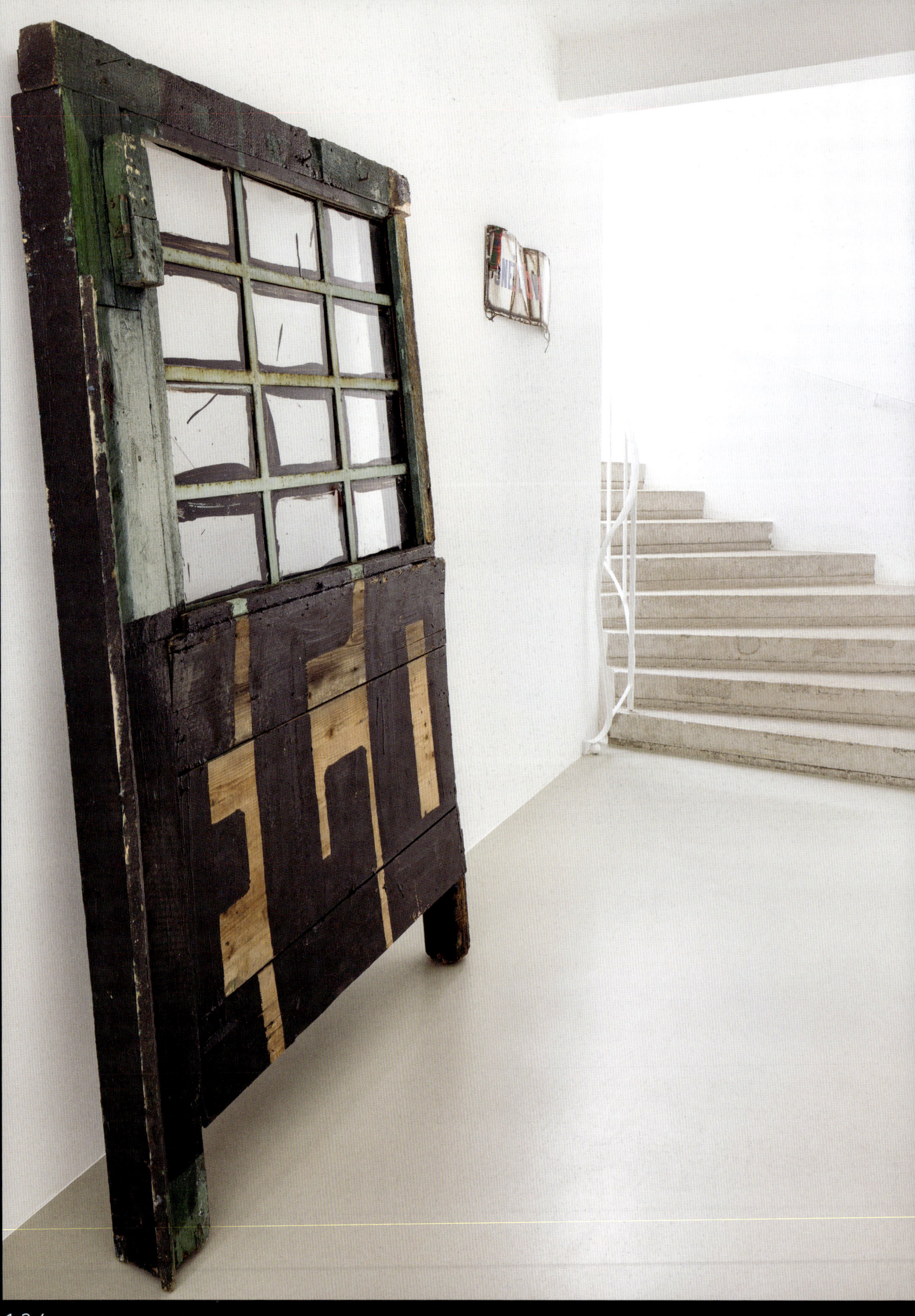

XIII

Archive SF / Archív SF

After his return from the USA in 1990, Filko's *System SF* became more and more of a sprawling meta-system by means of which he re-arranged and reconsidered the entirety of his artistic work. A dynamic was set in motion that led to Filko reworking and redating many earlier works. In this process the *Archive SF* came about, an ongoing depot with about 80 different ordering components and a comprehensive system for cataloging sketches, smaller objects, text art, photographs, and many archive materials.

In the archive room in the exhibition, a large number of items that provide insight into this fascinating ordering and semiotic system and other physical objects that are situatively interconnected with it, is presented. Art and life here form an indivisible unity, as becomes immediately clear at the entrance to the archive, which consists of two doors painted by Filko. [01] [09]

Nach der Rückkehr aus den USA im Jahr 1990 entwickelte sich Filkos *System SF* zunehmend zu einem unüberschaubaren Metasystem, durch das er die Gesamtheit seines Schaffens und Lebens neu anordnet und überdenkt. Eine Dynamik entsteht, unter deren Einfluss Filko frühere Werke vielfach überabeitet und neu datiert. In diesem Prozess entsteht das *Archív SF*, ein in einer rund 80-teiligen Ordnerstruktur kontinuierlich aufgebautes Magazin und umfassender Verweiszusammenhang an Skizzen, kleineren Objekten, Textkunst, Fotografien und zahlreichem Archivmaterial.

Im Archivraum der Ausstellung wird verschiedenes Material gezeigt, um Aufschluss über dieses faszinierende Ordnungs- und Zeichensystem wie situativ damit verbundene räumliche Elemente zu geben. Kunst und Leben bilden hier eine untrennbare Einheit, was bereits durch den Eingang des Archivs deutlich wird, der aus zwei bemalten Türarbeiten von Filko besteht. [01] [09]

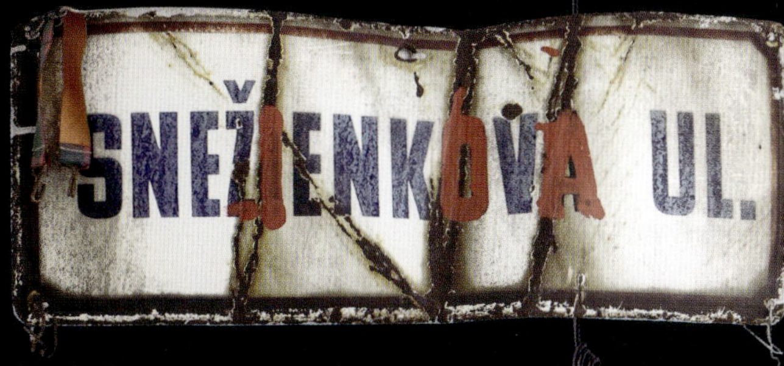

[03A] *Subject – Object / Subjekt – Objekt*, c. 1995

[04] *Street name sign Snežienková Street / Uličná tabuľa Snežienková ulica*, c. 1990

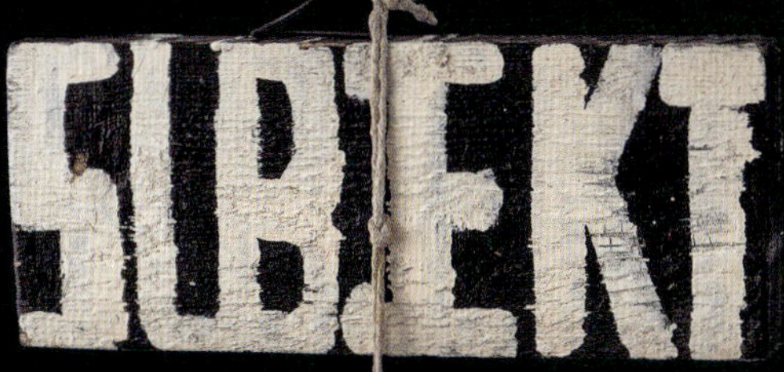

Visitors can use a screen to gain further insight into selected archive material. Various thematically connected objects are displayed in this room, supplemented by projections of historical exhibition views and further images from the archive. The text-images "Subject" and "Object" are written in white and black on wooden boards, and also the word "EGO." *Archive SF* is situated in the realm between the totality of the ego (black) and self-dissolution of the artistic self through transcendence (white). Two photographs from a vernissage are also characterized by these two opposites, showing visitors overpainted in white and Filko as the only person in black. [14] Filko saw his entire system as "psychophilosophy," whereby material forms of expression are reconceived as mirrors of psychic states of mind.

An einem selbst bedienbaren Bildschirm lässt sich Einblick in ausgewähltes Archivmaterial verschaffen. Diverse thematisch assoziierte Objekte breiten sich im Raum aus und werden durch eine Projektion aus historischen Ausstellungssituationen und weiteren Bildern aus dem Archiv ergänzt. Auf mehreren Holzplatten sind die Schriftbilder „Subjekt" und „Objekt" in weißer und schwarzer Farbe geschrieben, auch die Aufschrift „EGO" ist zu sehen. Das *Archív SF* erscheint im Spannungsfeld zwischen der Totalität des Egos (Schwarz) und der Selbstauflösung des künstlerischen Ichs durch die Transzendenz (Weiß). Von diesen Gegensätzen sind auch zwei Fotografien einer Vernissage bestimmt, auf welchen Besucher*innen in weiß übermalt sind, während Filko als einzige Person in schwarz zu sehen ist. [14] Filkos gesamtes System wird von ihm als Psychophilosophie aufgefasst, wobei der materielle Ausdruck als Spiegel von psychischen Dispositionen neu imaginiert wird.

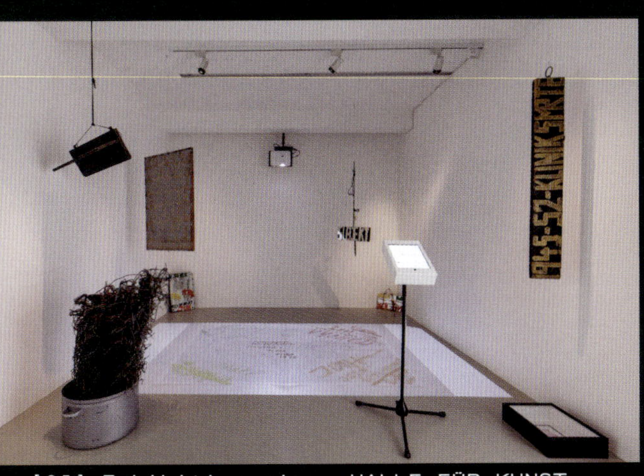

[05] *Exhibition view, HALLE FÜR KUNST Steiermark, Graz, 2022*

→[02A] *Birth of SF / Narodenie SF*, c. 1960

←[01] *Door (UISFO EGOQ) / Dvere (UISFO EGOQ)*, c. 2000

There are also works here that present text in each of the first four colors of the fully developed *System SF*, red, orange, yellow, and green. The two smaller ones show the links between the four colors and the four elements [07] [11], while the largest of these three works also links the colors up with the signs of the compass: red (first chakra, earth/east), orange (second chakra, fire/south), yellow (third chakra, air/west), green (fourth chakra, water/north). [08]

A further larger work also contains different dates that are each connected with the three "clinical deaths" that Filko himself said he experienced after serious accidents. Filko presented this story of his clinical deaths with great conviction, but also to add to the mythical construction of his artistic personality. [10] [12]

Weiters sind Arbeiten zu sehen, die vier Schriftzüge in den jeweiligen ersten Farben des voll ausgereiften *System SF* zeigen, die Farben Rot, Orange, Gelb und Grün. Die zwei kleineren Arbeiten verdeutlichen die Verknüpfung der vier Farben mit den vier Elementen [07] [11], während die größte der drei Arbeiten die Farben mit den Himmelrichtungen verbindet: Rot (1. Chakra, Erde/Osten), Orange (2. Chakra, Feuer/Süden), Gelb (3. Chakra, Luft/Westen), Grün (4. Chakra, Wasser/Norden). [08]

Eine mehrteilige Arbeit enthält außerdem verschiedene Jahresangaben, die mit insgesamt drei „klinischen Toden" zusammenhängen, die Filko nach eigener Aussage durch schwere Unfälle erlebt haben soll. Filko benutzt das Narrativ der klinischen Tode aus Überzeugung, aber wohl auch um zur mythischen Konstruktion seiner Künstlerpersönlichkeit beizutragen. [10] [12]

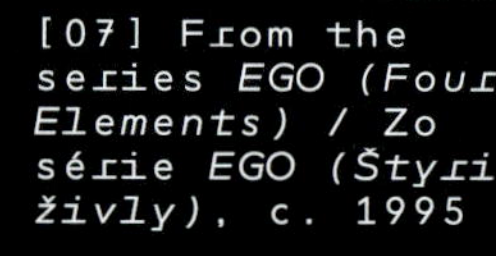

[06] From the cycle *EGO* / *Z cyklu EGO*, c. 1995

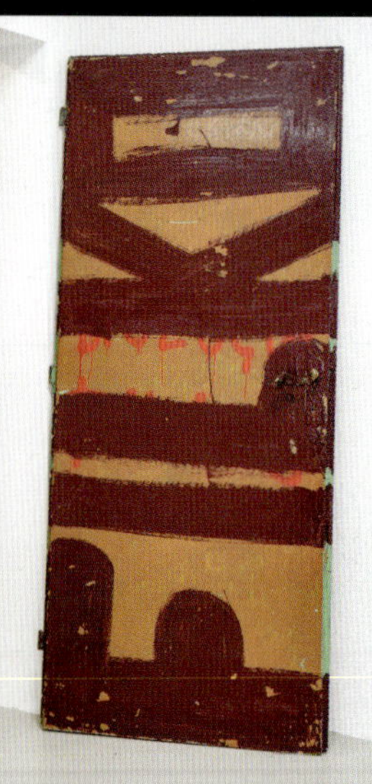

[07] From the series *EGO (Four Elements)* / *Zo série EGO (Štyri živly)*, c. 1995

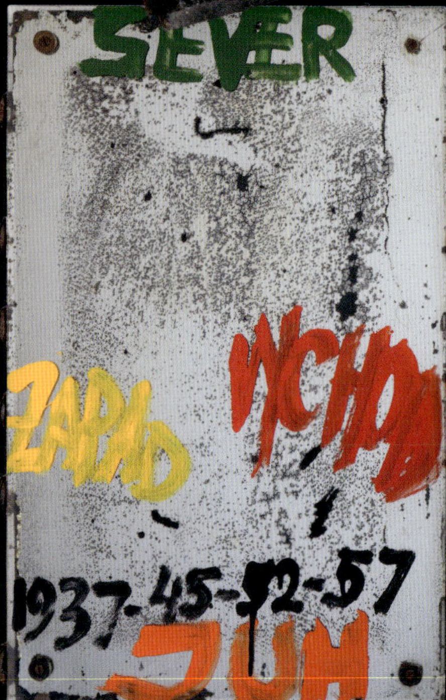

[08] From the series *EGO (Four Sides of the World)* / *Zo série EGO (Štyri svetové strany)*, c. 1995

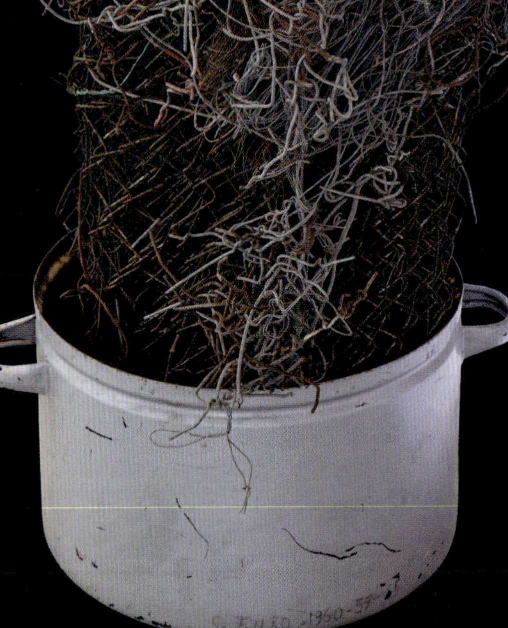

[02B] *Birth of SF* / *Narodenie SF*, c. 1960

[09] *FILKO*, c. 1995

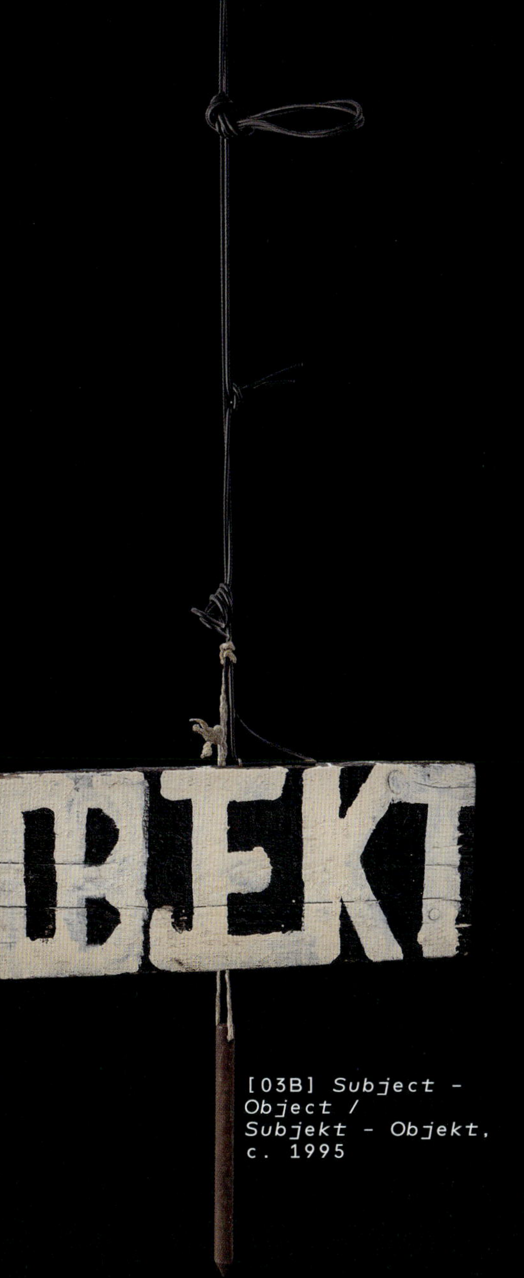

[03B] *Subject – Object / Subjekt – Objekt*, c. 1995

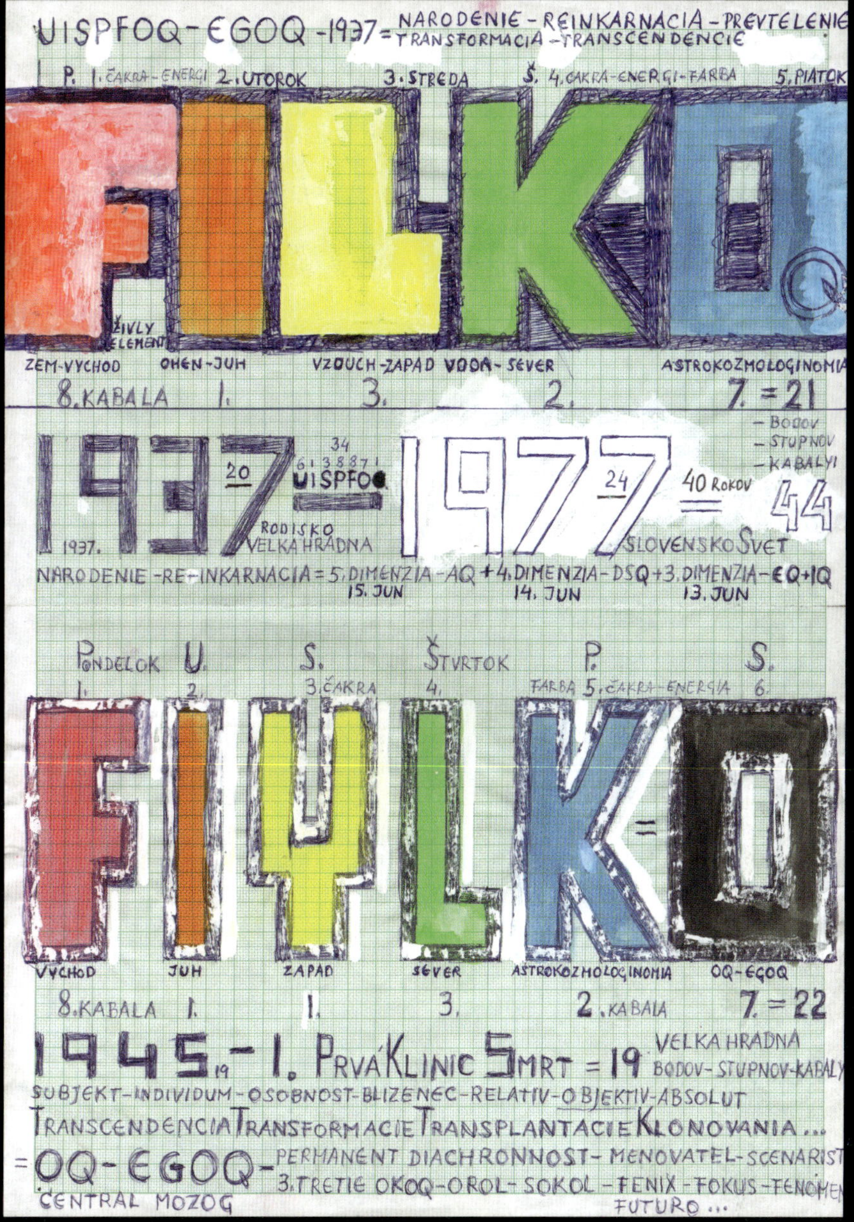

[10] *SF Clinical Deaths / SF Klinické smrte*, 1995

Other works address Filko's famous artist's studio Snežienková, in the northern outskirts of Bratislava. A marginally reworked street sign [04] becomes an autonomous work, presenting the three colors of Filko's dimensions, red, white, and blue. The artist himself can be seen on the roof of his studio in two photographs, while other pictures show the interior. All of the studio's rooms are arranged according to the colors and phases of Filko's work, so that they themselves are an integral part of the *Archive SF*. Many works are laid out on the floor, walls, and ceiling, forming a total work of art in conjunction with the building itself, permitting no separation between art and life. Filko's studio is a clear impression of the totality and universal approach of his artistic personality. [17]

Andere Arbeiten beschäftigen sich mit Filkos berühmtem Künstleratelier Snežienková, das sich in der nördlichen Peripherie von Bratislava befindet. Ein geringfügig bearbeitetes Straßenschild [04] wird zum autonomen Werk und zeigt in Rot, Weiß und Blau die drei Farben von Filkos Dimensionen. Der Künstler ist auf zwei Fotografien auf dem Dach seines Ateliers zu sehen, wobei die Innenräume des Künstlerstudios auf fotografischen Arbeiten gezeigt werden. Die gesamten Räume des Studios sind nach Farben und Werkphasen geordnet und bilden einen integralen Bestandteil des *Archív SF*. Zahlreiche Werke befinden sich verteilt am Boden, an Wand und Decke und bilden zusammen mit der Architektur ein Gesamtkunstwerk, das keine Trennung zwischen Kunst und Leben mehr zulässt. Durch Filkos Studio tritt die Totalität und universelle Haltung seiner künstlerischen Persönlichkeit klar in Erscheinung. [17]

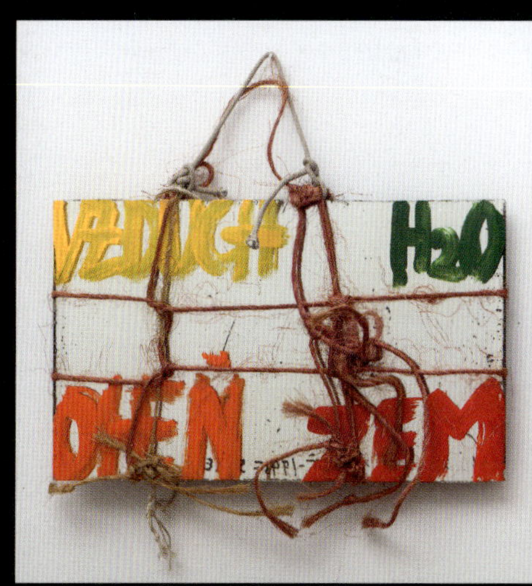

[11] *From the series Four Elements (Earth, Air, Fire, Water) / Zo série Štyri živly (Zem, Vzduch, Oheň, Voda)*, c. 1990

The artworks in the archive space as well as the digital video archive were compiled especially for this exhibition by Lucia Gregorová Stach, chief curator at the Slovak National Gallery in Bratislava.

Die Gestaltung des Archivraumes sowie das digitale Videoarchiv wurde von Lucia Gregorová Stach, Chefkuratorin an der Slovak National Gallery in Bratislava, eigens für diese Ausstellung zusammengestellt.

Stano Filko
maliar, multimedialista (tvorca enviromentov a inštalácií)

Stano Filko (1937) sa narodil vo Veľkej Hradnej, rokom svojho narodenia datuje autor aj vznik Geminy – Triada – Quadrofonia – Asymetria. V rokoch 1953 – 1958 študoval na Strednej škole umeleckého priemyslu v Bratislave a pokračoval na Vysokej škole výtvarných umení v špeciálke monumentálnej tvorby u prof. P. Matejku, prof. D. Milly (maľba).
Autor patrí k prvej generácii slovenských kontextuálnych konceptualistov, akcionistov a predstaviteľov nových médií (svetlo, zvuk, verbál, vizuál v paralelno-synchrónnej kontextualnosti).
Po počiatočných expresívnych a kubizujúcich maľbách realizoval štrukturálne asambláže, koláže a objekty (napr. Oltáre súčasnosti, 1960 – 1965), ktorých poetika súvisela napr. aj s informelom (Stary a Novy zakon). V autorovej tvorbe z rokov 1960-65-67 – 1969 môžeme nájsť náznaky viacerých otázok, ktorými sa neskôr zaoberali autori týchto tendencií (napr. koncept ... v bielom priestore, 1973 – 1974, kolektívne spolu s M. Lakym... je idei nekonečného priestoru a jeho interpretácia prost... 60.rokov Filko ako ... individuálna piata dime...

Spolu s A. Mlynárči... deklarácie HAPPSO... určitého výseku sku... k vyjadreniu vlastný... PSOC-e IV (1967, pozvánka na vesmír... návštevníka. Autor... antropocentrická a...
Človek v ňom nevy... v ňom samom, sám sa stáva miest... smeruje nielen k de...dencii štvrtej dimenzie 4D, ale k n... objektívna:...
V jeho dielach exis... movesmíru (napr. cez Moje rodisko, 196... futurológa, smrť – nirvána)...
V roku 1966 napísal ... vlastné názory na umelecku tvorbu a (... V roku 1969 vychádzať ďalšieho mani... jekte, ktorý po prvé je jedným z posledných prúdo... existenciou anti-post... happeningov ako kontemplatívn...
Približne od polovice 70. rokov opäť prenášal svoju tvorbu v troch paralelne synchrónnych cestách ako: piata dimenzia (5D) = BIELA: jedenásta čakra (11 č.), transparentná (12 č.), zlatá (10 č.) energie, absolútna duša objektiv... infinity... entita – súcno, psycho – filozofia; štvrtá dimenzia (4D) = MODRÁ: fyzický časopriestor, kozmológia, kozmo – vesmír... loginom... (v 3D zastupuje DSUQ – ... duch, spirit, universe, Q – ako čistý/čas); tretia dimenzia (3D) = ČERVENÁ: space... time, ktorý vznikol v našom kozmovesmíre po = post „Veľkom tresku" (dal vznik...
= 12 – 1. = čakier – energetického spektra farieb SF + 8 až 9 abecedného numerologie... (kybernetika)... Postupne stále viac upúšťal od manuálnych zásahov do diel a tvoril projekty... a inštalácie nielen v štýle technicistickom, ale až existenčného postmaterializmu...

[13] AUTENTKSF I., Text-art, 2005-12

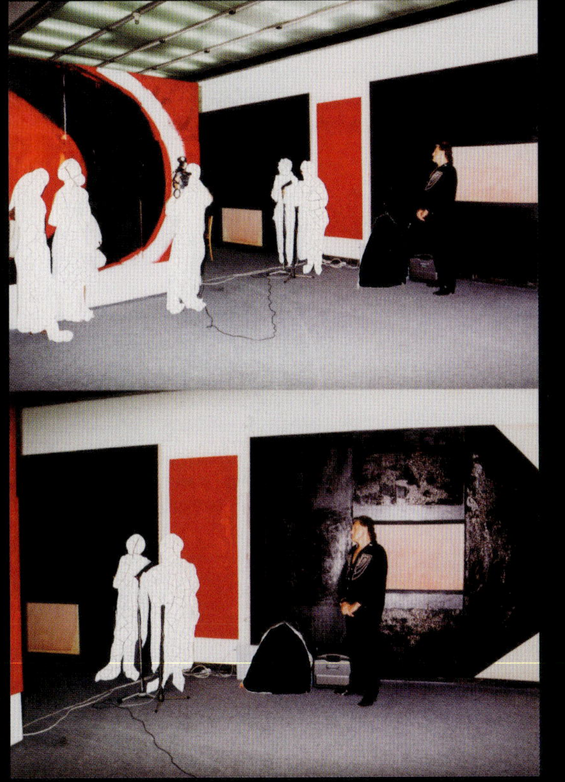

[14] *PHYLKO - 1993 - VERNISSAGE / PHYLKO - 1993 - VERNISÁŽ*, 1993

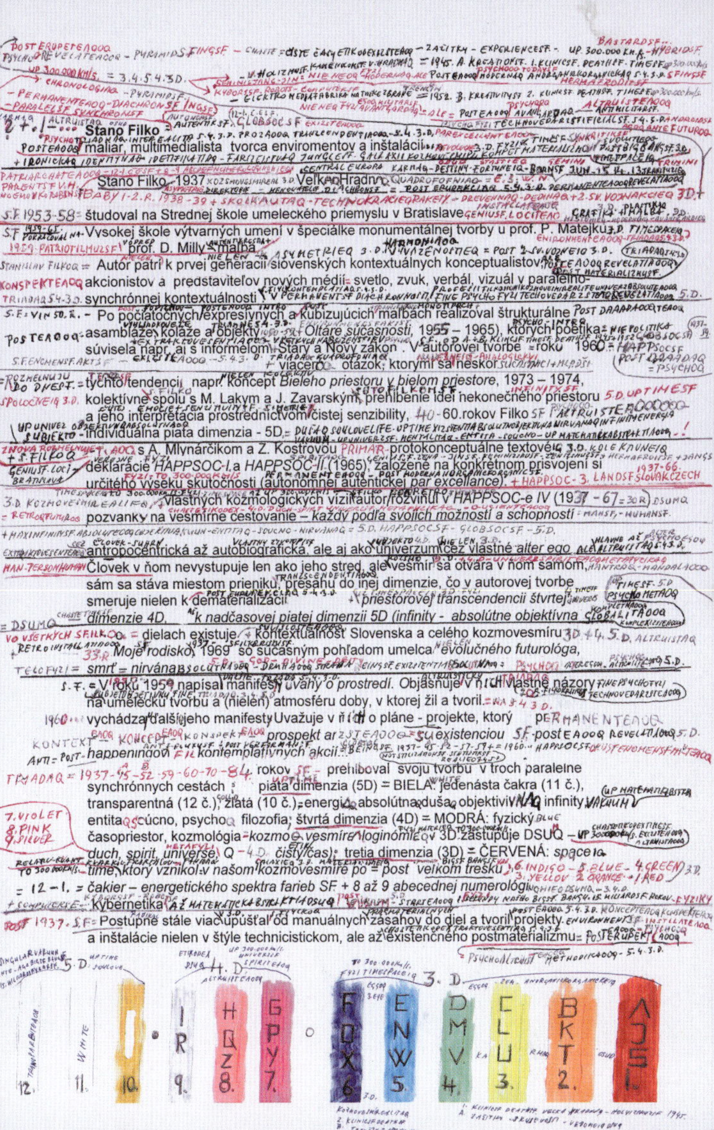

[15] *AUTENTKSF Biography / AUTENTKSF Biografia*, 2005-12

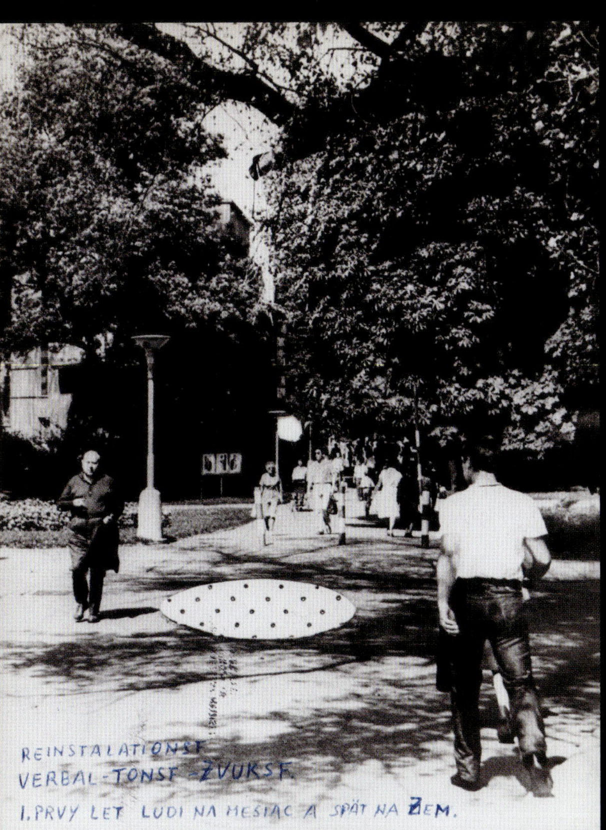

[16] *Flight of Cosmonauts to the Moon in Stages and their Return to the Earth / Let kozmonautov na Mesiac po etapách a ich návrat na Zem*, 1969

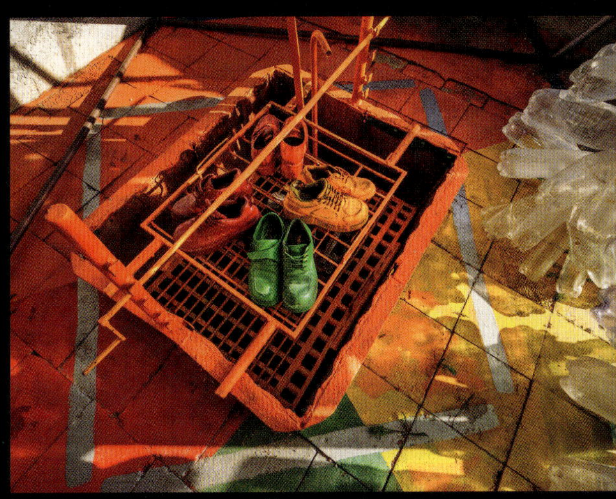

[17] *Artist's studio Snežienková /*

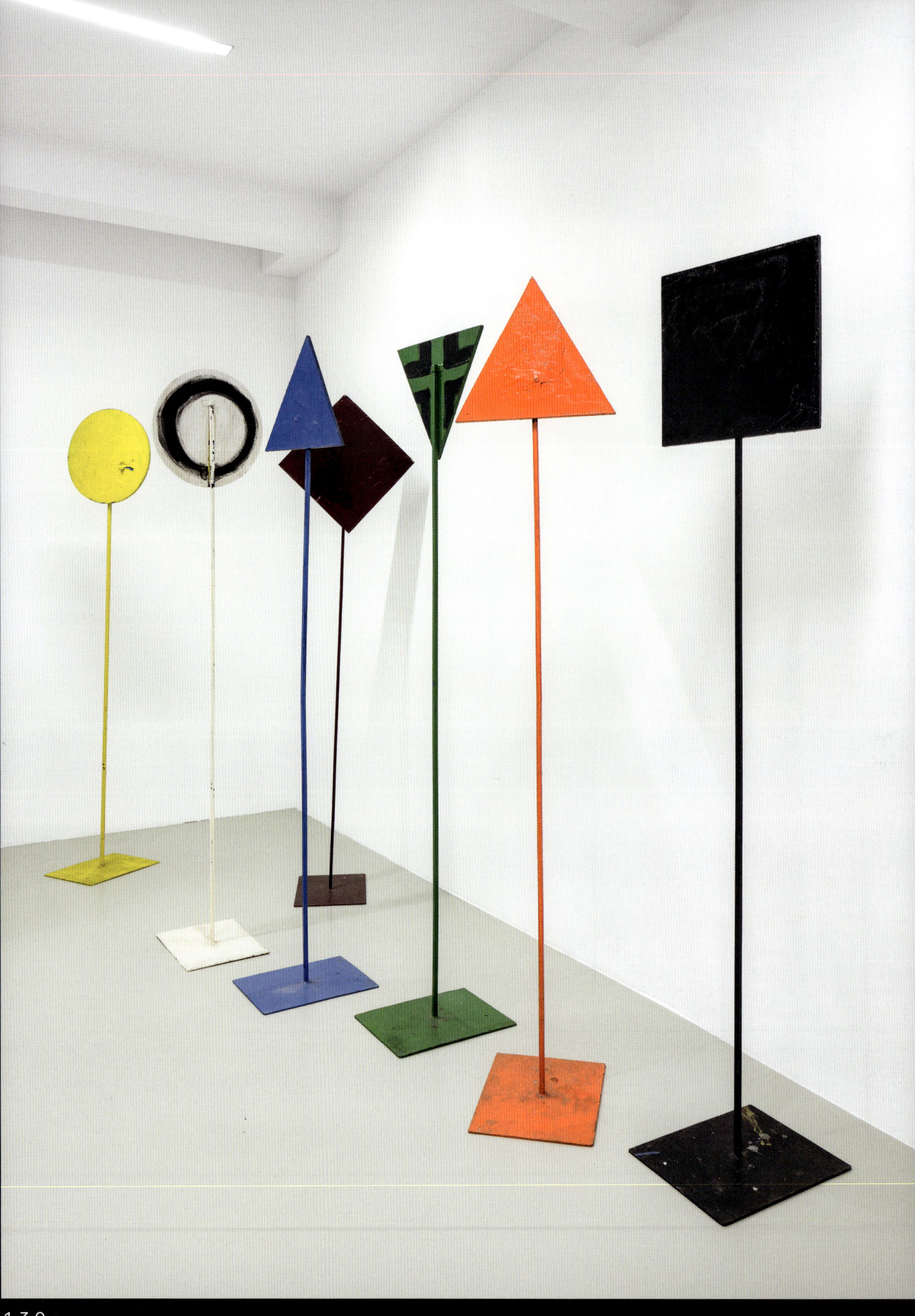

XIV

System SF: Identity and Guiding System / Identität und Leitlinien

Moving from the archive room, there are a number of works that present important continuities in the *Archive SF*. Here again it becomes clear how Filko combined the different levels of meaning in his work over many years with everyday objects, using these as a kind of guiding system, also in spatial terms. This guiding system is seen in the form of street signs that Filko overpainted in *Monument to Traffic Signs. External Environment – Communication / Pomník značkám. Externé prostredie – komunikácia* (c. 1990) [01], using one color from his seven phase chakra system for each. The structures in the way the paint is applied and the traces of the material beneath unfold a performative aspect that at the same time recalls an iconoclastic gesture. The usual function of these signs is made invisible with paint, and their symbolism is brought into Filko's own system that now transfers them into a human dimension related to our own bodies.

Vom Archivraum ausgehend werden eine Reihe von Arbeiten gezeigt, die wichtige Konstanten des *Archiv SF* aufspannen. Hier wird noch einmal deutlich, wie Filko die verschiedenen Bedeutungsebenen seiner langjährigen Arbeit mit alltäglichen Gegenständen verbindet und diese als eine Art Leitsystem, auch räumlich verstanden, ausbreitet. Dieses Leitsystem tritt anhand einiger Straßenschilder in Erscheinung, die Filko in *Monument to Traffic Signs. External Environment – Communication / Pomník značkám. Externé prostredie – komunikácia* (ca. 1990) [01] mit jeweils einer Farbe des siebenstufigen Chakrensystems übermalt hat. Die Strukturen des Farbauftrages, sowie die Spuren des darunterliegenden Materials entfalten einen performativen Aspekt, der gleichzeitig an eine ikonoklastische Geste erinnert. Die gewohnheitsgemäße Funktion der Schilder ist mit Farbe unkenntlich gemacht und deren Zeichenhaftigkeit in Filkos eigenes System umgewandelt worden, das sich nun in eine körperbezogene, menschliche Dimension transferiert.

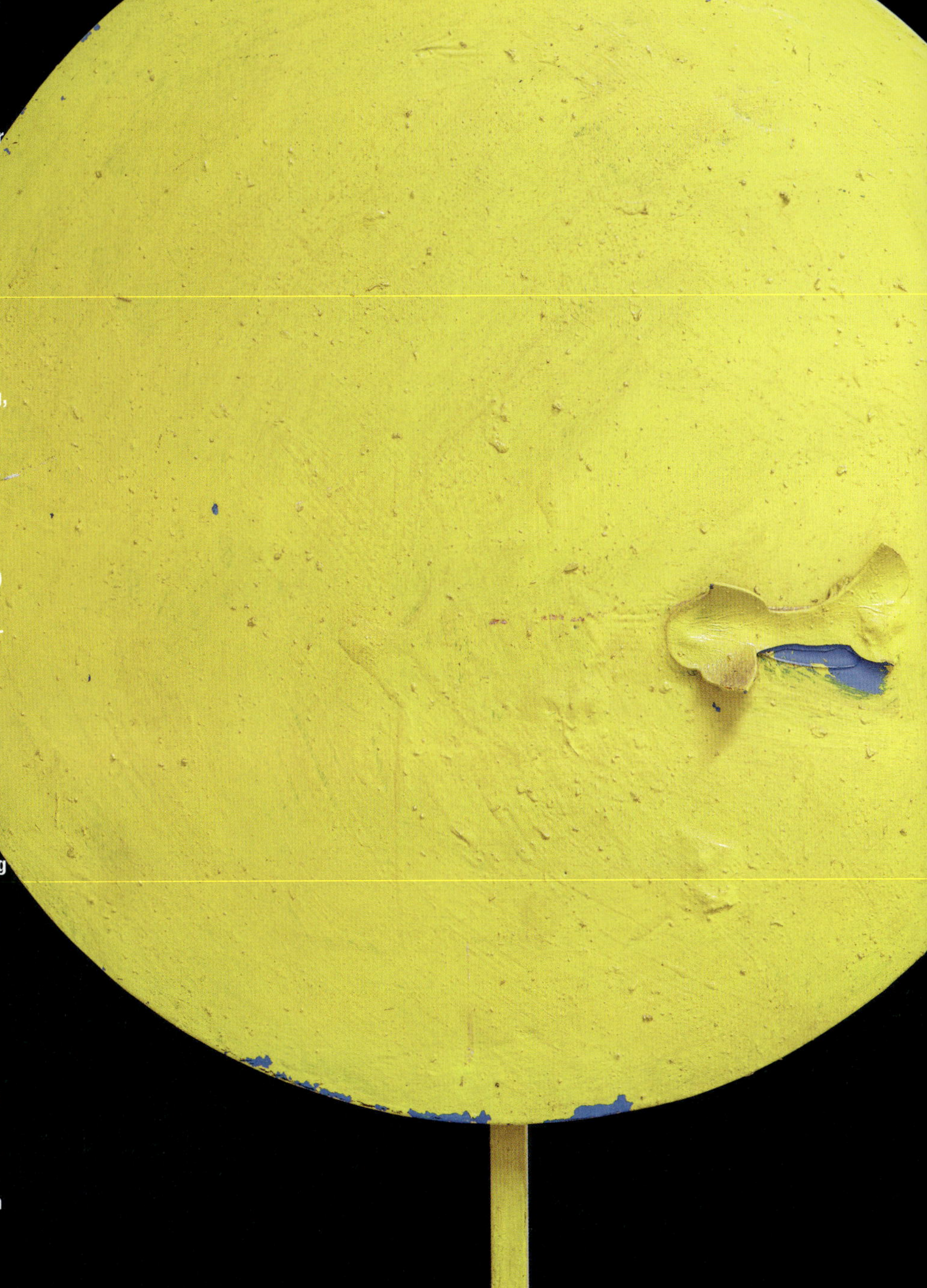

In the archive room the three-part installation *SF Clinical Deaths / SF Klinické smrte* (1995) is presented, which consists of two drawings and a wooden plank with text, where the years 1945 and 1952 are shown as important cornerstones in Filko's biography. Filko often told a mythical story about "clinical deaths" that he said he experienced after serious accidents several times in his life. Clinical death is also illustrated in the work on paper where a red figure seems to be lying in a coffin and the word "EGO" is added. The periods of time between Filko's clinical deaths might also represent different states of consciousness, as Filko often hinted when he spoke of different "clones" of his artistic ego. He also expresses this division of his life into different identities with different ways of writing his own name ("Filko," "Phylko," "Phys"), as shown on a related work on paper.

Im Archivraum ist die mehrteilige Arbeit *SF Clinical Deaths / SF Klinické smrte* (1995) zu sehen, welche aus zwei Zeichnungen und einer beschriebenen Holzplanke besteht. Das Holzstück offenbart die Jahreszahlen 1945 sowie 1952 als wichtige Eckpunkte in Filkos Biografie. Filko entfaltet immer wieder eine mystische Erzählung über „klinische Tode", die er mehrfach während seines Lebens durch schwere Unfälle erlebt haben soll. Der klinische Tod wird auch bildlich auf der Papierarbeit verdeutlicht, auf der eine rote Figur mit der Aufschrift „EGO" wie in einem Sarg zu liegen scheint. Parallel dazu könnten die Zeitspannen zwischen den klinischen Toden auch unterschiedliche Bewusstseinszustände symbolisieren, was Filko immer wieder andeutet, indem er von verschiedenen „Klonen" seines künstlerischen Egos spricht. Diese Unterteilung seines Lebens anhand verschiedener Identitäten bringt er zudem durch unterschiedliche Schreibweisen seines eigenen Namens wie „Filko", „Phylko", „Phys" zum Ausdruck, wie auf einer zugehörigen Papierarbeit ersichtlich wird.

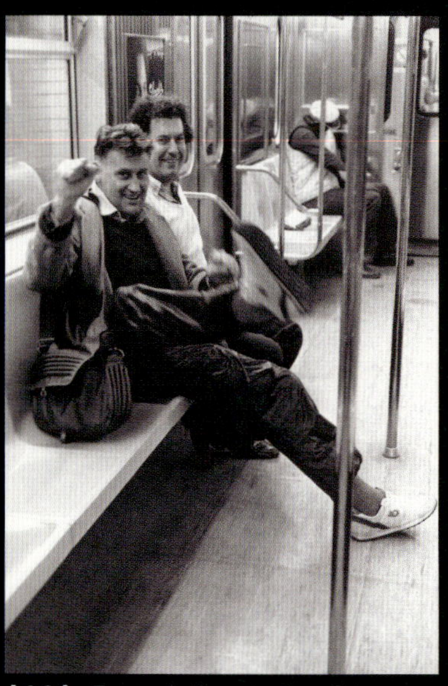
[02] Juraj Bartoš, Stano Filko, New York, 1984

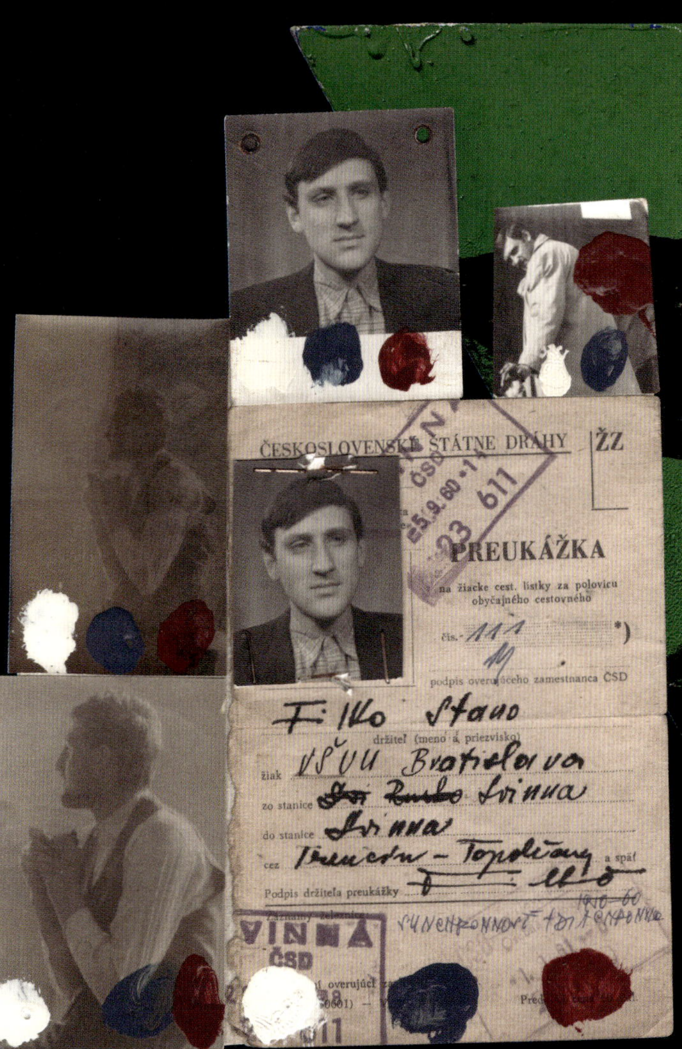
[03] *SF Railway Customer Card / SF Železničná preukážka*, 1964

The work *SF Railway Customer Card / SF Železničná preukážka* (1964) [03] shows an officially approved Slovak identity card of Stano Filko to which he added several photo portraits. Filko can be seen in different poses, and both the document and the photographs have additional round spots of paint in white, blue, and red. The three main colors of his system are also the colors of the Slovak national flag, which raises basic questions as to the interpretative authority of the artistic system. Does this represent a fundamental rewriting of the symbolism, an ironic approach, or the affirmation of nationalism?

Die Arbeit *SF Railway Customer Card / SF Železničná preukážka* (1964) [03] zeigt einen amtlich bescheinigten, slowakischen Identitätsnachweis von Stano Filko, dem er mehrere Fotoporträts hinzugefügt hat. Filko ist in unterschiedlichen Posen zu sehen und sowohl das Dokument als auch die Fotografien sind mit rundlichen Farbtupfen in den Farben Weiß, Blau und Rot versehen. Die drei Hauptfarben seines Systems stellen gleichzeitig die Farben der slowakischen Nationalflagge dar, was grundsätzliche Fragen nach der Deutungsmacht von künstlerischen Systemen aufwirft: Bedeutet die Übernahme eine grundlegende Umschreibung der Symbolik, eine Ironisierung oder Affirmation von Nationalismus?

→[01C] *Monument to Traffic Signs. External Environment – Communication / Pomník značkám. Externé prostredie – komunikácia, 1967/c. 1990*

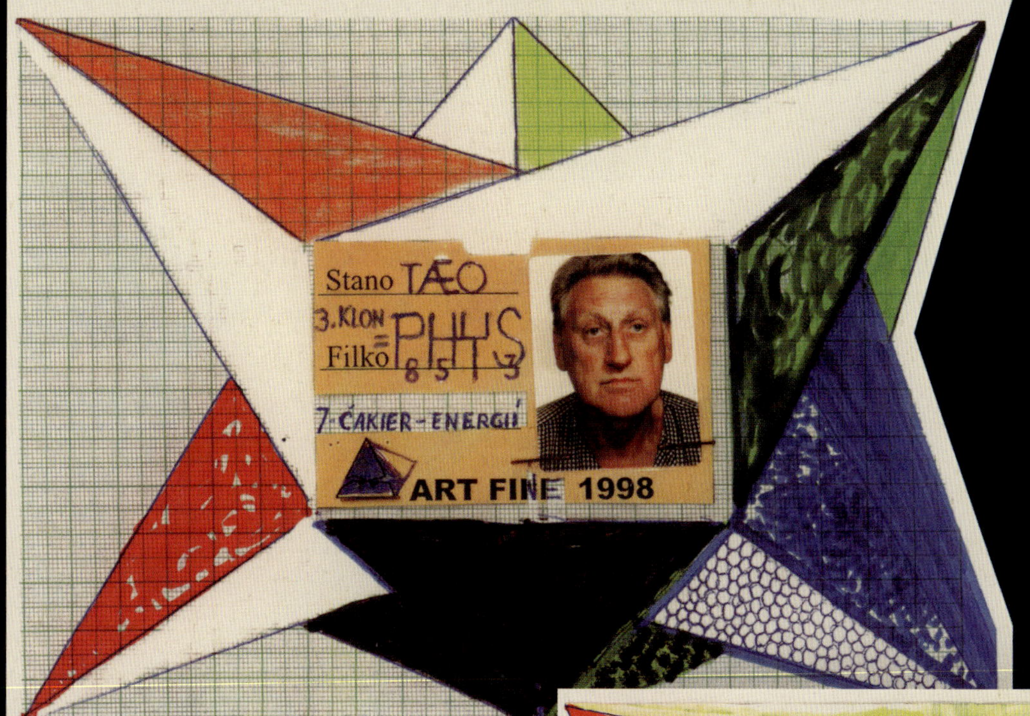

[04] Untitled, 1971–c. 2010

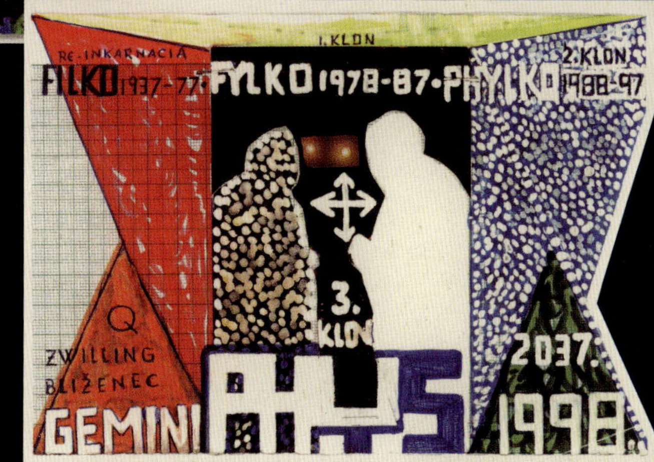

Finally visitors see a further element of the guidance system: seven wooden boards entitled *7 Chakra Colors (Wooden Formwork) / 7 farieb čakier (Drevené debnenie)* (c. 1995) [06], each of them displaying a number in the colors of the chakra system.

Schließlich begegnen den Besucher*innen als weiteres Element des Leitsystems sieben Holztafeln, *7 Chakra Colors (Wooden Formwork) / 7 farieb čakier (Drevené debnenie)* (ca. 1995) [06], auf welchen jeweils eine Zahl in den Farben des Chakrensystems zu sehen ist.

[05] Untitled, 1971–c. 2010

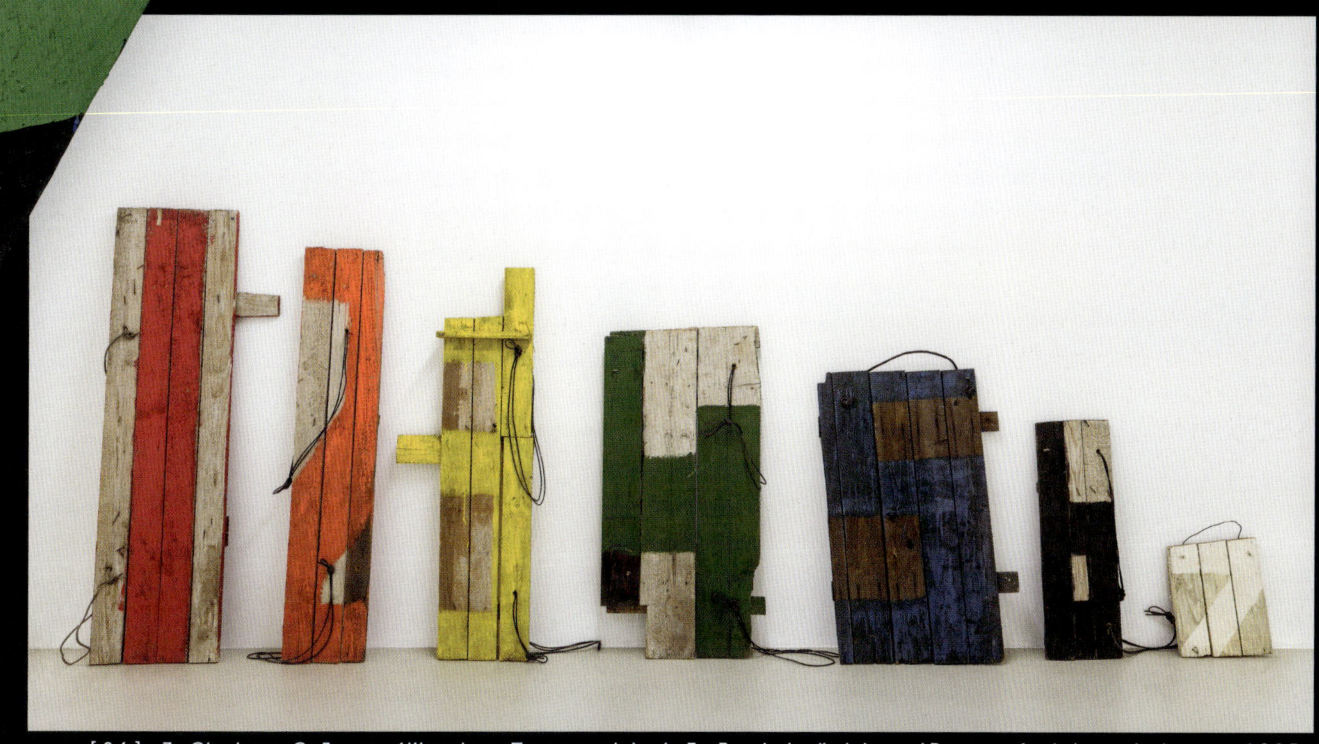

[06] *7 Chakra Colors (Wooden Formwork) / 7 farieb čakier (Drevené debnenie)*, c. 1995

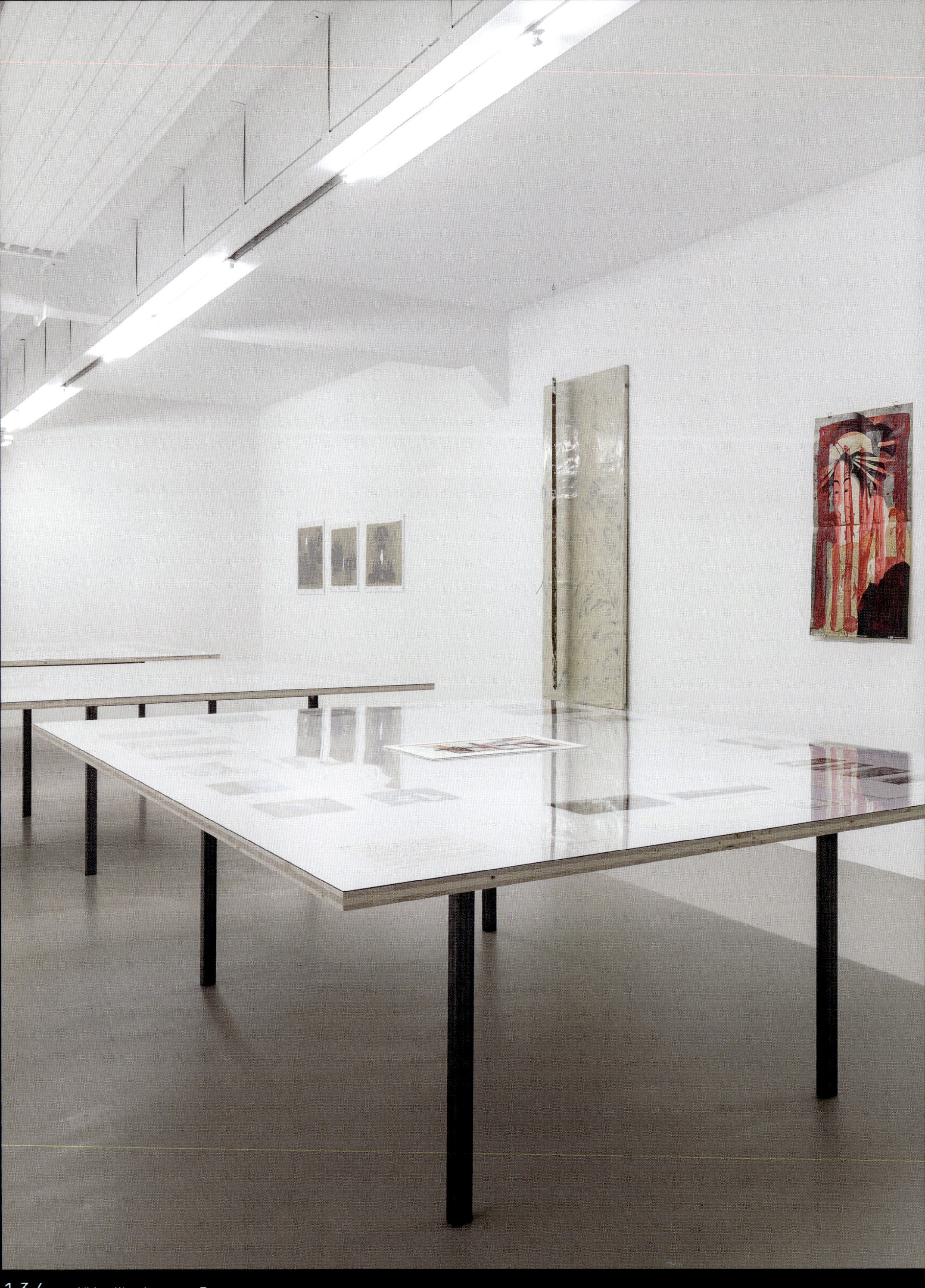

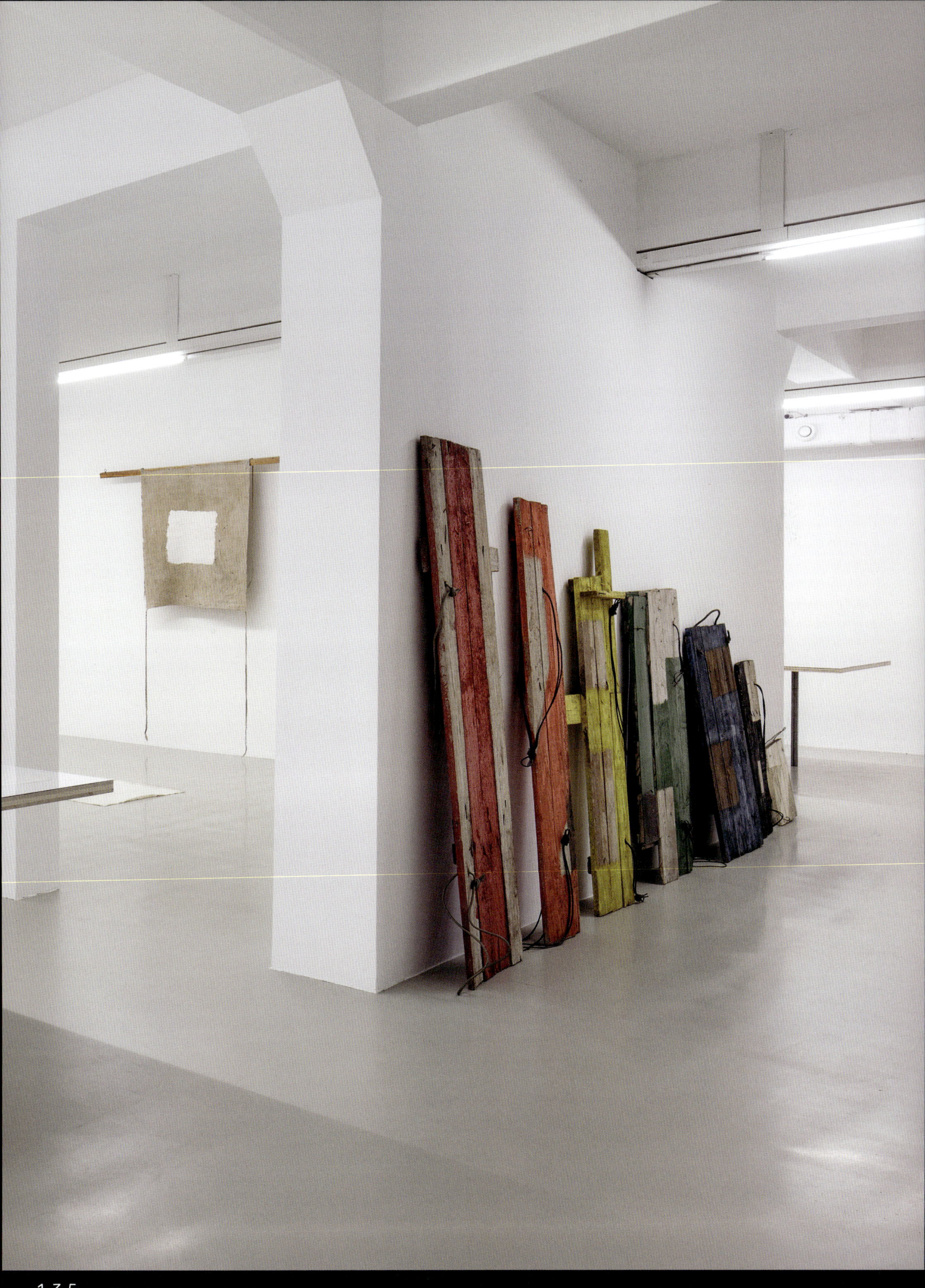

XV. Works on Paper / Papierarbeiten

Works on paper actually give an impression of how Stano Filko continuously developed his *System SF* over the decades. It is apparent that *System SF* is a metaphysical system in which Filko combines fragments from scientific disciplines such as philosophy, astronomy, and physics with pseudo-scientific theories. He uses the system to develop a visual form of thinking that crosses borders in different ways, among them the borders between art and life, subjectivity and objectivity, east and west, and material and cognition, to name only the most important.

Two sheets show *EXIZSTEAOQ = HAPPSOCSF System / ANTE BIGBANGSF 5.D.* (1995–2005) [02] and *RETROQ System SF* (1995–2005) [03] colored numbered columns that clearly illustrate the distinctions in *System SF*. Each column is devoted to one of twelve colors or chakras and presents the connections to different areas of being, senses, elements, signs of the compass, and dimensions. Filko also attributes a specific philosophical doctrine or school to the features of each chakra, ranging from Heidegger, Wittgenstein, and Kant to Aristotle. The system cannot be grasped through a knowledge of rational sources alone, however, but must be seen as a paradoxical order shaped also in many ways by emotional components.

Gerade Papierarbeiten geben einen Einblick darüber, wie Stano Filko sein *System SF* über Jahrzehnte hinweg kontinuierlich ausgearbeitet hat. Deutlich wird, dass es sich beim *System SF* um ein metaphysisches System handelt, in dem Filko Versatzstücke aus wissenschaftlichen Disziplinen wie Philosophie, Astronomie und Physik mit pseudo-wissenschaftlichen Theorien verbindet. Er nutzt das System um eine visuelle Form des Denkens zu entwickeln, die vielfach Grenzen überwindet, Grenzen zwischen Kunst und Leben, Subjektivität und Objektivität, Ost und West sowie Materie und Kognition, um nur die wesentlichsten zu nennen.

Die zwei Blätter *EXIZSTEAOQ = HAPPSOCSF System / ANTE BIGBANGSF 5.D.* (1995–2005) [02] und *RETROQ System SF* (1995–2005) [03] zeigen farbig nummerierte Spalten und veranschaulichen das *System SF* in maximaler Differenzierung. Jede Spalte widmet sich einer von zwölf Farben bzw. Chakren und offenbart Verbindungen zu bestimmten Daseins- und Sinnesbereichen, Elementen, Himmelsrichtungen und Dimensionen. Der Charakteristik jedes Chakras ordnet Filko jeweils auch eine bestimmte philosophische Lehre zu, diese reichen von Heidegger, Wittgenstein und Kant bis hin zu Aristoteles. Nichtsdestotrotz lässt sich das System nicht allein durch die Kenntnis rationaler Quellen verstehen, sondern muss als eine paradoxe Ordnung begriffen werden, die auch vielfach von emotionalen Komponenten bestimmt ist.

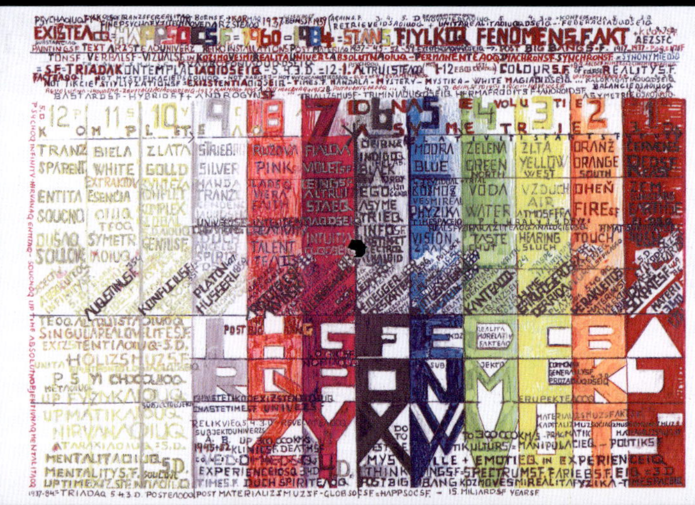

[02] *EXIZSTEAOQ = HAPPSOCSF System / ANTE BIGBANGSF 5.D.*, 1995–2005

[03] *RETROQ System SF*, 1995–2005

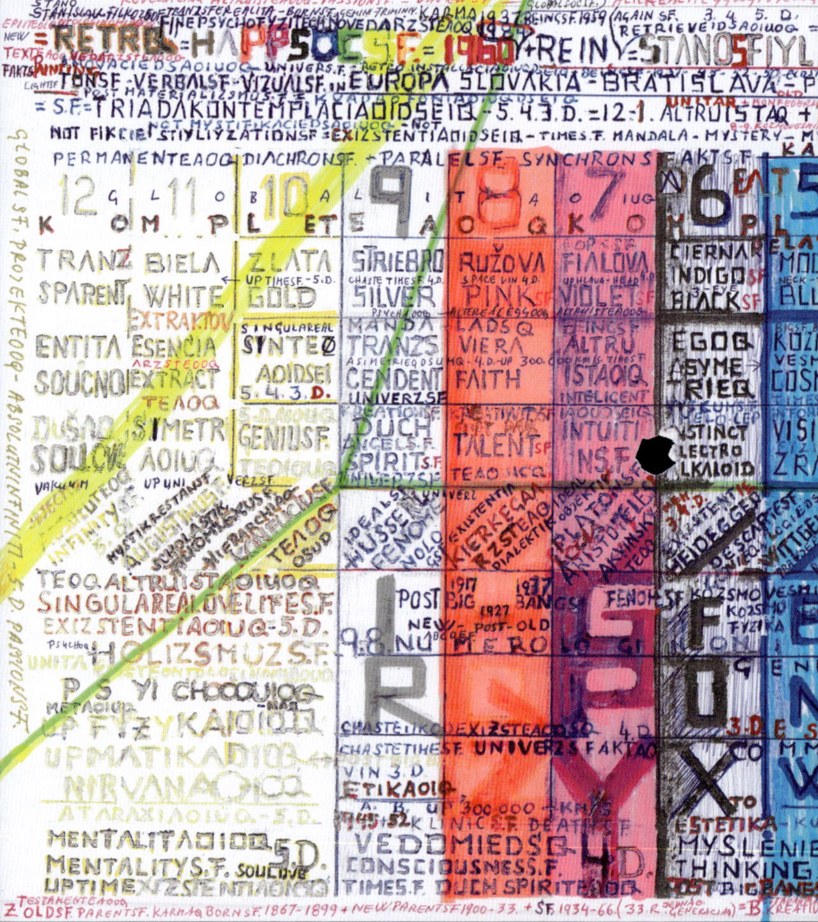

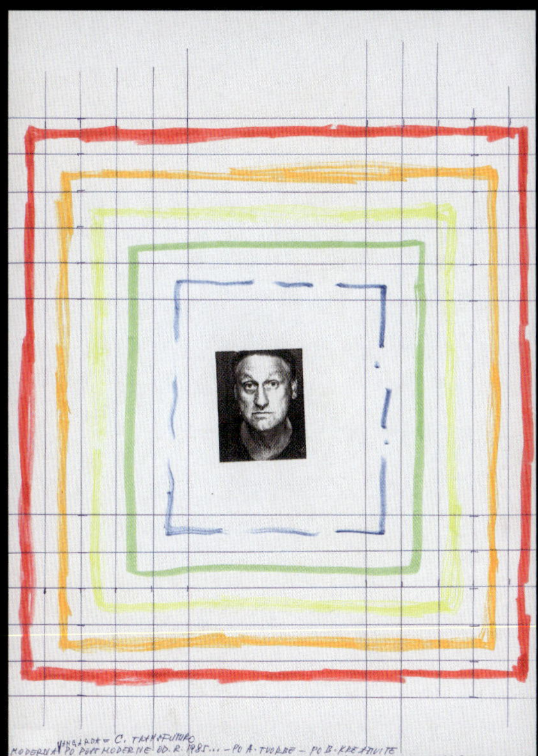

[04] *Self-Portrait – Phylko / Autoportrét – Phylko 1988–90*, 1985–95

Another sheet entitled *Self-Portrait – Phylko / Autoportrét – Phylko 1988–90* (1985–95) [04] illustrates this connection: In the center of a rectangular colored field there is a photo self-portrait of Filko, by means of which the artistic ego appears as the starting point of the system. This ego is not to be seen as unified, however, but consists of various "cloned" identities that Filko draws on another sheet in graffiti-like forms. In six different colors this work shows arrangements of letters that are all permutations of Filko's name. Filko accords these different periods of time, and they seem to express different clones of his own identity, as in his own narrative about his "clinical deaths."

It is typical in Filko's *System SF* that very different fields of knowledge are drawn on, and that these gain a subjective component through their artistic appropriation. The sheet *The Lost World of Mammoths in Slovakia / Stratený svet mamutov na Slovensku* (1985–95) [05] uses a newspaper article about mammoths in Slovakia to show how far artistic appropriation can go and how improbable it is that this system could ever produce any kind of unified and rationalist whole.

Ein anderes Blatt mit dem Titel *Self-Portrait – Phylko / Autoportrét – Phylko 1988–90* (1985–1995) [04] verdeutlicht diese Verbindung: In der Mitte eines rechteckig angeordneten und durch Farbe markierten Bereiches befindet sich ein fotografisches Selbstporträt von Filko, durch welches das künstlerische Ego als Ausgangspunkt des Systems erscheint. Dieses Ego ist aber nicht als einheitlich zu betrachten, sondern besteht aus verschiedenen „geklonten" Identitäten, die Filko auf einem weiteren Blatt in Graffito-ähnlicher Gestalt ausarbeitet. In sechs verschiedenen Farben sind auf der Arbeit Anordnungen von Buchstaben zu sehen, die Permutationen von Filkos Namen bilden. Diese werden von Filko mit unterschiedlichen Zeitspannen versehen und scheinen verschiedene Klone seiner Identität auszudrücken, wie auch in seiner Erzählung über die „klinischen Tode".

Typisch für Filkos *System SF* ist das Aufgreifen ganz unterschiedlicher Wissensbereiche, die dann durch die künstlerische Bearbeitung eine subjektive Komponente erhalten. Das Blatt *The Lost World of Mammoths in Slovakia / Stratený svet mamutov na Slovensku* (1985–1995) [05] zeigt mittels eines Zeitungsartikels über Mammuts in der Slowakei, wie weit die künstlerische Aneignung reicht und wie unwahrscheinlich es gleichzeitig ist, dass aus dem System ein einheitlich-rationalisierbarer Zusammenhang wird.

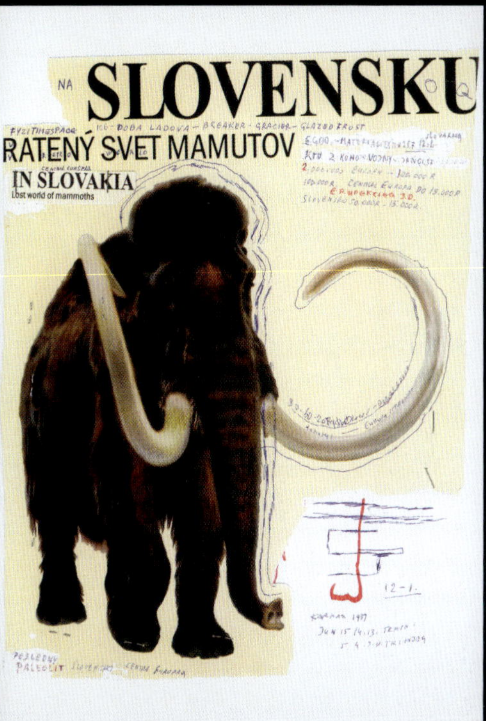

[05] *The Lost World of Mammoths in Slovakia / Stratený svet mamutov na Slovensku*, 1985–95

[06] Untitled, 1971–c. 2010

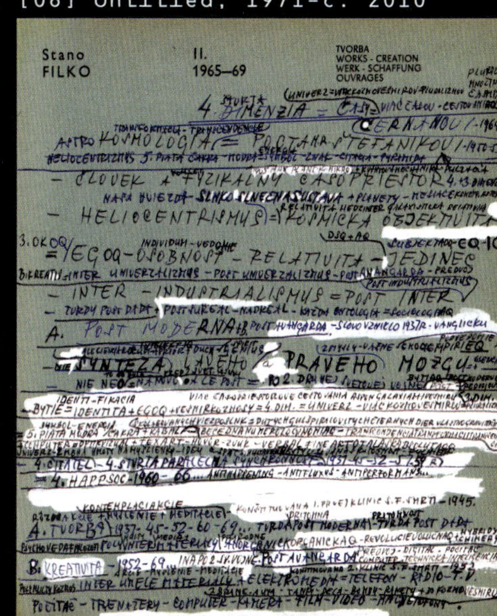

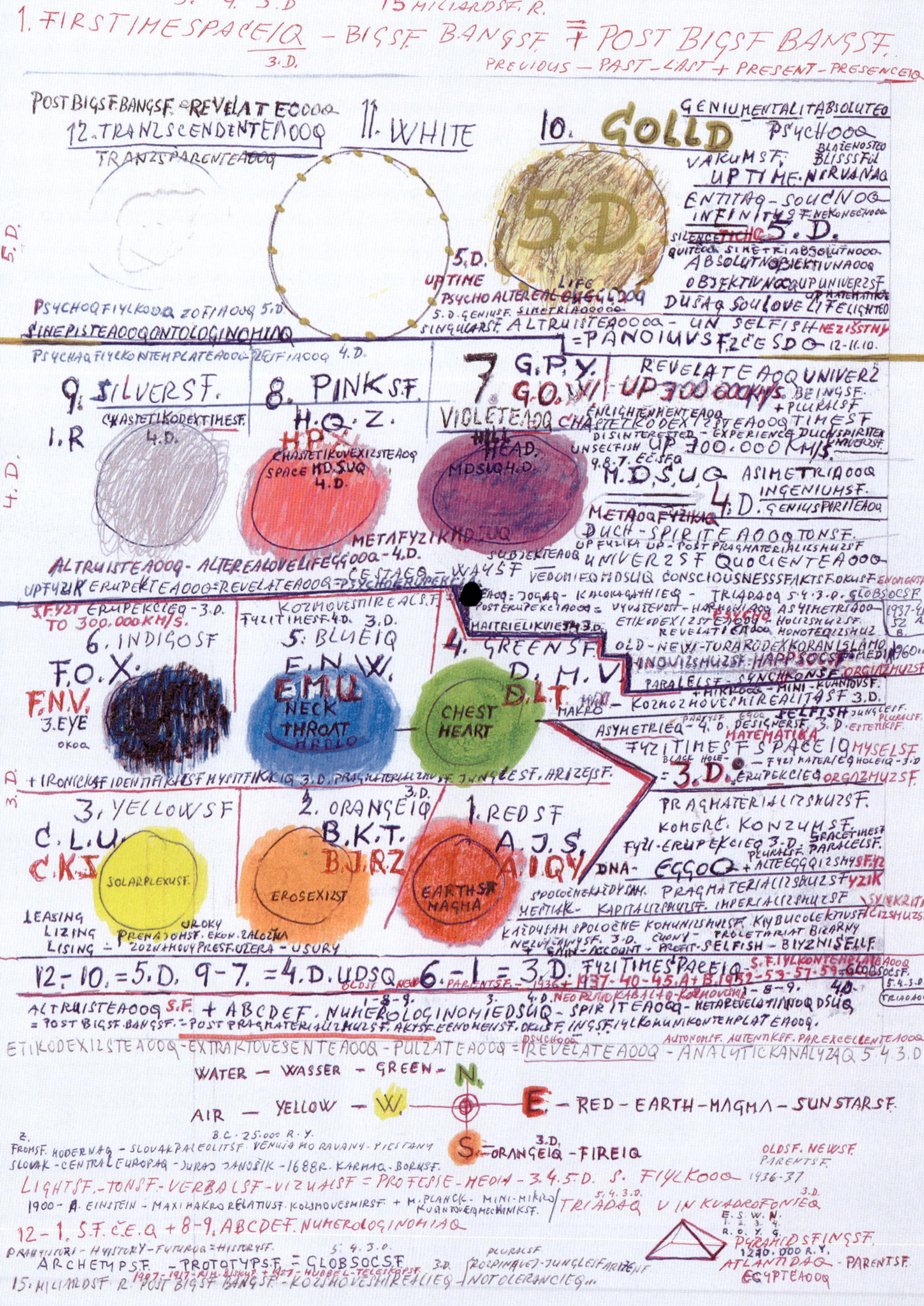
N.
5. 4. 3. D   15 MILIARDSF. R.
1. FIRSTIMESPACEIQ — BIGSF. BANGSF. ⇌ POST BIGSF. BANGSF.
3. D.
PREVIOUS — PAST — LAST + PRESENT — PRESENCEIQ
POST BIGSF. BANGSF. — REVELATECOOQ
12. TRANZSCENDENTEAOOQ
TRANZSPARENTEAOOQ
11. WHITE
10. COLLD
5. D.
GENIUMENTALITABSOLUTEO
PSYCHOOQ
VAKUMSF.   BLAZENOSTCO
BLISSSFUL
UP TIME. NIRVANAQ
ENTITAQ — SOUCNOQ
INFINITY — NEKONECNOOQ
SILENCETICHO 5. D.
QUITECO SINCETRIABSOLUTNOOQ
ABSOLUTNOBJEKTIVNAOOQ
OBJEKTIVNOQ UP UNIVERZSF.
DUSAQ SOULOVE LIFELIGHTEO
5. D.
UPTIME
PSYCHO ALTEREALOHGGLLOOQ
5. D. GENIUSF. SINCETRIAOOOOO
SINGUIARSF. ALTRUISTEAOOQ — UN SELFISH NEZISSTNY
= PANOIUVSF. 2°ČESDO 12-11.10.
PSYCHOOQFIYLKOOQ ZOFIAOOQ 5. D.
SINEPISTEAOOQONTOLOGINOHIAQ
PSYCHAQ FIYLKONTEHPLATEAOOQ ZOFIAOOQ 4. D.
9. SILVERSF.
I. R
4. D.
CHASTETIKODEXTIMESF.
8. PINK SF.
H. Q. Z.
HPX
CHASTETIKOVEXIZSTEAOOQ
SPACE H.D.S.U.Q
4. D.
7. G. P. Y.
G. O. W.
VIOLETEAOQ CHAPTE
HILL
HEAD.
MDSUQ 4. D.
METAFYZIKHD.UQ
UP 300.000 KM/S
REVELATEAOQ UNIVERZ
BEINGSF.
+ PLURALSF.
ENLIGHTENHENTEAOQ
CHAPTEKODEX 2 STEAOOQ TIMESF.
DISINTERESTED — EXPERIENCE DUCHSPIRITEH
UNSELFISH UP 300.000 KM/S
9.8.7. ĚČSFQ
M.D.S.U.Q ASIMETRIAOOQ
INGENIUHSF.
4. D. GENIUSPIRITEAOQ
DUCH — SPIRITEAOOQ TONSF.
UPFUZIA UP — POST PRAGHATERIALISHUZSF
UNIVERZSF QUOCIENTEAOOQ
CONSCIOUSNESSSFAKTSF.OKUSF. EVONGHSF.
TRIAQAOQ 5.4.3.0. GLOBSOCSF.
ETIKODEX12STEAOOQ ASYHETRIAOO
HOLIZHUZSF
OLD — NEWI — TURAKODEXKORANISLAMO
INOVIZSHUZSF. HAPPSOCSF.
PARALELSF. — SYNCHRONSE ORGIZHUZSF
+ HIKROSF. — MINI — KVANTOVSF.
— KOZHOZHOVESHIREALITASF 3. D.
ASYHETRIEQ — 4. D. DESIGNERSF. MATEHATIKA
FYZI TIMESF SPACE IQ MYSELSF.
BLACK HOLE — FYZI HATERIEQHOLEIQ 3. D.
= 3. D. ERUPEKCIEQ ORGOZHUZSF.
6. INDIGOSF
F. O. X.
F. N. V.
3. EYE
5. BLUEIQ
E. N. W.
EMU
NECK
THROAT
HRDLO
4. GREENSF.
D. M. V
D. LT
CHEST
HEART
+ IRONICKAF IDENTIFIKATESF HYSTIFIKAIQ 3. D. PRAGHATERIALIZHUVSF. JUNGLESF. ARIZEISF.
PRAGHATERIALIZSHUZSF.
KOHERĚ. KONZUMSF.
SPACETIMESF
FYZI-ERUPEKCIEQ 3. D. PLURALSF. PARALELSF.
+ ALTEREQQIZSHYSFYZIK
3, YELLOWSF
C. L. U.
C. K. J
SOLARPLEXUSF.
2. ORANGEIQ
3. D.
B. K. T.
B. J. R. Z
EROSEXIZST
1. RED SF
A. J. S.
A. I. Q. Y
EARTHSF
MAGHA
DNA — EGGOQ
SPOLOČENSKÝDYSAH. PRAGHATERIALIZSHUZSF FYZIK
HEHIAK — KAPITALIZHUZSF. IMPERIALIZSHUZSF SYNKRITI
KAŽDÝSAH SPOLOČNE KOMUNIZHUSF. KYBUCOLEKTIVSFCIZSHUZSF
NERVIHANYSF. 3. D. CUONY — PROLETARIAT BIZARNY
+ GAIN — ACCOUNT — PROFIT-SELFISH — BIYZNISEILF.
LEASING
LIZING
LISING — ŽROKY
PRENAJOHSF. EKON.ZALOŽNA
ŽOZNAKHOVYPRESF.UŽERA — USURY
12 — 10. = 5. D. 9 — 7. = 4. D. UDSQ
6 — 1 = 3. D. FYZI TIMESPACEIQ
ALTRUISTEAOOQ S.F. + ABCDEF. NUHEROLOGINOHIEDSUQ
= POST BIGSF. BANGSF. — POST PRAGHATERIALIZHUZSF. AKTSF.EENOHENSF.OKUSF. INGSF.FIYLKOMUNIKONTEHPLATEAOOQ.
ETIKODEXIZSTEAOOQ — EXTRAKTOVESENTEAOOQ — PULZATEAOOQ
REVELATEAOOQ — ANALYTICKANALYZAQ 5 4 3. D.
WATER — WASSER — GREEN —
N.
AIR — YELLOW — W — E — RED — EARTH — HAGHA — SUN STARSF.
S — ORANGEIQ — FIREIQ
B.C. 25.000 R. Y.
FROMSF. HODERNAQ — SLOVAKPALEOLITSF. VENUJA HORAVANY — PIESTANY
SLOVAK — CENTRALEUROPAQ — JURAJ JANOSIK — 1688R. KARHAQ. BORKSF.
OLDSF. NEWSF
PARENTSF.
LIGHTSF. — TONSF. — VERBALSF. — VIZUALSF = PROFESSIE — HEDIA — 3.4.5.D. S. FIYLKOOQ 1936-37
1900 — A. EINSTEIN — MAXI HAKRO RELATIUSF. KOSHOVESHIRSF. + H. PLANCK — MINI — HIKRO
KUAHTOVEHHECHINKSF. TRIADAQ V IN KUADROFONIEQ
12 — 1. S.F. ČE.Q + 8-9. ABCDEF. NUHEROLOGINOHIAQ
PRAHYIIORI — HYSTORY — FUTURAQ = HISTORYSF.
ARCHETYPSF. — PROTOTYPSF. = GLOBSOCSF.
PRZPINAVEJ — JUNGLEIFARIEIHT
PYRAHID SFINGSF.
1230.000 R. Y.
ATLANTIDAQ — PARENTSF.
EGYPTEAOOQ
15. HILIARDSF. R. POST BIGSF. BANGSF. — KOZHOVESHIREALIEQ — NOTOLERANCIEQ...

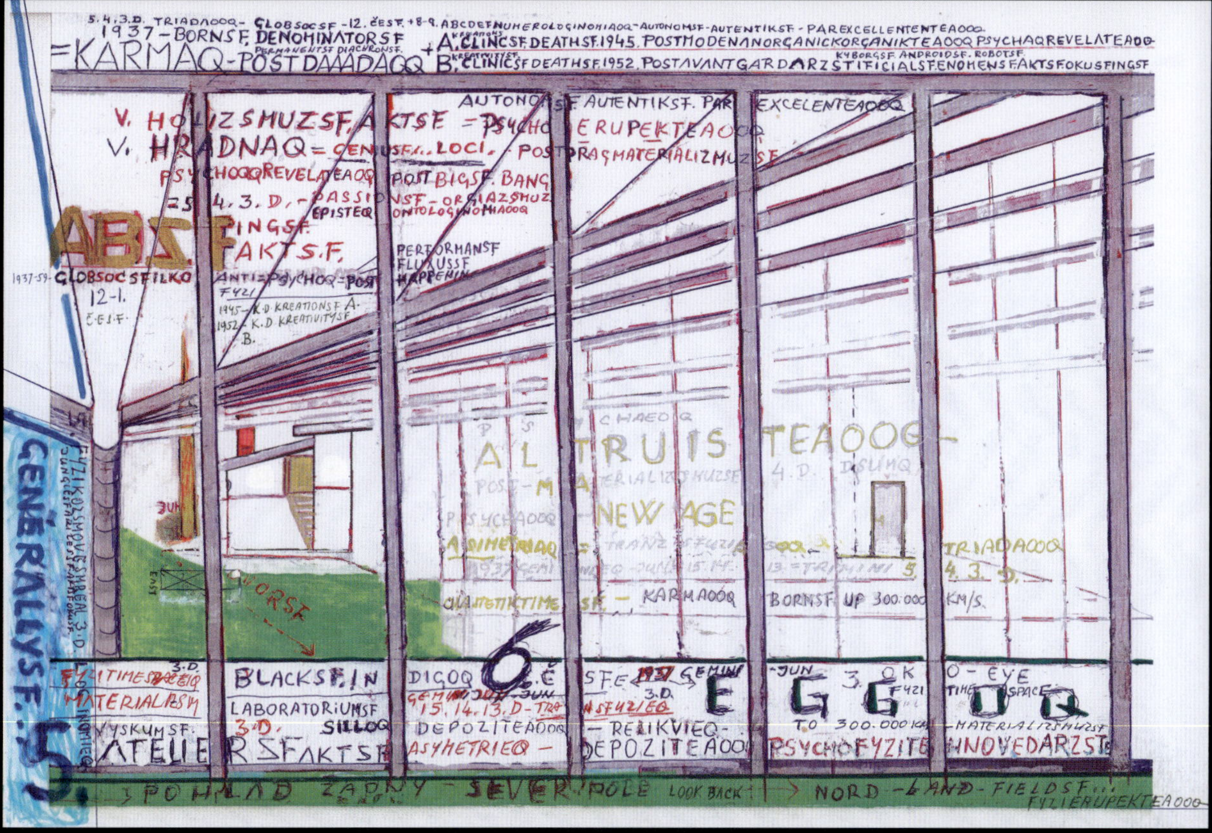

[08] *S.FYILKORAB VELKA HRADNAQ I., 2000–10*

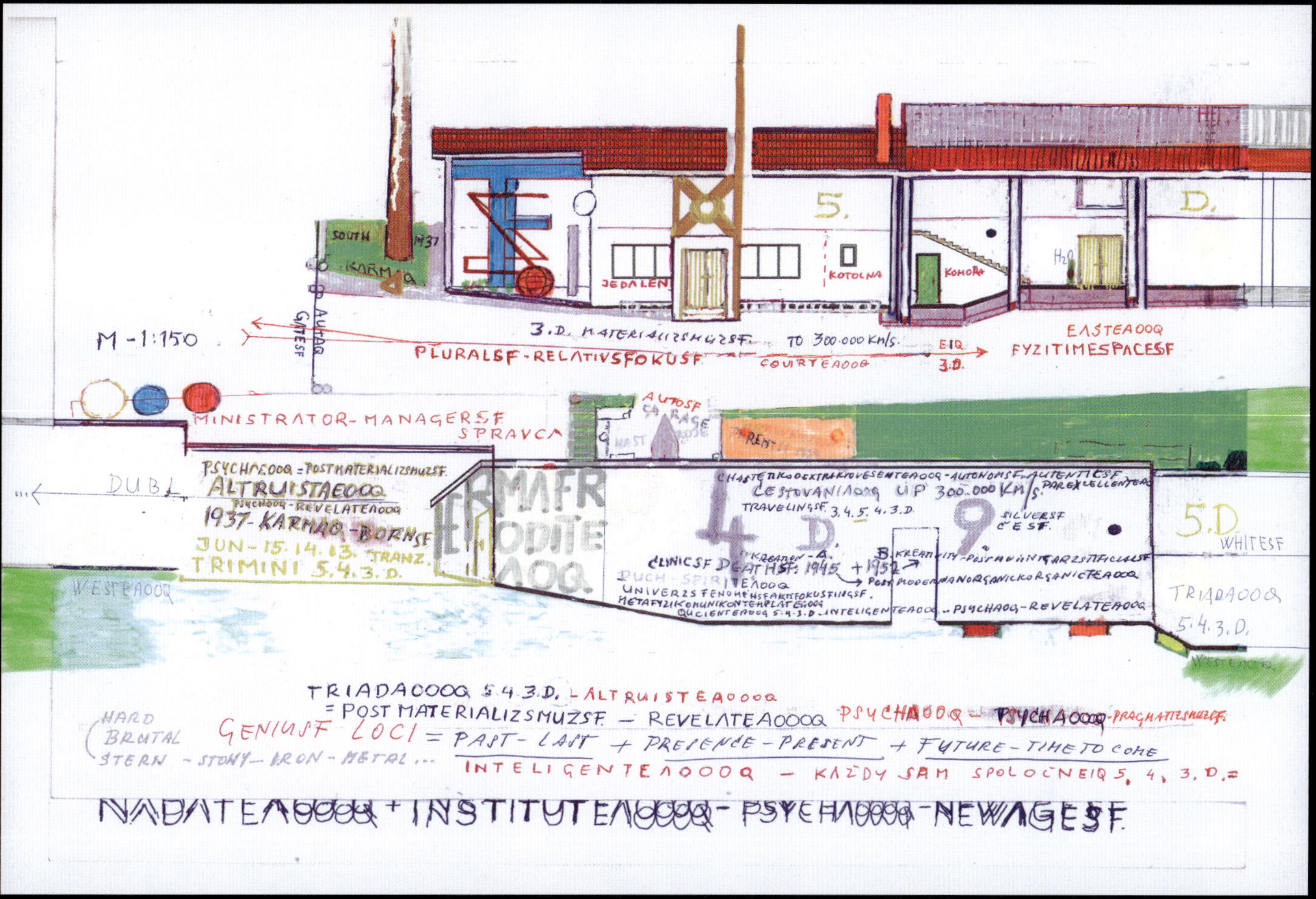

[09] *INSTITUTEAOOQ – Project Velká Hradná I. / INSTITUTEAOOQ Projekt Velká Hradná I., 2000–10*

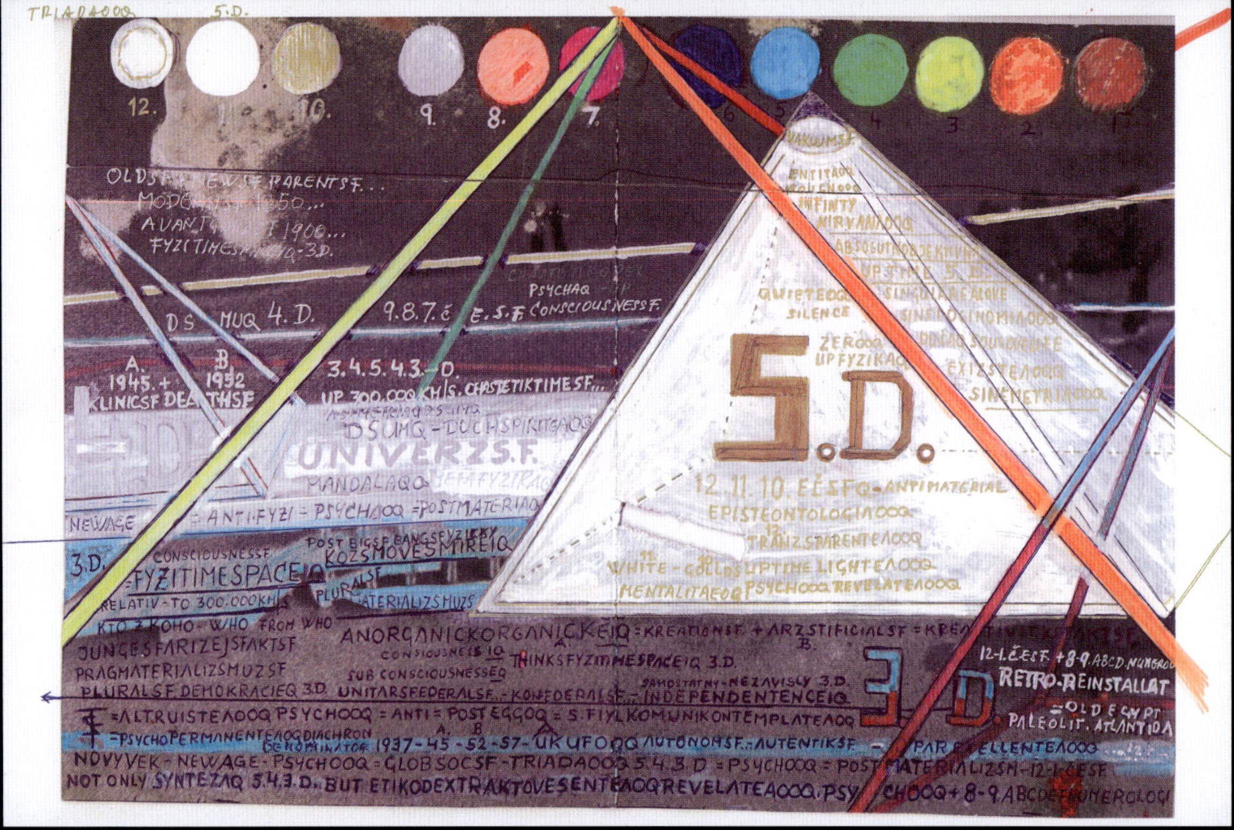

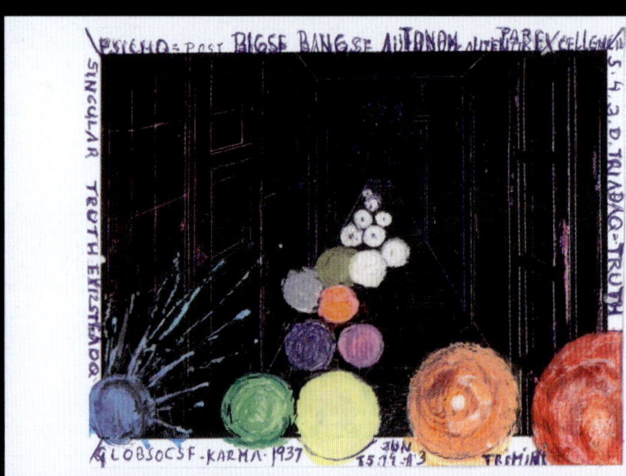

[10] *5.D. UNIVERSESF Pyramid I. / 5.D. UNIVERZSF Pyramída I.*, 1995–2005

It is very clear that Filko's interest in the cosmic space and in aviation and space exploration were very important for his *System SF*. Several sheets allude to outer space, with the colors and chakras of the system presented as spheres on a black background, reminiscent of both color samples and planets. [07] On one of these works the system is linked with a pyramid [10], a symbol that Filko saw as representing the ideal form of the universe and that he also placed on the roof of his studio. In his famous artist's studio Snežienková Filko also implemented his system in the arrangement of real rooms. *System SF* became a comprehensive ordering principle and an archive of Filko's own life. He also had the idea of devoting an entire museum in his home town of Veľká Hradná to the system, which was sadly not realized. His plans for this are presented in two project sketches. [09] [14]

Klar erkennbar ist jedoch, wie wichtig Filkos Interesse am kosmischen Raum und der Luft- und Raumfahrt für das *System SF* gewesen sein muss. Mehrere Blätter zeigen Anklänge an das Weltall, die Farben bzw. Chakren des Systems sind in sphärischer Form vor schwarzem Hintergrund zu sehen und erinnern gleichzeitig an Farbsamples und Planeten. [07] Auf einer dieser Arbeiten wird das System mit einer Pyramide verbunden [10], ein Symbol, das für Filko die ideale Form des Universums darstellt und sich auch auf dem Dach seines Ateliers wiederfindet. In seinem berühmten Künstleratelier Snežienková hat Filko das System zudem durch die Anordnung realer Räume ausgearbeitet. Das *System SF* wurde zu einem umfassenden Ordnungsprinzip und Archiv von Filkos Leben. Filko hatte auch die Idee, dem System ein ganzes Museum in seinem Heimatort Veľká Hradná zu widmen, was leider nicht realisiert werden konnte. Zwei Projektskizzen geben über seine Planungen Auskunft. [09] [14]

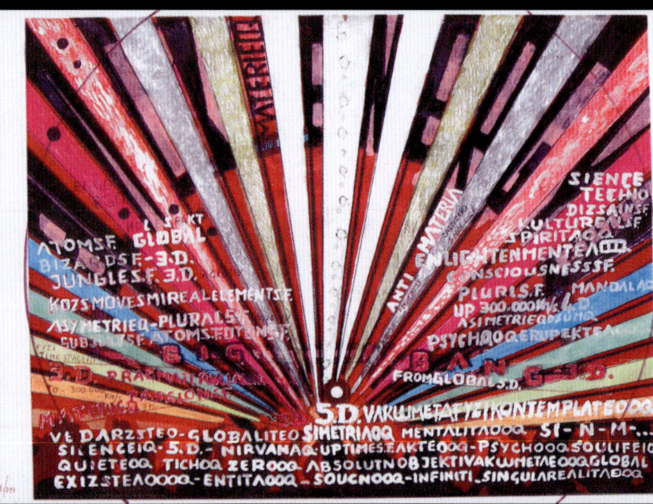

[11] *SINGULAR TRUTH / Stano Filko Master's Studio*, 1995–2005

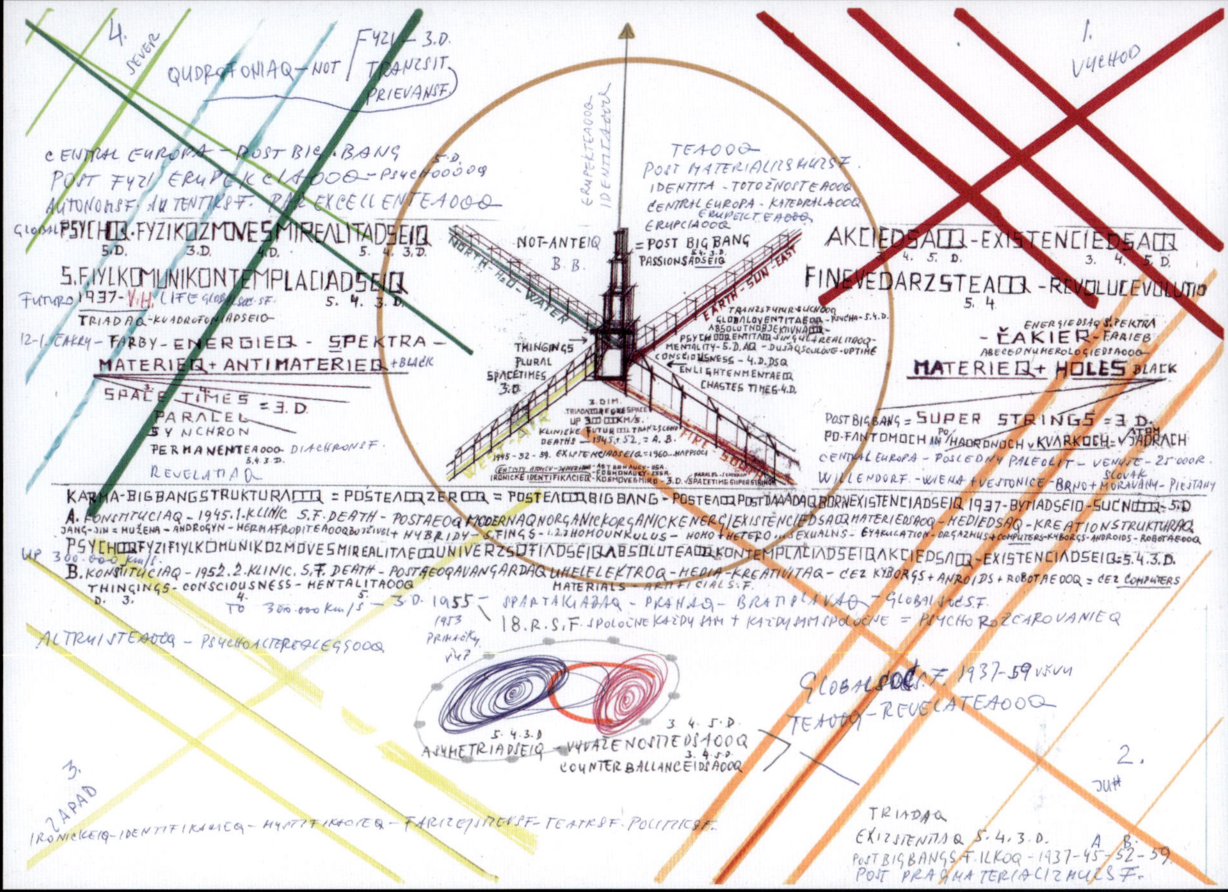

[13] *TRANZSIT PRIEVANSF II. Project Tranzit / TRANZSIT PRIEVANSF II. Projekt Tranzit, 2005–10*

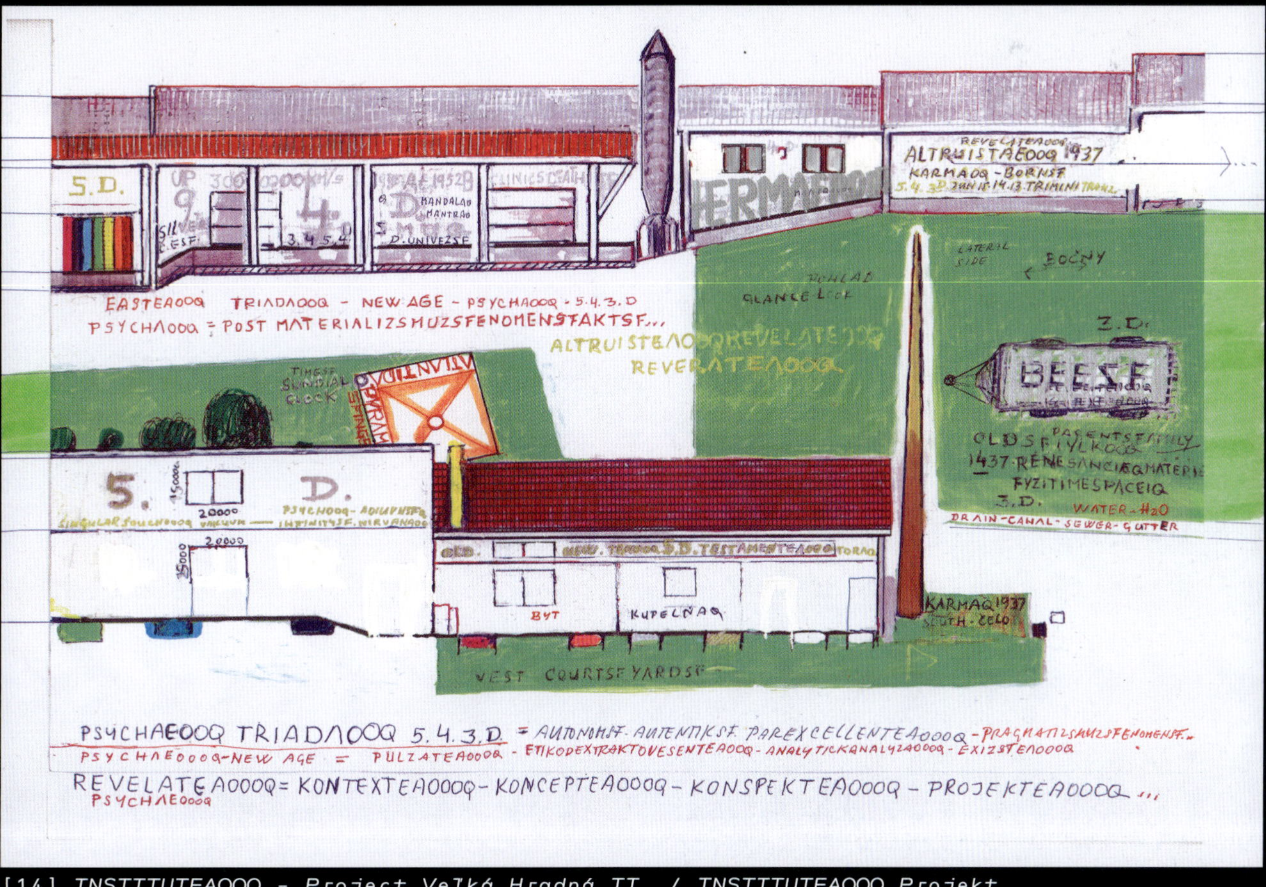

[14] *INSTITUTEAOOQ – Project Veľká Hradná II. / INSTITUTEAOOQ Projekt*

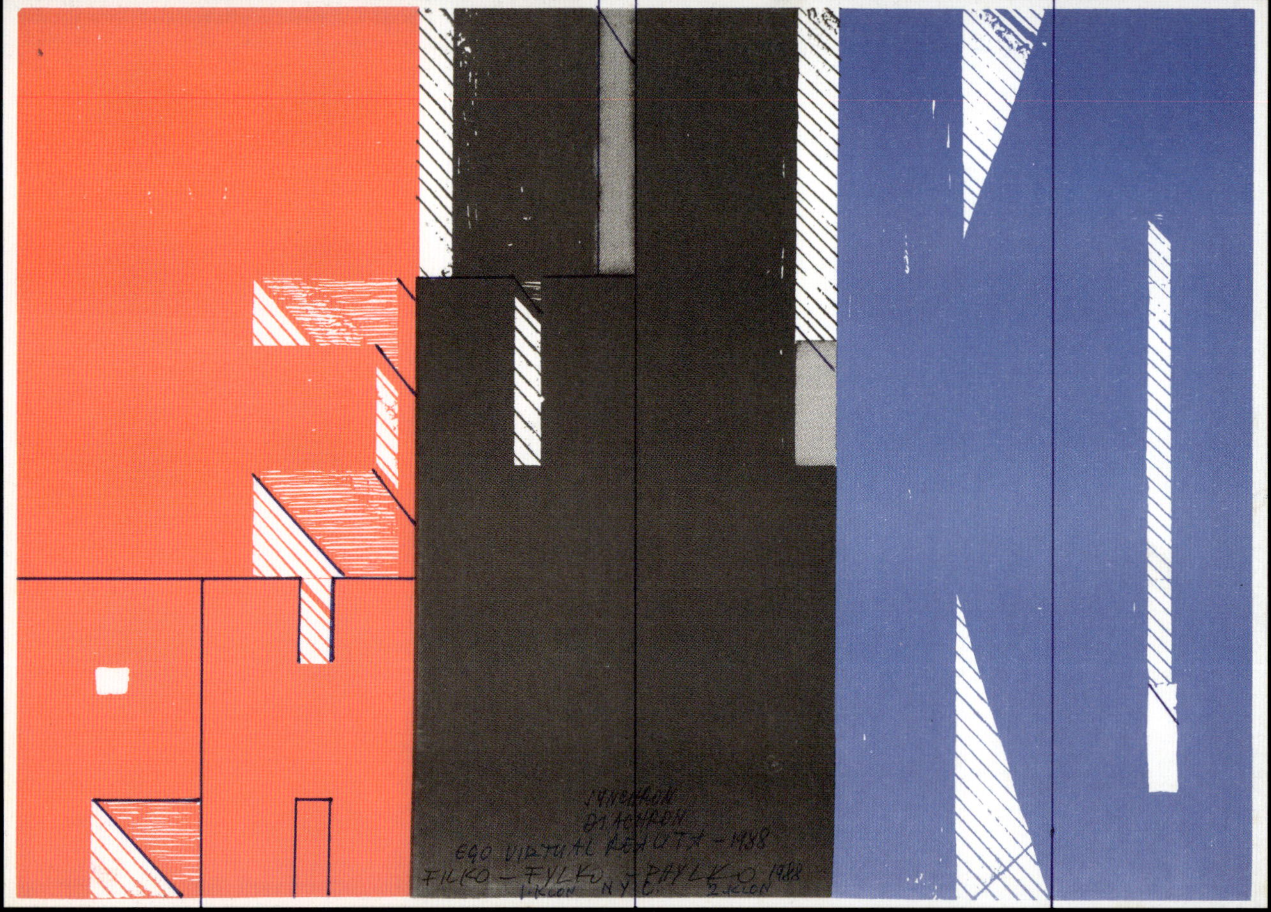

[15] *Phylko – Synchron – Diachron, 1985–95*

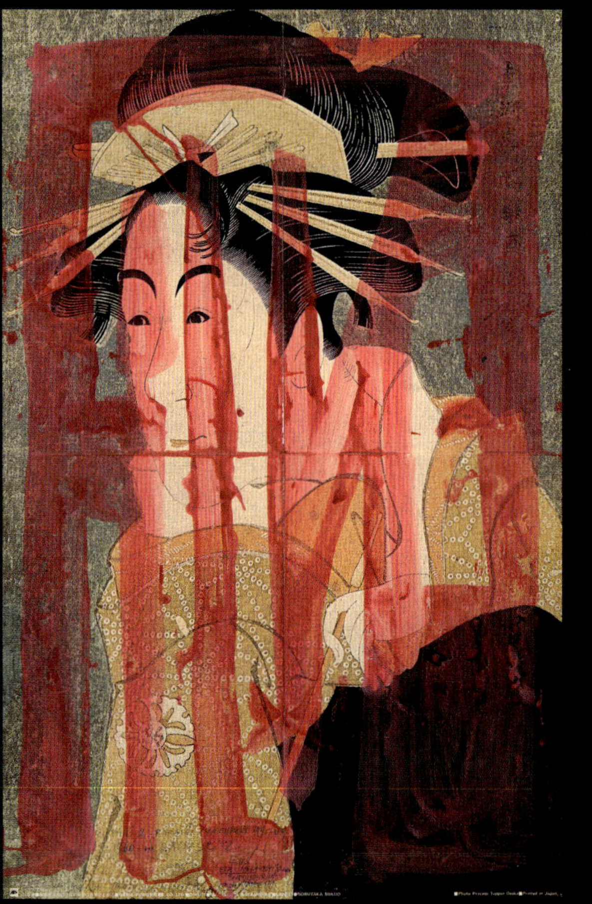

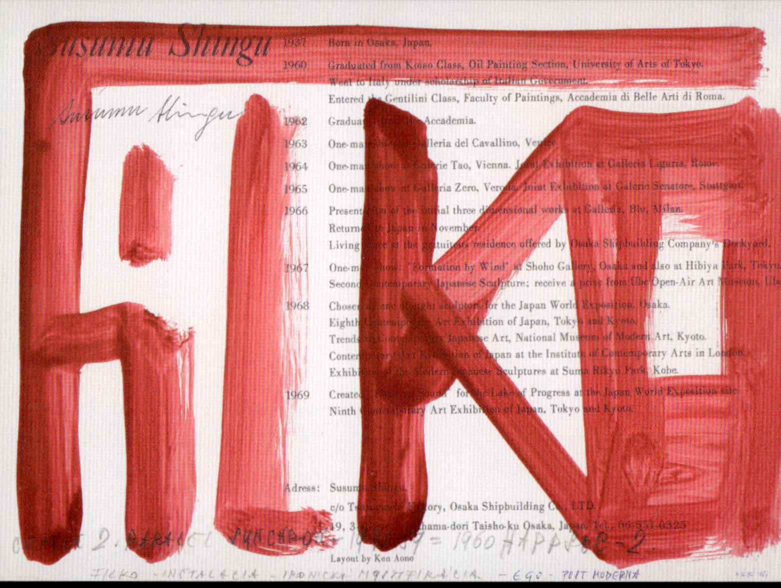

[17] *Filko on the Susumu Shingu Poster /
Filko na plagáte Susumu Shingu, 1970/c. 2000*

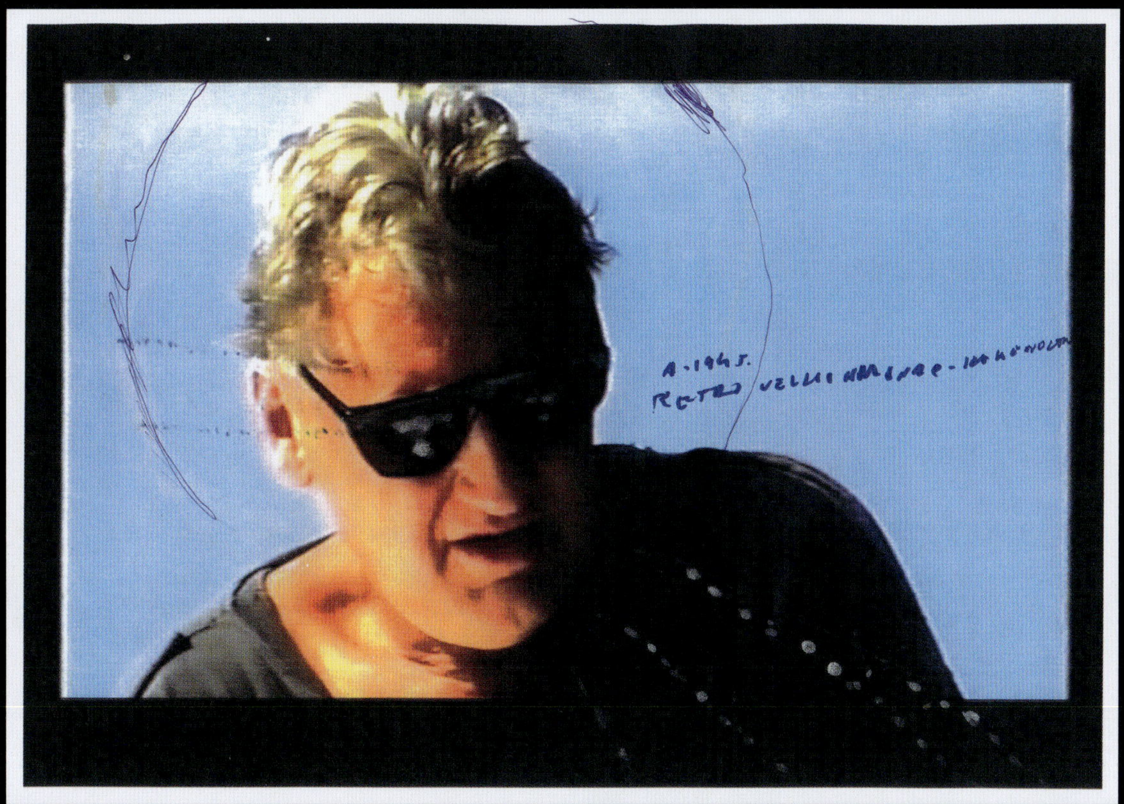

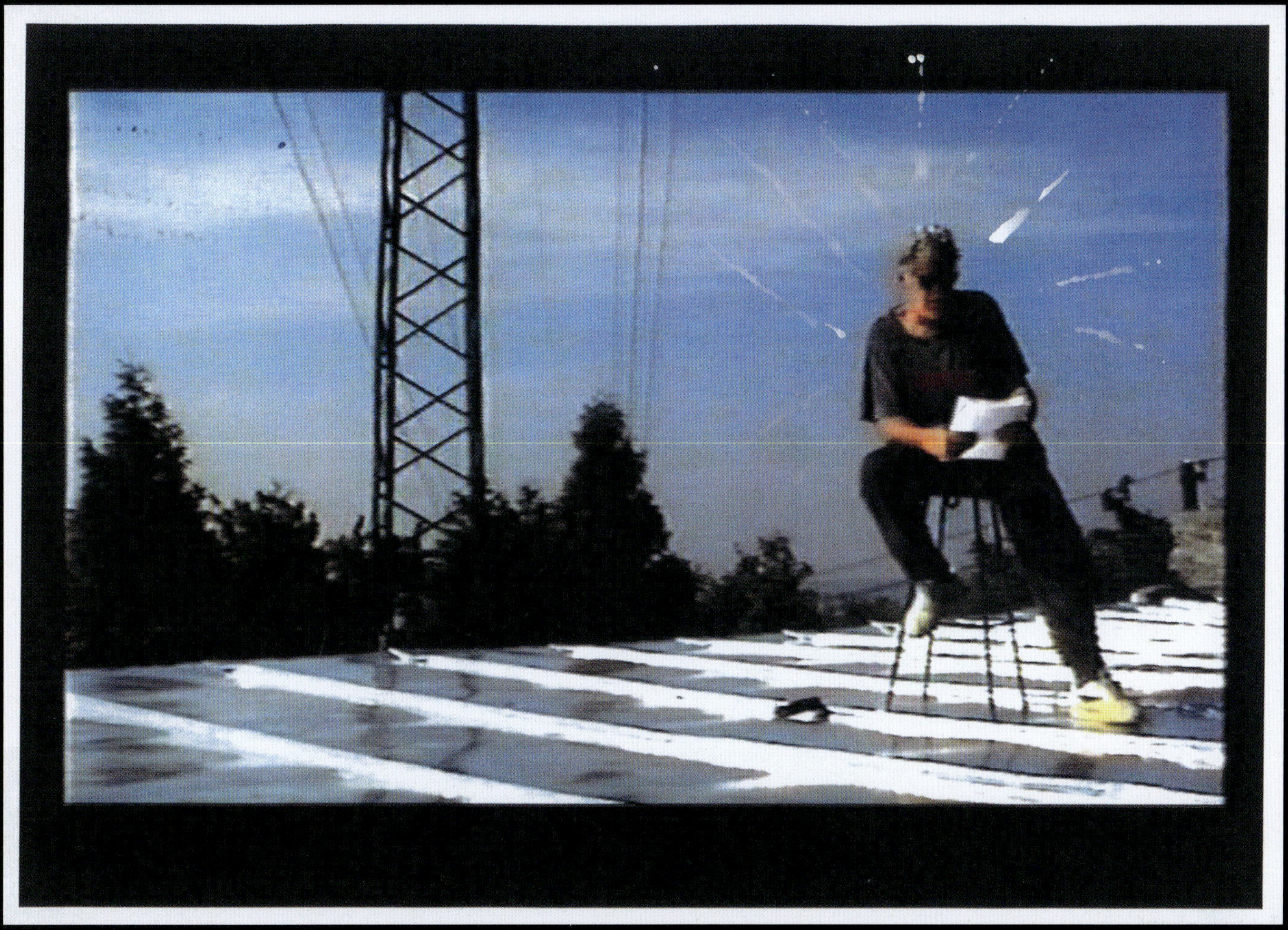

[19] *RETRO VELKAQ HRADNAQ II., 1995–2005*

Blue Ladders in the Universe: Space and Cosmos as Sensual Topoi in the Work of Stano Filko. Or: A System by Filko on *PSYCHOQFYZIKOZMOVESMIREALUNVERZABSOLUTEAQ – FIYLKOMUNIKONTEMPLACIEDSAOQ*

Patricia Grzonka

The retrospective of the work of Slovak artist Stano Filko in Graz is a good opportunity to take a look back at the "cosmos"[1] of this artist. An increasing body of literature on Filko notwithstanding, there are still many gaps in our knowledge of his eclectic oeuvre, raising the question as to which paradigms have hitherto been applied in the mechanisms evaluating his art. The following is not intended as a new interpretation of Filko's work, and instead I would like to suggest a reading based on a certain approach to the themes of space and place that places his relations to the context and the reality of post-socialist art in a new focus. [01–02]

Retrospective

Stano Filko (1937–2015) was and is certainly no unknown in Slovak and central European art, but the sheer magnitude of his transgressive artistic oeuvre has made it difficult to approximate his work and has meant that art scholarship has hitherto only focused on specific aspects. In the context of Slovak art history his works seem very much unique, as they depart from the parameters of both post-conceptual and post-socialist art. It is no coincidence therefore that today Stano Filko is primarily associated with works that can be inscribed into the narrative of Western art and that thus a large part of his opulent oeuvre is neglected. The conceptual works (such as the *HAPPSOC* series in the 1960s, the environments from the same period, and the metaphysical and transcendental gestures of his *White Space* project in the 1970s) have attracted most attention to date. These work groups can be seamlessly connected to the context of the avant-garde and the neo-avant-garde in the European metropolises of Paris and Milan at the time, or the New York art scene—and these are also the places to which Filko created or sought his own major artistic relations.[2] One might also say that Stano Filko very purposefully made these connections to a Western art scene while he was still operating under the system of a socialist state.[3]

Blaue Leitern im Universum: Raum und Kosmos als sinnliche Topoi bei Stano Filko. Oder: Ein System von Filko zu *PSYCHOQ-FYZIKOZMOVESMIREALUNVERZ-ABSOLUTEAQ – FIYLKOMUNIKON-TEMPLACIEDSAOQ*

Patricia Grzonka

Die Retrospektive über den slowakischen Künstler Stano Filko in Graz ist eine gute Gelegenheit, sich dem „Kosmos"[1] dieses Künstlers aus einer rückblickenden Perspektive zu nähern. Nach wie vor existieren trotz einer zusehends wachsenden *Filko-Literatur* viele Leerstellen in Bezug auf sein eklektisches Werk, die die Frage aufwerfen, welche Paradigmen bisher im Verwertungsmechanismus seines Œuvres geltend wurden. In diesem Text soll es nicht um eine Neuinterpretation von Filkos Werk gehen, vielmehr möchte ich auf der Basis seines spezifischen Zugangs zu Themen des Raums und des Ortes eine Lektüre vorschlagen, die sein Verhältnis zum Kontext und zur Realität post-sozialistischer Kunst neu in den Fokus rückt. [01-02]

Retrospektiv

Stano Filko (1937–2015) war und ist zwar in der slowakischen und mittelosteuropäischen Kunst kein Unbekannter, aber der schiere Umfang seines transgressiven künstlerischen Werks erschwerte bisher den Zugang zu diesem und brachte es mit sich, dass sich die Kunstwissenschaft nur mit einzelnen Aspekten seines Werks befasst hat. Im Kontext der slowakischen Kunstgeschichte etwa erscheinen seine Arbeiten singulär, indem sie sowohl aus dem Rahmen einer post-konzeptuellen als auch einer post-sozialistischen Kunst fallen. So ist es kein Zufall, dass Stano Filko heute vor allem mit Arbeiten assoziiert wird, die sich ins Narrativ einer westlich geprägten Kunsterzählung einschreiben lassen und dem gegenüber ein Großteil seines opulenten Werks ausgeblendet wird. Die konzeptuellen Arbeiten (etwa die Serien zu *HAPPSOC* der 1960er-Jahre, die Environments aus derselben Zeit oder die metaphysisch-transzendentalen Gesten des *White Space*-Projekts aus den 1970er-Jahren) erfuhren bisher die meiste Aufmerksamkeit. Diese Werkgruppen können nahtlos an den Kontext von Avantgarde und Neo-Avantgarde in den damaligen europäischen Metropolen Paris und Mailand oder an die New Yorker

He certainly never held back his own personal motivation for gaining recognitions and *success* (whatever that might be) in the context of an international art world.[4]

The art-historical reception that set in after the end of the real-socialist empire, and that in particular grew during the last ten years of the artist's life from 2005, has hitherto mainly concentrated on this particular accessibility to discourse appertaining to his conceptual works. At the same time his late work, which came across as colorful, raw, crazy, and *regressive* in comparison to his *cool* early days, received little attention. This has now changed in recent years, initially thanks to an unconventionally done show in Brno[5] [03] and the retrospective in Graz.[6] These exhibitions on the one hand are not afraid of works that show Filko as an expressive painter and as an *arrangeur*, a bricoleur of different found objects, or as a mystical and introverted *shaman*, and they at the same time pay due attention to Filko as an artist who developed his own independent conceptual idioms within a monochrome complex of works.

The sixth solo exhibition in the Vienna gallery Layr also broke with the reluctance to address Filko's expressive late work from the 1990s on. In their exhibition *RED EXILE*, curators Søren Grammel and Jan Verwoert look at precisely that critical phase in Filko's oeuvre in which the artist became *physical* and *materialist* in the name of a pure anti-metaphysical understanding of the body, a phase that seemed to bid farewell to the earlier conceptual periods.[7] With a good deal of humor—an aspect that has also not been sufficiently addressed in studies on the artist to date—Filko's work is presented to us as not caring for any borders between genres and whose anarchist gesture appropriates objects that do not seem to fit into the clean cosmos of an artist of the neo-avant-garde: a caricature of a self-portrait, monumental gestural painting, a shovel as an accessory, AIDS, assemblages, and a pink pepper mill put together from spray cans and painter's rollers. The presentation of an anarchic and inverted cosmos on the basis of the emotional color red.

Priestor – Space

But within these presentations overarching themes in emergent "Filkology" have so far hardly played any role. This will be attempted in the following, establishing a consistent line of content that runs through both Filko's early and late work as well as the various intermediary phases, and that represents something of a constant within this so frequently diffuse and seemingly contradictory oeuvre. This line is the idea of space. [04]

The idea of space, the direct or indirect thematization of space (in Slovak *priestor*) is present in nearly all of Filko's works. It crosses genres just as his work does, it comprises many "dimensions" that are expressed in his late work in the form of a timeless multi-layered abstract system and that also operate as metaphors. Many works already contain the naming of space in their titles, often in several languages. Space is immaterially connoted in the ascriptions to the "cosmos" as a symbolic utopian place and a social vision. [05] But the idea of space can also be located in concrete physical terms: in Bratislava as a point of reference, for example, where Filko's artistic socialization began and where after his return from American exile he bought a plot of land on Kamzík hill and established his studio there. In this studio that he called "deposit" Filko realized his artistic visions from the mid-1990s as a Foucaultian heterotopia,[8] by transforming the profane building and garden into a placeless and timeless structure. The arrangements he implemented there are solely bound to his own *System SF*. Antennae on the roof and various self-made scaffold-like constructions symbolize the connection of this location of inspiration and artistic production with the rest of the universe.

The significance of space-time structures in contemporary art and more generally in the culture of the twentieth century has many connotations. The question as to the ways in which *space* is made productive in art and theory has been completely reconfigured since the middle of the twentieth century and above all in recent decades. We are no longer living in a homogeneous space, but in a space that is charged with qualities. Our idea of space is liberated from its role within the concept of location that remained valid for centuries, and now tends to entail the integration of psychological, social, economic, nuclear-age, and finally also emancipatory perspectives. Including political and gender issues also particularly indicates that space is understood as a "relational and not just as an absolute category" especially also in art.[9]

The manifesto-like actions of the *HAPPSOC* (happy socialism) series are among Stano Filko's earliest conceptual works. They are all immaterial conceptions of geographical-spatial dispositions. *HAPPSOC I.* (1965, together with the artist Alex Mlynárčik and the theorist Zita Kostrová) comprises the *awareness* of the sociopolitical space of the city of Bratislava—a *Situations-Readymade* that evokes life in Bratislava during the period from May 2 to 8, 1965, the days between Labor Day (May 1) and the day commemorating the end of the war (May 9). The manifesto for this action declares the different elements of this awareness: 138,036 women, 128,727 men, 49,991 dogs, 18,009 buildings, 165,236 balconies 40,070 water pipes in apartments, 35,060 washing machines, 1 castle, 1 Danube, 22 theaters, 6 cemeteries, 1,000,801 tulips, etc. This bureaucratic list of in total 23 items amounts to a kind of hymn to the materialist "reality" (Filko) of the city of Bratislava, which in the late 1960s was still part of the Socialist Republic of Czechoslovakia ČSSR. The further actions (strictly speaking they were mainly declarations in verbal and written form, Filko's *Anti-Happenings* that took place away from public attention in order to avoid the censors) clearly included the broader geopolitical environment. *HAPPSOC II.* (1965) was a seven-day "creation" on Bratislava station, while Filko called *HAPPSOC III.* (*Altar of Contemporaneity*, 1966) an immaterial invitation that included the population of the country and thus the suggestion that they explore the territory of the state.[10] It is not just the artefacts and objects that are part of this reality, but also spatial structures, *relations* and *relational structures* that represent the aggregate of an abstract object-subject relationship.[11]

Modern Tower of Space

The blue sculpture entitled *Modern Tower of Space / Moderná veža vesmíru* (1967–68),[12] [06] also from the late 1960s, possibly refers to a planned installation for public space, or to an official commission, and it is thus to be understood as a model. The construction consists of a tower that can be entered from

Kunstszene anschließen – und dies sind auch die Orte, zu denen Filko seine künstlerischen Hauptbeziehungen knüpfte oder suchte.[2] Man könnte vielleicht auch sagen, dass Stano Filko sehr bewusst diesen Anschluss an eine westlich orientierte Kunstszene noch unter einem sozialistischen Staatssystem gesucht hat.[3] Seine persönliche Motivation, im Kontext eines internationalen Kunstgeschehens Anerkennung und *Erfolg* – was auch immer damit gemeint sein mag – zu erlangen, hat er selbst jedenfalls nie zurückgehalten.[4]

Die kunsthistorische Rezeption, die nach dem Zerfall des real-sozialistischen Imperiums einsetzte und die sich besonders in den letzten zehn Lebensjahren des Künstlers ab 2005 verstärkte, konzentrierte sich bisher vorwiegend auf diese besondere Diskursfähigkeit seiner konzeptuellen Werke. Gleichzeitig wurde seinem Spätwerk, das dem *coolen* Frühwerk gegenüber bunt, roh, crazy und *regressiv* wirkte, wenig Aufmerksamkeit zuteil. Dies änderte sich jedoch in den letzten Jahren zunächst mit einer unüblich *gebürsteten* Werkpräsentation in Brno[5] [03] sowie mit der Retrospektive in Graz.[6] Diese Ausstellungen schrecken einerseits nicht vor Arbeiten zurück, die Filko als expressiven Maler und Arrangeur, als *Bricoleur* verschiedener vorgefundener Objekte oder als mystisch-introvertierten *Schamanen* zeigen und würdigen ihn gleichzeitig als einen Künstler, der in einem monochromen Werkkomplex eine eigenständige konzeptualistische Sprache entwickelte.

Aber auch die sechste Einzelausstellung in der Wiener Galerie Layr bricht mit der *Scham*, sich mit Filkos expressivem Spätwerk ab den 1990er-Jahren zu beschäftigen. In ihrer Ausstellung *RED EXILE* widmen sich die Kuratoren Søren Grammel und Jan Verwoert genau jener kritischen Phase in Filkos Werk, in der der Künstler *physisch-materialistisch* wird im Namen eines puren anti-metaphysischen Körperverständnisses, das die früheren konzeptuellen Perioden scheinbar ablöste.[7] Mit nicht geringem Humor – ein Aspekt, der in den bisherigen Annäherungen zum Künstler auch zu kurz gekommen ist – wird uns Filkos Werk präsentiert als eines, das sich nicht um Genregrenzen kümmert und dessen anarchischer Gestus sich Objekten bemächtigt, die scheinbar auch nicht in den cleanen Kosmos eines Künstlers der Neo-Avantgarde passen: ein karikaturhaftes Selbstporträt, monumentale gestische Malerei, eine Schaufel als Accessoire, AIDS-Assemblagen oder eine pinke Pfeffermühle, die aus Sprühdosen und Malerrollen gebastelt wurde. Die Präsentation eines anarchistisch-verdrehten Kosmos auf der Basis der emotionalen Farbe Rot.

Priestor – Space

Innerhalb dieser Präsentationen jedoch haben übergreifende Thematiken in der einsetzenden „Filkologie" bisher kaum eine Rolle gespielt. Darum soll es aber im Folgenden gehen, um die Etablierung einer inhaltlichen Linie, die Filkos Früh- und Spätwerk, genauso wie seine unterschiedlichen Zwischenphasen durchzieht und die so etwas wie eine Konstante in seinem oft diffusen und widersprüchlich wirkenden Werk darstellt: Die Idee von Raum. [04]

Die Idee von Raum, die direkte oder indirekte Adressierung des Raumes, Slowakisch *priestor*, Englisch *space*, ist in nahezu allen Werken Filkos präsent. Sie ist genreübergreifend wie sein Werk auch, sie umfasst viele „Dimensionen", die in seinem Spätwerk in der Form eines überzeitlichen, mehrstufigen abstrakten Systems zum Ausdruck kommen

und metaphorisch funktionieren. Viele Arbeiten enthalten bereits im Titel die Nennung von Raum, oft in mehreren Sprachen. Raum ist als symbolischer Ort der Utopie und der gesellschaftlichen Vision in den Zuschreibungen zum „Kosmos" immateriell konnotiert. [05] Aber die Idee von Raum ist auch konkret physisch lokalisierbar: im Bezugsort Bratislava etwa, wo Filkos künstlerische Sozialisation begann und wo er nach seiner Rückkehr aus dem amerikanischen Exil ein Grundstück in der Sneženková-Straße am Kamzík-Hügel erwarb und darauf sein Atelier errichtete. In diesem „deposit" genannten Atelier hat Filko seine künstlerischen Visionen ab Mitte der 1990er-Jahre als eine Foucault'sche Heterotopie realisiert,[8] indem er das profane Gebäude samt Garten in eine ort- und zeitlose Struktur überführte. Die Zuordnungen, die er dort vornahm, sind allein an sein eigenes *System SF* gebunden. Antennen auf dem Dach und diverse selbstgebaute, gerüstähnliche Konstruktionen symbolisieren dabei die Verbindung des Ortes der Inspiration und der künstlerischen Produktion zum Rest des Universums.

Die Bedeutung der Raum-Zeit-Struktur in der zeitgenössischen Kunst und generell in der Kultur des 20. Jahrhunderts ist vielfältig konnotiert. Die Frage, wofür *Raum* heute in Kunst und Theorie produktiv gemacht wird, hat sich seit der Mitte des 20. Jahrhunderts, vor allem aber in den letzten Jahrzehnten völlig neu gestellt. Wir leben nicht mehr in einem homogenen Raum, sondern in einem Raum, der mit Qualitäten aufgeladen ist. Unsere Vorstellung von Raum ist aus ihrer über die Jahrhunderte gültigen gebundenen Rolle an das Konzept der Ortung entlassen und bewegt sich hin zu einer Integration von psychologischen, sozialen, ökonomischen, atomzeitlichen und schließlich auch emanzipatorischen Auffassungen. Die Einbeziehung vor allem auch politischer und genderorientierter Ansätze verdeutlicht dabei, dass „Raum als relationale und nicht nur als absolute Kategorie" gerade auch in der Kunst verstanden wird.[9]

Zu Stano Filkos frühesten konzeptuellen Arbeiten zählen die manifestartigen Aktionen der Reihe *HAPPSOC* (Happy Socialism). Sie alle sind immaterielle Konzeptionen von geografisch-räumlichen Dispositionen: *HAPPSOC I.* (1965, gemeinsam mit dem Künstler Alex Mlynárčik und der Theoretikerin Zita Kostrová) bildet die *Vergegenwärtigung* des soziopolitischen Raums der Stadt Bratislava – ein *Situations-Readymade*, das den Lebensraum von Bratislava während der Zeit vom 2. bis zum 8. Mai 1965, in der Zeit zwischen dem Tag der Arbeit (1. Mai) bis zum Tag des Gedenkens an das Kriegsende (9. Mai) evoziert. Im Manifest der Aktion werden die einzelnen Elemente dieser Vergegenwärtigung deklariert: 138.036 Frauen, 128.727 Männer, 49.991 Hunde, 18.009 Häuser, 165.236 Balkone, 40.070 Wasserleitungen in Wohnungen, 35.060 Waschmaschinen, 1 Burg, 1 Donau, 22 Theater, 6 Friedhöfe, 1.000.801 Tulpen, usw. Hinter dieser bürokratischen Aufzählung mit 23 Punkten verbirgt sich eine Art Hymnus an die materialistische „Realität" (Filko) der Stadt Bratislava, die in den späten 1960er-Jahren noch Teil der Tschechoslowakischen Sozialistischen Republik ČSSR war. Die weiteren Aktionen (im strengen Sinne waren es vorwiegend verbale und schriftlich fixierte Deklarationen, Filkos „Anti-Happenings", die abseits der Öffentlichkeit stattfanden, um der Zensur zu entgehen) bezogen zusehends den geopolitischen Umraum mit ein. *HAPPSOC II.* (1965) umfasste die siebentägige *Kreation* auf dem Bahnhof Bratislava,

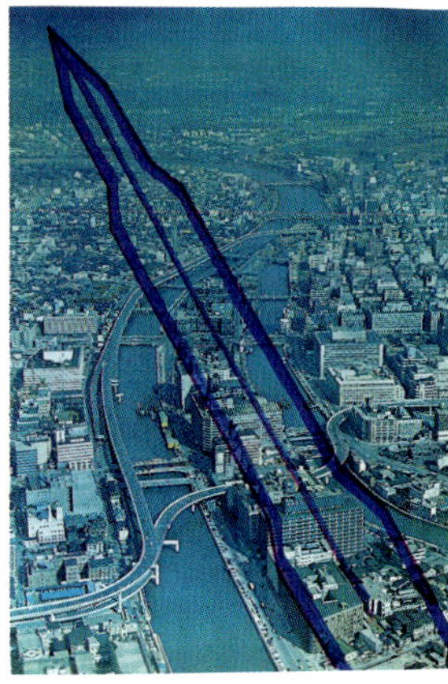

[01] From the series *Sculptures of the Twentieth century IV. / Zo série Sochy XX. storočia IV.*, 1968–69

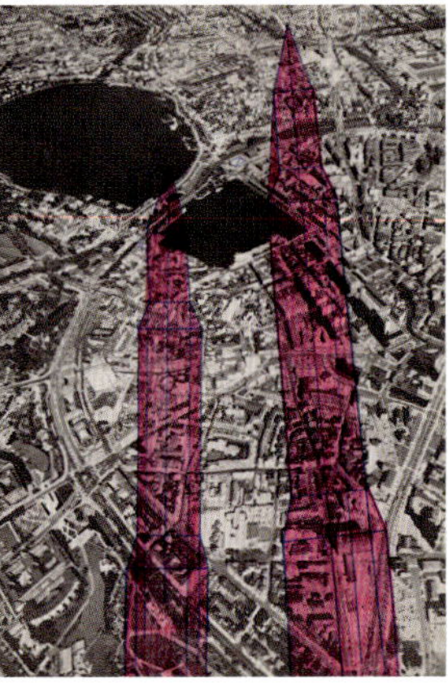

[02] From the series *Sculptures of the Twentieth century / Zo série Sochy XX. storočia*, 1968

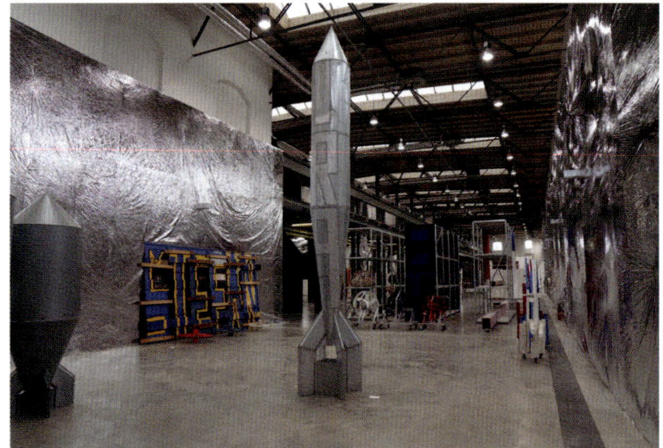

[03] *Registration of Stano Filko / Registrace Stana Filka, Fait Gallery, Brno, 2022*

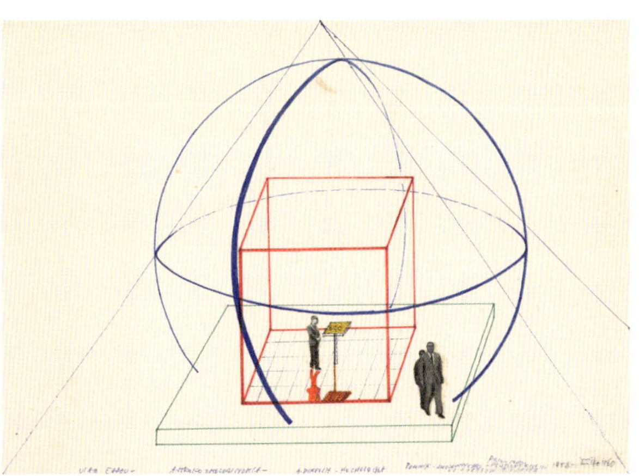

[04] From the series *Monuments of Contemporary Space I. / Zo série Pomníky súčasného priestoru I.*, 1967–68/1995

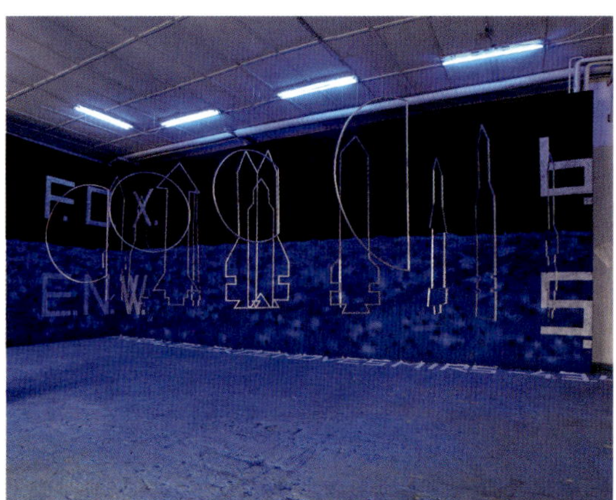

[05] *UP 300000 KM/S, tranzit.sk, Bratislava, 2005*

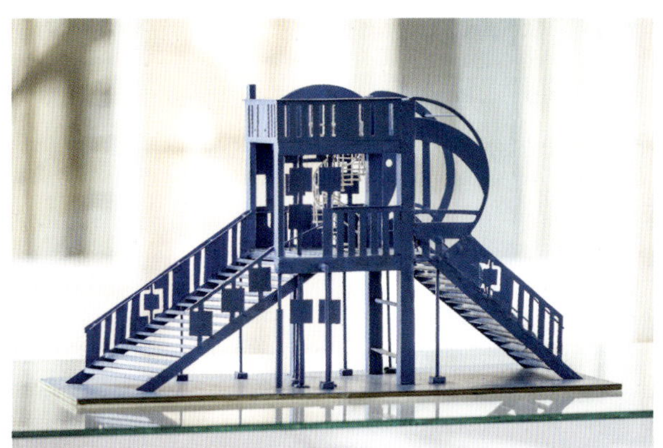

[06] *Modern Tower of Space / Moderná veža vesmíru*, 1966–67

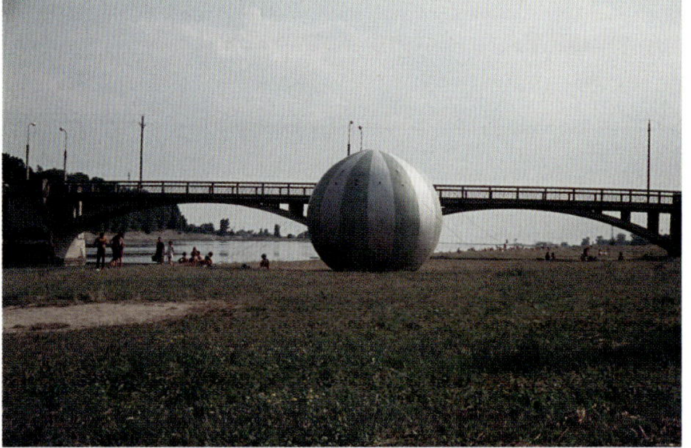

[07] *Breathing – The Celebration of Air / Dýchanie – oslava vzduchu*, 1970

HAPPSOC III. (*Altar of Contemporaneity*, 1966) nannte Filko eine immaterielle Einladung, die über die Einbeziehung der Bevölkerung des Landes die Aufforderung zur Erkundung des Staatsterritoriums enthielt.[10] Nicht nur die Artefakte und Objekte gehören zu dieser Realität, sondern auch räumliche Strukturen, die als *Relationen, relational structures*, das Aggregat einer abstrakten Objekt-Subjekt-Beziehung darstellen.[11]

Modern Tower of Space

Die blaue Skulptur mit dem Titel *Modern Tower of Space / Moderná veža vesmíru* (1967/1968)[12] [06], ebenfalls aus den späten 1960er-Jahren, verweist möglicherweise auf eine geplante Installation für den öffentlichen Raum, beziehungsweise auf einen offiziellen Auftrag und ist demzufolge als Modell zu verstehen. Die Konstruktion besteht aus einem von zwei Seiten begehbaren Turm, dessen hinauf- bzw. hinabführende Treppen so breit sind, dass sie bequem bestiegen werden können. Geländer und Turmüberdachung sind durch verschiedene ornamentale geometrische Platten betont, die Assoziation zum Thema Raum wird einerseits durch das Blau des Stahls, andererseits durch die Symboliken von Kreis, bzw. Halbkreis hervorgerufen, die an Planetenkonstellationen erinnern. Der Titel wiederum wirkt – ähnlich wie bei *HAPPSOC* – hymnisch. In der Evokation eines Seinszustands (Ontologie) liegt der versteckte Symbolismus dieser Arbeit: Die Anrufung der wichtigsten modernistischen Topoi von Raum und Kosmos. Der starke Bezug zum Monumentalen resultiert aus Filkos Ausbildungszeit an der Hochschule für Bildende Künste Bratislava, wo er die Abteilung für Monumentalmalerei unter Dezider Milly und Peter Matejka besuchte. Diese Ausbildung hat es Stano Filko in seiner Anfangszeit erleichtert, großformatige offizielle Auftragsprojekte auszuführen, sie half aber auch, schwierige räumliche Situationen zu bewältigen, und generell scheint sie seinen Hang zu räumlicher Expansion und seine Vorliebe für Großformate, die vor allem ab den 1980er-Jahren bemerkbar wurde, beeinflusst zu haben.

Auch die Environments sind in mehrfacher Hinsicht räumliche Systeme: dreidimensionale Installationen als begehbare Kunsträume. Allen Environments ist ein besonderes Raum-Objekt-Verhältnis eigen; hier möchte ich mich nur auf diejenigen konzentrieren, denen eine räumliche Ästhetik dezidiert eingeschrieben ist. *Cosmos I. / Kozmos I.* (1968) ist eine pneumatische Struktur in Form einer Dreiviertel-Kugel mit zwei Ein- bzw. Ausgängen, innen finden sich Projektionen von Raumfahrt und Weltall: Der Weg zum Kosmos ist ein Gang in einen dunklen Raum mit der flackernden Projektion technischer Errungenschaften wie Raketen, Weltraumkapseln etc. Platons idealistische Höhle wird hier zum popkulturellen Ereignis mit sakralem Touch heruntergefahren, in dem die Betrachter*innen zum Staunen angehalten werden. Mit der Installation *Breathing – The Celebration of Air / Dýchanie – oslava vzduchu* (1970) [07] konzipierte Stano Filko ein weiteres aufblasbares Environment, das im Entstehungsjahr in Bratislava am Ufer der Donau aufgestellt war.[13] Dieses Environment ist ebenso symptomatisch für Filkos nicht-materielle Kunstauffassung: Es erfüllt keinen besonderen Zweck und dient sich nirgends an, es kommuniziert elementare physische Prozesse und spielt mit den Elementen, in diesem Fall mit Luft. Anders also als bei vergleichbaren pneumatischen Objekten von der anderen Seite des Eisernen Vorhangs – Walter Pichlers *Großer Raum (Prototyp 3)* (1966) etwa –, die im Kontext von optimierenden Tools zu verstehen sind, geht es hier nicht um die „Verbesserung des Alltags". Vielmehr ist diesem Environment ein quasi-religiöses Moment der Andacht eingeschrieben, das im Titel angedeutet wird: Der Atem ist die immaterielle Substanz, die gepriesen wird. Es ist eine Kunst, die völlig im Hier und Jetzt verhandelt wird.

Diese „Vergegenwärtigungen", wie Filko sie bezeichnete, finden sich in vielen seiner Arbeiten wieder – von den Assemblagen aus Stadtansichten und Beobachtungstürmen (*Models of Observation Towers / Modely pozorovacích veží*, 1966–1967), der Umleitung von Donauwasser durch ein selbstentwickeltes Röhrensystem, bis zum mehrstufigen, multikoloristischen Konzept der Chakren. Sie alle rücken ein sehr körperliches, tätiges Subjekt ins Zentrum einer Weltbetrachtung, die zwar mit metaphysischen Konzepten operiert – wie der Transzendenz des *White Space* –, die gleichzeitig immer konkret räumlich und objektbezogen fundiert ist. Dies ist eminent widersprüchlich, aber es entspricht genau der unterschiedlichen Auffassung von Körperlichkeit zwischen Filko und „Phylko".[14] So ist auch der weiße Škoda 120SL, den Stano Filko 1982 auf der documenta 7 zeigte und mit dem er ein Jahr zuvor in den kapitalistischen Westen geflohen war, ein Vehikel des Materials, das im Akt des Übermalens vernichtet wird. Filko nennt diesen Akt *Love of Ontology / Liebe zur Ontologie / Láska k ontológii* (1982) [08].

Kosmos – Kosmismus

Um den Widerspruch dieser Geste des Ineinanderfallens entgegengesetzter Enden, die nicht nur im Akt der Übermalung eines Autos steckt – der im übrigen ein Transzendieren eines x-beliebigen Massenprodukts in ein Kunstobjekt ist – würdigen zu können, ist ein Exkurs über den weiteren Kontext von Filkos Arbeiten notwendig. Wie ein Großteil der Kunst, die im Kalten Krieg entstanden ist – einer Zeit der Kybernetik, der forcierten Technologieentwicklung und der Abenteuer im Weltall –, so ist auch das Werk des slowakischen Künstlers geprägt von einem Wissens- und Expansionsparadigma, das im globalen Westen und im globalen Osten zwar unterschiedlich konnotiert war, das aber beidseits des Eisernen Vorhangs *vergleichbare* künstlerische Erzeugnisse hervorbrachte.[15] Die Beschäftigung mit den Themen von Raumfahrt und Weltall war eines der zentralen Momente einer spätmodernistischen Zivilisation, in der die Technikbegeisterung sich auch in den visuellen Metaphern der Maschinenästhetik niederschlug. Der Topos der Raumfahrt als symbolische Setzung des Fortschritts hatte dabei auch ältere Konzepte einer abstrakten, in die Zukunft gerichteten Utopie verdrängt. Darin waren sich die kulturellen Ausprägungen in den Ländern des sogenannten Kommunismus und des Kapitalismus ähnlich. Nicht aber in der Verdinglichung dieser Errungenschaften zu Instrumenten der Popkultur. So klärt sich auch das Verhältnis von künstlerischen Produktionen einer westlich-kapitalistischen und einer sozialistischen, nicht-marktwirtschaftlich orientierten Moderne: im Formenrepertoire und im Produktekanon durchaus vergleichbar, klaffen die Intentionen auseinander. In den ehemaligen Staaten der sowjetischen Einflusssphäre war die Technikbegeisterung dabei immer mit einer besonderen Form des utopischen Futurismus gekoppelt, der als Kosmismus in der Kunst Spuren hinterlassen hat.[16] [09-10]

two sides, with stairs leading up (and down again) that are wide enough to be able to walk comfortably. The railings and roof are embellished by various ornamental geometrical plates, and associations to the theme of space are raised on the one hand by the blue color of the steel, and on the other by the symbols of the circle and semicircle that recall constellations of planets. The title on the other hand seems hymnal—here similar to *HAPPSOC*. The hidden symbolism of this work is in the evocation of a state of being (ontology), an appeal to the most important modernist topoi of space and cosmos. The strong reference to the monumental results from Filko's time as a student at the Bratislava University of the Fine Arts, where he attended the department for monumental painting under Dezider Milly and Peter Matejka. In his early years, these studies made it easier for Stano Filko to take on large-format official commissions, and it also helped him to manage difficult spatial situations, and in general it seems to have influenced his interest in spatial expansion and his preference for large formats, which became evident above all from the 1980s on.

The environments are also spatial systems in several ways: three-dimensional installations as walk-in art spaces. All of the environments have their own specific relationship between space and object, and here I would like to concentrate on those that are very clearly inscribed with a spatial aesthetic. *Cosmos I. / Kozmos I.* (1968) is a pneumatic structure in the form of a three-quarter sphere with two entrances or exits and with projections of space travel and outer space in the interior. The path to the cosmos is a walk into a dark room with the flickering projection of technical achievements such as rockets, space capsules, etc. Plato's idealist cave is here brought down to a pop-cultural event with a sacred touch, whereby the viewers are invited to be amazed. With the installation *Breathing – The Celebration of Air / Dýchanie – oslava vzduchu* (1970) [07] Stano Filko conceived a further blow-up environment, which was erected on the banks of the Danube in Bratislava in the year it was created.[13] This environment is also symptomatic for Filko's non-material view of art, which fulfills no particular purpose and serves no one and nothing, but communicates elementary physical processes and plays with the elements, in this case with air. Unlike comparable pneumatic objects from the other side of the Iron Curtain, such as Walter Pichler's *Großer Raum (Prototyp 3) / Large Room (Prototype 3)* (1966), that should be understood in the context of optimizing tools, this work is not about the "improvement of everyday life." Instead this environment has a quasi-religious moment of devotion, as implied in its title. Breath is the immaterial substance that is praised, and this is an art that is negotiated completely in the here and now.

This consciousness-raising as Filko aimed for, are found in many of his works—from the assemblages of city views and observation towers (*Models of Observation Towers / Modely pozorovacích veží*, 1966–67), to the redirection of the Danube by means of a system of pipes, to the multi-layered and multicolored concept of the chakra. All of these place a very physical and active subject in the center of a perspective on the world, which, while it operates with metaphysical concepts such as the transcendence of the white space, is also always specifically spatial and based on reference to objects. This is highly contradictory but it corresponds precisely to the different views of the physical held by Filko and "Phylko."[14]

Thus the white Škoda 120SL that Stano Filko showed at documenta 7 in 1982, and in which he had fled to the capitalist West the previous year, is a vehicle of the material that is destroyed in the act of overpainting. Filko calls this act *Love of Ontology / Liebe zur Ontologie / Láska k ontológii* (1982) [08].

Cosmos – Cosmism

In order to appreciate the contradiction inherent in this gesture of opposite ends falling together, which is not only seen in the act of overpainting a car (which is also a transcendence of an arbitrary mass product by making it an art object), we require a look at the further context of Filko's works. Like most of the art that was produced during the Cold War, an age of cybernetics, of the forced development of technologies, and of adventures in space, the work of this Slovak artist is shaped by a paradigm of knowledge and expansion that was differently connoted in the global West and the global East but nonetheless led to *comparable* artistic products on both sides of the Iron Curtain.[15] The interest in the themes of space travel and outer space was one of the key moments in late-modernist civilization, in which enthusiasm for technology was also expressed in the visual metaphors of a machine aesthetics. The topos of space travel as a symbolic assertion of progress thereby replaced older concepts of an abstract future-looking utopia. In this, the cultural formations in the states of so-called communism and capitalism resembled each other. But not in the objectification of these achievements as instruments of popular culture. Here the relationship between the artistic production of Western and capitalist and a socialist non-market-oriented modernism becomes clear: in the repertoire of forms and in the canon of products they were certainly comparable, but their intentions were far apart. In the former states in the Soviet sphere of influence, enthusiasm for technology was always linked to a particular form of utopian futurism, which left its traces in art as cosmism.[16] [09–10]

This goes back to the early twentieth century, to philosophers and authors in the circle of Russian anarchism. They included Nikolaj Fyodorov (1829–1903), who in his posthumously published major work, *The Philosophy of the Common Task* (1906/1913), called on the whole of humanity to "unite in the shared task of the total treatment and transformation of the universe, in combating and overcoming death, in resurrection and the complete restitution of all the dead." After the philosopher's death his work was widely disseminated, although primarily restricted to a Russian readership. Put briefly, the project of the common task consists "in creating the technological, social, and political conditions under which it is possible for all people who have ever lived to be resurrected through technical and artificial means."[17] Fyodorov did not believe in the immortality of the soul outside of the body, but in the body itself. And he firmly believed in technology; because all things are material and physical, then everything is feasible and can be technically manipulated. And he believed in the power of social organization. Based on the ideas of Fyodorov, in 1922 the first biocosmistic manifesto of Aleksandr Svjatogor also addressed the problem of resurrection and immortality via freedom of movement in the cosmic space. Like Fyodorov, Svjatogor saw immortality as the goal and the precondition

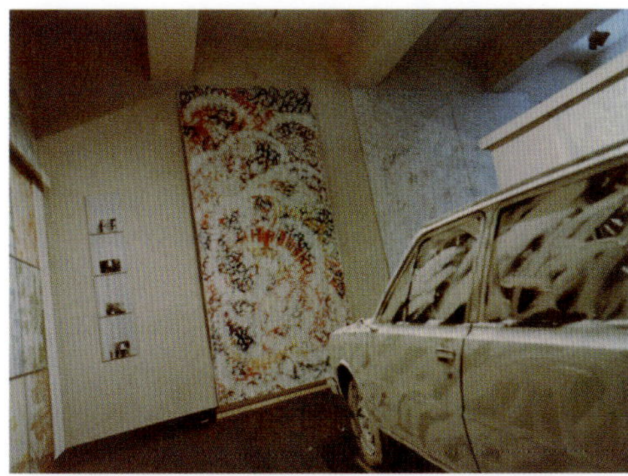

[08] *Love of Ontology / Láska k ontológii*, documenta 7, Neue Galerie, Kassel, 1982

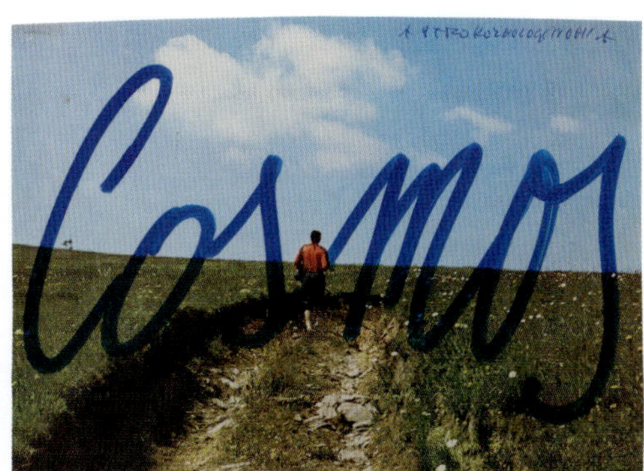

[09] *Cosmos - Man / Cosmos - Človek*, 1968

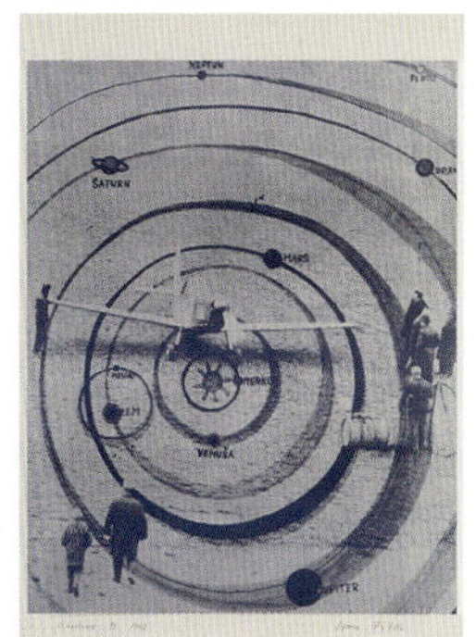

[10] *Associations III. / Asociácie III.*, 1968

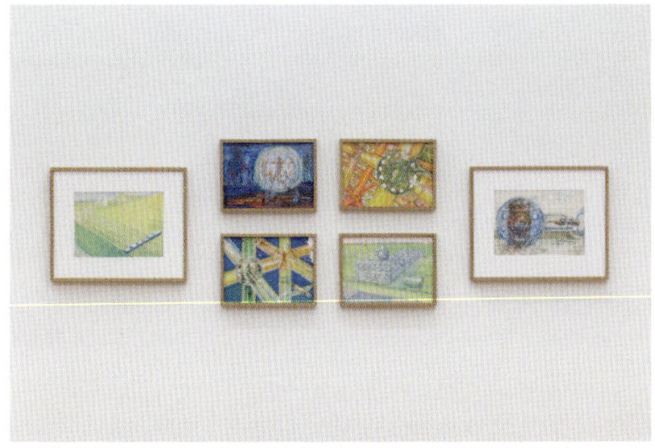

[11] Fedir Tetyanych, Croy Nielsen, Vienna, 2022

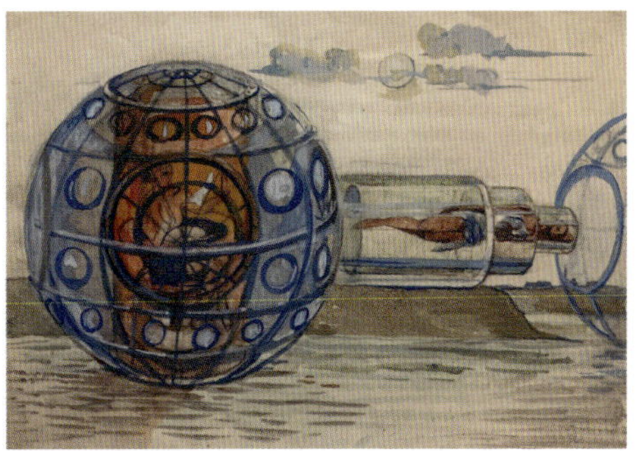

[12] Fedir Tetyanych, *Biotechnosphere with Man-Conduits* (Biotechnospheres. Cities of Future.), 1980s

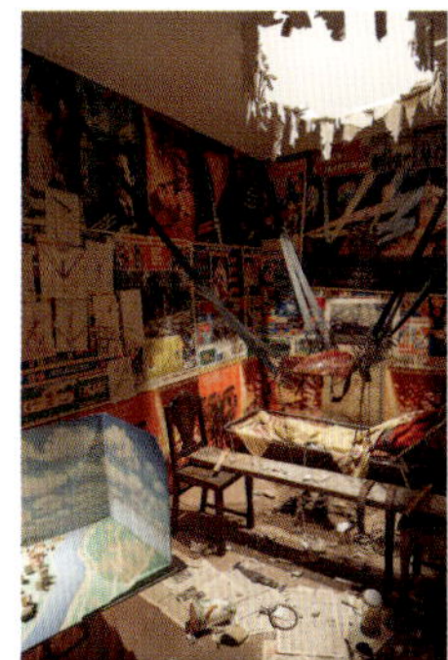

[13] Ilya und Emilia Kabakov, *The Man Who Flew Into Space From His Apartment*, 1985

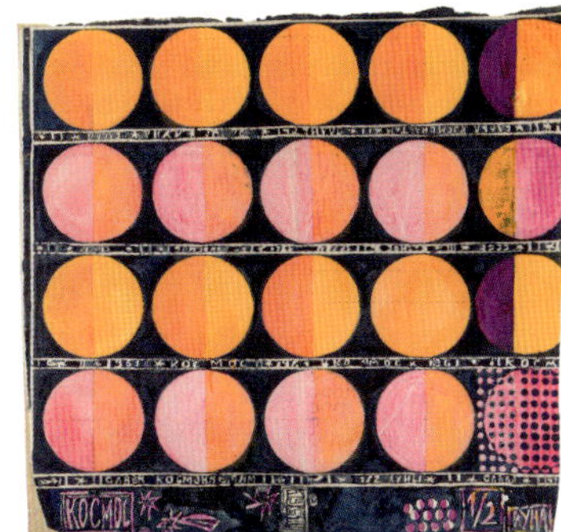

[14] Anna Andreeva, *1/2 of the Moon*, 1961

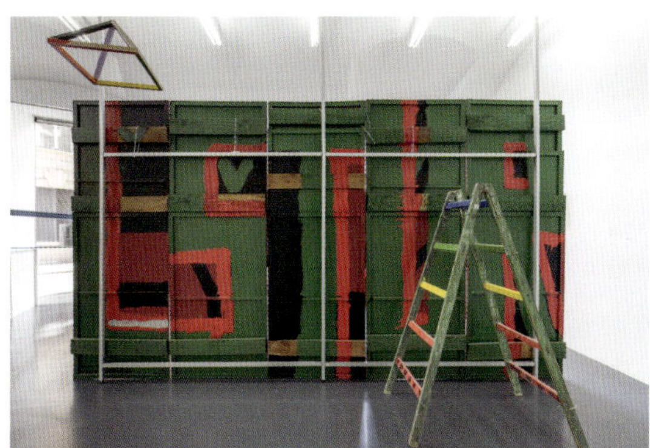

[15] Stano Filko *RED EXILE*, Layr, Vienna, 2022

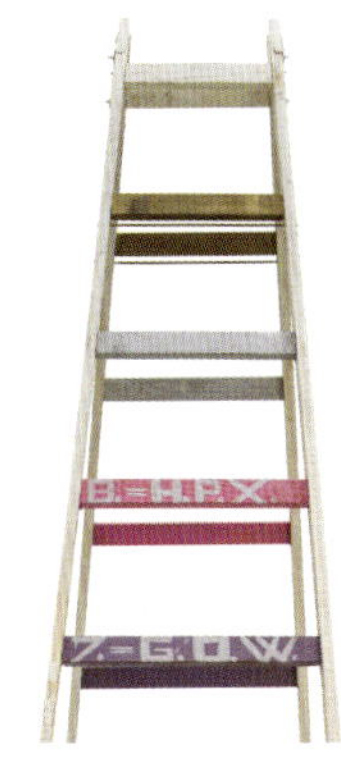

[16] *12 Chakra Colors Ladder / Rebrík vo farbách 12 čakier*, c. 2005

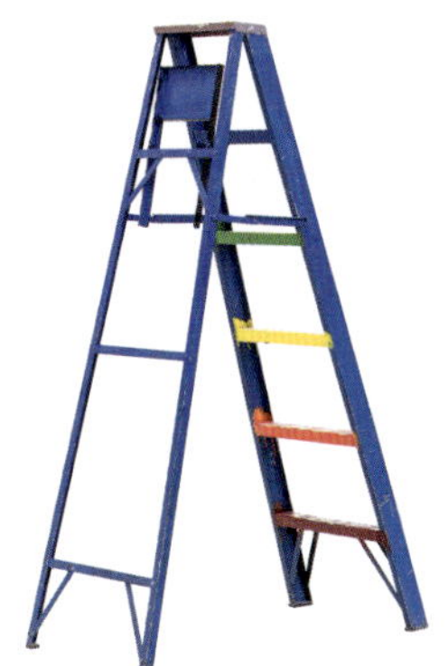

[17] *7 Chakra Colors Ladder / Rebrík vo farbách 7 čakier*, c. 1995

of the future communist society, by means of total bio-power and the collectivization of space and time.

Without being able to go into further detail here, it can be said that Russian cosmism has been influential on art to this day. The Ukrainian Fedir Tetyanych (1942–2007), for example, operated like Filko eclectically in various genres, also beginning as a painter and producing wall reliefs for the official Soviet Union. He also expanded the basis of his art with performative practices in the 1960s and 1970s. And in particular there was a specific connection to cosmist art. Tetyanych also constructed environments from trash and found footage, always with reference to a better society, because in the future, as is particularly evident in his space capsules *Biotechnospheres* (1980–2000).[18] [11-12]

In his installation *The Man Who Flew Into Space From His Apartment* (1985) [13], Ilya Kabakov, from the circle around the Moscow Conceptualists, and who moved to the West in 1988, created a vision of a man who built a machine that catapulted him into space. The energy of the machine derives from the cumulative existence of all Russian art. With a direct connection to the official space program of the Soviet Union, Russian artist Anna Andreeva designed textiles with cosmonaut motifs that were used as official souvenirs for state occasions.[19] [14] And if we go back to the origins of this cosmist sphere, then we can also see Vladimir Tatlin's experimental *Letatlin* flying objects from the 1920s in the same context.

The greater the distance from the epicenter of the Soviet sphere of influence, the more diverse the ideas of cosmic art also become. In Bratislava, a particularly vital focal point of this trend, the cosmist idea merged with Western views of conceptual art, such as in the work of Juliús Koller and his *Ufonaut* series, and also Rudolf Sikora, who designed a questionnaire on the universe in collaboration with Koller, Filko and Igor Gazdik.[20] The reflex of this art can even be seen in a younger generation, such as the artist Roman Ondák, who was born in 1966. Cosmism was not just the inversion of outside and inside and the falling together of the ends, it was also a manifest visualization of escape as an escapist opportunity to meld reality and fiction. During the *monolithic* communist period the motifs of flying and other escapists elements were used in art as ways to abandon the present.[21] Stano Filko's own system of *self-stylization* could on the surface be compared with these approaches, just as it could be mistaken for an "individual mythology," to use the term coined by Harald Szeemann.[22] But Filko's *System SF* in his final years was not so much a drift into his personal ego than more an attempt to universalize his person by integrating pseudo- or para-scientific categories and also his doctrine of the chakras.[23] The *System SF* is called "Filcault."

Blue Ladders in Space

There is much more to be said about this artist. To finish, I would like to draw attention to one object that is seen in very different constellations throughout Filko's entire oeuvre: the ladder. [15] In many works that refer to outer space or to space in general, the ladder is a symbolic link between the Earth and the universe. Filko always used an A-frame ladder made of two ladders joined at the top. [16-17] As the ladder stands alone, it is a mediator between above and below, a sensual object, a readymade that was not created by the artist but was invented before him: typologically in the form of steps. In the work of Stano Filko the ladder stands paradigmatically for an overcoming of physical existence, the power of transformation, and the creation of a new transcendental sphere of being, Filko's "ontology." In a particularly attractive drawing of 1966–67, *Blue Ladders in Space / Modré rebríky v priestore*, he captured this state. As if just breathed onto the paper, in a finely drawn interior space with a deep perspective, there are nine A-frame ladders of different sizes in black and indigo blue. In Filko's color system these stand for the spaces of death and the ego. The ladders seem to be being pulled from above, but are somehow still clinging to the ground. In this state of near suspension they are reminiscent of rockets about to take off: they will soon set off. [18-20]

1   Filko used the term "cosmos" to denote certain groups of works and portfolios. This term runs through all the phases of his work like a topos and is here used to stand for Filko's exploration of the theme of space.

2   After early contact with the work of the French Nouveau Réaliste theorist Pierre Restany, from 1982 Stano Filko lived after his emigration in his self-chosen exile in New York. Pierre Restany, "Stanislav Filko, Architect information," in *Stano FILKO 1965/69* (Bratislava, 1970), n. p.

3   Daniel Grúň, "Notes of a Belated Viewer: Revisiting *White Space in White Space*," in *White Space in White Space. Biely priestor v bielom priestore, 1973–1982. Stano Filko, Miloš Laky, Ján Zavarský* (Vienna, 2021), p. 29.

4   I met Stano Filko when I was working on the text of my monograph about his work, which was published in 2005 (*Stano Filko*, Prague, 2005), a book that was initiated by Dušan Brozman, the head of the Pro Helvetia office in Bratislava at the time. That essay was based on around fifteen studio visits in Bratislava, which I still remember very vividly. I found Stano Filko to be a very sensitive and also very self-confident person.

5   *Registrace Stana Filka / Registration of Stano Filko*, Fait Gallery, Brno, October 6, 2021–January 8, 2022.

6   *Stano Filko, A Retrospective*, HALLE FÜR KUNST Steiermark, Graz, March 19–June 5, 2022.

7   *RED EXILE*, Layr, Vienna, March 26–May 21, 2022.

8   For Michel Foucault heterotopias are places that represent not realized utopias in our Western civilization, a kind of counter to real built manifestations. Michel Foucault, "Of Other Spaces: Utopias and Heterotopias," in *Rethinking Architecture: A Reader in Cultural Theory*, ed. Neil Leach (New York, 1997), pp. 330–36.

9   Sabine Hark, "Gendered Spaces – Spatialized Gender: Synthese und Perspektiven der Konstitution von Raum und Geschlecht," conference report, October 24–26, 2013, Kassel, in *H-Soz-Kult*, January 16, 2014, www.hsozkult.de/conferencereport/id/tagungsberichte-5200 (accessed July 10, 2022) (trans.).

10   A total of five actions are known under the title *HAPPSOC*. Action IV. included extension into the cosmos, *HAPPSOC V.* contains all the works on *White Space*. Patricia Grzonka, *Stano Filko* (Prague, 2005), p. 106.

11   On the concept of relational aesthetics with reference to *HAPPSOC III.* see Bojana Piškur, in *2000+ Art East Collection, The Art of Eastern Europe*, eds. Zdenka Badovinac and Peter Weibel (Innsbruck, 2001): "It differed from a happening by its appropriation of *found society* and the participation of ordinary people, without any intervention by the artist. The manifesto *What is HAPPSOC?* states that it is 'an event inciting the perception of reality removed from the stereotype of its existence.' It is defined as 'a universally valid and *living* way of changing found reality into an artefact, in which not only the immediate surroundings of the participant, but also the aggregate of relations evoked by the things viewed become the *object* …,'" p. 87.

12   Shown in the exhibition *RED EXILE*, Layr, Vienna, 2022.

13   Re-enacted at the HALLE FÜR KUNST Steiermark, Graz, 2022.

14   Stano Filko adapts his name to these levels of being: in the often excessive associations of the titles and labels of his works, the spectrum ranges from Filko to "Phylko" with numerous variations: *PSYCHOQFYZIKOZMOVESMIREALUNVERZABSOLUTEAQ – FIYLKOMUNIKONTEMPLACIEDSAOQ*, see the flyer for tranzit.sk, Bratislava, 2005.

15   On the *comparability* of different art systems see Piotr Piotrowski, "How to Write a History of Central East European Art?," in *Third Text* 23, 1, 2009. Referring to Piotrowski, in 2021 Raino Isto proposed an update of his idea of moderate regionalism, suggesting the concept of a "weakened history of modernism," which essentially includes marginalized regions. Raino Isto, "Towards a Weakened History of Modernisms," in *UMĚNÍ ART* 2, 69, 2021, pp. 193–95.

16   The Institute of the Cosmos: www.cosmos.art (accessed July 10, 2022).

17   Boris Groys and Michael Hagemeister, eds., *Die Neue Menschheit. Biopolitische Utopien in Russland zu Beginn des 20. Jahrhunderts* (Frankfurt, 2005), p. 10 (trans.).

18   Fedir Tetyanych, *Biotechnospheres*, 1980–2000, pinchukartcentre.org/en/exhibitions/doslidnitska-platforma_-kanon-fripulya (accessed June 8, 2022).

19   www.russianartandculture.com/anna-andreeva-and-her-experimental-designs/ (accessed June 5, 2022). The examples presented here, also from the Moscow Conceptualists group, could be complemented by many more.

20   Igor Gazdik, Stano Filko, Július Koller, Rudolf Sikora, *?!+… (questionnaire)*, 1972.

21   Boris Groys and Ilya Kabakov, eds., *Die Kunst des Fliehens. Dialoge über Angst, das heilige Weiß und den sowjetischen Müll* (Munich and Vienna, 1991).

22   See Harald Szeemann, *Individuelle Mythologien*, originally used as an exhibition title at Kunsthalle Bern in 1972.

23   Patricia Grzonka, "Stano Filko: Künstlerische Selbstkonstruktion zwischen Ost und West," in *Paradigmenwechsel. Ost- und Mitteleuropa im 20. Jahrhundert, Kunstgeschichte im Wandel der politischen Verhältnisse*, conference proceedings of the fifteenth conference of the Association of Austrian Art Historians (Hohenems, 2011).

Dieser geht zurück auf das frühe 20. Jahrhundert, auf Philosophen und Autoren im Umfeld des russischen Anarchismus. Zu ihnen gehört Nikolaj Fedorov (1829–1903), der in seinem Hauptwerk, der nach seinem Tod veröffentlichten *Philosophie des gemeinsamen Werkes* (1906/1913), die gesamte Menschheit dazu aufrief, „sich zu vereinigen im ‚gemeinsamen Werk' der totalen Behandlung und Verwandlung des Universums, der Bekämpfung und Überwindung des Todes und der Auferweckung – der vollkommenen Wiederherstellung aller Verstorbenen". Nach dem Tod des Philosophen fand sein Werk immer größere Verbreitung, die allerdings im Wesentlichen auf die russische Leserschaft begrenzt war. Das Projekt der gemeinsamen Tat besteht, kurz formuliert, „in der Schaffung der technologischen, sozialen und politischen Bedingungen, unter denen es möglich ist, alle Menschen, die je gelebt haben, auf technische und künstliche Weise wiederauferstehen zu lassen."[17] Fedorov glaubte nicht an die Unsterblichkeit der Seele jenseits des Körpers; er glaubte an den Körper selbst. Genauso fest glaubte Fedorov an die Technik: Weil alles materiell und körperlich ist, ist alles machbar, technisch manipulierbar. Und er glaubte an die Kraft der sozialen Organisation. Von Fedorov ausgehend, behandelte auch das erste biokosmistische Manifest von Aleksandr Svjatogor von 1922 das Problem der Auferweckung und der Unsterblichkeit über die Bewegungsfreiheit im kosmischen Raum. Ähnlich wie Fedorov hielt Svjatogor Unsterblichkeit für das Ziel und für die Voraussetzung der zukünftigen kommunistischen Gesellschaft, durch die totale Biomacht über die Kollektivierung des Raumes und auch der Zeit.

Ohne hier weiter ins Detail gehen zu können, kann behauptet werden, dass der russische Kosmismus bis heute eine Einflusssphäre auf die Kunst behalten hat. Der Ukrainer Fedir Tetyanych beispielsweise (1942–2007), bewegte sich ähnlich eklektisch wie Filko in unterschiedlichen Sparten: So hat er ebenfalls als Maler begonnen und führte für die offizielle Sowjetunion Wandreliefs aus. Ebenso erweiterte er die Basis seiner Kunst mit performativen Praktiken in den 1960er- und 70er-Jahren. Aber ganz besonders gab es auch den spezifischen Zusammenhang mit kosmistischer Kunst: Auch Tetyanych baute seine Environments aus Trash und *Found Footage* stets im Bezug auf die Entstehung einer besseren, weil zukünftigen Gesellschaft, besonders gut nachvollziehbar in seinen Raumkapseln *Biotechnospheres* (1980–2000).[18] [11-12]

Der aus dem Kreis des Moskauer Konzeptualismus stammende Ilya Kabakov, der 1988 in den Westen übersiedelte, entwarf in der Installation *The Man Who Flew Into Space From His Apartment* (1985) [13] die Vision eines Mannes, der sich einen Apparat konstruierte, um sich ins Weltall zu katapultieren. Die Energie des Apparates basiert auf der kumulierten Existenz der gesamten russischen Kunst. In direkter Verbindung zum offiziellen Raumfahrtprogramm der Sowjetunion entwarf die russische Künstlerin Anna Andreeva Stoffdesigns mit Kosmonautensujets, die als offizielle Souvenirs bei Staatsanlässen verteilt wurden.[19] [14] Und wenn wir zum Ursprung dieser kosmistischen Sphäre zurückgehen, so können die experimentellen, *Letatlin* genannten Flugkörper Wladimir Tatlins aus den 1920er-Jahren genau in dem Kontext verstanden werden.

Mit zunehmender Distanz vom Epizentrum der sowjetischen Einflusssphäre diversifizieren sich auch die Ideen der kosmistischen Kunst. In Bratislava, einem besonders vitalen Brennpunkt dieser Richtung, vermischte sich die kosmistische Idee mit westlichen Auffassungen der Konzeptkunst, wie bei Juliús Koller und seinen Ufonauten-Serien, oder Rudolf Sikora, die in Zusammenarbeit mit Filko und Igor Gazdik einen Fragebogen zum Universum entwarfen.[20] Selbst bei einer jüngeren Generation, so beim 1966 geborenen Künstler Roman Ondák, ist der Reflex dieser Kunst spürbar. Im Kosmismus erfolgte nicht nur die Inversion von Außen und Innen, vom Zusammenfallen der Enden, er war auch eine manifeste Vergegenwärtigung der Flucht, als eskapistische Möglichkeit, Realität und Fiktion in eins zu setzen. Während der „monolithischen" kommunistischen Periode wiederum, waren Fliegen und eskapistische Elemente in der Kunst übliche Motive, die Gegenwart zu verlassen.[21] Stano Filkos eigenes System der *Selbststilisierung* könnte an der Oberfläche mit diesen Ansätzen verglichen werden, genauso wie es mit der „Individuellen Mythologie", um den Begriff Harald Szeemanns zu verwenden, verwechselt werden kann.[22] Dabei stellt Filkos *System SF* der letzten Jahre nicht so sehr ein Abtauchen ins persönliche Ego dar, als einen Versuch, seine Person zu universalisieren, indem er pseudo- oder parawissenschaftliche Kategorien, wie eben die Chakrenlehre darin integrierte.[23] Das *System SF* heißt „Filcault".

Blaue Leitern im Raum

Es ist noch lange nicht alles gesagt zu diesem Künstler. Zum Schluss jedoch möchte ich die Aufmerksamkeit auf ein Objekt lenken, das sich in ganz unterschiedlichen Konstellationen durch Filkos ganzes Werk zieht: die Leiter. [15] In vielen Arbeiten mit Bezug zum Weltall oder generell zum Raum stellt sie symbolisch die Verbindung zwischen Erde und Universum her. Filko verwendete immer eine sogenannte Bockleiter mit zwei am oberen Ende ineinander verschränkten Einzelleitern. [16-17] Da sie alleine steht, ist sie Mittlerin zwischen oben und unten, ein sinnliches Objekt, ein Readymade, das nicht vom Künstler geschaffen wurde, sondern bereits vor ihm erfunden war – typologisch eine Treppe. Im Werk Stano Filkos steht die Leiter paradigmatisch für die Überwindung der körperlichen Existenz, die Kraft der Verwandlung und der Schaffung einer neuen transzendenten Seinssphäre, Filkos „Ontologie". In einer besonders schönen Zeichnung aus dem Jahr 1966/67, *Blue Ladders in Space / Modré rebríky v priestore*, hielt er diesen Zustand fest. Fast nur hingehaucht, in einem fein angedeuteten, perspektivisch wiedergegebenen Innenraum stehen neun Bockleitern unterschiedlicher Größe in den Farben Schwarz und Indigoblau. In Filkos Farbsystem symbolisieren diese den Raum des Todes und des Egos. Die Leitern scheinen von oben gezogen zu werden, hängen aber dennoch irgendwie am Boden fest. In diesem Quasi-Schwebezustand erinnern sie an Raketen kurz vor dem Start: Gleich heben sie ab. [18-20]

1 Mit „Kosmos" bezeichnete Filko bestimmte Werkgruppen und Mappen, die dem Thema zugeordnet waren. Dieser Begriff zieht sich durch alle Phasen wie ein Topos und wird hier stellvertretend für Filkos Beschäftigung mit Raumthemen verwendet.
2 Nachdem er noch in Bratislava früh mit dem Theoretiker der französischen Nouveau Réalistes, Pierre Restany, in Kontakt kam, lebte Filko nach seiner Emigration ab 1982 im selbstgewählten Exil in New York. Pierre Restany, „Stanislav Filko, Architekt der Information", in: *Stano FILKO 1965/69*, Bratislava 1970, o. S.
3 Daniel Grúň, „Notes of a Belated Viewer. Revisiting White Space in White Space", in: *White Space in White Space. Biely priestor v bielom priestore, 1973–1982. Stano Filko, Miloš Laky, Ján Zavarský*, Wien 2021, S. 29 ff.
4 Ich habe Stano Filko im Zuge der Vorbereitungen meines Textes zur 2005 erschienen Monografie (*Stano Filko*, Prag 2005) kennengelernt, einem Buch, das auf Initiative von

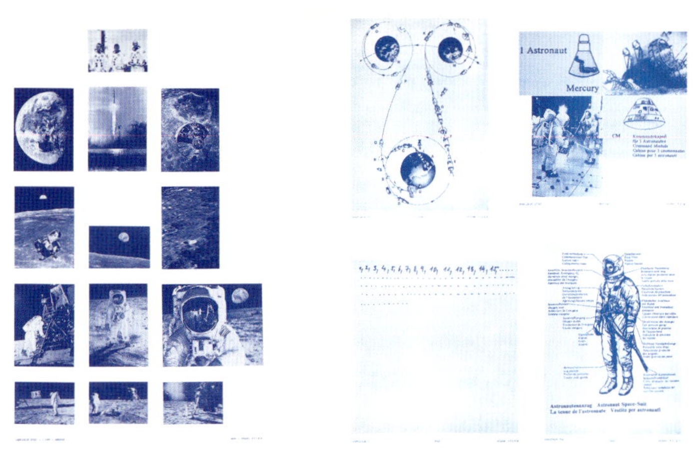

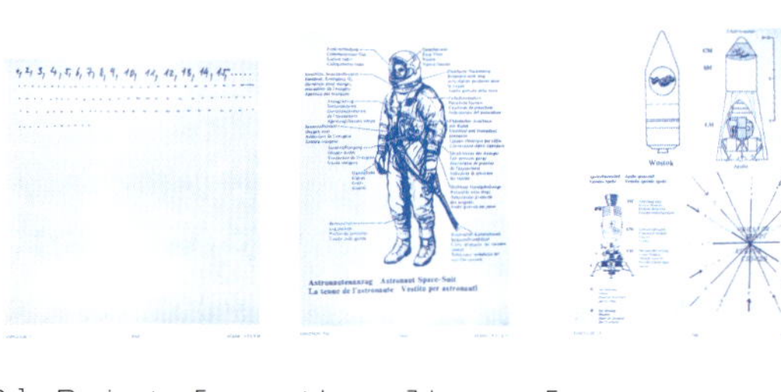

[18] *Associations XXXI. - I. Flight - Moon / Asociácie XXXI. - I. let - mesiac, 1969*

[19] Print from the album of *Associations II. / List z albumu Asociácie II.,* 1968-69

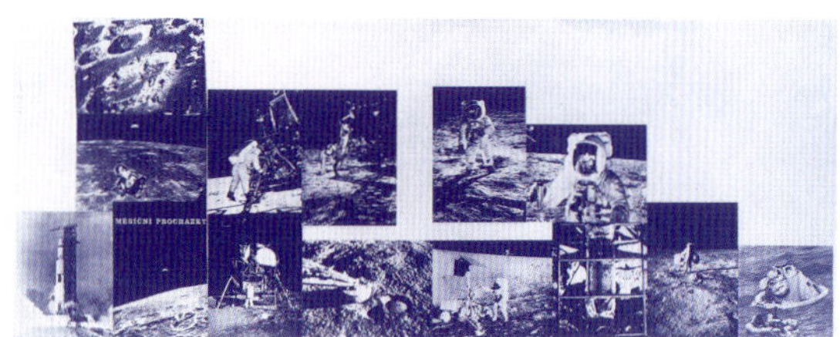

[20] *Associations XXX. - A / Asociácie XXX. - A,* 1968-69

Dušan Brozman, dem damaligen Leiter des Pro Helvetia-Büros in Bratislava, entstanden ist. Der Essay ist damals auf der Grundlage von etwa fünfzehn Atelierbesuchen in Bratislava entstanden – Besuche, die mir immer noch sehr präsent sind. Stano Filko habe ich dabei als sensiblen und gleichzeitig sehr selbstbewussten Menschen kennengelernt.

5   *Registrace Stana Filka / Registration of Stano Filko*, Fait Gallery, Brno, 6.10.2021 – 8.1.2022.

6   *Stano Filko, A Retrospective*, HALLE FÜR KUNST Steiermark, Graz, 19.3. – 5.6.2022.

7   *RED EXILE*, Layr, Wien, 26.3. – 21.5.2022.

8   Als Heterotopie bezeichnet Michel Foucault diejenigen Orte, die in unserer westlichen Zivilisation nicht realisierte Utopien darstellen, eine Art *Gegenplatzierungen* zu den realen gebauten Manifestationen. Michel Foucault, „Andere Räume", in: *Aisthesis, Wahrnehmung heute oder Perspektiven einer anderen Ästhetik*, Leipzig 1990.

9   Sabine Hark, „Gendered Spaces – Spatialized Gender: Synthese und Perspektiven der Konstitution von Raum und Geschlecht", Tagungsbericht, 24.10. – 26.10.2013, Kassel, in: *H-Soz-Kult*, 16.1.2014, www.hsozkult.de/conferencereport/id/tagungsberichte-5200 (10.7.2022).

10   Insgesamt fünf Aktionen sind unter dem Titel *HAPPSOC* bekannt. Die IV. Aktion umfasste die Ausweitung in den Kosmos, *HAPPSOC V.* beinhaltet alle Arbeiten zum *White Space* (siehe Patricia Grzonka, *Stano Filko*, Prag 2005, S. 106.)

11   Zum Begriff der *relational aesthetics* in Bezug auf *HAPPSOC III.* siehe Bojana Piškur, in: *2000+ Art East Collection, The Art of Eastern Europe*, hrsg. von Zdenka Badovinac und Peter Weibel, Innsbruck 2001: „It differed from a happening by its appropriation of *found society* and the participation of ordinary people, without any intervention by the artist. The manifesto *What is HAPPSOC?* states that it is 'an event inciting the perception of reality removed from the stereotype of its existence.' It is defined as 'a universally valid and *living* way of changing found reality into an artefact, in which not only the immediate surroundings of the participant, but also the aggregate of relations evoked by the things viewed become the *object* …'", S. 87.

12   Gezeigt in der Ausstellung *RED EXILE*, Layr, Wien 2022.

13   Re-enacted in der HALLE FÜR KUNST Steiermark, Graz, 2022.

14   So gleicht Stano Filko seinen Namen diesen Seinsebenen an: in den bisweilen vor Assoziationen überbordenden Beschriftungen seiner Arbeiten geht das Spektrum von Filko zu „Phylko" mit zahlreichen Variationen einher: *PSYCHOQFYZIKOZMOVESMIREAL-UNVERZABSOLUTEAQ – FIYLKOMUNIKONTEMPLACIEDSAOQ*, siehe Flyer zur Ausstellung bei tranzit.sk, Bratislava 2005.

15   Zur Vergleichbarkeit verschiedener Kunstsysteme: Piotr Piotrowski, „How to Write a History of Central East European Art?", in: *Third Text*, 23, 1, 2009. Mit Bezug auf Piotrowski hat Raino Isto 2021 eine Aktualisierung von dessen Position eines moderaten Regionalismus mit dem Konzept einer *weakened history of modernisms* vorgeschlagen, dem wesentlich auch die Berücksichtigung von marginalisierten Regionen eingeschrieben ist: „Towards a Weakened History of Modernisms", Raino Isto, in: *UMĚNÍ ART* 2, 69, 2021, S. 193–195.

16   The Institute of the Cosmos: www.cosmos.art (10.7.2022).

17   *Die Neue Menschheit. Biopolitische Utopien in Russland zu Beginn des 20. Jahrhunderts*, hrsg. von Boris Groys und Michael Hagemeister, Frankfurt am Main 2005, S. 10.

18   Fedir Tetyanych, *Biotechnospheres*, 1980–2000, pinchukartcentre.org/en/exhibitions/doslidnitska-platforma_-kanon-fripulya (8.6.2022).

19   www.russianartandculture.com/anna-andreeva-and-her-experimental-designs/ (5.6.2022). Die hier vorgestellten Beispiele, auch aus der Gruppe der Moskauer Konzeptualisten, wären um viele zu erweitern.

20   Igor Gazdik, Stano Filko, Július Koller, Rudolf Sikora, *?!+… (questionnaire)*, 1972.

21   *Die Kunst des Fliehens. Dialoge über Angst, das heilige Weiß und den sowjetischen Müll*, hrsg. von Boris Groys und Ilya Kabakov, München und Wien 1991.

22   Harald Szeemann, *Individuelle Mythologien*, ursprünglich als Ausstellungstitel in der Kunsthalle Bern 1972 verwendet.

23   Patricia Grzonka, „Stano Filko: Künstlerische Selbstkonstruktion zwischen Ost und West", in: *Paradigmenwechsel. Ost- und Mitteleuropa im 20. Jahrhundert, Kunstgeschichte im Wandel der politischen Verhältnisse*. Tagungsband zur 15. Tagung des Verbands österreichischer Kunsthistorikerinnen und Kunsthistoriker, Hohenems 2011.

XVI

Interventions on Works on Paper / Interventionen auf Papierarbeiten

Alongside his important contribution to installation and object art, Stano Filko began in the 1960s to undertake artistic interventions by means of smaller works, including collages, works on paper, and photographs. The gradual development of his *System SF* led to an increased reuse and adaptation of this material. Especially the photographic works say much about Filko's artistic strategies when using fragments of found reality.

Neben seinen wichtigen Beiträgen zur Installations- und Objektkunst beginnt Stano Filko während der 1960er-Jahre künstlerische Interventionen anhand von kleineren Arbeiten vorzunehmen, darunter Collagen, Papierarbeiten und Fotografien. Die schrittweise Herausbildung von Filkos *System SF* führte zu einer ausgeweiteten Wiederverwendung und nachträglichen Bearbeitungen dieses Materials. Vor allem anhand der fotografischen Arbeiten lässt sich viel über Filkos künstlerische Strategien im Umgang mit Versatzstücken vorgefundener Wirklichkeit erfahren.

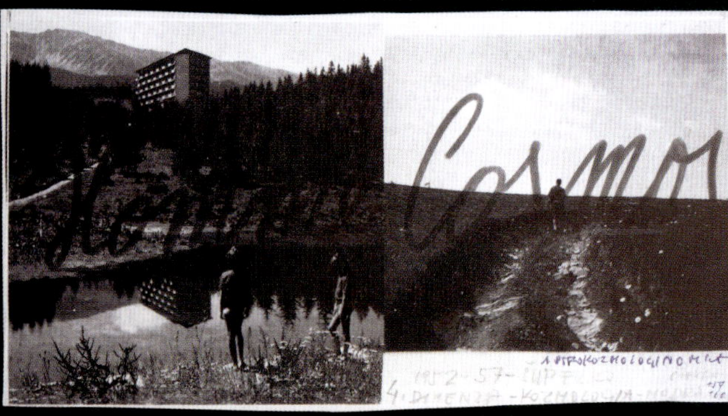

[01] *Cosmos – Man / Cosmos – Človek*, 1968

[02] From the series *Monuments of the Solar System / Zo série Pomníky slnečnej sústavy*, 1967

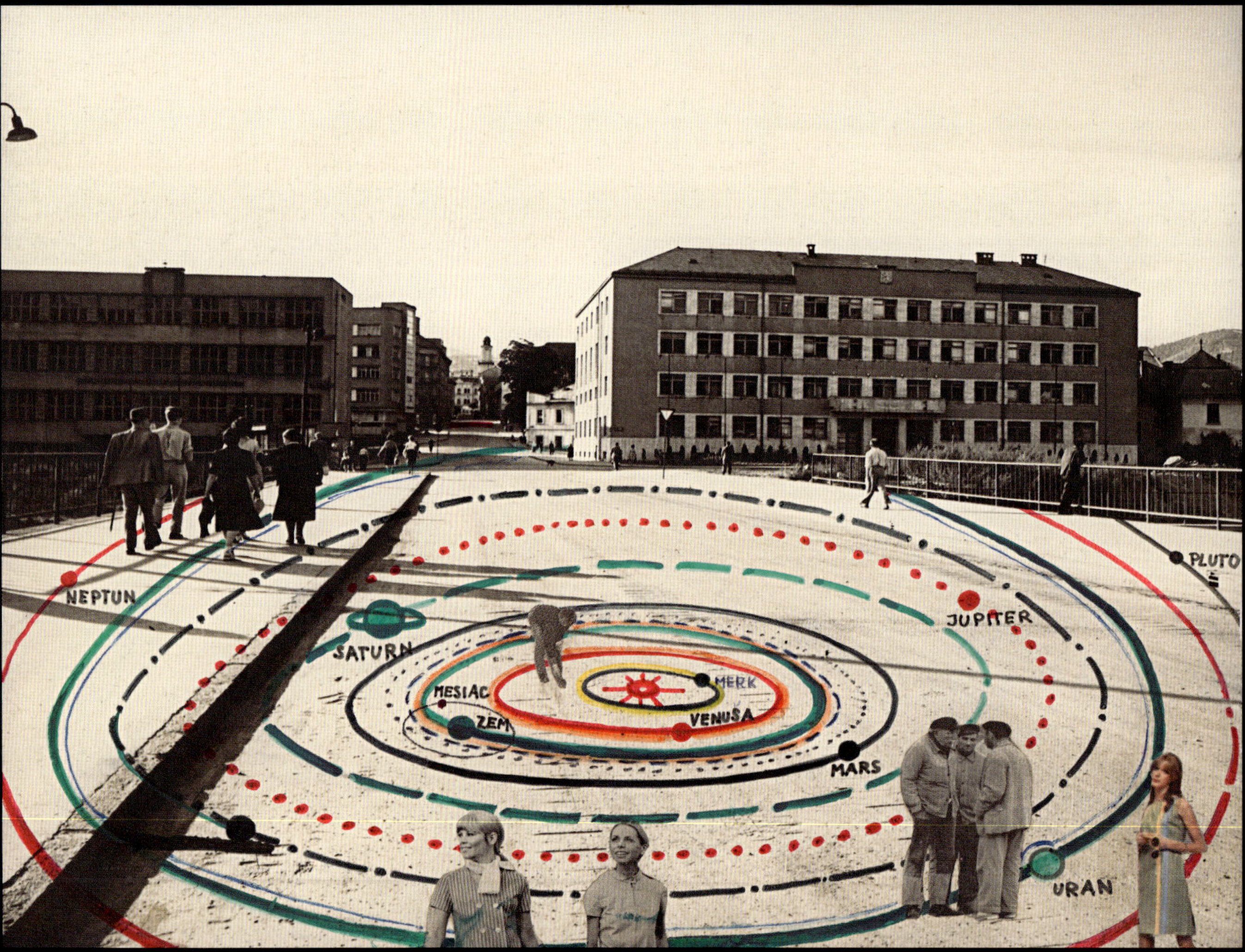

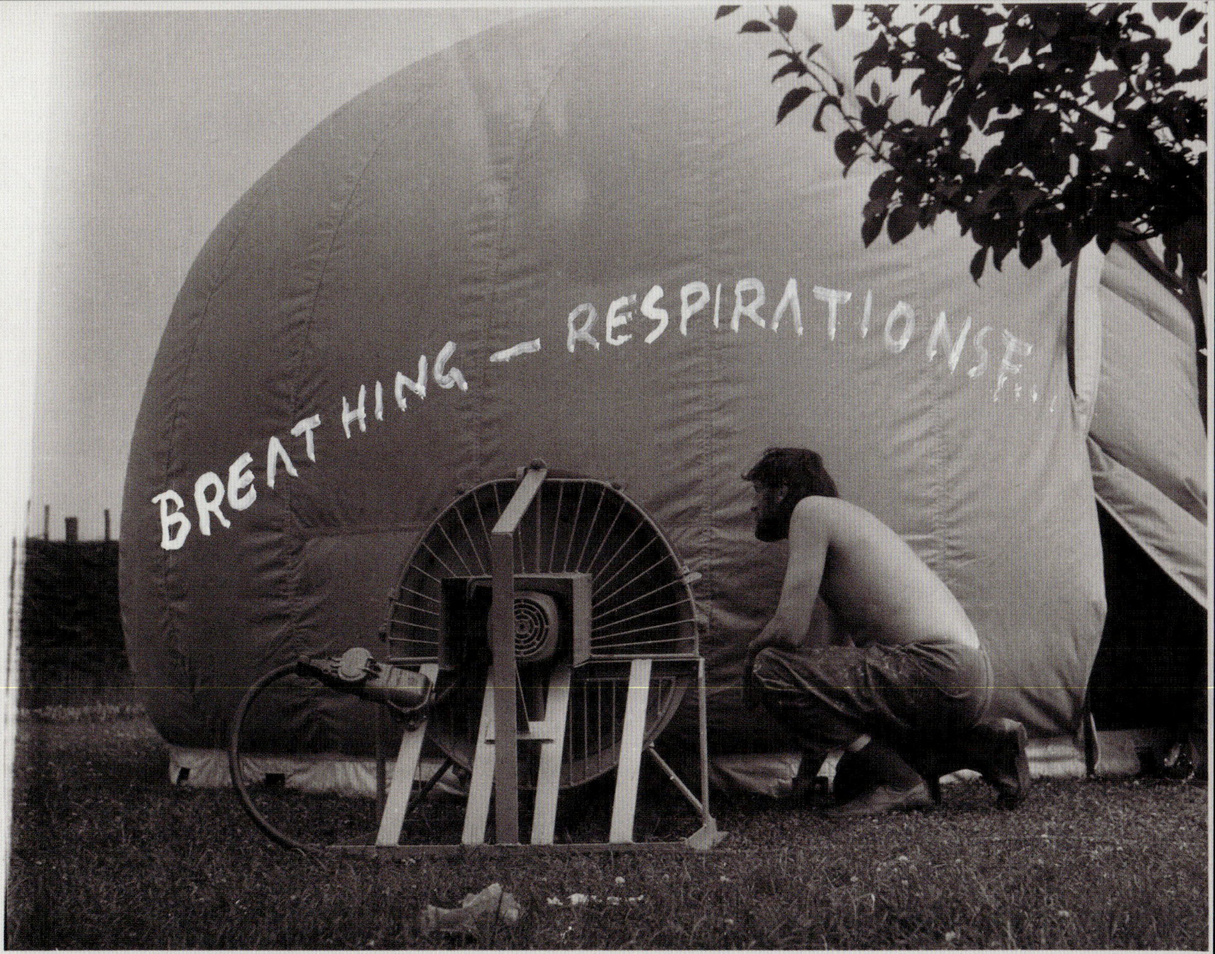

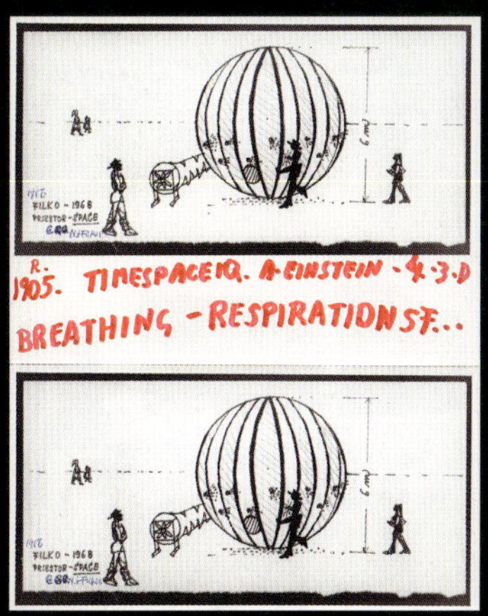

[03] Cosmos. BREATHING - RESPIRATIONSF / Kozmos. BREATHING - RESPIRATIONSF, 1967/c. 2000

Filko begins with the depicted reality of photography, then alters the specific constellation of space and time by confronting the work with elements of an expanded and abstract understanding of space. This is most apparent in the two works *Cosmos – Man / Cosmos – Človek* (1968) [01] and *Monuments of the Solar System / Pomníky slnečnej sústavy* (1967) [02]. In the first one, the added element is the word "cosmos" above a figure on the firmament, and in the second there is an orbital system that has penetrated the collage-like real space. In both works we see human realities that Filko's interventions cause to meld with an abstract cosmic reality which he called "Super-Space-Time." This experience is the focus of two works that each show an important balloon sculpture by Filko, *Cosmos. / Kozmos. BREATHING – RESPIRATIONSF* (1967/c. 2000) [03] and *BREATHING – RESPIRATIONSF* (1968/c. 2000) [04]. Here Filko's artistic exploration addresses the subject of breathing, which brings the human organism into constant harmony with the movement of the universe expanding and contracting. As so often, Filko is concerned to establish a new perspective on reality, which in these cases leads to the overarching space of the cosmos.

Filko geht von der abgebildeten Wirklichkeit der Fotografie aus, verändert das konkret dargestellte Raum-Zeit-Gefüge aber durch die Konfrontation mit Elementen eines erweiterten und abstrakten Raumverständnisses. Am offensichtlichsten tritt dies in den beiden Arbeiten *Cosmos – Man / Cosmos – Človek* (1968) [01] und *Monuments of the Solar System / Pomníky slnečnej sústavy* (1967) [02] zutage. Auf der ersten Arbeit stellt dieses Element das Wort „Cosmos" über einer Figur auf dem Firmament dar, auf der zweiten Arbeit zeigt sich ein orbitales System, das in den collagenhaften Realitätsraum eingedrungen ist. In beiden Arbeiten sind menschliche Realitäten zu sehen, die durch Filkos Intervention mit einer abstrakten, kosmischen Realität verschmelzen, die er als „Super-Space-Time" (Super-Raum-Zeit) bezeichnet hat. Um diese Erfahrung drehen sich auch zwei Arbeiten, auf welchen jeweils eine wichtige Ballonskulptur von Filko zu sehen ist, *Cosmos. / Kozmos. BREATHING – RESPIRATIONSF* (1967/ca. 2000) [03] und *BREATHING – RESPIRATIONSF* (1968/ca. 2000) [04]. Die künstlerische Auseinandersetzung Filkos stellt hier das Atmen in den Mittelpunkt, durch das sich der menschliche Organismus im ständigen Übereinklang mit der Bewegung des Ausdehnens und Zusammenziehens des Universums befindet. Wie so oft geht es Filko darum, einen neuen Blick auf die Realität zu etablieren, der in diesen Fällen zum übergeordneten Raum des Kosmos führt.

[04] BREATHING – RESPIRATIONSF, 1968/c. 2000

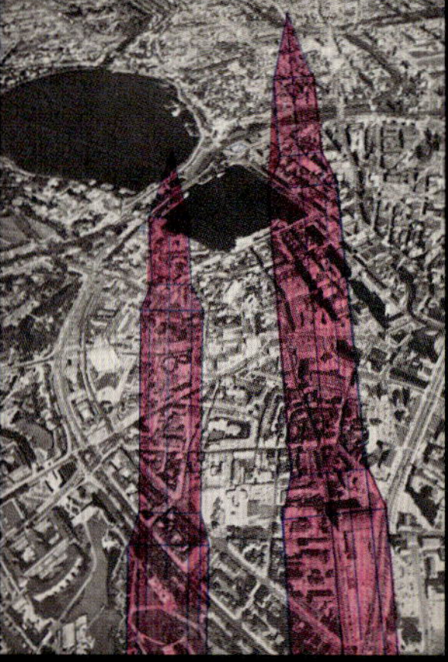

The works of the series *Sculptures of the Twentieth Century / Sochy XX. storočia* (1968–69) [05–06] [09] consist of photographic depictions of urban areas and also photographs from popular magazines that Filko has overwritten with elongated outlines. These lines partly allude to the shapes of space rockets, but they are also strongly reminiscent of military rockets and projectiles. A superior reality is exchanged, and the cosmic space gives way to a symbolism that seems to embody the contemporary reality of the Cold War. The territorial rationale of the superpowers USA and Russia and the arms race come to mind. Filko's interventions thus also address the political space. This is particularly obvious when looking at works like *Occupation of the Czechoslovak Socialist Republic – Pink Heart / Okupácia ČSSR – Ružové srdce* (1968/1978) [07] and *EGOQ with Alexander Dubček / EGOQ s Alexandrom Dubčekom* (1968/c. 1995) [08], which are about the events of the Prague Spring in 1968. Filko's adaptations add a subjective component to the concrete, historical snapshots. In the first work he places pink hearts into the picture, and in the second the letters "EGOQ" are placed over the politicians depicted. These subjective components are seen as the projection of Filko's artistic principle of the ego, which manifested itself in a public action in which he undertook a measurement of the distance between trees. As an artistic document the work *The Space among Trees – The Masses. Plan-Projectart / Priestor medzi stromami – hmotami. Plán-projektart* (1969) [10] recalls this kind of nonconformist behavior which the regime at the time most likely would have seen to be suspicious.

Die Arbeiten der Serie *Sculptures of the Twentieth Century / Sochy XX. storočia* (1968–69) [05–06] [09] beinhalten fotografische Aufnahmen von Stadtgebieten, aber auch Fotografien aus populären Magazinen, die Filko mit langgezogenen Umrissen überschrieben hat. Die Umrisse sind teilweise an die Form von Weltraumraketen angelehnt, erinnern aber auch stark an militärische Raketengeschosse und Projektile. Das übergeordnete Gefüge der Realität wird ausgetauscht, der kosmische Raum weicht einer Symbolik, welche die damalige Weltordnung des kalten Krieges zu verkörpern scheint. Das territoriale Denken der Großmächte USA und Russland, sowie die militärische Aufrüstung kommen in den Sinn. Die Interventionen Filkos beschäftigen sich demnach auch mit dem politischen Raum. Dies wird vor allem offensichtlich, wenn man sich Arbeiten wie *Occupation of the Czechoslovak Socialist Republic – Pink Heart / Okupácia ČSSR – Ružové srdce* (1968/1978) [07] oder *EGOQ with Alexander Dubček / EGOQ s Alexandrom Dubčekom* (1968/ca. 1995) [08] zuwendet, die sich um die Ereignisse des Prager Frühlings im Jahr 1968 drehen. Durch Filkos Bearbeitung wird den konkreten, historischen Momentaufnahmen gleichzeitig eine subjektive Komponente hinzugefügt. Bei der ersten Arbeit setzt Filko pinke Herzen in den Bildraum, auf der zweiten Fotografie breitet sich vor den damals beteiligten Politikern der Schriftzug „EGOQ" aus. Diese subjektiven Komponenten werden als Projektion von Filkos künstlerischem Prinzip des Egos aufgefasst, welches sich auch in einer öffentlichen Aktion manifestiert hat, in der er eine Messung der Abstände zwischen Bäumen vorgenommen hat. Als künstlerisches Dokument erinnert die Arbeit *The Space among Trees – The Masses. Plan-Projectart / Priestor medzi stromami – hmotami. Plán-projektart* (1969) [10] an diese Art des non-konformen Verhaltens, das unter dem damaligen Regime wahrscheinlich als verdächtig wahrgenommen wurde.

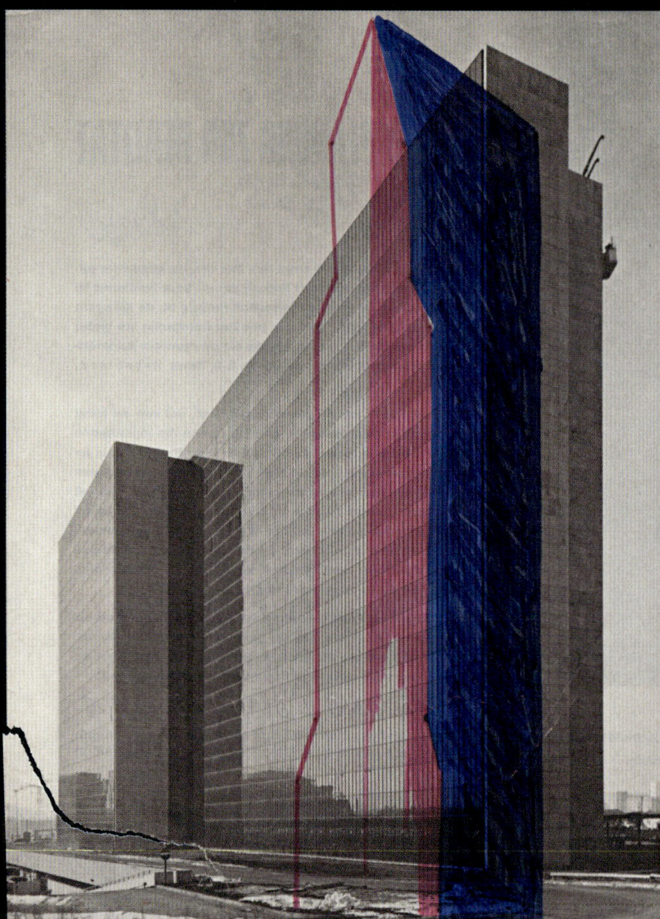

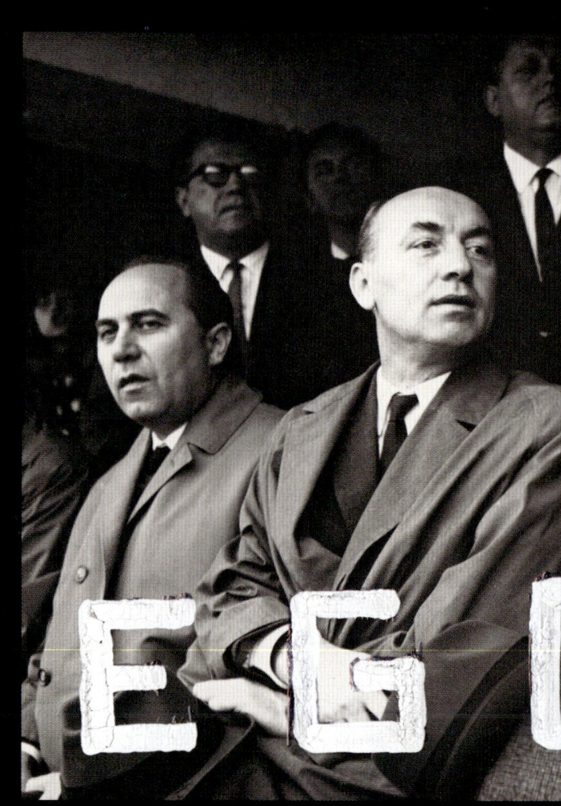

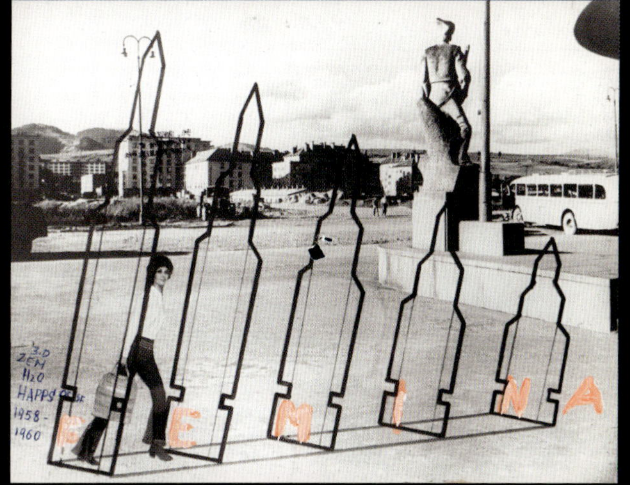

[09] From the series *Sculptures of the Twentieth Century (FEMINA)* / Zo série *Sochy XX. storočia (FEMINA)*, 1968/c. 1995

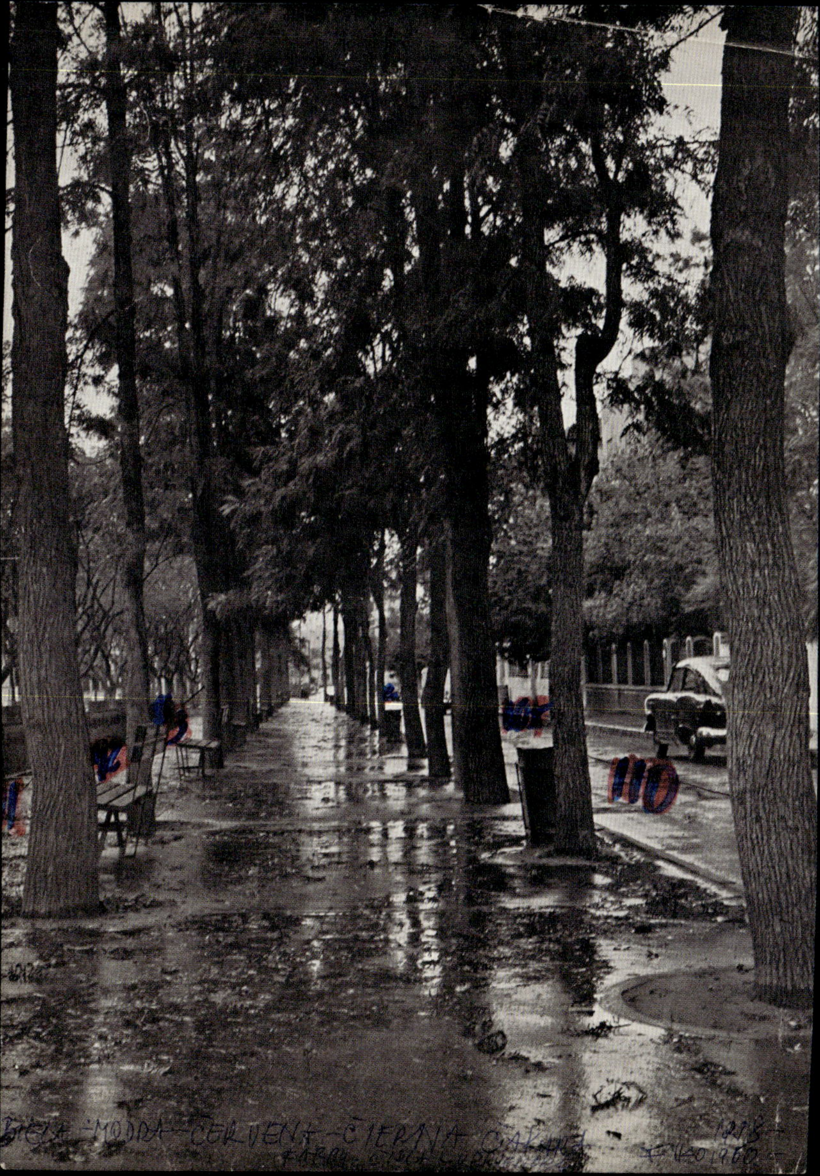

[10] *The Space among Trees – The Masses. Plan-Projectart* / *Priestor medzi stromami – hmotami.*

XVII

HAPPSOC: Happening and Society / Happy Socialism

Many of the addressees of this message in Bratislava in 1965 had no idea at all what it was all about. They received a strangely printed invitation card to a series of happenings entitled "HAPPSOC" and due to take place in the city between May 1 and 9. [01] Each of these days was proclaimed an independent part of this action, and there was an added appendix that looked like some kind of statistical report and seemingly arbitrarily listed numerous features of the city. This document begins with a list of the numbers of all women, men, dogs, and apartments in the city, and becomes particularly paradoxical with its final elements "entire Bratislava 1" and "Castle 1." [02]

Viele Adressat*innen der Nachricht im Bratislava des Jahres 1965 wussten ganz einfach nicht, was damit anzufangen sei: Sie erhielten eine eigenartig bedruckte Einladungskarte, die eine Reihe an Happenings zwischen dem 1. und 9. Mai in Bratislava unter dem Namen „HAPPSOC" ausrief. [01] Jeder Tag wurde als eigener Teil der Aktion proklamiert und das Ganze enthielt einen Anhang, der an einen statistischen Report erinnerte und scheinbar willkürlich zahlreiche Elemente um die Stadt Bratislava aufzählte. Das Dokument fängt mit einer Auflistung der Anzahl aller Frauen, Männer, Hunde und Wohnungen der Stadt an und wird letztendlich durch die Elemente „ganz Bratislava 1" und „Burg 1" paradox. [02]

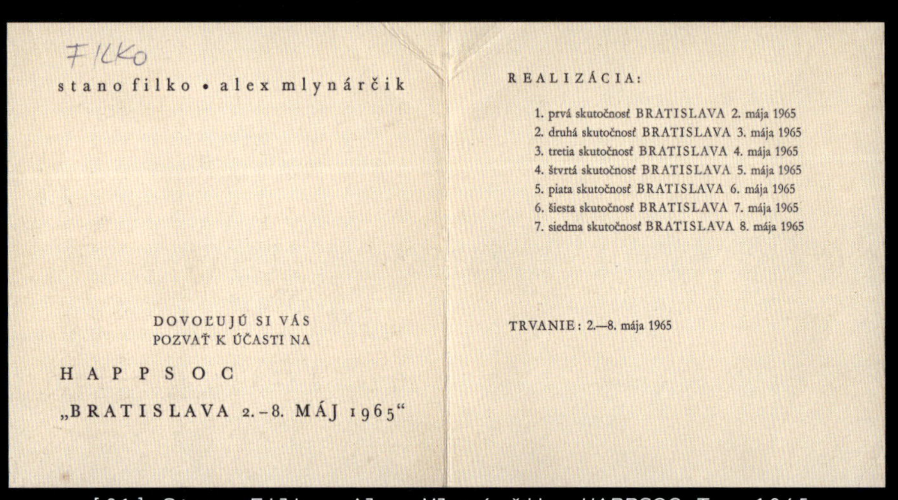

[01] Stano Filko, Alex Mlynárčik, *HAPPSOC I.*, 1965

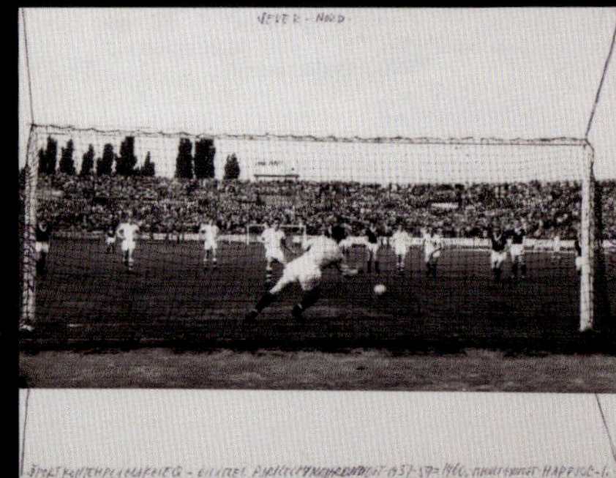

[03] *HAPPSOC I. (SPORT) / HAPPSOC I. (ŠPORT)*, 1965/c. 2000

It was also for this notable action that Filko became more widely known in the 1960s. He conducted it together with Alex Mlynárčik. The term "HAPPSOC" is an artistic assertion, presumably put together from parts of the words "happening" and "society," or "happy socialism" and can be seen as a genre akin to conceptual art, action art, and Fluxus. Shortly after the action the explanatory *HAPPSOC Manifesto / HAPPSOC Manifest* (1965) was published, declaring that the action intended to observe "found reality." Within a limited spatial and temporal framework, "activities to recognize the limitless scope of existing coherence" were set in motion.

Neben seiner frühen Beschäftigung mit der Installationskunst wurde Filko in den 1960er-Jahren durch diese bemerkenswerte Aktion bekannt, die er zusammen mit Alex Mlynárčik verantwortete. Der Begriff „HAPPSOC" ist eine künstlerische Behauptung, setzt sich wohl aus Wortteilen von *happening* und *society* zusammen oder steht für *happy socialism* und ist zwischen Konzept- und Aktionskunst hin zu Fluxus angesiedelt. Kurz nach der Aktion wurde das *HAPPSOC Manifesto / HAPPSOC Manifest* (1965) herausgegeben, das als eine Art Erklärung diente. Demnach handelt es sich um eine Aktion, welche die Betrachtung „vorgefundener Wirklichkeit" zum Ziel hat. In einem begrenzten raumzeitlichen Rahmen werden „Aktivitäten des Erkennens der grenzenlosen Spannweite der bestehenden Kohärenz" in Gang gesetzt.

OBJEKTY:	
1. Ženy	137.936
2. Muži	128.727
3. Psi	48.991
4. Domy /s provizóriami/	18.009
5. Balkóny	165.236
6. Poľnohospodárske usadlosti	22
7. Prevádzkové budovy	525
8. Byty	64.725
9. Vodovody v bytoch	40.070
10. Vodovody mimo bytov	944
11. Sporáky elektrické	3.505
12. " plynové	37.804
13. Práčky	35.060
14. Chladničky	17.534
15. Celá Bratislava	1
16. Hrad	1
17. Dunaj /v Bratislave/	1
18. Pouličné lampy	142.090
19. Televízne antény	128.726
20. Cintoríny	6
21. Tulipány	1,000.801
22. Divadlá /aj ochotnícke/	9
23. Kiná,komíny,električky,viechy,autá, trolejbusy,písacie stroje,rádiá,obchody, knižnice,nemocnice,atď.	

FILKO

[02] Stano Filko, Alex Mlynárčik, *HAPPSOC I.*, 1965

FILKO STANO

Roku 1966 a ďalšie roky Vás pozývam k účasti na

En 1966 et dans les années suivantes je Vous invite à vouloir bien participier au

AKCIE UNIVERZÁL

SKUTOČNO

Priestor:
ÚZEMIE ČSSR · ČESKOSLOVENSKO

Skutočnosti:

a. Život, situácie, vzťahy, atmosféra v ČSSR.
b. V neobmedzenom čase budúcom i minulom.
c. Životné pocity: subjektívne i spoločné.
d. Miesto a čas individuálny, na hociktorom malom či väčšom priestore
e. Ľudia, mestá, dediny, príroda, zvieratá, technika, veda, šport, ročné obdobie, umenie, literatúra, hudba, budúcnosť...

ACTION UNIVERSELLE

RÉALITÉ

Lieu:
Territoire de la ČSSR (Tchécoslovaquie)

FAITS:

a. Vie, situation, rapports, atmosphère en ČSSR.
b. Dans le temp futur et passé illimité.
c. Sentiments vécus: subjectifs et sociaux.
d. Lieu et temps individuel, au quelconque petite ou grande place.
e. Hommes, villes, villages, nature, animaux, technique, science, sport, saisons, art, littérature, musique, future...

[05A] *HAPPSOC III. The Altar of the Present / HAPPSOC III. Oltár súčasnosti, 1966*

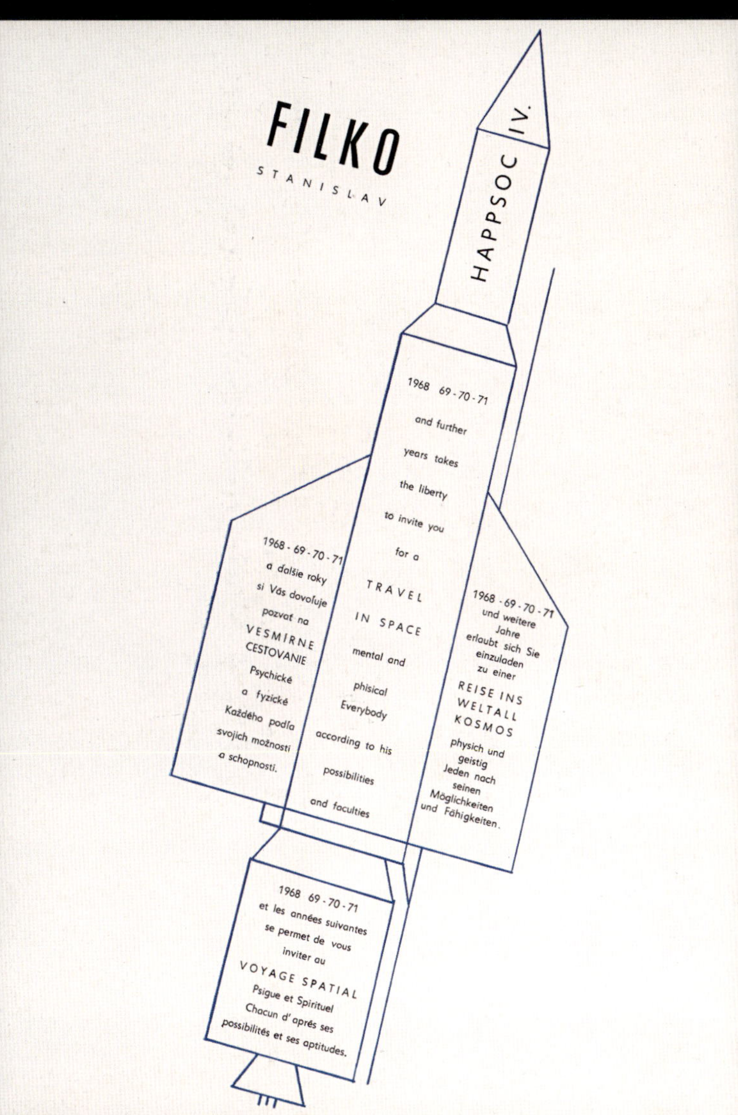

[04] *HAPPSOC IV. Travel in Space / HAPPSOC IV. Vesmírne cestovanie, 1967*

This project developed to become a series over several years, with three further editions and various spin-offs. *HAPPSOC II.* (1965) entailed the paradoxical demand to spend a from day to day increasing period of time during the days between Christmas Day and New Year in a not clearly determined train station in Bratislava. *HAPPSOC IV.* (1967) [04] demanded going as best as possible into outer space, both in mind and body, so that here the project finally left behind any real spatial context. Like the artistic practice of Joseph Beuys, this group of works is based on a very broad concept of art that above all refers to an understanding and shaping of social conditions.

Es entwickelte sich eine mehrjährige Programmabfolge, auf die ursprüngliche Version folgten weitere drei Ausgaben, aber auch diverse Nebenprodukte. *HAPPSOC II.* (1965) beinhaltet die paradoxe Aufforderung, an den Tagen zwischen erstem Weihnachtstag und Neujahr eine mit den Tagen zunehmende Verweildauer an einer nicht näher spezifizierten Zugstation in Bratislava zu verbringen. *HAPPSOC IV.* (1967) [04] bildet eine Aufforderung sich nach bester Möglichkeit gedanklich und physisch in den Weltraum zu begeben, womit sich das Konzept endgültig von einem realen und räumlichen Zusammenhang befreit. Ähnlich der künstlerischen Praxis von Joseph Beuys bildet diese Werkgruppe eine sehr weitläufige Auffassung von Kunst, die sich vor allem auf die Erfassung und Formung sozialer Zusammenhänge bezieht.

HAPPSOC I. (1965) is above all a space of opportunity, whereby the time period given is key. Both of these days were national holidays in real-socialist Czechoslovakia and they were politically connoted. May 1 is Labor Day, and on May 9, the date of the liberation of Czechoslovakia by the Red Army, large military parades took place. "HAPPSOC" resists this ubiquitous political interpretation and instead emphasizes the everyday reality of life beyond demonstrations of political power.

HAPPSOC I. (1965) ist vor allem ein Raum der Möglichkeit, wobei der angegebene Zeitraum wesentlich ist. Beide Tage sind in der real-sozialistischen Tschechoslowakei Nationalfeiertage gewesen und dadurch politisch konnotiert: der 1. Mai ist der Tag der Arbeit, am 9. Mai, dem Tag der Befreiung der Tschechoslowakei durch die rote Armee, fanden repräsentative Militärparaden statt. „HAPPSOC" widersetzt sich der allgegenwärtigen politischen Vereinnahmung und betont die alltägliche Realität abseits der Zurschaustellung politischer Macht.

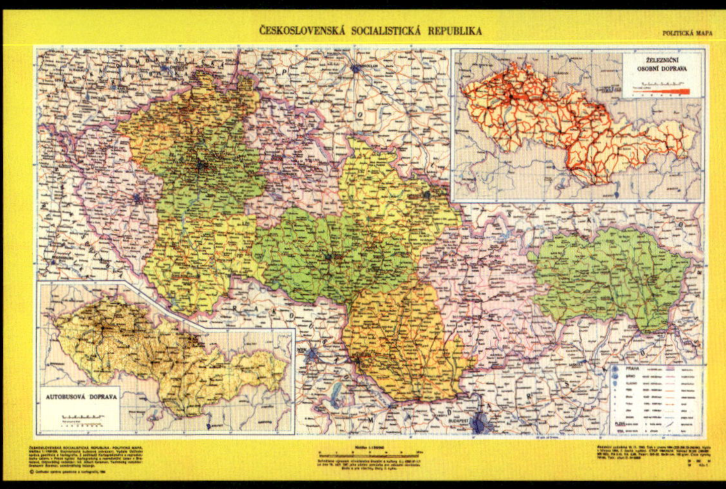

[05B] *HAPPSOC III. The Altar of the Present / HAPPSOC III. Oltár súčasnosti, 1966*

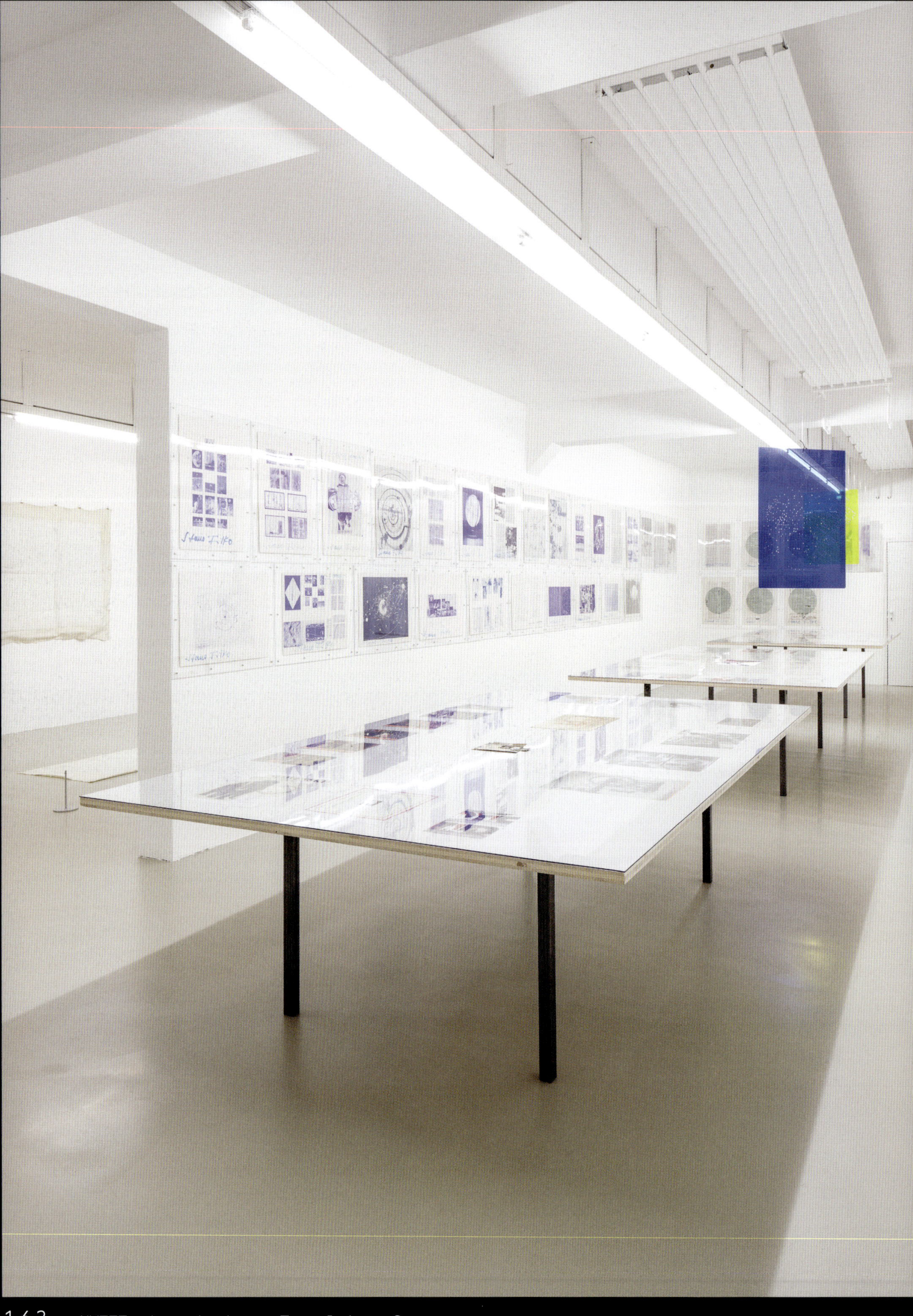

XVIII

Associations: Travel into Space / Reise ins All

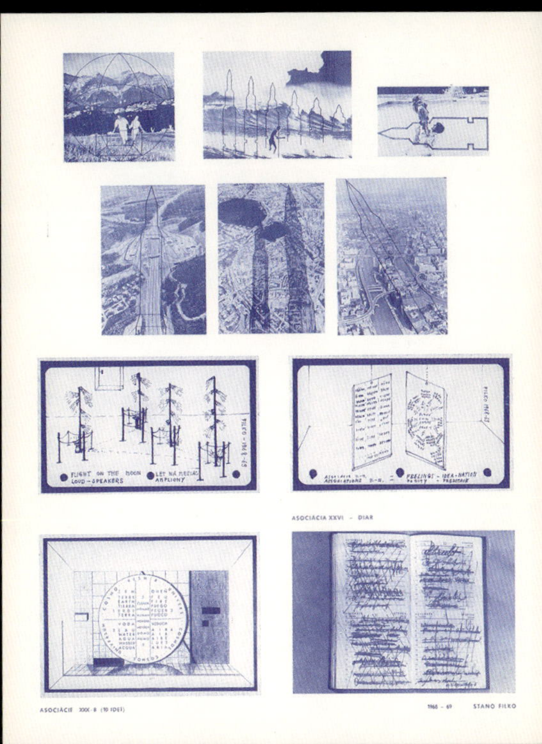

[02] *Associations XXX. - B / Asociácie XXX. - B*, 1968-69; from the series *Associations / zo série Asociácie*, 1967-70

Stano Filko addressed the theme of the cosmos very early in his career, and between 1967 and 1970 he explored it in depth in his series *Associations / Asociácie* (1967–70) [01-22]. In an early part of the series, he works on the theme in a way that resembles the activities of an archivist. Filko collected various diagrams, texts, and photographs, and then worked on them artistically, thereby appropriating them. Connecting elements are the color blue, which is the color of the cosmos in his system, and various cosmic motifs such as star signs, space expeditions, and the structure of the universe. He employed a graphic poster style, using silkscreen and offset printing, media that seem to suit the technical and thematic orientation on the idea of progress, and also the fact that the theme itself featured strongly in the press and media. Sometimes motifs and texts are crossed out or a signature is added, so that the structures of the cosmos are reworked and transferred into the artistic system.

Stano Filko hat den Kosmos schon früh künstlerisch aufgegriffen und sich zudem fortwährend zwischen 1967 und 1970 in der Serie *Associations / Asociácie* (1967–1970) [01-22] damit auseinandergesetzt. In einem frühen Teil der Serie bearbeitet er das Thema in einer Form, die an die Tätigkeit eines Archivars erinnert. Filko sammelt verschiedene Diagramme, Schriftstücke und Fotografien, bearbeitet diese aber gleichzeitig künstlerisch und eignet sie sich an. Verbindende Elemente sind dabei die Farbe Blau, in seinem System die Farbe des Kosmos, sowie unterschiedliche kosmische Motive wie Sternenbilder, Weltraumexpeditionen und die Struktur des Universums. Dabei verwendet er eine grafische, plakative Auseinandersetzung unter Verwendung von Sieb- und Offsetdruck, die der technisch wie inhaltlich fortschrittsorientierten, aber auch stark durch die Presse medialisierten Thematik äquivalent erscheint. Bisweilen werden Motive und Texte nachträglich durchgestrichen oder mit einer Signatur versehen, womit die Strukturen des Kosmos überarbeitet und in das künstlerische System überführt werden.

[04] *Associations - The Celestial Globe / Asociácie - Glóbus vesmíru*, 1966-67; from the series *Associations / zo série Asociácie*, 1967-70

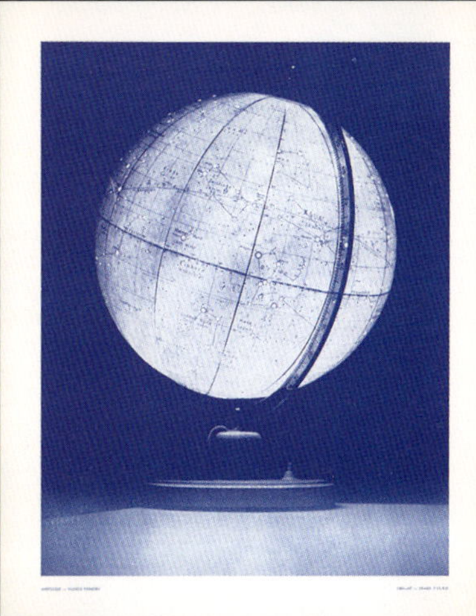

[03] *Concept - 1968 - Cosmos / Koncept - 1968 - Cosmos*, 1968; from the series *Associations / zo série Asociácie*, 1967-70

←[01] Exhibition view, HALLE FÜR KUNST Steiermark, Graz, 2022

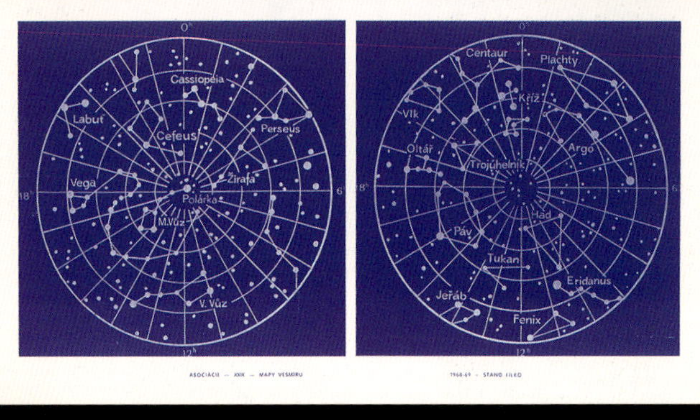

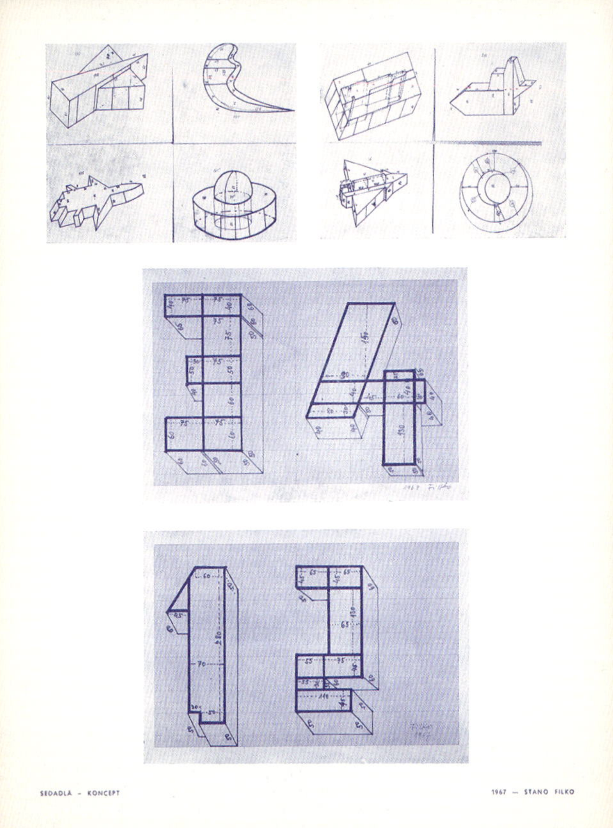

[05] *Seats - Concept / Sedadlá - Koncept,
1967; from the series Associations /
zo série Asociácie, 1967-70*

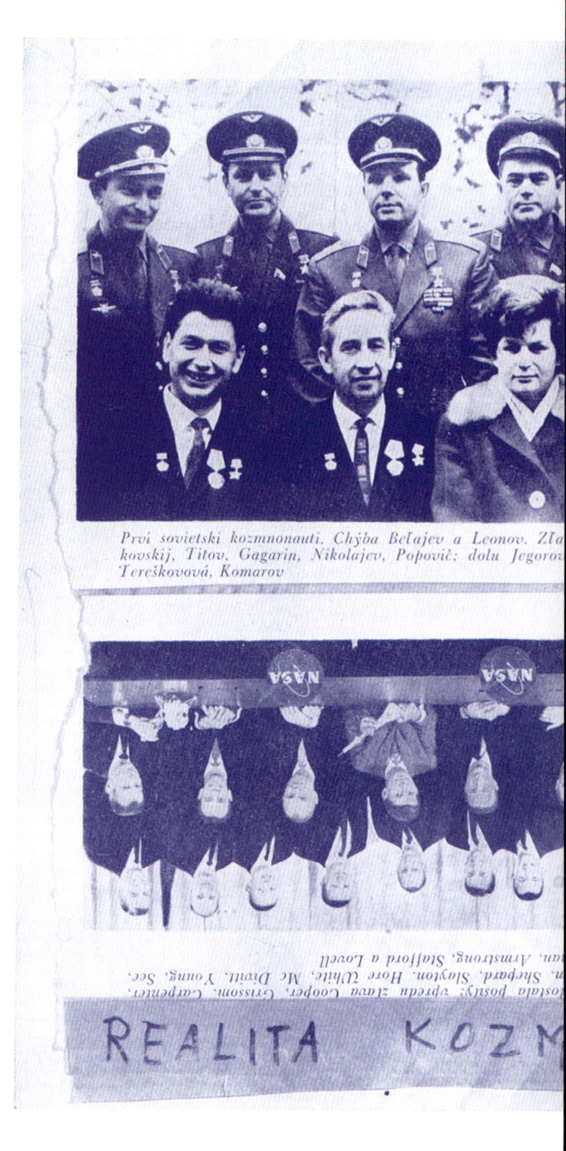

[08] *Reality of the Cosmos - B /
Realita kozmu - B, 1968-69;
from the series Associations /
zo série Asociácie, 1967-70*

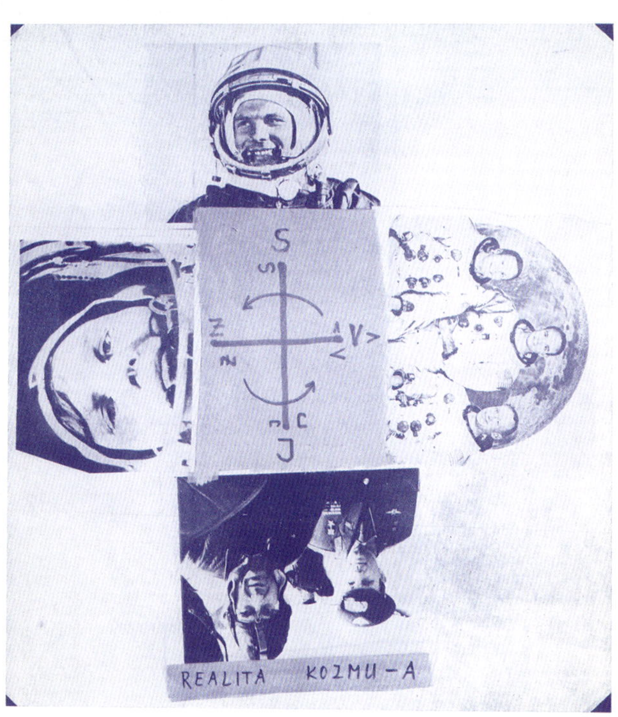

[07] *Reality of the Cosmos - A / Realita kozmu - A,
1968-69; from the series Associations / zo série
Asociácie, 1967-70*

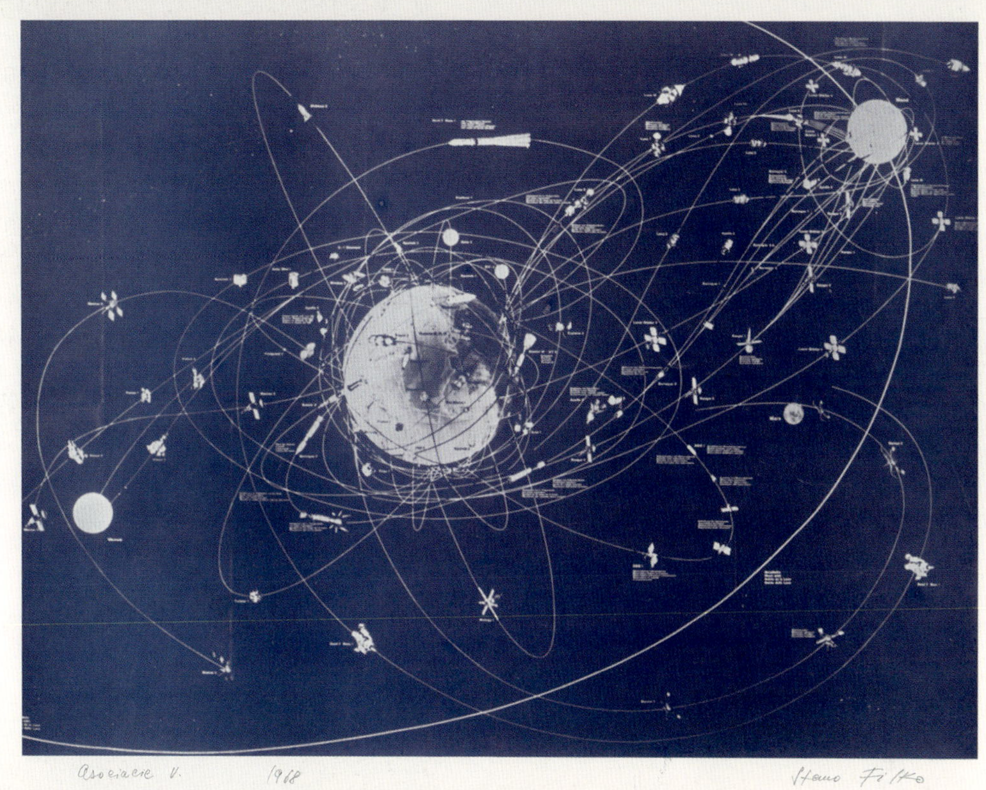

[09] *Associations V. / Asociácie V.*; from the series *Associations /
zo série Asociácie*, 1967–70

[10] *Associations XV. / Asociácie XV.*, 1968–69; from the series
Associations XXXX. / zo série Asociácie XXXX., 1970

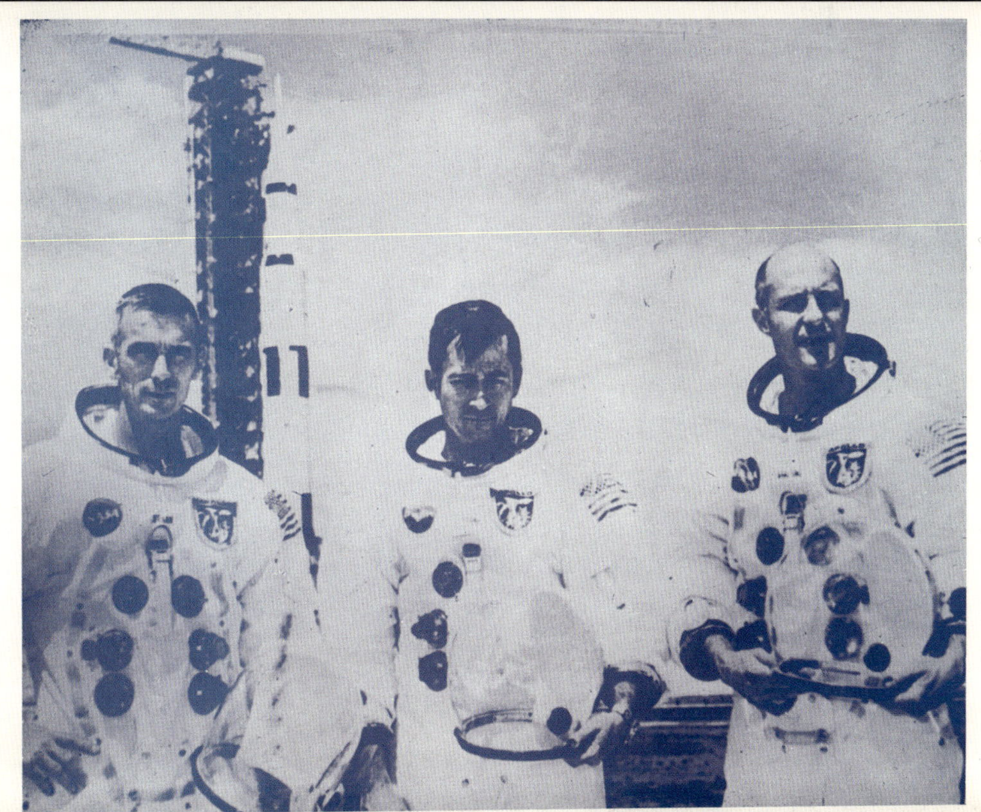

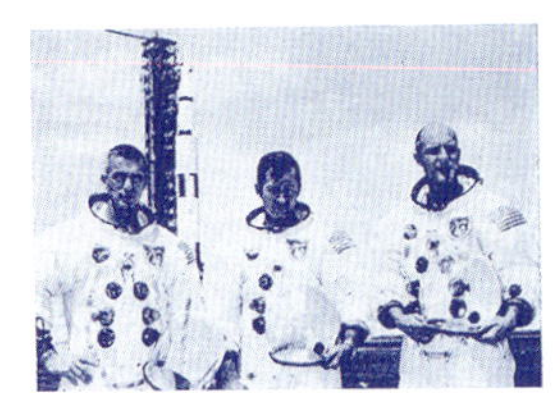

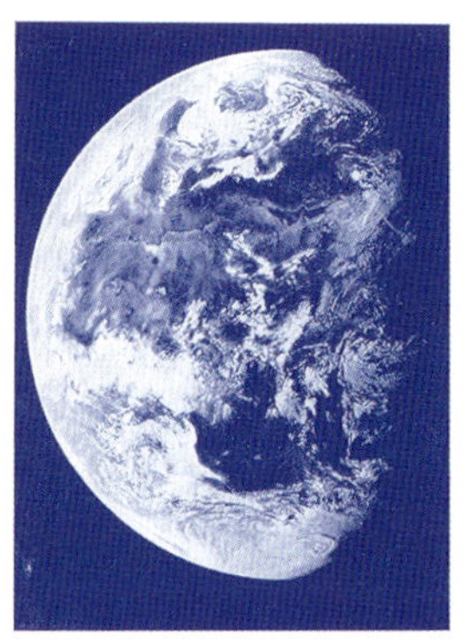
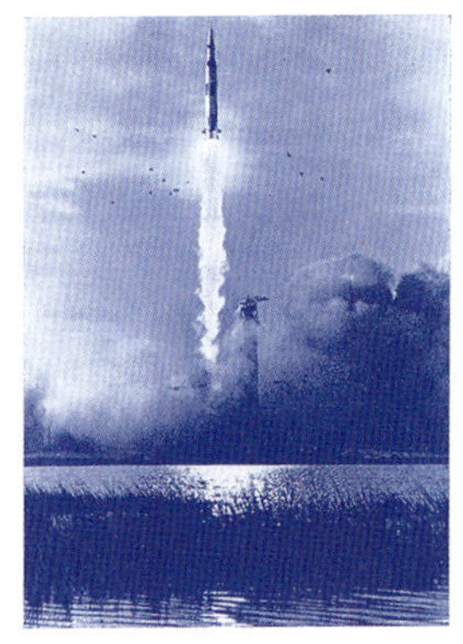
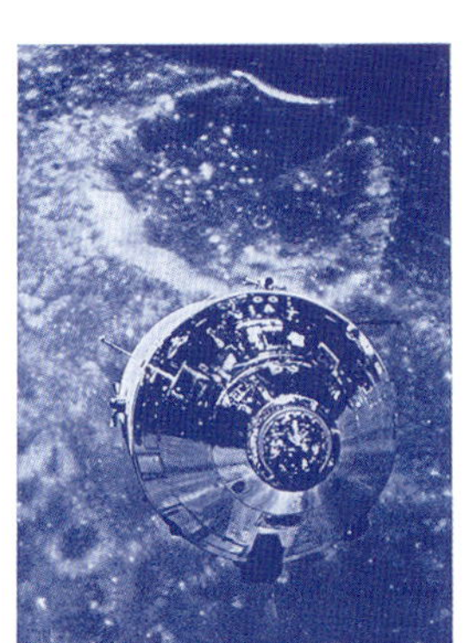

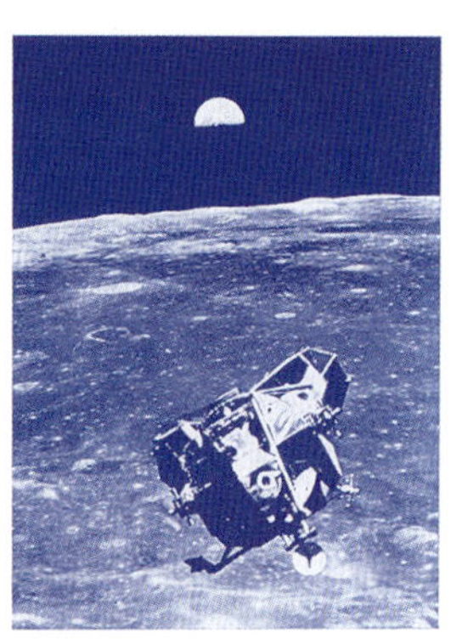
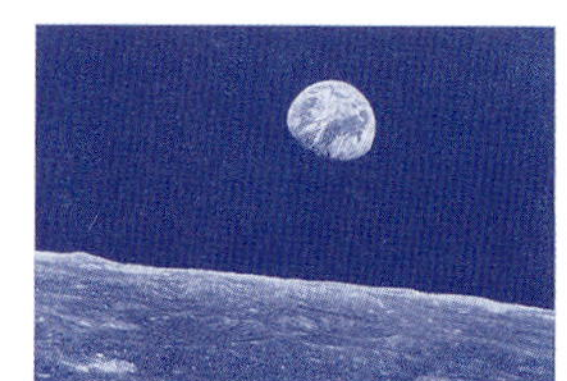
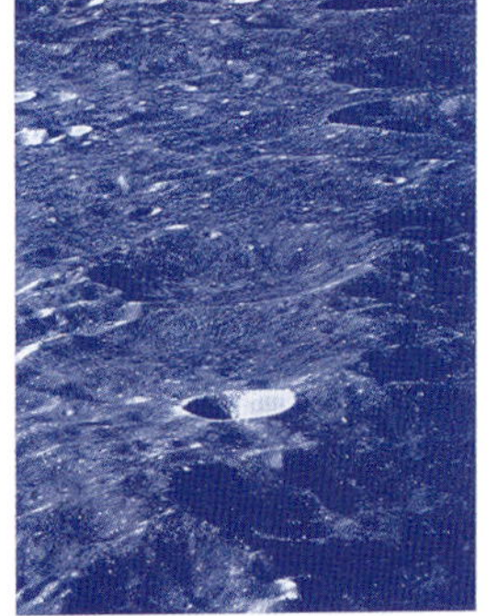

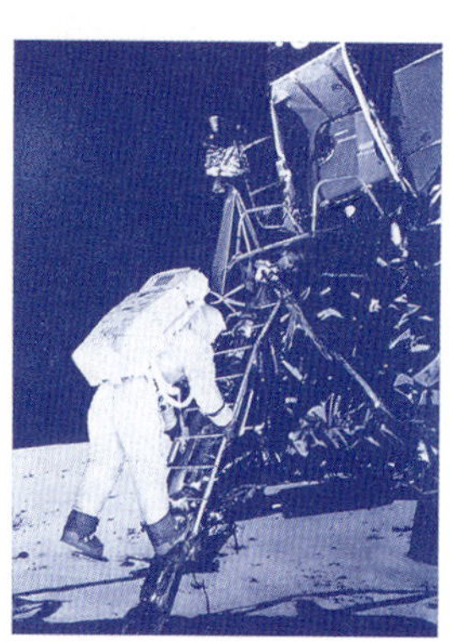
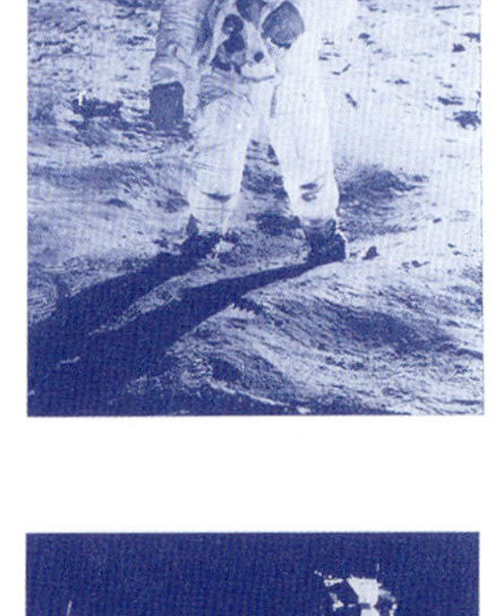
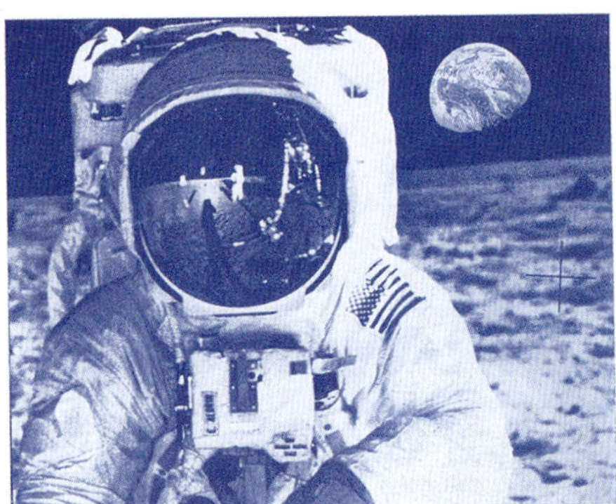

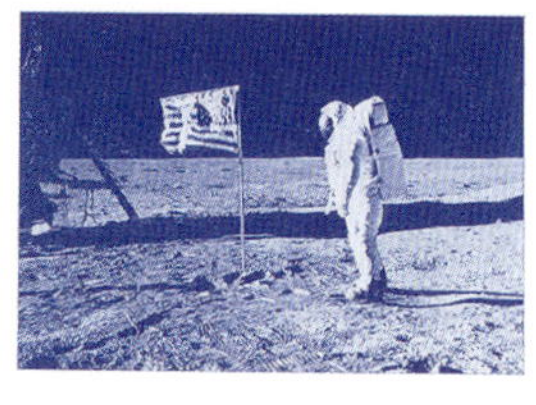
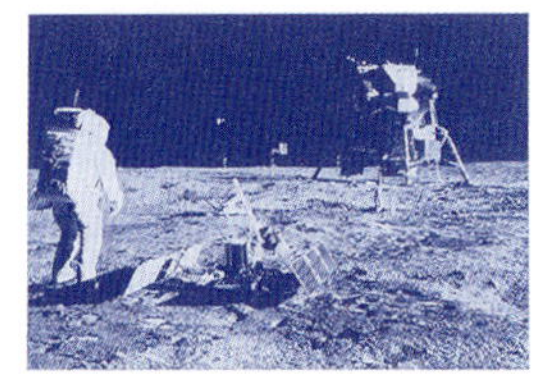
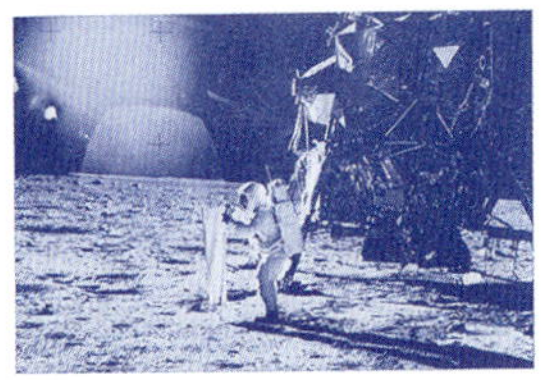

ASOCIÁCIE XXXI. — I. LET — MESIAC   1969 — STANO FILKO

[12] Associations XIII. - B /
Asociácie XIII. - B, 1969;
from the series Associations /
zo série Asociácie, 1967-70

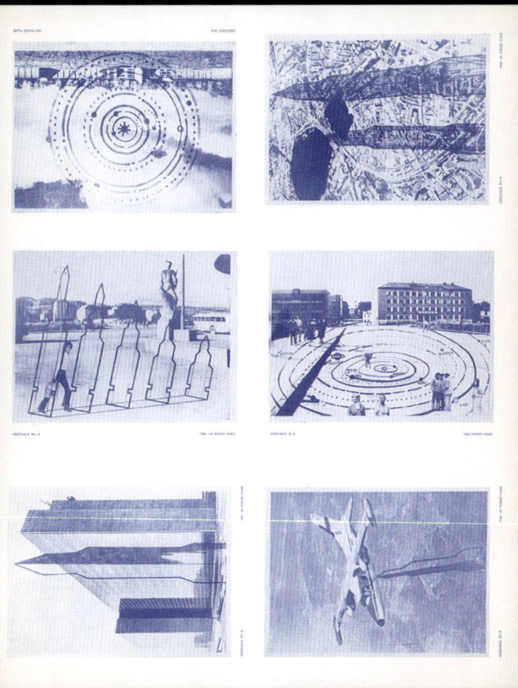

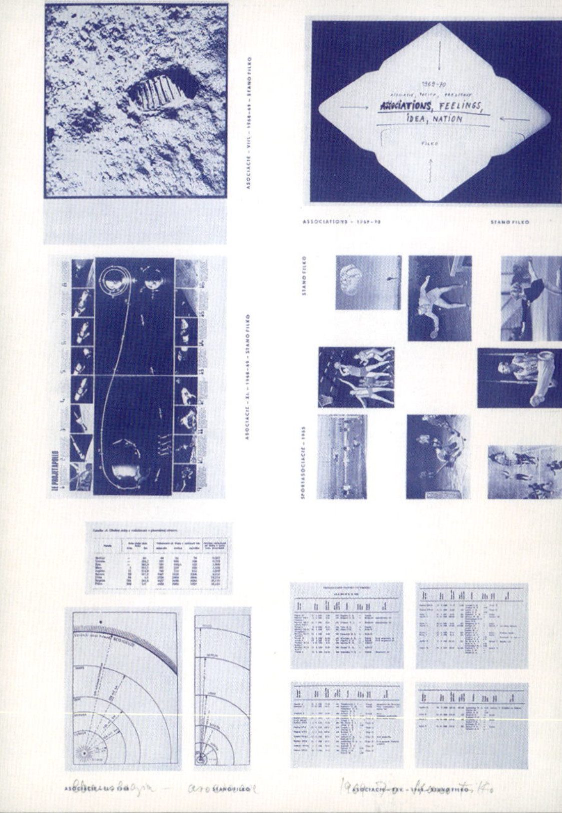

[13] Chronology - Associations /
Chronológia - Asociácie, 1969-70; from
the series Associations / zo série
Asociácie, 1967-70

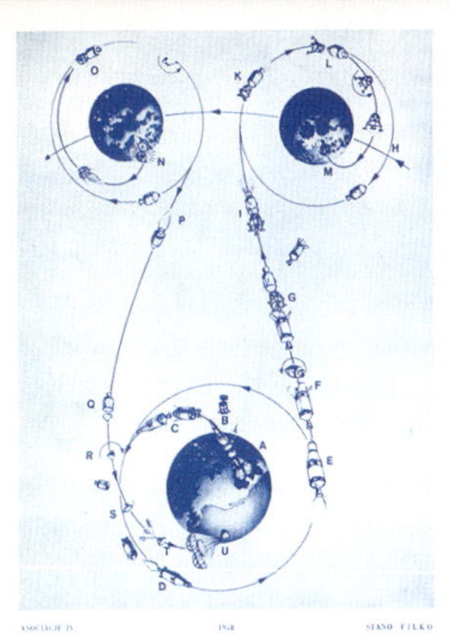

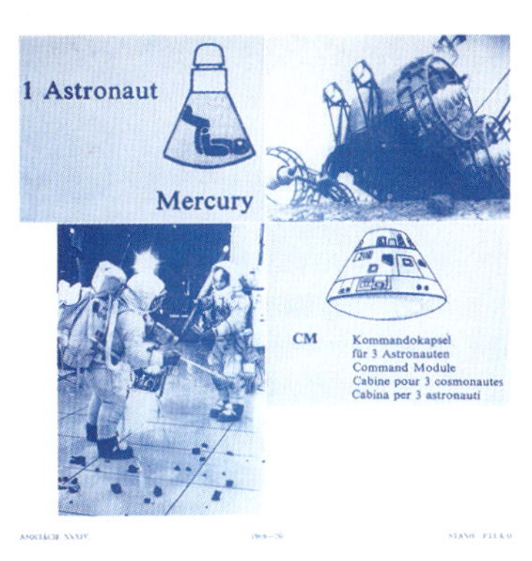

1 Astronaut

Mercury

CM   Kommandokapsel
      für 3 Astronauten
      Command Module
      Cabine pour 3 cosmonautes
      Cabina per 3 astronauti

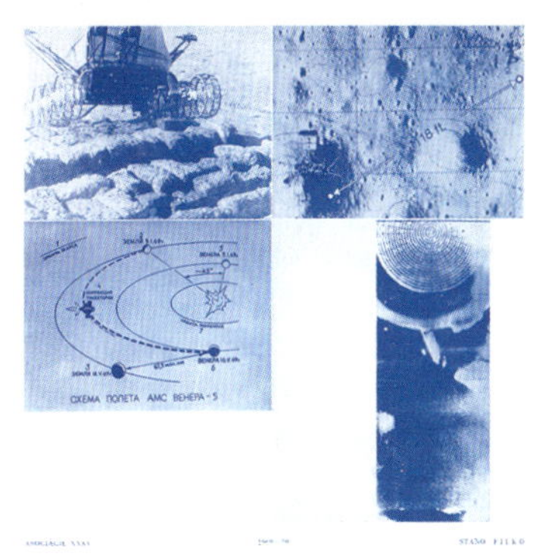

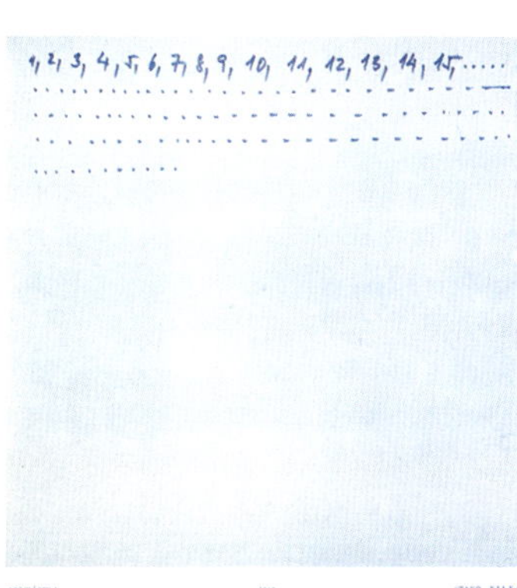

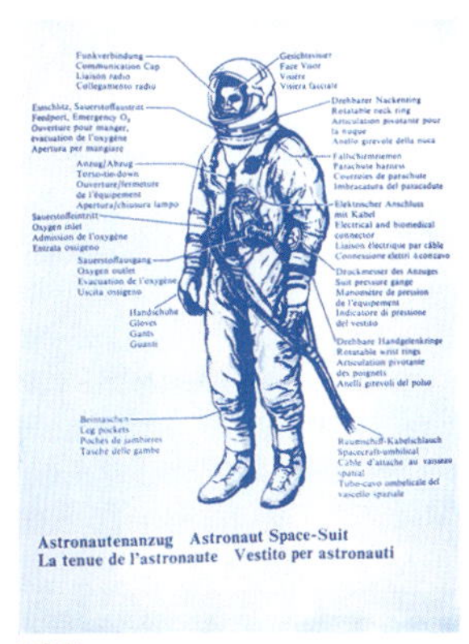

Astronautenanzug   Astronaut Space-Suit
La tenue de l'astronaute   Vestito per astronauti

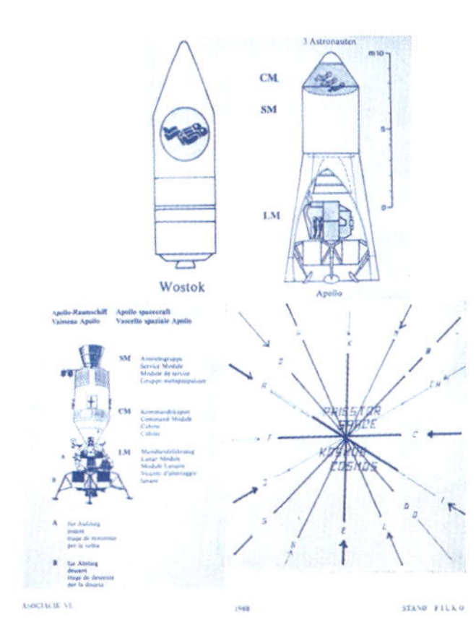

Wostok

Apollo

In both material and spatial terms, Filko's interest in the cosmos in the later works in the *Associations* series are quite different. He uses yellow Plexiglas and polished aluminum sheets into which he inserts circular holes, thus suggesting a machine-made aesthetics. Filko drew here on new spatial concepts in painting, incorporating the surrounding space into the work. By restricting gestural means and using industrial materials he also connected with the Western trends in Minimal Art that were current at the time.

In materieller wie räumlicher Hinsicht stellt sich Filkos Beschäftigung mit dem Kosmos in den späteren Arbeiten der Serie *Associations* noch einmal anders dar. Filko verwendet gelbe Plexiglasplatten, sowie polierte Aluminiumblätter und durchdringt diese mit kreisrunden Löchern, wodurch eine maschinengefertigte Ästhetik hervorgerufen wird. Filko lehnt sich an neue räumliche Konzepte in der Malerei an, und bezieht den umliegenden Raum mit ein. Durch die Zurückdrängung des Gestischen und das Verwenden von Industriematerial knüpft er außerdem an damals aktuelle, westliche Tendenzen der Minimal Art an.

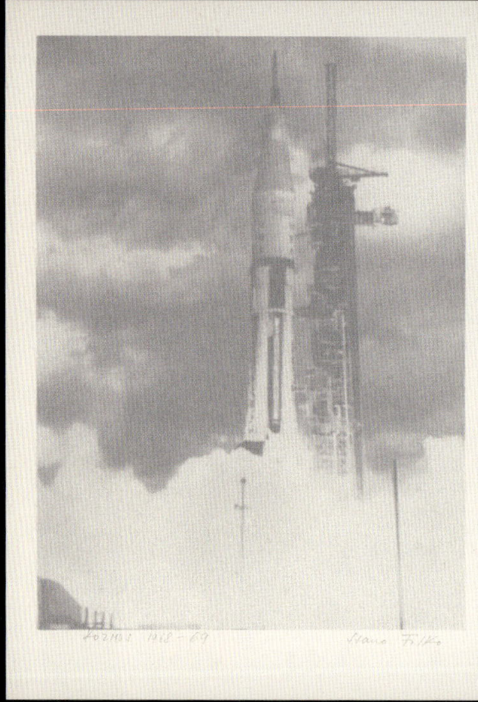

[15] *Cosmos / Kozmos*, 1968–69; from the series *Associations / zo série Asociácie*, 1967–70

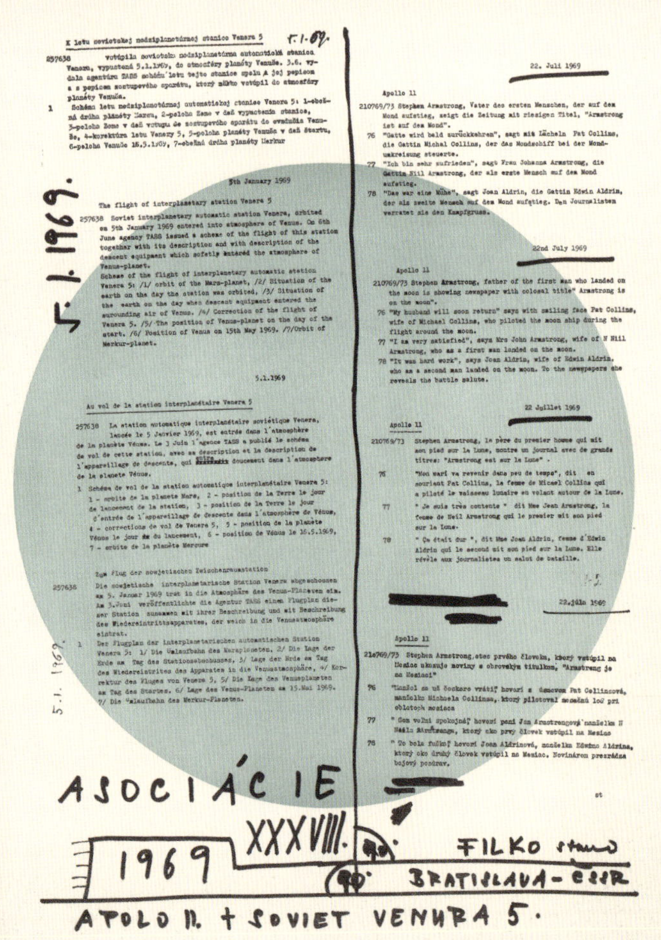

[16] *Associations XXXVIII. / Asociácie XXXVIII.*, 1969; from the series *Associations / zo série Asociácie*, 1967–70

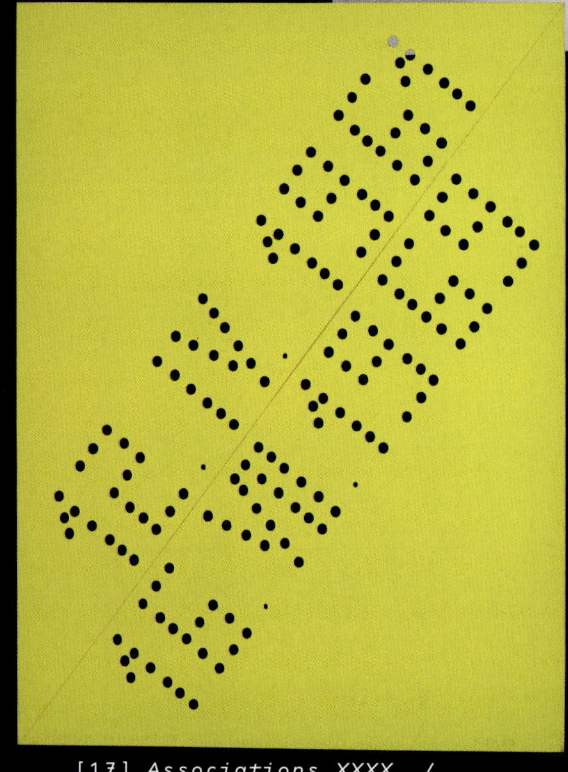

[17] *Associations XXXX. / Asociácie XXXX.*, 1970

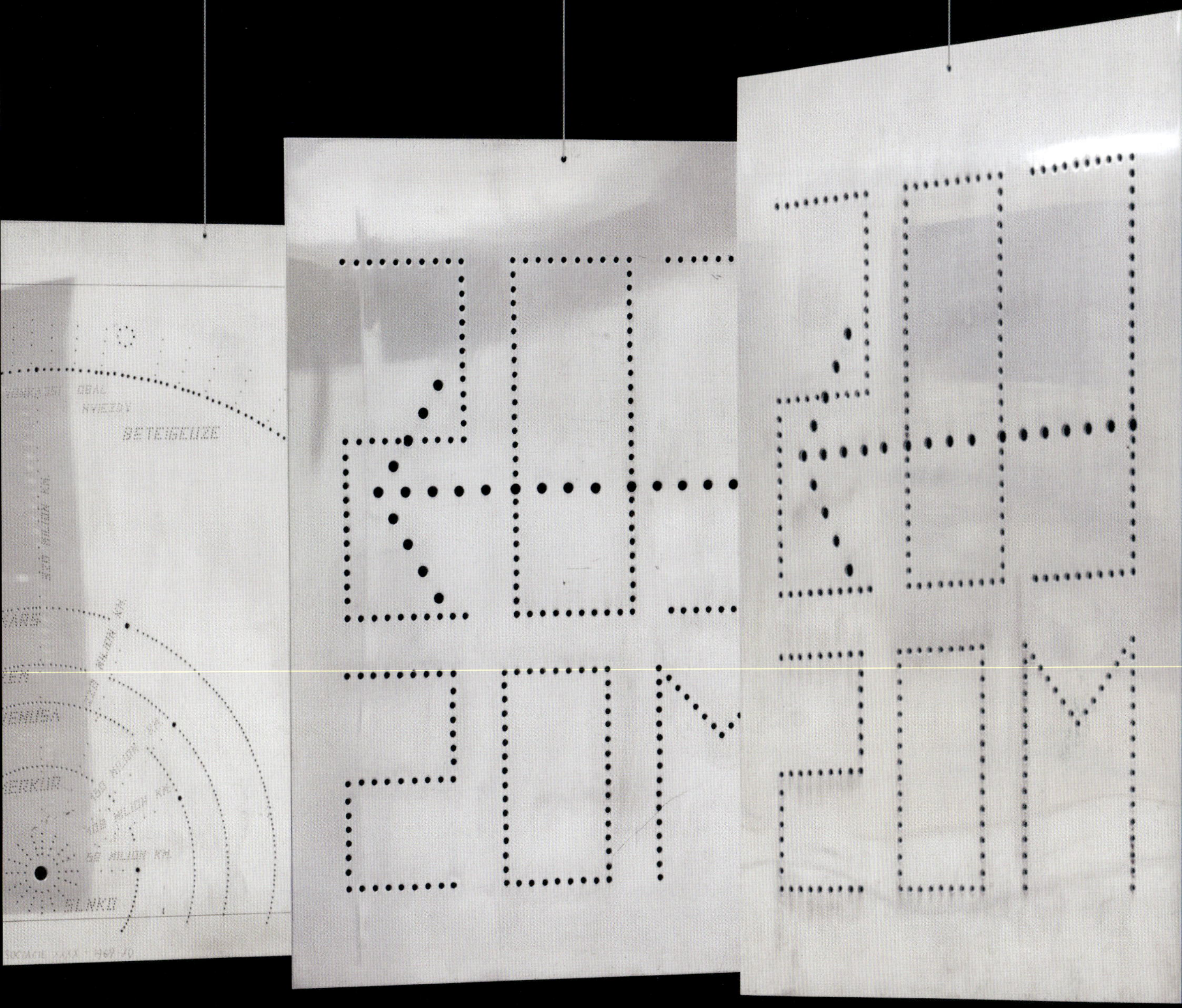

[18–20] *Associations XXXX. /
Asociácie XXXX.*, 1969–70

[21] *Associations XXXX. (COS-MOS) /
Asociácie XXXX. (COS-MOS)*, 1969–70

Filko wished to avoid disturbing his presentation of the cosmos with any subjective expression. In some of these works the perforations represent connections between numbers that seem to recall encoded communication in space. In other places the perforations illustrate the structure of the galactic system. Two specific rows of numbers can be more precisely explained. One yellow Plexiglas sheet has two dates from the history of space exploration. [17] On April 12, 1961, Russian astronaut Yuri Gagarin became the first man to orbit our planet, while July 16, 1969, is the date of the take-off of the American Apollo 11 mission, which put the first men on the moon.

Filko war es wichtig, die Mediatisierung des Kosmos nicht durch den subjektiven Ausdruck zu stören. Auf manchen Werken stellen die Perforationen Verbindungen zwischen Zahlen dar, die an die Kommunikation im Weltraum mittels Codes zu erinnern scheinen. An anderer Stelle verdeutlichen die Perforationen den Aufbau des galaktischen Systems. Zwei Zahlenreihen lassen sich an dieser Stelle noch näher benennen – eine gelbe Plexiglasplatte ist mit zwei wichtigen Zeitangaben der Astronautik versehen. [17] Am 12. 4. 1961 hat der Russe Juri Gagarin als erster Mensch den Orbit unseres Planeten umkreist. Der 16. 7. 1969 verweist auf den Start der amerikanischen Apollo 11-Mission, worauf die erste Mondlandung folgte.

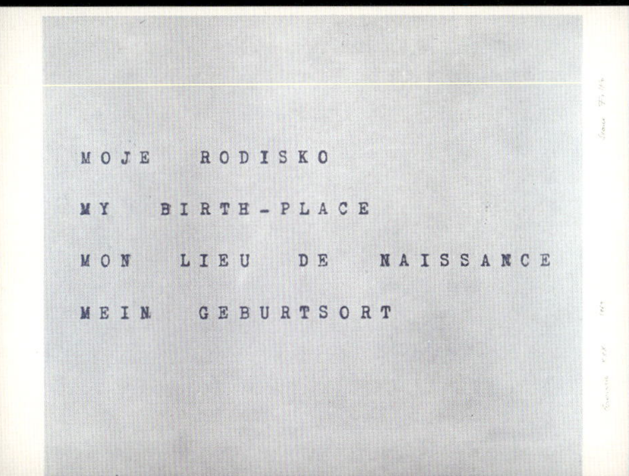

[22] *Associations XXX. / Asociácie XXX.*,
1969; from the series *Associations /
zo série Asociácie*, 1967–70

Genealogy of Modernist Essentialism

Mira Keratová

Stano Filko belongs to the generation of Slovak 1960s neo-avant-gardists including Alex Mlynárčik, Július Koller and Peter Bartoš[1] who explored the performance of life in its everydayness. With Mlynárčik (along with Zita Kostrová), Filko worked on a manifesto project and the readymade-event *HAPPSOC I., BRATISLAVA 2.–8. MAY, 1965 / HAPPSOC I. BRATISLAVA 2.–8. MÁJ 1965*, which they distributed as an invitation for participation with a statistical register of "objects" (men, women, dogs, etc.), located at that time in Bratislava. It was created through the appropriation of the temporally and spatially defined reality of the city of Bratislava in the midst of the socialist celebrations of Labor Day and of the anniversary of the end of World War Two (according to the Soviet doctrine). Through Mlynárčik's connections to the Paris Nouveau Réalisme movement, Pierre Restany reported on the manifesto on the international scene. Accordingly, Filko's work was historically seen together with global conceptual trends, which, however, were occurring in different parts of the world and under different conditions, within which they had their specific forms.[2] Its continuation was *HAPPSOC II. 7 DAYS OF CREATION / HAPPSOC II. 7 DNÍ STVORENIA*, between December 25 and 31, 1965. Filko further developed this "social happening" model independently; in a third series with the title, *ACTION UNIVERSAL. HAPPSOC III. ALTAR OF CONTEMPORANEITY / AKCIA UNIVERZÁL. HAPPSOC III. OLTÁR SÚČASNOSTI* (1966) he appropriated the so-called reality of Czechoslovakia with its life, past, and future in space and time. This was followed by *HAPPSOC IV. TRAVEL IN SPACE / HAPPSOC IV. VESMÍRNE CESTOVANIE* (1967) in the dimensions of the entire universe. [01]

In reviews from the time, Filko's works of the 1960s, with their theatrically compounded elements from everyday life (see for example the environment of the housing inventory *Dwelling 1966 of Contemporaneity – Reality / Obydlie 1966 súčasnosti – skutočnosti* of 1966 [02], exhibited at the Gallery on Charles Square [Galerie na Karlově náměstí] in Prague in 1967, where he staged a series of thirty *Altars of Contemporaneity / Oltáre súčasnosti* from 1963–66), were primarily analyzed in relation to Surrealism and Art Informel.[3] The critic Jiří Padrta also saw a "certain romantic feature" in Filko's staged rituals, in which "there takes place more an absurd ceremony rather than a theatre-life and event."[4] He explained the authentic position of Filko's critique of consumerism, expressed through the elevation of material welfare into ethical and spiritual frameworks, by reminiscences to folklore and liturgy. Tomáš Štraus spoke about the "nationally distinctive editing of the world Pop Art movement."[5] Apart from art-historical references, the period critics also searched for new understandings; the often-quoted Pierre Restany called Filko "an architect of information."[6]

The exhibition *Dwelling 1966 of Contemporaneity – Reality / Obydlie 1966 súčasnosti – skutočnosti* (1967) was widely received in the Czechoslovak press. In this performative environment, Filko presented naked models in the roles of so-called living sculptures. [03] From the viewpoint of Linda Nochlin's "politics of vision,"[7] analyzing the modes of representation of female subjects and bodies, their position within the installation was constructed patriarchally: through the idea of the private world as a quasi *mise-en-scène* of a household that is traditionally a man's property. Non-individualized naked women in gas masks were, in Restany's words, conceived as "objects of aesthetic contemplation."[8] They were reduced to alienated subjects. In the context of the post-war world of the Cold War, the unsettling element of the gas mask appears as a reference to the threat of nuclear or chemical weapons; in a feminist perspective, as a controlling male principle.

The curator Zdeněk Félix moved around wearing a gas mask among the passive and fetishized bodies of the models. His speech explaining the situation was played from a tape recorder.[9] The audience was also supposed to join the hierarchized "living sculptures"[10] (*Waiting objects – actions / Čakacie objekty – akcie*). Their changing into special clothes with slippers (Štraus called these elements "props of

Genealogie eines modernistischen Essentialismus

Mira Keratová

Stano Filko gehört mit Alex Mlynárčik, Július Koller und Peter Bartoš[1] jener Generation der slowakischen Neoavantgarde an, die den Lauf des Lebens anhand ihres Alltagslebens thematisierten. Gemeinsam mit Mlynárčik (und Zita Kostrová) erarbeitete Filko Mitte der 1960er-Jahre das Manifest mit dem dazugehörigen Readymade-Event *HAPPSOC I., BRATISLAVA 2.–8 MAY, 1965 / HAPPSOC I. BRATISLAVA 2.–8. MÁJ 1965.* Dafür verteilten die Künstler*innen Einladungen zur Teilnahme, die unter anderem ein statistisches Verzeichnis der „Objekte" (Männer, Frauen, Hunde usw.), die sich zu jener Zeit in Bratislava befanden, enthielten. So stand das Happening mit einer Aneignung der zeitlich und räumlich aufgenommenen Wirklichkeit der Stadt für die sozialistischen Feierlichkeiten zum Tag der Arbeit und zur Beendigung des Zweiten Weltkriegs (gemäß der sowjetischen Doktrin) im Zusammenhang. Da Mlynárčik mit dem Nouveau Réalisme-Kreis in Paris in Verbindung stand, berichtete Pierre Restany über das Manifest auf internationaler Bühne. In der Folge wurde auch Filkos Kunst historisch zu den globalen konzeptuellen Tendenzen gezählt, die jedoch in verschiedenen Teilen der Welt unter unterschiedlichen Bedingungen entstanden und jeweils spezifische Formen annahmen.[2] Filkos Nachfolgeaktion hieß *HAPPSOC II. 7 DAYS OF CREATION / HAPPSOC II. 7 DNÍ STVORENIA* und fand vom 25. bis 31. Dezember 1965 statt. Der Künstler entwickelte damit das „soziale Happening"-Konzept eigenständig weiter. In der dritten Serie mit dem Titel *ACTION UNIVERSAL. HAPPSOC III. ALTAR OF CONTEMPORANEITY / AKCIA UNIVERZÁL. HAPPSOC III. OLTÁR SÚČASNOSTI* (1966) eignete er sich gleich die ganze sogenannte Realität der Tschechoslowakei mit all ihrem Leben, ihrer Vergangenheit und ihrer Zukunft in Raum und Zeit an. Sodann folgte *HAPPSOC IV. TRAVEL IN SPACE / HAPPSOC IV. VESMÍRNE CESTOVANIE* (1967) in den Dimensionen des gesamten Universums. [01]

Filkos Werke aus den 1960er-Jahren (siehe zum Beispiel das Environment mit Wohnungsinventar *Dwelling 1966 of Contemporaneity – Reality / Obydlie 1966 súčasnosti – skutočnosti* aus 1966 [02], das 1967 in der Galerie am Karlsplatz [Galerie na Karlově náměstí] in Prag ausgestellt wurde, wo er bereits 1963–1966 eine Serie von dreißig *Altars of the Present / Oltáre súčasnosti* in Szene gesetzt hatte) mit ihren theatralisch kombinierten Elementen aus seinem Alltagsleben wurden in den damaligen Rezensionen vorwiegend in Bezug auf den Surrealismus und die informelle Kunst analysiert.[3] Auch der Kritiker Jiří Padrta attestierte dem inszenierten Ritual vor Ort, das seiner Meinung nach „eher einer absurden Zeremonie als einem Theaterereignis gleichkam", einen „gewissen romantischen Zug".[4] Die authentische Pose der Konsumkritik Filkos, die sich in der Überhöhung des materiellen Wohlstands in den ethischen und spirituellen Bereich ausdrückte, erklärte Padrta indes durch Reminiszenzen an die Folklore und die Liturgie. Zum selben Anlass sprach Tomáš Štraus wiederum von einer „national geprägten Variante der weltweiten Pop-Art-Bewegung".[5] Neben solchen kunsthistorischen Bezügen suchten die damaligen Kritiker aber auch nach neuen Deutungen. So nannte der vielzitierte Pierre Restany Filko einen „Architekten der Information".[6]

Die Ausstellung *Dwelling 1966 of Contemporaneity – Reality / Obydlie 1966 súčasnosti – skutočnosti* (1967) fand in der tschechoslowakischen Presse großen Widerhall. Im Rahmen eines performativen Environments präsentierte Filko hier nackte Models als sogenannte lebende Skulpturen. [03] Unter dem Gesichtspunkt von Linda Nochlins „Politik des Blicks",[7] mit der sie die Repräsentationen von Frauen und ihren Körpern analysierte, war deren Position innerhalb der Installation freilich patriarchalisch angelegt, wurde doch die private Welt hier gleichsam als Haushalt inszeniert, den ganz traditionell der Mann besitzt. Die anonymen Nacktmodelle in Gasmasken wurden von Filko, um mit Restany zu sprechen, als „Objekte der ästhetischen Kontemplation" konzipiert.[8] Sie wurden auf entfremdete Subjekte reduziert. Vor dem Hintergrund des Kalten Kriegs erscheint das beunruhigende Element der Gasmaske zwar als Verweis auf die Bedrohung durch nukleare oder chemische Waffen, aus feministischer Perspektive hingegen als Prinzip männlicher Herrschaft.

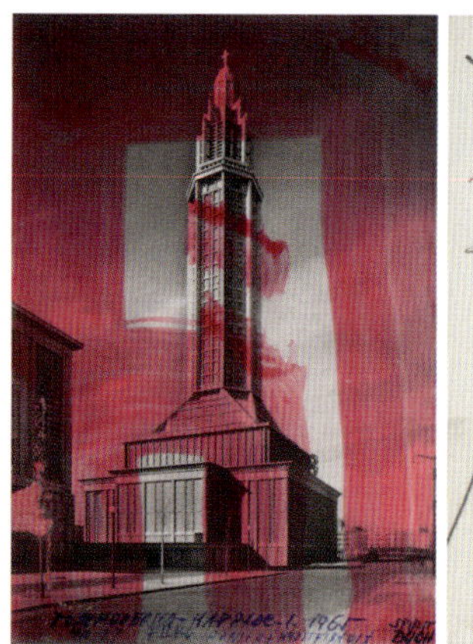 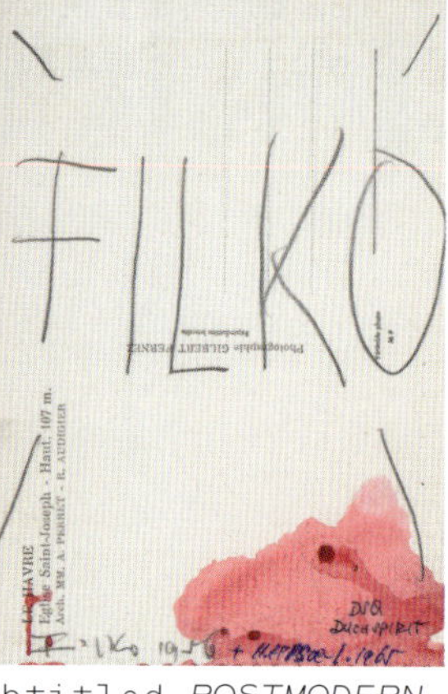

[01A–B] Untitled (subtitled *POSTMODERN HAPPSOC-I. 1965 – DSQ SPIRIT / Postmoderna Happsoc-I. 1965 – DSQ Duch Spirit*), c. 1990s

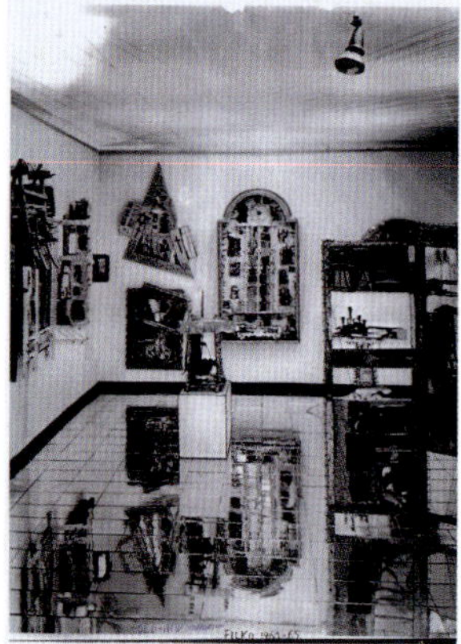

[02] Dwelling 1966 of Contemporaneity – Reality / Obydlie 1966 súčasnosti – skutočnosti, 1967

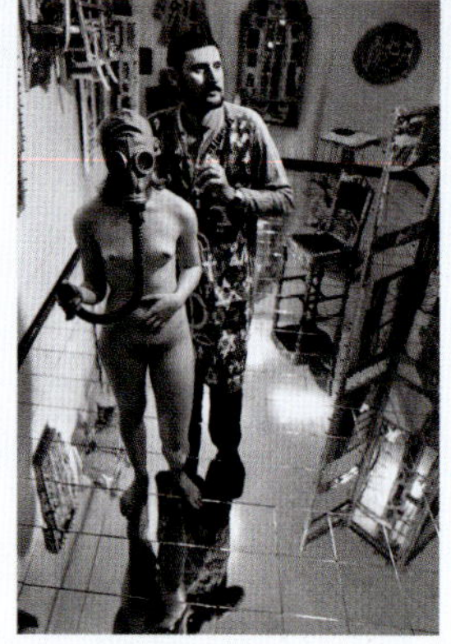

[03] Stano Filko with model at Dwelling 1966 of Contemporaneity – Reality / Obydlie 1966 súčasnosti – skutočnosti, 1967

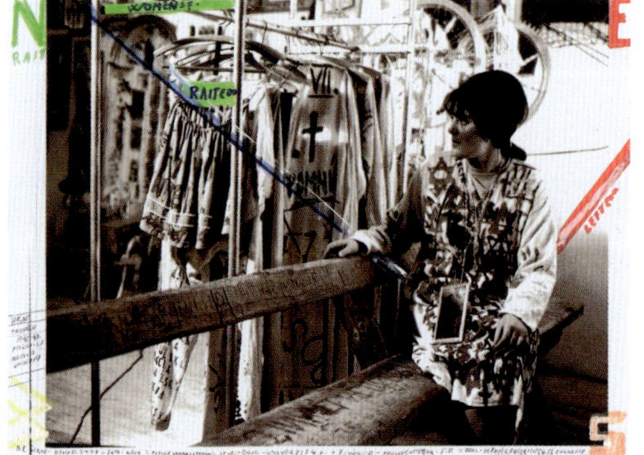

[04] Clothes from the exhibition *Dwelling 1966 of Contemporaneity – Reality / Obydlie 1966 súčasnosti – skutočnosti*, 1967

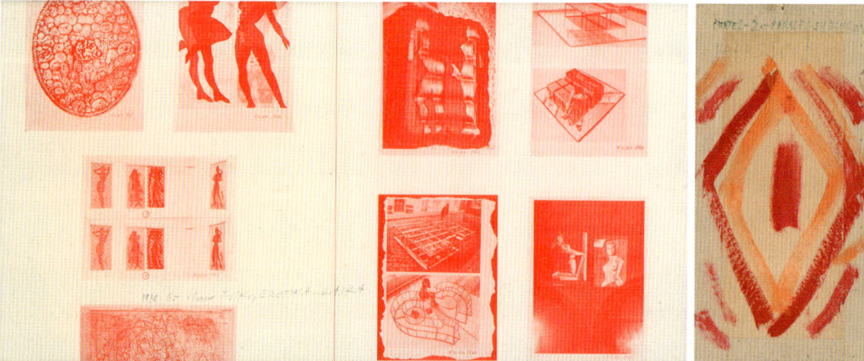

[05A–B] *EROTIC – LOVE / EROTIKA – LÁSKA*, late 1960s

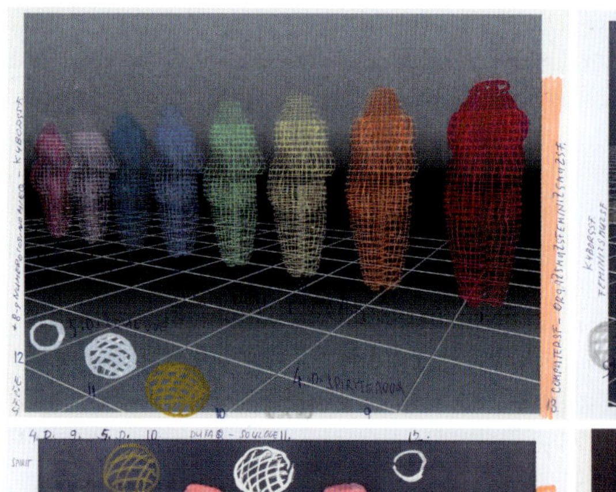

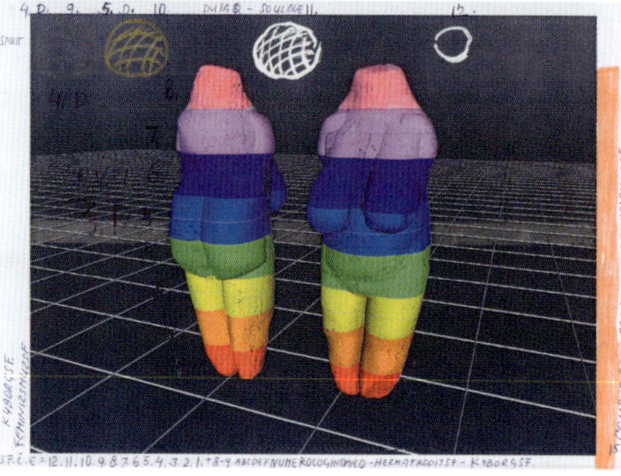

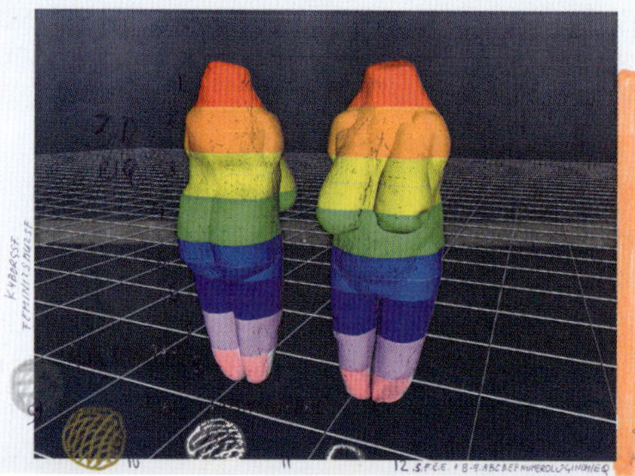

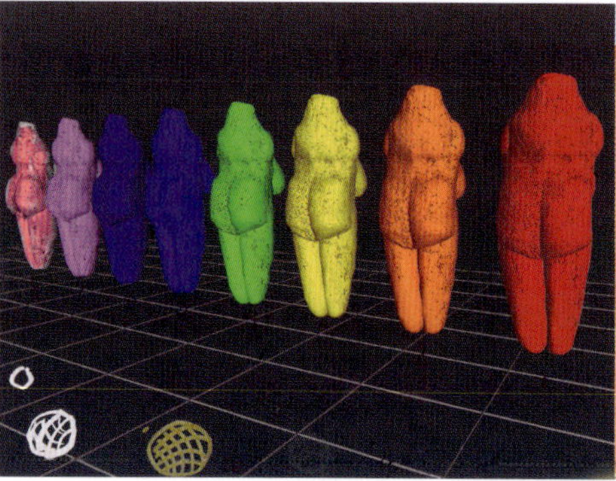

[06–09] Untitled (series subtitled *FEMINISMANSF / FEMINIZMUZSF*), 1990s

Der Kurator Zdeněk Félix mischte sich, ebenfalls eine Gasmaske über seinem Gesicht, zwischen die passiv fetischisierten Models. Seine die Situation erläuternde Eröffnungsrede wurde währenddessen von einem Tonband abgespielt.[9] Ein andermal sollte auch das Publikum sich den hierarchisierten „lebenden Skulpturen"[10] (*Waiting objects – actions / Čakacie objekty – akcie*) anschließen. Die Leute sollten spezielle Gewänder samt Hausschuhe anlegen (Štraus nannte diese Elemente „Requisiten der Intimität")[11], was ihre Körperlichkeit unterstreichen, sie aber auch im inszenierten Privatraum verorten sollte. Die Gewänder waren mit Davidsternen und Christuskreuzen bemalt [04] (auch später entnahm Filko seine Lieblingssymbolik dem Alten und Neuen Testament) und verwiesen damit auf die jüdisch-christliche Zivilisation, zwangsweise aber auch auf deren patriarchale Geschichte der sexuellen Unterdrückung und dem dualistischen Konzept von Kultur und Natur. Das Spiegeln einer privaten „Realität" in einen halböffentlichen Raum sollte durch ein Radio (*Playing Altar Contemporaneity / Hrací oltár súčasnosti*) und durch eine partizipative Installation, in der man selbst Stempel verwenden durfte (*Table for Anonymous Graphics / Stôl pre anonymnú grafiku*), weiter akzentuiert werden.

Die Altare aus der Serie *Altars of Contemporaneity / Oltáre súčasnosti* (1963–1966) aus alten Industrieholzmöbeln, für die Filko in seinem Œuvre mehrmals Verwendung fand, waren auch Teil der Ausstellung *Dwelling 1966 of Contemporaneity – Reality*. Der Künstler zimmerte sie zu teils symmetrischen, teils asymmetrischen Formen und bemalte sie dann mit weißem, silbernem oder goldenem Pigment. Dann gestaltete er sie mit alten Nägeln, leeren Patronenhülsen, Kruzifixen und Drähten zu Reliefs und fügte kleine Spiegel ein. Zusammen mit dem für ihn typischen Spiegelboden, den er hier erstmals verwendete, sollten sie in kinematografisch-illusionärer Weise Körper in Teilperspektiven fragmentieren, und zwar ganz im Sinn des sogenannten skopophilen (oder sogar perversen) Vergnügens, das Laura Mulvey unter den Blickwinkeln von Freud und Lacan analysierte.[12] Dementsprechend hat Filko seine „Altare" auch mit erotischen Fotos beklebt. Auch sie wählte er mit dem sogenannten männlichen Blick aus, der sich laut Mulvey dadurch auszeichnet, dass der Mann der Träger der Subjektivität ist, während das unbedeutende Weibliche zum Objekt degradiert wird.[13] Kritiken von damals deuteten Filkos Sujetwahl indes als Kritik am neuen kulturellen Fetisch. Neben den heteronormativ stereotypen Pin-up-Girls verwendete er nämlich beispielsweise auch das Bild des Film-Sexsymbols Brigitte Bardot und kontrastierte provokante, von Männern choreografierte Frauenposen mit Reproduktionen christlicher Heiliger oder Madonnen. Durch diese streng moralisierende Komponente lud er das Werk mit einer, sagen wir, Pseudospiritualität auf. (So hatten Filko und Mlynárčik schon in *HAPPSOC II.* das Publikum während der Weihnachtszeit in einen Stripteaseclub eingeladen.)

Im Übrigen treffen die meisten der Klischees, die von der feministischen Kritik der 1970er-Jahre aufs Korn genommen wurden, auf das Werk Filkos geradezu lehrbuchhaft zu. Dazu gehört die dichotome Sicht des aktiven Mannes als Vertreter des Fortschritts gegenüber der passiven Frau, die bei Filko in den 1960er-Jahren für Lust und Liebe und in den 1980er-Jahren dann für Fruchtbarkeit und Mutterschaft steht. Der Prager Schau folgte *External Environment – Communication / Externé prostredie – komunikácia* (1967) in der Galerie Cyprián

Majerník in Bratislava, wo der Künstler so genannte „Skulpturen-Architekturen" (oder „Skulpturen-Wolkenkratzer-Aussichtstürme") ausstellte. Das männliche Prinzip dieses Environments wurde im Gegensatz zur *Behausung* nicht mehr als privater, sondern gleichsam als öffentlicher „Fetisch" artikuliert. Im Gegensatz zur „inneren Umwelt" der *Dwelling of Reality – Contemporaneity* Ausstellung schuf Filko hier als Pendant eine äußere Umwelt, die er dann zur Installation *Universal Environment / Univerzálne prostredie* (1966–1967) weiter ausarbeitete. Jedoch hatte er schon zuvor deutliche geschlechtsspezifische Rollenverteilungen erkennen lassen, zum Beispiel in der Assemblage *Grandpa and Grandma Are Listening to the Radio / Dedko – babka počúvajú rádio* (1965), für die er die einen Gegenstände der Frau, die anderen dem Mann zuordnete (so beispielsweise einen Weidenkorb oder einen Topf im Gegensatz zu einem Rad). Auch hier stellte Filko mit seiner penibel dichotom ausgeführten Ikonographie klar, dass Gegensätzliches immer aufeinander bezogen ist.

Die Assemblage-Altar-Objekte gehörten einem Diskurstypus in der sozialistischen Gesellschaft an, der, wie Texte aus jener Zeit belegen, „Problematik der zivilisatorischen Umwelt" genannt wurde. Er hing eng mit den Umständen der sozialistischen Moderne zusammen, die „den Ausdruck eines neuen Verhältnisses von Künstler und Realität" für notwendig erachtete. So war dieser Diskurs vor allem von sozialen Fragen geprägt, in deren Zusammenhang ja auch der Wohnbau massiv vorangetrieben wurde. Dadurch entwickelte sich eine breitere gesellschaftliche Debatte über die angemessene Lebensqualität in einem sich verändernden städtischen Umfeld und somit auch im modernen Haushalt. Die Debatte wurde also nicht primär wie im Westen als Kritik an der Konsumgesellschaft geführt. Sie war nicht durch Überfluss, sondern durch Mangel gekennzeichnet.[14]

Von dem *Universal Environment*, das 1968 auf der bedeutenden Ausstellung *Cinematism, Spectacle, Environment* im Maison de la Culture in Grenoble, vorher jedoch schon 1967 auf der Ausstellung *Situácie / Situations* im Verband der slowakischen bildenden Künstler (Spolok slovenských výtvarných umelcov) in Bratislava gezeigt wurde, existierten mehrere Ausführungen. Es war Filkos erstes architektonisch konzipiertes multimediales Environment,[15] die vorigen waren durch die schlichte Kombination mehrerer Elemente entstanden. Als externalisiertes Environment sollte es *Dwelling 1966 of Contemporaneity – Reality* austarieren, und so kommentierte Filko,[16] dass er hier Erotik und Technologie gegenüberstelle. Das nachfolgende Environment *Poetry about Space and Cosmos / Poézia o priestore a kozme* (1967–1968), ausgestellt auf der Expo in Osaka 1970) war hingegen bereits als schieres Fest des (internationalen) Raums konzipiert, in dem durch Pop-Anklänge gleichsam nach Tatlin-Manier Technik und Kunst verschmolzen wurden (in Filkos Worten: „die Folklore der industriellen Zivilisation"[17]). In seiner Interpretation der historischen Avantgarden als neuer künstlerischer Praxis, die sich als Reaktion auf die moderne Technik von der Tradition absetzte, brachte Boris Groys diese Metapher auf den Punkt: Kunst = Maschine.[18] Auch im slowakischen oder, genauer gesagt, tschechoslowakischen Kontext wurde das Vermächtnis der sowjetischen Avantgarden in der zweiten Hälfte der 1960er-Jahre durch die Neuauflage wichtiger Primärdokumente, etwa vom slowakischen Theoretiker Oskar Čepan oder dem tschechischen Kritiker Jiří Padrta, erneut aktuell.[19]

intimacy"[11]), was supposed to enhance their embodiment, as was their situating themselves in a staged private area. The robes were painted with Stars of David and Crosses of Christ [04] (see also Filko's later favorite symbolism of the Old and New Testament) as a reference to Judeo-Christian civilization and, necessarily, also its patriarchal history of sexual repression within the dualist concept of culture and nature. The reflection of a private "reality" shared in a semi-public space was to be heightened by a radio playing (*Playing Altar of Contemporaneity / Hrací oltár súčasnosti*), or by the participatory installation for stamping (*Table for Anonymous Graphics / Stôl pre anonymnú grafiku*).

The altars form the series *Altars of Contemporaneity / Oltáre súčasnosti* (1963–66) in the recycled industrially manufactured wood furniture which Filko used throughout his work, were part of the *Dwelling 1966 of Contemporaneity – Reality* show. They were compounded into symmetrical and asymmetrical formats painted in white, silver, and golden pigments. They were assembled into reliefs from beaten nails, empty cartridge cases, crucifixes, and wires. Filko inserted small mirrors into them. Together with the typical mirror floor, which he used here for the first time, and in a cinematographic-illusional way, they were supposed to fragment bodies and multiply perspectives, as well as provide so-called scopophilic (even reverse) pleasure, analyzed by Laura Mulvey from Freudian-Lacanian positions.[12] Filko further collaged the surfaces of the altars with erotic reproductions. These were selected from the position of a so-called male gaze, in which, according to Mulvey,[13] the masculine is the bearer of subjectivity, while the feminine, not being a maker of meaning, is objectified. Period reviews interpreted the setting of the work as a critique of the new cultural fetish. In addition to the heteronormatively stereotyped pin-up girls, Filko also used, for example, the image of the film sex symbol Brigitte Bardot. Male-choreographed laszivious female poses in the pictures were contrasted with reproductions of Christian saints or Madonnas. With such a rigid moralizing component, he built up the tension of the image of, let's say, false spirituality. (Similarly, earlier in *HAPPSOC II.*, Filko and Mlynárčik had invited the audience to a visit to a strip club during the Christian Christmas season.)

Most of the stereotypes that were articulated by feminist criticism from the 1970s apply in textbook fashion to Filko's work. These include a bipolar view of the active man as the representative of progress, and the passive woman, who in the case of Filko represented pleasure and love in the 1960s and fertility and motherhood in the 1980s. The Prague show was followed by the exhibition *External Environment – Communication / Externé prostredie – komunikácia* (1967) at the Bratislava Cyprián Majerník Gallery, where Filko presented so-called "sculptures-architectures" (also "sculptures-skyscrapers-observation towers"). The masculine principle of this environment was semantically articulated, as opposed to the *Dwelling 1966 of Contemporaneity – Reality* show, no longer as a private, but, so to speak, as a public "fetish." In contrast to this "internal" environment, Filko thus created its pendant, the external environment, which he further elaborated in the installation *Universal Environment / Univerzálne prostredie* (1966–67). But he had already constructed clear gender-differentiated roles before; e.g. as part of the assemblage *Grandpa – Grandma Are Listening to the*

Radio / Dedko – babka počúvajú rádio (1965), in which he attributed some found objects to the woman, others to the man (see wicker basket or pot versus wheel). Here too Filko was dealing with the relationality of contradictory positions through binary chiseled iconography.

Assemblage-altar objects followed a type of discourse in socialist society that was, as period texts affirm, formulated as "problematics of the civilizational environment." This was embedded in the conditions of socialist modernism, which considered "the expression of a new relationship of the artist to reality" as a necessity. It was framed mainly by addressing social issues (in the course of which massive housing constructions were carried out). In relation to this a wider social debate on the requirements for the quality of life in a changing urban environment, and thus in a modern household, was also developed. This debate was not primarily conducted from the position of a critique of consumer society as in the West, meaning not through the surplus, but rather the lack.[14]

Universal Environment, shown at the influential exhibition *Cinematism, Spectacle, Environment* at the House of Culture (Maison de la Culture) in Grenoble, 1968 (originally at the *Situations / Situácie* exhibit held in the Association of Slovak Visual Artists [Spolok slovenských výtvarných umelcov] in Bratislava, in 1967), existed in a number of variations. It was Filko's first architecturally conceived multimedia environment.[15] Previous ones were constructed by the installation of several elements. As an externalized environment that was meant to compensate for the *Dwelling 1966 of Contemporaneity – Reality* show, Filko commented on it by saying that here he put erotica and technology into juxtaposition.[16] His next environment, *Poetry about Space and Cosmos / Poézia o priestore a kozme* (1967–68, exhibited at the Expo in Osaka, 1970), was already conceived only as a celebration of the (international) space to which, through pop adaptions, so to speak, in a Tatlin-esque manner, technology was incorporated into art (in Filko's words, as "the folklore of industrial civilization").[17] In his interpretation of the historical avant-gardes as a new type of artistic practice, which diverged from tradition in response to contemporary technologies, Boris Groys formulated the realization of the metaphor, Art = Machine.[18] Also in the Slovak or let's say Czechoslovak context, the legacy of the Soviet avant-gardes in the second half of the 1960s was updated anew by influential editions of primary documents, for example by the Slovak theorist Oskar Čepan or the Czech critic Jiří Padrta.[19]

Also, the program of the East-European neo-avant-garde, although politically inconsistent and methodologically inaccurate, was declared to be an attempt at objectivism as a counter-example to the subjectivity of private aesthetic taste. Whether directly in his statements or in text records, in the course of his work Filko too criticized the bourgeois habitus which, however, he viewed mainly as a lifestyle, but did not see it through a structural critique of a system, in which lifestyle would be understood perhaps in the sense of Bourdieu way as a class expression. Edit András stated that "while conceptualism played an active role in the criticism of modernism in Western countries, its local Eastern variants were firmly anchored in it."[20] So it was only those who approached the period's technocratic enthusiasm either skeptically or even dismissively who polemicized to a

Auch das Programm der osteuropäischen Neo-Avantgarde deklarierte sich, wenngleich politisch unschlüssig und methodisch ungenau, als Versuch eines Objektivismus gegen die Subjektivität des privaten ästhetischen Geschmacks. Ob nun in seinen belegten Äußerungen oder in seinen Textprotokollen, auch Filko kritisierte mit seinem Werk den bürgerlichen Habitus, den er jedoch in erster Linie als Lebensstil verstand. Seine Kritik war also keine strukturelle Systemkritik, in der der Lebensstil im Sinne von, sagen wir, Bourdieu als Ausdruck einer Klasse verstanden wird. So stellte Edit András fest, dass „der Konzeptualismus in den westlichen Ländern zwar eine aktive Rolle in der Kritik der Moderne spielte, seine lokalen östlichen Varianten aber fest in derselben verankert waren".[20] Es blieben also nur diejenigen, die dem technokratischen Enthusiasmus der Zeit skeptisch oder gar ablehnend gegenüberstanden und daher gewissermaßen gegen das modernistische Ethos polemisierten. Zu ihnen gehörte Peter Bartoš, der abseits des Mainstreams sein Programm einer sogenannten ökologischen Kultur im städtischen Lebensraum formulierte. Július Koller zum Beispiel war, wie aus seinem Nachlass hervorgeht, ein langjähriger Kritiker Filkos. Laut Aurel Hrabušický erkannte er in dessen Versuchen, die Kunst zeitlos zu machen,[21] einen „Mangel an Realitätssinn" sowie eine „Flucht vor den Verpflichtungen gegenüber der Welt".[22]

In seinen interaktiven Environments im menschlichen Maß (ca. 5×5 Meter bei 3 Metern Höhe[23]) war das Publikum, wie Filko in vielen Äußerungen aus dieser Zeit betonte, Teil des Werks. Die Kunst sollte ein Abbild der Realität sein, während das Publikum im Zuge der Aneignung dieser Realität in ein *tableau vivant* integriert wurde (vgl. Filkos Ausdruck „Spiegelrealität"). Typische Elemente dieser Environments waren neben dem Spiegelboden (den er bei *Dwelling 1966 of Contemporaneity – Reality* zum ersten Mal verwendet hatte) auch audiovisuelle Elemente wie ein laufendes Radio, ein Tonband oder eine Diashow. Filko dockte seine Environments also auch an die Lichtkunst und kinetische Kunst der Zeit an. Im Zusammenhang sowohl mit McLuhans Medientheorien über die Erweiterung menschlicher Fähigkeiten und psychischer oder sozialer Komplexität durch das Medium, als auch mit dem genannten Postulat von Groys, bezeichnete Georg Schöllhammer sie auch als „visuelle Metaphern für den Zustand des Subjekts in der Moderne". Schöllhammer interpretierte Filkos Environments unter dem Aspekt des Spektakels als Werke, die im Kontext „der Fragmentierung der Subjektivität durch die bürokratischen und organisatorischen Apparate der realsozialistischen Gesellschaften eine kritische Analyse" möglich machten. In ihrer Präsenz gestatten sie „sozusagen die Übertragung dieser Kritik vom Realen ins Symbolische".[24]

Zusätzlich zu den für Filko charakteristischen Bodenspiegeln umfassten diese Environments aber auch weiche Wände aus Kunstgewebe, die performativ um den Raum angeordnet waren. Filko experimentierte also mit taktilen Qualitäten schon vor seinen monumentalen weichen Architekturen *Cosmos / Kozmos* (1967–1969) und *Breathing – The Celebration of Air / Dýchanie – Oslava vzduchu* (1970). In *Universal Environment* baute der Künstler neben Raketen und Himmelskörpern auch Silhouetten weiblicher Akte ein, die er mit einer elektrischen Spritzpistole, Acetonfarben und einer Schablone auf durchscheinende Vorhänge aufbrachte. Die weiblichen Figuren sind hier nicht nur durch ihre Stilisierung zu erotischen Fetischen aufgeladen, sondern auch durch das

gesamte Konzept der performativen Installation. Die außen gehängten Transparentstoffbahnen evozieren gleichsam eine Projektionsfläche voyeuristischer Phantasien. So wird die Installation mit all ihren Wunsch- und Traumbildern zu einem lasziven Schattenspiel. Die Anonymisierung der Akte, die auch eine symbolische Kastration der Frau implizieren, reizte also zur visuellen Lust, wie Laura Mulvey es nannte.[25]

In seinem Künstlerbuch *Stano FILKO II. 1965/69* deutete Filko dieses Ensemble selbst im Rahmen der Symbolik von Mensch und Technik. Neben der großen Erzählung von der Eroberung des Kosmos stellte er dazu eine Diashow mit spießigen Bildern aus der Massenkultur zusammen, die die „Sehnsüchte der Menschheit" kontrollierten. Filko ergänzte diese um Bilder von rasanten Autos und idolisierten Pin-ups, die hier als sogenannte Signifikanten des männlichen Anderen firmieren. Diese Bilder einer normativen Sexualität waren für ihn „kalte Erotika des Weltraumzeitalters". Die folgende Installation *Poetry about Space and the Cosmos* (1967–1968, auf der Expo 1970 in Osaka ausgestellt) knüpfte, was die Materialien betrifft, an das *Universal Environment* an. Filko widmete sie bereits ausschließlich den Themen der Zeit und der menschlichen Expansion in den Weltraum (siehe die schematisierten Mond- und Raketenmotive). Im Rahmen seiner Methode, immer Gegenstücke zu inszenieren, verwendete Filko parallel ähnliche Formate und Materialien sowohl im kosmologischen als auch im erotischen Teil seiner Installationen dieser Zeit. [05A] Das Gleiche gilt für die Grafikserien und Serigrafie- und Monotypie-Multiples von Akten und Raketen, die er auf Landkarten druckte (zum Beispiel *Map of the World (Women) / Mapa sveta (Ženy)*, 1966–1967; *Map of the World (Rockets) / Mapa sveta (Rakety)*, 1967). Auch hier akzentuierte er seine Einstellung durch generative Ästhetik, Serialität, Multiples und Wiederverwendung. Ab den 1990er-Jahren erweiterte er diese Methoden durchaus schlüssig auf digitale Experimente. Außerdem schuf er mit der Textilarbeit *Blinds / Rolety* (1966) Acrylsprühbilder schematisierter lebensgroßer weiblicher Silhouetten. Auch zum Zwecke der fotografischen Dokumentation installierte er diese dann als konzeptuelles Environment eines „erotischen Büros" im tatsächlichen Büro des einflussreichen tschechischen Kritikers Jindřich Chalupecký,[26] wobei er die Fotos dann vermutlich in der Prager Galerie Václav Špála zeigte. In dieser Dokumentation, die 1970 in Filkos Künstlerbuch gedruckt wurde, wirkt die Kunst wie ein spielerischer Eingriff in ein rationalisiertes, funktionalistisches Umfeld.

Ebenso druckte der Künstler die Silhouetten von Frauenakten auf seine sogenannten pneumatischen Skulpturen, die ruhende Venusfiguren darstellen sollten.[27] Obwohl sich seine Ikonografie allmählich in Richtung ödipaler Mutteridole weiterentwickelte, diente die Urversion auch als Vorbild des späteren Typus der sogenannten „Scheherazade". Einige der pneumatischen Skulpturen fungierten auch als Matratzen, Aufblasskulpturen oder Kissen (1966–1967). Hier arbeitete Filko mit abstrahierten Geschlechtersymbolen. Beispiele dafür sind Geräte zur Erholung wie aufblasbare Bälle (in Filkos Worten „Nüsse"), die er zu einer phallischen Komposition arrangierte, oder ein Multiple weiblicher Brüste aus blau und rot transparentem Plexiglas aus derselben Zeit, dem letzten Drittel der 1960er-Jahre. Wenn auch nicht mehr explizit, blieb die Geschlechtlichkeit 1968 auch in dem Environment *Pneumatic Wheels / Pneumatické kolesá* noch angedeutet. Seine früheren

  Genealogie eines modernistischen Essentialismus

certain extent against the modernistic ethos. Among them was Peter Bartoš, who worked out his program of the "ecological culture" of the urban living environment outside the mainstream. On the basis of sources from his estate, Július Koller, for example, was a long-term Filko critic. According to Aurel Hrabušický, he saw in his attempts at what Filko called the timelessness[21] of art a "lack of a sense of reality" and an "escape from commitments towards the world."[22]

In interactive environments on a human scale (c. 5 × 5 meters at a height of 3 meters)[23], as Filko emphasized in many statements from that time, the spectator was a part of the work, which was supposed to be a reflection of reality, while in the process of appropriating this reality, the viewer became at the same time part of the living picture (see Filko's term "mirror reality"). The typical elements of these environments were, in addition to the structure of the mirror floor (which he used for the first time as part of *Dwelling 1966 of Contemporaneity – Reality*), also other dynamic audio-visual features like a radio playing, tape sound, and a slide-show. These environments were therefore seen within the context of light-kinetic art. In connection with McLuhan's media theories about the medium expanding human capacities and psychic or social complexities, and in connection with Groys's postulates, Georg Schöllhammer called them "visual metaphors of the status of the subject in modernity," interpreting them from the position of a spectacle, as environments that in the context of "the fragmentation of subjectivity by the bureaucratic and organizational apparatuses of real socialist societies, form a critical analysis," and through embodiment, enable "the transfer of this criticism, so to speak, from the real to the symbolic."[24]

In addition to the typical mirror structures on the floor, these environments also included soft walls made of faux-mesh, performatively layered in rows around the perimeter. Filko was experimenting with their sensual qualities even before his monumental soft architectures, *Cosmos / Kozmos* (1967–69) and *Breathing – The Celebration of Air / Dýchanie – Oslava vzduchu* (1970). In *Universal Environment*, along with rockets and space bodies, mechanically rendered Pop Art images of female nudes, sprayed with acetone paints with an electric pistol according to a template, were also placed on transparent curtains. The female characters were erotically fetishized not only through their stylization, but also by the whole concept of the performative installation in general. The enclosing anchored transparent fabric evoked a quasi-projection screen with voyeuristic qualities. The installation was composed of images of the desired or dreamt-of scenes of a lascivious shadow-play. Their anonymized notions, conditioned by the symbolic castration of the woman, aimed for visual delight, as Laura Mulvey referred to it.[25]

According to his artist's book *Stano FILKO II. 1965/69*, Filko saw the symbolism of humanity and technology in this complementarity. In addition to the grand narrative of the conquest of the cosmos, a slideshow was composed of the petty aesthetics of mass culture that governs the "desires of mankind." Filko outlined this with images of fast cars and idolized pin-up girls as the so-called signifiers of the male other. The images of generalized sexuality were supposed to represent the "cold erotica of the space age." In terms of material, the installation *Poetry about Space and the Cosmos* (1967–68, exhibited at the Expo in Osaka in 1970) is linked to *Universal Environment*. It was already devoted exclusively to the theme of the time, the expansion into space (see the schematized motif of the moon and rockets). As part of his strategy of creating counterparts, Filko used in parallel similar formats and materials in the cosmological and erotic part of his work from this period. [05A] The same was the case in the graphic series and multiples of serigraphs or monotypes of nudes and rockets which he printed on found maps (e.g. *Map of the World (Women) / Mapa sveta (Ženy)*, 1966–67; *Map of the World (Rockets) / Mapa sveta (Rakety)*, 1967). He continuously supported his positions through the generative aesthetics of his works and the seriality of their multiples or recycles, which, from the 1990s, he expanded through digital experiments. With acrylic over a template, he sprayed schematized life-size female silhouettes onto the fabric *Blinds / Rolety* (1966). In order to photo-document this series, and at the same time to show the blinds in their intended use, he installed them as an environment of an "erotic office" in the real office of an influential Czech critic, Jindřich Chalupecký,[26] presumably in the Prague Václav Špála Gallery. In the photo-documentation published in his artist's book (1970), this appears as a playboyish intervention in a rationalized, functionalist setting.

Filko similarly printed the silhouettes of female figures on his so-called pneumatic sculptures, which were supposed to represent resting Venuses.[27] Although his iconography gradually developed toward maternal idols, its initial version also led to the later type of the "Scheherazade." Some of the pneumatic sculptures simultaneously served as mattresses, inflatables, or cushions (1966–67). Within them, he worked with abstracted gender signs. Examples include tools for relaxation activities like inflated balls (or "nuts" in Filko's words), arranged into a phallic composition, or a multiple of the female breast made of blue and red transparent plexiglass from the same period, the last third of the 1960s. Although already absent, gender was still implied in the environment *Pneumatic Wheels / Pneumatické kolesá* (1968). His previous participatory environments *The Room of Love / Izba lásky* and *Heart of Love / Srdce lásky* (1966) in turn present a sexist representation of a love relationship. Their abbreviated expression through formal and content simplifications of primary sexual signs was also applied by Filko in the synthesizing period of the 1980s and 1990s. At that time, he mainly used a rhombic pictogram rendered in paint to denote female genitalia. [05B] Within the motif of paleolithic Venuses from that time, he also used their iconic signs of fertility (e.g. accentuated hips and breasts), through which he reduced the female figures to their sex, as Simone de Beauvoir describes in her book *The Second Sex* (1949), the translation of which was published in Czechoslovakia in 1967.[28] [06-09]

As he did from transhumanist aspirations in the 1990s, in the 1960s Filko drew inspiration from the progressive technocratic perspective of industrial civilization. This also influenced modernist architecture in Slovakia and its utopian heights from this period, when it was equally defining itself against the assumptions of Leninist materialism. His ironic inflatable environments such as *Cosmos* (exhibited at the *6th Youth Biennale* in Paris in 1969) or *Breathing – The Celebration of Air* (also referred to under its original name, *Wind in a 6 Meter Compression Sphere / Vietor v 6 m pretlakovej guli*,

partizipatorischen Environments *Room of Love / Izba lásky* und *Heart of Love / Srdce lásky* (1966) wiederum waren sexistische Darstellungen einer Liebesbeziehung. Die formale und inhaltliche Verkürzung der Sexualität auf primärsexuelle Merkmale setzte Filko auch in seiner synthetisierenden Periode in den 1980er- und 1990er-Jahren fort. Nunmehr stellte er weibliche Genitalien vor allem durch ein mit Farbe aufgetragenes Rauten-Piktogramm dar. [05B] Da damals paläolithische Venusfiguren entdeckt wurden, übernahm er nun auch deren sexuelle Merkmale als ikonenhafte Darstellungen der Fruchtbarkeit (beispielsweise betonte Hüften und Busen). Auch hier reduzierte Filko Frauen wieder auf ihr Geschlecht, wie es Simone de Beauvoir in ihrem Buch „Das andere Geschlecht" 1949 beschreibt, dessen Übersetzung 1967 in der Tschechoslowakei erschien.[28] [06–09]

Wie der spätere Transhumanismus der 1990er-Jahre ließ sich Filko schon in den 1960er-Jahren vom technokratischen Fortschritt der industriellen Zivilisation inspirieren. Auch die modernistische Architektur in der Slowakei erreichte damals utopisch lichte Höhen, stellte sie sich doch ebenfalls gegen die Prämissen des leninistischen Materialismus. Filkos ironische aufblasbare Environments vom Ende der 1960er-Jahre wie *Cosmos* (ausgestellt auf der 6. Jugendbiennale in Paris 1969) oder *Breathing – The Celebration of Air* (auch unter seinem ursprünglichen Namen *Wind in a 6 Meter Compression Sphere / Vietor v 6 m pretlakovej guli*, ausgestellt auf der Veranstaltung *Polymusic space / Polymúzický priestor* in Piešťany, 1970)[29] finden ihr Gegenstück wiederum in der sogenannten weichen Architektur, die der Künstler experimentell im Kontext der Hippie-Gegenkultur realisierte und die politisch eher in der anarchistischen als in der modernistischen Tradition steht (beispielsweise mobile aufblasbare Objekte, Kapseln und Zellen, oder auch die Auflösung von Städten in eine offene nomadische Bauweise, die sich auf die Umwelt und das Gemeinwohl bezogen). Diese Architektur, die sich unter anderem durch ihre Weichheit auszeichnet, wurde daher nicht nur im Hinblick auf die materielle Formgebung analysiert, sondern hinsichtlich ihrer Flexibilität und Sensibilität bzw. ihrer sinnlichen Reaktionsmöglichkeiten auf Berührung und Druck. Immerhin besaßen Filkos interaktive Environments eine weiche Oberfläche, die nicht als Wand, sondern vielmehr durch die Sinneseindrücke des Publikums definiert wurde.

Zu Filkos politisch engagierteren Werken gehört ein heute nicht mehr existentes Environment, nämlich die *Cathedral of Humanism / Katedrála humanizmu* (1968), deren Architektur er wahrscheinlich in der ersten Hälfte der 1990er-Jahre zu einem neuen Environment, dem *CosmosSpaceUniverse / Kozmovesmírunivers*, umbaute. Präsentiert wurde es auf der bedeutenden internationalen Ausstellung *Danuvius* in Bratislava, die als für lange Zeit letzte Schau zeitgenössischer experimenteller Kunst unmittelbar nach dem Einmarsch der Armeen der Sowjetunion und des Warschauer Paktes in die Tschechoslowakei im Jahr 1968 großes öffentliches Interesse erregte. Zu der Installation gehörte auch eine Diashow mit Presseporträts – unter anderen von Politikern, darunter des Reformsozialisten Alexander Dubček –, die Filko internationalen Medien entnommen hatte. [10–14] Die Aufnahmen zeigten den damals bekanntesten Politiker (in seiner Rolle im Rahmen eines nationalen Traumas mittlerweile mit dem heutigen ukrainischen Präsidenten Zelensky vergleichbar) bei offiziellen Besuchen als sogenannter Repräsentant eines „Sozialismus mit menschlichem Antlitz" (siehe Prager Frühling 1968), aber auch informell in der Freizeit, zum Beispiel in einem Schwimmbad.

Im letzten Drittel der 1970er-Jahre, während des Konsolidierungsprozesses, der in der Tschechoslowakei „Normalisierung" genannt wurde, übermalte Filko diese Fotoporträts für seine Serie *Transcendency / Transcendencia* im Zusammenhang mit der Thematik des weißen Raumes. Da wir heute für die damaligen Tendenzen der indirekten Politisierung ästhetischer Fragen sensibilisiert sind, könnte man sagen, dass Filko damit (wie auch mit den übermalten Fotografien aus seinem persönlichen Archiv) so etwas wie die ohnmächtige Macht seiner Epoche eingefangen hat, in der das Regime zwar bereits ethisch geschwächt war, de facto aber weiter bestand. In ganz Europa werden die 1970er-Jahre mit einem konservativen Wertewandel in Verbindung gebracht, einem kulturellen Konservatismus, der sich indes nicht nur in der offiziellen Kultur, sondern als Dissens manifestierte. Die Liberalisierung führte zu einer Formalisierung reformistischer Parolen wie auch zur zunehmenden Bürokratisierung, die mit einer verstärkten Kontrolle der staatlichen Kulturpolitik durch die Parteien einherging.

Mit Ausnahme der Umbruchszeiten hat Filko also keine klare Haltung zum politischen Leben eingenommen. Sein Universalismus wurzelte fest in der bipolaren Welt der Moderne, ob es nun um körperliche Lust versus geistige Pein oder um „the West and the Rest" ging, also um die geopolitische Rivalität im Kalten Krieg. In der Spätphase seines Œuvres, das der Systematisierung galt, nahm er sogar eine noch essentialistischere Haltung ein. Filko deutete nun die Entwicklung der Zivilisation und das evolutionäre Modell der Welt unter einer begrifflich singulären transhistorischen Perspektive, in die er auch einzelne kreationistische Elemente einbezog.

FILKO WHITE SPACE 1970er-Jahre

In einem „Brief an die Freunde" (List priateľom, 1970)[30] beschrieb Filko seine Kunst als „Erschaffung dreier Wege". Er meinte sinngemäß, dass wir nunmehr, nachdem wir die Grenze zwischen der objektiven und der nicht-objektiven Welt überschritten hätten, bei etwas anlangten, das man nur mehr erahnen könne. Dies zeige, sei er überzeugt, dass unser Weg der richtige sei, und er nennt ihn Physik und Metaphysik bzw. Bewusstsein und Unterbewusstsein. Die von ihm formulierte Triade sollte die Essenz des Lebens auch mit religiösen Heilsvorstellungen in Zusammenhang bringen, die er als „Extrakt" seines „Farbsystems" betrachtete. Filko übernahm also eine religiöse Dreieinigkeitslehre, im Besonderen die biblische Trinität von „KÖRPER – GEIST – SEELE". So ordnete er seine Werke, wenn sie einen anthropozentrischen Aspekt hatten, der Farbe Rot („BIOLOGIE"), wenn sie einen kosmischen Aspekt hatten, der Farbe Blau („KOSMOLOGIE"), und, wenn sie die Grenzen des Bewusstseins überschritten, der Farbe Weiß („ONTOLOGIE") zu. Diese Farbtriade hatte er bereits in einigen Werken aus dem letzten Drittel der 1960er-Jahre verwendet.[31] Während sich Filko in den 1960er-Jahren mit seiner Kunst an den Zeitgeist anlehnte, so verortete er sie ab den 1970er-Jahren in einem autonomen Feld entgegen dem Zeitgeist.

Das Konzept von *White Space in White Space / Biely priestor v bielom priestore* (1973–1982) wurde gemeinsam mit Miloš Laky (1948–1975) und Ján Zavarský (1948–2022) realisiert.

exhibited at the *Polymusic space / Polymúzický priestor* event in Piešťany, 1970) from the end of the 1960s,[29] have an analogy in the so-called soft architecture which, on an experimental level, was realized in the cultural context of hippy counterculture, and politically more in an anarchist than a modernistic tradition (e.g. mobile inflated objects, capsules and cells or the urbanist resolution of open structures of nomadic cities, all of which concentrated on environmental relations and the forming of communities). The material qualities of this architecture, expressed by softness, were therefore explored not only for their material potential, but also due to the flexibility of the given system and its sensitivity or sensory response capabilities in response to touch and tension. The architecture of such interactive environments was a soft surface that is not defined by solid walls, but by the sensual experience of the viewer.

A no-longer existant environment, *Cathedral of Humanism / Katedrála humanizmu* (1968), is among Filko's more politically committed works. He probably recycled the architecture of this work in the first half of the 1990s to create a new environment, *CosmosSpaceUniverse / Kozmovesmírunivers.* He presented it at the important international exhibition *Danuvius* in Bratislava, which met with great public interest as the last exhibition of contemporary experimental art for a long time, just after the intervention of armies from the Soviet Union and the Warsaw Pact into Czechoslovakia in 1968. Included in the installation was a slideshow with journalistic portraits of, among others, politicians, including the representative of reform socialism, Alexander Dubček, which Filko had taken from the world media of the time. [10–14] The shots showed the politician being followed by the media (in his role within a national trauma comparable to today's Ukrainian President Zelensky) during official visits within the so-called post-January political representation (see the Prague Spring 1968 period), and even in informal leisure-time situations, for example at a swimming pool.

In the last third of the 1970s, during the consolidation process of so-called Czechoslovak "normalization," Filko repainted these slides in the physical form of analog photographs related to the *Transcendency / Transcendencia* series, in the context of solving the so-called *White Space* issue. From the contemporary view, sensitized to the period's tendencies of the implicit politicization of aesthetic issues, we can say that Filko here captured (as in the case of the repainted photographs from his personal archive) a kind of impotent potentiality of his era, in which, although the regime was ethically weakened it continued on in the form of a de facto regime. All over Europe, the 1970s were generally associated with a conservative overturning of values, a cultural conservatism which manifested itself both in official culture and in dissent. Liberalization processes resulted in the formalization of reformist slogans and increasing bureaucratization, tied in with increased party control over the state's culture policy.

Apart from his statements during periods of upheaval, Filko did not adopt a more articulated attitude to political life. His universalism was anchored in the modernist bipolar world, whether bodily indulgence versus spiritual torment, or the "West and the rest," which was set in the geopolitical rivalry of the Cold War. In his late period of the systematization of his work, Filko took an even more essentialist stance

wherein he interpreted the development of civilization and the evolutionary model of the world in a singularly conceived, transhistorical perspective, in which he also included specific creationist moments.

FILKO WHITE SPACE 1970s

In his "Letter to Friends" (List priateľom, 1970),[30] Filko described his work as the "creation of three roads." He said that after having crossed the border of the objective and the non-objective world, we get to what is only guessed at; this should show the path that, as he was convinced, is the right one, and he named it as physics and metaphysics, as consciousness and subconsciousness. The triad that he formulated was intended to effect the essence of life also in connection with the religious ideas of salvation, and he considered it to be the "extract" of his "Color System," into which he adapted religious trinitarianism, especially the biblical idea of the trinity of "BODY – SPIRIT – SOUL." He thus classified his work, in the case of its anthropocentric dimensions, to the color red ("BIOLOGY"), if it concerned the cosmic scale, into blue ("COSMOLOGY") and if it crossed into spiritual limits, then into white ("ONTOLOGY"). He had used this color triad already in several of his works from the last third of the 1960s.[31] While in the 1960s, Filko's production was linked to the period culture, in the 1970s by contrast it defined itself in an autonomous field against it.

The concept of *White Space in White Space / Biely priestor v bielom priestore* (1973–82) was carried out as a part of a collective author's subject together with Miloš Laky (1948–1975) and Ján Zavarský (1948–2022). This was preceded by their collaboration within projects connecting art with science like the albums from 1973 *Time I. / Čas I.* and *Time II. / Čas II.* (together with Július Koller and Rudolf Sikora), or *Cosmic Messages / Vesmírne posolstvá* (together with Peter Bartoš, Michal Kern and the critic Tomáš Štraus), which were inspired by the development of the *Voyager* space probes program and the global discussion on intergalactic communications and repetitive structures of the so-called active messaging. This type of thinking, inspired by, let's say, the scientific conception of objectivity, built on quantitative analysis, the systematization and generalization of facts about the world abstracted from an individual's perspective, was also taken up by *White Space in White Space.*

The concept of the manifesto *White Immaterial Space in a Pure White Infinite Space / Biely nehmotný priestor v čistom bielom nekonečnom priestore* (1973) was doubtlessly influenced mainly by monochromatic reduced painting, either by Kazimir Malevich, whose work and theoretic texts were at that time again being published in Czechoslovakia,[32] or by Yves Klein, whose work was also known in the local environment through contacts with the New Realists. In contrast to Malevich's understanding of the subject of abstraction, which was removed from regular relations with the concrete, while the supremacy of pure feeling was to be mediated exclusively by sensual perception, Klein empathically explored the sensible properties of real space, the walls of which he painted with a white paint-roller (see *The Void* at the Paris Iris Clert Gallery).[33]

Through research procedures within the *White Space* series since the 1970s, as opposed to the cultural survey of

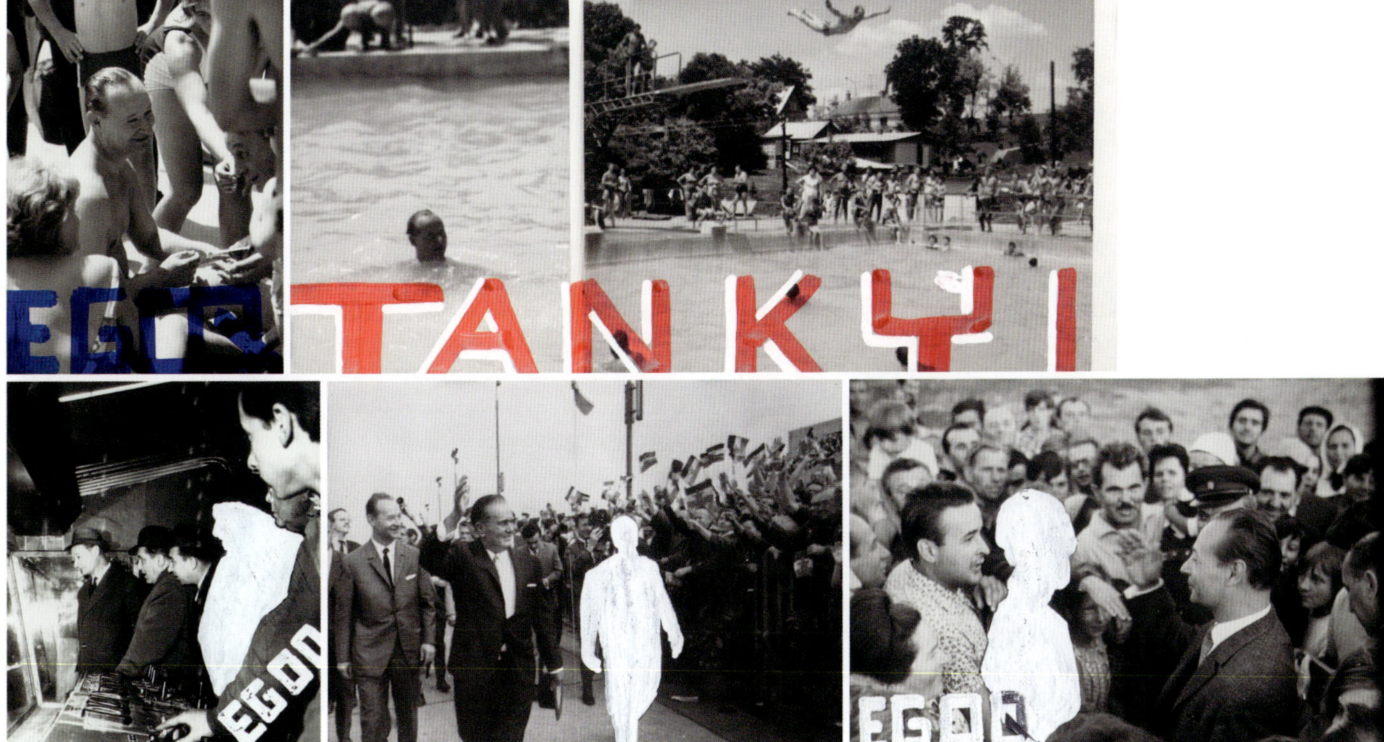

[10–14] Untitled (*Cathedral of Humanism* with Alexander Dubček, adapted for the competition for the memorial of the anti-totalitarian demonstration of 1968 and Dubček's late 80th birthday / *Katedrála humanizmu* s Alexandrom Dubčekom prispôsobená pre súťaž na pamätník proti-totalitnej demonštrácie v roku 1968 a Dubčekovým nedožitým osemdesiatym narodeninám), 1968/2001

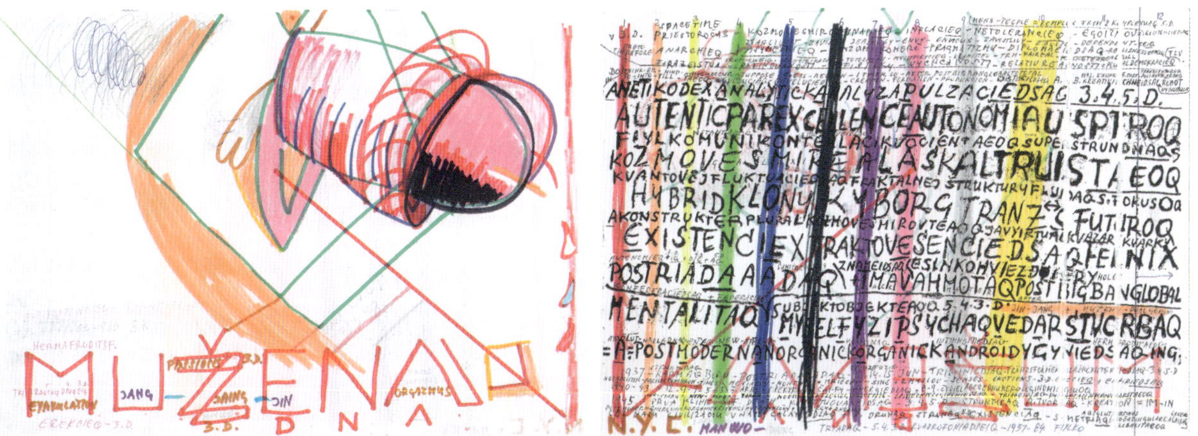

[15A–B] Untitled (subtitled *HERMAPHRODITSF - MALEFEMALE - ERECTION - 3.D. - DNA / HERMAFRODITSF - MUŽENA - EREKCIEQ - 3.D. - DNA*), 1990s

the known physical world within the *HAPPSOC* program, Filko refined the idea of non-representational transcendence which, together with Laky and Zavarský, he formulated as "pure emotion." In line with the program declarations and exhibition experiments, Filko later systematized the collective and individual parts of the *White Space in White Space / Biely priestor v bielom priestore* into four phases: 1. *SENSIBILITY / SENZIBILITA* (1973–74, the group manifesto *White Immaterial Space in a Pure White Infinite Space / Biely nehmotný priestor v čistom bielom nekonečnom priestore* realized in the Brno House of Art / Dům umění města Brna, 18. 2. 1974); 2. *SENSITIVITY / SENZITIVITA* (1974–76, joint *Manifesto of Pure Sensitivity / Manifest čistej senzitivity*, 1974–75), which also included reinstallations at the 9th Biennial of Young Artists in Paris in 1975 and at the Club of Young Artists in Budapest, 1977. The project of an infinite surface of mechanic painting with a paint-roller thus developed out of so-called *PURE SENSIBILITY* with its horizontally formatted and serial works (e.g. materially structured white folded strips of canvas or cylinders with a colored layer) which, for the needs of photo documentation, were to evoke in the closed gallery an installation space into the vertical lines of so-called *PURE SENSITIVITY* (e.g. latex paintings on linen strips or seemingly unstructured felts). According to Tomáš Štraus, the concept of the *White Space* underwent an evolution from an engineering to a poetic approach.[34]

After Laky's death and Zavarský's re-orientation to scenography work,[35] Filko formulated other postulates of *White Space* individually. In the subsequent stages, 3. *EMOTION / EMÓCIA* (1977, realization at Gallery LDK Labirynt, Lublin 1977–78) and 4. *TRANSCENDENCE / TRANSCENDENCIA* (1978, Gallery gn ZPAF, Gdansk 1978, and the Mala Galeria Warsaw, 1978–79), he further defined sensuality with reference to Kant and a priori knowledge.[36] He later wrote a handwritten annotation, "KONTEXT ART," in the artist's publications *Emotion* and *Transcendence*. It can be assumed that he saw them as a contextualization of the project, as part of which, during several public or private performances painting a white ceiling with a white roller, in Poland or the former Yugoslavia, he transferred *White Space in White Space* from the original ideal space into a specific one.

Similar to *HAPPSOC*, the concept of *White Space* (also originally a collective project) became a life project for Filko. He gradually included it in his system, in which he elaborated it in new meanings throughout his life as avant-garde *idée fixe*. From its initial materialization in the 1970s, he developed it in the direction of gradual and repeated sublimation in the 1990s in a range of works listed under varied titles: *White – Ontology – Transcendence – Metaphysics / Biela – Ontológia – Transcendencia – Metafyzika*, up to the *Model of the World/ Quadrophony* project as part of the Czechoslovak Pavilion at the 51st Biennale di Venezia, 2005 (with Ján Mančuška and Boris Ondreička), which he realized in the syncretic phase of his work. He set the *Big Bang* as the zero point, as a landmark of the historical and ahistorical, an intermediate stage between the physical and the transcendental. *White Space*, like *HAPPSOC*, has always fascinated the imagination of researchers; they have examined declarations and photographs related to it, interpretations of the rhythm of the folding of stripes or the scenic composition of the space, even though few had their own experience with the original

work. Filko himself handled it at the level of relics, which he freely replicated and gradually mythologized.

Filko's imaginative philosophy was thus formed in the dichotomous interrelationship of non-referential spirituality ("WHITE SPACE") and everyday materiality ("HAPPSOC"), thus with both views beyond the visible world and views of real sensual experience, which Filko often portrayed by masculinizing gender identity. [15A] In this sense, as Carol Duncan puts it, for modern artists "the quest for spiritual transcendence on the one hand and the obsession with a sexualized female body on the other, rather than appearing unrelated or contradictory, can be seen as parts of a larger, psychologically integrated whole."[37] Thus, in the cultural tradition of dualism, Filko developed his concept of the world born from the collision of the earthly biological realm with the immaterial realm of the higher spheres. [16A] In his late manuscripts, he referred to his work from the 1960s and 1970s as "constituted creation," and his later continuation in the 1980s and 1990s as "creativity," which, from his point of view, explained his transition from a discursive to an outsider practice.

FYLKO NYC 1980s

In 1981, Filko emigrated from socialist Czechoslovakia to West Germany, living primarily in Düsseldorf, and came into contact with, among others, Joseph Beuys, with whom he was most likely connected by the Slovak critic Tomáš Štraus, who was also an emigrant. According to the testimonies of Filko's contemporaries, the impulse for his emigration was mainly the ever-worsening conditions of exhibition presentation in the Czechoslovak Socialist Republic, where in 1972 he was expelled from the Union of Slovak Visual Artists and from the official scene.[38] He repainted the Škoda automobile in which he had fled the country white and exhibited it at documenta 7 in Kassel in 1982 together with large-format paintings of the tire prints (*The Living / Das Leben*), by which he followed up on roller paintings of *White Space*. He referred to it with an original fragment, which he included into the overall spatial installation entitled *Love of Ontology / Liebe zur Ontologie*. This can be regarded as the demise of the original *White Space* on a normative level.

Later, at the end of 1982, Filko left for New York, where he met artists like Keith Haring and Andy Warhol, with whom he already had contact from his earlier career. According to the findings from his estate, in the processes of self-historization he also appropriated and repainted the works by these artists, as he did with his own student works, documents, and family photographs. It is said that in New York he worked as a house painter and out of solidarity was steadily employed in auxiliary works by the circle of Czechoslovak emigrants. According to several testimonies, despite a number of opportunities, he was unable to participate in the commercial gallery system, although he seems to have originally envisaged this; this could also be related to his immense demands for gallery service.[39] At the end, in the transition period of the 1990s, other Eastern European artists also experienced great disillusionment with the orientation of the gallery operation to profit. Although many of them had been part of the counterculture in the era of state socialism, if they had an academic education they had also been able

Vorausgegangen waren bereits Kollaborationsprojekte, die Kunst und Wissenschaft verbanden, wie die Zyklen aus 1973 *Time I. / Čas I.* und *Time II. / Čas II.* (gemeinsam mit Július Koller und Rudolf Sikora) oder *Cosmic Messages / Vesmírne posolstvá* (gemeinsam mit Peter Bartoš, Michal Kern und dem Kritiker Tomáš Štraus), die vom *Voyager*-Raumsondenprogramm und der weltweiten Debatte über intergalaktische Kommunikation und repetitiven Signalen aus dem All, dem sogenannten *active messaging* angeregt wurden. Die zugrunde liegende Denkweise war, könnte man sagen, von der wissenschaftlichen Objektivitätsauffassung inspiriert, die auf quantitativer Analyse, Systematisierung und Verallgemeinerung von Tatsachen beruht und damit von der subjektiven Sicht abstrahiert. Sie wurde auch bei *White Space in White Space* verfolgt.

In erster Linie war das Manifest *White Immaterial Space in a Pure White Infinite Space / Biely nehmotný priestor v čistom bielom nekonečnom priestore* (1973) ohne Zweifel von der reduzierten monochromen Malerei beeinflusst – also von Kasimir Malewitsch, dessen Kunst und theoretische Texte zu dieser Zeit in der Tschechoslowakei gerade neuveröffentlicht wurden,[32] aber auch von Yves Klein, der durch persönliche Kontakte mit den Nouveau Réalistes bekannt war. Im Gegensatz zu Malewitschs Verständnis der Abstraktion, das von normalen Zusammenhängen mit konkreten Objekten absah und die Überlegenheit des reinen Gefühls ausschließlich über die sinnliche Wahrnehmung vermitteln wollte, erforschte Klein empathisch die wahrnehmbaren Eigenschaften realer Räume, deren Wände er mit einer Rolle weiß strich (so bei *The Void* in der Pariser Galerie Iris Clert).[33]

Im Gegensatz zur kulturellen Protokollierung der materiellen Welt im Rahmen des *HAPPSOC*-Programms kultivierte Filko seit den 1970er-Jahren in der *White Space*-Serie durch Forschungsverfahren die Idee einer ungegenständlichen Transzendenz, die er mit Laky und Zavarský gemeinsam „reine Emotion" nannte. In Übereinstimmung mit seinen programmatischen Erklärungen und Ausstellungsexperimenten systematisierte Filko später sowohl den kollektiven als auch seinen individuellen Teil des *White Space in White Space / Biely priestor v bielom priestore* zu vier Phasen. Die ersten beiden waren: 1. *SENSIBILITY / Senzibilita* (1973/74, Gruppenmanifest *White Immaterial Space in a Pure White Infinite Space / Biely nehmotný priestor v čistom bielom nekonečnom priestore*, realisiert im Haus der Kunst in Brünn [Dom umění města Brna] am 18. 2. 1974), 2. *SENSITIVITY / Senzitivita* (1974–1976, gemeinsames *Manifesto of Pure Sensitivity / Manifest čistej senzitivity*, 1974–1975), wozu zum Beispiel auch die erneute Installationen auf der 9th Biennial of Young Artists 1975 oder im Club of Young Artists in Budapest 1977 zählen. Das Projekt einer unendlichen Fläche, die maschinell mit einer Walze gestrichen wird, entwickelte sich also von der sogenannten *PURE SENSIBILITY* horizontal formatierter Serien (zum Beispiel direkt gefaltete weiße Leinwandstreifen oder Zylinder mit einer Farbschicht), die zum Zweck der Fotodokumentation in einer geschlossenen Galerie installiert werden sollten, zu den vertikalen Linien der sogenannten *PURE SENSITIVITY* (zum Beispiel Latexmalereien auf Leinenbahnen oder offenbar texturlosen Filzen). Laut Tomáš Štraus ging Filko bei der Konzeption des *White Space* also von einem technischen zu einem poetischen Ansatz über.[34]

Nachdem Laky verstorben und Zavarský sich auf die Arbeit als Ausstatter umorientiert hatte,[35] formulierte Filko im Alleingang weitere Postulate des *White Space*. Die zwei folgenden Phasen hießen 3. *EMOTION / Emócia* (1977, in der Galerie LDK Labirynt in Lublin 1977/78 realisiert) und 4. *TRANSCENDENCE / Transcendencia* (1978, Galerie gn ZPAF in Danzig 1978 sowie Mala Galeria in Warschau 1978/79). Mit ihnen definierte der Künstler Sinnlichkeit unter Bezugnahme auf Kant und das Wissen *a priori*.[36] In den Künstlerbüchern *Emotion* und *Transcendence* fügte Filko später handschriftlich die Gattungsbezeichnung „KONTEXT ART" hinzu. Man darf annehmen, dass er damit die Kontextualisierung des Projekts meinte, da er nämlich anlässlich mehrerer öffentlicher und privater Mal-Performances in Polen und im ehemaligen Jugoslawien, wo er den Plafond mit einer weißen Farbwalze strich, den *White Space in White Space* vom ursprünglich idealen in den konkreten Raum überführte.

Wie schon *HAPPSOC* wurde das Konzept des *White Space* (das ebenfalls als Gemeinschaftsprojekt begonnen wurde) für Filko zu einem Lebensprojekt. Nach und nach bezog er es in sein Gesamtsystem ein, wo er es im Sinne einer avantgardistischen *idée fixe* zeitlebens mit neuen Bedeutungen auflud. Von den anfänglichen Umsetzungen in den 1970er-Jahren entwickelte Filko den *White Space* bis in die 1990er-Jahre allmählich stufenweise in Richtung Sublimierung. Dazu gehören eine Reihe von Werken, die er unter variablen Titeln *White – Ontology – Transcendence – Metaphysics / Biela – Ontológia – Transcendencia – Metafyzika* ausführte, aber auch das Projekt *Model of the World/Quadrophony* als Teil des tschechoslowakischen Pavillons auf der 51. Biennale von Venedig 2005 (mit Ján Mančuška und Boris Ondreička), das bereits der synkretistischen Phase seines Œuvres zuzuordnen ist. Der Urknall war für ihn nun der Nullpunkt – ein Anker des Historischen und Ahistorischen, zugleich aber auch ein Zwischending zwischen dem Materiellen und dem Transzendenten.

Wie *HAPPSOC* hat auch der *White Space* stets die Phantasie von Forscher*innen angeregt. Sie sichteten Erklärungen und Fotos, deuteten den Faltrhythmus der Streifen oder die szenische Komposition des Raums, wenngleich nur wenige das Originalwerk sahen. Filko selbst behandelte es wie eine Reliquie, die er nach Lust und Laune reproduzierte und nach und nach zum Mythos machte.

Filkos phantastische Philosophie formte sich durch die Wechselbeziehung der Pole nicht-referentieller Spiritualität („WHITE SPACE") einerseits und alltäglicher Materialität („HAPPSOC") andererseits, zwischen Ausblicken über die sichtbare Welt hinaus und sinnlichem Erleben, das er oft durch die Maskulinisierung der Geschlechtsidentität darstellte. [15A] In diesem Sinne kann bei modernen Künstlern wohl allgemein, wie Carol Duncan schrieb, „die Suche nach spiritueller Transzendenz einerseits und die Besessenheit vom sexualisierten Frauenkörper andererseits als integrale Bestandteile eines umfassenderen psychologischen Ganzen und nicht verbindungslos oder widersprüchlich verstanden werden".[37] Auf diese Weise entwickelte Filko seine Weltanschauung, die als Zusammenprall des irdischen Biologischen mit dem Immateriellen höherer Sphären durchaus in der kulturellen Tradition des Dualismus stand. [16A] In seinen späten Manuskripten bezeichnete er seine Kunst aus den 1960er- und 1970er-Jahren dementsprechend als „konstituierte Schöpfung" und die aus den 1980er- und 1990er-Jahren als „Kreativität", was – aus seiner Sicht – auch seinen Übergang von einer diskursiven zu einer außenseiterischen Praxis erklärte.

      Genealogie eines modernistischen Essentialismus

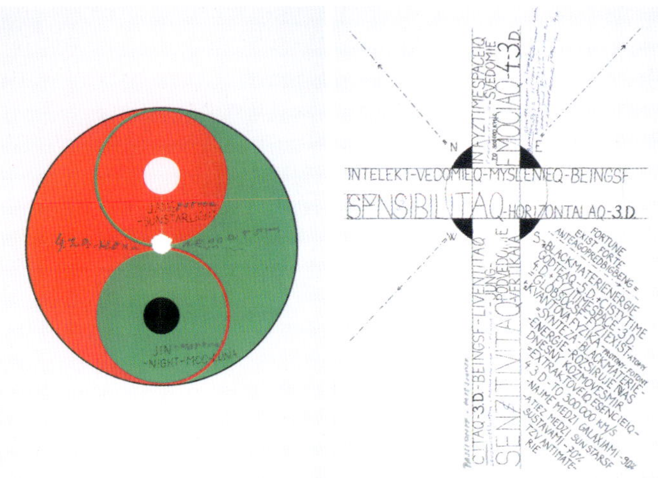

[16A-B] Untitled, after 2005

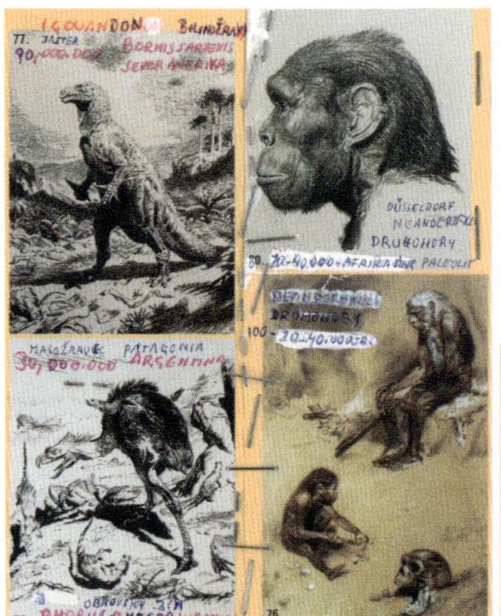
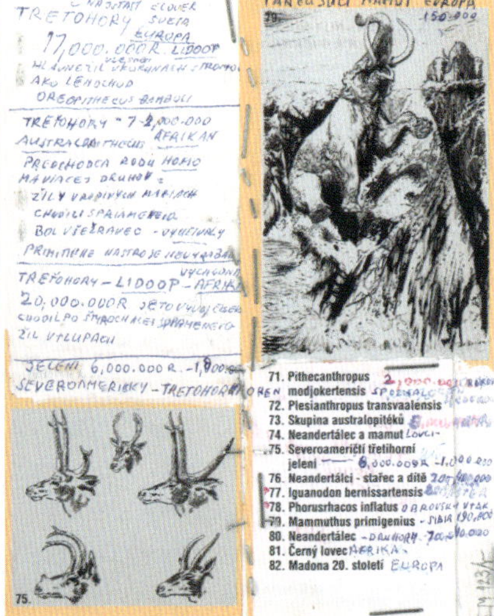
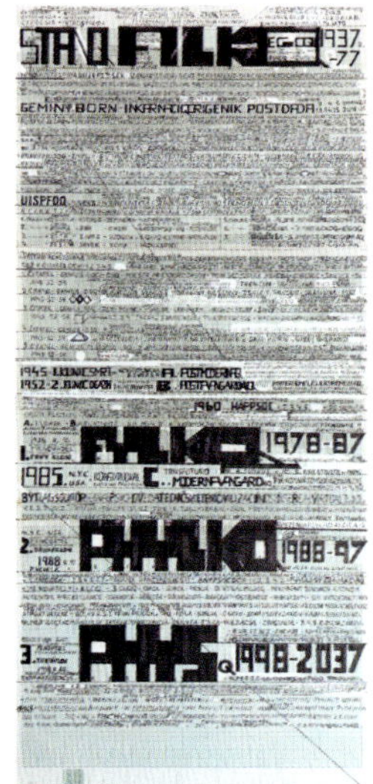

[17A-B] Untitled, 2000s

[18] Untitled,
c. 1997

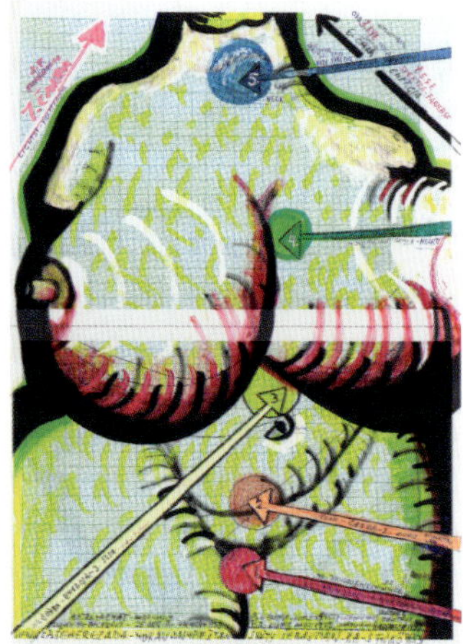
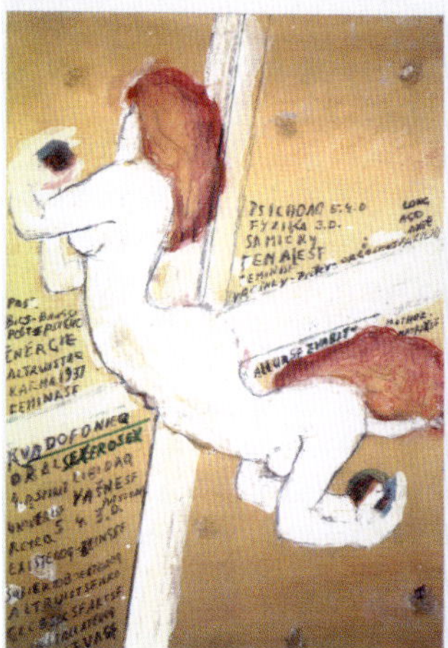

[19] Untitled
(subtitled
*VENUSSHEHERAZADE –
MORAVANYPIEŠŤANY –
SAINT SEBASTIAN –
SHE – SFILKO 1953 /
VENUŠAŠEHEREZADA –
MORAVANYPIEŠŤANY –
SVÄTÝ ŠEBASTIAN –
KA – SFILKO 1953)*,
early 1990s

[20A-B] Untitled (subtitled *PSYCHOAQ
5.4.D. – PHYSICS 3.D. – FEMALES – FEMALESF –
FEMINISF – VAGINES – PUSSIES / PSICHOAQ
5.4.D. – FYZIKA 3.D. – SAMIČKY – FEMALESF –
FEMINISF – VAGINKY – PIČKY)*, 2000s

1981 wanderte Filko aus der kommunistischen Tschechoslowakei nach Westdeutschland aus, wo er die meiste Zeit in Düsseldorf lebte und unter anderem mit Joseph Beuys in Kontakt kam, mit dem ihn wahrscheinlich der slowakische Kritiker Tomáš Štraus, ebenfalls ein Emigrant, bekannt machte. Nach Aussagen von Filkos Zeitgenoss*innen waren der Auslöser für seine Emigration vor allem die sich ständig verschlechternden Ausstellungsbedingungen in der Tschechoslowakei, wo er 1972 aus dem Verband der bildenden Künstler der Slowakei und damit aus dem offiziellen Kunstbetrieb ausgeschlossen wurde.[38] Den Škoda, mit dem er aus dem Land geflohen war, lackierte er weiß, um ihn 1982 auf der documenta 7 in Kassel zusammen mit großformatigen Gemälden von Reifenabdrücken (*The Living / Das Leben*) auszustellen, wobei er mit letzteren an die Walzenbilder des *White Space* anknüpfte. Darauf bezog er sich in einem Originalfragment, das er in die Rauminstallation mit dem Titel *Liebe zur Ontologie / Love of Ontology* einbezog. Dies kann wohl als ein Abrücken vom ursprünglichen *White Space* auf der normativen Ebene betrachtet werden.

Gegen Ende 1982 zog es Filko weiter nach New York, wo er unter anderem Keith Haring und Andy Warhol traf, mit denen er bereits in früherer Zeit Kontakt gehabt hatte. Nach Erkenntnissen aus seinem Nachlass hat er sich Werke dieser Künstler ebenso wie seine eigenen Studentenarbeiten oder Dokumente und Familienfotos für die eigene Selbsthistorisierung angeeignet und übermalt. In New York soll er als Anstreicher gearbeitet haben und wurde vom Kreis der tschechoslowakischen Emigrant*innen aus Solidarität immer wieder zu Hilfsarbeiten herangezogen. Mehreren Zeugnissen zufolge konnte er sich trotz zahlreicher Gelegenheiten nicht im kommerziellen Galeriesystem etablieren, obwohl er dies ursprünglich wohl vorhatte. Dies könnte aber auch mit den immensen Ansprüchen zusammenhängen, die Filko an Galerien stellte.[39] Schließlich trat in der Übergangszeit der 1990er-Jahre auch bei anderen osteuropäischen Künstler*innen eine große Ernüchterung über die Profitorientierung des Kunstbetriebs ein. Obwohl viele von ihnen in der kommunistischen Zeit zur Gegenkultur gehört hatten, so hatten sie doch, jedenfalls wenn sie eine akademische Ausbildung hatten, bis zu einem gewissen Grad an den sozialen Vorteilen teilgehabt, die mit dem staatlich geförderten Status des freischaffenden Künstlers oder der freischaffenden Künstlerin verbunden waren.

Auf die Frage, warum er Amerika verlassen habe und 1990 in die Slowakei zurückgekehrt sei, antwortete Filko in einem undatierten Arbeitsgespräch mit Fedor Blaščák Folgendes: „Weil ich enttäuscht war. Von Amerika und von der westlichen Marktwirtschaft. Ich bin vor dem Kommunismus geflohen, habe dabei aber nur den Materialismus (das heißt den marxistischen) gegen den Marktmaterialismus/Pragmatismus getauscht …" In seinen Kunsttexten hat Filko mehrfach seine Ablehnung von Überbaukonzepten kundgetan. So stellte er beispielsweise fest: „Es gibt nur einen Materialismus, ob kapitalistisch oder kommunistisch, das ist dasselbe", oder „EGO-Pragmatismus im Kapitalismus – dialektischer Materialismus im Kommunismus." Filko gehörte zu jener tschechoslowakischen Generation, bei der sich (wie die Historikerin Kristína Andělová zusammenfasste[40]) sogar potenziell linke Regimekritik meist in vorpolitischen, allgemeinen politischen oder in Menschenrechtsthemen auflöste, um bis in die 1990er-Jahre und darüber hinaus als Vorstellung einer Art unpolitischen Zivilgesellschaft fortzuleben. Dieses vage kritische Denken führte während der neoliberal-ideologischen Gehirnwäsche der 1990er-Jahre zum Verlust aller kritischen Werkzeuge gegen den fortschreitenden Kapitalismus. Im ehemaligen Ostblock war linke Klassenkritik delegitimiert, hatte doch der real existierende Sozialismus jahrzehntelang ein Monopol auf sie gehabt. Nach 1989, als marxistische Ideen wie Gespenster durch die ehemals kommunistischen Staaten geisterten, erschien sie dann, um mit Derrida zu sprechen, nur noch als „Heimsuchung" (l'hantologie). [17A-B]

Während seiner sogenannten amerikanischen Periode in den 1980er-Jahren konzentrierte sich Filko vor allem auf neoexpressive Malerei in Assemblage-Installationen sowie großformatige Serien, die er oft mit Buchstaben, zum Beispiel Variationen seines Namens oder der Abkürzung AIDS, das er als spezifisches Merkmal der New Yorker Kulturkämpfe verstand, versah. Im Zusammenhang mit der *Altars*-Serie aus den 1960er-Jahren interpretierte er diese Kämpfe als Leviathan, als makabren Tanz einer neuen Zivilisationskrise. Davon ausgehend führte er mit sich selbst einen widersprüchlichen Dialog zwischen Altruismus und Egoismus, der von der christlichen Lehre der „gottgegebenen Tugenden" beeinflusst war.

In diese Zeit fiel auch Filkos Beschäftigung mit der gegenständlichen Malerei. Einmal mehr im Konflikt mit der konventionellen Moral schuf er zum Beispiel animalistische Frontalszenen von Matronen [19], die er gesichts- und geschlechtslos im Graffiti-Stil auf anatomische Darstellungen von Gebärmüttern oder Vaginen (unter anderem auch in der Objektform eines Schranks mit den Geburtsdaten seiner Mutter), bisweilen auch sogenannte „vaginae dentatae" reduzierte. Darüber hinaus malte er aber auch laszive Männer, die er als mythischen *Pan* oder als vergnügungssuchende barocke alte Männer darstellte. Aurel Hrabušický verstand Filkos großformatige Serien aufgesperrter Münder mit Zähnen (zum Beispiel in der Serie *Spirit*) als von Gottheiten indianischer Kulturen inspiriert.[41] Jedenfalls glichen einige dieser Motive gefährlichen, potenziell verschlingenden oder kastrierenden Wesen mit pornografischen Zügen [20A], die er mehr oder weniger in der künstlerischen Tradition matriarchal orientierter Medusa-Gorgonen als blutrünstige, zugleich aber beschützende, monströse und doch burleske, erotisch selbstentblößte und doch mädchenhafte Muttergöttinnen durchaus patriarchal anlegte. Es sind Frauen, wie sie in den Werken moderner Künstler oft erscheinen, aber auch vom Feminismus kritisiert wurden.[42]

Zeitkritiker*innen wie Štraus stimmten überein, dass Filko transavantgardistische Kulturströmungen aufnahm und sich von den Neuen Wilden in Deutschland anregen ließ. Zugleich griff er mit seinen Gemälden auch selbsthistorisierend auf die eigenen Anfänge im Post-Informel und in der Assemblage-Kunst der 1960er-Jahre zurück. Schon in dieser Phase hatte er zum Beispiel ein kulturspezifisches Readymade geschaffen, das er allerdings „Zivilisationsmüll" nannte, ließ Leerstellen zu, und wenn er Farbe, Isolierschaum oder dergleichen verwendete, dann brachte er diese mit der vollen Dose oder Spraypistole auf. Gleichzeitig arbeitete Filko an der – seiner Meinung nach – gegensätzlichen Position

to enjoy to some extent the social benefits associated with the state-supported status of a freelance artist.

On the question of why he left America to return to Slovakia in 1990, in a conversation with Fedor Blaščák (undated) Filko said the following: "Because I was disappointed. By America and by the Western market economy. I went away from communism here and exchanged materialism (that is, Marxist) for market materialism/pragmatism." He formulated his disagreement with superstructure concepts several times in his text-arts, in which he noted, for example, that "materialism is one, whether capitalist or communist, it's all the same," or "EGO pragmatism in capitalism— dialectic materialism in communism." Filko belonged to the Czechoslovak generation in which (as the historian Kristína Andělová summarized it[40]) even potentially leftist criticism of the regime was mostly dissolved in pre-political or a universal framing of political questions, or in human rights issues, which still in the 1990s and even later persisted as an idea of a kind of non-political civil society. This unarticulated form of critical thinking then resulted, in the neoliberal ideological brainwashing period of the 1990s, in the loss of the tools of criticism for emerging capitalism. In the former socialist block, leftist class criticism was then definitively delegitimized by being monopolized by the regime for decades. After 1989, it appeared, to use a term of Derrida's, only at the level of a kind of "hauntology," in which Marxist ideas returned to the former Eastern bloc in the form of ghosts. [17A-B]

In the 1980s, during his "American period," Filko concentrated mostly on neo-expressive painting of assemblage installations and large-format image sets, often with lettric transcriptions, for example variations of his name or the acronym AIDS, which he used as an attribute of the New York culture wars. He drew connections with his series of *Altars* from the 1960s, interpreting his actual works in a Leviathan way, as a dance macabre of a new civilizational crisis. From there, he led a contradictory dialog between altruism and egoism, influenced by the Christian doctrine of "virtues given from above."

During this period, Filko also devoted himself to figurative painting. Again, in a conflicting position with conventional morality, he created, for example, animalistic frontal scenes of matrons [19] with no closer identity, and women reduced in a graffiti style to anatomical figures of wombs or vaginas (also, for example, in the object form of a closet with the dates of his mother's birth) or in a version of the so-called "vagina dentata." But he also depicted the figures of lewd men, imagined by figures of the mythological *Pan* or pleasure-seeking baroque old men. Aurel Hrabušický saw in his series of close-ups of gaping mouths and teeth (e.g. the *Spirit* series) inspiration from the deities of native American cultures.[41] Anyway, several of these motifs were apparitions of dangerous-looking beings, potentially devouring or castrating, with pornographic features [20A] that he constructed patriarchally, more or less in the artistic tradition of Medusa Gorgons, bloodthirsty and at the same time accepting matrifocal mother goddesses, monstrous yet burlesque, erotically self-exposed, and girlish too. These are women as they appear in the works of modern artists, and which were thematized by feminist culture.[42]

Period critics such as Štraus agreed that Filko was here absorbing trans-avant-garde cultural trends and was inspired by the German Neue Wilde. But this was also a self-historicizing return to his own Post-Informel and assemblage beginnings from the 1960s. Even in this phase, for example, he composed a culturally framed readymade (he called it "civilizational waste") or he admitted material joints, and if, for example, he used paint, insulation foam, and the like, then also with the whole can or spray container. At the same time, he worked (from his point of view) on the contrasting position of non-concrete two-sided polyptychs (he called them "mobiles" and "curtains"), which were part of large-scale spatial installations with monochromatic surfaces and mirror foils.

On the ruins of the *White Space*, Filko began to concentrate more intensively on his ever-present retrospection. Within this, he began to phenomenalize selected historical experiences of the world, even using specific Slavic symbols related to the prehistory of Slovakia. After his arrival to Slovakia, he summarized it in a profile text in a newspaper with the words: "In the long march from the Slovakian Palaeolithic in 25,000 BC and from the cave paintings to the Egyptian pyramids up to the works of Malevich and Brancusi, art has been torn between the iconoclastic and the image-constructing myth."[43] A period newspaper critique stated that the motif of Slovakia's oldest art artifact, the Paleolithic goddess of fertility, the *Moravian Venus*, became one of Filko's reliquaries in America.[44] This female mammoth tusk torso from around 22,800 BC was dug up in 1930 in a field in the region of Filko's birthplace, in Moravany nad Váhom. [21–22] The headless sculpture, which therefore cannot threaten anyone with its own erotic power, was then included in the next androcentric alternation of Filko's universalist triad in the form: "Woman – Scheherazade – Venus."

PHYLKO BRATISLAVA 1990s

Filko associated the gender-determined concept of the female principle with the basic colors red, yellow, and orange. [23] In the spirit of biological essentialism, he meant these colors to represent a biological foundation and eroticism. And while he moved toward a greater diversity of representations as a result of his stay in New York in the 1980s, he never attained a truly de-essentialized queer approach. Anyway, from the non-specific sexualized models of the popular magazines of the 1960s (see WOMAN or BIOLOGY), he moved to a more non-normative and raw position in which he already depicted, for example, a hermaphrodite body, even though not constructed in an asexualized or cross-gendered way. It remained rather more or less anchored in the dominant mode of heteropatriarchal representation as an image filtered by male fantasies of cuddly lesbians and embodied kinky dominatrixes. Finally, such imaginaries commonly framed all kinds of otherness and representations of non-normative gender. Moments of the possible surpassing of singularity appeared in Filko's work in the portrayal of female characters inspired by mythological beings such as the Amazons or the Sphinx that are defined against men, and others that were eventually subdued and killed such as the Hydra and the Chimera. Since they are combinations of multiple fearsome animals, they no longer have singularity. Filko even selectively used references to radical democratic discourse, and he even incorporated

    Genealogy of Modernist Essentialism

abstrakter doppelseitiger Polyptychen, die er „Mobiles" und „Vorhänge" nannte und die er in große Rauminstallationen mit monochromen Oberflächen und Spiegelfolien einbaute.

Auf den Ruinen des *White Space* beschäftigte sich Filko nun intensiver mit der ohnehin immer latent gewesenen Rückschau. Er begann damit, ausgewählte historische Ereignisse aus seiner Sicht darzustellen, wobei er sogar auf slawische Symbole aus der Vorgeschichte der Slowakei zurückgriff. Nach seiner Rückkehr in die Slowakei fasste er dieses Thema in einer Zeitung wie folgt zusammen: „Auf dem langen Weg vom slowakischen Paläolithikum 25.000 v. Chr. über die Höhlenmalereien bis zu den ägyptischen Pyramiden und den Werken von Malewitsch und Brancusi wurde die Kunst immer zwischen einem ikonoklastischen und einem ikonischen Mythos hin- und hergeworfen."[43] Eine Zeitungskritik aus dieser Zeit erwähnt, dass der älteste Kultgegenstand in der Slowakei eine paläolithische Fruchtbarkeitsgöttin, die *Venus von Mähren*, sei und dass sie für Filko in den USA zu einer Reliquie geworden war.[44] Dieser weibliche Torso aus dem Stoßzahn eines Mammuts aus der Zeit um 22.800 v. Chr. wurde 1930 auf einem Feld in der Region von Filkos Geburtsort Moravany nad Váhom ausgegraben. [21-22] Filko jedenfalls konnte mit dieser kopflosen Skulptur, deren erotische Kraft heute wohl niemanden mehr bedrohlich erscheint, seine nächste androzentrische Universaltriade vervollständigen. Sie hieß „Frau – Scheherazade – Venus".

PHYLKO BRATISLAVA 1990er

Filko verband seine geschlechtlich determinierte Vorstellung des weiblichen Prinzips mit drei Grundfarben – Rot, Gelb und Orange. [23] Ganz im Sinne des biologischen Essentialismus stellte er mit ihnen ein biologisches Prinzip und die Erotik dar. Obwohl er seit seinem Aufenthalt in New York in den 1980er-Jahren sein künstlerisches Vokabular geöffnet hatte, fand er nie zu einer wirklich antiessentialistisch queeren Einstellung. Immerhin ging er aber von unspezifisch sexualisierten Modellen aus populären Magazinen der 1960er-Jahre (siehe WOMAN oder BIOLOGY) zu einer undifferenziert nicht-normativen Position über, wenn er beispielsweise bereits einen hermaphroditischen Körper darstellte, der ihm allerdings weder unsexualisiert noch gender-übergreifend gelang. Das Bild blieb mehr oder weniger im vorherrschenden Modus heteropatriarchaler Repräsentation verwurzelt, filterte der Künstler es doch durch seine männliche Phantasien von zärtlichen Lesben und einer perversen Domina. Schließlich wirkten sich solche Fantasien ganz generell auf seine Wahrnehmung jeglicher Form des Andersseins und des nicht-normativen Geschlechts aus. Momente, in denen Filko über solche Eindeutigkeiten hinausging, finden sich nur in Darstellungen weiblicher Figuren, die von mythologischen, sich gegen Männer abgrenzenden Wesen inspiriert sind – wie Amazonen oder Sphingen –, oder die letztlich unterworfen und getötet werden – wie die Hydra oder die Chimära. Sie sind nicht mehr eindeutig, weil sie Mischwesen aus verschiedenen furchterregenden Tieren darstellen. Darüber hinaus zog Filko sehr wohl selektive Verbindungen zum radikaldemokratischen Diskurs. So bezog er sogar den Schwarzen Feminismus in eine Version der Triade „Feminism – Womanism – Femaleism" (Slowakisch Feminizmus – Womanizmus – Ženizmus) ein. [24-25]

Dennoch blieb seine sexuell imaginierte Frau mythisiert eingebettet in eine spekulativ universalistische und kosmologische Sichtweise (vgl. „SCHEHERAZADE" abwechselnd mit „KOSMOLOGIE"). Letztlich mündeten nach Filkos Übergangsstadium der 4. Dimension, nach der Idee einer nicht-individualisierten, dominanten und bedrohlichen Scheherazade, die in der amerikanischen Periode auftaucht, alle Frauensujets schließlich in der Fruchtbarkeit grenzenloser Matriarchatsarchetypen (so verkörpert beispielsweise „VENUS" die „METAPHYSIK"). Viele der Frauendarstellungen Filkos behielten also ihre Bedeutung, obwohl sie nun gewissermaßen übermenschliche abstrakte Konzepte verkörperten (so die Mutter aller Mütter als Inbegriff der Fruchtbarkeit oder die Freiheitsstatue als Inbegriff der Gerechtigkeit usw.). [26] Der Künstler band sie in eine Art höheres überirdisches System ein, wodurch ihre Körperlichkeit zu abstrakten Begriffen transzendiert scheint. Gleichzeitig bleiben sie aber auch unverständlich, als seien sie Schatten von Frauen, keine wirklichen Menschen, sondern bloß vervielfältigbare Zeichen. Und so ist das Publikum in vielen von Filkos Werken zwar von Frauen umringt, kann sie aber weder berühren noch begehren. Die Frauen bleiben Schatten ihrer selbst, Schatten ihrer wirklichen Sexualität. [27]

In den 1990er-Jahren überwand Filko schließlich seine starre allgemeine Vorstellung binärer Gegensätze und stabiler Identitäten. Dies führte ihn zur postmodernen Idee eines post-geschlechtlichen Cyborgs, der indes wie im New Age eine Art Gedächtnis seiner vergangenen Körper behält. Er ist nicht mehr nur Mensch, sondern mehr als ein Mensch, nicht nur eine Maschine, sondern mehr als eine Maschine. Er ist ein Hybrid aus Maschine und Organismus, das die Dialektik von Materialismus und Idealismus scheinbar überwunden hat. So formulierte es bereits Donna Haraway zu Beginn des posthumanistischen Diskurses in ihrem „Cyborg Manifesto" (1985): „Cyborgs sind nicht mehr durch die Polarität von öffentlich und privat strukturiert, Cyborgs definieren eine technologische Polis, die zum großen Teil auf einer Revolution der sozialen Beziehungen im ‚oikos', dem Haushalt, beruht. Natur und Kultur werden neu definiert. Die eine stellt nicht mehr die Ressource für die Aneignung und Einverleibung durch die andere dar".[45] Zu dieser Zeit beschäftigte sich Filko, wenn auch nur auf der simplen Ebene der magischen Medizin, mit der Chakrenlehre, die er als seine innere Mystik präsentierte. Ähnlich wie in den 1960er-Jahren, als er die Welt als biologisches und technisches Kontinuum gesehen hatte, interessierte ihn der technische Fortschritt und der banale Alltag zugleich. Filkos Computergrafiken aus den 1990er- und frühen 2000er-Jahren sind wohl von den computergenerierten Bildern der frühen 1980er-Jahre wie beispielsweise dem berühmten Film *Tron* (1982) inspiriert. Dies betraf unter anderem auch die Serie nicht-binärer Cyborg-Tier-Bricolagen der *Mährischen Venus* von der Wende der 1990er-Jahre, die er mit „FEMINIZMUZSF" beschriftete [28-29] (in der Zerlegung des Wortes auf Slowakisch FEMINI-Z-MUŽ, übersetzt Weibliches-aus-Männlichem, bedeutet das: die Frau, die vom Mann kam, also Eva und nicht Lilith), oder seine Tunnelanimationen, die Filko von Beschreibungen von Nahtoderlebnissen kannte, an denen er nun Interesse fand. (In den späten 1990er-Jahren zählte *Leben nach dem Tod* von Raymond A. Moody zu den populärsten Büchern in der Slowakei, obwohl es mit einer ganzen Flut esoterischer Selbsthilfeliteratur

Black feminism into a version of his trilogy: "Feminism − Womanism − Femaleism" (trans. from Slovak Feminizmus − Womanizmus − Ženizmus). [24-25]

But Filko's sexually imagined women remained mythicized, embedded in a speculative universalist cosmological perspective (see "SCHEHERAZADE" alternating with "COSMOLOGY"). In the end, through the transitional stage of his fourth dimension, and through the idea of the non-individualized subject of the dominant and threatening female Scheherazade, which appeared in Filko's American period, these women figures eventually flowed into the fertile powers of the infinite beings of archetypal matriarchal figures (see "VENUS" personifying "METAPHYSICS"). Many of Filko's depictions of women's bodies thus retained their meanings in a kind of embodiment of superhuman abstract concepts (see the mother of mothers as an etalon of fertility or the Statue of Liberty as an etalon of justice, etc.). [26] They are incorporated into a kind of higher superterrestrial system, and their corporeal element seems to transcend abstract concepts. At the same time, however, they remain incomprehensible, like clusters of shadows of women, not real women, just signs that multiply. And so, although in many of Filko's works the viewer is surrounded by a woman, there is no way to touch her, nor to be able to desire her. She only is a shadow of herself, only a shadow of true sexuality. [27]

In the 1990s, Filko overcame the rigidity of the universal validity of binary oppositions and stable identity, which eventually resulted in a postmodern idea of a postgender cyborg (which in a New-Ageist way also composed a kind of memory of old bodies), who is no longer just a man, but more than a man, and not just a machine, but more than a machine: a hybrid of machine and organism, seemingly overcoming the dialectic of materialism and idealism. As Donna Haraway put it in the early days of posthumanist discourse in her "Cyborg Manifesto" (1985): "No longer structured by the polarity of public and private, the cyborg defines a technological polis based partly on a revolution of social relations in 'the oikos,' the household. Nature and culture are reimagined; the one can no longer be the resource for appropriation or incorporation by the other."[45] Filko, even if only at the level of folk healing, was at that time also simultaneously dealing with the theory of chakras, which he presented as his inner mysticism. This is similar to when in the 1960s, set in the perspective of the world as a biological and technical continuum, he was simultaneously interested in technological progress and the everyday banality of the household. Filko's computer graphics from the 1990s and early 2000s seem to be informed by early CGI, experiments with computer-generated imagery from the early 1980s, such as the iconic *Tron* (1982). This concerned, among others, for example, the series of nonbinary cyborg-animal bricolages of *Moravian Venus* from the turn of the 1990s, annotated "FEMINIZMUSSF" [28-29] (in the decomposition of the word in Slovak translated as femine-from-male, i.e. biblical Eve and not Lilith), and the tunnel animations based on clinical death experiences, which Filko was also interested in. (In the transitional 1990s, one of the most popular books in Slovakia was *Life after Life* by Raymond A. Moody, published in a flood of esoterically tuned self-help literature, obviously often related to a mystique about how to make money, but generally aimed at setting some kind of new mindset for a new era).

At that time, Filko also reconstructed his own identity. Initially, in the "HERMAFRODITSF" version, he considered parallel timelines. [30] He also articulated changes in his artistic positions through his altering identities. His later concepts of "POSTBIGBANG" and "ANTEBIGBANG" did not refer exclusively to the creation and transformation of life, or life after life. They also corresponded to the alleged details of Filko's incarnations, including his reported clinical deaths.[46] As he expressed it in a number of works and records, in a version from the late 1990s, he recognized several of his identities, to which he also referred as "CLONES: FILKO (1937–77) − FYLKO (1978–87) − PHYLKO (1988–97) − PHYS (1998–2037)."[47] [18] He also spoke of himself as a so-called "TRIMINI," in place of the dualist Zodiac sign, Gemini. He stated that he had been born three times: on June 13, 1937, after a blood transfusion, on June 14, 1937, and again on June 15, 1937, as was recorded in his documents, albeit erroneously. Then, according to his own statements, he was incarnated two more times. He should have survived the first clinical death in 1945 following a fall in a quarry while pasturing cows; a second time in 1952 after an electric shock in a weapon factory near Trenčín.[48] In preserved manuscripts, and also in his *Memories of Clinical Deaths*, he describes these experiences in an almost Steinerian manner.[49]

After the change of the regime and his return to Slovakia in 1990, Filko also absorbed the nationalist narratives of identity politics that, along with a politics of memory, dominated throughout the 1990s in culturally conservative post-Communist countries. He began to assemble the conceptual classification of his work according to the color triad of the Czechoslovak tricolor, then, after the division of the country since 1993, to the Slovak flag. On the invitation to his apparently first Bratislava exhibition after his return from emigration was stated: "The identity of my work is conceptual: it has three directions or routes of equal energy, just like the Slovak flag: biology/red, cosmology/blue, ontology/white. This division is at the same time international and cosmological."[50] [31]

By way of reference to the decades-old debate on the asymmetrical relations between Czechs and Slovaks, Filko no longer used the name *Československo* (Czechoslovakia) in his works, but *Slovenskočesko* (Slovakbohemia). Then he annotated his name, Stanislav, as: "SUBJEKT − SLÁVA − SLOVÁK − SLAVIAN − SVET − SLOBODA" (Subject − Glory − Slovak − Slavic − World − Freedom). He also made reference to several political figures who historically had a formative influence on the building of the national identity, such as the representative of reform socialism in the 1960s, Alexander Dubček, the cofounder of the interwar first Czechoslovak republic, Milan Rastislav Štefánik, and the representative of the national revivalist movement from the nineteenth century, Ľudovít Štúr. In the face of the growing liberal nationalism of the 1990s, however, he spoke from a kind of patriotic position of a historical democrat. According to him: "Nationality − genealogy − identity is important, necessary, what supports and strengthens self-esteem; all the people on the globe do it, but some hide it more, some less. We exist in a physical time-space, a pragmatic reality. If only we were all cosmopolitans, but even then we would all be a bit different … The whole world, all people, have not and will not go beyond their nationality − identity so quickly in

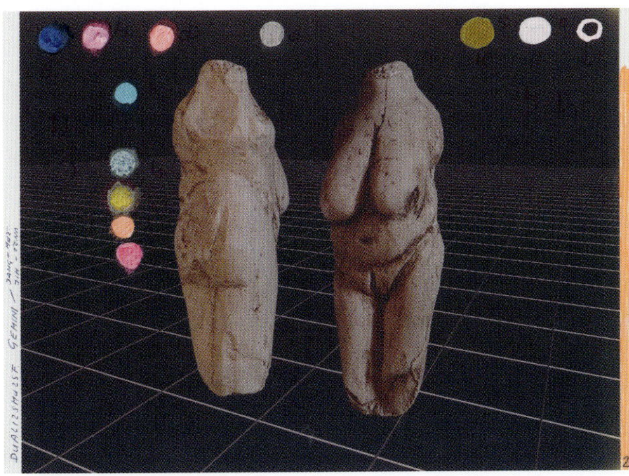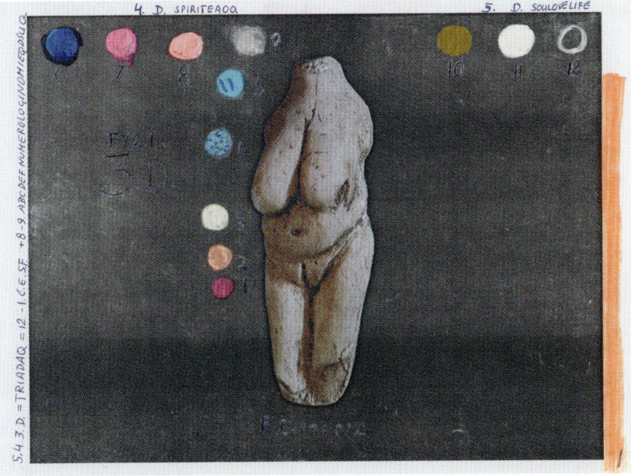

[21-22] Untitled (series subtitled *FEMINISMANSF / FEMINIZMUZSF*), 1990s

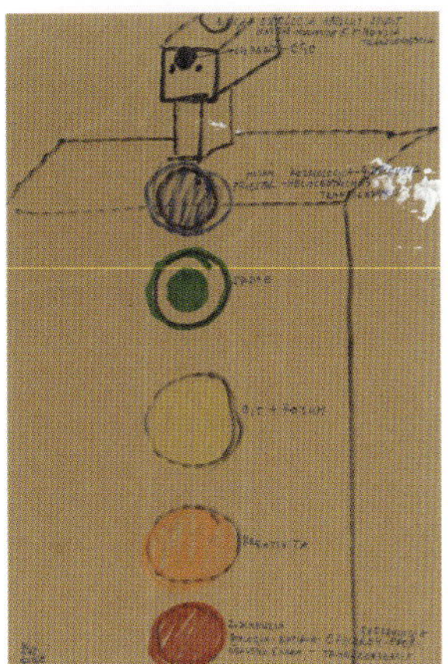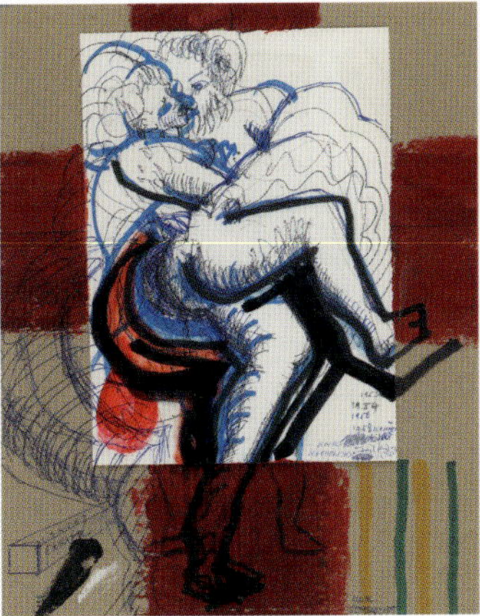

[23] Untitled
(subtitled
*High School of
Art INDUSTRY +
Academy of Fine
Arts - 7 CHAKRAS -
ENERGIES - FILKO
1950-59 / ŠUP +
VŠVU - 7 čakier -
energii - filko
1950-59*), 1992

[24-25] Untitled (subtitled *SLOVAK PALEOLITH -
VENUS - SHEHERAZADE = MORAVANY - PIEŠTANY -
25,000 BC - DISCOVERED 1937 / SLOVAK
PALEOLIT - VENUŠA - ŠEHEREZADA = MORAVANY -
PIEŠTANY - 25.000 B.C. - OBJ. 1937*), 1990s

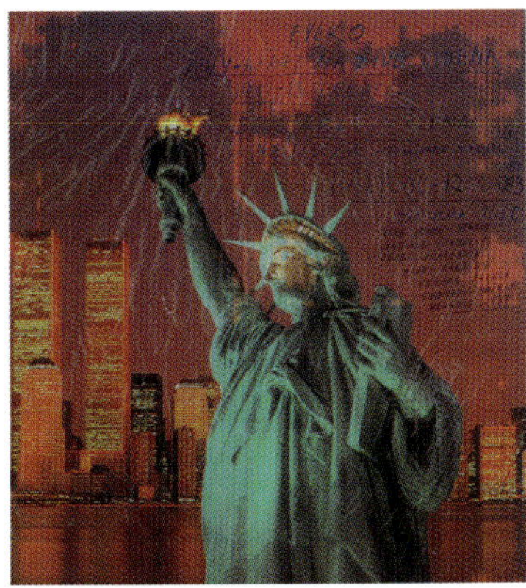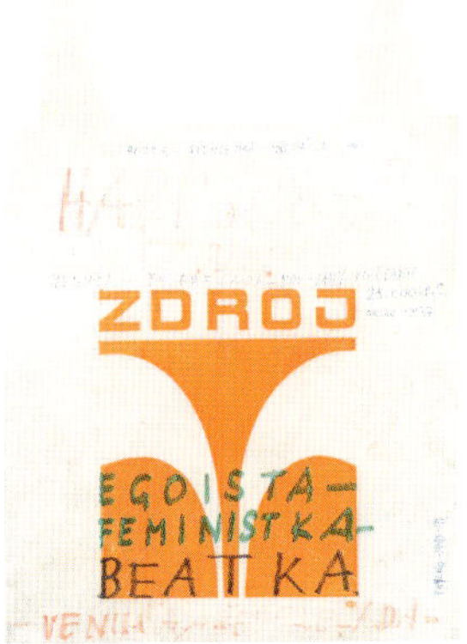

[26] Untitled (subtitled
*FYLKO, FIRST SEEN LIVE
1982-13. DECEMBER,
SHEHERAZADE - WOMAN
VENUS - MEMORY OF
HAPPSOC - 1.-2. 1965-
1983, BRATISLAVA - NYC /
Fyilko, prvý-1.krát na
živo videná 1982-13.
December, Šeherezáda -
Žena Venuša - spomienka
na Happsoc - 1.-2. 1965-
1983, BRATISLAVA - NYC*),
1980s

[27] Untitled
(subtitled *SCOURCE
(company called
Zdroj) - EGOIST -
FEMINIST -
BEATA - VENUS -
SHEHERAZADE /
Zdroj - Egoista -
Feministka -
Beatka - Venuša -
Šeherezáda*), early
1990s

   Genealogie eines modernistischen Essentialismus

this time and space." And he continues more critically: "The uncertainty of the world and of the individual in life is felt as an emptiness, and that is why so many people … substitute it with a father, God, Jesus, or faith in something else. Trust in authority? Thus personal, state, international, national insecurity."[51] Also in several of his statements from the early 1990s, Filko clearly spoke in favor of a local culture and shared national tradition. Besides specific Slovak modernist artists (namely Miloš Bazovský, Ľudovít Fulla, and Mikuláš Galanda) he also referred to folk art.[52]

PHYS POST/ANTE−BIGBANG 2000s

Filko's work moved continuously from the declared solving of "current problems of human society" in the 1960s to a more subjective level of work with myth. He created his terminological "PSYCHOPHILOSOPHICAL SYSTEM," which he structured with verticals of colors and horizontals of dimensions. From the initial three colors that his work contained from the 1960s to the 1980s, he came by continuous structuring to seven colors in the 1990s and, a decade later, to twelve. [15B] This scheme was progressively condensed so that in the last phase, the "Color System" (in Slovak Systém Farieb in initials SF) had twenty or more colors, while the thirteenth to the twentieth colors were specifications of the twelfth, transcendent. They were the content of: "indefinite metaphysical-ontological space" (fifth dimension) − "timespace of the after-life" (fourth dimension) − "timespace of the physical world" (third dimension), with each color extending only to a certain dimension, while each higher dimension contained everything from the previous lower levels.[53] As evidenced by Filko's diagram *Association XVIII. / Asociácie XVIII.* (1968−69) within the wider cycle with the same name, in the 1960s he was following the Aristotelian anthropocentric model of the modern concept of holism. Colors could represent and could even be substituted by the four elements (fire, water, air, earth), which classical philosophy, or also alchemy and the like for example, identified as the basic components of the world; they could be further substituted, for example, by the cardinal directions (east, west, north, south), etc. [32]

Filko's "System" was constructed as a structuralist model of a system of mutual relations, and their dynamics. The structuralist tendencies marginalized under socialism, and their subsequent post-structuralist revival in 1990s Slovakia may have influenced its construction. Filko used it to explain various phenomena, either defined by known systems of knowledge or newly formulated ones. With the help of an eclectic mix of various philosophical, scientific, mystical, and esoteric sources, Filko, who had never learnt English,[54] created his own international newspeak, in which neologisms had their place. Georg Schöllhammer called it a meta-disciplinary language,[55] through which he para-scientifically interpreted his overall concept of the world. He developed its inner dialectics in a binary conceptual logic, for example through "Symmetry" (attributed to 5.D.) versus "Asymmetry" (4.D.), "Diachrony" versus "Synchrony," or "Altruism" (4.D.) versus "Egoism" (3.D.). [20B] In a modernistic attempt to arrive at some kind of final algorithm ("Singular Truths" against "Pluralistic Relativity") which would explain the endless transformations of life, he pursued a universalistic world-view (see "Absolute Objectivity"). In connection to this, Július

Koller noted Filko's statement related to the transformations of *White Space* from 1978, when Filko testified that he "wants to do such art that represents a substance" that would be timeless in the face of the developmental turns in art history. According to Koller, this "arises from the false basis of some 'art.' and moreover, 'eternal.'" which he considered a "stupid and naive mistake."[56]

In his "System," Filko also developed all the potentialities contained in his previous work. He conceptualized the temporal dimension, and included the cosmological line of his creation to the "POSTBIGBANG" part of his work, in which he dealt with the physical space-time of the third dimension. He schematized it as "Materialization − History − Ratio − Ego." This related to *HAPPSOC* from the 1960s up to Filko's very last works. On the other hand, the "ANTEBIGBANG" part referred to the metaphysical world of the fifth dimension. To this parallel universe, with which our known world of the third dimension is connected by means of the dimension, so-called "Pure Time" (through "Sensuality − Sensibility − Emotion − Spirituality"), he associated works related with *White Space* from the 1970s to the end of his career. As a representation of this dichotomy, he used for example the sign of the cross. The horizontal arm ("IQ = Intellect − Reason") represented the rational level of understanding of the world ("Sensibility"). The vertical arm ("CQ = Feeling − Passion") as the irrational principle ("Sensitivity") runs through all the dimensions up to the transcendent. [16B] This comes out of the formal typology of the original *White Space* system.

As in a sci-fi dialectic, with Filko too, introspection intertwined with retrospection. Within the dynamics of developmental ruptures, it alternated with an intense presence in the current cultural situation. In an attempt to avoid a meaning-reductive reading of his work, he strove to make it difficult to sort it into classic categories, e.g. styles or techniques. His way of extricating himself from normative interpretations led through self-actualizing processes. As a painter trained in the 1950s, when emphasis was on craftsmanship, he had an intensive experimental practice combined with a systematic unlearning of both academic teaching and artistic skill. From avantgarde positions through what Groys has called a reactionary shift toward traditional forms, he arrived at specifically outsider Art Brutist positions at the time when he was systematizing his work into a superior "system of everything." One closely related example of this type of practice is Arthur Bispo do Rosário's way of describing the world. But, at the same time, Filko invented his own classification, as well as methods of making it unclear; through multiple reworking, layering, and antedating, when instead of the date of the physical production, he stated the time of the creation of the idea (or the birth of the concept or the date of its revision), linked to a personal curriculum. Near the end of his life, he was dating his works only by the year of his birth as a medium, 1937.

The neo-avantgarde of the 1960s defined its concept of art in respect to the limits of traditional media, therefore it used complex appropriation to transfer the readymade from real life into the imaginary world of art, in which it had to recontextualize it anew.[57] An elaborate theoretical system was used for this. In the 1990s, after the eclectic phase of the American period of the 1980s, Filko systematized his work. At the same time, he retrospectively included older works into

angespült kam, die nur allzu oft die neue Mystik des Geldverdienens thematisierte, allgemein jedoch darauf abzielte, eine neue Einstellung zu fördern.)

Zur selben Zeit gestaltete Filko auch seine eigene Identität um. Als „HERMAFRODITSF" ging es ihm zunächst um parallele Zeitläufe. [30] Hier motivierte er die Veränderungen seiner künstlerischen Positionen auch mit einem Identitätswandel. So bezogen sich die späteren Konzepte von „POSTBIGBANG" und „ANTEBIGBANG" nicht nur auf die Erschaffung und den Wandel des Lebens bzw. das Leben nach dem Tod, sondern auch auf fiktive Details seiner Inkarnationen als Künstler, darunter die von ihm berichteten klinischen Tode.[46] Wie an zahlreichen Werken und Aufzeichnungen ablesbar, postulierte er mit einem Werk aus den späten 1990er-Jahren gleich mehrere Identitäten, die er als „CLONES: FILKO (1937–1977) – FYLKO (1978–1987) – PHYLKO (1988–1997) – PHYS (1998–2037)",[47] [18] also als Klone seiner selbst bezeichnete. In Erweiterung des Tierkreiszeichens Zwillinge (Gemini) nannte sich der Künstler aber auch „TRIMINI". So gab er an, dreimal geboren worden zu sein, nämlich am 13. Juni 1937 nach einer Bluttransfusion, am 14. Juni 1937 und nochmals am 15. Juni 1937, wie in seinen Urkunden auch, allerdings fälschlicherweise vermerkt worden sein soll. Danach inkarnierte er angeblich sogar noch zweimal. Den ersten klinischen Tod 1945 soll er nach einem Sturz in einen Steinbruch überlebt haben, als er Kühe retten wollte, den zweiten 1952 nach einem Stromschlag in einer Waffenfabrik bei Trenčín.[48] In erhaltenen Manuskripten und auch in seinen *Memories of Clinical Deaths* beschreibt er diese Erlebnisse beinahe im Stile Rudolf Steiners.[49]

Nach der Wende und seiner Rückkehr in die Slowakei im Jahr 1990 eignete sich Filko auch die nationalistischen Narrative der neuen Identitätspolitik an, die in den kulturell konservativen postkommunistischen Ländern neben der Erinnerungspolitik die 1990er-Jahre beherrschten. Er begann also, sein Werk konzeptionell nach der Farbtriade der tschechoslowakischen Fahne und, nach der Teilung des Landes im Jahr 1992, nach der slowakischen Flagge zu ordnen. Auf der Einladung zu seiner offenbar ersten Ausstellung in Bratislava nach der Rückkehr aus der Emigration hieß es: „Die Identität meiner Arbeit ist konzeptuell: Sie folgt drei Richtungen oder Wegen gleicher Energie wie die slowakische Flagge: Biologie/Rot, Kosmologie/Blau, Ontologie/Weiß. Diese Dreiteilung ist international und kosmologisch zugleich".[50] [31]

Im Hinblick auf die jahrzehntelange Debatte über die asymmetrische Beziehung von Tschech*innen und Slowak*innen verwendete Filko in seinen Werken nun nicht mehr den Namen Tschechoslowakei (Československo), sondern *Slovakočesko* (Slowakisch-Böhmen). Weiters deutete er seinen Vornamen Stanislav als „SUBJEKT – SLÁVA – SLOVÁK – SLAVIAN – SVET – SLOBODA" (Subjekt – Glorie – Slowakisch – Slawisch – Welt – Freiheit). Zudem verwies er auf politische Persönlichkeiten, die historisch die Herausbildung der nationalen Identität geprägt hatten, so auf den Reformsozialisten der 1960er-Jahre Alexander Dubček, den Mitbegründer der ersten tschechoslowakischen Republik in der Zwischenkriegszeit Milan Rastislav Štefánik oder den Vertreter der nationalen Erweckungsbewegung im 19. Jahrhundert Ľudovít Štúr. Über den aufkommenden liberalen Nationalismus der 1990er-Jahre sprach Filko indessen aus einer Art patriotischen Haltung als historischer Demokrat. In seinen Worten klang das so: „Nationalität – Genealogie – Identität

sind wichtig, notwendig, sie stützen und stärken das Selbstwertgefühl; alle Menschen weltweit haben sie, doch manche verbergen sie mehr, manche weniger. Wir leben in einem physischen Zeit-Raum, einer pragmatischen Realität. Selbst wenn wir alle Kosmopoliten wären, so unterschieden wir uns doch alle ein wenig… In unserer Zeit und unserem Raum wird die ganze Welt, werden alle Völker nicht so bald über ihre Nationalidentität hinwegkommen." Etwas kritischer fährt er fort: „Die Ungewissheit der Welt und des Einzelnen in seinem Leben wird als Leere empfunden, die so viele Menschen […] mit einem Vater, Gott, Jesus oder dem Glauben an etwas anderes füllen. Sollen sie auf Autoritäten vertrauen? Folglich persönliche, staatliche, internationale, nationale Unsicherheit…"[51] In den frühen 1990er-Jahren sprach sich Filko mehrmals klar für die lokale Kultur und eine gemeinsame nationale Tradition aus. Neben einigen anderen modernen Künstlern (namentlich Miloš Bazovský, Ľudovít Fulla und Mikuláš Galanda) bezog er sich dabei auch auf die slowakische Folklore.[52]

PHYS POST/ANTE–BIGBANG 2000s

Filkos Werk bewegte sich kontinuierlich weg von der expliziten Lösung „aktueller Probleme der menschlichen Gesellschaft" in den 1960er-Jahren und hin zu einer subjektiveren Arbeit am Mythos. So schuf er ein terminologisches „PSYCHOPHILOSOPHISCHES SYSTEM", das er vertikal nach Farben und horizontal nach Dimensionen ordnete. Von den anfänglichen drei Farben, die sein Werk von den 1960er- bis in die 1980er-Jahre auszeichneten, kam er in den 1990er-Jahren durch Ausdifferenzierung auf sieben, und zehn Jahre später schließlich auf zwölf Farben. [15B] Dieses Schema verdichtete Filko nach und nach, so dass sein „Farbsystem" (Systém Farieb oder abgekürzt SF) in der letzten Phase zwanzig oder mehr Farben umfasste, wobei die dreizehnte bis zwanzigste Farbe die zwölfte – Transzendenz – weiter unterteilte. Ihre Bedeutung reichte von „unbestimmter metaphysischontologischer Raum" (5. Dimension), über „Zeitraum des Jenseits" (4. Dimension) bis zum „Zeitraum der physischen Welt" (3. Dimension), wobei sich jede Farbe nur auf eine dieser Dimensionen bezieht, und jede höhere Dimension alle niedrigeren enthält.[53] Wie aus dem Diagramm *Association XVIII. / Asociácie XVIII.* (1968/69) im gleichnamigen Zyklus ablesbar ist, folgte Filko in den 1960er-Jahren dem anthropozentrischen Modell des Aristoteles, das für ihn zur Grundlage eines modernen Holismusbegriffs wurde. Die Farben konnten die vier Elemente (Feuer, Wasser, Luft, Erde), die in der klassischen Philosophie, aber auch in der Alchemie und ähnlichem als die Grundbestandteile der Welt angesehen wurden, darstellen und sogar durch sie ersetzt werden. Zudem konnten sie zum Beispiel mit den Himmelsrichtungen (Ost, West, Nord, Süd) ausgetauscht werden. [32]

Filko baute sein „System" als strukturalistisches Modell gegenseitiger Beziehungen und ihrer Dynamik auf. Auch die im Kommunismus an den Rand gedrängten strukturalistischen Tendenzen und anschließend das post-strukturalistische Revival in der Slowakei der 1990er-Jahre könnten seinen Aufbau beeinflusst haben. Filko nutzte sein System, um Phänomene zu erklären, die entweder durch schon bekanntes Wissen abgesteckt oder von ihm neu formuliert wurden. Durch eine eklektische Mischung aus diversen philosophischen, wissenschaftlichen, mystischen und esoterischen Quellen

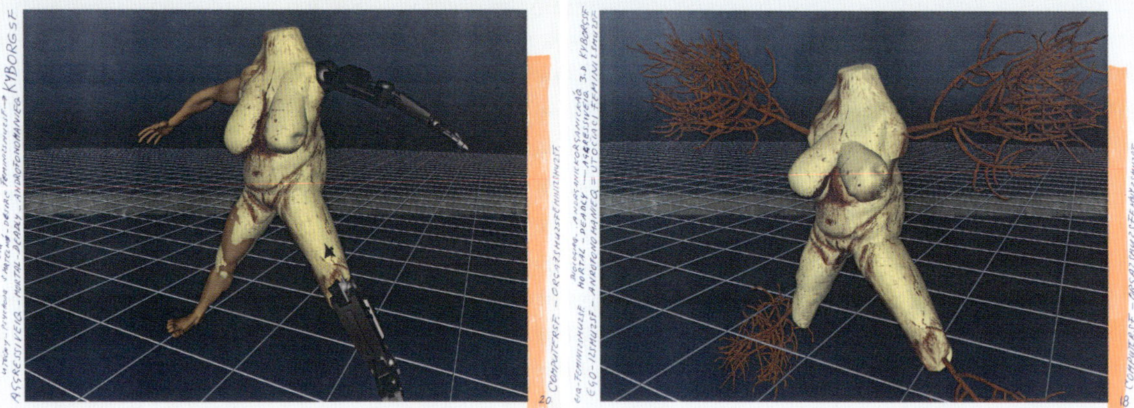

[28–29] Untitled (series subtitled *FEMINISMANSF / FEMINIZMUZSF*), 1990s

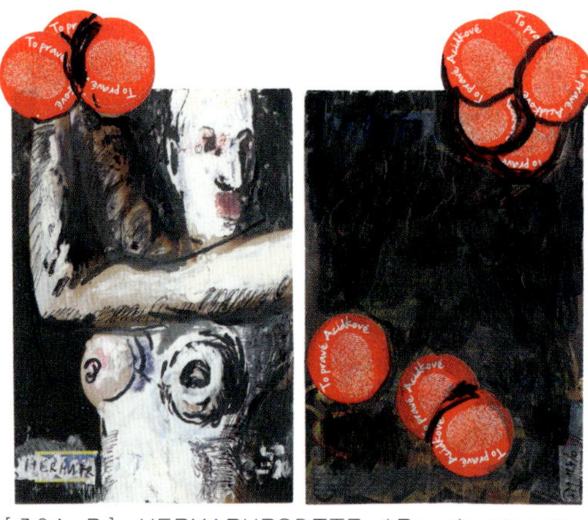

[30A–B] *HERMAPHRODITE* (Projectart *The Real Acidko*) / *HERMAFRODIT* (Projektart *To pravé acidkové*), after 2006

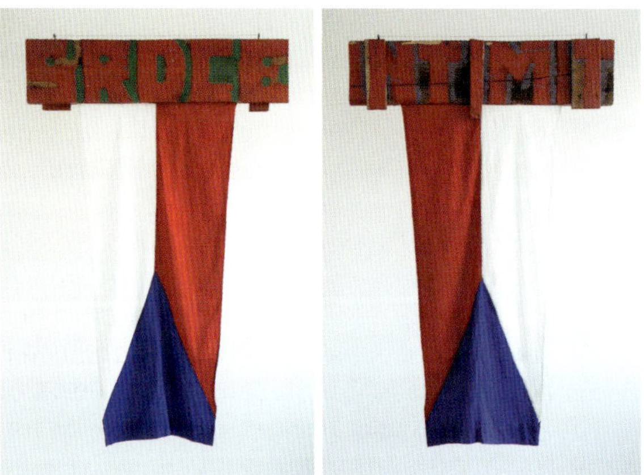

[31A–B] From the series *Heart/ Intimacy* / *Zo série Srdce/Intimita*, 1995

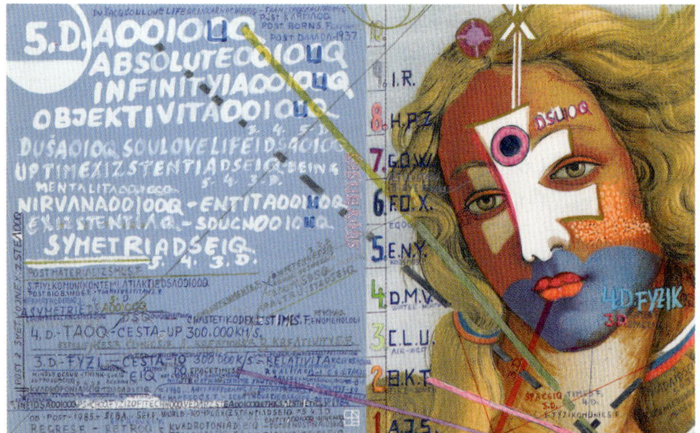

[32] Untitled (Projectart *Renaissance masters*), after 2005

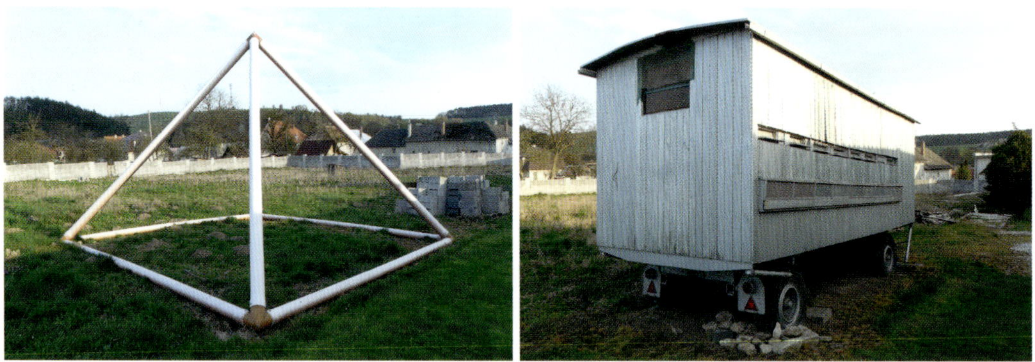

[33–34] View of Stano Filko's studio environment in Veľká Hradná, 2011

schuf Filko, der nie Englisch lernte,[54] damit sein eigenes internationales Neusprech, in dem auch Neologismen ihren Platz fanden. Georg Schöllhammer nannte diese Kunstsprache, mit der Filko die gesamte Welt parawissenschaftlich deutete, metadisziplinär.[55] Die innere Dialektik des Systems entwickelte er gemäß einer Logik begrifflicher Gegenpole, zum Beispiel „Symmetrie" (5.D. zugeordnet) versus „Asymmetrie" (4.D.), „Diachronie" versus „Synchronie" oder „Altruismus" (4.D.) versus „Egoismus" (3.D.). [20B] Sein modernistisch angelegter Versuch, so etwas wie einen endgültigen Algorithmus (mit „einer Wahrheit" statt „pluralistischer Relativität") zu finden, der die endlosen Veränderungen des Lebens erklären sollte, fußte auf einer universalistischen Weltsicht („absolute Objektivität"). In diesem Zusammenhang verwies Koller auf Filkos Auskunft über die Transformationen seines *White Space* aus dem Jahr 1978, er wolle „Kunst machen, die eine Substanz darstellt" und damit angesichts der kunsthistorischen Entwicklungen zeitlos sei. Dies, kommentierte Koller, „kam von der falschen Grundannahme einer ‚Kunst', noch dazu einer ‚ewigen'", was er für einen „idiotischen und naiven Fehler" hielt.[56]

Filko bildete in seinem „System" auch sämtliche Möglichkeiten ab, die in seinem früheren Werk angelegt waren. Bei der Konzeption seiner Zeitdimension bezog er die kosmologische Schöpfungslinie in den „POSTBIGBANG"-Teil seines Œuvres ein, in dem er sich mit der physikalischen Raumzeit der 3. Dimension befasste. Sein Zeitschema lautete nunmehr „Materialisierung – Geschichte – Ratio – Ego". Damit umfasste er nun alles von *HAPPSOC* aus den 1960er-Jahren bis hin zu den neuesten Werken. Der „ANTEBIGBANG"-Teil hingegen galt der metaphysischen Welt der 5. Dimension. Zu diesem Paralleluniversum – in dem unsere gewöhnliche dreidimensionale Welt mit der Dimension der so genannten „reinen Zeit" (durch „Sinnlichkeit – Auffassung – Gefühl – Spiritualität") verbunden ist – gehörten alle Arbeiten im Zusammenhang mit dem *White Space* von den 1970er-Jahren bis zu Filkos Lebensende. Zur Darstellung dieser Dichotomie verwendete er zum Beispiel das Kreuzzeichen, dessen waagrechter Balken („IQ = Intellekt – Vernunft") für die rationale Ebene des Weltverständnisses („Sensibility") und dessen vertikaler Balken („CQ = Gefühl – Leidenschaft") für das irrationale Prinzip („Sensitivity") stand. [16B] Dieser Gegensatz zieht sich durch alle Dimensionen bis hin zum Transzendenten, wie aus der formalen Typologie des ursprünglichen Systems des *White Space* hervorgeht.

Wie bei der Dialektik von Science-Fiction mischte sich auch bei Filko Innenschau mit Rückschau. Durch die Dynamik der Brüche in der äußeren Entwicklung alternierten beide jedoch mit einer intensiven Präsenz in der aktuellen Kulturöffentlichkeit. Um eine reduktionistische Deutung seines Werks zu verhindern, versuchte Filko, die Einordnung seiner Kunst in klassische Kategorien, zum Beispiel nach Stil oder Technik, zu erschweren. Sein Versuch, sich normativen Interpretationen zu entziehen, führte über die Selbstverwirklichung. Als Maler, der in den 1950er-Jahren ausgebildet wurde, als noch das Handwerkliche im Vordergrund stand, entwickelte er eine dichte experimentelle Praxis, die mit dem systematischen Verlernen sowohl der akademischen Lehre als auch des künstlerischen Könnens verbunden war. Von einer ursprünglich avantgardistischen Position gelangte er über etwas, das Groys später als reaktionäre Hinwendung zu traditionellen Formen

bezeichnete, letztlich zu einer ganz eigenen außerkünstlerischen, brutistischen Position, aus der heraus er sein Werk zu einem übergeordneten „System von allem" systematisierte. (Ein eng verwandtes Beispiel für eine Kunst dieses Typs wäre Arthur Bispo do Rosários Weltbeschreibung.) Gleichzeitig jedoch erfand Filko eine eigene Klassifikation sowie Methoden, diese zu verunklaren. Dazu gehörten die mehrfache Neubearbeitung von Werken, die Übereinanderschichtung oder die Vordatierung, wenn er statt des Datums der eigentlichen Fertigstellung den Zeitpunkt der Ideenfindung (oder der Geburt des Konzepts oder der Überarbeitung) angab und die Kunst damit mit dem persönlichen Lebenslauf kurzschloss. Gegen Ende seines Lebens datierte er seine Werke überhaupt nur noch mit dem Jahr seiner Geburt, nämlich 1937.

Die Neo-Avantgarde der 1960er-Jahre definierte ihren Kunstbegriff im Bezug auf die Grenzen der traditionellen Medien. So eignete sie sich auf komplexe Weise Alltagsgegenstände an, um sie in der imaginäre Welt der Kunst zum Readymade zu erheben, das dort neu kontextualisiert werden musste.[57] Dazu entwickelte sie ein vertracktes theoretisches System. In den 1990er-Jahren, also nach seiner eklektischen Phase in den USA, systematisierte auch Filko sein Werk und bezog dabei ältere Arbeiten rückwirkend in jede Neuerung in seinem Systems mit ein. Man könnte sagen, dass *Dwelling 1966 of Contemporaneity – Reality*, das seinen künstlerischen Erfolg in den 1960er-Jahren beflügelt hatte, in diesem Sinn sein Werk prägte, wenngleich die nachfolgende politische Situation ihm stark zu schaffen machte. Die ikonografischen und auch semiotischen Prinzipien, die er dort zur Anwendung brachte, übernahm er jedenfalls in die kommenden Jahrzehnte. Immer wieder thematisierte Filko Konsumwahn und Überfluss, die er sexualisiert als Raffgier und Oberflächlichkeit darstellte und die im Gegensatz zur Spiritualität seiner Farben Gold und Weiß standen. In diesem Sinne standen seine Raketen und Bomben aus der zweiten Hälfte der 1980er-Jahre, die rosa und in den Farben der Chakren bemalt waren, mit den Gasmasken zwanzig Jahre zuvor in Verbindung usw.

Ausgehend von seiner Privatmythologie schuf sich Filko eine ganz eigenständige Ikonographie. Auf ihrer Grundlage verwendete er wiederholt spezifische Elemente wie Spiegel, Globen, Pyramiden, Radios, Fernseher oder mit dem klinischen Tod verbundene Elemente wie Bomben, Leitern, Raketenmodelle, einen Tunnel in eine andere Dimension oder Ventilatoren, deren Deutungen er von den späten 1960er-Jahren an immer weiter entwickelte. So begriff er diese Ventilatoren später als Zeitportale und nicht mehr bloß als Windmaschinen. Auch Verweise auf das ländliche Umfeld, aus dem Filko stammte, sind sehr häufig. In der letzten Phase seines Schaffens bezog der Künstler praktisch alles aus seinem Alltag in seine Werke ein – Medikamentenschachteln oder auch einen probiotischen Joghurt der Marke Acidko, den er gerade verspeist hatte. Dabei verwendete nicht nur konkrete Gegenstände, sondern wählte aufgrund ihrer numerologischen Geheimbedeutungen[58] auch Zahlen aus und integrierte sie in sein Werk.

Filkos legendäres Atelier in der Snežienková-Straße unterhalb des modernistischen Fernsehturms auf dem Kamzík-Hügel bei Bratislava war ursprünglich ein Gartenhäuschen, das er ab den 1990er-Jahren allseitig erweiterte. So nahm es nach und nach die Form eines Gesamtkunstwerks an, das er mit neuen und archivierten Sammlungsobjekten sowie deren

   Mira Keratová   Genealogie eines modernistischen Essentialismus

each new update of his system. It could be said that in a sense *Dwelling 1966 of Contemporaneity – Reality*, which spurred his huge artistic success in the 1960s, was a defining work for him, although the subsequent political situation took a toll on him. He carried over the iconographic and also semiotic principles that he used there to the following decades. He constantly thematized over-consumption and over-indulgence, which was depicted in a sexualized position as greed and shallowness, in contrast to the spirituality of gold and white colors. In this sense, his rockets and bombs from the second half of the 1980s, painted pink and in the colors of the chakras, were linked with gas masks from twenty years before, and so on.

With reference to his personal mythology, Filko created a unique iconography for himself. On its basis, he took the repetition of specific elements such as mirrors, globes, pyramids, radios, televisions, and elements from clinical deaths such as bombs, ladders, rocket models, or tunnels to another dimension, or, to give another example, he later staged blowing ventilators, whose interpretations had been evolving since the late 1960s, like fans as time portals rather than as wind machines. He also made continuous references to the rural environment he came from. In the concluding phase of his work, he included practically anything from his everyday life into his works, the packaging of the medicines he used, or a probiotic yoghurt called Acidko that he was eating. He used not only concrete objects, but even selected numbers for their hidden meanings,[58] since he took an interest in numerological concepts and also integrated them into his work.

The legendary studio on Snežienková street beneath the modernist Kamzík TV tower was originally a garden cottage that since the 1990s Filko had been constantly expanding in all directions. It took on the form of a total installation in which he constantly recomposed current and cumulatively archived historical objects and their documentation. He introduced his tours by saying that it was not just a studio where (contemporary) art was created, but also a depository of historical works.[59] The environment was reminiscent of everything possible, including the synesthetic exhibitions of Paul Thek, Kurt Schwitters's *Merzbau*, and even the *Junkspace* of Rem Koolhaas; the developmentally non-linear and associatively ordered collection of works followed the Aby Warburg imaginative model by marking the works and sorting them into the color spaces according to a "Psychophilosophical System." In its systemization, Filko achieved a kind of New Ageist obscurity of a cabinet of curiosities. Its conception corresponded with the character of his creation, in which each single work is part of a single lifelong work. At the same time, each work is equipped with a specific predisposition, which allows the determination of its intended placement within the whole.

In 2005 in his native village of Veľká Hradná near Trenčín, Filko began to realize his monumental complex *Ark / Archa*. He built its premises around his grandparents' farmhouse; his grandfather, to whom he referred several times, was a particularly influential figure for him. The conception of a sort of *Gesamtkunstwerk*, with the thoughtful placement of selected elements (pyramid, beehive, and others), was to define Filko's personal and at the same time cosmic dialectic. [33–34] *Ark* was to absorb all his works on the level

of an archive, workshop, laboratory, and institute. Here he also planned to concentrate works that he had been storing from the mid-1960s (partly still in time layers) in the Bratislava studio on Snežienková. After his death, already after his works were moved to Veľká Hradná in his last years, they were taken away by the family. The original *Ark* project, which was supposed to be a guide for the interpretation of Filko's works, as well as a tool for maintaining control over their interpretation, or a spatial catalog raisonné, thus ultimately remained an unrealized "Prospect-art," [32] open to multiple perspectives of reading and vulnerable to the polysemantic nature of interpretation.

HARD–POST–MODERN ± HARD–POST–AVANTGARDE

1   During the reform years in the 1960s, the generation of Slovak authors who lived in centralized Czechoslovakia, outside the center of Prague and who were referred to as "l'école de Bratislava," enjoyed unprecedented international success unlike anything before or after.
2   Filko's participation in the Conceptual Art exhibition *Plans and Projects as Art* (Pläne und Projekte als Kunst) at Kunsthalle Bern in 1969, and the publication and exhibition *Global Conceptualism: Points of Origin, 1950s–1980s* at Queens Museum of Art in New York in 1999. Tomáš Pospiszyl for example states that the work of Stano Filko (and also Július Koller) "contained within itself elements that we do not usually associate with Conceptual Art. Both their approaches and results insist that only through an irrational perception of the world can we achieve new knowledge and experiences." Tomáš Pospiszyl, *Asociativní dějepis umění* (Associative Art History), ed. tranzit.cz (Prague, 2014), p. 84.
3   Filko's assemblages, such as *Grandpa – Grandma Are Listening to the Radio / Dedko – babka počúvajú rádio* (1965) are related with conceptual objects of a rediscovered Marcel Duchamp in the 1960s, but can also be associated, for example, with the surrealist *Poème-Objet* (1930s) of André Breton or *Spirit of Our Age: Mechanical Head* (1919) by Raoul Hausmann. The period critic Jiří Padrta, in connection with Filko's "profane altars-fetishes," spoke of a legacy of Surrealism rather than Dadaism, since, according to him, their intention is "the apotheosis of banality that wants to become a new ritual, legible in very demonstrative, purposefully trivial and provocative symbols." Jiří Padrta, "Stano Filko," in *Výtvarná práce* 5 (Art Work) (1967), p. 5.
4   Ibid.
5   Tomáš Štraus, "Filkovo slovo k architektúre" (Filko's Word on Architecture), in *Výtvarná práce* 16 (Art Work) (1967).
6   Pierre Restany, "Architect of Information," in *Stano FILKO II. 1965/69. Tvorba / Works – Creation / Werk – Schaffung / Ouvrages*, ed. Stano Filko (Bratislava, 1970), n. p.
7   Linda Nochlin, "Why Have There Been No Great Women Artists?" in *ARTnews* (1971).
8   Restany, "Architect of Information" (see note 6).
9   From the exhibition also came the now lost film recording *Dwelling 1966 of Contemporaneity – Reality / Obydlie 1966 súčasnosti – skutočnosti* (B/W film, approx. 10 min., 1967) by the authors Tibor Borský and Dušan Trančík, as states Lucia Gregorová Stach, "Filkova mladá tvorba" (Filko's Young Work). *Stano Filko 1*, eds. Lucia Gregorová Stach and Aurel Hrabušický, exh. cat. Slovak National Gallery (Slovenská národná galéria) (Bratislava, 2018), p. 25.
10   The concept of the so-called living sculpture was further developed by Filko not only as part of mirror images of his performative environments but also through elaborated figurative staffages in collages, connected for example with *Monuments of Contemporary Space / Pomníky súčasného priestoru* or *Monuments of Contemporary Civilization / Pomníky súčasnej civilizácie*, or *Statues of XX. Century / Sochy XX. storočia*, etc., some of which were included in the well-known album *Associations / Asociácie* (1967–70).
11   Štraus, "Filkovo slovo k architektúre" (Filko's Word on Architecture) (see note 5).
12   Laura Mulvey, "Visual Pleasure and Narrative Cinema" (1975), in *Feminism and Film Theory*, ed. Constance Penley (New York and London, 1988), pp. 57–68.
13   Ibid.
14   Much later in 2008, Filko exhibited the series of *Altars of Contemporaneity / Oltáre súčasnosti* (1963–66) at the Bratislava City Gallery (Galéria mesta Bratislavy) as part of the exhibition *Filko's Ark and Altars of Contemporaneity* (Filkova archa a oltáre súčasnosti). As a self-historicizing reference, he related them directly to the Old Testament prophetic texts about Noah's Ark. The exhibition's curator, Ivan Jančár, stated in the catalog that the connection with this particular biblical theme came out of Filko's conversations with his grandfather during his childhood.
15   In an international context, the format of the environment was popularized e.g. by documenta 4, 1968.
16   Juraj Fuchs, "Na výstavu svetového umenia v Ósake. Dielo Stanislava Filku" (At the World Art Symposium in Osaka. Work by Stanislav Filko), in *Práca* (January 31, 1970).
17   "Filko – tvorba 1963–66" (Filko – Work 1963–66), in *Smena* (February 4, 1967).
18   Boris Groys, "Das Kunstwerk als nichtfunktionelle Maschine" (The Work of Art as Non-functioning Machine), in *Vladimir Tatlin. Leben, Werk, Wirkung. Ein internationales Symposium* (Vladimir Tatlin. Life, Work, Impact. An International Symposium), ed. Jürgen Harten (Cologne, 1993).
19   *O nepredmetnom svete/Kazimír S. Malevič* (On a Non-Objective World/Kazimir S. Malevich), ed. Oskar Čepan (Bratislava, 1968); and Čepan's book *Tatlinova iniciatíva* (Tatlin's Initiative) of 1971; a publication whose printing was stopped and banned in the so-called normalization era; and the publications of Jiří Padrta in the magazines *Výtvarné umění* (Fine Arts) and *Výtvarná práce* (Art Work) in the 1960s. Padrta's estate later published his manuscript from that period *Kazimír Malevič a suprematismus* (Kazimir Malevich and Suprematism) (Prague, 1996).
20   According to Edit András, for example, the lack of criticism of modernism in Hungary was related to the fact that it played a significant opposition role against official culture. Edit András, "Transgressing Boundaries (Even Those Marked Out by the Predecessors) in New Genre Conceptual Art," in *Art After Conceptual Art*, eds. Alexander Alberro and Sabeth Buchmann (Vienna, 2006), p. 166.

Dokumentationen laufend umarrangierte. Seine Atelierbesucher*innen instruierte er immer, dass es sich nicht nur um ein Atelier handle, in dem (zeitgenössische) Kunst geschaffen werde, sondern auch um ein Depot für historische Werke.[59] Das Haus erinnerte an alles mögliche – an die synästhetischen Ausstellungen Paul Theks, den *Merzbau* von Kurt Schwitters oder auch den *Junkspace* von Rem Koolhaas. Die nicht chronologisch, sondern nach einem „Psychophilosophischen System" assoziativ geordnete Werksammlung wiederum folgte eher dem Ideenmodell Aby Warburgs. So markierte er die Objekte und sortierte sie nach einem System in die jeweiligen Farbräume ein. Mit seiner Systematisierung erreichte Filko indes die Obskurität eines Kuriositätenkabinetts im New-Age-Stil. Diese Konzeption entsprach indes dem Charakter seines Œuvres, in dem jedes einzelne Werk Teil des Lebenswerkes wurde. Zugleich war jedes Werk auch mit einer spezifischen Prädisposition ausgestattet, die es dem Künstler erlaubte, ihm seinen Platz im Ganzen zuzuweisen.

2005 begann Filko in seinem Heimatdorf Veľká Hradná bei Trenčín mit der Realisierung seines monumentalen Komplexes *Archa* (Arche), den er um das Bauernhaus seiner Großeltern herum geplant hatte. Besonders sein Großvater, auf den er sich mehrfach berief, war für ihn eine prägende Figur gewesen. Die Konzeption dieses Gesamtkunstwerks mit der durchdachten Platzierung ausgewählter Elemente (Pyramide, Bienenstock und andere) sollte Filkos private und zugleich kosmische Dialektik endgültig verkörpern. [33-34] In *Archa* wollte er alle seine Arbeiten zu einem Archiv, einer Werkstatt, einem Labor und einem Institut zusammenführen. Hierhin wollte er auch jene Werke transferieren, die er seit Mitte der 1960er-Jahre (zum Teil immer noch wie in Zeitschichten) in seinem Atelier in der Snežienková-Straße aufbewahrte. Nach Filkos Tod und dem Transfer seiner Werke nach Veľká Hradná wurden sie von der Familie mitgenommen. Das ursprüngliche *Archa*-Projekt, das gleichzeitig ein Leitfaden zur Deutung der Werke Filkos und ein Instrument zur Beibehaltung der Kontrolle über diese Deutung und ein räumliches Werkverzeichnis werden sollte, blieb somit letztlich unrealisierte „Prospect-Art" [32] und als solche offen für alle Lesarten sowie die polysemantische Natur der Interpretation.

HARD–POST–MODERN ± HARD–POST–AVANTGARDE

1   Die Generation slowakischer Künstler*innen, die in der zentralisierten Tschechoslowakei außerhalb des Zentrums von Prag lebte und als „l'école de Bratislava" bekannt wurde, feierte in den 1960er-Jahren einen beispiellosen internationalen Erfolg, der weder in der vorangegangenen noch in der nachfolgenden Ära erreicht wurde.

2   Man denke an Filkos Teilnahme an der Konzeptkunst-Ausstellung *Pläne und Projekte als Kunst* 1969 in der Kunsthalle Bern oder an die Publikation und Ausstellung *Global Conceptualism: Points of Origin, 1950s–1980s* im Queens Museum of Art in New York 1999. Tomáš Pospiszyl zum Beispiel hielt fest, dass das Werk von Stano Filko (aber auch von Július Koller) „Elemente enthält, die wir normalerweise nicht mit Konzeptkunst verbinden. Beide beharren in ihrer Einstellung und ihren Werken darauf, dass wir nur durch die irrationale Wahrnehmung der Welt zu neuen Erkenntnissen und Erlebnissen gelangen können". Tomáš Pospiszyl, *Asociativní dějepis umění* (Assoziative Kunstgeschichte), tranzit.cz, Prag 2014, S. 84.

3   Filkos Assemblagen wie *Grandpa – Grandma Are Listening to the Radio / Dedko – babka počúvajú rádio* (1965) sind in der Tat mit den konzeptuellen Objekten des in den 1960er-Jahren wiederentdeckten Marcel Duchamp verwandt, lassen sich aber auch beispielsweise mit dem surrealistischen *Poème-Objet* von André Breton (1930er-Jahre) oder mit *Spirit of Our Age: Mechanical Head* (1919) von Raoul Hausmann in Verbindung bringen. Der Kritiker Jiří Padrta stellte zu jener Zeit Filkos „profane Altar-Fetische" eher in die Tradition des Surrealismus als des Dadaismus, denn ihm zufolge war Filkos Absicht „die Apotheose der Banalität, die zu einem neuen Ritual werden soll, das sich in sehr demonstrativen, absichtlich trivialen und provokanten Symbolen ausformt". Jiří Padrta, „Stano Filko", in: *Výtvarná práce* (Kunstwerk), 5, 1967, S. 5.

4   Ebd.

5   Tomáš Štraus, „Filkovo slovo k architektúre" (Filkos Wort zur Architektur), in: *Výtvarná práce* (Art Work), 15/16, 1967.

6   Pierre Restany, „Architect of Information", in: *Stano FILKO II. 1965/69. Tvorba / Works – Creation / Werk – Schaffung / Ouvrages*, hrsg. von Stano Filko, Bratislava 1970, o. S.

7   Linda Nochlin, „Why Have There Been No Great Women Artists?", in: *ARTnews*, 1971.

8   Restany 1970 (wie Anm. 6).

9   Von der Ausstellung stammt auch die heute verschollene Filmaufnahme *Dwelling 1966 of Contemporaneity – Reality / Obydlie 1966 súčasnosti – skutočnosti* (S/W-Film, ca. 10 Min., 1967) von Tibor Borský, Dušan Trančík, schreibt Lucia Gregorová Stach in *Filko's Young Work. Stano Filko 1*, hrsg. von Lucia Gregorová Stach und Aurel Hrabušický, Ausst.-Kat. Slovak National Gallery (Slovenská národná galéria), Bratislava 2018, S. 25.

10   Das Konzept der sogenannten lebenden Skulptur wurde von Filko nicht nur im Rahmen der Spiegelbilder in seinen performativen Environments weiterentwickelt, sondern auch durch aufwändige figurative Collagen, zum Beispiel bei den *Monuments of Contemporary Space / Pomníky súčasného priestoru*, den *Monuments of Contemporary Civilization / Pomníky súčasnej civilizácie* oder *Statues of XX. Century / Sochy XX. storočia* usw., von denen er einige in den bekannte Zyklus *Associations / Asociácie* (1967–1970) aufnahm.

11   Štraus 1967 (wie Anm. 5).

12   Laura Mulvey, „Visual Pleasure and Narrative Cinema" (1975), in: *Feminism and Film Theory*, hrsg. von Constance Penley, New York/London 1988, S. 57–68.

13   Ebd.

14   Erst viel später, nämlich 2008, stellte Filko in der Städtischen Galerie Bratislava (Galéria mesta Bratislavy) die Serie *Altars of Contemporaneity / Oltáre súčasnosti* (1963–1966) im Rahmen der Ausstellung *Filkova archa a oltáre súčasnosti* (Filko's Ark und *Altars of Contemporaneity*) aus. Selbsthistorisierend stellte er sie gleich in eine Linie zur alttestamentarischen Arche Noah. Der Kurator der Ausstellung Ivan Jančár erläuterte dazu im Katalog, dass die Verbindung zu diesem biblischen Thema von Gesprächen Filkos mit seinem Großvater während der Kindheit rührte.

15   International wurde das Environment z. B. durch die documenta 4 (1968) populär.

16   Juraj Fuchs, „Na výstavu svetového umenia v Ósake. Dielo Stanislava Filku" (Auf dem Weltkunstsymposium in Osaka. Werke von Stanislav Filko), in: *Práca*, 31. Januar 1970.

17   „Filko – tvorba 1963–66" (Filko – Arbeiten 1963–66), in: *Smena*, 4. Februar, 1967.

18   Boris Groys, „Das Kunstwerk als nichtfunktionelle Maschine", in: *Vladimir Tatlin. Leben, Werk, Wirkung. Ein internationales Symposium*, hrsg. von Jürgen Harten, Köln 1993.

19   *O nepredmetnom svete/Kazimir S. Malevič* (Über eine nicht-objektive Welt/Kasimir S. Malewitsch), hrsg von Oskar Čepan, Bratislava 1968; und auch Čepans Buch *Tatlinova iniciatíva* (Tatlins Initiative) aus dem Jahr 1971, dessen Druck in der sogenannten Normalisierungszeit eingestellt und verboten wurde; vgl. weiters die Veröffentlichungen von Jiří Padrta in den Zeitschriften *Výtvarné umění* (Schöne Künste) und *Výtvarná práce* (Kunstwerk) aus den 1960er-Jahren. Aus Padrtas Nachlass erschien ein Manuskript aus derselben Zeit mit dem Titel *Kazimír Malevič a suprematismus* (Kasimir Malewitsch und der Suprematismus), Prag 1996.

20   Laut Edit András hing die mangelnde Kritik an der Moderne in Ungarn beispielsweise damit zusammen, dass letztere eine so bedeutende Oppositionsrolle gegenüber der offiziellen Kultur spielte. Edit András, „Transgressing Boundaries (Even Those Marked Out by the Predecessors)", in: *Art After Conceptual Art*, hrsg. von Alexander Alberro und Sabeth Buchmann, Wien 2006, S. 166.

21   Filkos Lieblingsausdruck dafür war „uptime", eine ungenaue englische Übersetzung des von ihm verwendeten slowakischen Begriffs „nadčas" (Überzeit) oder „nadčasovost" (Überzeitlichkeit) im Gegensatz zu Zeitlichkeit. In diesem Sinne lautete der Titel seiner retrospektiven Ausstellung bei den Tranzit-Workshops in Bratislava *UP 300000 km/s* (2005).

22   Aurel Hrabušický verweist neben mehreren anderen Zeitzeug*innen immer wieder auf Kollers Ablehnung des Manifests *White Immaterial Space in a Pure White Infinite Space / Biely nehmotný priestor v čistom bielom nekonečno priestore* (1973/74), in dem Filko wiederholt von „reiner Kunst" als sogenannte Sensibilität spricht. Laut Hrabušický bezeichnete Koller dieses Manifest zusammenfassend als „Chaos idealistischer, naiver und materialistischer Pseudo-Ideen". Ähnlich scharf kritisierte er Filkos Künstlerheft *Emotion / Emócia* (1977) als „pures idealistisches Geschwafel". Hrabušický gibt an, dass Koller bereits Filkos Künstlerbuch *Stano FILKO II. 1965/69* von 1970 auf die Schaufel genommen habe und von „oberflächliche Bilder der Welt und banale Elemente" bescheinigte, die bloß ein „Volkstheater für die Massen" ergäben und die er als „Gestaltungskunst" abstempelte, wo Filko selbst sie doch so gerne als angewandte Kunst begriff. Zu Filkos Zyklus *Associations / Asociácie* (1968/69) schrieb Koller von „langweiliger Information und Pseudodokumentation in einer Zeit, in der es an echter Information und zwischenmenschlicher Kommunikation mangelt". Aurel Hrabušický, „O zrozumiteľnom Kollerovi a nezrozumiteľnom Filkovi" (Über den verständlichen Koller und den unverständlichen Filko), überarbeiteter Vortrag von der Konferenz *Július Koller U.F.O.-naut?* in der Slovak National Gallery, Bratislava 2009, in: *Jazdec*, 3, 2012, S. 4.

23   Viele von Filkos immersiven konzeptuellen Environments blieben unrealisiert und überlebten nur im Nachlass als sogenannte „Plan-Projektkunst" oder „prospectart". Aurel Hrabušický, „Kinetické environmenty a projekty fiktívnych architektonických konštrukcií" (Kinetische Environments und Projekte fiktiver architektonischer Konstruktionen), hrsg. von Gregorová Stach und Hrabušický 2018 (wie Anm. 9), S. 199–202.

24   Georg Schöllhammer, „Leben in der 5.4.3. Dimension. Eine Retrospektive in Bratislava entdeckt ein Werk von Stano Filko neu", in: *Springerin*, 12/2, 2006, S. 49.

25   Vgl. die symbolische Kastration der Frau, die mit Lacans Kastrationsangst des Mannes durch Macht- oder Kontrollverlust korrespondiert. Mulvey 1975/1988 (wie Anm. 12), S. 64.

26   Persönliches Gespräch mit Stano Filko im August 2011.

27   Den erhaltenen Skizzen zufolge wollte er diese offenbar zu einem Environment verbinden, das aber letztlich nicht realisiert wurde.

28   Lucia Gregorová Stach zufolge führte die tschechoslowakische Ausgabe des Buchs von de Beauvoir „die grundlegende Formulierung der Differenz zwischen biologischem Geschlecht und sozialem Geschlecht in den lokalen kulturellen Diskurs ein. Als Folge sei es „zur Formulierung neuer visueller Strategien aus weiblicher Perspektive und zu einer teilweise geschlechtsspezifischen Neuschreibung der Avantgarde gekommen (siehe Mária Bartuszová, Eva Kmentová, Jana Želibská). Lucia Gregorová Stach, „Eros a civilizácia" (Eros und Zivilisation), in: Gregorová Stach und Hrabušický 2018 (wie Anm. 9), S. 65; zu diesem Thema, auch im Zusammenhang mit Filkos Kunst, schrieb Zora Rusinová „Reč tela alebo iné čítanie (K zrodu problému tela a pohlavia v slovenskom výtvarnom umení)" (Körpersprache oder andere Lesarten [Über den Ursprung des Problems des Körpers und des Geschlechts in der slowakischen Bildkunst]), in: *Galéria – Ročenka SNG 2003* (Galerie-Jahrbuch SNG 2003), hrsg. von Slovak National Gallery, Bratislava 2004, S. 9–30.

29   Manchen erinnern diese Werke auch an Walter Pichlers Arbeiten aus derselben Zeit.

30   Filkos Profilseite mit einer Einführung von Ján Kamenistý und mit einem Abdruck einiger älterer und neuer Künstlertexte finden sich in *Smena* vom 26. Juli 1991, S. 5.

21   Filko's favorite term was "uptime" as an inaccurate English translation of the Slovak term "nadčas" (overtime) that he used, or "nadčasovosť" (timelessness), as opposed to temporality. In this sense, the title of his retrospective exhibition in the Bratislava tranzit workshops was *UP 300000 km/s* (2005).

22   Aurel Hrabušický, as well as a number of contemporary witnesses, often quote, for example, Koller's rejection of the manifesto *White Immaterial Space in a Pure White Infinite Space / Biely nehmotný priestor v čistom bielom nekonečnom priestore* of 1973–74, in which "pure art" is repeatedly mentioned as the so-called sensibility. According to Hrabušický, in connection with this manifesto, Koller summarily wrote about "the chaos of idealist, naive, and materialistic pseudo-ideas." He similarly commented on Filko's artist's booklet *Emotion / Emócia* (1977) as "pure idealistic gibberish." Hrabušický states that Koller already criticized Filko's artist's publication, *Stano FILKO II. 1965/69* (1970), which he referred to as "superficial images of the world, banal elements" resulting in "popular theatre for the masses" and called it "the art of arrangement." (Comparison to applied art was also Filko's own favorite judgement upon others.) On Filko's cycle, *Associations / Asociácie* (1968–69), Koller wrote about "boring information and pseudo-documentation in a time when there is a lack of real information and communication among people." Hrabušický, "O zrozumiteľnom Kollerovi a nezrozumiteľnom Filkovi" (On the Understandable Koller and the Non-understandable Filko), re-edited paper from the conference *Július Koller U.F.O.-naut?*, Slovak National Gallery, Bratislava, 2009, in *Jazdec* (March 2012), p. 4.

23   Many of Filko's conceptual immersive environments remained unrealized and survived only in project documentation as so-called *plan-projectart* or *prospectart*. See Aurel Hrabušický, "Kinetické environment a projekty fiktívnych architektonických konštrukcií" (Kinetic environments and projects of fictitious architectural constructions) (see note 9), pp. 199–202.

24   Georg Schöllhammer, "Leben in der 5.4.3. Dimension. Eine Retrospektive in Bratislava entdeckt das Werk von Stano Filko neu" (Life in the 5.4.3. Dimension. A Retrospective in Bratislava Rediscovers the Work of Stano Filko), in *springerin* (February 2006), p. 49.

25   See the symbolic castration of a woman related to the Lacanian castration anxiety of a man due to the loss of power, or control; Mulvey, "Visual Pleasure and Narrative Cinema" (see note 12), p. 64.

26   From a personal conversation with Stano Filko in August 2011.

27   According to preserved sketches, Filko apparently intended to compound them in an environment which in the end was not brought about.

28   According to Lucia Gregorová Stach, the Czechoslovak edition of de Beauvoir brought "a fundamental formulation of the difference between biological sex and social gender" to the local cultural discourse. According to her, in relation to that there arose "the formulation of new visual strategies from the female gender perspective, and a partial gender rewriting of the avant-garde (see Mária Bartuszová, Eva Kmentová, Jana Želibská)." Gregorová Stach, "Eros a civilizácia" (Eros and Civilization) (see note 9), p. 65; on this topic, also in relation to Filko's work, see the text of Zora Rusinová, "Reč tela alebo iné čítanie (K zrodu problému tela a pohlavia v slovenskom výtvarnom umení)" (Body Language or Other Readings [On the Origin of the Issue of the Body and Gender in Slovak Visual Art]), in *Galéria – Ročenka SNG 2003* (Gallery – SNG Yearbook 2003), ed. Slovak National Gallery (Bratislava, 2004), pp. 9–30.

29   To many, these works are also reminiscent of the works of Walter Pichler from that period.

30   Filko's profile page, with an introduction by Ján Kamenistý, and with a reprint of several older and current authorial texts, see *Smena* (July 26, 1991), p. 5.

31   For example, in his three blocks on a turntable project *Nothing on a Rotating Electric Pedestal / Nič na točitom elektrickom podstavci* as part of the tricolored chandelier in *Universal Environment* from the late 1960s.

32   Filko, Laky, and Zavarský originally used the concept of "sensibility" in the *White Space* manifesto instead of "pure emotion," which could have come out of Malevich's essay *Die gegenstandslose Welt* (Object-free World) (1927), which was translated and published in Czechoslovakia at that time (for details, see note 19). The influence of Malevich's postulations was also confirmed by Ján Zavarský in several statements; the interview by Fedor Blaščák, "Stano Filko v Žiline 2. V spomienkach kolegov" (Stano Filko in Žilina 2. In Memory of Colleagues) (2016), https://www.youtube.com/watch?v=SMY1O3hFPMU; the interview by Beata Jablonská "Ján Zavarský, Biely priestor v bielom priestore" (White Space in White Space), part I. and II. (2019), https://www.youtube.com/watch?v=mfuuMSpJK4Y, and https://www.youtube.com/watch?v=iOgDvnEVjrk (all accessed May 20, 2022).

33   Yves Klein, *The Specialization of Sensibility in the Raw Material State into Stabilized Pictorial Sensibility, The Void* (La spécialisation de la sensibilité à l'état matière première en sensibilité picturale stabilisée, Le Vide), exhibition at Iris Clert Gallery (Paris 1958).

34   Tomáš Štraus, *Stano Filko – Miloš Laky – Ján Zavarský*, exh. cat. Fiatal müvészek klubja (Budapest, 1977), n. p.

35   According to Zavarský, Filko requested his permission to continue independently on the project, see published video interviews with Ján Zavarský from 2016 and 2019 (see note 32).

36   Stanislav Filko, "Transcendentálna meditácia 1980" (Transcendental Meditation 1980), in *Text-Art*, self-published 1980, n. p.

37   Carol Duncan, "The MoMA's Hot Mamas," in *Art Journal* 48 (1989), p. 172.

38   Monumental realizations in architecture, which he also partially involved himself in, remained a relatively free area. From the point of view of the government, Filko's situation was significantly worsened by his critical commentary on the events of 1968, which he gave as part of his work *Cathedral* at the Bratislava *Danuvius* exhibition. Apparently, in order to keep his passport, Filko signed a cooperation agreement with the secret police, State Security (Štátna bezpečnosť), and was registered in their records as a collaborator from 1973 to 1975, although purportedly to Fedor Blaščák, this did not lead to real active collaboration. See Fedor Blaščák, "Esej / MILOŠ LAKY (1948–1975). Biografická skica a príspevok k sociálnym dejinám slovenskej neoavantgardy na začiatku sedemdesiatych rokov" (Essay / MILOŠ LAKY [1948–1975]. Biographical sketch and contribution to social history of the Slovak neo-avant-garde in the early 1970s), in *MAG D A* (Bratislava, 2022), https://magdamag.sk/2022/06/26/esej-milos-laky-1948-1975/?fbclid=IwAR1YQ6T_9IhVDAxn-1ih9pCf-ScoZJLj8scRGkRDvWX-H0Gp8fcCRaN09g7E (accessed June 27, 2022). In his manuscript from the 1990s, Filko stated the situation of the time: "Where they—adequately, above the party—do not value my work or my personality … conceal my work = structure, glaze it over—to the underground, out of envy … I am disappointed—offended—disillusioned before leaving for Expo 70 Osaka…."

39   He was reportedly employed by, for example, the Czech post-war emigrant and patroness, Meda Mládková. He was also in contact with other emigrants from the former Czechoslovakia. Apparently, they all provided him with contact to galleries, but he was unable to arrange cooperation with any of them. This was privately remarked on by, for example, Charlotta Kotik in an interview in 2014, and also Tomáš Štraus in 2008 with respect to Filko's time in Germany, on which he also partially published correspondence. During his emigration, Filko also had some existential support however. According to his own statement, Beuys too

purchased his works. According to documents from his estate, he even gained some stipends, e.g. from the A. and E. Gottlieb Foundation (1986) and the Pollock-Krasner Foundation (1986, 1989) during his stay in the USA.

40   "Levicovému disentu chybělo živější napojení na kontrakulturu, říká historička Andělová" (Left-wing dissent lacked a more lively connection to the counter culture, said historian Andělová), the podcast Kolaps, in *Alarm* (Prague, January 27, 2022), https://a2larm.cz/2022/01/levicovemu-disentu-chybelo-zivejsi-napojeni-na-kontrakulturu-rika-historicka-andelova/ (accessed June 20, 2022).

41   Aurel Hrabušický, "Filkova Novosvětská 1982–1990" (Filko's Novosvětská 1982–1990), in *Stano Filko '80s in N.Y.C. Paintings & Objects*, eds. Aurel Hrabušický and Nina Vrbanová, *Art Capital* (Bratislava 2014), p. 7.

42   For example, Susan R. Bowers, "Medusa and the Female Gaze," in *NWSA Journal* 2 (Spring 1990), pp. 217–235.

43   *Smena* 1991 (see note 30), p. 5.

44   Filko expressed himself inaccurately with the words: "She became fatal to me, because in the year I was born, she herself was born (or appeared)." Ľudo Petránsky, "K výstave Stana Filka v SNG, *Červená – modrá – biela*" (On The Stano Filko Exhibition at the Slovak National Gallery, *Red – Blue – White*), in *SME Daily* (March 24, 1993).

45   Donna Haraway, "A Manifesto for Cyborgs: Science, Technology, and Socialist Feminism in the 1980s," in *Socialist Review* 80 (1985), p. 67.

46   As part of his newspaper profile Filko, after his return from emigration, published the text "Poetry = Prose from Clinical Death" within the larger elaboration *Memories of Clinical Death*, which at that time he dated to 1946 and 1951. Filko's contemporaries agree that prior to his emigration he had not yet worked with this concept, in *Smena* 1991 (see note 30), p. 5.

47   Back in 1991, the last phase of Filko's developmental perspective remained open and the phasing took the form of: "Stanislav Filko 1937–1977; Stan Fylko 1978–1987; Stan Phylko 1988–…"

48   According to Filko's texts and statements, he allegedly was trying to save cows from falling into a five-meter quarry, and so broke his arm and some ribs. The reported second clinical death could have happened in the newly nationalized munitions factory Zbrojovka in Považská Bystrica, which was renamed Považské strojárne after the war. Filko was there on a job and according to Fedor Blaščák's recollection of an interview with Filko, he was putting up a propaganda poster that read: "March, a month without swearing." In his manuscripts from the estate, Filko described it such that when he was about to fall five or six meters from an indoor crane above high-voltage wires, he grabbed them and burnt his left wrist.

49   The manuscript from his estate with notes on a monograph at that time prepared but unpublished (by tranzit.cz, around 2010), where Filko wrote of a glow in the space where "the barefoot spirits of former physical bodies on Earth floated … they were all dressed in white tunics and stated that they were all naked underneath. He mentioned the music from the angelic trumpets and the spirits communicating with each other by means of mental energy, through their "conscience," which he interpreted as the messenger between the fifth and the third dimensions.

50   Invitation to Filko's exhibition at the no longer existing B & M Gallery, Obchodná st. 70, Bratislava, from the beginning of 1991. Later, in 1993, in Bratislava he presented his work from the American period in a series of three ongoing exhibitions. The "Red Part" was presented at the Slovak National Gallery (after the Slovak National Gallery transported his works from the USA to Slovakia); "Blue" at the former Expatriate Museum (Krajanské múzeum) of Matica slovenská; The "White Part" was planned for the Umelecká Beseda, but in the end he presented all three parts together in 1994 at the Slovak National Gallery at Zvolen Castle in Central Slovakia.

51   *Smena* 1991 (see note 30), p. 5.

52   Ibid.

53   According to Filko's model, the FIFTH DIMENSION is a "time non-specific metaphysical-ontological space," made up of: the 12. transparent color, which represented the absolute; the 11. white color, as essence, and the 10. golden color of the soul ("Duch/Spirit"). The FOURTH DIMENSION (Filko also called it "the postman") was supposed to be a connection of 3.D. and 5.D., and he defined it as "ALTRUISM." In contrast to 5.D., which was characterised by perfect SYMMETRY, here was the "ASYMMETRIC time-space of the afterlife," represented by the 9. silver color as the pinnacle of the spirit ("Spirit Universe"); the 8. pink color, which signifies not only falsehood, but also love, and the 7. purple color, which is supposed to be the destination of clinical death. The THIRD DIMENSION is "the time-space extent of the physical world" (the so-called "Cosmo-Universe"), which Filko associated with "EGOISM." Here belongs the 6. indigo/black color, representing the ego and black matter; the 5. blue color, which represented the cosmos and material reality; the 4. green color, affecting socio-political reality and social utopias; the 3. yellow color, which was characterized by dualism and which Filko associated with the birth of the so-called "Hermaphrodite" and the beginning of mankind; the 2. orange color, which meant eroticism and sex, and the 1. red color representing biology, as well as womanhood and so-called "Magma."

54   Lucia Gregorová Stach states that he allegedly suffered from dyslexia, and so did not learn even French when he was in Paris in 1968 on a six-month stay. See Lucia Gregorová Stach, "Inštalácie z mediálnych aparátov" (Installations from Media Apparatuses), Gregorová Stach, Hrabušický, 2018 (see note 9), p. 124.

55   Schöllhammer, 2006 (see note 24), p. 49.

56   Hrabušický, 2009/2012 (see note 22), p. 4.

57   In this way he dealt, for example, with the now iconic cosmological iconography, which he adopted in the 1960s and early 1970s from the time's propaganda of flights into space and from the popular press (e.g. the Czechoslovak magazine, *Letectví a kosmonautika* [Flight and Cosmonautics]), as well other symptomatic contexts. Filko's series of gramophone records with conceptual sound interpretations (*Cosmos – Cosmos Espace Univers*; *Cosmos – 9–1*; *Futúr – Cosmos Futúr*; *Atom – Reál*, 1970–1971), for example, may have been inspired by products of mass culture dedicated to the theme of the conquering of the cosmos like the popular brochure *Člověk v kozme* (Man in the Cosmos), 4/1966, which included flexible vinyl records with recordings, etc.

58   When his mobile phone was disconnected in the final years, it was important for him to keep the old digits for the new number to contain the fated years of his clinical deaths, and the date of his birth. His phone numbers therefore were: 09 48 54 1937, 0907 06 14 37, or variations like 0911 06 14 37.

59   Stano Filko's interview with Hans Ulrich Obrist and Roman Ondák (Bratislava 2005), https://halle-fuer-kunst.at/en/context/huo-interview/; see also "HAPPSOC," directed by Kvetoslav Hečko, Slovak Television (Bratislava 1997), https://vimeo.com/83386764 (accessed June 20, 2022).

31 Ende der 1960er-Jahre beispielsweise im Zuge des Projekts *Nothing on a Rotating Electric Pedestal / Nič na točitom elektrickom podstavci* beim dreifarbigen Kronleuchter, der zum *Universal Environment* gehörte.

32 Ursprünglich erwogen Filko, Laky und Zavarský für das Manifest des *White Space* anstelle der „reinen Emotion" den Ausdruck „Sensibilität", den sie aus Malewitschs Essay „Die gegenstandslose Welt" (1927) haben hätten können, der damals in der Tschechoslowakei in Übersetzung erschienen war (Einzelheiten Anm. 19). Ján Zavarský bestätigte in der Tat mehrfach einen Einfluss der Postulate Malewitschs, so im Interview von Fedor Blaščák „Stano Filko in Žilina 2. V spomienkach kolegov" (Stano Filko in Žilina 2. In Erinnerung an einen Kollegen), 2016, https://www.youtube.com/watch?v=SMYlO3hFPMU, oder im Interview von Beata Jablonská „Ján Zavarský, Biely priestor v bielom priestore" (Weißer Raum in weißem Raum, Teil I. und II.), 2019, https://www.youtube.com/watch?v=mfuuMSpJK4Y und https://www.youtube.com/watch?v=iOgDvnEVjrk) (Zugriff jeweils 20. Mai 2022).

33 Yves Klein, *The Specialization of Sensibility in the Raw Material State into Stabilized Pictorial Sensibility, The Void / La spécialisation de la sensibilité à l'état matière première en sensibilité picturale stabilisée, Le Vide*, Ausstellung in der Galerie Iris Clert, Paris 1958.

34 Tomáš Štraus, *Stano Filko – Miloš Laky – Ján Zavarský*, Ausst.-Kat. Fiatal müvészek klubja, Budapest 1977, o. S.

35 Zavarský berichtete, dass ihn Filko um Erlaubnis bat, das Projekt alleine fortzusetzen. Vgl. die veröffentlichten Videointerviews mit Ján Zavarský 2016 und 2019 (zitiert in Anm. 32).

36 Stanislav Filko, „Transcendentálna meditácia 1980" (Transzendentale Meditation 1980), in: *Text-Art*, Selbstverlag 1980, o. S.

37 Carol Duncan, „The MoMA's Hot Mamas", in: *Art Journal*, 48/2, 1989, S. 172.

38 Monumentalbauten, an denen er teilweise auch beteiligt war, blieben für ihn indes ein relativ freies Feld. Aus Behördensicht verschlechterte sich Filkos Lage erheblich wegen eines kritischen Kommentars zu den Ereignissen von 1968, den er im Zuge seiner Arbeit *Cathedral* auf der Ausstellung *Danuvius* in Bratislava geäußert hatte. Angeblich um seinen Reisepass behalten zu können, unterzeichnete Filko einen Kooperationsvertrag mit der Geheimpolizei, das heißt der Staatssicherheit (Štátna bezpečnosť), bei der er laut Akten von 1973 bis 1975 als Mitarbeiter eingetragen war. Fedor Blaščák hingegen meint, dass dieser Vertrag zu keiner wirklich aktiven Zusammenarbeit führte, siehe Fedor Blaščák, „Esej / MILOŠ LAKY (1948–1975). Biografická skica a príspevok k sociálnym dejinám slovenskej neoavantgardy na začiatku sedemdesiatych rokov" (Essay / MILOŠ LAKY [1948–1975]. Biografische Skizze und Beitrag zur Sozialgeschichte der slowakischen Neoavantgarde in den frühen 1970er-Jahren.), in: *MAG D A*, Bratislava 2022, https://magdamag.sk/2022/06/26/esej-milos-laky-1948-1975/?fbclid=IwAR1YQ6T_9IhVDAxn-1ih9pCf-ScoZJLj8scRGkRDvWXH0Gp8fcCRaNO9g7E (27. 6. 2022). In einem Manuskript aus den 1990er-Jahren hielt Filko seine damalige Lage fest: „Weil sie – eigentlich: die Parteiführung – meine Kunst und meine Person nicht schätzen […], verschweigen sie meine Arbeit = Struktur, verbannen diese – in den Untergrund, nur aus Neid … Ich bin enttäuscht – verletzt – desillusioniert vor meiner Abreise zur Expo 70 in Osaka …"

39 Berichten zufolge war Filko unter anderem bei der tschechischen Nachkriegsemigrantin und Mäzenin Meda Mládková beschäftigt. Zudem stand er mit anderen Emigrant*innen aus der ehemaligen Tschechoslowakei in Kontakt. Offenbar vermittelten diese ihm Kontakte zu Galerien, doch konnte er mit keiner eine Zusammenarbeit vereinbaren. Dies bemerkten zum Beispiel Charlotta Kotik in einem privaten Gespräch 2014, aber auch Tomáš Štraus 2008 hinsichtlich Filkos Deutschlandaufenthalts, über den er auch Teile der Korrespondenz veröffentlichte. Dennoch erfuhr Filko während seiner Emigration auch eine gewisse existenzielle Unterstützung. Seiner Angabe nach kaufte auch Beuys Werke an. Gemäß den Unterlagen aus seinem Nachlass erhielt Filko in den USA sogar einige Stipendien, zum Beispiel von der A. und E. Gottlieb-Stiftung (1986) oder der Pollock-Krasner-Stiftung (1986, 1989).

40 „Levicovému disentu chybělo živější napojení na kontrakulturu, říká historička Andělová" (Dem linken Widerstand fehlte eine direktere Verbindung zur Gegenkultur, sagt die Historikerin Andělová), im Podcast Kolaps, in: *Alarm*, Prag, 27. Januar 2022, https://a2larm.cz/2022/01/levicovemu-disentu-chybelo-zivejsi-napojeni-na-kontrakulturu-rika-historicka-andelova/ (20. 6. 2022).

41 Aurel Hrabušický, „Filkova Novosvětská 1982–1990" (Filko's Novosvětská 1982–1990), in: *Stano Filko '80s in N.Y.C. Paintings & Objects*, hrsg. von Aurel Hrabušický und Nina Vrbanová, Bratislava 2014, S. 7.

42 z. B. Susan R. Bowers, „Medusa and the Female Gaze", in: *NWSA Journal*, 2/2, Frühjahr 1990, S. 217–235.

43 *Smena* 1991 (wie Anm. 30), S. 5.

44 Filko drückte sich dabei ungenau aus: „Sie wurde mir zum Verhängnis, denn in dem Jahr, in dem ich geboren wurde, wurde sie selbst geboren (oder entdeckt)." Siehe Ľudo Petránsky, „K výstave Stana Filka v SNG, *Červená – modrá – biela*" (Über Stano Filkos Ausstellung *Red – Blue – White* in der Slowakischen Nationalgalerie), in: *SME Daily*, 24. März 1993.

45 Donna Haraway, „Ein Manifest für Cyborgs", in: *Die Neuerfindung der Natur: Primaten, Cyborgs und Frauen*, Frankfurt am Main/New York 1995, S. 34.

46 Mit seinem Zeitungsprofil veröffentlichte Filko nach seiner Rückkehr aus der Emigration den Text „Poesie = Prosa vom klinischen Tod" im Rahmen des größeren Projekts *Erinnerungen an den klinischen Tod*, das er auf 1946 und 1951 vordatierte. Filkos Zeitgenossen hingegen sind sich einig, dass er vor seiner Emigration solche Vorstellungen noch nicht hatte, vgl. *Smena* 1991 (zitiert in Anm. 30), S. 5.

47 1991 begann für Filko die letzte Phase seiner Entwicklung, und so nahm die Phaseneinteilung folgende Form an: „Stanislav Filko 1937–1977; Stan Fylko 1978–1987; Stan Phylko 1988–…"

48 Eigenen Texten und Aussagen zufolge will Filko versucht haben, die Kühe vor dem Sturz in einen fünf Meter tiefen Steinbruch zu retten, wobei er sich den Arm und einige Rippen gebrochen hätte. Der zweite klinische Tod soll sich in der eben verstaatlichten Munitionsfabrik Zbrojovka in Považská Bystrica zugetragen haben, die nach dem Krieg in Považské strojárne umbenannt wurde. Filko hatte dort einen Auftrag, und nach Fedor Blaščáks Erinnerung an ein Gespräch mit Filko hängte er gerade ein Propagandaplakat auf, auf dem stand: „März, ein Monat ohne Fluchen". In Manuskripten aus dem Nachlass hielt Filko fest, dass er, als er drohte, fünf oder sechs Meter von einem Hallenkran über Hochspannungsdrähten zu fallen, letztere ergriff und sich dabei das linke Handgelenk verbrannte.

49 Dieses Manuskript aus dem Nachlass enthält auch Notizen zu einer (von tranzit.cz 2010) geplanten, jedoch nie veröffentlichten Monografie, in denen Filko von einem Leuchten im Raum sprach, in dem „die barfuß laufenden Geister einstiger echter Menschen schwebten […] sie waren alle in weiße Tuniken gekleidet". Darüber hinaus erklärte er, dass diese alle darunter nackt gewesen seien. Filko erwähnte auch die Musik von Engelstrompeten und, dass die Geister miteinander durch mentale Energie kommunizierten, durch ihr „Gewissen", das er als Boten zwischen der 5. und der 3. Dimension interpretierte.

50 Zitat von der Einladung zu Filkos Ausstellung in der ehemaligen Galerie B & M, Obchodná st. 70, Bratislava, Anfang 1991. Im Jahr 1993 präsentierte er dann in Bratislava seine Arbeiten aus der amerikanischen Periode in einer Serie von drei Ausstellungen. Ihr „roter Teil" wurde in der Slowakischen Nationalgalerie gezeigt (nachdem diese seine Werke aus den USA in die Slowakei transportieren hatte lassen), „Blau" im ehemaligen Krajanské múzeum (Exilant*innenmuseum) im Matica slovenská, und der „weiße Teil" war für die Umelecká Beseda geplant. Schließlich jedoch präsentierte Filko alle drei Teile zusammen 1994 in der Slowakischen Nationalgalerie im Schloss Zvolen in der Zentralslowakei.

51 *Smena* 1991 (wie Anm. 30), S. 5.

52 Ebd.

53 In Filkos Modell ist die 5. DIMENSION ein „zeit-unspezifischer metaphysisch-ontologischer Raum", bestehend aus der 12. transparenten Farbe, die das Absolute darstellt, der 11. weißen Farbe als Essenz und der 10. goldenen Farbe der Seele („Duch/Geist"). Die 4. DIMENSION (Filko nannte sie auch „den Briefträger") sei eine Verbindung von 3.D. und 5.D., die er als „ALTRUISMUS" definierte. Im Gegensatz zur 5.D., die sich durch perfekte SYMMETRIE auszeichnete, befand sich hier der „ASYMMETRISCHE Zeit-Raum des Jenseits", repräsentiert durch die 9. silberne Farbe als Gipfel des Geistes („Geistuniversum"); die 8. rosa Farbe, die nicht nur die Lüge, sondern auch die Liebe bedeute, und die 7. violette Farbe, die das Schicksal des klinischen Todes sein soll. Die 3. DIMENSION wiederum sei „die zeitlich-räumliche Ausdehnung der physischen Welt" (das sogenannte „Kosmo-Universum"), die Filko mit „EGOISMUS" verband. Hierher gehören 6. die Farbe Indigo/Schwarz, die das Ego und die dunkle Materie repräsentiert, 5. die Farbe Blau, die den Kosmos und die materielle Realität darstellt, 4. die Farbe Grün, die die sozio-politische Realität und die sozialen Utopien meint, 3. die Farbe Gelb, die durch Dualismus gekennzeichnet ist und die Filko mit der Geburt des so genannten „Hermaphroditen" und dem Menschheitsbeginn verband, 2. die Farbe Orange, die Erotik und Sex bedeutet, sowie 1. die Farbe Rot, welche die Biologie sowie die Weiblichkeit, aber auch das sogenannte „Magma" darstellt.

54 Lucia Gregorová Stach erwähnt, dass Filko angeblich an Legasthenie litt und deshalb auch nicht Französisch lernte, als er 1968 für ein halbes Jahr in Paris weilte. Lucia Gregorová Stach, „Inštalácie z mediálnych aparátov" (Installationen aus Medienapparaten), Gregorová Stach, Hrabušický, 2018 (wie Anm. 9), S. 124.

55 Schöllhammer, 2006 (wie Anm. 24), S. 49.

56 Hrabušický, 2009/2012 (wie Anm. 22), S. 4.

57 So beschäftigte sich auch Filko mit einer nun für ihn typischen kosmologischen Ikonographie, die er in den 1960er- und frühen 1970er-Jahren nicht nur aus der damaligen Propaganda für Weltraumflüge und aus der populären Presse (zum Beispiel der tschechoslowakischen Zeitschrift *Letectví a kosmonautika* [Flug und Kosmonautik]), sondern auch aus anderen symptomatischen Kontexten übernahm. Filkos Serie von Grammophonplatten mit konzeptuellen Klanginterpretationen (*Cosmos – Cosmos Espace Univers*; *Cosmos – 9–1*; *Futúr – Cosmos Futúr*; *Atom – Reál*; alle 1970–1971) könnte wohl von Massenprodukten inspiriert worden sein, die sich der Eroberung des Kosmos widmeten. So war die populäre Broschüre *Člověk v kozme* (Der Mensch im Kosmos), 4/1966, die ebenfalls dünne Vinylplatten mit Tonaufnahmen usw. enthielt.

58 Als in den letzten Lebensjahren sein Mobiltelefon mehrmals abgedreht wurde, war ihm wichtig, dass die alte Telefonnummer innerhalb der neuen zu behalten, sodass die Schicksalsjahre seiner klinischen Tode und das Datum seiner Geburt erhalten blieb. Seine Nummern lauteten daher 09 48 54 1937, 0907 06 14 37, oder deren Abwandlungen wie 0911 06 14 37.

59 Stano Filkos Gespräch mit Hans Ulrich Obrist und Roman Ondák (Bratislava 2005), https://halle-fuer-kunst.at/en/context/huo-interview/; oder „HAPPSOC" unter der Regie von Kvetoslav Hečko, Slowakisches Fernsehen, Bratislava 1997, https://vimeo.com/83386764 (20. 6. 2022).

VERTIKAL

SENSITIVEN – 1974-1975-1976
(S. FILKO — M. LAKY — J. ZAVARSKÝ)

— Wir bekennen uns zur freien „reinen Sensitivität", die absolut ist und die einzige Möglichkeit „der reinen sensitiven Kunst".

— Wir distanzieren uns von allen Formen einer Erklärung der „reinen Sensitivität", weil die „reine Sensitivität" in ihrer reinen Aktivität absolut ist.

— Die „reine Sensitivität" mit ihrem absoluten Wesen ist die einzige Möglichkeit unsere reine Aktivität der „reinen sensitiven Kunst" zu entfalten.

— Wir verkünden die Inkompatibilität eines ideellen Ballastes mit unserer reinen Aktivität der „reinen Sensitivität".

— Es ist nicht möglich unsere reine Aktivität der „reinen Sensitivität" zu erklären, es ist nur möglich sie in der „reinen sensitiven Kunst" zu realisieren.

— Unsere „reine Sensitivität" trat aus dem Rahmen der rationalen Erkenntnis heraus, gelangte in die Sphäre der „reinen Sensitivität", mit deren Hilfe sie sich eröffnet und verständlich wird.

— Die „reine Sensitivität" ist infolge ihres Charakters verständlich, aber nicht erklärbar.

— Unsere reine Aktivität in ihrem übersubjektiven Wesen und die „reine Sensitivität" mit ihrem absoluten Charakter sind überzeitliche Formen der „reinen sensitiven Kunst".

— Wir sind gegen die Philosophie in der Kunst und bekennen uns nur zur „reinen Sensitivität", die absolut ist.

— Die „reine Sensitivität" ist eine absolute überzeitliche Bewegung in der Kunst und in ihrer reinen Aktivität unwiederholbar und ständig aktuell.

ONTOLOGI

SENSITIV – 1974-1975-1976
(S. FILKO — M. LAKY — J. ZAVARSKÝ)

— We professe the free „pur sensitivity" which is absolut and the unique possibility of the „pure sensitiv art".

— We keep aloof from all forms of explantation of the „pure sensitivity", for the „pure sensitivity", is absolut in its pure activity.

— The „pure sensitivity" in its absolute being is the unique possibility to display our pure activity of „pure sensitiv art".

— We proclaim the incompatibility of an ideal burden with our pure activity of „pure sensitivity".

— It's impossible to explain our pure activity of „pure sensitivity", it's only possible to realize it in the „pure sensitiv art".

— Our „pure sensitivity" stepped out from the frame of the rational knowledge and penetrated in the sphare of „pure sensitivity" with help of which it opens itself and gets intelligible.

— The „pure sensitivity" is considering its caracter intelligible, but can not be explained.

— Our pure activity, being super-subjectiv and the „pure sensitivity", being absolute, are super-timely forms of the „pure sensitiv art".

— We are againts the philosophy in the art and recognize only the „pure sensitivity" which is absolute.

— The „pure sensitivity" is a movement super-timely in the art and considerings its pure activity, can not be repeated and ever is current.

1974 – FILKO – 1976 – TEXTART

In the course of the installation *White Space in White Space / Biely priestor v bielom priestore* (1973–76) Filko commenced with a new form of text production, *Text-art*. An important first step was taken in the *White Space in White Space Manifesto / Biely priestor v bielom priestore Manifesto* (1973), which he published together with Miloš Laky and Ján Zavarský to accompany the installation. This manifesto was issued in four different languages at the same time, and it follows in the stylistic tradition of Kazimir Malevich, with very clearly formulated proclamations that are a linguistic companion to the dematerialization of art.

In the manifesto, Filko, Laky, and Zavarský proclaim absolute art, by means of which they wish to step beyond the limits of the material world and to get as close as possible to concepts like emptiness and infinity. These convictions are very clearly expressed and used by the artists to delineate and affirm their position. Absolute art is seen in the manifesto as the expression of "pure sensitivity," and then further developed as such in the publication *White Space in White Space, Pure Sensitivity / Biely priestor v bielom priestore, Čistá senzitivita* (1974–75) in nine languages. According to the artists, pure sensitivity cannot be explained, so that its proclamation in language becomes a paradox text. Pure sensitivity should be realized by artistic action, as "pure sensitive art."

Im Zuge der Installation *White Space in White Space / Biely priestor v bielom priestore* (1973–1976) beginnt für Filko in den 1970er-Jahren auch eine neue Form der Textproduktion, die *Text-art*. Ein wichtiger Anfang gelingt ihm durch das *White Space in White Space Manifesto / Biely priestor v bielom priestore Manifesto* (1973), welches er gemeinsam mit Miloš Laky und Ján Zavarský zur Installation veröffentlichte. Das Manifest wurde in vier verschiedenen Sprachen gleichzeitig herausgegeben und folgt der stilistischen Tradition Kazimir Malevichs: Es handelt sich dabei um klar formulierte Proklamationen, welche die Entmaterialisierung der Kunst sprachlich begleiten.

Im Manifest rufen Filko, Laky und Zavarský die absolute Kunst aus, mit welcher sie die Grenzen der materiellen Welt überschreiten wollen und sich Konzepten wie Leere und Unendlichkeit maximal annähern. Diese Überzeugungen werden klar zum Ausdruck gebracht und von den Künstlern benutzt, um ihre Position abzugrenzen und zu verfestigen. Die absolute Kunst wird in dem Manifest als Ausdruck der „reinen Sensibilität" begriffen und schließlich in der Veröffentlichung *White Space in White Space, Pure Sensitivity / Biely priestor v bielom priestore, Čistá senzitivita* (1974–1975) in neun Sprachen als „reine Sensitivität" weiter ausgebaut. Die reine Sensitivität kann laut den Aussagen der Künstler aber nicht erklärt werden, was die sprachliche Proklamation gleichzeitig zu einem paradoxen Text werden lässt. Die reine Sensitivität soll sich durch die künstlerische Aktivität selbst realisieren, als „reine sensitive Kunst".

[01] Stano Filko, Miloš Laky, Ján Zavarský, SENSITIVITY – Text-art / SENZITIVITA – Text-art, 1976

[02A]

1977 — STANISLAV FILKO

EMÓCIA

ČISTÁ EMÓCIA

BIELY PRIESTOR V BIELOM PRIESTORE

Senzibilita (1973) = vnímavo citový — inžinierska citovosť — horizontála

Senzitivita (1974, 75, 76) = citovo vnímavý — čistá citlivosť — vertikála

Emócia (1977) = duševne citový — citovo duševný

Čistá emócia je tretí stupeň Bieleho priestoru v bielom priestore — čistého umenia — nefyzikálneho umenia — absolútneho umenia — nadčasového umenia ...

Čistá emócia opustila — prekročila senzibilitu (plátno, papier) — horizontálu. Ďalej prekročila senzitivitu (filc biely), vertikálu. Čistá emócia nemá už žiaden materiál, ani zdanlivý, ani farbu, biela je tu ako pojem = nefarba, ako nadčasovosť, absolútnosť, centralizmus, nadsubjektívnosť, ..., kde ide o utópiu, nadbudúcnosť, nadčasové nekonečno, nadkozmičnosť, nadneviditeľnosť, nadinternacionálnosť, nadkozmopolitnosť, nadsenzibilnosť, nadsenzitívnosť, nadmaliarstvo, nadminulosť, nadprítomnosť, nadbudúcnosť, špeciálnosť, nadsubjektívnej čistej, absolútnej, čisto abstraktnej abstraktnosti — nadčasovosti. Táto čistá emócia je absolútnym tretím stupňom nefyzikálneho umenia, ktorá sa našim fyzikálnym umením nedá, ani nemôže vysvetľovať, (lebo v ňom neexistuje).

Čistá emócia je umenie nadčasové, nadkozmické, nadabsolútne, ... tuda i tento text taký je a bude.

Čistá emócia je umenie zároveň poetické, (vo svojej nefyzikálnosti).

Čisté umenie — emócia vo svojej nefyzikálnosti, nadčasovosti, absolútnosti, ... je umelecky špecificky obsahové, večné, absolútne, ... slobodné, ... Je to plánovaná emotívna nadkozmická citlivosť vo svojej nadsubjektívnosti, ktorá je nadvedecká — nevedecká, nevysvetliteľná, nefilozofická, neštylizovaná, nevedná, nesenzibilná, nesenzitívna, nefarebná, nevecná, nemateriálna, neidealistická, nepopulárna, tichá a zároveň netichá, nekonečná v nekonečnu, neexpresívna, neadaptateľná, neča-

sová, nekonkrétna, nekoštruktívna, nedekoratívna, neformová, neformálna, nehmotná, neabstrahovaná, nekarieristická, neaplikovateľná, nekomplikovateľná, nejednoduchá, nechudobná, nebohatá, nesubjektívna, neobjektívna, nemateriálna, nepozemská, neezemská, nenáboženská, neúniková, neúzka, neširoká, neideová, nezaužívaná, neakademická, nefilozofická podľa dnešných filozófii (na Zemi), je to nič a zároveň všetko, je neparadoxná, nesentimentálna, nežánrová, nepolitická, nehrubá, neideová, neformálna, nerytmická, netvarová, antisymetrická, antinedecentralizovaná, antineaktuálna, neaktuálna, neoslavná, nepátosná, nepoctivá, neformalistická, nekritičná, neľúbivá, neromantická, nepovrchová, nepesimistická, nežalmová, neošklivá, antinedušovná, nečasová, nepolopatična, nezváčšeninová, nezobrazovaná, neviditeľná o neviteľnej danosti vesmíru, nedejová, nežánrová, nesubjektívna, nadsubjektívna, absolútna DANOSŤ, nadčasovosť, nadobjektívnosť, čistá abstrakcia vo svojej abstrakcii, ... vo všetkých druhoch umenia. (ESENCIA)

Emócia je médium materiálnosti? Médium maliarstva? Médium filozofie umenia, umenia filozofie (totálnosti, nadčasovosti, absolútnosti, nemateriálnosti, nefyzičnosti, možnosti ...)

Je ďalším — III. predstupňom transcendencie.

Je internacionálna, kozmičná, slovanská ...

Je čiste absolútna, nadčasová, esencia, emócia...

Je to nadsubjektívna, nadobjetívna danosť.

Je maľovaná — realizovaná okrem TEXT-ARTU i maliarskym válkom.

Je maľovaná smerom do nekonečna, na plexisklách, na stenách, na plafónoch ...

Emócia je ako podmet — čistá absolútnosť, nie ako prívlastok;

Realizovaná bola a je, na plexisklách, stenách, plafónoch; po prvýkrát roku 1977 p. Kr. (p. n. let.).

TEXT-ART

[02A] *EMOTION. Pure Emotion. White Space in White Space - Text-art / EMÓCIA. Čistá Emócia. Biely priestor v bielom priestore - Text-art, Manifesto / Manifest, 1977*

[02B]

1977 — STANISLAV FILKO

EMOTION

PURE EMOTION

WHITE SPACE IN WHITE SPACE

Sensibility (1973) = perceiving sensitiv — engeener-sensitivity — horizontale

Sensitivity (1974, 75, 76) = sensitivly perceiving — pure sensitiveness — verticale

Emotion (1977) = spiritually sensitiv — sensitivly spiritual

Pure emotion is the third degree of White room in the white space — of pure art — notphysical art — absolute art — super--timely art...

The pure emotion abandoned — transgressed the sensibility (canvas, paper) — the Horizontale, besides it, transgressed the sensitivity (white felt), the Verticale. Pure emotion has no more material, not even apparent one, no colour, white is here as notion — not-colour, as super-timely character, absolute, centralism, supersubjectivity. ... where the question is the utopia, super-future, super-timely infinite, super cosmic character, superinvisibilty, super-internationalism, super-cosmopolitism, supersensibility, supersensitivity, super-painting, super-past, super-present, super-future, speciality, of supersubjective, pure, absolute, purely abstract abstrahation — of the super-timely character. This pure emotion is the absolute third degree of notphysical art, which one can not explainne by means of our physical art (because it dossnot exist in it).

Pure emotion is super-timely, supercosmic, superabsolute, ...art, therefore thus the text is and will be such.

Is pure emotion an art poetical simultaneously? (in its notphysicality).

Pure art — emotion, in its notphysicality, supertimely character, absolute character, ... is irartistically specifically full of content, it is objective, absolute, ... free, ... It is the planned emotional supercosmic sensitivity in its supersubjectivity, which is superscientific — not scientific, not explicable, notphilosophical, not stylized, not of scientific character, not sensible, not sensitic, not coloured, not objective, not materialistic, not idealistic, not popular, silent and in the same time not silent, infinite in the Infinite, not expressiv, not adaptable, not timely, not concrete, not constructive, not decorative, not formed, not formal, not materialistic, not abstrahated, not ambitious to career, not applicable, not complicable, not simple, not poor, not rich, not subjective, not objective, not materialistic, not from this world, not earthly, not religious, not flighting, not narrow, not wide, not ideel, not habitual, not academical, not philosophical according to philosophical systems up-to-day (in the world), it is nothing and simultaneously all, it is not-paradoxe, not sentimental, not of any genre, not political, not big, not ideell, not formal, not rhythmical, not formed, antisymmetrical, antinot-decentralized, anti-not-current, not-current, not glorificative, not pathetic, not respectful, not formalistic, not critical, not attractive, not romantic, not superficial, not pessimistic, not a kind of psalms, not ugly, anti-not-spiritual, timeless, not vulgar, not exaggereting, not described, invisible about the invisible faculty of the Universe, not happening, not a kind of genre, notsubjective, supersubjective, the absolut FACULTY, supertimely character, superobjectivity, pure abstraction in its abstraction, ... in all kinds of art. (Essence)

Is the emotion the medium of materiality? and the medium of paiting? The medium of the philosophy of the art, of the arts and of the philosophy (of the totality, the super-timely, absolute, immateriality, no-physicality, possibility...)

It is the further — III before degree of transcendence, it ist international, cosmic, Slav... Roman, German, Anglo...

It is the purely absolute, super-timely, essence, emotion...

It is the super-subjectiv, super-objective faculty.

It is painted — realised beyond the TEXT-ART with the painters-roller, too.

It is painted towards the infinite, on plexiglass, on walls, on ceiling...

Emotion as subject is the pure absolute, not as attribute;

It was realised and now it is too, on plexiglasses, walls, ceilings: the first time in the Year 1977 after Christ (in our era).

TEXT-ART

[02B] *EMOTION. Pure Emotion. White Space in White Space - Text-art / EMÓCIA. Čistá Emócia. Biely priestor v bielom priestore - Text-art, Manifesto / Manifest, 1977*

These important texts are the starting point for Filko's later independently written *Text-art* works, by means of which he transferred his earlier textual production into his own *White Ontology* phase and also reevaluated it. Filko initiated his independent work here with his performative concept of *EMOTION – EMÓCIA (Text-art)* (1977) [0 2], but was also still drawing on questions concerning materiality and transcendence in art. He uses the concept of "pure emotion" as a further (third) form of transcendence.

Diese wichtigen Texte bildeten den Ausgang für Filkos spätere und eigenständig verfassten *Text-art* Schriften, durch deren Ausarbeitung er die vorangegangenen, textlichen Produktionen in seine eigene Werkphase der *Weißen Ontologie* überführte und damit noch einmal neu bewertete. Mit dem performativen Konzept *EMOTION – EMÓCIA (Text-art)* (1977) [0 2] initiierte Filko das alleinige Kapitel, schließt aber weiter an Fragen nach der Materialität und der Transzendenz in der Kunst an. Er verwendet den Begriff der „reinen Emotion" als eine weitere (dritte) Ausprägung des Transzendenten.

TRANSCENDENCIA
(Nadzmyslovosť — naddimenzionálnosť)

Tvorba 1978—79 atď. je zrkadlom transcendencie.

Je to čistá absolútne nadabsolútna špecifická vo svojej špecifickosti nadčasová, večná, prapodstatná, nadsubjektívna, nadobjektívna danosť vo svojom čistom umení. Môže sa pochopiť len na vnútornej hodnote a slobode absolútnosti človeka, ale nie naukovo vedecky vysvetliť.

Nie je len vedomie subjektu, alebo objektu, ale je to uvedomenie si...

Je to boj za totalizovanie absolútnej danosti, večnosti pre človeka, ktoré bolo, je a bude, treba ho len...(nie náboženstvo — nie relígia), kde nejde len o absolútnu krásu, ale o čistú prapodstatu — je to čisté ego, teda nie je to len sebarealizácia človeka, možno i tam transcendencia začína.

Nie je to žiaden žáner, ani fyzikálna filozofia, nie je to len obohatenie vnútornej duchovnej estetiky človeka, ale je to uvedomenie si samej prapodstaty, čistoty, absolútnosti, čistého absolútneho umenia — esencia. Nie je to žiadna tzv. figurácia ani tzv. abstrakcia, ani tzv. abstrahovanosť, ani tá najabstrahovanejšia, ale v skutočnosti je ponad alebo ak chceme poza za ňu. Teda je to ponad absolútna, ponad objektívna, nefyzikálna nadčasová danosť.

Absolútny je i „Biely priestor v bielom priestore", ktorý má tri stupne svojej danosti: 1. senzibilita, 2. senzitivita, 3. emócia.

Transcendencia vo fyzikálnom svete, v živote, vo vede, v náuke sa zdá byť bláznovstvom, ale akým bláznovstvom, to záleží všetko na našej vnútornej úrovni, duchovnosti, slobode, ...a na každom absolútnom ponad absolútnom...

Transcendencia je realizovaná viacerými formami, výtvarnými atribútmi, či už slovnejšie, obraznejšie, optickejšie, menej optickejšie, materiálnejšie, menej materiálnejšie, atď....

V skutočnosti je najlepšie zrušiť materiálnosť, optickosť, slovnosť, atď....

Transcendencia je predstavená pre konzumenta — diváka: 1. slovne — zrkadlovo, 2. na vlastnej osobe vytiahnutá z kruhu — prúdu každodennej existencie?

Pojem predmetnosť, nepredmetnosť, konkrétnosť, nekonkrétnosť, abstrahovanosť, čistá abstrakcia, tvarovosť, netvarovosť, symetria, asymetria, porovnanie, neporovnanie, ...tu už nemá žiaden zmysel ani význam.

TRANSCENDENTION
(Oversensuality)

Creation 1978—79 etc. is the mirror of transcendention.

It is pure absolute overabsolute, specific in its specify, overtemporal, overlasting, essentiality, oversubjective, overobjective existence, in its pure art. It can be understood only in the internal value and freedom of the absolutness of a man, but not doctrinaly, scientificaly explained.

It is not only consciousness of subject or object, but it is the realization...

It is the fight for totalizing of absolute existence, eternity for the man, which was, is and will be, it only is to be... (no religion), where is not only a way of absolute beauty, but the way of pure essentiality — that is the pure ego.

So that is not only a selfrealization of a man, the transcendention may start there, too.

It is neither genre, nor physical philosophy, it is not only enrichness of internal spiritual aesthetic, of a man, but the realization of the essentiality itself, cleanliness, absolutness, pure absolute art — essence. It neither is so called figuration or abstraction neither that the most abstractive, but it realy is above it or if we want around it.

So it is above absolutness, above objectivity, unphysical, overtemporal existence.

Transcendention in the physical world, in the life, in the science looks to be foolness, it all depends on our internal level, on spirit, freedom... and on each absolutness above absolutness.

Transcedention is realized by more of the fine art's atributions, more vocabulary, more metaphoricaly, more optical, less optical, more materialy, less materialy etc....

It is the best in reality to ban the materiality, vocabularity, etc....

The transcendention is served to the consumer — onlooker: 1. by mirrors, 2. on its own person pullerd out from the circle — of the stream of everyday's existence?

The notion — objectivity, unobjectivity, concretion, unconcretion, abstraction, pure abstraction, formness, unformness; symmetry, unsymmetry, compareness, uncompareness have neither sence nor importance here anymore.

[handwritten: Filko – 1976 1979 Textart]
[handwritten: 1978 – FILKO – TEXT ART – KONTEXT ART]

1978

Pomocou čistého, nefyzikálneho, nadčasového, nadsubjektívneho, absolútneho,... bieleho priestoru, v bielom priestore čistého umenia dostali sme sa do vnútornej premeny myslenia, s ktorou sa ďalej dostávame k hlbšiemu mysleniu... transcendenciou — čistého nefyzikálneho, nadsubjektívneho, nadčasového absolútneho... čistého umenia.

TRANSCENDENCIA

Transcendencia = predskúsenostný, nadzmyslový (podstata transcendenta = predskúsenosť — nadzmyslovosť [nie náboženstvo]).

Transcendencia je čistá, nadčasová, nadsubjektívna, nadobjektívna, absolútna,... podstatná danosť všetkých umení, vo filozofickom svete nevysvetliteľná, jej vnútorná podstata pozná, uvedomuje si extrát všetkých druhov umenia (doteraz na tejto Zemi vytvorených — fyzikálnych — i nefyzikálnych) a najmä ich objavenie, odhalenie podstaty, neviditeľnosti umenia, (fyzikálnych i nefyzikálnych) v nefyzikálnej nadčasovej skutočnosti...

Transcendentné umenie je umenie **nadnefyzikálne**, vychádza a pozná všetko, čo vlastní predchádzajúce nefyzikálne umenie, čisté umenie — Biely priestor v bielom priestore = senzibilita; senzitivita; emócia.

Transcendencia patrí a zároveň **je i štvrtý stupeň** nefyzikálneho absolútneho, nadčasového,... nadsubjektívneho,... čistého umenia, ktorá ale prekročila Biely priestor v bielom priestore.

Transcendencia je teda i extrát všetkých druhov Bieleho priestoru v bielom priestore (senzibilita, senzitivita, emócia).

Možná — možný začiatok, predchodca uvedomenia si čistého umenia je už i Platón, Aristoteles, Akvinský, Deskartes, Leibniz, Kant, Hegel,... Grédt, Mercier, Maritain, Gilson,... Gergaard,... čistá fenomenológia,...

Čistá transcendencia — čisté umenie nefyzikálne, nadčasové, nadsubjektívne, absolútne,... je a má možná výťažok — esenciu i z Husserlového transcendentálneho subjektu, treba ako sám Husserl tvrdí; poznať transcendentálny subjekt znamená preskúmať — premyslieť intencionálnu štruktúru vedomia. Sú to zákony absolútnej slobody, čo do presnosti a prísnosti, prekonávajú zákony exaktných vied.

Je to i výťažok, — esencia z umenia neviditeľného egyptského, paleolitického, neolitického, Leonarda da Vinciho...

Čisté umenie je večná, nefyzikálna (nie náboženská) nadčasová, nadsubjektívna, absolútna, nefyzikálna,... danosť. Je to absolútne nefyzikálno vo fyzikálnosti, skryté tajomstvo, je to totálna negácia (možná len zatiaľ) logických spôsobov myslenia. Zčasti ju objavujeme (možno) v tzv. druhej filozofii a najmä v čistom nefyzikálnom umení, ktorá je nadčasová, nadsubjektívna, absolútna,...

je to tajomný skrytý zdroj večného svetla, ktorá vyžaruje až do nadčasovosti, absolútnosti, nadsubjektívnosti,..., nedá sa deštrovať pomocou hociakej filozofie, jedine pomocou čistého transcendenta (nadčasová danosť sa nedá a nemôže redukovať, vysvetlovať poznaním — pomocou fyzikálneho sveta).

Čistá transcendencia čistého umenia prekročila čistú fenomenológiu, ontológiu, senzibilitu, senzitivitu, emóciu — je to totálna fyzikálna prázdnota a je večnou danosťou nadčasovosti, absolútnosti,...

Oproti senzibilite, senzitivite, emócii — Bieleho priestoru nefyzikálneho sveta, nehmotnosti, nepredmetnosti, netvarovosti, absolútnosti, má čistá transcendencia absolútnu nemateriálnosť i nefarebnosť, ktorá sa už neprejavuje ani ako pomocný dorozumievajúci — vysvetľujúci prostriedok.

Čistá transcendencia je objavenie a zároveň realizovanie absolútnej nadnefyzikálnej danosti, nadčasovosti, absolútnosti,... pomocou nadsubjektivizácie (vedomie a danosť — danosť a vedomie?).

Prostredníctvom subjektívneho myslenia uskutočňujeme fakt danosti, čím sa môžeme dostať do nadsubjektivizácie absolútnosti, nadčasovosti,... je to danosť, ktorú objavujeme (treba rozmýšľať, mať dušu, ducha, cit,... vedomie, podvedomie) nadsubjektívnou, nadobjektívnou aktívnosťou, tranzitívnosťou, cieľavedomosťou,... ???.

Transcendencia je nefyzikálne, nadnefyzikálne, nefilozofické, nadčasové, neobjektívne, absolútne, nadsubjektívne,... čisté umenie. Nie je to už Biely priestor v bielom priestore (senzibilita, senzitivita, emócia), je to i jeho výťažok — esencia, ktorá z neho vyšla a bez neho by možná nebola vznikla čistá nadsubjektívna, nadnefyzikálna, nadčasová, absolútna,... **transcendencia**.

[handwritten: Filko... 1976-77 +1978 Fylko]
[handwritten: TEXT ART – KONTEXT ART]

A larger shift came with the texts *TRANSCENDENCE / TRANSCENDENCIA* (1978) [03] [04] and *TRANSCENDENCE I., II. / TRANSCENDENCJA I., II.* (1979) [05], where he understood the essential element of the transcendent in art increasingly as an expression of his principle of the artistic ego. Here a critical view is called for, as this turns out to be a patriarchal perspective in which the "absolute existence of a man" becomes an all-encompassing principle of artistic creation. Filko himself developed a new self-awareness through his work on texts, further establishing his artistic identity.

Ein größerer Einschnitt folgt mit den Schriften *TRANSCENDENCE / TRANSCENDENCIA* (1978) [03] [04] und *TRANSCENDENCE I., II. / TRANSCENDENCJA I., II.* (1979) [05], wobei das so wesentliche Element des Transzendenten in der Kunst von Filko zunehmend als Ausdruck seines Prinzips des künstlerischen Egos verstanden wird. Ein kritischer Blick auf diese Entwicklung ist hier angebracht: Es offenbart sich eine patriarchale Perspektive, welche die „absolute Existenz eines Mannes" zum allumfassenden Prinzip der künstlerischen Schöpfung erklärt. Filko selbst entwickelt im Zuge der Textarbeit ein neues Selbstbewusstsein, mit dem er seine künstlerische Identität festigt.

STANISLAV FILKO – WORKS – ART

I.

TO BE, Nature, the Man, Father, Bible, History, Popular character .Sentiment, Rational, Individuum, Essention, Scholastika, Roman, Gothic, Romantic, Physical – to be, Subject, Concrete, Nature, Power, Absurdity, Nostalgic, Sensibility, Eensitivitet, Emotion, Spirit, Intelligent, Intellectuality...
1959 — Art painting real
1960–62 — Art nature, Art material, Art Slavic / Art Bible Action, Art Lettrism Action
1963 — Art Collage Action, Art Dressing Action / Art Assemblage Action
1964 — Art Pop Architecture
1963–65 — Art Ringing Action, Art Graphic Action / Art Cinema – Film, Art Mirror Action / Art Environments Action, Art Bible Action / Art Altars Action, Art erotic Action
1967–68 — Art My birthplace, Art Power / Art Land Action
1969 — Art Performance Action
1972 — Art Nature – Power – Collective

II.

TO BE, Technics XX.ST., the Man, Power, Son, Concrete, Elektronic, Sintes, Renaissance, Modern, Times, Space, Baroc, Individuum, Essention, Subject, Physical – to be, Industry, Technics, Universe, Objectiv, Sensibility, Optimism, Cosmos, Future, Spirit, Intelligent, Intellectuality...
1965–67 — Art Happsoc – Conspect Manifestation
1966 — Art erotic, Project, Concept
1966–67 — Art System Action, Art minimal / Art constructivism, Art sociological / Art Light Action, Art Cynetism Action / Art Cinema-Film Action, Art multiple

Art Ringing Action, Art Environmen[t] / Art Manifestation, Art Utopistic / **Art Real Cosmos Action**
1968–69 — Art Project Action – Manifestation / Concept Action – Manifestation, Art [...]pect, / Action Manifestation, Art real Cosm[os Ac]tion, / Art Television Action, Art Video Act[ion] / Art sociological, Art ringing Action, / Art Text, Art Cinema Film / Art Idea, Art Future
1970–72 — Art collective

III.

TO BE, nonphysical, the Man, Super, Ess[ention], Subject, Intelligent, Spirit, Pure Spir[it], Absolute, Super-timely, pure Intellectuality technics, PURE, Super, Esention...
1954–59 — Art phenomenological a) 1954–59 (p[...] design, graphics, partiture, text...)
1970–72 — Art phenomenological b) 1970–72 (p[...] graphics, partiture, text...)
1973–77 — Art white space in white space (p[...] graphics, design, partiture, text, [...] Art, Manifestation, Text Art...) / a) pure-sensibility – 1973 b) pure-se[...] 1974–5–6 c) pure-Emotion – 1977
1978–79 — Art Transcendency a) b) c) (p[...] graphics, partiture, ringing, Manife[...] Design, Text Art...)
1980 — Art Meditation Transcendency (p[...] sculpture, graphics, partiture, design[...] ing, Manifestation, Text Art...)

DIW CRIZ 756/80 500 O-4

The text *MEDITATION TRANSCENDENTAL – Text-art / TRANSCENDENTÁLNA MEDITÁCIA – Text-art* (1980) [06] is soberer in comparison to the other works. Filko summarizes his entire text-art production of the 1970s and derives abstract concepts from it, providing systematic definitions. Filko developed his *Text-art* through his whole career in parallel to his production of art-works, thereby strengthening his theoretical position and also then establishing his *Archive SF*.

Das Schriftstück *MEDITATION TRANSCENDENTAL – Text-art / TRANSCENDENTÁLNA MEDITÁCIA – Text-art* (1980) [06] ist im Vergleich wieder sachlicher gehalten. Filko fasst die gesamte Textkunst-Produktion der 1970er-Jahre zusammen und arbeitet abstrakte Begriffe heraus, die er systematisch definiert. Die *Text-art* hat Filko sein ganzes Leben über parallel zu seiner Werkproduktion immer weiter ausgebaut, um seine theoretische Position zu stärken und schließlich das *Archiv SF* zu etablieren.

STANISŁAW FILKO

I.

1978

TRANSCENDENCJA

1979

II.

MAŁA GALERIA PSP–ZPAF
00-277 WARSZAWA, PLAC ZAMKOWY 8
SIERPIEŃ 1980

STANISLAV FILKO
MEDITATION TRANSCENDENTAL
1980

TEXT—ART

Meditation transcendental is an art — no scientific, super-real, beyond the doctrine, beyond the reality, anticosmic, beyond the cosmic, super-sensuous, pure super-timely sense, purely abstract, beyond the time, absolut, unobservable, planned, unplanned, super-objectif, beyond the objectif, no-subjectif, beyond the subjectif, super-subjectif, conceivable, inconceivable, spirituel, logically spirituel, silent, pur, unrecognizable, recognizable, existing before the experience...

Passing the white space and all the three degrees of the white space in the white space and its super-subjectivity of the three autors Filko—Laky—Zavarský and its infinty (pure sensibility as subject and not as attribut, 1973) (sensitivity pure as subject and not as attribut, 1974, 75, 76) pure emotion as subject and not as attribut, 1977), which manifested itself also in the Text-Art of sensibility, 1973, Text-Art of the sensitivity, 1974, 75, 76; of the emotions — in the Text-Art 1977 and also sets aut — phylosophi — cally, spirituelly. in coeating manner and artistically from the transcendency I 1978 and the transcendency II 1979.

It is no-physical, beyond the physical, super-timely, beyond the time, absolut, supernatural... a phenomenon supernatural (it is possible that it is working among the centres of the nervous system).

The absolut character — transcendency — transcendental... it is meditation transcendental.

The transcendental meditation is above, over, beyond... the physical, material, objectif, psychic, subjectif, objectif character, assymetric, formed, rytmic, coloured, picturesque, geometric, antigeometric, expressive, antiexpressive, technic, antitechnic, industrial, antiindustrial, artisanal, antiartisanal, usuel, antiusuel, functionnel, antifunctionnel, ideal, antiideal, political, antipolitical, applicable, unapllicable, formalistic, no-formalistic in manner of genre, in manner of no genre, compository, anticompository, existentional, antiexistentional, expressive, antiexpressive occurence, thinking. super-thinking, antithinking. It is a pure necessity.. the meditation transcendental.

CONTEMPLATION
= (Latin) concontrated reflexion, meditation, consideration

CONTEMPLATIVE
= (Latin) meditative, considerative, profound

MEDITATION
= (Latin) consideration, meditation, reflexion

MEDITATIVE
= (Latin) meditative, profound, reflective, considerative

SPIRIT
= 1. spirituel, internal world of the the man; soul, the interior
2. (philosophically) the immaterial essence of the being (in metaphysical and religious sense)
3. (ecclesiastically) Saint Spirit, the third person of God in the christian doctrine

SUBJECT
= (Latin) 1. the perceiving, understanding, thinking and working being
2. person
3. (in the grammaire) the subject

ABSOLUTE =

THE ABSOLUTE
= (Latin) in the idealistic philosophy the eternal, unchanged, infinite ancestral base of the world, rejected by the dialectic materialism
= (Latin) significates it which exists beside whatever relation, is not attached to any condition, exists for itself, is unlimited and perfect and the cause of all other, In the different philosophic tendances as absolute is considered God, the material, life, existence a. s. f.

THE ABSOLUTE CHARACTER
= (Latin) in the philosophy — exclusive validity, independance, character non-conditional

ABSOLUTE
= (Latin)
1. no attached to condition, independant (contrast ist the relative)
2. complete, perfect, a hundred percent
3. unlimited
4. is generally valid, has a permanent worth, permanent

MÚSIKÉ
= (a Greek locution which passed almost to all languages)

MUSIC
= (a Latin, German word in the standard-language) Music

NERVOUS SYSTEM
= (the Slovakian word nervný becomed obsolete, used in the literature, right is nervový) mechanism in the organism which regulates the activity of all the organism mechanismes

CREATION
= 1. technical term (creation)
2. creature

CREATIONISM
= philosophical tendance idealiste which proclaims the creation of lining beings
= (from the Latin creatio — creation)
1. explanation of the origine of the world by a creating act of a supernatural being
2. literary tendance proclaiming the magic power of the poetry to creates a new, ideal world (founded by the Chilean Huidobre)

CREATIVE
= (setting out of the former words about) creative

INTELLINGENCE
= 1. intellectual power, talent; intellect
2. Stratum of the intellectual workers, educated men

MENTAL
= concerning the intellectual maturity, intellectual

MENTALITY
= (French) mental adaptation; character of thinking and feeling

NIVEAU
= (French) the level

PHENOMENOLOGY
= (Greek) doctrine reactionary, idealistic, which examines the natural and spirituel phenomenons and considers the phenomenons of the conscience as the sole reality
= theory, reactionary and subjective-idealistic, based on the description and analysis of the phenomenons of the „pure" transcendental conscience

PHENOMENON
= (Greek)
1. sign, phenomenon
2. (philosophically) reality as it seems to us, phenomenon, sign; in the idealistic philosophy a subjective phenomenon, existing only in the conscience, which does not reflect the reality; phenomenon of the conscience
= (greek: phainomenon) terme used by E. Kant for the objective reality, as it appaers in our experience (contrasting to the „thing in itself" (Ding an sich). It is used also in wider sense for somwhat phenomenon (artistic, culturel, a. s. f.)

PHENOMENALISM
= (Grek) reactionary idealistic tendance denying the existence of an objective world and recogrizing the phenomenons of the conscience, the phenomenons as unique reality
= tendance philosophical, according to which the things are recognized as they appaer and not so as they are in reality

ČISTA SVIEST =

CZYSTY
= (in Polish) clean, veritable, pure

VREME
= (probably) time

TRANSCENDENTAL
= (Latin) in the idealistic system of E. Kant what is in our recognizing aprioristic, that will say all which is preceding our experience and simultaneously makes possible it, resp. is its condition; „philosophy transcendental" the system of the aprioristic conscience on the base of „pure" notions independant — supposedly — of the experience
= it which is before the experience, above the senses

TRANSCENDANT
= (from Latin transcendere — transgress) it which is in relation to some thing (occurence) beside this thing (occurence), which surpasses it. The contrast is the imminent. E. g. Kant eÛplains the transcedant as sommething which depasses the limits of our experience, resp. of our recognizing based on the experience; that will say the unrecognizable world of the things on themwelves — Ding an sich super the senses

TRANSCENDENTALISM
= tendance examining the supersensuel phenomenons

XX

*Transcendency / **Transzendenz***

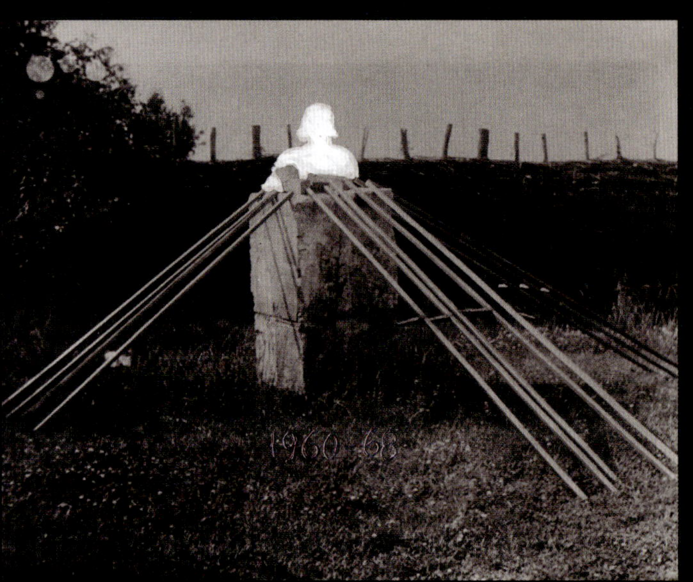

[01] *Interpretation HAPPSOC - Land Art from the series Transcendency / Interpretácia HAPPSOC - land art zo série Transcendencia, 1967/1978*

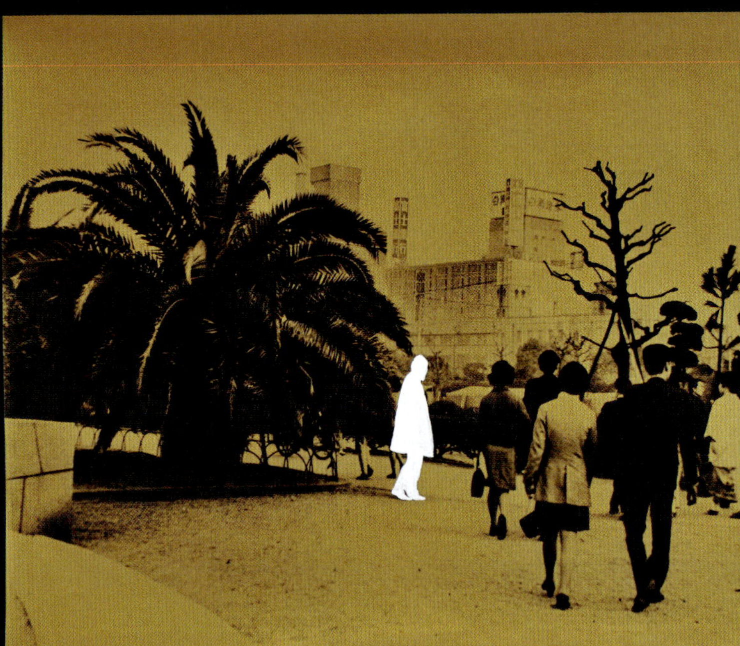

[02] From the cycle *Transcendency / Z cyklu Transcendencia, 1978-79*

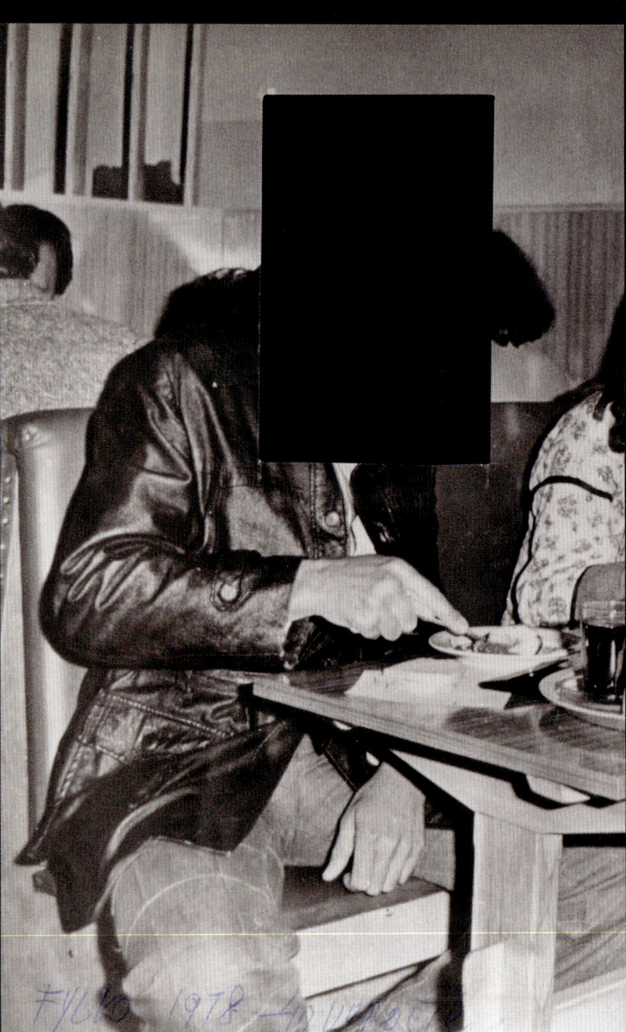

In the 1970s the themes of emptiness, transcendence, and the absolute played an important role in Filko's work. Transcendence addresses realms beyond material reality, and it entered into Filko's work in 1973 in the form of the color white in the installation *White Space in White Space / Biely priestor v bielom priestore*. This work was created in collaboration with Miloš Laky and Ján Zavarský, but thereafter Filko developed the theme alone, as in the *Transcendency / Transcendencia* cycle. In the course of his work, Filko brought all of the works exploring this theme together under the idea of *White Ontology*.

In den 1970er-Jahren spielen die Themenbereiche Leerheit, Transzendenz und das Absolute eine wichtige Rolle in Filkos Schaffen. Die Transzendenz thematisiert das über die stoffliche Wirklichkeit Hinausreichende und trat unter dem Zeichen der Farbe Weiß 1973 durch die Installation *White Space in White Space / Biely priestor v bielom priestore* innerhalb von Filkos Œuvre in Erscheinung. Aus dieser Zusammenarbeit mit Miloš Laky und Ján Zavarský entwickelte Filko den Themenbereich in späterer Folge alleine weiter, wie auch der Zyklus *Transcendency / Transcendencia* zeigt. Im Laufe seines Schaffens fasste Filko diesen weitreichenden Teil seines Werkes unter dem Stichwort *White Ontology* zusammen.

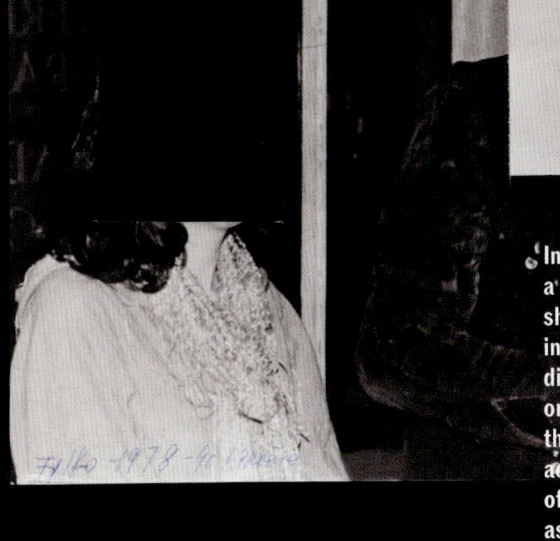

[03] From the cycle
*Transcendency III. / Z cyklu
Transcendencia III.*, 1979

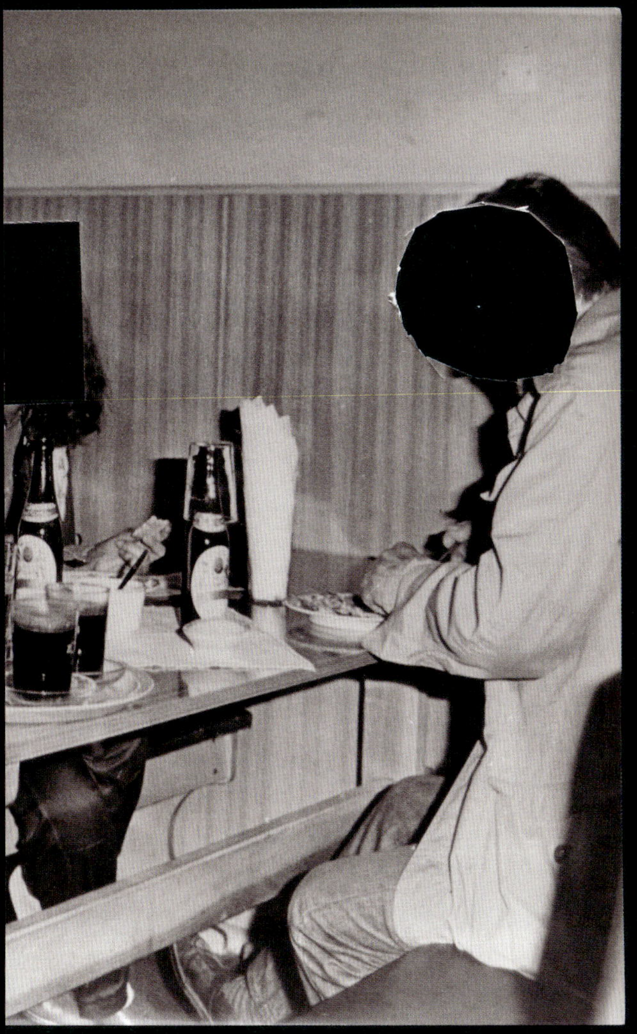

In this photo series, Filko again addresses a process of dematerializing art, here shifting it to different kinds of photographs in which he sets in motion a dynamics of disappearance. Filko removes faces or whole people from the pictures, either through overpainting them in white, or by actually cutting faces out of the paper of the photographs. Filko uses these works as mirrors of transcendence, as he himself put it. This would seem to be a form of the transformation of everyday life.

Some of the photographs have added golden pigment that makes them seem like sacred objects. This impression is heightened by the overpainting of entire figures in white, so that what remain are flat silhouettes that add a mysterious element to reality. On one photograph this is particularly conspicuous: a group of persons is leaning on a railing before a church, and between the church and these people is a figure seen from the front and overpainted in white [09]. White color fields in other works in the series clearly show their affinity to the aesthetics of *White Space in White Space / Biely priestor v bielom priestore*.

Filko greift den Prozess der Entmaterialisierung der Kunst in der Fotoserie wieder auf und verlagert diesen, indem er eine Dynamik der Auslöschung auf verschiedenartigen Fotografien in Gang setzt. Filko löscht Gesichter und einzelne Personen aus dem Bildzusammenhang, einerseits durch Übermalung mit weißer Farbe, andererseits werden viele Gesichter durch die stellenweise Entfernung des Bildmaterials selbst herausgelöst. Filko verwendet die Arbeiten als Spiegel der Transzendenz, so hat er es zumindest selbst ausgedrückt, es scheint dabei um eine Form der Umwandlung des Alltäglichen zu gehen.

Einige der Fotografien sind mit goldenem Pigment versehen und wirken dadurch sakral. Verstärkt wird der Eindruck durch das Übermalen ganzer Figuren in Weiß, woraufhin flache Silhouetten entstehen, die der Wirklichkeit eine mysteriöse Komponente hinzufügen. Auf einer Fotografie fällt dies ganz besonders auf: eine Gruppe von Personen lehnt an einem Geländer vor einer Kirchenfassade, darüber, hinter den Rücken der Personen, eine weißübermalte Figur in frontaler Ansicht [09]. Zudem wird auf anderen Arbeiten der Serie anhand weißer Farbfelder die Nähe zur Ästhetik von *White Space in White Space / Biely priestor v bielom priestore* offensichtlich.

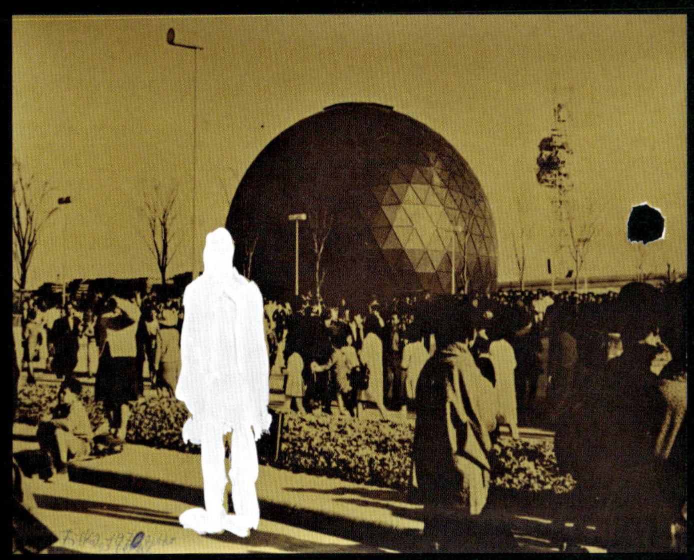

[05] From the cycle *Transcendency I. / Z cyklu Transcendencia I.*, 1970/1978

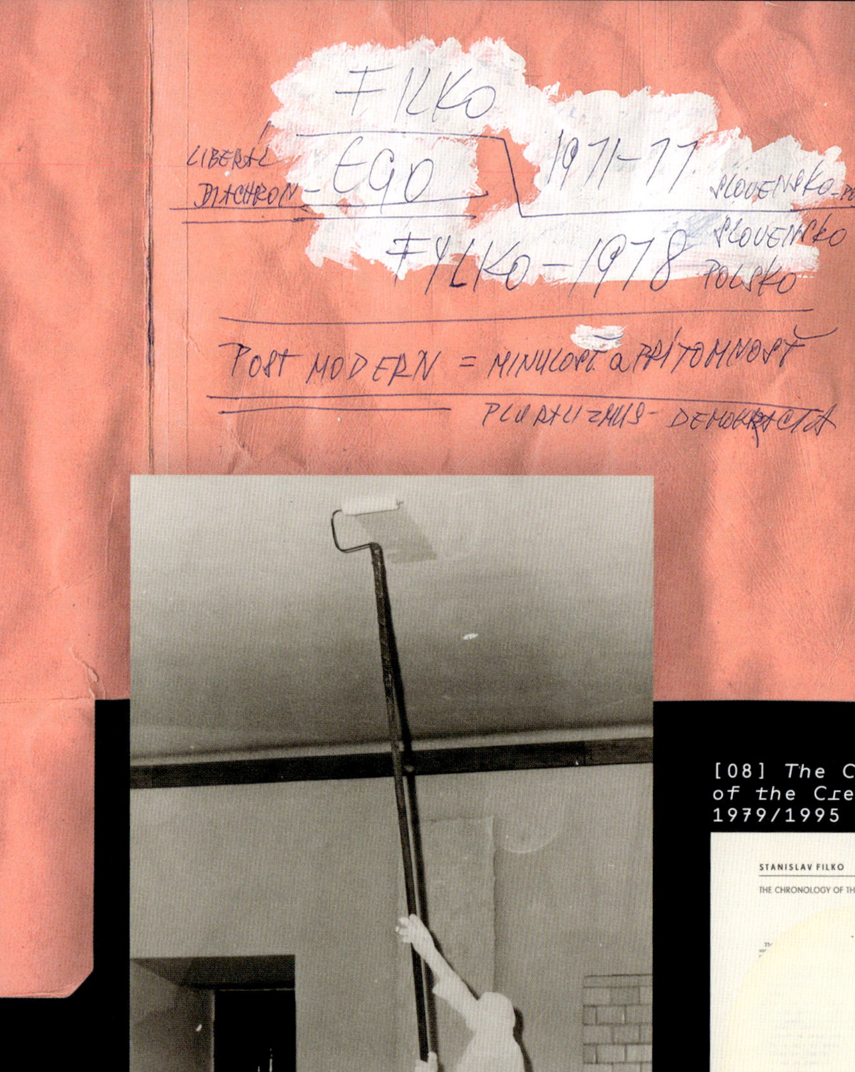

[07] *Emotion - Transcendency /
Emócia - Transcendencia, 1977-78*

[08] *The Chronology
of the Creation - Art,
1979/1995*

On some works Filko himself might be seen, but his face is always covered over in white. In others well-known people from history or Filko's friends are presented, but most of them have been made unrecognizable. The still visible features of buildings and landscape in two photographs suggest that these were taken in 1970 during Filko's trip to Japan to take part in the Expo in Osaka. The artist seems to transfer his own personal experience into the white of transcendence, addressing a different level of reality. The accompanying incorporeality recalls spiritual teachings and seems to propose a timeless perspective on life. In religious contexts leaving the real world behind is often associated with a kind of purity. Filko seems to be taking a more radical approach to his art here, with a new introspection and formlessness, and an awareness of an absolute existence which he repeatedly proclaimed through his own self. His fifth dimension stands at the center of it all, with the color white symbolizing this realm.

Auf manchen Arbeiten vermutet man Filko selbst, jedoch ist sein Gesicht immer mit weißer Farbe ausgelöscht, auf anderen sind historische Persönlichkeiten oder Freunde zumeist unkenntlich abgebildet. Anhand der verbliebenen architektonischen und landschaftlichen Details zweier Fotografien lässt sich vermuten, dass es sich um Aufnahmen handelt, die 1970 auf Filkos Japan-Reise entstanden sind. Diese stand auch im Zusammenhang seiner Teilnahme an der Expo in Osaka. Der Künstler scheint seine persönlichen Erfahrungen in das Weiß der Transzendenz zu überführen und thematisiert damit eine andere Ebene der Realität. Die damit verbundene Körperlosigkeit erinnert an spirituelles Gedankengut, wobei es um eine überzeitliche Perspektive auf das Leben zu gehen scheint. Im religiösen Kontext ist die Herauslösung aus der Realität oft mit einer Art „Reinheit" verbunden. Für Filko scheint sich das Ganze noch einmal radikaler darzustellen, als neue Innerlichkeit und Formlosigkeit in der Kunst, wie auch als Bewusstsein der absoluten Existenz, die er immer wieder durch die eigene Person proklamiert. In den Mittelpunkt der Überlegungen rückt Filkos 5. Dimension mit der Farbe Weiß als Symbolisierung für genau diesen Bereich.

[09] From the cycle Transcendency /
Z cyklu Transcendencia, 1978–79

Ciphers of Transcendency
Filko's Construct of a Universal Extrasensory Worldview

Christian Höller

"Transcendency is pure, super timely, super objective, absolute, … [an] essential faculty of all the arts, inexplicable in the philosophical world …." This is a statement from a manifesto of 1978, printed in the twenty-page exhibition publication on the occasion of Stano Filko's 1979 *Transcendencja* show at Galeria GN ZPAF in Gdańsk. The aim of all artistic endeavor, as the repeated mantra-like wording said, was "the transcendency of the pure, notphysical, supersubjective, supertimely, absolute … pure art." And, taking the claim to universality of this program a step further: "Pure art is eternal, notphysical …. It is the absolutely not-physical in the physicality, hided (hidden) secret, it is the total negation … of the logical manners of thinking."[1]

What drove Filko, aged forty, to posit such an exaggerated paradigm of universality, in view of the materialist worldview that was the official doctrine of the communist states at the time? How was this hyper-idealist program to be understood, one which left even the most vehement advocates of the transcendental and of knowledge far beyond the realm of the senses look rather timid. "Transcendency is before experiences, … supersensousness (not religion)," Filko said, here still certainly in line with idealist philosophy, but then not permitting art (whatever its specific approach at this particular historical moment might be) any sensual leeway whatsoever: "it is the total physical vacuum and eternal faculty of super timely, absolute character."[2] What might this art be like, which was completely immaterial, colorless (a matter of course), beyond time, and beyond all the parameters of the subjective and objective? A vacuum, pure negation, simply *absolute*, but without being equated with religious experience?

The manifesto included photographs, some of them of exhibits or exhibition views from the show in Gdańsk, all with one thing in common. They all had a figure that was painted over in white or cut out. These photographs showed scenes from Filko's life going back as far as 1945, including images of the artist installing his work. They all had these "white-outs," which for Filko signaled no less than the transition to the transcendental. "Breaking the intactness of the exhibition photos covering various periods in my life was a means of a transcendental change,"[3] he said looking back in an interview in 1991, then adding that the whole thing was strongly connected to transcendental philosophy, which he had got to know from his grandfather Paul. Already as a child he had conversations with his grandfather about the connection between the extrasensory (in a non-mystical sense) and the idea of the white space or the color white (which was not a color for him). It just took a long while, he said, into the 1970s, for him to begin to introduce this connection into his art. The manipulated photographs in the Gdańsk exhibition gave an impression of this or rather presented one possible version of how to implement the "change" to the transcendental—namely by attempting to destroy the trace of one's own presence, whether when working on the land, holding a lecture, or being together with others in a photo booth.

Of course this is no real erasure, as the whitening far too clearly indicates what has been whitened and thus makes it seem all the more interesting. Rather, this act expresses the "wish to disappear,"[4] the aim of leading one's own creation, even one's own existence, or at least elementary parts of these, toward the great all-encompassing universal void that precludes all physical or sensual articulation. In other words: striving for the supratemporal, supraobjective (and suprasubjective), the absolute that is the basis of everything earthly or that encompasses it from without.

Infinite Void

Of course Filko knew that it was not so easy to approach the extrasensory absolute, which is why it was all the more

Chiffren von Transzendenz
Filkos Konstrukt einer universellen übersinnlichen Anschauung

Christian Höller

„Transcendency is pure, super timely, super objective, absolute, … [an] essential faculty of all the arts, inexplicable in the philosophical world …" So lautet ein Eintrag in dem 1978 verfassten Manifest, abgedruckt in der zwanzigseitigen Ausstellungspublikation anlässlich von Stano Filkos Schau *Transcendencja* (1979) in der Galeria GN ZPAF in Gdańsk. Ziel jeder Kunstanstrengung, so die mantrahaft wiederkehrende Formel, sei „the transcendency of the pure, notphysical, supersubjective, supertimely, absolute […] pure art". Und um den Absolutheitsanspruch dieses Programms nochmals zu toppen: „Pure art is eternal, notphysical […]. It is the absolutely not-physical in the physicality, hided (hidden) secret, it is the total negation […] of the logical manners of thinking."[1]

Was hatte den damals vierzigjährigen Filko dazu getrieben, angesichts einer materialistischen Weltanschauung, wie sie in den kommunistischen Staaten damals offizielle Doktrin war, ein derart überspitztes Absolutheitsparadigma zu postulieren? Wie war dieses hyperidealistische Programm zu verstehen, das selbst die vehementesten Verfechter des Transzendentalen, einer über alles Sinnliche hinausgehenden Erkenntnis, alt aussehen ließ? „Transcendency is before experiences, […] supersensousness (not religion)", hieß es durchaus noch in Einklang mit der idealistischen Philosophie, um jedoch der Kunst – wie immer sie in diesem historischen Moment konkret ausgerichtet sein mochte – so gut wie keinen sinnlichen Spielraum mehr zu lassen: „pure transcendency has absolute immateriality and colorless character" – „it is the total physical vacuum and eternal faculty of super timely, absolute character."[2] Wie konnte diese Kunst beschaffen sein, die gänzlich immateriell, farblos (versteht sich von selber), noch dazu überzeitlich, jenseits aller Grenzen des Subjektiven und Objektiven, angesiedelt sein sollte? Ein Vakuum, pure Negation, *absolut* eben, ohne deshalb mit religiöser Erfahrung gleichgesetzt zu sein?

Beigefügt waren dem Manifest Fotografien, teils Exponate bzw. Ausstellungsansichten der Schau in Gdańsk, die eines miteinander verband: Es war stets eine Figur auf dem jeweiligen Bild weiß übermalt oder ausgeschnitten worden. Die Fotografien zeigten, zurückreichend bis ins Jahr 1945, Szenen aus Filkos Leben bzw. den Künstler beim Installieren der Arbeit – allesamt mit besagten „white-outs" versehen, die für Filko nichts weniger als den Übergang zum Transzendenten signalisierten. „Breaking the intactness of the exhibition photos covering various periods in my life was a means of a transcendental change"[3], sagte er rückklickend in einem Interview 1991, um sogleich hinzuzufügen, dass das Ganze stark mit der Transzendentalphilosophie, wie er sie von seinem Großvater Paul kennengelernt hatte, zusammenhing. Bereits als Kind sei er im Gespräch mit diesem auf den Zusammenhang zwischen dem Übersinnlichen (im nicht-mystischen Sinn) und der Idee des weißen Raums bzw. der Farbe Weiß (die für ihn keine Farbe war) gestoßen. Es habe nur lange gedauert, nämlich bis in die 1970er-Jahre, bis er diesen Konnex auch in seiner Kunst umzusetzen begann. Die bearbeiteten Fotografien der Gdańsk-Ausstellung vermittelten einen Eindruck davon bzw. stellten eine mögliche Variante dar, wie sich die „Veränderung" hin zum Transzendentalen bewerkstelligen ließ: nämlich indem die Spur seiner eigenen Präsenz, sei es bei der Arbeit auf dem Land, bei einem Vortrag, oder zusammen mit anderen Personen in einem Fotoautomat, zu tilgen versucht wird.

Selbstredend ist dies keine wirkliche Auslöschung – dafür deutet die Weißung zu sehr auf das Geweißte und damit umso interessanter Erscheinende hin. Vielmehr drückt sich in dem Akt der „Wunsch zu verschwinden"[4] aus: das Ansinnen, das eigene Schaffen, ja die eigene Existenz, oder zumindest elementare Teile davon, an die große, umfassende, universelle Leere heranzuführen, die jeglicher physischen oder sinnlichen

decidedly spoken of in the manifestos of this period. These manifestos began with the first formulation of the *White Space in White Space* concept in 1973 and then saw continuous adaptations and reformulations through the 1970s. In 1973, Filko had cooperated with Miloš Laky and Ján Zavarský, in order, as it was put in the first programmatic text on their jointly planned "creation," to make a "white unmaterialized space in a pure white infinite space." [01] (The three had already worked together, with further artists too, in the projects *…Time I… / …Čas I…* [1973] and *Time II. / Čas II.* [1973].[5]) *Biely priestor v bielom priestore*, the original title, was devoted to "pure sensibility," a concept that clearly displays references to Malevich (see for example his painting *White on White*, 1917)[6] and Yves Klein (particularly his installation *The Void*, 1958).[7] "Pure sensibility" was not explicitly connected to extrasensory absolutes (super timely, super objective, supersubjective, etc.) at this juncture, but it was nonetheless certainly aimed at going "beyond the world of reality" and accessing "internal dynamics being identical with infinitude."[8]

Now this going beyond objective (and also subjective) reality, this pretty-well obsessive reaching out for the infinite may well have been strongly determined by the situation in Czechoslovakia at the time, in particular the politics of the state. Research has often noted that the reduction to a zero point of white on white, and moreover in a spatial setting, that was intended to create a sense of immaterial endlessness, was a vehement and uncompromising counter-reaction to the materialist state doctrine (or in artistic terms socialist realism).[9] Filko and his comrades-in-arms repeatedly came into conflict with the authorities after the defeat of the Prague Spring in 1968, and he found very few opportunities to exhibit his work. This meant that it was necessary to devise a form of artistic articulation that avoided coming up against the powers-that-were, and also—and perhaps even more crucially—to search for a mode of transcendency that went beyond the unpleasant and highly restrictive (and also social) reality. The way out was "the idea of infinite emptiness," as the manifesto put it by way of a cipher for this transcendency, but that was also too intangible for the authorities for them to be able to identify it as an explicit violation of the dominant doctrine.

Filko, Laky, and Zavarský installed the first version of *White Space in White Space / Biely priestor v bielom priestore* pretty well overnight on February 18, 1974, in the Brno House of the Arts,[10] while also producing photographic documentation [02] that they then distributed together with the first manifesto as a samizdat self-publication—while hardly anyone had had a chance to actually see the exhibition. It was important here to avoid any form of individual signature, to use industrial materials, and to postulate collective authorship. In subsequent versions, such as at the Galéria mladých in Bratislava in 1974 or at the Paris Biennial in 1975, further elements were added to the original ensemble that adhered to these criteria and was made of white canvases rolled out or unfolded on the wall, whereby the folds had to be clearly visible as an integral component. These additions included free-standing cardboard rolls of differing heights and hanging felt strips of different lengths and painted white.[11] [03–04] This led to the second mainly *vertical* phase of *White Space in White Space / Biely priestor v bielom priestore,*

following on from the horizontal first phase, which was now entitled "pure sensitivity" in contrast to the original "pure sensibility." In terms of the idea of transcendence, going beyond the objective and subjective sensually perceivable space, it was said to make no real difference whether the accent was rather on sensibility or sensitivity. (From the present perspective too it is primarily the different focus on either the horizontal or the vertical that matters.) And when in 1977 "pure emotion" was added as a third level, now by Filko as the sole author,[12] this also seemed to be more a case of further emphasis of what had already been stated and less a principled new version of the underlying conceptual idea. [05]

The spatial and situational implementation was different, however, with the focus moving away from the form of an installation (which was not how it was denoted at the time), namely the presentation of a somehow already finished immaterial infinity, and toward a performative exploration of the same. This is well illustrated in a photograph that he used many times, showing Filko applying white paint using a roller attached to a rod, a performance that is illustrated in the catalog of the 1978 *Emotion – 1977* exhibition in Lublin and which Filko repeated a number of times, including in 1980 at Galeria SKC in Belgrade—Filko always referred to this as an "anti-performance." [06] While Július Koller had written of the "fiction of a space that de facto does not exist"[13] in a kind of counter-manifesto on the occasion of the original versions of *White Space*, it now seemed as if Filko wanted to provide active hints, again using art-based ciphers, as to how one might nonetheless gain proximity to such a space. The transcendency of immaterial infinity may well not have been immediately comprehensible, no matter how "sensibly," "sensitively," or "emotionally" you went about getting there. But some points of access could be created, certain secondary means established, even if these were then so matter-of-fact as dripping white paint on the extended arm of a painter's roller.

Transcendention

Art historian Ješa Denegri reported on Filko's "anti-performance" at SKC Belgrade in 1980, noting that the artist stood on a bench and applied white paint to the ceiling that was already painted white, using an extended roller, and doing this up to the point that this new coating, which initially was not visible, gradually began to appear in its own right. Like an apparition, or better a slow process of making it appear, come forward, define itself—all of which is again just an indirect aid to expressing the claim to the infinite that Filko was pursuing. It is also interesting that Denegri reported that during this action the artist's voice was heard from a cassette recorder, reciting a list of terms: "immateriality, informality, non-rhythmicity, non-abstractness, non-concreteness, non-constructiveness, non-decorativeness, non-applicability, non-subjectivity, non-objectivity, non-sentimentality, non-philosophicality, non-politicality" and so on.[14] That the absolute was strongly accompanied by the forced negation of everything finite and determined had already been clear in the Gdańsk manifesto ("the total negation of the logical manners of thinking"). But that this Hegelian construct also referred quite directly to the aesthetic implementation,

Artikulation vorausgeht. In anderen Worten: jenes Überzeitliche, Überobjektive (und Übersubjektive), sprich Absolute anzustreben, das allem Irdischen zugrunde liegt bzw. es von außen her einfasst.

Unendliche Leere

Dass dem übersinnlichen Absoluten nicht so leicht beizukommen ist, war Filko selbstverständlich klar. Deswegen wurde es in den zu dieser Zeit produzierten Manifesten auch umso eindringlicher beschworen. Manifeste, die 1973 in der ersten Formulierung des *White Space in White Space*-Konzepts ihren Ausgang nahmen und die gesamten 1970er-Jahre hindurch kontinuierliche Um- bzw. Neuformulierungen erfuhren. 1973 hatte sich Filko mit Miloš Laky und Ján Zavarský zusammengetan, um, wie es im ersten programmatischen Text zu der gemeinsam geplanten „Schöpfung" hieß, einen „weißen immateriellen Raum im weißen unendlichen Raum" zu schaffen. [01] (Die drei hatten zuvor, zusammen mit weiteren Künstlern, bei den Projekten *...Time I... / ...Čas I...* [1973] und *Time II. / Čas II.* [1973] zusammengearbeitet.[5]) *Biely priestor v bielom priestore*, so der Originaltitel, sollte der „reinen Sensibilität" gewidmet sein – ein Konzept, an dem sich unschwer Bezüge zu Malewitsch (vgl. etwa sein Bild *Weißes Quadrat auf weißem Grund*, 1917)[6] oder Yves Klein (vor allem dessen Installation *The Void*, 1958)[7] ablesen lassen. Die „reine Sensibilität" wurde auf dieser ersten Stufe noch nicht explizit mit übersinnlicher Absolutheit (super timely, super objective, supersubjective, etc.) in Verbindung gebracht, war aber nichtsdestotrotz bereits dezidiert auf eine „Überschreitung der Welt der Realität", ja eine Erschließung der „inneren Dynamik der Unendlichkeit" angelegt.[8]

Nun mag diese Überschreitung der objektiven (wie auch subjektiven) Realität, dieses geradezu besessene Schielen nach Unendlichkeit, stark von der gesellschafts- und vor allem auch staatspolitischen Situation in der damaligen Tschechoslowakei beeinflusst gewesen sein. Vielfach wurde in der Forschung angemerkt, dass die Reduktion auf diese Art Nullpunkt – Weiß auf Weiß, noch dazu in einem räumlichen Setting, das den Anschein immaterieller Grenzenlosigkeit vermitteln sollte – eine vehemente und kompromisslose Gegenreaktion auf die materialistische Staatsdoktrin (bzw. in künstlerischer Hinsicht auf den sozialistischen Realismus) darstellte.[9] Filko, wie auch seine Mitstreiter, war nach der Niederschlagung des Prager Frühlings 1968 wiederholt mit den Behörden in Konflikt geraten und fand kaum noch Ausstellungsmöglichkeiten vor – was es zum einen nötig machte, eine Form der künstlerischen Artikulation zu finden, der dieser Zusammenprall mit der politischen Obrigkeit erspart blieb; und zum anderen, vielleicht noch entscheidender, nach einem Modus der Transzendenz zu suchen, der über die unliebsame und höchst restriktiv materielle (bzw. auch soziale) Realität hinausging. Den Ausweg bot „die Idee der unendlichen Leere", wie es in dem Manifest hieß und als welche diese Transzendenz chiffriert war, die aber auch für die Autoritäten so wenig greifbar war als dass man daran einen expliziten Verstoß gegen die herrschende Doktrin hätte festmachen können.

Filko, Laky und Zavarský installierten die erste Version des „Weißen Raums im weißen Raum" in einer Art Nacht- und Nebelaktion am 18. Februar 1974 im Haus der Künste in Brno,[10] fertigten davon eine fotografische Dokumentation an [02], welche sie anschließend – die Ausstellung hat sonst niemand wirklich gesehen – zusammen mit dem ersten Manifest als Samisdat-Eigenpublikation in Umlauf brachten. Wichtig war bei der Realisierung die Vermeidung jeglicher individuellen Handschrift, die Verwendung industrieller Materialien sowie das Postulat einer kollektiven Autorschaft. In darauffolgenden Versionen, etwa in der Galéria mladých in Bratislava 1974 oder auf der Paris-Biennale 1975, wurden dem solcherart fabrizierten ursprünglichen Ensemble aus ausgerollten, an den Wänden hängenden bzw. ausgefalteten weißen Leinwänden (die Faltungen sollten als integraler Bestandteil gut erkennbar sein) weitere Elemente hinzugefügt: etwa unterschiedlich hohe, stehende Kartonrollen oder unterschiedlich lange, hängende Filzstreifen, allesamt weiß bemalt.[11] [03-04] Dies führte zur zweiten – nach der ersten, *horizontalen* – vorwiegend *vertikalen* Phase von *White Space in White Space / Biely priestor v bielom priestore*, welche im Unterschied zur „reinen Sensibilität" der ersten Version mit dem Begriff „reine Sensitivität" betitelt war. In Bezug auf den Transzendenzgedanken – dem Überschreiten der objektiven und subjektiven, sinnlich wahrnehmbaren Realität – machte es vermeintlich keinen allzu großen Unterschied, ob der Akzent eher auf Sensibilität oder auf Sensitivität lag. (Auch aus heutiger Sicht ist diesbezüglich primär die unterschiedliche Konzentration auf das Horizontale bzw. Vertikale ausschlaggebend.) Und als 1977, diesmal vom Alleinautor Filko verfasst, die „reine Emotion" als dritte Stufe hinzukam,[12] wirkte auch das mehr wie eine nachdrückliche Betonung des bereits Gesagten denn wie eine prinzipielle Neufassung der zugrundeliegenden Konzeptidee. [05]

Verschoben hatte sich hingegen die räumlich-situative Umsetzung: So verlagerte sich der Fokus vom Installativen (als welches es damals nicht bezeichnet wurde), sprich der Präsentation einer gleichsam fertigen immateriellen Unendlichkeit, hin zu einer eher performativen Erschließung derselben. Idealtypisch dafür ist ein mehrfach verwendetes Foto, das Filko beim Auftragen weißer Farbe mittels einer an einer Stange befestigten Farbwalze zeigt – eine Performance, die beispielsweise im Katalog zur Ausstellung *Emotion – 1977* (1978) in Lublin abgebildet ist, und die Filko unter anderem 1980 in der Galeria SKC in Belgrad wiederholte (von Filko stets als „Anti-Performance" bezeichnet) [06]. Hatte Július Koller anlässlich der anfänglichen Versionen von „White Space" in einer Art Gegenmanifest von der „Fiktion eines Raums, der de facto gar nicht existiert"[13], gesprochen, so schien es, als wolle Filko – erneut über chiffrenhafte Kunstgriffe – aktive Hinweise liefern, wie man trotz allem in die Nähe eines solchen Raumes gelangen könne. Die Transzendenz der immateriellen Unendlichkeit mochte nicht auf Anhieb – egal wie „sensibilisiert", „sensitiv" oder „emotional" man an die Sache heranging – einsehbar sein. Dennoch ließen sich Zugänge herstellen, Hilfskonstruktionen schaffen, auch wenn diese so lapidar sein mochten wie die tropfende weiße Farbe am verlängerten Arm einer Malerwalze.

Transzendention

Der Kunsthistoriker Ješa Denegri berichtete von Filkos „Anti-Performance" im SKC Belgrad 1980, dass der Künstler, auf einer Bank stehend, so lange weiße Farbe mit einem verlängerten Farbroller auf die weiß gestrichene Decke auftrug, bis

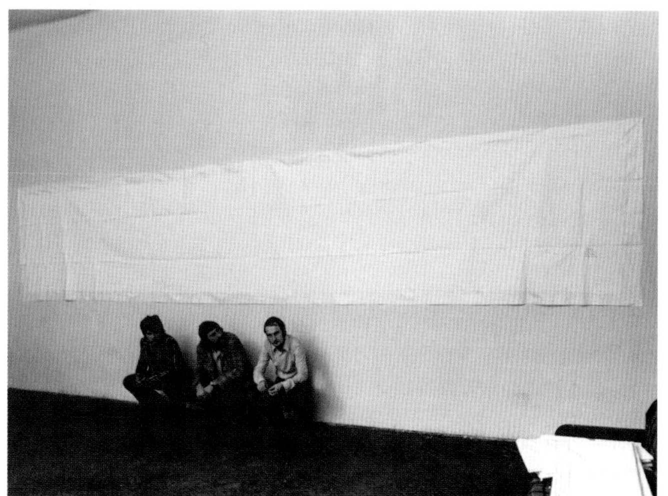

[01] Stano Filko, Miloš Laky, Ján Zavarský (from left to right), *White Space in White Space / Biely priestor v bielom priestore*, Academy of Fine Arts Bratislava, 1973

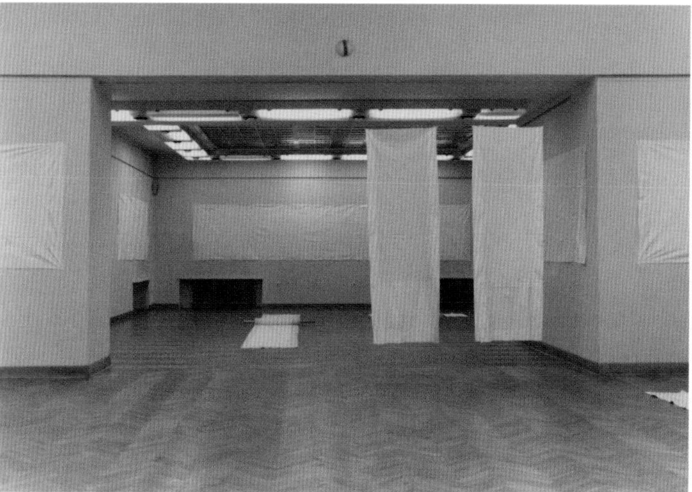

[02] Stano Filko, Miloš Laky, Ján Zavarský, *White Space in White Space / Biely priestor v bielom priestore*, House of Arts Brno, 1974

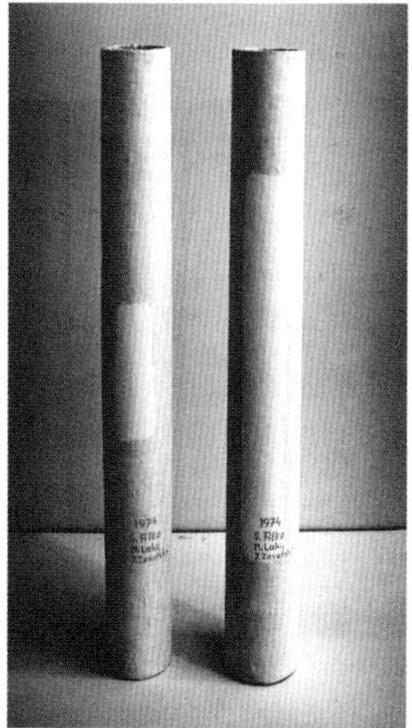

[03] Stano Filko, Miloš Laky, Ján Zavarský, *White Space in White Space / Biely priestor v bielom priestore*, 1974

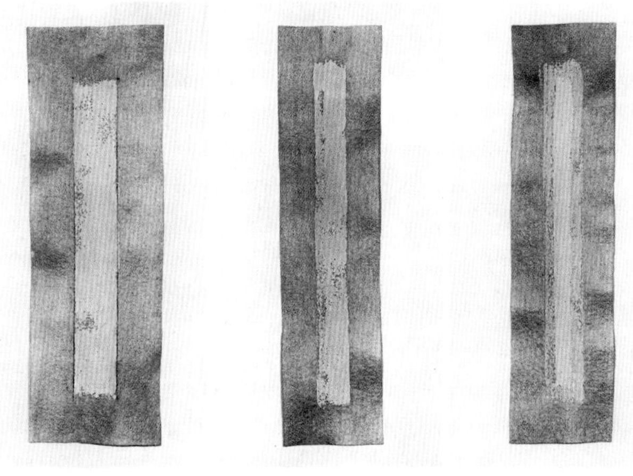

[04] *Stano Filko – Miloš Laky – Ján Zavarský*, Fiatal Müvészek Klubja / Young Artists' Club Budapest, exhibition catalog, 1977, right page *Sensitivity Manifesto*, 1974–1975–1976

sich dieser Auftrag, anfänglich nicht wahrnehmbar, allmählich von der Umgebung abzuheben begann. Wie eine Erscheinung, oder besser: ein langsames Erscheinen-Lassen, Hervortreten, Sich-Abzeichnen, was erneut alles nur Behelfsausdrücke sind für den Unendlichkeitsanspruch, den Filko damit verfolgte. Interessant ist zudem, dass laut Denegri während der Aktion die Stimme des Künstlers aus einem Kassettenrekorder zu vernehmen war, wie sie eine Liste von Begriffen aufsagte: „immateriality, informality, non-rhythmicity, non-abstractness, non-concreteness, non-constructiveness, non-decorativeness, non-applicability, non-subjectivity, non-objectivity, non-sentimentality, non-philosophicality, non-politicality" und so fort.[14] Dass das Absolute stark mit einer forcierten Negation alles Endlichen und Bedingten einherging, war schon aus dem Gdańsk-Manifest hervorgegangen („the total negation of the logical manners of thinking"). Dass diese Hegel'sche Denkfigur aber auch ganz unmittelbar auf die ästhetische Umsetzung, mithin den behelfsmäßigen, zuletzt aber immer noch sinnlichen Brückenschlag hin zum Unendlichen bezogen war, überraschte nichtsdestotrotz: Legte die Einfachheit der verwendeten Mittel (weiße Malerfarbe, handelsüblicher Farbroller) doch eher eine „Verklärung des Gewöhnlichen" nahe als den Durchbruch zu wahrer Transzendenz. Am Ende nahm Filko laut Denegris Schilderung ein Stück weiße Kreide und schrieb das Wort „Emotion"[15] an die weiße Wand – auch das eher der lapidare Ausdruck einer elementaren Spur, eines Zeichens, dessen Signifikat in dem damit angepeilten „inalienable spiritual state" (Denegri) lag.

Doch diese Spur konnte auch andere Formen annehmen, wie Filkos Ausstellung 1980 in der Warschauer Mała Galeria PSP-ZPAF zeigte. [07] *Transcendence I. / Transcendencja I.* (1978) und *Transcendence II. / Transcendencja II.* (1979) [08] griff zum einem auf einige der „geweißten" Fotografien zurück, die bereits in der Gdańsk-Schau ein Jahr zuvor enthalten gewesen waren. Neben dem konturgenauen Ausblocken – einer Art umrisshaftem *Evakuieren* – von einzelnen abgebildeten Figuren (meist handelte es sich um Filko selbst) trat in *Transcendence II.* aber auch eine neue Methode auf den Plan: das Unkenntlichmachen mittels weißer Rechtecke und Quadrate sowie, in unzweifelhaft ironischem Bezug auf Malewitsch, weiße Quadrate auf weißem (rechteckigem) Grund. Das betreffende Foto, in dem dies zur Anwendung kommt, zeigt Menschen, die einem Vortrag lauschen. Einer davon, vermutlich Filko selber, ist von besagtem weißem Quadrat auf weißem Grund überdeckt – eine Art doppelte Tilgung also, als müsse der Verschiebung des Sinnlichen ins Vor- bzw. Übersinnliche noch eins draufgesetzt werden. Auf der Seite davor sind im Katalog die Köpfe zweier Personen (Filko und einer weiblichen Begleiterin) durch ein größeres und ein kleineres Rechteck weggeblockt [09-10]. Auf der Seite nach dem Vortragsbild ist das weiße Rechteck auf weißem Grund über den Kopf einer im Stehen vortragenden Person gestülpt (vermutlich wieder Filko selbst), während sein gesamter Torso in gleißendes weißes Licht getaucht ist. Das letzte Bild des Katalogs schließlich zeigt das weiße Rechteck zum Wandbild mutiert, wo es von nicht identifizierbaren Personen begutachtet wird.

Aber es gibt noch weitere Ausgestaltungen der Transzendenz-Idee, ablesbar an Fotobearbeitungen der Jahre 1978–1980.[16] Teils erfolgte dies, zusätzlich zu den konturgenauen bzw. orthogonalen Weißungen, durch amorphere weiße Flecken, teils auch durch Kreise, die bisweilen auf die Rechtecke

erneut Weiß auf Weiß, aufgetragen sind. Filkos „Text-Art"-Komponente, wie sie auch in dem Warschau-Katalog unter dem Titel *Transcendention (Oversensuality)* (1979) enthalten war, ließ in ihrer Apodiktik keinen Zweifel am – auch diese Steigerungsform war möglich – *Über*absolutheitsanspruch der Unternehmung: „Creation 1978–1979 etc. is the mirror of transcendention. It is pure absolute overabsolute, specific in its specificity, overtemporal, overlasting, essentiality, oversubjective existence, in its pure art. […] [It] is above absoluteness, above objectivity, unphysical, overtemporal existence."[17] Einen Schlüsselbegriff im Schielen nach dem Überabsoluten bildete der „Spiegel der Transzendention", womit erneut ein vermeintlich triviales Hilfsmittel angesprochen war, mit dem man seiner selbst gewahr werden kann – aber nicht wie üblich seiner sonst nicht wahrnehmbaren (physischen) Seite, sondern viel elementarer: seiner übersubjektiven Existenz, ja der Bedingung dieser Existenz bzw. *deren* Gewahrwerdens. Dass sich die Farbe Weiß besonders für diese Spiegelfunktion anbot,[18] lag insofern nahe, als Weiß als das Unbeschriebene schlechthin und zugleich als unendlich Beschreibbares eine im positiven Sinn grenzwertige Position in Bezug auf das Farbspektrum einnimmt. Dass sich darin das Existenzielle per se, das jeder konkreten Verkörperung Vorausgehende, gleichsam *idealiter* spiegeln konnte, kam dem Transzendenzgedanken sichtlich entgegen. Wobei dieses Spiegelmoment auch mit trivialen Mitteln – als Spur, Fingerzeig, Chiffre – herstellbar war, ohne (zunächst noch) auf „großkünstlerische" Methoden zurückgreifen zu müssen.

Weiße Ontologie

1980 produzierte Filko ein weiteres „Text-Art"-Manifest mit dem Titel *Meditation Transcendental / Transcendentálna meditácia* (1980), erneut in mehreren Sprachen herausgegeben, im Unterschied zu den beiden vorangegangenen Katalogen aber ohne begleitendes Bildmaterial. Geplant war, einen entsprechenden Korpus von Arbeiten beim Festival 3SD (Three Sunny Days) zu zeigen, das der Kurator (und heutige Umweltminister der Slowakei) Ján Budaj organisiert hatte, das jedoch kurzerhand von den Behörden untersagt wurde.[19] Das gleichnamige Manifest rekapitulierte das Transzendenzansinnen Filkos nochmals in Form eines Lexikons – von A wie „Absolut" bis T wie „Transzendentalismus" – und enthielt erneut eine programmatische Erklärung, wie sie vom Duktus her alle seine Manifeste seit 1973 gekennzeichnet hatte: „Transzendentale Meditation ist eine Kunst, nicht gelehrt, überreal, jenseits des Realen, antikosmisch, jenseits des Kosmischen, übersinnlich, jenseits des Sinnlichen, rein, ist überzeitlicher Sinn, rein abstrakt, jenseits der Zeit, absolut, unbeobachtbar, geplant, nicht geplant, überobjektiv, jenseits des Objektiven, nicht subjektiv, jenseits des Subjektiven, übersubjektiv, erreichbar, unerreichbar, geistig, logisch-geistig, still, rein, unerkennbar, liegt vor der Erfahrung …"[20]

Interessant ist hier nicht allein die versuchte (gleichsam performative) Aufhebung des Widerspruchprinzips, Basis jeglicher „logisch-geistigen" Aspiration (geplant, nicht geplant […] erreichbar, nicht erreichbar …). Vielmehr war in dem Text noch ein weiteres Transzendenzmoment benannt, nämlich die „Überschreitung des weißen Raumes und seiner sämtlichen drei Grade des weißen Raumes im weißen Raum und seiner Übersubjektivität …"[21] Mit den drei Graden waren

no matter how much this was just a crutch (so to speak), and ultimately also a sensual path forged toward the infinite, was nonetheless surprising, as the simplicity of the means employed (white industrial paint, ordinary painter's rollers) rather suggested an "idealization of the habitual" than any breakthrough to true transcendency. At the end of the performance, according to Denegri's description, Filko took a piece of white chalk and wrote the word "emotion"[15] on the white wall—this too as a rather matter-of-fact expression of an elementary trace, a sign that signified lay in the "inalienable spiritual state" (Denegri) it aspired to.

But this trace could also assume other forms, as Filko's 1980 exhibition in the Warsaw Mała Galeria PSP-ZPAF showed. [07] *Transcendence I. / Transcendencja I.* (1978) and *Transcendencja II.* (1979) [08] on the one hand took recourse to some of the "whitened" photographs blocking out precisely along the contours (a kind of outline "evacuation") of certain depicted figures (mostly this was Filko himself), *Transcendence II.* also used a new method. This was making things unrecognizable by using white squares and rectangles, and, in an unmistakably ironic reference to Malevich, white squares on a white (rectangular) background. The photograph where all of this is deployed shows people listening to a lecture. One of them, probably Filko himself, is covered by the white square on a white background, so that this is a kind of double erasure, as if it was necessary to add a further level to the shifting of the sensual into the pre- or extrasensory realm. On the previous page in the catalog the heads of two people (Filko and a female accompaniment) are blocked out by a larger and a smaller rectangle. [09-10] On the page after the photograph of the lecture, the white rectangle on a white background is placed over the head of a person standing and lecturing (again presumably Filko himself), while his entire torso is illuminated by bright white light. The last picture in the catalog then shows the white rectangle transformed into an image on a wall, where it is being inspected by a person who is not identifiable.

There are further expressions of the idea of transcendence, as we can see from manipulated photos from the years 1978–80.[16] In addition to whitening along contours or in orthogonal forms, these new manipulations entailed the use of amorphous white spots or circles that are applied to the rectangles, again white on white. Filko's "text-art" component, as also included in the Warsaw catalog under the title *Transcendention (Oversensuality)* (1979), was so apodictic as to permit no doubt about the *over*-absolute (this form of superlative was possible too) claims of the endeavor: "Creation 1978–1979 etc. is the mirror of transcendention. It is pure absolute overabsolute, specific in its specificity, overtemporal, overlasting, essentiality, oversubjective existence, in its pure art. … [It] is above absoluteness, above objectivity, unphysical, overtemporal existence."[17] A key concept in this act of peering toward the over-absolute was the "mirror of transcendention," which again denoted an allegedly trivial aid by means of which one could become aware of oneself, but not as usually one's otherwise not perceivable (physical) side, but something far more elemental: one's supra-subjective existence, the very condition of this existence or the act of becoming aware of it. That the color white was particularly suited to this mirror function[18] made sense because white can be seen as the epitome of the unwritten and at the same time as an infinitely "writable" medium that has a positively connoted marginal position within the spectrum of colors. That the existential per se, which precludes all concrete embodiment, could be mirrored as an *ideal* form here, certainly meant that this came close to the concept of the transcendental. This mirror moment could, however, be established using trivial means too, as a trace, a pointer, a cipher, without (at least initially) having to take recourse to "major artistic" methods.

White Ontology

In 1980 Filko produced a further "text-art" manifesto entitled *Meditation Transcendental / Transcendentálna meditácia* (1980), initially published in several languages, but in contrast to two prior catalogs without any accompanying images. The plan was to show a corresponding body of works at the 3SD (Three Sunny Days) Festival, which the curator Ján Budaj (today minister of the environment in Slovakia) had organized, but which was forbidden by the authorities as short notice.[19] The manifesto recapitulated Filko's aspirations to transcendence in the form of an encylopedia, from A for absolute to T for transcendentalism, and again contained a programmatic declaration in the same tone that had featured in all of Filko's manifestos since 1973: "Meditation transcendental is an art—no scientific, super-real, beyond the doctrine, beyond the reality, anticosmic, beyond the cosmic, super-sensuous, pure super-timely sense, purely abstract, beyond the time, absolut, unobservable, planned, unplanned, super-objectif, beyond the objectif, no-subjectif, beyond the subjectif, super-subjectif, conceivable, inconceivable, spirituel, logically spirituel, silent, pur, unrecognizable, recognizable, existing before the experience …."[20]

It is not only the attempt to overcome—performatively, as it were—the principle of contradiction and the basis of every "logically spirituel" aspiration ("planned, unplanned," "conceivable, inconceivable") that is of interest here. The text also names a further moment of transcendence, namely "[p]assing the white space and all the three degrees of the white space in the white space and its super-subjectivity."[21] The three degrees of sensibility, sensitivity, and emotion denoted the stages of the *White Space* project hitherto given, and they corresponded in geometrical terms to horizontality and verticality, and, in reference to emotion, the at first sight less clearly apparent increasing *spiritualization* of all of these forms of perception. In any case, Filko's next project, his participation in documenta 7 following his emigration from at that time Czechoslovak Socialist Republic ČSSR, was devoted to the *Love of Ontology / Liebe zur Ontologie / Láska k ontológii* (1982) [11], as the name of his contribution put it. The mix of older works (from the *Sensitivity* and *Transcendency* series) with newer large-format paintings, and (not to be forgotten) the "escape car" from Czechoslovakia that was overpainted in white, produced an eclectic and formally hybrid combination that in terms of genre diverged in all kinds of directions.[22] Again the artefacts that were at the location and were sensually tangible operated more like ciphers, behind—or better *over*—which the true content of this art situated: an ontology as the essential basis of all being, empty in itself, infinite (but also open to being filled in infinite ways), white in white (infinitely mirroring itself), ultimately the transgression of every transgression.

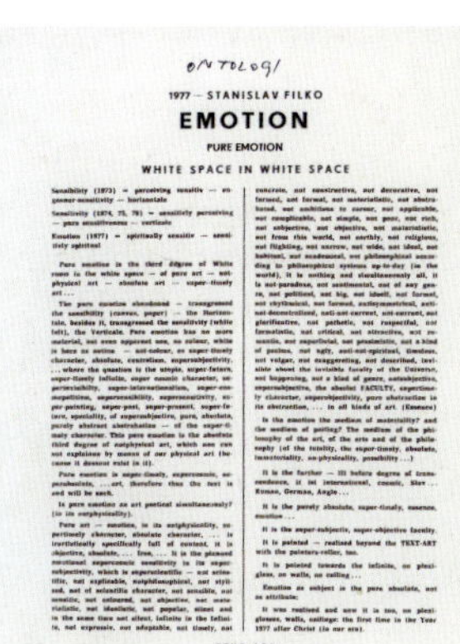
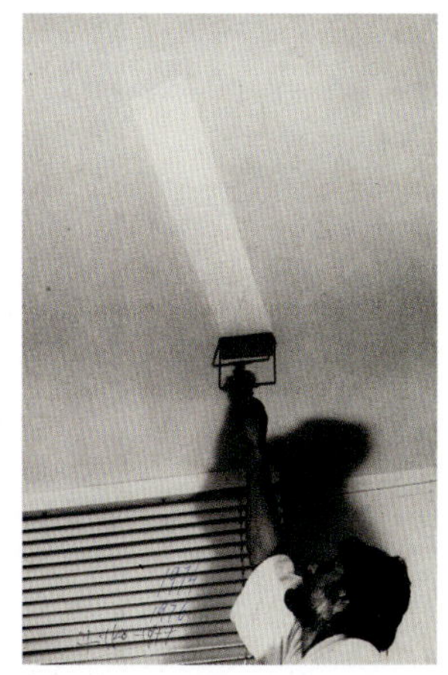

[05A] *EMÓCIA. Čistá Emócia. Biely priestor v bielom priestore – Text-art / Emotion. Pure Emotion. White Space in White Space – Text-art*, Manifesto / Manifest, 1977
[05B] *EMOTION. Pure Emotion. White Space in White Space – Text-art / Emócia. Čistá Emócia. Biely priestor v bielom priestore – Text-art*, Manifesto / Manifest, 1977
[05C] *EMOTION. Reine Emotion. Weisser Raum im Weissen Raum – Text-art / Emócia. Čistá Emócia. Biely priestor v bielom priestore – Text-art*, Manifesto / Manifest, 1977

[06] *Emotion / Emócia, Anti-performance*, 1977

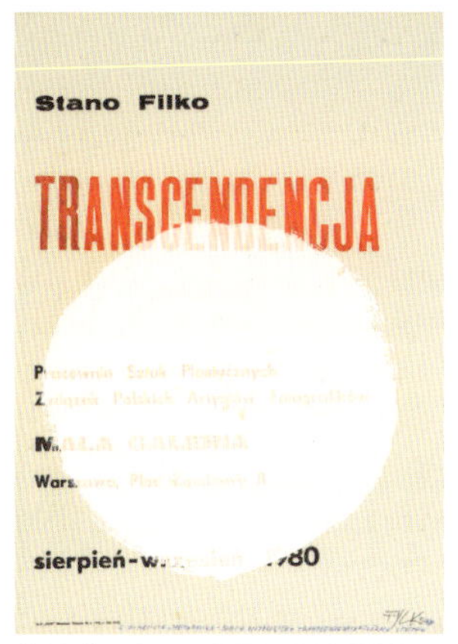

[07] *5th DIMENSION WHITE ONTOLOGIC TRANSCENDENCE DEVOURED EVERYTHING / 5. DIMENZIA BIELA ONTOLOGICKÁ TRANSCENDENCIA – ZOŽRALA VŠETKO*, 1980–95

[08] *TRANSCENDENCE I., II. / TRANSCENDENCJA I., II.*, 1978–79

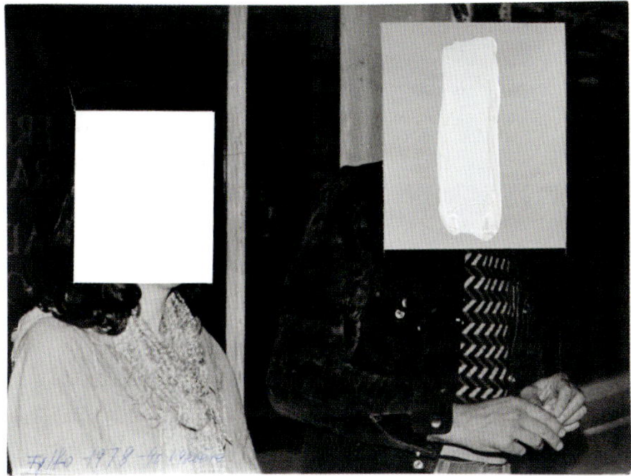
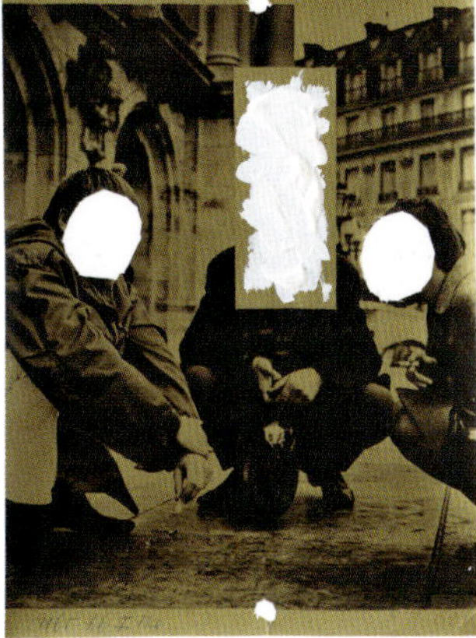
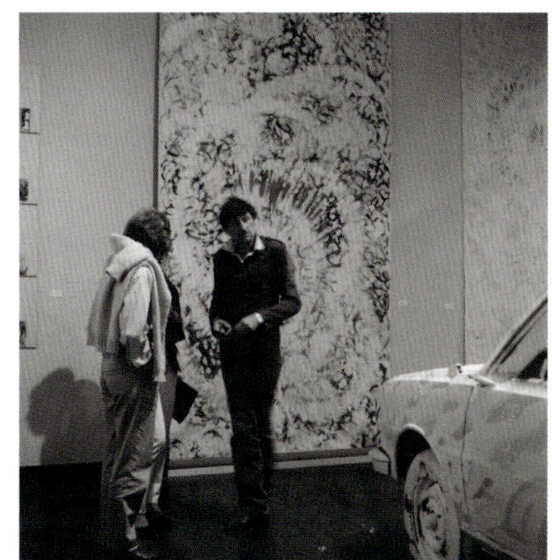

[09] *From the cycle Transcendency III. / Z cyklu Transcendencia III.*, 1979

[10] *From the cycle Transcendency / Z cyklu Transcendencia*, 1978–80

[11] *Love of Ontology / Láska k ontológii*, documenta 7, Neue Galerie, Kassel, 1982

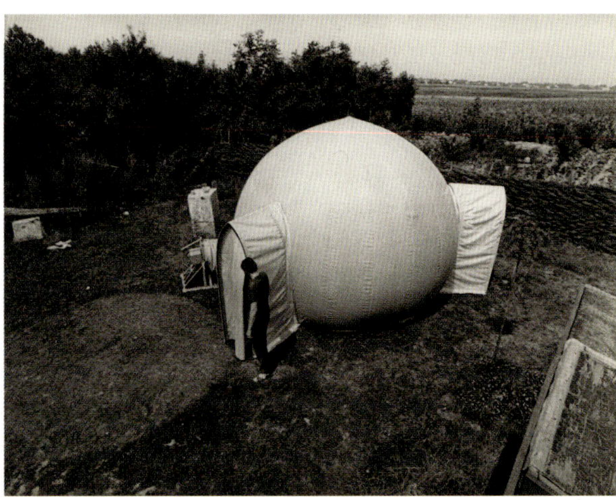

[12] *Cosmos II. – Environment / Kozmos II. – environment,* 1968, 1968

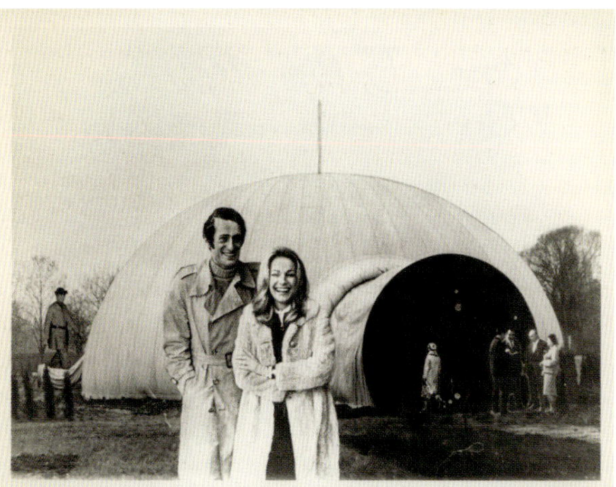

[13] *Cosmos II. – Environment / Kozmos II. – environment,* 1968

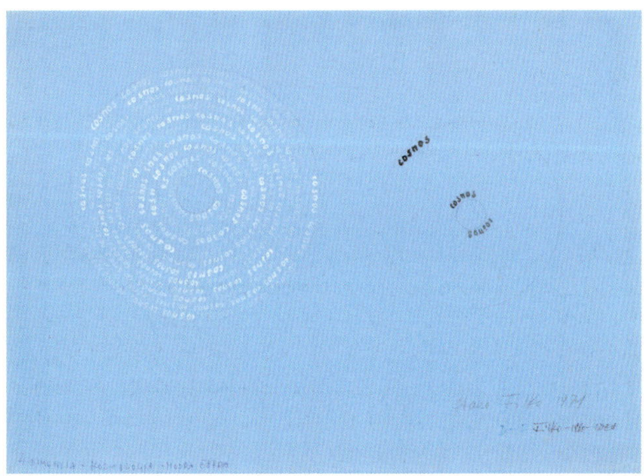

[14] *Cosmos I.,* 1971

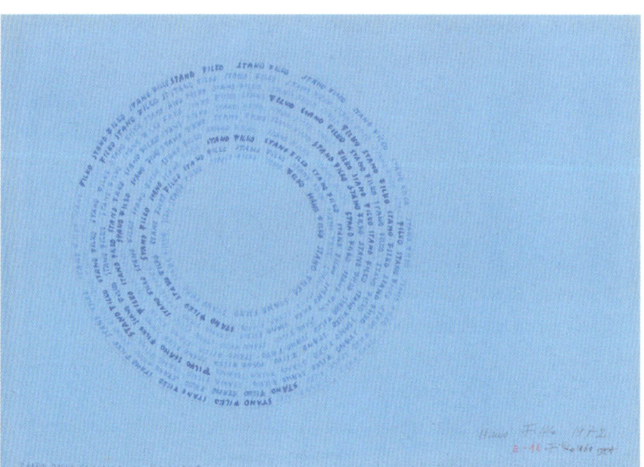

[15] *Cosmos II.,* 1971

die bisherigen Stufen des *White Space*-Projekts gemeint, also Sensibilität, Sensitivität und Emotion, denen in geometrischer Hinsicht Horizontalität und Vertikalität sowie (in Bezug auf Emotion zunächst weniger klar ersichtlich) die zunehmende *Vergeistigung* all dieser Anschauungsformen entsprachen. Jedenfalls war sein nächstes Projekt die auf seine Emigration aus der damaligen Tschechoslowakischen Sozialistischen Republik ČSSR folgende documenta 7-Teilnahme, der *Love of Ontology / Liebe zur Ontologie / Láska k ontológii* (1982) [11], so der Titel des Beitrags, gewidmet. In der Mischung von älteren Arbeiten (aus der *Sensitivity*- bzw. *Transcendency*-Reihe) mit neueren, großformatigen Malereien und, nicht zu vergessen, dem weiß übertünchten „Fluchtauto" aus der ČSSR lag eine eklektische, formal hybride Zusammenstellung vor, die genremäßig in alle möglichen Richtungen ausscherte.[22] Erneut fungierten die vor Ort, sinnlich wahrnehmbaren Artefakte mehr wie Chiffren, hinter – oder besser: *über* – denen der wahre Gehalt dieser Kunst angesiedelt war: eine Ontologie als Wesensgrund allen Seins, in sich selber leer, unendlich (aber auch unendlich variabel befüllbar), Weiß in Weiß (unendlich in sich gespiegelt), letztlich die Überschreitung jeglicher Überschreitung.

Dass Filko dieser „superlativen" Kunst schlussendlich den Titel „weiße Ontologie"[23] gab, überrascht nicht, insofern hier nochmals die Eckpfeiler seines Denkens – die spirituelle Erfahrbarkeit von Leere und Unendlichkeit zum einen, die beständige Suche nach Transzendenz und dem Grund allen Seins zum anderen – kongenial zusammengeführt wurden. Bekanntlich entwickelte Filko ab diesem Zeitpunkt (den späten 1970er-Jahren) seine bis zu seinem Lebensende 2015 maßgebliche Dimensionen- bzw. Chakren-Lehre. Das fortwährend komplexer werdende Konstrukt[24] lässt sich von seinen Grundkonstanten her auf die allem zugrundeliegende Unterscheidung von Biologie (3. Dimension, Rot), Kosmos (4. Dimension, Blau) und Ontologie (5. Dimension, Weiß) zurückführen[25] – ungeachtet der darüber hinausgehenden Farbzuordnungen und Miniverästelungen, denen das *System SF* in späteren Jahren unterlag. Wesentlich in diesem Zusammenhang ist, dass die 5. (und höchste) Dimension indirekt selbst von anderen Grenzwerten *ausgeblockt* ist, also gleichsam ex negativo, wiewohl nicht von diesen bedingt, abgesteckt wird. Es sind dies abgesehen vom Körperlichen/Biologischen (Rot) die Dimensionen des Ego (Schwarz/Indigo), gleichsam der Nullpunkt alles Transzendentalen, und, an das Weiße unterhalb angrenzend, jene des Kosmos (Blau).

Die unendliche übersinnliche Anschauung ist von diesen Extrempolen oder besser gesagt andersfarbigen Dimensionalitäten her eingefasst – was sie als Wegweiser, ja als eine Art Steigbügelhalter für das Absolute in Filkos Kunst gleichermaßen spannend macht. Ego und Kosmos finden ihre wichtigsten Artikulationen im unmittelbaren Vorfeld des *White Space*-Projekts, aber zum Teil auch weit darüber hinaus: das Kosmische etwa mit den ausladenden Environments rund um das Jahr 1969 [12-13], später dann auch in Richtung Bildentleerung gehenden Bleistiftzeichnungen, die zartest ausgeführte konzentrische Kreise zeigen (*Cosmos*, 1971/72) [14-15]; das Ich beginnend bei den konzeptuellen Selbstporträts der 1960er-Jahre bis hin zu den später immer wieder in Pyramidenform auftretenden Ego-Surrogaten (einem Platzhalter für das allwissende Auge, etwa in *Arte de Sistemas – EGO*, 1971/ca. 1980). Beide Eckpfeiler, Ich und Kosmos, weisen in

Richtung Absolutheit, unterliegen aber in ihrer Weltlichkeit und Physikalität anderen Dimensionalitäten. Weswegen auch sie bestenfalls Fingerzeige, Chiffren, im Hinblick auf eine wahrlich übersinnliche Anschauung, fassbar einzig über die „transzendentale Meditation", liefern können.

Š(Koda)

Dass die „transzendentale Meditation" selbst letzten Endes mit sehr weltlichen, um nicht zu sagen profanen Mitteln operieren musste, belegen zahlreiche Beispiele quer durch die Jahrzehnte, in denen Filko auch abseits des *White Space*-Projekts nach dem Absoluten angelte. Bereits 1967, also lange vor Letzterem, aber auch vor der historischen Phase der sogenannten „Normalisierung"[26], hatte er ein Konzept entwickelt, bei dem es um die mehrlagige Faltung von weißem, semitransparentem Seidenpapier ging. *Nothing at all / Vôbec nič* (1967/ca. 1990) [16], so der Titel der erst in den 1990er-Jahren ausgeführten Serie, gab – zumindest ideell – einen Vorgeschmack auf die kommende „weiße Ontologie". Bis zu sieben und mehr unterschiedliche Weiß-Schattierungen ließen sich durch einen simplen Kunstgriff, die Faltung eben, erzielen. Es war dies ein deutlicher Vorbote auf die unendliche Vielfalt, die in der Transzendenz – chiffriert durch „das Weiße" – angelegt war. *Transcendence / Transcendencia* (1967/1978/ca. 2000) titelt auch ein Double von zwei bearbeiteten Fotografien aus dem Jahr 1967, von denen eine später in der Gdańsk-Ausstellung 1979 auftauchte. Zu sehen ist ein in der Landschaft platzierter Betonsockel, auf dem eine – nachträglich „geweißte" – Büste platziert ist. An den Sockel sind in allen vier Richtungen Holzstangen in schrägem Winkel angelehnt, was dem Ensemble eine pyramidale Anmutung verleiht. In der zweiten Variante des Foto-Doubles ist das skulpturale Arrangement mit einem aufgemalten weißen Kreis umschrieben, daneben eine Aufschrift, die beginnt mit „5. DIMENZIA – ABSOLUT – [...]".[27] [17] Wiewohl diese textliche Kontextualisierung vermutlich erst im Jahr 2000 hinzugefügt wurde, lässt sich auch hieran ablesen, wie ernst es Filko mit dem Anpeilen der 5. Dimension, sprich der Überschreitung hin zum Unbedingten, Absoluten war. Simples Seidenpapier, richtig gefaltet, konnte ebenso eine Pforte zum Übersinnlichen darstellen wie alte Fotografien, die nur entsprechend präpariert werden mussten, damit aus ihnen der absolute Geist sprach. Oder wenn schon nicht sprach, so zumindest *emanierte*, ausstrahlte – für jene, die antimaterialistischen Sinnes genug waren, um dies tatsächlich auch wahrzunehmen.

Filkos „Fluchtauto", ein Škoda 120SL, den er für die documenta 7 in wildem Farbauftrag weiß bepinselte, konnte in dieser genealogischen Reihe „irdischer" Chiffren für das Absolute genauso eine Rolle spielen wie eine senkrecht im Schnee (weiß!) stehende Kiste, die ein wundersames Sammelsurium enthielt. *White Space on Snow, Open Installation / Biely priestor na snehu, otvorená inštalácia* (1993–1995)[28] [18], so der Titel, enthielt allerlei Krempel, von leeren Plastikflaschen über zusammengerollte Planen bis hin zu Gasflaschen und Kanistern – nicht einmal durchgehend weiß alles, aber vielleicht war das zu dem Zeitpunkt auch gar nicht mehr nötig. In den 1990er-Jahren hatte das „System Filko" und vor allem auch die 5. Dimension der weißen Ontologie einen derartigen Vollendungsgrad erreicht, dass die anvisierte

    Christian Höller   Chiffren von Transzendenz

That Filko then finally gave this "superlative" art the name "white ontology"[23] was not a surprise, as here again the cornerstones of his thinking—the ability to spiritually experience emptiness and infinity on the one hand and the constant search for transcendence and the basis of all being on the other—were masterfully conjoined. It is well known that from this point on (the late 1970s) and up to the end of his life in 2015 Filko developed his decisive doctrine of the dimensions or chakras. The fundamental and unchanging pillars of this increasingly complex construct[24] can be seen in the underlying distinctions between biology (third dimension, red), cosmos (fourth dimension, blue), and ontology (fifth dimension, white),[25] irrespective of the further color ascriptions and mini-branches that the *System SF* was accorded in later years. In this context the key is that the fifth (and highest) dimension is *blocked out* indirectly by two other limits, and is thus defined *ex negativo*, even if it is not determined by these others. Apart from the physical/biological (red) these are the dimensions of the ego (black/indigo), amounting to the zero point of everything transcendental, and, bordering on the white from below, the cosmos (blue).

The endless extrasensory is spanned by these two extreme poles, or better put: these two dimensions of different colors, which makes them equally exciting in their function as pointers or stepping stones to the absolute in Filko's art. Ego und cosmos find their most important articulations in the immediate vicinity of the *White Space* project, but also partly far beyond this: the cosmic, for example, with the expansive environments around the year 1969 [12-13], and later in the pencil drawings that tended to empty pictures showing the most delicately drawn concentric circles (*Cosmos,* 1971–72) [14-15]; the ego beginning with the conceptual self-portraits of the 1960s and up to the later ego surrogates that recurred in the shape of a pyramid (a placeholder for the omniscient eye, as in *Arte de Sistemas – EGO*, 1971/c. 1980). Both corner pieces, ego and cosmos, point in the direction of the absolute, but are subject in their this-worldliness and physicality to other dimensions. Which is why they can at best offer pointers and ciphers in terms of a true extrasensory perception, graspable solely by means of "transcendental meditation."

Š(Koda)

That "transcendental meditation" itself ultimately had to operate with very worldly, if not to say profane means, is shown by numerous examples over all the decades during which Filko was also fishing for the absolute beyond the *White Space* project. As early as 1967, long before the latter, and also before the historical phase of a so-called "normalization,"[26] he had developed a concept based on several layers of folding of white semi-transparent silk paper. *Nothing at all / Vôbec nič* (1967/c. 1990) [16] was the title of this series, which was not implemented until in the 1990s, and it was a foretaste, at least in ideal terms, of the "white ontology" to come. Up to seven and more different shades of white could be created by using a simple trick—namely folding. This was a clear precursor of the infinite variety that the transcendental and its cipher "white" promised. *Transcendence / Transcendencia* (1967/1978/c. 2000) is also the title of a double made of two manipulated photographs of 1967, one of

which reappeared in the Gdańsk exhibition in 1979. It shows a concrete plinth set in a landscape, with a bust that has been whitened placed upon it. On all four sides of the plinth wooden rods have been attached at sloping angles, giving the ensemble the impression of a pyramid. In the second variant of this photo double the sculptural arrangement is expressed by means of a painted white circle, and an adjacent text beginning with "5. DIMENZIA – ABSOLUT – …"[27] [17] Although the textual contextualization was not added until the year 2000, it still can be seen to show how seriously Filko was in wishing to target the fifth dimension, namely to step over to the unconditional and absolute. Simple silk paper, correctly folded, could just as well represent a gateway to the extrasensory as could old photographs, which just needed to be correspondingly treated so that the absolute spirit could speak from them. Or if it did not speak, then at least it *emanated* and radiated—for those who had sufficient anti-materialist sense to actually notice this.

Filko's "escape car," a Škoda 120SL, which he painted a disorderly white for documenta 7, was in a just as good a position to play a role in this genealogical series of "earthly" ciphers for the absolute as a box standing vertically in snow (white), inside of which was a marvelous collection of objects. This work named *White Space on Snow, Open Installation / Biely priestor na snehu, otvorená inštalácia* (1993–95)[28] [18] contained all sorts of stuff, from empty plastic bottles to rolled-up plastic sheets and gas bottles and canisters, not all of them entirely white, but perhaps at this juncture this was no longer necessary. In the 1990s the "System Filko" and above all the fifth dimension of white ontology had achieved such a state of completion that the transcendence aspired for was now given rather by the system as a whole than any individual artifacts. The place that was excluded *ex negativo* by the other dimensions (and color chakras) no longer needed to be evidenced independently, such as by means of apodictic and mantra-like repeated manifestos. The system began to carry itself, as Filko's increasingly expansive exhibitions at the time and his studio with the character of a total work of art impressively showed.[29] [19] On the way there many small signs and wonders were still required—ciphers of transcendence that were planned like the proverbial ladder that can be pushed aside once the highest level was attained. And even if the ultimate metaphysical result of this endeavor might not seem to be so immediately evident to everyone today, Filko's ciphers are nonetheless among the most radical steps taken in the twentieth century toward a *liberating* and not just ominous esoteric transcendence.

1   Cited from *White Space in White Space. Biely priestor v bielom priestore, 1973–1982. Stano Filko, Miloš Laky, Ján Zavarský,* eds. Daniel Grúň, Christian Höller, Kathrin Rhomberg (Vienna, 2021), p. 158. Further Filko manifestos also cited from here. These were usually published in several languages at the same time.

2   Ibid., p. 159.

3   "Jana Geržová – Stano Filko: The Identity of My Creation is Conceptual," in *Profil* 4, 1991, p. 15.

4   Lucia Gregorová Stach, "Example Filko: Themes and Contexts in His Work," in *STANO FILKO 1.*, eds. Lucia Gregorová Stach, Aurel Hrabušický, exh. cat. Slovak National Gallery (Bratislava, 2018), English version on academia.edu; and Noit Banai, "*White Space in White Space* in Contexts," in *White Space in White Space* (see note 1), p. 203; a dialectic reading of the "whiteout" practice that leads to a similarly strong reinforcement of the artistic act is given by Jan Verwoert, "World as Medium: On the Art of Stano Filko," in *e-flux* 28, October 2011, https://www.e-flux.com/journal/28/68020/world-as-medium-on-the-work-of-stano-filko/ (accessed April 24, 2022).

5   *White Space in White Space* (see note 1), pp. 24–27; and Lisa Grünwald, "At a Given Time and in a Given Place: A Chronology of *White Space in White Space*," in *White Space in White Space* (see note 1), p. 211.

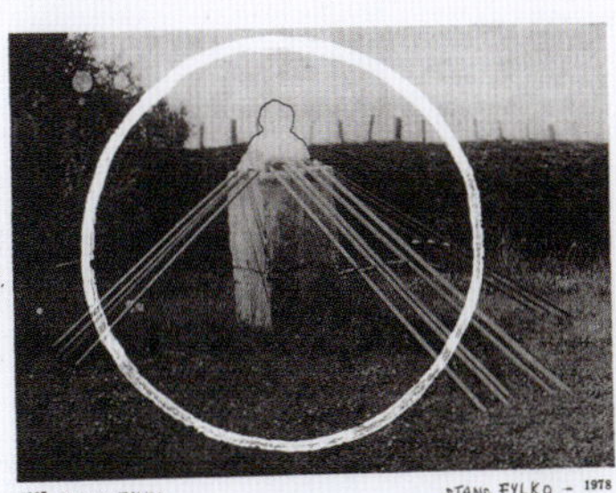

[16] Concept - Nothing at all /
Koncept - Vôbec nič, 1967

[17] Transcendence. 5. DIMENSION
ABSOLUT - AQ - Timelessness - HAPPSOC 5. /
Transcendencia. 5. DIMENZIA ABSOLUT - AQ -
Nadčasovosť - HAPPSOC 5., 1967/1978/2000

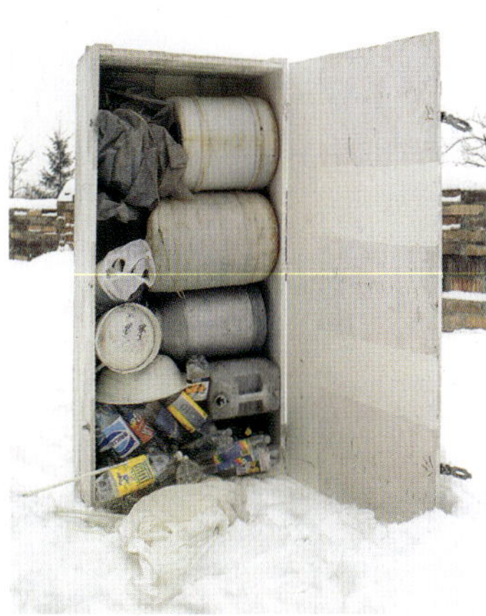

[18] White Space
on Snow, Open
Installation / Biely
priestor na snehu,
otvorená inštalácia,
1993-1995

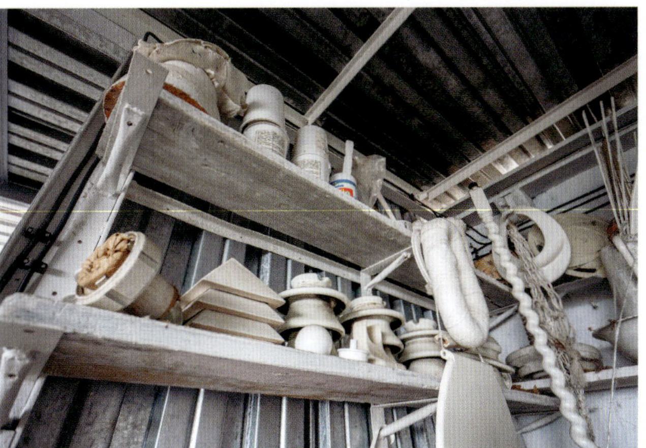

[19] Artist's studio Snežienková /
Umelcov ateliér Snežienková, 2007

6	Daniel Grúň, "Notes of a Belated Viewer: Revisiting *White Space in White Space*," in *White Space in White Space* (see note 1), pp. 32–33.

7	Vít Havránek, "The Emergence of Pure *EMOTION* through Repetition," in *White Space in White Space* (see note 1), pp. 154–55; and Banai, "*White Space in White Space* in Contexts" (see note 4), pp. 199–201.

8	This was the formulation in the first manifesto of 1973–74, in *White Space in White Space* (see note 1), p. 54.

9	Patricia Grzonka's untitled monographic essay in *STANO FILKO* (Prague, 2005), pp. 113–14; and Jan Verwoert, "Liebe zur Ontologie," *Texte zur Kunst*, September 1, 2021, https://www.textezurkunst.de/articles/jan-verwoert-liebe-zur-ontologie/?highlight=verwoert (accessed April 21, 2022).

10	Documentation in *White Space in White Space* (see note 1), pp. 37–51, and Grúň, "Notes of a Belated Viewer" (see note 6), pp. 29–34.

11	*White Space in White Space* (see note 1), pp. 75–82.

12	*White Space in White Space* (see note 1), p. 145; and Havránek, "The Emergence of Pure *EMOTION* through Repetition" (see note 7).

13	Július Koller, "The Fiction of a Space That De Facto Does Not Exist," in *White Space in White Space* (see note 1), pp. 85–88.

14	Cited from Ješa Denegri, "Stano Filko," in *White Space in White Space* (see note 1), p. 174.

15	Ibid.

16	*White Space in White Space* (see note 1), pp. 187–93.

17	Ibid., p. 167.

18	Gregorová Stach, "Example Filko: Themes and Contexts in His Work" (see note 4), n. p.

19	"3SD – Interview after a Year: Stano Filko in Conversation with Ján Budaj (1981)," in *White Space in White Space* (see note 1), pp. 183–86.

20	*White Space in White Space* (see note 1), p. 178.

21	Ibid.

22	Banai, "White Space in White Space in Contexts" (see note 4), pp. 204–07; and Grünwald, "At a Given Time and in a Given Place" (see note 5), p. 215.

23	"*STANO FILKO – POETRY ON SPACE – COSMOS*," exh. cat. Slovak National Gallery (Bratislava, 2016), pp. 75–76.

24	Grzonka, (untitled monographic essay) (see note 9), p. 98; Georg Schöllhammer, "Leben in der 5.4.3. Dimension," in *springerin* 2, 2006; Boris Ondreička, "*MULTIMODAL GOOGLIFICATION OF COSMOLOGY-ORIENTED DIAGRAMMATIC EXPERIMENTATIONS OF STANO FILKO* (2019)," May 2019, https://emanuellayr.com/exhibitions/multimodal-googlification-of-cosmology-oriented-diagrammatic-experimentations-of-stano-filko/ (accessed April 24, 2022); and Boris Ondreička, "Filko's *Albedo*," in *White Space in White Space* (see note 1), pp. 129–31.

25	When exactly Filko began to work with the color triad red – blue – white is difficult to reconstruct from today's perspective. It is interesting, however, that these are also the national colors of the ČSSR and their use can be understood as an indirect reflection on the 1968 invasion of the Red Army. (The color combination red – white – blue is found in numerous national flags; an irony of history would have it that Filko's superimposition of red, blue and white corresponds exactly to today's flag of the Russian Federation).

26	Jana Geržová, "The Myths and Reality of Conceptual Art in Slovakia," in *Konceptuálne umenie na zlome tisícročí / Conceptual Art at the Turn of Millennium* (Bratislava and Budapest, 2002), pp. 32–42; and Grúň, "Notes of a Belated Viewer" (see note 6), p. 34.

27	"*STANO FILKO – POETRY ON SPACE – COSMOS*" (see note 23), p. 95.

28	Reproduced in *STANO FILKO*, eds. Patricia Grzonka, Stano Filko (Prague, 2005), p. 69.

29	Description in Grzonka (see note 9), pp. 98–102; and Boris Ondreička, "Filko's *Albedo*" (see note 24).

Transzendenz mehr vom Gesamtsystem her als von einzelnen Artefakten darin gewährleistet war. Der von den anderen
Dimensionen (und Farb-Chakren) *ex negativo* ausgesparte
Ort des Absoluten musste nicht mehr eigens, etwa durch
apodiktische, mantrahaft wiederholte Manifeste, unter Beweis
gestellt werden. Das System begann sich gleichsam selbst
zu tragen, wie Filkos zu dem Zeitpunkt immer ausladender
werdende Ausstellungen bzw. sein immer „Gesamtkunst-
werk-artigeres" Atelier eindrucksvoll belegten.[29] [19] Auf
dem Weg dorthin bedurfte es jedoch vieler kleiner Zeichen
und Wunder – Chiffren von Transzendenz, die wie die be-
rühmte Leiter konzipiert waren, die man wegstoßen konnte,
sobald man die höchste Stufe erlangt hatte. Auch wenn der
letztendliche metaphysische Ertrag dieser Unternehmung
aus heutiger Sicht nicht jedem/jeder auf Anhieb einleuchten
mag, so zählen Filkos Chiffren mithin zu den konsequen-
testen Schritten, die im 20. Jahrhundert in Richtung einer
befreienden und nicht bloß ominös esoterischen Transzendenz
gesetzt wurden.

1   Zitiert so wie alle weiteren Passagen aus diversen Manifesten nach *White Space in White Space. Biely priestor v bielom priestore, 1973–1982. Stano Filko, Miloš Laky, Ján Zavarský*, hrsg. von Daniel Grúň, Christian Höller, Kathrin Rhomberg, Wien 2021, S. 158. Filkos Mani-feste wurden meist in mehreren Sprachen zugleich publiziert; in diesem Aufsatz wird, falls vorhanden, auf die deutsche Fassung, oder wenn diese nicht vorliegt, auf die englische Fassung zurückgegriffen.
2   Ebd., S. 159.
3   „Jana Geržová – Stano Filko: The Identity of My Creation is Conceptual", in: *Profil*, 4, April 1991, S. 15.
4   Lucia Gregorová Stach, „Example Filko: Themes and Contexts in His Work", in: *STANO FILKO 1.*, hrsg. von Lucia Gregorová Stach, Aurel Hrabušický, Ausst.-Kat. Slovak National Gallery, Bratislava 2018, englische Version auf academia.edu, o. S.; sowie Noit Banai, „*White Space in White Space* in Contexts", in: *White Space in White Space* (wie Anm. 1), S. 203; eine dialektische Lesart der „Whiteout"-Praxis, die auf eine umso stärkere Bekräftigung des künstlerischen Akts hinausläuft, findet sich bei Jan Verwoert, „World as Medium: On the Art of Stano Filko", in: *e-flux*, 28.10.2011, https://www.e-flux.com/journal/28/68020/world-as-medium-on-the-work-of-stano-filko/ (24.4.2022).
5   *White Space in White Space*, S. 24 ff.; sowie Lisa Grünwald, „At a Given Time and in a Given Place: A Chronology of *White Space in White Space*", in: ebd., S. 211.
6   Daniel Grúň, „Notes of a Belated Viewer: Revisiting *White Space in White Space*", in: ebd., S. 32 f.
7   Vít Havránek, „The Emergence of Pure *EMOTION* through Repetition", in: ebd., S. 154 ff.; sowie Banai, „*White Space in White Space* in Contexts", S. 199 ff.
8   So die Formulierung in der deutschen Fassung des ersten Manifests 1973/74.
9   Patricia Grzonka, (titelloser monografischer Essay), in: *STANO FILKO*, Prag 2005, S. 113 ff.; sowie Jan Verwoert, „Liebe zur Ontologie", in: *Texte zur Kunst*, 1. September 2021, https://www.textezurkunst.de/articles/jan-verwoert-liebe-zur-ontologie/?highlight=verwoert (21.4.2022).
10   Dokumentation in *White Space in White Space* (wie Anm. 1), S. 37 ff.; sowie Grúň, „Notes of a Belated Viewer" (wie Anm. 6), S. 29 ff.
11   *White Space in White Space* (wie Anm. 1), S. 75 ff.
12   Ebd., S. 145; sowie Havránek, „The Emergence of Pure *EMOTION* through Repetition".
13   Július Koller, „The Fiction of a Space That De Facto Does Not Exist", in: *White Space in White Space* (wie Anm. 1), S. 85 ff.
14   Zit. n. „Ješa Denegri – Stano Filko (Review, 1980)", in: *White Space in White Space* (wie Anm. 1), S. 174.
15   Ebd.
16   *White Space in White Space* (wie Anm. 1), S. 187 ff.
17   Ebd., S. 167.
18   Gregorová Stach, „Example Filko: Themes and Contexts in His Work" (wie Anm. 4), o. S.
19   „3SD – Interview after a Year: Stano Filko in Conversation with Ján Budaj (1981)", in: *White Space in White Space* (wie Anm. 1), S. 183 ff.
20   *White Space in White Space* (wie Anm. 1), S. 180.
21   Ebd.
22   Banai, „*White Space in White Space* in Contexts" (wie Anm. 4), S. 204 ff; sowie Grün-wald, „At a Given Time and in a Given Place" (wie Anm. 5), S. 215.
23   *STANO FILKO – POETRY ON SPACE – COSMOS*, hrsg. von Slovak National Gallery, Bratislava 2016, S. 75 ff.
24   Grzonka, (titelloser monografischer Essay) (wie Anm. 9), S. 98 f.; Georg Schöllhammer, „Leben in der 5.4.3. Dimension", in: *springerin*, 2, 2006; Boris Ondreička, „*MULTIMODAL GOOGLIFICATION OF COSMOLOGY-ORIENTED DIAGRAMMATIC EXPERIMENTA-TIONS OF STANO FILKO* (2019)", Mai 2019, https://emanuellayr.com/exhibitions/multi-modal-googlification-of-cosmology-oriented-diagrammatic-experimentations-of-stano-filko/ (24.4.2022); sowie ders., „Filko's *Albedo*", in: *White Space in White Space* (wie Anm. 1), S. 129 ff.
25   Wann Filko genau mit der Farbtrias Rot–Blau–Weiß zu arbeiten begann, lässt sich aus heutiger Sicht nur schwer rekonstruieren. Interessant ist aber, dass dies auch die National-farben der ČSSR sind und ihre Verwendung als indirekter Reflex auf den Einmarsch der Roten Armee 1968 verstanden werden kann. (Die Farbkombination Rot–Weiß–Blau findet sich in zahlreichen Nationalflaggen wieder; eine Ironie der Geschichte will es, dass Filkos Übereinanderschichtung von Rot, Blau und Weiß exakt der heutigen Fahne der Russischen Föderation entspricht.)
26   Jana Geržová, „The Myths and Reality of Conceptual Art in Slovakia", in: *Konceptuálne umenie na zlome tisícročí / Conceptual art at the turn of millennium*, Bratislava/Budapest 2002, S. 32 ff.; sowie Grúň, „Notes of a Belated Viewer" (wie Anm. 6), S. 34.
27   *STANO FILKO – POETRY ON SPACE – COSMOS* (wie Anm. 23), S. 95.
28   Abgebildet in *STANO FILKO*, hrg. von Patricia Grzonka, Stano Filko, Prag 2005, S. 69.
29   Vgl. die Beschreibung bei Grzonka, (titelloser monografischer Essay) (wie Anm. 9), S. 98 ff.; sowie Ondreička, „Filko's *Albedo*" (wie Anm. 24), S. 129 ff.

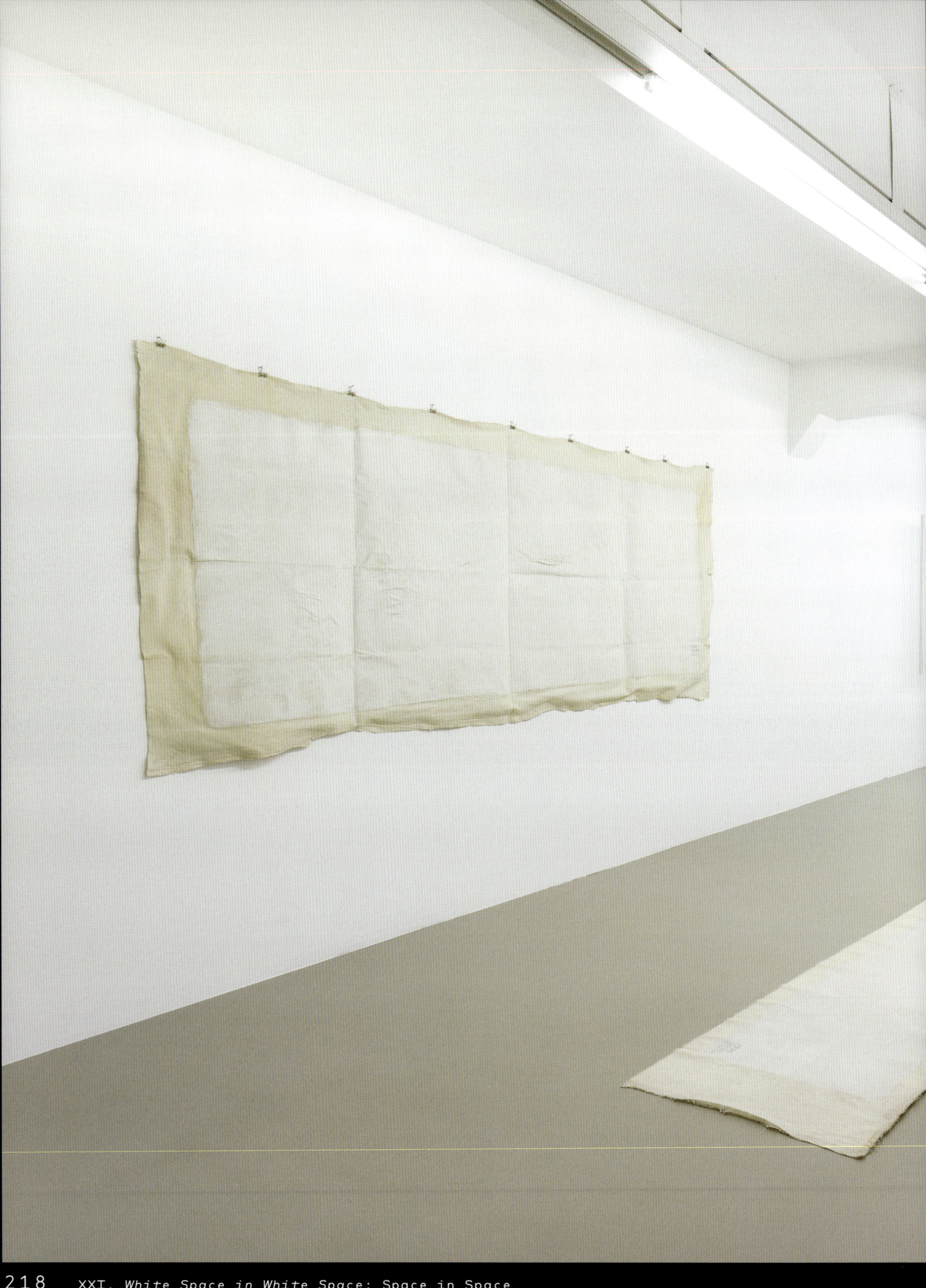

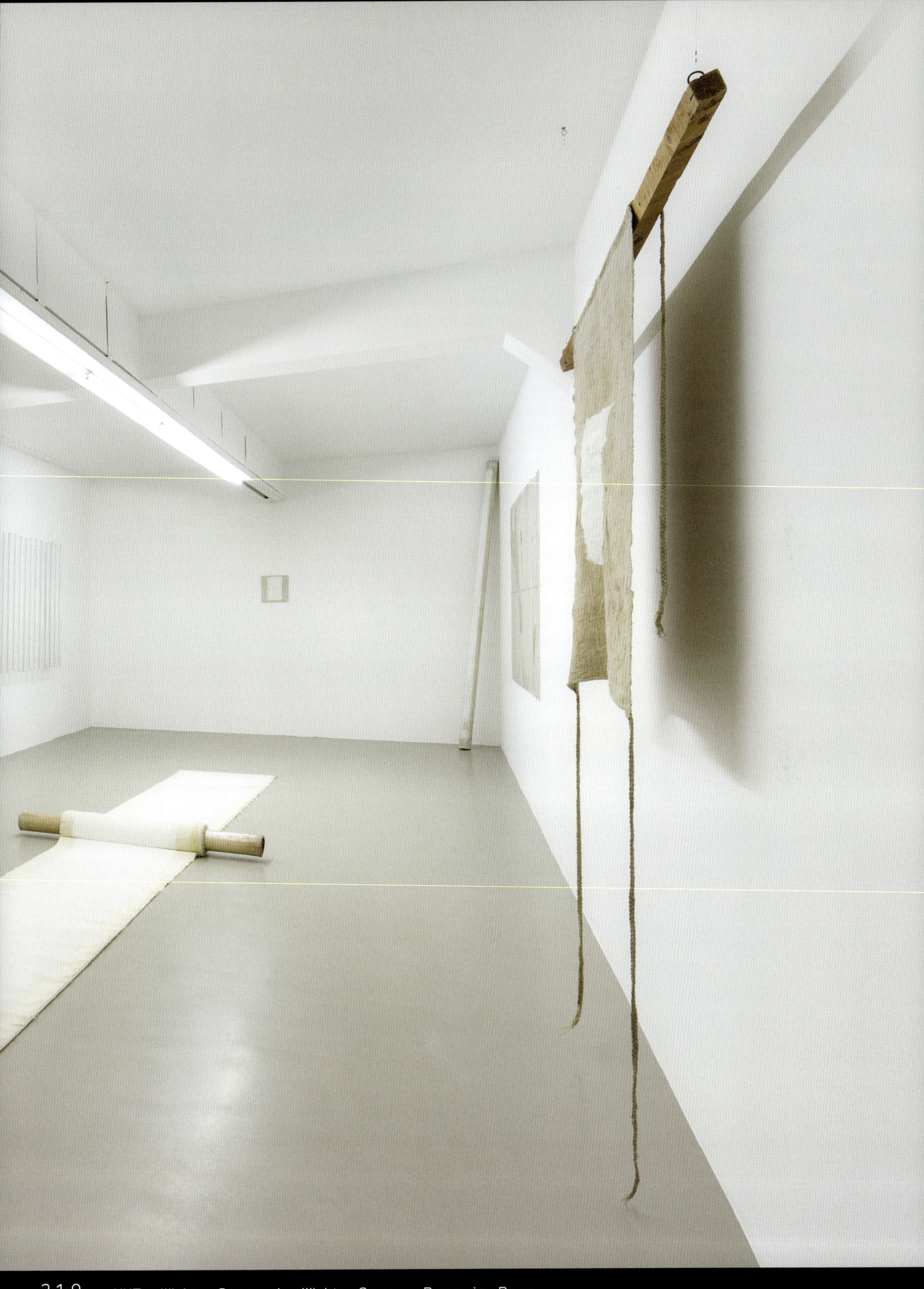

XXI

White Space in White Space:
Space in Space / Raum im Raum

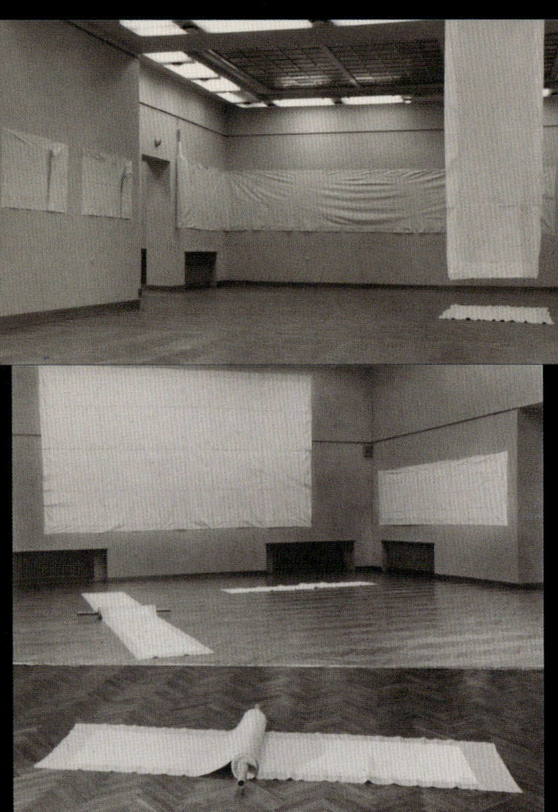

[02] Stano Filko, Miloš Laky, Ján Zavarský, *White Space in White Space / Biely priestor v bielom priestore*, 1974, House of Arts, Brno, 1974

After the defeat of the Prague Spring by the Red Army in August 1968 and the totalitarian phase of "normalization" that quickly followed this, Czechoslovakia saw increased uniformity in society and long-term restrictions on personal freedoms. In 1972 Stano Filko was expelled from the Czechoslovak association of fine artists, which amounted to a prohibition to work. This made collective work with his artist friends and intensive exchange away from the public eye all the more important. It was during this phase that the project *White Space in White Space / Biely priestor v bielom priestore* began, which Filko developed over several years together with Miloš Laky and Ján Zavarský. [17]

White Space in White Space was realized in different forms as installations. The first legendary event took place on February 18, 1974, for just a few hours in private at the Dům umění (House of Arts) in Brno. [02–03] [16] *White Space in White Space* was presented as a large installation with objects and canvases that had been painted with white angular latex stripes using rollers, aiming at least on the surface for a non-artistic impression, whereby references to Western Minimal and Conceptual Art are nonetheless clearly evident. The central element was the plentiful use of loose-hanging linen, suspended from the ceiling in long strips, and also placed on the floor and walls. This all-over suspended the "laws" of the space and confronted visitors with a radical emptiness heading toward nothing.

Infolge der Niederschlagung des Prager Frühling durch die sowjetische Armee im August 1968 und der bald darauf einsetzenden totalitären Phase der „Normalisation" kam es in der Tschechoslowakei zu einer zunehmenden Gleichschaltung der Gesellschaft und einer nachhaltigen Einengung der persönlichen Freiheiten. Stano Filko wurde 1972 aus der Vereinigung der bildenden Künstler*innen der Tschechoslowakei ausgeschlossen, was einem Berufsverbot gleich kam. Daraufhin wurde das kollektive Arbeiten mit befreundeten Kunstschaffenden und der intensive Austausch abseits der Öffentlichkeit zunehmend wichtiger. In dieser Phase entstand auch das Projekt *White Space in White Space / Biely priestor v bielom priestore*, welches Filko über mehrere Jahre gemeinsam mit Miloš Laky und Ján Zavarský entwickelt hat. [17]

White Space in White Space wurde in unterschiedlichen Ausführungen als Installation realisiert. Die erste, legendäre Realisation fand am 18. Februar 1974 für die Dauer von ein paar Stunden abseits der Öffentlichkeit im Dům umění (House of Arts), Brno statt. [02–03] [16] *White Space in White Space* wurde als eine umfassende Installation aus Objekten und Leinwänden präsentiert, die durch Farbwalzen mit weißem, rechteckigen Latexanstrich bemalt wurden und einen vorderhand nicht-künstlerischen Ausdruck anstrebten, wobei Bezüge zur Minimal Art und Concept Art westlicher Prägung offensichtlich sind. Das zentrale Element war die ausgiebige Verwendung von unbespanntem Leinen, welches in langen Bahnen von der Decke hing, sowie an Boden und Wänden platziert wurde. Dieses *All-over* setzte die Gesetze des Raumes außer Kraft und konfrontierte die Besucher*innen mit einer radikalen Leerheit, die auf das Nichts zusteuert.

[05] Stano Filko, Miloš Laky, Ján Zavarský, *White Space in White Space / Biely priestor v bielom priestore*, 1974

[04] Stano Filko, Miloš Laky, Ján Zavarský, *From the series Sensitivity. White Space in White Space / Zo série Senzitivita. Biely priestor v bielom priestore*, 1973–75

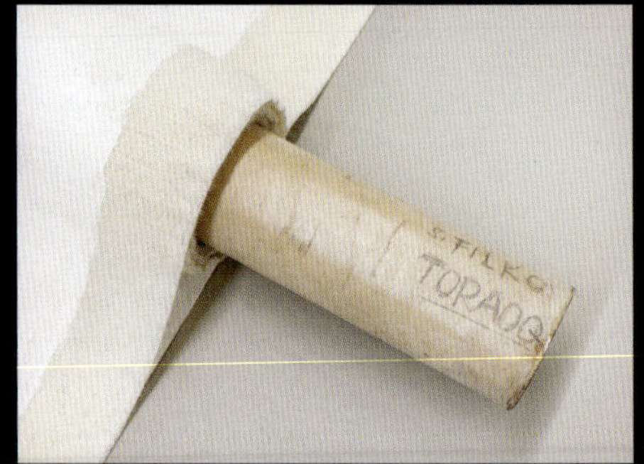

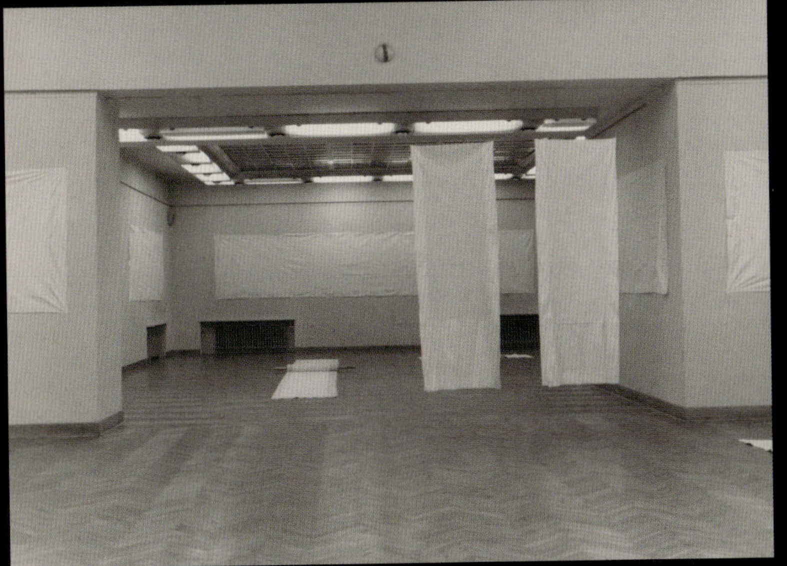

[03] Stano Filko, Miloš Laky, Ján Zavarský, *White Space in White Space / Biely priestor v bielom priestore*, 1974, House of Arts, Brno, 1974

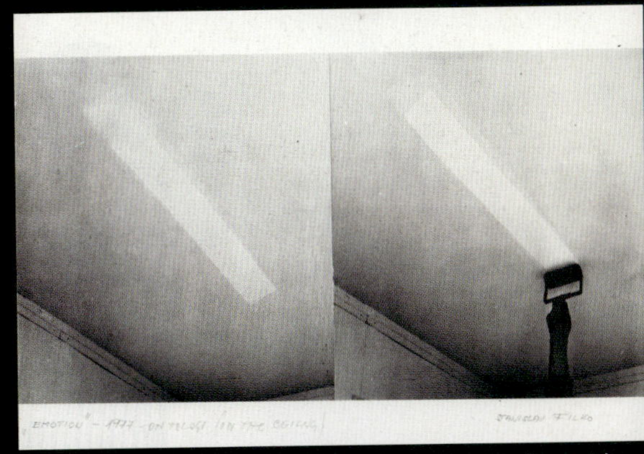

[06] *Emotion - 1977 - Ontology (on the Ceiling)*, 1977

[07] *White Square / Biely štvorec*, c. 1995

The original 1974 version of *White Space in White Space* was followed by versions for further exhibitions that were adapted by the artists to the different spatial conditions. Here felt strips and cardboard rolls were used as bearers of the white color fields. This further expanded the vertical structure of the installation, bestowed a strong rhythm onto the rooms, and further emphasized the gap between art and reality.

White Space in White Space asks as to the relationship between art and space, both in social and in material terms. To what extent is art dependent on a specific form, a certain material, or established institutions? In the tradition of Kazimir Malevich, Filko, Laky, and Zavarský pursue a process of dematerialization and transcendence, and they wish to hereby create an art of "pure sensitivity."

Auf die Ursprungsversion 1974 von *White Space in White Space* folgten Realisationen für weitere Ausstellungen, die von den Künstlern jeweils an die räumlichen Gegebenheiten angepasst wurden. Nun kamen vermehrt Filzbänder und Kartonrollen als Träger der weißen Farbfelder zum Einsatz. Dadurch wurde die vertikale Struktur der Installation ausgebaut, die Räume mit einem stärkeren Rhythmus versehen und die Lücke zwischen Kunst und Realität noch einmal stärker betont.

White Space in White Space stellt Fragen nach der Beziehung zwischen Kunst und Raum, sowohl in gesellschaftlicher als auch in materieller Hinsicht. Inwieweit ist die Kunst auf eine konkrete Form, ein bestimmtes Material oder auf etablierte Institutionen angewiesen? In der Tradition Kazimir Malevichs folgen Filko, Laky und Zavarský einem Prozess der Dematerialisierung und der Transzendenz und wollen damit eine Kunst der „reinen Sensibilität" erschaffen.

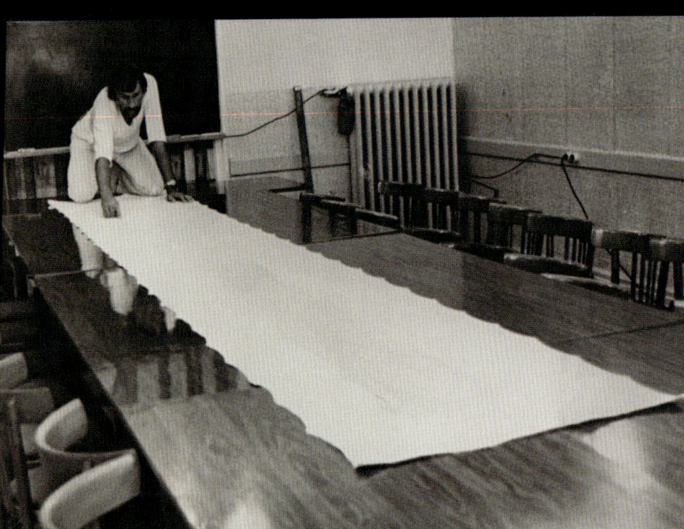

[08] *White Space – Anti-performance Behind Closed Doors / Biely priestor – Anti-performance za zavretými dverami, 1978*

White Space in White Space had a significant influence on the Czechoslovak art scene in the 1970s. To accompany their various versions, Filko, Laky, and Zavarský also published several manifestos and statements. For Filko the work on the manifestos marks an important step in his oeuvre toward conceptual and text-art, which he continued to pursue alone after 1976. He also addressed the performance as artistic medium, rejecting it as *Anti-performance* by using a canvas painted in white. [08] Following on from his artistic self-reflection of this collaboration, Filko continued to drive his own projects forward, leading to further concepts and actions such as *EMOTION – EMÓCIA (Text-art)* (1977), and *TRANSCENDENCE I., II. / TRANSCENDENCJA I., II.* (1979). This whole creative period stands under the auspices of *White Space in White Space*, and Filko later called it *White Ontology*.

White Space in White Space übte großen Einfluss auf die tschechoslowakische Kunstszene der 1970er-Jahre aus. Im Zuge der unterschiedlichen Realisierungen haben Filko, Laky und Zavarský auch mehrere Manifeste und Proklamationen veröffentlicht. Für Filko markiert die Arbeit an den Manifesten einen wichtigen Schritt in seinem Œurvre hin zur Konzept- und Textkunst, die er nach 1976 wieder alleine weiterverfolgt. Auch der Performance als künstlerisches Medium widmete sich Filko, indem er diese unter Verwendung einer weiß bemalten Leinwand als *Anti-performance* von sich wies. [08] Aus der künstlerischen Selbstreflexion der Zusammenarbeit heraus treibt Filko seine eigenen Projekte weiter an, was zu Folgekonzepten und Aktionen wie *EMOTION – EMÓCIA (Text-art)* (1977), und *TRANSCENDENCE I., II. / TRANSCENDENCJA I., II.* (1979) führt. Diese gesamte Schaffensperiode steht unter dem Vorzeichen von *White Space in White Space* und wird später von Filko mit dem Begriff *White Ontology* überschrieben.

[09] Stano Filko, Miloš Laky, Ján Zavarský, *White Space in White Space / Biely priestor v bielom priestore, 1973*

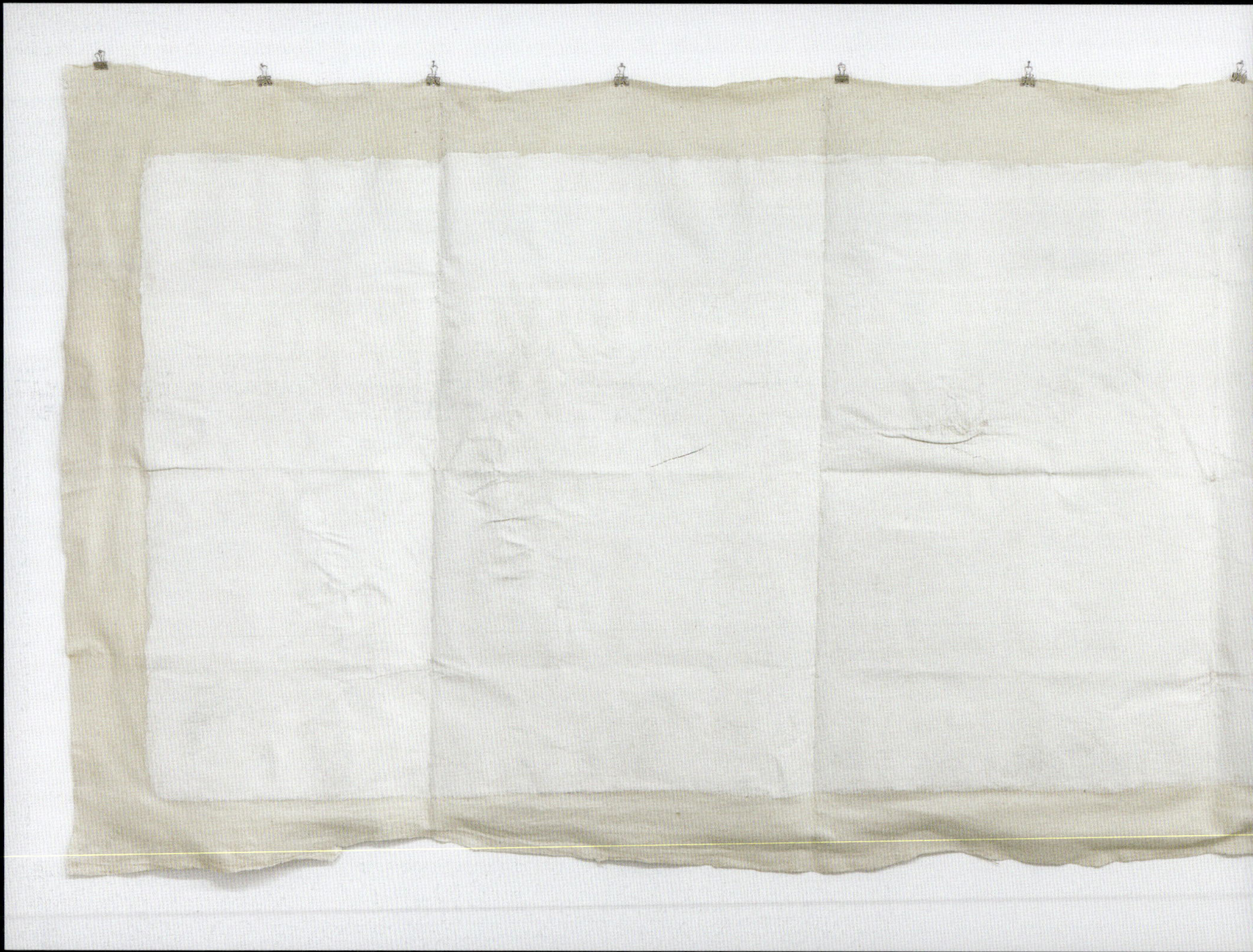

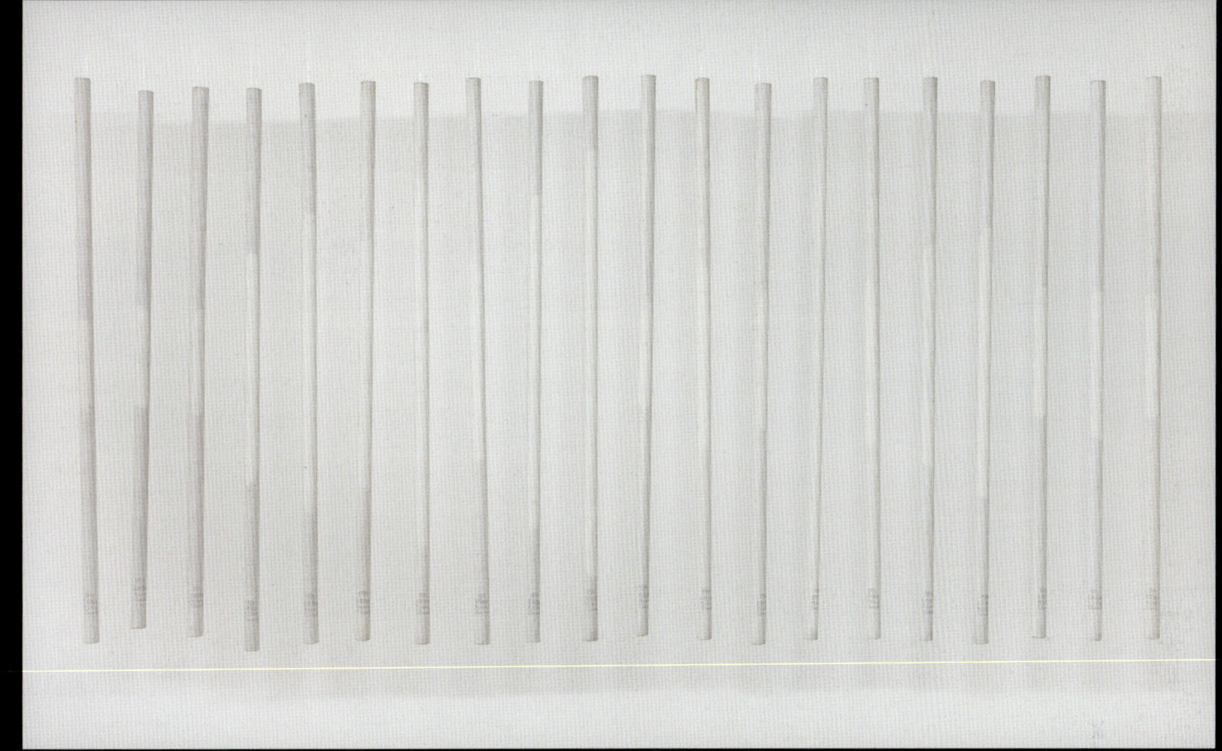

[10A] Stano Filko, Miloš Laky, Ján Zavarský, *White Space in White Space / Biely priestor v bielom priestore*, 1974

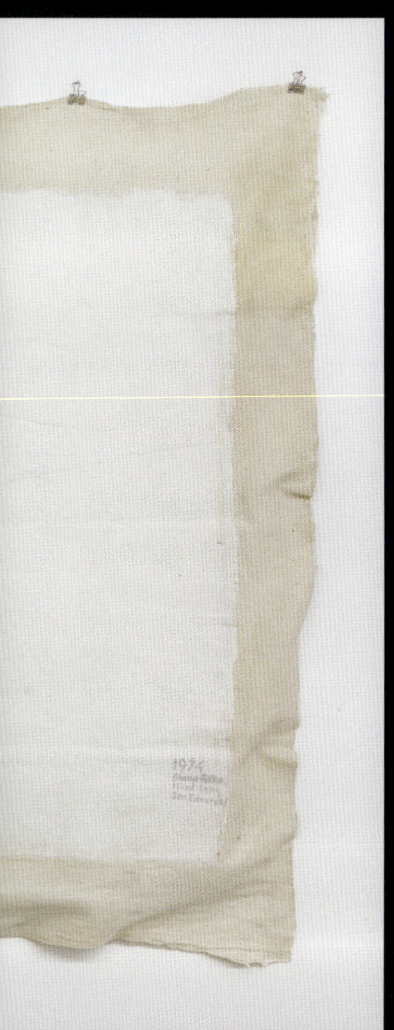

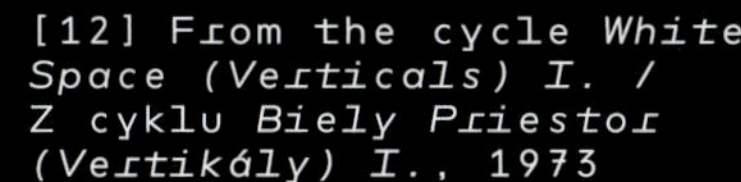

[11] From the series *Verticals for Realization in Architecture /* Zo série *Vertikály na realizáciu v architecture*, 1977

[12] From the cycle *White Space (Verticals) I. /* Z cyklu *Biely Priestor (Vertikály) I.*, 1973

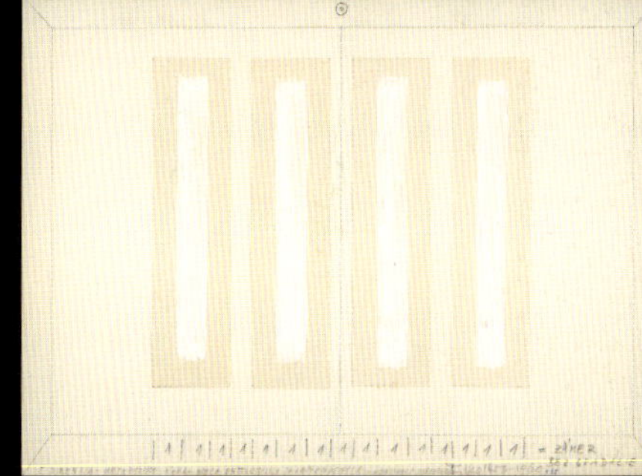

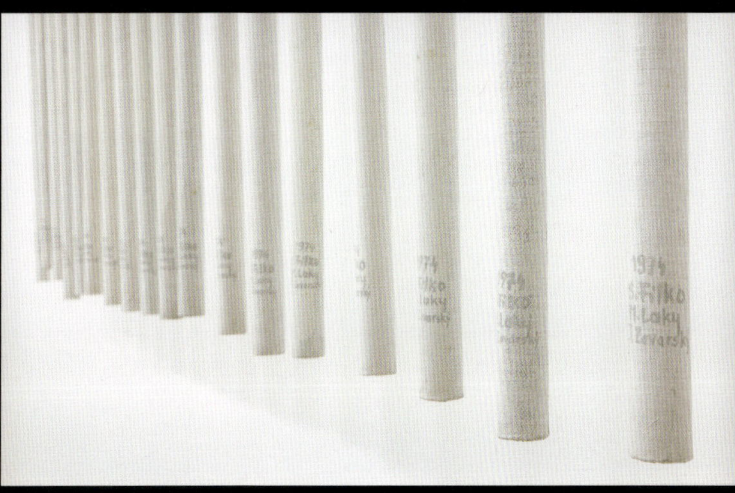

[10B] Stano Filko, Miloš Laky, Ján Zavarský, *White Space in White Space / Biely priestor v bielom priestore*, 1974

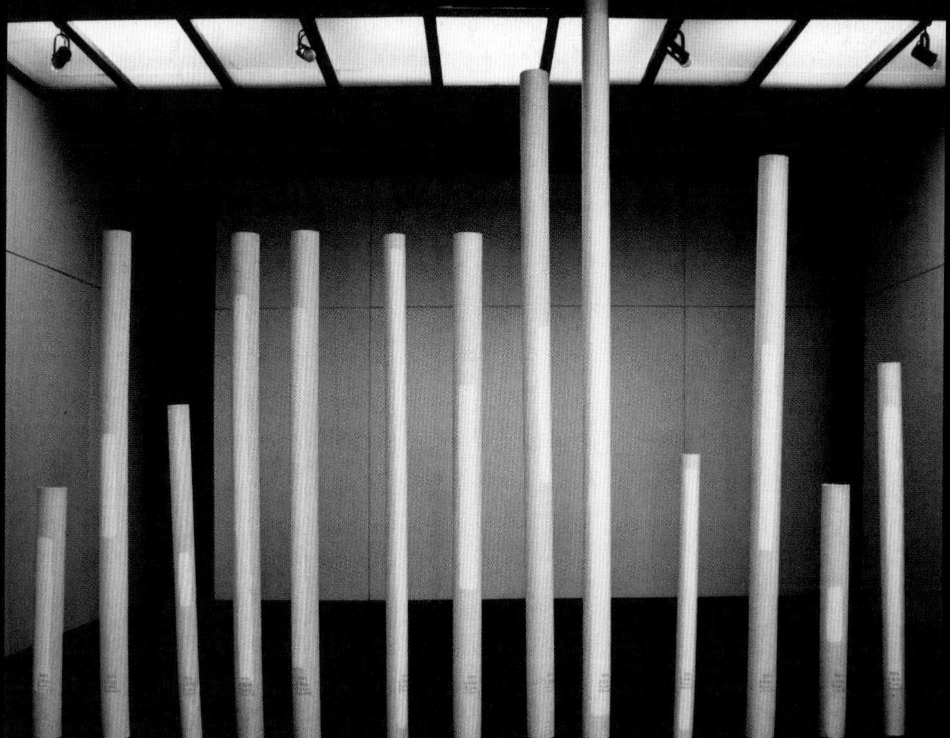

[14] Stano Filko, Miloš Laky, Ján Zavarský, *White Space in White Space / Biely priestor v bielom priestore*, Gallery of Youth / Galéria mladých, Bratislava, 1974

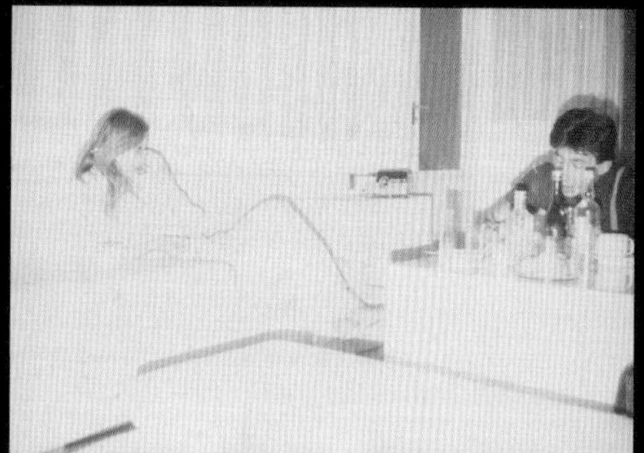

[15] Miloš Laky's apartment with Hana Lakyová and Ján Budaj, 1970s

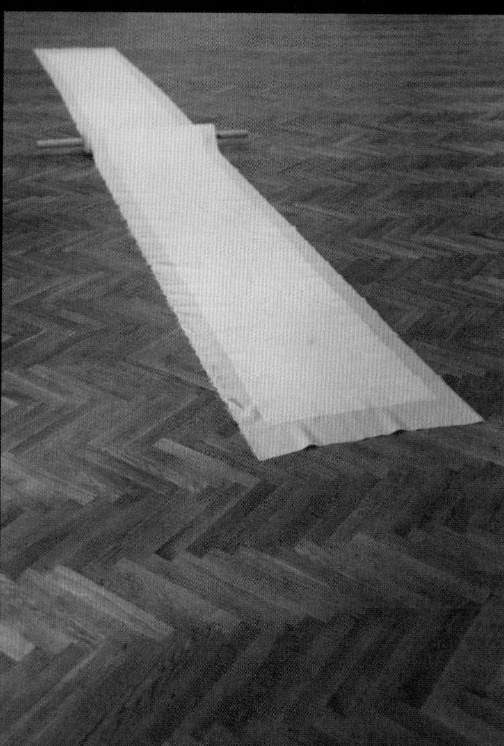

[16] Stano Filko, Miloš Laky, Ján Zavarský, *White Space in White Space / Biely priestor v bielom priestore*, 1974, House of Arts, Brno, 1974

This presentation does not recreate a specific historical continuity or a specific version of the work series, but rather presents the themes of these works as a space within a space, showing various items and elements from the different exhibitions and some of the accompanying texts, as well as other related works.

Die Präsentation folgt keiner historischen Kontinuität oder einer bestimmten Version der Werkreihe, vielmehr führt sie den Themenkomplex als Raum im Raum auf, indem verschiedene Versatzstücke und Elemente aus den unterschiedlichen Ausstellungen sowie einige der dazugehörigen Textdokumente, aber auch Arbeiten im Kontext lose präsentiert werden.

←[13] Stano Filko, Miloš Laky, Ján Zavarský, *White Space in White Space / Biely priestor v bielom priestore*, 1974

MANIFEST
(weisser immaterieller Raum im weissen unendlichen Raum)

1. Unsere Schöpfung ist im Gegensatz zur Kunst des Objekts, Environments, Konzepts, zum Hyperrealismus, Minimalart, zur lyrischen und postgeometrischen Abstraktion, sie verläst die Gegenstandrealität und gibt sich keine Mühe irgendein Erkenntnis über diese Welt zu erlangen.

2. Mit der Überschreitung der Grenzen der objektiven Welt werden wir der unendlichen Leere bewusst, in der wir unser Denken entfalten.

3. Wenn man den reinen weissen Raum mit einem weisen Raum bemalt, ensteht eine Spannung, die die innere Dynamik der Unendlichkeit vorstellt.

4. Die zentrale Spannung zweier weissen Räume veranlasst die unbegrenzte Expansivität im Unendlichen.

5. Unser Schaffen der reinen Kunst ist scheinbar entgültig, seine innere Dynamik ist mit dem Unendlichen identisch.

6. Unsere subjektive Darstellung der inneren Unendlichkeits dynamik ist rhytmuslos und deshalb sieht sie keiner bildenden Darstellung der objektiven Realität änlich.

7. Die Dynamik des Endlosen wird in jedem von uns ausgerüktem Original aus der unendlichen Möglichkeitsmenge dargestellt.

8. Die Idee der unendlichen Leere ist ein allgemeines Medium, das wir mittels der reinen Senzibilität in die Schöpfung der reinen Kunst interpretieren.

9. Mit Hilfe der reinen Senzibilität gestalten wir künstlerisch die unendliche Leere – wir schaffen einen weissen immateriellen Raum im reinen weissen unendlichen Raum.

10. Die reine Sensibilität ist unsere Schöpfungmetode.

11. Mit unserem Schaffen haben wir die Erforschung der objektiven Realität überschritten und verlassen und sind in die Sphäre des Unerkenntlichen geraten, das nur die reine Sensibilität darstellen kann.

12. Unsere schöpferische Bestrebung ist eine Überschreitung der Welt der Realität und der erste Schritt in die Welt der reinen Senzibilität. Die reine Kunst ist Kunst dieser Sensibilität.

1973–74
Stano FILKO
Miloš LAKY
Ján ZAVARSKÝ

Stano FILKO
Na Hrebienku 43, 80100 Bra
Miloš LAKY
Brnianska 83, 80100 Bratisl
Ján ZAVARSKÝ
Palisády 53/a, 80100 Bratisl

MANIFESTO

(A white unmaterialized space in a pure white infinite space.)

1. In its very nature our creative work is in contrast with the art of the object, the environment, the concept, the hyperrealism, the minimalart, the lyric and postgeometric abstraction, it leaves the objective reality and does not try to gain any knowledge about this world.

2. By crossing the boundary of the objective world we become conscious of the infinite emptiness we develop our thinking in.

3. By painting a pure white space on another white space a tension representing the internal dynamics of the infinitude arises.

4. The central tension of two white spaces instigates the unlimited expansiveness in the infinitude.

5. Our creative work of pure art is seemingly finite, its internal dynamics being identical with infinitude.

6. Our subjektive depiction of the inner dynamics of the infinitude is without rhythm therefore it does not resemble any creative representation of the objektive reality.

7. The dynamics of infinitude is expressed in every original work created by us from an infinite amount of posibilities.

8. The idea of infinite emptiness is the general medium transferred to the creative work of pure art by means of pure sensibility.

9. By means of pure sensibility we make creative art out of infinite emptiness. We create a white unmaterialized space in a pure white infinite space.

10. Pure sensibility is the metod of our creation.

11. Whith our creative work we have exceeded and left the research of the objektive world and got to the sphere of the unknown that can be expressed only by pure sensibility.

12. Our creative aim is to go beyond the world of reality, it is the first step into the world of pure sensibility. Pure art is the art of this sensibility.

1973–74

Stano FILKO
Miloš LAKY
Ján ZAVARSKÝ

MANIFEST

(biely nehmotný priestor v čistom bie

1. Naša tvorba je v protiklade k u hyperrealizmu, minimalartu, lyri predmetnú realitu a nesnaží sa z

2. Prekročením hraníc predmetnéh no, v ktorom rozvíjame naše mys

3. Pomaľovaním čistého bieleho p ktoré predstavuje vnútornú dyna

4. Centrálne napätie dvoch bielych navosť v nekonečne.

5. Naša tvorba čistého umenia je z totožná s nekonečnom.

6. Naše subjektívne zobrazenie vnu a preto sa nepodobá na žiadne v

7. Dynamika nekonečna je vyjadre z nekonečného množstva možno

8. Idea nekonečného prázdna je v senzibility interpretujeme do tvo

9. Pomocou čistej senzibility zvýtva biely nehmotný priestor v čistom

10. Čistá senzibilita je metódou naše

11. Našou tvorbou sme prekročili a o sme sa do sféry nepoznaného, k

12. Našou tvorivou snahou je prekroč senzibility. Čisté umenie je umen

onečnom priestore)

bjektu, environmentu, konceptu,
stgeometrickej abstrakcii, opúšťa
ké poznanie o tomto svete.

vedomujeme si nekonečné prázd-

bielym priestorom vzniká napätie,
konečna.

ov navodzuje neohraničenú rozpí-

onečná, jej vnútorná dynamika je

ynamiky nekonečna je bez rytmu
zobrazenie predmetnej reality.

ždom nami vytvorenom originále

é médium, ktoré pomocou čistej
ho umenia.

nekonečnú prázdnotu. Vytvárame
nekonečnom priestore.

skum predmetného sveta a dostali
e zobraziť iba čistá senzibilita.
ta reality a prvý krok do sveta čistej
senzibility.

1973–74

Stano FILKO
Miloš LAKY
Ján ZAVARSKÝ

MANIFESTE

(un espace blanc immatériel dans l'espace blanc pur et infini)

1. Notre création est en opposition avec l'art de l'objet, l'environnement, le concept, l'hyperréalisme, le minimalart, l'abstraction lyrique et postgéométrique; elle abandonne la réalité objective et elle ne s'efforce pas d'acquérir aucune connaissance sur ce monde.

2. En dépassant les limites du monde objectif nous nous rendons compte du vide infini ou se developpe notre pensée.

3. Une fois l'espace blanc superposé à l'espace blanc pur, il se produit une tension représentant le dynamisme intérieur de l'infini.

4. La tension existante entre les deux espaces blancs établit une expansion sans limites dans l'infini.

5. Notre création de l'art pur est définitive en apparence, par son dynamisme intérieur elle est identique à l'infini.

6. Notre figuration subjective du dynamisme intérieur de l'infini est privé du rythme quelconque, c'est pour cela qu'elle ne ressemble pas à aucune représentation plastique de la réalité objective.

7. Le dynamisme de l'infini s'exprime dans chaque oeuvre originale créée par nous et tirée d'un nombre infini des possibilités.

8. L'idée du vide infini, c'est le médium interprété par nous dans la création de l'art pur au moyen de la sensibilité pure.

9. Au moyen de la sensibilité pure nous représentons plastiquement le vide infini. Nous créons un espace blanc immatériel dans l'espace blanc pur et infini.

10. La méthode de notre création, c'est la sensibilité pure.

11. Avec notre création nous avons dépassé et abandonné l'exploration du monde objectif et nous avons abordé le domaine de l'inconnu qui ne peut être représenté que par la sensibilité pure.

12. Notre engagement créateur est de dépasser le monde de la réalité et de faire le premier pas dans le monde de la sensibilité pure. L'art pur, c'est l'art de la sensibilité ainsi comprise.

1973–74

Stano FILKO
Miloš LAKY
Ján ZAVARSKÝ

List of Works / Werkliste
Exhibition / Ausstellung

Page / Seite 12-15
I. *System SF:*
System Stano Filko

[01]
VACUUMDREAMSEXISTENCEDSAOOQ,
2000-10
   Print, paper, ink, felt-
   tip pen / Druck, Papier
   Zeichentusche, Filzstift
   29.7×42cm
   Courtesy Slovak National
   Gallery, Bratislava

[02]
Untitled (subtitled
*PSYCHOAQ 5.4.D. – PHYSICS
3.D. – FEMALES – FEMALESF –
FEMINISF – VAGINES – PUSSIES /
PSICHOAQ 5.4.D. – FYZIKA
3.D. – SAMIČKY – FEMALESF –
FEMINISF – VAGINKY – PIČKY)*,
2000s
   Double-sided color print,
   paper / Doppelseitiger
   Farbdruck, Papier
   42×29.7cm
   Courtesy Collection of
   Central Slovakian Gallery /
   Stredoslovenská galéria,
   Banská Bystrica

[03]
RETROQ System SF, 1995-2005
   Print, paper, mixed
   media, felt-tip pen, pen,
   perforation / Druck, Papier,
   Mixed Media, Filzstift,
   Stift, Perforation
   29.7×42.1cm
   Courtesy Slovak National
   Gallery, Bratislava

[04]
*Cosmos. Associations XVII. /
Cosmos. Asociácie XVII.*, 1969
   Serigraph, plastic /
   Serigrafie, Plastik
   54.2×54.2cm
   Courtesy Slovak National
   Gallery, Bratislava

[05]
*Associations XXII. / Asociácie
XXII.*, 1968-69
   White cardboard, printed /
   Weißer Karton, bedruckt
   70×50cm
   Courtesy Slovak National
   Gallery, Bratislava

[06]
*Associations XIX. / Asociácie
XIX.*, 1968-69
   White cardboard, printed /
   Weißer Karton, bedruckt
   70×49.9cm
   Courtesy Slovak National
   Gallery, Bratislava

[07]
*Artist's studio Snežienková /
Umelcov ateliér Snežienková*,
2007
   Photo / Foto: Pato Safko

[08]
*7 Chakra Colors Ladder /
Rebrík vo farbách 7 čakier*,
c. 2000
   Found object, acrylic, wood,
   metal / Gefundenes Objekt,
   Acryl, Holz, Metall
   174×63cm
   Courtesy Layr Vienna / Wien

Page / Seite 16-19
II. Interventions in Public
Space / Interventionen im
öffentlichen Raum

[01A-C]
*Breathing – The Celebration
of Air / Dýchanie – oslava
vzduchu*, 1970
HALLE FÜR KUNST Steiermark,
Graz, 2022
   Photos / Fotos: kunst-
   dokumentation.com

[02]
*Breathing – The Celebration
of Air / Dýchanie – oslava
vzduchu*, 1970
   Tarpaulin, electric motor,
   fan / Plane, elektrischer
   Motor, Ventilator
   ø 550cm
   Courtesy Slovak National
   Gallery, Bratislava

[03A-B]
*12 Colors of Reality
(Balloons) / 12 farieb reality
(Balóny)*, 1978-2011
HALLE FÜR KUNST Steiermark,
Graz, 2022
   Fabric and other materials,
   electric motor, fan / Stoff
   und andere Materialien,
   elektrischer Motor,
   Ventilator
   12 pieces, each / 12 Stück,
   je ø 300cm
   Courtesy Slovak National
   Gallery, Bratislava
   Photos / Fotos: HALLE FÜR
   KUNST Steiermark, Graz

[04A-B]
*SP Record / SP gramoplatňa
KOZMOS – 9-1; FUTÚR – COSMOS
FUTÜR; ATOM – REÁL; COSMOS –
COSMOS ESPACE UNIVERSE*,
1970-71
   Digitized sound transferred
   from 4 vinyl records /
   Digitalisierter Sound aus 4
   Vinyl-Schallplatten
   Loop
   Courtesy Linea Collection,
   Bratislava; Layr, Vienna /
   Wien
   Photos / Fotos: Slovak
   National Gallery, Bratislava

[05A]
Pyramid / Pyramída, c. 1995
   Lichtenfels Sculpture, 2021
   Photo / Foto: Layr, Vienna /
   Wien

[05B]
Pyramid / Pyramída, c. 1995
HALLE FÜR KUNST Steiermark,
Graz, 2022
   Plastic tubes, paint /
   Kunststoffrohre, Farbe
   390×550×550cm
   Courtesy Linea Collection,
   Bratislava; Layr, Vienna /
   Wien
   Photo / Foto: kunst-
   dokumentation.com

Page / Seite 20-23
III. First Insight /
Erste Annäherung

[01A]
Wind / Vietor, 1967/c. 1995
HALLE FÜR KUNST Steiermark,
Graz, 2022
   Photo / Foto: kunst-
   dokumentation.com

[01B]
Wind / Vietor, 1967/c. 1995
   Metal, synthetic paint,
   electric cable / Metall,
   synthetische Farbe,
   elektrisches Kabel
   3 objects, each / 3 Objekte,
   je 120×135×135cm
   Courtesy Linea Collection,
   Bratislava; Layr, Vienna /
   Wien
   Photo / Foto: kunst-
   dokumentation.com

[02]
Wind / Vietor, 1967/c. 1995
   tranzit.sk, Bratislava, 2005
   Photo / Foto: Martin
   Marenčin

[03]
*7 Chakra Colors Bench /
Lavička vo farbách 7 čakier*,
c. 2000
   Found object, wood,
   acrylic / Gefundenes Objekt,
   Holz, Acryl
   107×30×80cm
   Courtesy Linea Collection,
   Bratislava; Layr, Vienna /
   Wien
   Photo / Foto: kunst-
   dokumentation.com

[04A-B]
*Monument – Czechoslovak
Flag / Pomník – zástava
Československa*, 1968/1993
   Metal, paint / Metall, Farbe
   220×80×50cm
   Courtesy Linea Collection,
   Bratislava; Layr, Vienna /
   Wien
   Photos / Fotos: kunst-
   dokumentation.com

[05]
Monument – Czechoslovak Flag / Pomník - zástava Československa, 1968/1993
Facsimile, B/W photograph (24×9cm) enlargened/framed, paper, whitening liquid, felt-tip pen / Faksimile, S/W-Fotografie (24×9cm) vergrößert/gerahmt, Papier, weißfärbende Flüssigkeit, Filzstift
60×23cm
Courtesy Linea Collection, Bratislava; Layr, Vienna / Wien
Photo / Foto: kunst-dokumentation.com

[06A–B]
Priestor - Space X. - Rockets / Priestor - Space X. - Rakety, 1967
Metal, paint / Metall, Farbe
15 objects, variable dimensions / 15 Objekte, variable Maße
Courtesy Linea Collection, Bratislava; Layr, Vienna / Wien
Photos / Fotos: kunst-dokumentation.com

Page / Seite 24-31
IV. Colors and Dimensions / Farbe und Dimensionen

[01–02] [10]
Exhibition view / Ausstellungsansicht, HALLE FÜR KUNST Steiermark, Graz, 2022
Photos / Fotos: kunst-dokumentation.com

[03]
7 Chakra Colors / 7 farieb čakier, c. 1995
Found Material, wood, acrylic / Gefundenes Material, Holz, Acryl
430×11×2cm
Courtesy Linea Collection, Bratislava; Layr, Vienna / Wien
Photo / Foto: kunst-dokumentation.com

[04]
EGO - Gemini - Reincarnation (5.4.3.D.) / EGO - Blíženci - Reinkarnácia (5.4.3.D.), c. 1995
Wood, paint / Holz, Farbe
3 parts, each / 3 Teile, je 200×150×40cm
Courtesy Linea Collection, Bratislava; Layr, Vienna / Wien
Photo / Foto: kunst-dokumentation.com

[05]
From the series *EGO 4.5.3.D. TRIADAQ / Zo série EGO 4.5.3.D. TRIADAQ*, c. 1992
Paper, watercolor, pen, white paint / Aquarell, Papier, Stift, weiße Farbe
32.5×47.5cm
Courtesy Linea Collection, Bratislava; Layr, Vienna / Wien
Photo / Foto: kunst-dokumentation.com

[06]
Central Brain / Centrálny mozog, c. 2000
Found objects, fabric, plastic cord, wire / Gefundene Objekte, Stoff, Plastikschnur, Draht
70×55×55cm
Courtesy Linea Collection, Bratislava; Layr, Vienna / Wien
Photo / Foto: Martin Marenčin

[07A–C]
Three Women (3.4.5.D.) / Tri ženy (3.4.5.D.), c. 1995
Wood, paint / Holz, Farbe
3 objects, each / 3 Objekte, je 225×222×227cm
Courtesy Linea Collection, Bratislava; Layr, Vienna / Wien
Photos / Fotos: kunst-dokumentation.com

[08A–C]
Wooden Poles in Chakra Colors / Drevené tyče vo farbách čakier, c. 2005
Wood, paint / Holz, Farbe
9 pieces, each 400cm long / 9 Stück, je 400cm lang
Courtesy Linea Collection, Bratislava; Layr, Vienna / Wien
Photos / Fotos: kunst-dokumentation.com

[09]
Wardrobe in 7 Chakra Colors / Skriňa vo farbách 7 čakier, c. 1995
Found object, wood, paint / Gefundenes Objekt, Holz, Farbe
250×120×135cm
Courtesy Peter Petrička, Bratislava

[11]
7 Chakra Colors Ladder / Rebrík vo farbách 7 čakier, c. 1995
Found objects, metal, acrylic / Gefundene Objekte, Metall, Acryl
188cm×94×41cm
Courtesy Linea Collection, Bratislava; Layr, Vienna / Wien
Photo / Foto: kunst-dokumentation.com

[12]
12 Chakra Colors Ladder / Rebrík vo farbách 12 čakier, c. 2005
Found object, wood, acrylic / Gefundenes Objekt, Holz, Acryl
400×133×80cm
Courtesy Linea Collection, Bratislava; Layr, Vienna / Wien
Photo / Foto: kunst-dokumentation.com

[13A–B]
5.4.3.D., c. 2000
Found objects, wood, acrylic / Gefundene Objekte, Holz, Acryl
2 objects / 2 Objekte, 42×52×11cm; 56×52×11cm
Courtesy Linea Collection, Bratislava; Layr, Vienna / Wien
Photos / Fotos: kunst-dokumentation.com

Page / Seite 52-57
V. *Clinical Death Tunnel* and Balloon Works / und Ballon-Arbeiten

[01–03] [06]
Exhibition view / Ausstellungsansicht, HALLE FÜR KUNST Steiermark, Graz, 2022
Photos / Fotos: kunst-dokumentation.com

[04A–B]
Clinical Death Tunnel / Tunel klinickej smrti, c. 2010
Metal, paint / Metall, Farbe
2000×ø 35.2cm
Courtesy Linea Collection, Bratislava; Layr, Vienna / Wien
Photos / Fotos: kunst-dokumentation.com

[05]
Rotated Pyramid - Woman / Otočená pyramída - Žena, 2000-06
Metal, perforation, paint / Metall, Perforation, Farbe
115×150×150cm
Courtesy Linea Collection, Bratislava; Layr, Vienna / Wien
Photo / Foto: kunst-dokumentation.com

[07]
ALTRUISTADSEIQ 5.4.3.D. (EGO Balloon) / ALTRUISTADSEIQ 5.4.3.D. (EGO Balón), c. 2005
Inflatable balloon, paint / Aufblasbarer Ballon, Farbe
ø c. 200cm
Courtesy Linea Collection, Bratislava; Layr, Vienna / Wien
Photo / Foto: Martin Marenčin

[08]
Globe in the Transparent Color Chakra / Gula vo farbe transparentnej čakry, c. 2005
Plastic, fan, electric cable / Plastik, Ventilator, elektrisches Kabel
ø 260cm
Courtesy Linea Collection, Bratislava; Layr, Vienna / Wien
Photo / Foto: kunst-dokumentation.com

[09]
25,000 BC-1937, c. 1995
  Fabric, paint / Stoff, Farbe
  130×1500cm
  Courtesy Linea Collection,
  Bratislava; Layr, Vienna /
  Wien
  Photo / Foto: kunst-
  dokumentation.com

Page / Seite 58-61
VI. Rockets and Space /
Raketen und Weltraum

[01]
*Tenth Chakra Rocket / Raketa
desiatej čakry; DSUQ 4.D.
Rocket / DSUQ 4.D. Raketa*,
c. 2005; 2000
  Metal sheet, acrylic /
  Metallblech, Acryl
  400×83×83cm; 400×49×49cm
  Courtesy Linea Collection,
  Bratislava; Layr, Vienna /
  Wien
  Photo / Foto: kunst-
  dokumentation.com

[02]
*Rockets 5.4.3.D. / Rakety
5.4.3.D.*, 2000
  Welded metal sheet,
  acrylic / Geschweißtes
  Blech, Metall, Acryl
  3 objects, each / 3 Objekte,
  je 200×30×30cm
  Courtesy Linea Collection,
  Bratislava; Layr, Vienna /
  Wien
  Photo / Foto: kunst-
  dokumentation.com

[03]
*Chakra Colors Rockets -
Bombs / Rakety - bomby vo
farbách čakier*, c. 1985
  Found objects, metal, oil
  paint / Gefundene Objekte,
  Metall, Ölfarbe
  7 objects, each / 7 Objekte,
  je 107×35×35cm
  Courtesy Linea Collection,
  Bratislava; Layr, Vienna /
  Wien
  Photo / Foto: kunst-
  dokumentation.com

[04]
From the series *Sculptures of
the Twentieth century IV. /
Zo série Sochy XX. storočia
IV.*, 1968-69
  Found printed material,
  paper, felt-tip pen, pen /
  Gefundene Druckerzeugnisse,
  Papier, Filzstift, Stift
  25.7×18cm
  Courtesy Linea Collection,
  Bratislava; Layr, Vienna /
  Wien
  Photo / Foto: Slovak
  National Gallery, Bratislava

[05]
*Priestor - Space X. -
Rockets / Priestor -
Space X. - Rakety*, 1967
  Metal, paint / Metall, Farbe
  15 objects, variable
  dimensions / 15 Objekte,
  variable Maße
  Courtesy Linea Collection,
  Bratislava; Layr, Vienna /
  Wien
  Photo / Foto: kunst-
  dokumentation.com

[06]
*First Chakra Rocket / Raketa
prvej čakry*, c. 2005
  Metal sheet, paint /
  Metallblech, Acryl
  300×100×100cm
  Courtesy Linea Collection,
  Bratislava; Layr, Vienna /
  Wien
  Photo / Foto: kunst-
  dokumentation.com

[07]
*DSUQ 4.D. Rocket / DSUQ 4.D.
Raketa*, 2000
  Metal sheet, acrylic,
  perforation / Metallblech,
  Acryl, Perforation
  600×67×67cm
  Courtesy Linea Collection,
  Bratislava; Layr, Vienna /
  Wien
  Photo / Foto: kunst-
  dokumentation.com

[08]
*TIMESPACE - 4.3.D. (Rockets) /
TIMESPACE - 4.3.D. (Rakety)*,
1968/1993
  Wood, acrylic and other
  materials / Holz, Acryl und
  andere Materialien
  3 objects / 3 Objekte,
  180×108×12cm; 208×108×11cm;
  197×104×8cm
  Courtesy Linea Collection,
  Bratislava; Layr, Vienna /
  Wien
  Photo / Foto: kunst-
  dokumentation.com

[09]
*DSQ 4.D. Bomb / DSQ 4.D.
Bomba*, 1985-95
  Print, paper, pen / Druck,
  Papier, Kugelschreiber
  29.7×42cm
  Courtesy Slovak National
  Gallery, Bratislava

[10]
From the series *Map of the
World (Rockets) / Zo série
Mapa sveta (Rakety)*, 1967
  Found cartographic print,
  paper, printing from a lino
  stamper, pen / Gefundener
  kartographischer Druck,
  Papier, Linoldruck,
  Kugelschreiber
  95×39.2cm

[11]
*Living Art - On the Edge of
Europe*, Kröller-Müller Museum,
Otterlo, 2006
  Photo / Foto: Fedor Blaščák

Page / Seite 62-63
VII. *Shooting Range* and /
und *Constellations*

[01A-C]
*Shooting Range - Target
Universe / Strelnica-terč -
vesmír*, 1966-67/2005
  Object, collage, wood,
  acrylic, two rifles /
  Objekt, Collage, Holz,
  Acryl, zwei Gewehre
  350×180cm
  Courtesy Linea Collection,
  Bratislava; Layr, Vienna /
  Wien
  Photos / Fotos: kunst-
  dokumentation.com

[02A-B]
Constellations / Súhvezdia,
1968-69
  Copper sheets, perforation /
  Kupferbleche, Perforierung
  7 pieces, each / 7 Stück, je
  50.5×30cm
  Courtesy Linea Collection,
  Bratislava; Layr, Vienna /
  Wien
  Photos / Fotos: kunst-
  dokumentation.com

Page / Seite 64-65
VIII. (Model) Architecture
as Artistic Utopia /
(Modell-)Architektur als
künstlerische Utopie

[01A-D]
*Models of Observation Towers /
Modely pozorovacích veží*,
1966-67
  Print on cardboard; mirrors;
  5 objects / Druck auf
  Karton; Spiegel; 5 Objekte
  2 pieces, each / 2 Stück, je
  100×100cm; 32 pieces, each /
  32 Stück, je 50.5×30cm;
  variable dimensions /
  variable Maße
  Courtesy Linea Collection,
  Bratislava; Layr, Vienna /
  Wien
  Photo / Foto: kunst-
  dokumentation.com

[01A]
*Model of Observation Tower /
Model pozorovacej veže*, 1967
  Metal, paint / Metall, Farbe
  66×19×23cm
  Courtesy Linea Collection,
  Bratislava; Layr, Vienna /
  Wien
  Photo / Foto: kunst-
  dokumentation.com

[01B] [03]
*Model of Observation Tower /
Model pozorovacej veže*, 1966
  Found objects, metal /
  Gefundene Objekte, Metall
  82×19×23cm
  Courtesy Linea Collection,
  Bratislava; Layr, Vienna /
  Wien
  Photos / Fotos: kunst-
  dokumentation.com

[01C]
*Model of Observation Tower /
Model pozorovacej veže*, 1967
Metal, industrial paint /
Metall, Industriefarbe
93×55cm×28cm
Courtesy Linea Collection,
Bratislava; Layr, Vienna /
Wien
Photo / Foto: kunst-
dokumentation.com

[01D] [02]
*Model of Observation Tower /
Model pozorovacej veže*, 1967
Found object, metal, paint /
Gefundenes Objekt, Metall,
Farbe
60×29×21cm
Courtesy Linea Collection,
Bratislava; Layr, Vienna /
Wien
Photos / Fotos: kunst-
dokumentation.com

[01E]
Monster II. / Monštrum II.,
1963
Metal / Metall
113×34×32cm
Courtesy Slovak National
Gallery, Bratislava
Photo / Foto: kunst-
dokumentation.com

[04-05]
*Pneumatic Circles I. - XXXX. /
Pneumatické kolesá I. - XXXX.*,
1968
Orange and red inflatable
wheels; mirrors / Orange
und rote aufblasbare Reifen;
Spiegel
34 pieces and 12 pieces;
81 pieces, each 50.5×30cm /
34 Stück und 12 Stück;
81 Stück, je 50.5×30cm;
variable dimensions /
variable Maße
Courtesy Linea Collection,
Bratislava; Layr, Vienna /
Wien
Photos / Fotos: Slovak
National Gallery,
Bratislava; kunst-
dokumentation.com

Page / Seite 66-71
IX. Painting in the American
Period / Malerei in der
amerikanischen Periode

[01] [05]
Exhibition view /
Ausstellungsansicht, HALLE FÜR
KUNST Steiermark, Graz, 2022
Photo / Foto: kunst-
dokumentation.com

[02A-B]
SLOVAK, 1985
Canvas, acrylic / Leinwand,
Acryl
153×91cm
Courtesy Linea Collection,
Bratislava; Layr, Vienna /
Wien
Photos / Fotos: Martin
Marenčin

[03A-B]
AIDS - STAN, 1983
Canvas, acrylic / Leinwand,
Acryl
91×152cm
Courtesy Linea Collection,
Bratislava; Layr, Vienna /
Wien
Photos / Fotos: Martin
Marenčin

[04]
Self-Portrait / Autoportrét,
1982
Collage, cardboard, paint /
Collage, Karton, Farbe
100×70cm
Courtesy Linea Collection,
Bratislava; Layr, Vienna /
Wien
Photo / Foto: kunst-
dokumentation.com

[06A-C]
Štefánik/Čerňan, 1985-90
Wood, canvas, acrylic /
Holz, Leinwand, Acryl
6 pieces / 6 Stück, variable
dimensions / variable Maße
Courtesy Linea Collection,
Bratislava; Layr, Vienna /
Wien
Photos / Fotos: Martin
Marenčin

[07]
*Filko - Name Pink - Eight
Chakra / Filko - Meno Ružová -
Ôsma Čakra*, 1983-86
Canvas, acrylic / Leinwand,
Acryl
320×400cm
Courtesy Linea Collection,
Bratislava; Layr, Vienna /
Wien
Photo / Foto: Martin
Marenčin

[08]
*Contemplation in the Chakra
Color Spectrum / Kontemplácia
vo farbách čakier-spektier*,
c. 1993-95
Canvas, acrylic / Leinwand,
Acryl
2 parts / 2 Teile,
240×100×5cm; 197×100×5cm
Courtesy Linea Collection,
Bratislava; Layr, Vienna /
Wien
Photo / Foto: kunst-
dokumentation.com

[09A-B]
*The Old and New Testament /
Starý a Nový Zákon*, c. 1995
Hardboard, acrylic, oil,
putty / Hartfaserplatte,
Acryl, Öl, Kitt
243×122cm
Courtesy Linea Collection,
Bratislava; Layr, Vienna /
Wien
Photos / Fotos: kunst-
dokumentation.com

[10]
DSQ, c. 2000
Metal sheet, acrylic /
Metallplatte, Acryl
200×100cm
Courtesy Linea Collection,
Bratislava; Layr, Vienna /
Wien
Photo / Foto: Daša Barteková

Page / Seite 92-97
X. *Heart of Love*: Romance
and Eroticism / Liebe und
Erotik

[01]
Exhibition view /
Ausstellungsansicht, HALLE FÜR
KUNST Steiermark, Graz, 2022
Photo / Foto: kunst-
dokumentation.com

[02]
Venus / Venuša, c. 1995
Wood, paint / Holz, Farbe
113×27×4.5cm
Courtesy Linea Collection,
Bratislava; Layr, Vienna /
Wien
Photo / Foto: kunst-
dokumentation.com

[03]
From the series *Slovak Venus /
Zo série Slovenská Venuša*,
1958/c. 1995
Cardboard, mixed media /
Karton, Mixed Media
72.5×52cm
Courtesy Linea Collection,
Bratislava; Layr, Vienna /
Wien
Photo / Foto: Daša Barteková

[04A-B]
Heart of Love / Srdce lásky,
1966
Metal construction, plastic
strings, mirrors, found
object (ventilator) /
Metallkonstruktion,
Kunststoffseil, Spiegel,
gefundenes Objekt
(Ventilator)
280×244×52cm
Courtesy Linea Collection,
Bratislava; Layr, Vienna /
Wien
Photos / Fotos: kunst-
dokumentation.com

[05]
*Room of Love - Environment /
Izba lásky - environment*, 1966
Photo / Foto: Archive /
Archiv Hans Ulrich Obrist

[06]
From the series *EGO - ON -
IN - RED / Zo série EGO - ON -
IN - RED*, c. 1990
Paper, mixed media / Papier,
Mixed Media
70 × 50cm
Courtesy Linea Collection,
Bratislava; Layr, Vienna /
Wien
Photo / Foto: kunst-
dokumentation.com

[07]
From the series *Subject/EGO
GEMINI / Zo série Subjekt/EGO
GEMINI*, 1963/c. 1990
Watercolor paper, tempera,
watercolor, acrylic,
scratching / Aquarellpapier,
Tempera, Aquarell, Acryl,
Kratzer
42×30cm
Courtesy Linea Collection,
Bratislava; Layr, Vienna /
Wien
Photo / Foto: kunst-
dokumentation.com

[08]
*Heart of Love I. - II. / Srdce
lásky I. - II.*, 1966
 Offset, paper, pen, marker /
 Offset, Papier, Stift,
 Marker
 20.1×15cm
 Courtesy Linea Collection,
 Bratislava; Layr, Vienna /
 Wien
 Photo / Foto: Slovak
 National Gallery, Bratislava

[09]
Exhibition view /
Ausstellungsansicht, HALLE FÜR
KUNST Steiermark, Graz, 2022
 Photo / Foto: kunst-
 dokumentation.com

[10]
From the series *Female Breast
I. - X. (Blue/Red) / Zo série
Ženský prsník I. - X. (Modrý/
Červený)*, 1966
 Object, multiple, red
 Plexiglas, cord / Objekt,
 Multiple, rotes Plexiglas,
 Schnur
 74.5×56.5×17cm;
 74.5×56.5×17cm
 Courtesy Linea Collection,
 Bratislava; Layr, Vienna /
 Wien
 Photo / Foto: kunst-
 dokumentation.com

[11A-B]
*The Old and New Testament /
Starý a Nový Zákon*, 1983
 Diptych, assemblage, found
 objects, cardboard, paint /
 Diptychon, Assemblage,
 gefundene Objekte, Karton,
 Farbe
 165×200×35cm
 Courtesy Linea Collection,
 Bratislava; Layr, Vienna /
 Wien
 Photos / Fotos: kunst-
 dokumentation.com

[12A-B]
*Woman - Venus - Scheherazade -
Abstract / Žena - Venuša -
Šeherezáda - Abstrakt*, 1985
 Holz, Folie, Farbe / Wood,
 foil, paint
 210×120cm
 Courtesy Linea Collection,
 Bratislava; Layr, Vienna /
 Wien
 Photos / Fotos: kunst-
 dokumentation.com

[13A-B]
*SPIRIT - Shadow Super Head
Baby*, c. 1985
 Assemblage, found objects,
 paint / Assemblage,
 gefundene Objekte, Farbe
 140×78×50cm
 Courtesy Linea Collection,
 Bratislava; Layr, Vienna /
 Wien
 Photos / Fotos: kunst-
 dokumentation.com

[14A-B]
AIDS - STAN, 1983
 Canvas, acrylic / Leinwand,
 Acryl
 91×152cm
 Courtesy Linea Collection,
 Bratislava; Layr, Vienna /
 Wien
 Photos / Fotos: kunst-
 dokumentation.com

[15]
SPIRIT BABY, 1985
 Found objects, paint /
 Gefundene Objekte, Farbe
 160×70cm
 Courtesy Linea Collection,
 Bratislava; Layr, Vienna /
 Wien
 Photo / Foto: kunst-
 dokumentation.com

[16]
Axe in Pink / Ružová sekera,
c. 1990
 Found object, paint /
 Gefundenes Objekt, Farbe
 97×30cm
 Courtesy Linea Collection,
 Bratislava; Layr, Vienna /
 Wien
 Photo / Foto: kunst-
 dokumentation.com

[17]
Pink / Ružová, 1984
 Assemblage, found
 objects, canvas, acrylic /
 Assemblage, gefundene
 Objekte, Leinwand, Acryl
 92×152cm
 Courtesy Linea Collection,
 Bratislava; Layr, Vienna /
 Wien
 Photo / Foto: Martin
 Marenčin

Page / Seite 98-101
XI. *Universal Environment*

[01]
*Universal Environment /
Univerzálne prostredie*,
1966-67
 Environment, plastic
 structure, plastic mesh
 screens with airbrush
 stencils, acetone paints,
 terrestrial and celestial
 globes, mirrors, projector,
 projection of slides on a
 screen, chess table, board
 and pawns / Environment,
 Konstruktion aus Kunststoff,
 Maschensieb aus Kunststoff
 mit Airbrush auf Schablone,
 Aceton-Farbe, Globen der
 Erde und des Himmels,
 Spiegel, Projektor,
 Projektion von überspielten
 Diapositiven auf Leinwand,
 Schachtisch, Schachbrett und
 Schachfiguren
 300×400×400cm
 Courtesy Slovak National
 Gallery, Bratislava
 Photo / Foto: kunst-
 dokumentation.com

[02-03]
Exhibition view /
Ausstellungsansicht, HALLE FÜR
KUNST Steiermark, Graz, 2022
 Photos / Fotos: kunst-
 dokumentation.com

[04]
*Meditation of 7 Chakras.
Red - Blue - White 3.4.5.D. /
Meditácia 7 čakier. Červená -
modrá - biela 3.4.5.D.*,
c. 1985
 Mixed media, color slide in
 plastic, 5×5cm, *Archive SF /
 Mischtechnik, Farbdia in
 Plastik, 5×5cm, *Archív SF*
 5×5cm
 Courtesy Slovak National
 Gallery, Bratislava

[05]
*Space X. - Rockets /
Priestor X. - Rakety*, 1967
 Collage, paper, pen, pencil,
 marker / Collage, Papier,
 Stift, Bleistift, Marker
 33×45cm
 Photo / Foto: Archive /
 Archiv Hans Ulrich Obrist

[06]
From the series *Hemispheres
of Earth / Zo série Zemské
pologule*, 1967
 Monotype / Monotypie
 87×56cm
 Courtesy Slovak National
 Gallery, Bratislava

[07]
From the series *Map of the
World (Women) / Zo série Mapa
sveta (Ženy)*, 1966-67
 Found cartographic printing,
 paper, printing ink pressure
 sprayed through a stencil /
 Gefundener kartographischer
 Druck, Papier, mittels
 Schablone und Druck
 aufgebrachte Druckfarbe
 120.5×79cm

[08]
From the series *Map of the
World (Women) / Zo série Mapa
sveta (Ženy)*, 1967
 Found cartographic print,
 paper, printing from a lino
 stamper, pen / Gefundener
 kartographischer Druck,
 Papier, Linoldruck,
 Kugelschreiber
 95×42cm
 Courtesy Linea Collection,
 Bratislava; Layr, Vienna /
 Wien

[09] [13]
Exhibition view /
Ausstellungsansicht, HALLE FÜR
KUNST Steiermark, Graz, 2022
 Photos / Fotos: kunst-
 dokumentation.com

[10]
Reality III. / Realita III.,
1966
 Serigraph, etching /
 Serigrafie, Radierung
 52.3×33cm
 Courtesy Slovak National
 Gallery, Bratislava

[11]
Reality I. / Realita I., 1966
 Serigraph, etching /
 Serigrafie, Radierung
 33.6×49.2cm
 Courtesy Slovak National
 Gallery, Bratislava

[12]
Reality II. / Realita II.,
1966
  Serigraph, etching /
  Serigrafie, Radierung
  32.5×49cm
  Courtesy Slovak National
  Gallery, Bratislava

[14]
From the series *Map of the
World (Rockets) / Zo série
Mapa sveta (Rakety)*, 1967
  Found cartographic print,
  paper, printing from a lino
  stamper, pen / Gefundener
  kartographischer Druck,
  Papier, Linoldruck,
  Kugelschreiber
  95×39.2cm

  Page / Seite 102–109
  XII. Altars and / Altäre
  und *Grandpa – Grandma Are
  Listening to the Radio*

[01] [21]
Exhibition view /
Ausstellungsansicht, HALLE FÜR
KUNST Steiermark, Graz, 2022
  Photos / Fotos: kunst-
  dokumentation.com

[02]
From the cycle *S.F. EGOQ /
Z cyklu S.F. EGOQ*, c. 1995
Wood, acrylic, cord / Holz,
Acryl, Schnur
65×88×90cm
Courtesy Linea Collection,
Bratislava; Layr, Vienna /
Wien
Photo / Foto: kunst-
dokumentation.com

[03]
*Dwelling 1966 of
Contemporaneity – Reality /
Obydlie 1966 súčasnosti –
skutočnosti*, Poster / Plagát,
1967/c. 2000
  Paper, ink, pen,
  whitening liquid, felt-
  tip pen / Papier, Tinte,
  Kugelschreiber, weißfärbende
  Flüssigkeit, Filzstift
  69.3×99cm
  Courtesy Linea Collection,
  Bratislava; Layr, Vienna /
  Wien
  Photo / Foto: Slovak
  National Gallery, Bratislava

[04A–B]
From the series *Altars of
Contemporaneity (Chair) /
Zo série Oltáre súčasnosti
(Stolička)*, 1965
  Assemblage, collage, found
  objects, metal, wood, golden
  pigment / Assemblage,
  Collage, gefundene Objekte,
  Metall, Holz, Goldpigment
  92×45×58cm
  Courtesy Linea Collection,
  Bratislava; Layr, Vienna /
  Wien
  Photos / Fotos: kunst-
  dokumentation.com

[05A–B]
*Grandpa – Grandma Are
Listening to the Radio /
Dedko – babka počúvajú rádio*,
1965
  Assemblage, ready-made,
  found objects / Assemblage,
  Readymade, gefundene Objekte
  Variable dimensions /
  Variable Maße
  Courtesy Slovak National
  Gallery, Bratislava (donated
  by / gestiftet von Linea
  Collection, Bratislava,
  2018)
  Photos / Fotos: kunst-
  dokumentation.com

[06]
From the series *Altars of
Contemporaneity / Zo série
Oltáre súčasnosti*, 1965–66
  Assemblage, paper, mirror,
  wood, textile, metal, oil,
  acrylic / Assemblage,
  Papier, Spiegel, Holz,
  Textil, Metall, Öl, Acryl
  170×68×10cm
  Courtesy Slovak National
  Gallery, Bratislava
  Photo / Foto: kunst-
  dokumentation.com

[07]
From the series *Altars of
Contemporaneity / Zo série
Oltáre súčasnosti*, 1965
  Assemblage, collage, wire,
  mirror, metal, wood, golden
  pigment / Assemblage,
  Collage, Draht, Spiegel,
  Metall, Holz, Goldpigment
  113×77×10cm
  Courtesy Linea Collection,
  Bratislava; Layr, Vienna /
  Wien
  Photo / Foto: kunst-
  dokumentation.com

[08A–B]
From the series *Altars of
Contemporaneity (Chair) /
Zo série Oltáre súčasnosti
(Stolička)*, 1965
  Assemblage, collage,
  mirror, metal, wood, golden
  pigment / Assemblage,
  Collage, Metall, Spiegel,
  Metall, Holz, Goldpigment
  90×60×55cm
  Courtesy Linea Collection,
  Bratislava; Layr, Vienna /
  Wien
  Photos / Fotos: kunst-
  dokumentation.com

[09]
Gas mask from the
exhibition *Dwelling 1966 of
Contemporaneity – Reality /
Plynová maska z výstavy
Obydlie 1966 súčasnosti –
skutočnosti*, 1967
  Found object / Gefundenes
  Objekt
  Variable dimensions /
  Variable Maße
  Courtesy Linea Collection,
  Bratislava; Layr, Vienna /
  Wien
  Photo / Foto: kunst-
  dokumentation.com

[10A–B]
From the series *Altars of
Contemporaneity / Zo série
Oltáre súčasnosti*, 1964–65
  Assemblage, collage,
  mirror, metal, wood, golden
  pigment / Assemblage,
  Collage, Spiegel, Metall,
  Holz, Goldpigment
  120×84×22cm
  Courtesy Linea Collection,
  Bratislava; Layr, Vienna /
  Wien
  Photos / Fotos: kunst-
  dokumentation.com

[11]
From the series *Altars of
Contemporaneity / Zo série
Oltáre súčasnosti*, 1965
  Assemblage, collage, wire,
  mirror, metal, wood, golden
  pigment / Assemblage,
  Collage, Draht, Spiegel,
  Metall, Holz, Goldpigment
  88×52×8cm
  Courtesy Linea Collection,
  Bratislava; Layr, Vienna /
  Wien
  Photo / Foto: kunst-
  dokumentation.com

[12A–B]
Mobile III. / Mobil III., 1964
  Ready-made, wood, wire,
  paint / Readymade, Holz,
  Draht, Farbe
  74×82×48cm
  Courtesy Slovak National
  Gallery, Bratislava
  Photos / Fotos: kunst-
  dokumentation.com

[13]
From the series *Altars of
Contemporaneity / Zo série
Oltáre súčasnosti*, 1964–65
  Assemblage, collage,
  mirror, metal, wood, golden
  pigment / Assemblage,
  Collage, Spiegel, Metall,
  Holz, Goldpigment
  130×72×8cm
  Courtesy Linea Collection,
  Bratislava; Layr, Vienna /
  Wien
  Photo / Foto: kunst-
  dokumentation.com

[14]
From the series *Altars of
Contemporaneity / Zo série
Oltáre súčasnosti*, 1965
  Assemblage, found objects,
  wood, wire / Assemblage,
  gefundene Objekte, Holz,
  Draht
  150×80×15cm
  Courtesy Slovak National
  Gallery, Bratislava
  Photo / Foto: kunst-
  dokumentation.com

[15]
From the series *Altars of
Contemporaneity / Zo série
Oltáre súčasnosti*, 1965
  Assemblage, paper, mirror,
  wood, textile, metal,
  acrylic / Assemblage,
  Papier, Spiegel, Holz,
  Textil, Metall, Acryl
  161×83×25cm
  Courtesy Slovak National
  Gallery, Bratislava
  Photo / Foto: kunst-
  dokumentation.com

[16]
Object (Reliquary) / Objekt (Relikviár), 1964
Found objects, glass, wire, metal, wood, acrylic / Gefundene Objekte, Glas, Draht, Metall, Holz, Acryl
54×40×30cm
Courtesy Linea Collection, Bratislava; Layr, Vienna / Wien
Photo / Foto: kunst-dokumentation.com

[17]
From the series *Altars of Contemporaneity / Zo série Oltáre súčasnosti*, 1964–65
Assemblage, collage, mirror, metal, wood, golden pigment / Assemblage, Collage, Spiegel, Metall, Holz, Goldpigment
130×92×8cm
Courtesy Linea Collection, Bratislava; Layr, Vienna / Wien
Photo / Foto: kunst-dokumentation.com

[18]
Shattered Reality / Rozbitá skutočnosť, 1960–65
Assemblage, wood, metal / Assemblage, Holz, Metall
91×69.8cm
Courtesy Slovak National Gallery, Bratislava
Photo / Foto: kunst-dokumentation.com

[19]
From the series *Altars of Contemporaneity / Zo série Oltáre súčasnosti*, 1965
Assemblage, collage, mirror, metal, wood, paint / Assemblage, Collage, Spiegel, Metall, Holz, Farbe
143×127×31.5cm
Courtesy Linea Collection, Bratislava; Layr, Vienna / Wien
Photo / Foto: kunst-dokumentation.com

[20]
Dresses from the exhibition *Dwelling 1966 of Contemporaneity – Reality / Obydlie 1966 súčasnosti – skutočnosti*, 1967
Found objects, fabric, paint / Gefundene Objekte, Stoff, Farbe
4 pieces, variable dimensions / 4 Teile, variable Maße
Courtesy Linea Collection, Bratislava; Layr, Vienna / Wien
Photo / Foto: kunst-dokumentation.com

[22]
Clothes from the exhibition *Dwelling 1966 of Contemporaneity – Reality / Obydlie 1966 súčasnosti – skutočnosti*, 1967
Print on paper, felt-tip pen / Druck auf Papier, Filzstift
30×42cm
Courtesy Linea Collection, Bratislava; Layr, Vienna / Wien
Photo / Foto: kunst-dokumentation.com

[23]
SLOVAK ENTITAQ 4.D. Mobil III., 1964/c. 2010
Digital print, pen, felt-tip pen, whitening liquid, perforation / Digitaldruck, Stift, Filzstift, weißfärbende Flüssigkeit, Perforation
42×29.6cm
Courtesy Linea Collection, Bratislava; Layr, Vienna / Wien
Photo / Foto: Slovak National Gallery, Bratislava

Page / Seite 124–129
XIII. *Archive SF / Archív SF*

[01]
Door (UISFO EGOQ) / Dvere (UISFO EGOQ), c. 2000
Found object, mixed media, wood, glass, acrylic / Gefundenes Objekt, Mixed Media, Holz, Glas, Acryl
190.5×120×10cm
Courtesy Linea Collection, Bratislava; Layr, Vienna / Wien
Photo / Foto: kunst-dokumentation.com

[02A–B]
Birth of SF / Narodenie SF, 1960s
Found objects, mixed media / Gefundene Objekte, Mixed Media
110×60×60cm
Courtesy Linea Collection, Bratislava; Layr, Vienna / Wien
Photos / Fotos: kunst-dokumentation.com

[03A–B]
Subject – Object / Subjekt – Objekt, c. 1995
Wood, acrylic, cord, steel plummet / Holz, Acryl, Schnur, Stahllot
120×39×8cm
Courtesy Linea Collection, Bratislava; Layr, Vienna / Wien
Photos / Fotos: Martin Marenčin

[04]
Street name sign *Snežienková Street / Uličná tabuľa Snežienková ulica*, c. 1990
Found material, metal, paint / Gefundenes Material, Metall, Farbe
30×70cm
Courtesy Linea Collection, Bratislava; Layr, Vienna / Wien
Photo / Foto: kunst-dokumentation.com

[05]
Exhibition view / Ausstellungsansicht, HALLE FÜR KUNST Steiermark, Graz, 2022
Photo / Foto: kunst-dokumentation.com

[06]
From the cycle *EGO / Z cyklu EGO*, c. 1995
Wood, acrylic, cord / Holz, Acryl, Schnur
60×23×25cm
Courtesy Linea Collection, Bratislava; Layr, Vienna / Wien
Photo / Foto: Daša Barteková

[07]
From the series *EGO (Four Elements) / Zo série EGO (Štyri živly)*, c. 1995
Plastic, acrylic, cord / Kunststoff, Acryl, Schnur
30.5×30.5cm; 36×32cm
Courtesy Linea Collection, Bratislava; Layr, Vienna / Wien
Photo / Foto: kunst-dokumentation.com

[08]
From the series *EGO (Four Sides of the World) / Zo série EGO (Štyri svetové strany)*, c. 1995
Found material, acrylic / Gefundenes Material, Acryl
61×41cm
Courtesy Linea Collection, Bratislava; Layr, Vienna / Wien
Photo / Foto: Daša Barteková

[09]
FILKO, c. 1995
Found object, wood, paint / Gefundenes Objekt, Holz, Farbe
198×85×4.5cm
Courtesy Peter Petrička, Bratislava
Photo / Foto: kunst-dokumentation.com

[10]
SF Clinical Deaths / SF Klinické smrte, 1995
Drawing, paper, pen, felt-tip pen / Zeichnung, Papier, Stift, Filzstift
42×29.7cm
Courtesy Linea Collection, Bratislava; Layr, Vienna / Wien

[11]
From the series *Four Elements (Earth, Air, Fire, Water) / Zo série Štyri živly (Zem, Vzduch, Oheň, Voda)*, c. 1990
Mirror, paint, cord / Spiegel, Farbe, Schnur
26×42cm
Courtesy Linea Collection, Bratislava; Layr, Vienna / Wien
Photo / Foto: Daša Barteková

[12]
SF Clinical Deaths / SF Klinické smrte, 1995
Wood, paint / Holz, Farbe
122×18×4cm
Courtesy Linea Collection, Bratislava; Layr, Vienna / Wien
Photo / Foto: kunst-dokumentation.com

[13]
AUTENTKSF I., Text-art,
2005-12
    Print, paper, pen, felt-tip
    pen, perforation / Druck,
    Papier, Stift, Filzstift,
    Papier, Perforation
    42×29.7cm
    Courtesy Slovak National
    Gallery, Bratislava

[14]
PHYLKO - 1993 - VERNISSAGE /
PHYLKO - 1993 - VERNISÁŽ, 1993
    Montage, paper, photography,
    whitening liquid,
    perforation / Montage,
    Papier, Fotografie,
    weißfärbende Flüssigkeit,
    Perforation
    25.3×18cm
    Courtesy Linea Collection,
    Bratislava; Layr, Vienna /
    Wien
    Photo / Foto: Daša Barteková

[15]
AUTENTKSF Biography /
AUTENTKSF Biografia, 2005-12
    Print, paper, mixed media /
    Druck, Papier, Mixed Media
    46×30.6cm
    Courtesy Slovak National
    Gallery, Bratislava

[16]
Flight of Cosmonauts to the
Moon in Stages and their
Return to the Earth / Let
kozmonautov na Mesiac po
etapách a ich návrat na Zem,
1969
    B/W photograph, photographic
    paper, pen, perforation /
    S/W-Fotografie, Fotopapier,
    Stift, Perforation
    23.5×18cm
    Courtesy Linea Collection,
    Bratislava; Layr, Vienna /
    Wien
    Photo / Foto: Daša Barteková

[17]
Artist's studio Snežienková /
Umelcov ateliér Snežienková,
2007
    Photo / Foto: Pato Safko

    Page / Seite 130-133
    XIV. *System SF*: Identity and
    Guiding System / Identität
    und Leitlinien

[01A-C]
Monument to Traffic Signs.
External Environment -
Communication / Pomník
značkám. Externé prostredie -
komunikácia, 1967/c. 1990
    Installation, paint, wood,
    metal / Installation, Farbe,
    Holz, Metall
    Variable dimensions /
    Variable Maße
    Courtesy Linea Collection,
    Bratislava; Layr, Vienna /
    Wien
    Photos / Fotos: kunst-
    dokumentation.com

[02]
Juraj Bartoš, Stano Filko, New
York, 1984
    Photo / Foto: Juraj Bartoš

[03]
SF Railway Customer Card / SF
Železničná preukážka, 1964
    Collage, B/W photograph,
    latex paint, paper /
    Collage, S/W-Fotografie,
    Latexfarbe, Papier
    21.7×16.6cm
    Courtesy Linea Collection,
    Bratislava; Layr, Vienna /
    Wien
    Photo / Foto: Slovak
    National Gallery, Bratislava

[04-05]
Untitled, 1971-c. 2010
    Text-art, pen, acrylic on
    printed paper from the
    publication *Stano FILKO*
    II. / Text-Kunst, Stift,
    Acryl auf bedrucktem Papier
    aus der Publikation *Stano*
    FILKO II.
    Photos / Fotos: Archive /
    Archiv Hans Ulrich Obrist

[06]
7 Chakra Colors (Wooden
Formwork) / 7 farieb čakier
(Drevené debnenie), c. 1995
    Installation, found wooden
    objects, acrylic, wire /
    Installation, gefundene
    Holzobjekte, Acryl, Draht
    Variable dimensions /
    Variable Maße
    Courtesy Linea Collection,
    Bratislava; Layr, Vienna /
    Wien
    Photo / Foto: kunst-
    dokumentation.com

    Page / Seite 134-143
    XV. Works on Paper /
    Papierarbeiten

[01]
Exhibition view /
Ausstellungsansicht, HALLE FÜR
KUNST Steiermark, Graz, 2022
    Photo / Foto: kunst-
    dokumentation.com

[02]
EXIZSTEAOQ = HAPPSOCSF
System / ANTE BIGBANGSF 5.D.,
1995-2005
    Print, paper, mixed media,
    felt-tip pen / Druck,
    Papier, Mixed Media,
    Filzstift
    30.6×46cm
    Courtesy Slovak National
    Gallery, Bratislava

[03]
RETROQ System SF, 1995-2005
    Print, paper, mixed
    media, felt-tip pen, pen,
    perforation / Druck, Papier,
    Mixed Media, Filzstift,
    Stift, Perforation
    29.7×42.1cm
    Courtesy Slovak National
    Gallery, Bratislava

[04]
Self-Portrait - Phylko 1988-
90 / Autoportrét - Phylko
1988-90, 1985-95
    Xerocopy, paper, pen, felt-
    tip pen / Xerokopie, Papier,
    Stift, Filzstift
    42×29.7cm
    Courtesy Slovak National
    Gallery, Bratislava

[05]
The Lost World of Mammoths
in Slovakia / Stratený svet
mamutov na Slovensku, 1985-95
    Print, paper / Druck, Papier
    42×29.7cm
    Courtesy Slovak National
    Gallery, Bratislava

[06]
Untitled, 1971-c. 2010
    Text-art, pen, acrylic on
    printed paper from the
    publication *Stano FILKO*
    II. / Text-Kunst, Stift,
    Acryl auf bedrucktem Papier
    aus der Publikation *Stano*
    FILKO II.
    Photo / Foto: Archive /
    Archiv Hans Ulrich Obrist

[07]
FIRSTIMESPACEIQ, 1995-2005
    Print, paper, perforation /
    Druck, Papier, Perforation
    46×30.5cm
    Courtesy Slovak National
    Gallery, Bratislava

[08]
S.FYILKORAB VELKA HRADNAQ I.,
2000-10
    Xerox, print, mixed media,
    pen, marker, whitening
    liquid / Xerox, Druck,
    Mixed Media, Stift, Marker,
    weißfärbende Flüssigkeit
    30.6×46cm
    Courtesy Slovak National
    Gallery, Bratislava

[09]
INSTITUTEAOOQ - Project Velká
Hradná I. / INSTITUTEAOOQ
Projekt Velká Hradná I.,
2000-10
    Xerocopy, paper, print,
    felt-tip pen, pen, white
    paint / Xerokopie, Papier,
    Druck, Filzstift, Stift,
    weiße Farbe
    30.6×46cm
    Courtesy Slovak National
    Gallery, Bratislava

[10]
5.D. UNIVERSESF Pyramid I. /
5.D. UNIVERZSF Pyramída I.,
1995-2005
    Xerocopy, paper, mixed
    media, felt-tip pen,
    pen, perforation /
    Xerokopie, Papier, Mixed
    Media, Filzstift, Stift,
    Perforation
    30.5×46cm
    Courtesy Slovak National
    Gallery, Bratislava

[11]
SINGULAR TRUTH / Stano Filko
Master's Studio, 1995-2005
    Xerocopy, paper, print /
    Xerokopie, Papier, Druck
    29.7×42cm
    Courtesy Slovak National
    Gallery, Bratislava

[12]
*BIGSF BANGSF SUNSTARSF
SYSTEMSF*, 1995–2005
Xerocopy, paper, print,
felt-tip pen, perforation /
Xerokopie, Papier, Druck,
Filzstift, Perforation
29.7×42cm
Courtesy Slovak National
Gallery, Bratislava

[13]
*TRANZSIT PRIEVANSF II. Project
Tranzit*, 2005–10
Xerocopy, paper, print,
felt-tip pen, pen, white
paint / Xerokopie, Papier,
Druck, Filzstift, Stift,
weiße Farbe
29.7×42cm
Courtesy Slovak National
Gallery, Bratislava

[14]
*INSTITUTEAOOQ – Project Veľká
Hradná II.* / *INSTITUTEAOOQ
Projekt Veľká Hradná II.*,
2000–10
Print, paper, felt-tip pen,
pen, white paint / Druck,
Papier, Filzstift, Stift,
weiße Farbe
30.6×46cm
Courtesy Slovak National
Gallery, Bratislava

[15]
Phylko – Synchron – Diachron,
1985–95
Print, pen, paper / Druck,
Stift, Papier
25×35cm
Courtesy Slovak National
Gallery, Bratislava

[16]
*Filko on the Poster from
Osaka* / *Filko na plagáte z
Osaky*, 1970/c. 2000
Print, paper, watercolor,
pencil, pen / Aquarell,
Druck, Papier, Bleistift,
Stift
103×68cm
Courtesy Linea Collection,
Bratislava; Layr, Vienna /
Wien
Photo / Foto: Slovak
National Gallery, Bratislava

[17]
*Filko on the Susumu Shingu
Poster* / *Filko na plagáte
Susumu Shingu*, 1970/c. 2000
Print, paper, watercolor,
pencil, pen / Aquarell,
Druck, Papier, Bleistift,
Stift
36.5×51.3cm
Courtesy Linea Collection,
Bratislava; Layr, Vienna /
Wien
Photo / Foto: Slovak
National Gallery, Bratislava

[18]
RETRO VELKAQ HRADNAQ I.,
1995–2005
Print, paper, felt-tip pen /
Druck, Papier, Filzstift
29.7×42.1cm
Courtesy Slovak National
Gallery, Bratislava

[19]
RETRO VELKAQ HRADNAQ II.,
1995–2005
Print, paper, felt-tip
pen, pen / Druck, Papier,
Filzstift, Stift
29.7×42.1cm
Courtesy Slovak National
Gallery, Bratislava

Page / Seite 156–159
XVI. Interventions on Works
on Paper / Interventionen
auf Papierarbeiten

[01]
Cosmos – Man / *Cosmos –
Človek*, 1968
Found printed material,
felt-tip pen, pen /
Gefundenes bedrucktes
Material, Filzstift, Stift
14.2×20.2cm
Courtesy Linea Collection,
Bratislava; Layr, Vienna /
Wien

[02]
From the series *Monuments of
the Solar System* / Zo série
Pomníky slnečnej sústavy, 1967
Collage, pen, ink, felt-tip
pen, paper / Collage, Stift,
Tinte, Filzstift, Papier
24.5×30cm
Courtesy Linea Collection,
Bratislava; Layr, Vienna /
Wien
Photo / Foto: Slovak
National Gallery, Bratislava

[03]
*Cosmos. BREATHING –
RESPIRATIONSF* / *Kozmos.
BREATHING – RESPIRATIONSF*,
1967/c. 2000
B/W photograph, whitening
liquid, paper / S/W-
Fotografie, weißfärbende
Flüssigkeit, Papier
18.2×24cm
Courtesy Linea Collection,
Bratislava; Layr, Vienna /
Wien
Photo / Foto: Slovak
National Gallery, Bratislava

[04]
BREATHING – RESPIRATIONSF,
1968/c. 2000
B/W photograph, felt-tip
pen, pen, paper / S/W-
Fotografie, Filzstift,
Stift, Papier
22.2×18.2cm
Courtesy Linea Collection,
Bratislava; Layr, Vienna /
Wien
Photo / Foto: Slovak
National Gallery, Bratislava

[05]
From the series *Sculptures
of the Twentieth Century* /
Zo série *Sochy XX. storočia*,
1968
Found print, felt-tip pen,
pen, paper / Gefundener
Druck, Filzstift, Stift,
Papier
29.7×21cm
Courtesy Linea Collection,
Bratislava; Layr, Vienna /
Wien
Photo / Foto: Slovak
National Gallery, Bratislava

[06]
From the series *Sculptures
of the Twentieth Century* /
Zo série *Sochy XX. storočia*,
1968
Found print, felt-tip pen,
paper / Gefundener Druck,
Filzstift, Papier
21×17cm
Courtesy Linea Collection,
Bratislava; Layr, Vienna /
Wien
Photo / Foto: Slovak
National Gallery, Bratislava

[07]
*Occupation of the Czechoslovak
Socialist Republic – Pink
Heart* / *Okupácia ČSSR – Ružové
srdce*, 1968/1978
Intervention in photographs
by Ladislav Bielik, montage,
B/W photograph, tempera,
paper / Intervention in
Fotografien von Ladislav
Bielik, Montage, S/W-
Fotografie, Tempera, Papier
25×17.5cm
Courtesy Linea Collection,
Bratislava; Layr, Vienna /
Wien
Photo / Foto: Slovak
National Gallery, Bratislava

[08]
From the cycle / *EGOQ with
Alexander Dubček* / *Z cyklu
EGOQ s Alexandrom Dubčekom*,
1968/c. 1995
B/W photograph, whitening
liquid, paper / S/W-
Fotografie, weißfärbende
Flüssigkeit, Papier
13×18.3cm
Courtesy Linea Collection,
Bratislava; Layr, Vienna /
Wien
Photo / Foto: Slovak
National Gallery, Bratislava

[09]
From the series *Sculptures
of the Twentieth Century
(FEMINA)* / Zo série *Sochy
XX. storočia (FEMINA)*,
1968/c. 1995
B/W photograph, felt-tip
pen, pen, perforation,
paper / S/W-Fotografie,
Filzstift, Stift,
Perforation, Papier
17.4×22.7cm
Courtesy Slovak National
Gallery, Bratislava

[10]
*The Space among Trees - The
Masses. Plan-Projectart /
Priestor medzi stromami -
hmotami. Plán-projektart*, 1969
  Found printed material,
  felt-tip pen, pen /
  Gefundenes bedrucktes
  Material, Filzstift, Stift
  28.8×20.8cm
  Courtesy Linea Collection,
  Bratislava; Layr, Vienna /
  Wien
  Photo / Foto: Slovak
  National Gallery, Bratislava

Page / Seite 160-161
XVII. *HAPPSOC: Happening and
Society / Happy Socialism*

[01-02]
Stano Filko, Alex Mlynárčik,
HAPPSOC I., 1965
  Invitation card, offset,
  typescript, paper /
  Einladungskarte, Offset,
  Maschinenschrift, Papier
  14×13.7; 15×30cm
  Courtesy Linea Collection,
  Bratislava; Layr, Vienna /
  Wien
  Photos / Fotos: Slovak
  National Gallery, Bratislava

[03]
*HAPPSOC I. (SPORT) / HAPPSOC
I. (ŠPORT)*, 1965/c. 2000
  B/W photograph, pen, paper /
  S/W-Fotografie, Stift,
  Papier
  14.7×24cm
  Courtesy Linea Collection,
  Bratislava; Layr, Vienna /
  Wien
  Photo / Foto: Daša Barteková

[04]
*HAPPSOC IV. Travel in
Space / HAPPSOC IV. Vesmírne
cestovanie*, 1967
  Offset print, pen, paper /
  Offset-Druck, Stift, Papier
  30.5×21cm
  Courtesy Linea Collection,
  Bratislava; Layr, Vienna /
  Wien
  Photo / Foto: Slovak
  National Gallery, Bratislava

[05A-B]
*HAPPSOC III. The Altar of the
Present / HAPPSOC III. Oltár
súčasnosti*, 1966
  Object, watercolor,
  synthetic silk, mirror,
  offset; cartography /
  Objekt, Aquarell,
  synthetische Seide, Spiegel,
  Offset; Kartografie
  23.7×57.5cm; 40×40cm
  Courtesy Slovak National
  Gallery, Bratislava
  Photos / Fotos: Archive /
  Archiv Hans Ulrich Obrist

Page / Seite 162-196
XVIII. *Associations: Travel
into Space / Reise ins All*

[01]
Exhibition view /
Ausstellungsansicht, HALLE FÜR
KUNST Steiermark, Graz, 2022
Photo / Foto: kunst-
dokumentation.com

[02]
*Associations XXX. - B /
Asociácie XXX. - B*, 1968-69;
from the series *Associations /
zo série Asociácie*, 1969-70
  White plain cardboard,
  print / Weißer Karton, Druck
  70×50cm
  Courtesy Slovak National
  Gallery, Bratislava

[03]
*Concept - 1968 - Cosmos /
Koncept - 1968 - Cosmos*, 1968;
from the series *Associations /
Zo série Asociácie*, 1967-70
  White plain cardboard,
  print / Weißer Karton, Druck
  49.5×70cm
  Courtesy Slovak National
  Gallery, Bratislava

[04]
*Associations - The Celestial
Globe / Asociácie - Glóbus
vesmíru*, 1966-67; from the
series *Associations / zo série
Asociácie*, 1967-70
  White plain cardboard,
  print / Weißer Karton, Druck
  70.1×49.5cm
  Courtesy Slovak National
  Gallery, Bratislava

[05]
*Seats - Concept / Sedadlá -
Koncept*, 1967; from the
series *Associations / Zo série
Asociácie*, 1967-70
  White plain cardboard,
  print / Weißer Karton, Druck
  70×49.8cm
  Courtesy Slovak National
  Gallery, Bratislava

[06]
*Associations XXIX. - Maps
of the Universe / Asociácie
XXIX.- Mapy vesmíru*, 1968-69;
from the series *Associations /
zo série Asociácie*, 1967- 70
  White plain cardboard,
  print / Weißer Karton, Druck
  49.8×69.9cm
  Courtesy Slovak National
  Gallery, Bratislava

[07]
*Reality of the Cosmos - A /
Realita kozmu - A*, 1968-69;
from the series *Associations /
zo série Asociácie*, 1967-70
  White plain cardboard,
  print / Weißer Karton, Druck
  70.1×49.9cm
  Courtesy Slovak National
  Gallery, Bratislava

[08]
*Reality of the Cosmos - B /
Realita kozmu - B*, 1968-69;
from the series *Associations /
zo série Asociácie*, 1967-70
  White plain cardboard,
  print / Weißer Karton, Druck
  70.1×49.8cm
  Courtesy Slovak National
  Gallery, Bratislava

[09]
*Associations V. / Asociácie
V.*; from the series
*Associations / zo série
Asociácie*, 1967-70
  White handmade paper,
  autotype / Weißes
  Büttenpapier, Autotypie
  50×69.9cm
  Courtesy Slovak National
  Gallery, Bratislava

[10]
*Associations XV. / Asociácie
XV.*, 1968-69; from the series
*Associations XXXX. / zo série
Asociácie XXXX.*, 1970
  White handmade paper,
  autotype / Weißes
  Büttenpapier, Autotypie
  50×69.9cm
  Courtesy Slovak National
  Gallery, Bratislava

[11]
*Associations XXXI. - I.
Flight - Moon / Asociácie
XXXI. - I. let - mesiac*, 1969
  White plain cardboard,
  print / Weißer Karton, Druck
  70×49.5cm
  Courtesy Slovak National
  Gallery, Bratislava

[12]
*Associations XIII. - B /
Asociácie XIII. - B*, 1969;
from the series *Associations /
zo série Asociácie*, 1967-70
  Offset, Papier / Offset,
  Papier
  70×49.8cm
  Courtesy Slovak National
  Gallery, Bratislava

[13]
*Chronology - Associations /
Chronológia - Asociácie*,
1969-70; from the series
*Associations / zo série
Asociácie*, 1967-70
  Offset, paper / Offset,
  Papier
  66.9×49.3cm
  Courtesy Slovak National
  Gallery, Bratislava

[14]
Print from the album of
*Associations II. / List z
albumu Asociácie II.*, 1968-69
  White cardboard / Weißer
  Karton, Druck
  50×70.1
  Courtesy Slovak National
  Gallery, Bratislava

[15]
Cosmos / Kozmos, 1968-69; from
the series *Associations /
zo série Asociácie*, 1967-70
  White plain cardboard,
  print / Weißer Karton, Druck
  69.5×49.5cm
  Courtesy Slovak National
  Gallery, Bratislava

[16]
*Associations XXXVIII. /
Asociácie XXXVIII.*, 1969;
from the series *Associations /
zo série Asociácie*, 1967-70
   White paper, print / Weißes
   Papier, Druck
   70.1×50.1cm
   Courtesy Slovak National
   Gallery, Bratislava

[17]
*Associations XXXX. / Asociácie
XXXX.*, 1970
   Yellow Plexiglas,
   perforations / Gelbes
   Plexiglas, Perforationen
   72.5×50.5cm
   Courtesy Linea Collection,
   Bratislava; Layr, Vienna /
   Wien
   Photo / Foto: kunst-
   dokumentation.com

[18-20]
*Associations XXXX. / Asociácie
XXXX.*, 1969-70
   Aluminum, perforations,
   polish / Aluminum,
   Perforationen, Polierung
   59.5×42.4cm
   Courtesy Slovak National
   Gallery, Bratislava
   Photos / Fotos: kunst-
   dokumentation.com

[21]
*Associations XXXX. (COS-MOS) /
Asociácie XXXX. (COS-MOS)*,
1969-70
   Aluminum, perforations,
   polish / Aluminum,
   Perforationen, Polierung
   59.5×42.4cm
   Courtesy Linea Collection,
   Bratislava; Layr, Vienna /
   Wien
   Photo / Foto: kunst-
   dokumentation.com

[22]
*Associations XXX. / Asociácie
XXX.*, 1969; from the series
*Associations / zo série
Asociácie*, 1967-70
   White coated paper,
   autotype, typescript /
   Weißes gestrichenes Papier,
   Autotypie, Maschinenschrift
   50×70cm
   Courtesy Slovak National
   Gallery, Bratislava

Page / Seite 196-199
XIX. *Text-art*

[01]
Stano Filko, Miloš Laky,
Ján Zavarský, *SENSITIVITY -
Text-art / SENZITIVITA - Text-
art*, 1976
   Offset print, pen, paper /
   Offset-Druck, Stift, Papier
   30×13.4cm
   Courtesy Linea Collection,
   Bratislava; Layr, Vienna /
   Wien
   Photo / Foto: Archive /
   Archiv Hans Ulrich Obrist

[02A-B]
*EMOTION. Pure Emotion. White
Space in White Space -
Text-art / EMÓCIA. Čistá
Emócia. Biely priestor v
bielom priestore - Text-art*,
Manifesto / Manifest, 1977
   Pen, print, felt-tip pen /
   Stift, Druck, Filzstift
   29×40cm
   Courtesy Slovak National
   Gallery, Bratislava

[03]
*TRANSCENDENCE /
TRANSCENDENCIA*, 1978
   Print, pencil, pen, paper /
   Druck, Bleistift, Stift,
   Papier
   23.5×18.1cm
   Courtesy Slovak National
   Gallery, Bratislava

[04]
*TRANSCENDENCE /
TRANSCENDENCIA*, 1978
   Print, pencil, pen, paper /
   Druck, Bleistift, Stift,
   Papier
   23.5×18.1cm
   Courtesy Slovak National
   Gallery, Bratislava

[05]
*TRANSCENDENCE I., II. /
TRANSCENDENCJA I., II.*,
1978-79
   Print, pencil, pen, felt-
   tip pen, paper / Druck,
   Bleistift, Stift, Filzstift,
   Papier
   19.1×35.3cm
   Courtesy Slovak National
   Gallery, Bratislava

[06]
*MEDITATION TRANSCENDENTAL -
Text-art / TRANSCENDENTÁLNA
MEDITÁCIA - Text-art*,
Manifesto / Manifest, 1980
   Offset print, paper /
   Offset-Druck, Papier
   60×41.8cm
   Courtesy Slovak National
   Gallery, Bratislava

Page / Seite 200-203
XX. *Transcendency /
Transzendenz*

[01]
*Interpretation HAPPSOC -
Land Art from the series
Transcendency / Interpretácia
HAPPSOC - land art zo série
Transcendencia*, 1967/1978
   B/W photograph, whitening
   liquid, pen, paper / S/W-
   Fotografie, weißfärbende
   Flüssigkeit, Stift, Papier
   17.2×21.7cm
   Courtesy Linea Collection,
   Bratislava; Layr, Vienna /
   Wien
   Photo / Foto: Slovak
   National Gallery, Bratislava

[02]
*From the cycle Transcendency /
Z cyklu Transcendencia*,
1978-79
   Gold pigment photograph,
   whitening liquid, paper /
   Goldpigment-Fotografie,
   weißfärbende Flüssigkeit,
   Papier
   51×69cm
   Courtesy Linea Collection,
   Bratislava; Layr, Vienna /
   Wien
   Photo / Foto: Martin
   Marenčin

[03]
*From the cycle Transcendency
III. / Z cyklu Transcendencia
III.*, 1979
   B/W photograph, pen,
   perforation, paper /
   S/W-Fotografie, Stift,
   Perforation, Papier
   18×24cm
   Courtesy Linea Collection,
   Bratislava; Layr, Vienna /
   Wien
   Photo / Foto: Martin
   Marenčin

[04]
*From the cycle Transcendency
III. / Z cyklu Transcendencia
III.*, 1979
   B/W photograph, whitening
   liquid, pen, perforation,
   paper / S/W-Fotografie,
   weißfärbende Flüssigkeit,
   Stift, Perforation, Papier
   18×24cm
   Courtesy Linea Collection,
   Bratislava; Layr, Vienna /
   Wien
   Photo / Foto: Martin
   Marenčin

[05]
*From the cycle Transcendency
I. / Z cyklu Transcendencia
I.*, 1970/1978
   Gold pigment photograph,
   whitening liquid,
   perforation, paper /
   Goldpigment-Fotografie,
   weißfärbende Flüssigkeit,
   Perforation, Papier
   18×24cm
   Courtesy Linea Collection,
   Bratislava; Layr, Vienna /
   Wien
   Photo / Foto: Martin
   Marenčin

[06A-B]
*From the series Transcendency/
Filko EGO / Zo série
Transcendencia/Filko EGO*,
1978-79/c. 1990
   Collage, B/W photograph,
   golden pigment, whitening
   liquid, pen, found paper
   cover / Collage, S/W-
   Fotografie, Goldpigment,
   weißfärbende Flüssigkeit,
   Stift, gefundener
   Papierumschlag
   48.6×54.2cm
   Courtesy Linea Collection,
   Bratislava; Layr, Vienna /
   Wien
   Photos / Fotos: Martin
   Marenčin

[07]
*Emotion - Transcendency /
Emócia - Transcendencia*,
1977-78
  B/W photograph, pen / S/W-
  Fotografie, Stift
  24×18.2cm
  Courtesy Linea Collection,
  Bratislava; Layr, Vienna /
  Wien
  Photo / Foto: Daša Barteková

[08]
*The Chronology of the
Creation - Art*, 1979/1995
  Print, pen, white latex,
  pencil, paper / Druck,
  Stift, weißes Latex,
  Bleistift, Papier
  23.1×17.9cm
  Courtesy Slovak National
  Gallery, Bratislava

[09]
*From the cycle Transcendency /
Z cyklu Transcendencia*,
1978-79
  Gold pigment photograph,
  paper / Goldpigment-
  Fotografie, Papier
  59×74.6cm
  Courtesy Linea Collection,
  Bratislava; Layr, Vienna /
  Wien
  Photo / Foto: Martin
  Marenčin

Page / Seite 218-227
XXI. *White Space in White
Space*: Space in Space / Raum
im Raum

[01]
Exhibition view /
Ausstellungsansicht, HALLE FÜR
KUNST Steiermark, Graz, 2022
  Photo / Foto: kunst-
  dokumentation.com

[02-03]
Stano Filko, Miloš Laky,
Ján Zavarský, *White Space in
White Space / Biely priestor
v bielom priestore*, House of
Arts, Brno, 1974
  Courtesy Linea Collection,
  Bratislava; Layr, Vienna /
  Wien
  Photos / Fotos: Slovak
  National Gallery, Bratislava

[04]
*From the series Sensitivity.
White Space in White Space /
Zo série Senzitivita. Biely
priestor v bielom priestore*,
1973-75
  Felt, Plexiglas / Filz,
  Plexiglas
  10 pieces, each / 10 Stück,
  je 149×20cm
  Courtesy Slovak National
  Gallery, Bratislava
  Photo / Foto: kunst-
  dokumentation.com

[05]
Stano Filko, Miloš Laky,
Ján Zavarský, *White Space in
White Space / Biely priestor v
bielom priestore*, 1974
  White paint, canvas,
  cardboard / Weiße Farbe,
  Leinwand, Karton
  2800×85cm; tube / Röhre
  153cm
  Courtesy Linea Collection,
  Bratislava; Layr, Vienna /
  Wien
  Photo / Foto: kunst-
  dokumentation.com

[06]
*Emotion - 1977 - Ontology
(on the Ceiling)*, Anti-
performance, 1977
  Print, pencil, paper /
  Druck, Bleistift, Papier
  19 × 28.7cm
  Courtesy Slovak National
  Gallery, Bratislava

[07]
White Square / Biely štvorec,
1995
  Wood, white paint, canvas /
  Holz, weiße Farbe, Leinwand
  117×200×102cm
  Courtesy Linea Collection,
  Bratislava; Layr, Vienna /
  Wien
  Photo / Foto: kunst-
  dokumentation.com

[08]
*White Space - Anti-performance
Behind Closed Doors / Biely
priestor - Anti-performance za
zavretými dverami*, 1978
  B/W photograph, paper / S/W-
  Fotografie, Papier
  20×24.2cm
  Courtesy Linea Collection,
  Bratislava; Layr, Vienna /
  Wien
  Photo / Foto: Slovak
  National Gallery, Bratislava

[09]
Stano Filko, Miloš Laky,
Ján Zavarský, *White Space in
White Space / Biely priestor v
bielom priestore*, 1973
  Felt, white paint / Filz,
  weiße Farbe
  300×140cm
  Courtesy Linea Collection,
  Bratislava; Layr, Vienna /
  Wien
  Photo / Foto: kunst-
  dokumentation.com

[10A-B]
Stano Filko, Miloš Laky,
Ján Zavarský, *White Space in
White Space / Biely priestor v
bielom priestore*, 1974
  Canvas, cardboard, paint /
  Leinwand, Karton, Farbe
  20 tubes, each / 20 Röhren,
  je 135cm, ø 3.5cm
  Courtesy Slovak National
  Gallery, Bratislava
  Photos / Fotos: kunst-
  dokumentation.com

[11]
*From the series Verticals for
Realization in Architecture /
Zo série Vertikály na
realizáciu v architecture*,
1977
  Collage, paper, pencil,
  ink / Collage, Papier,
  Bleistift, Tusche
  29.5×42cm
  Courtesy Linea Collection,
  Bratislava; Layr, Vienna /
  Wien
  Photo / Foto: Slovak
  National Gallery, Bratislava

[12]
*From the cycle White Space
(Verticals) I. / Z cyklu Biely
Priestor (Vertikály) I.*, 1973
  Collage, paper, pencil,
  tempera / Collage, Papier,
  Bleistift, Tempera
  30.1×41.8cm
  Courtesy Slovak National
  Gallery, Bratislava

[13]
Stano Filko, Miloš Laky,
Ján Zavarský, *White Space in
White Space / Biely priestor v
bielom priestore*, 1974
  Cardboard tube, white
  paint / Kartonröhre, weiße
  Farbe
  300cm, ø 12cm
  Courtesy Linea Collection,
  Bratislava; Layr, Vienna /
  Wien
  Photo / Foto: kunst-
  dokumentation.com

[14]
Stano Filko, Miloš Laky,
Ján Zavarský, *White Space in
White Space / Biely priestor
v bielom priestore*, Gallery
of Youth / Galéria mladých,
Bratislava, 1974
  Courtesy Slovak National
  Gallery, Bratislava

[15]
Miloš Laky's apartment with
Hana Lakyová and Ján Budaj,
1970s
  B/W analog photograph /
  Analoge S/W-Fotografie
  18×24.7cm
  Courtesy Private Collection
  Photo / Foto: Archive /
  Archiv Ján Budaj

[16]
Stano Filko, Miloš Laky,
Ján Zavarský, *White Space in
White Space / Biely priestor
v bielom priestore*, House of
Arts, Brno, 1974
  Courtesy Linea Collection,
  Bratislava; Layr, Vienna /
  Wien
  Photo / Foto: Slovak
  National Gallery, Bratislava

[17A-B]
Stano Filko, Miloš Laky,
Ján Zavarský, *White Space in
White Space / Biely priestor v
bielom priestore*, Manifesto /
Manifest, 1973-74
  Samizdat, offset, inserted
  printed B/W-photographs /
  Samisdat, Offset, eingelegte
  gedruckte S/W-Fotografien
  A4 folded / gefaltet
  Courtesy Linea Collection,
  Bratislava; Layr, Vienna /
  Wien
  Photos / Fotos: Slovak
  National Gallery, Bratislava

Page / Seite 240
Stano FILKO II. 1965/69, 1970,
Cover of the publication by
the artist / Cover der vom
Künstler herausgegebenen
Publikation
  Photo / Foto: Archive /
  Archiv Hans Ulrich Obrist

Page / Seite 247
From the series *In the Pyramid
(Memories of HAPPSOC I.)* /
Zo série *V pyramíde (Spomienky
na HAPPSOC I.)*, c. 1995
  Felt-tip pencil, pencil,
  paper / Filzstift,
  Bleistift, Papier
  29.5×21cm
  Courtesy Christian Winkler
  Collection, Vienna / Wien

Page / Seite 251
From the series *Self-Portrait
SF* / Zo série *Autoportrét SF*,
1970-80
  Montage, B/W photograph,
  acrylic, pencil, xerocopy,
  paper / Montage, Xerokopie,
  Acryl, Bleistift, Xero-
  Kopie, Papier
  29.5×21cm
  Courtesy Private Collection

Page / Seite 255
*ADVERTISEMENT CAUSES OZON
DEPLETION / REKLAMA ZPUSOBÚJE
OZÓNOVOU DÍRU*
  Photo / Foto: Archive /
  Archiv Hans Ulrich Obrist

Page / Seite 256
*Intimacy - Self-Portrait -
Filko / Intimita -
Autoportrét - Filko*, c. 1970
  Etching, aluminium sheet /
  Radierung, Aluminiumblech
  30×20cm
  Courtesy Layr, Vienna / Wien

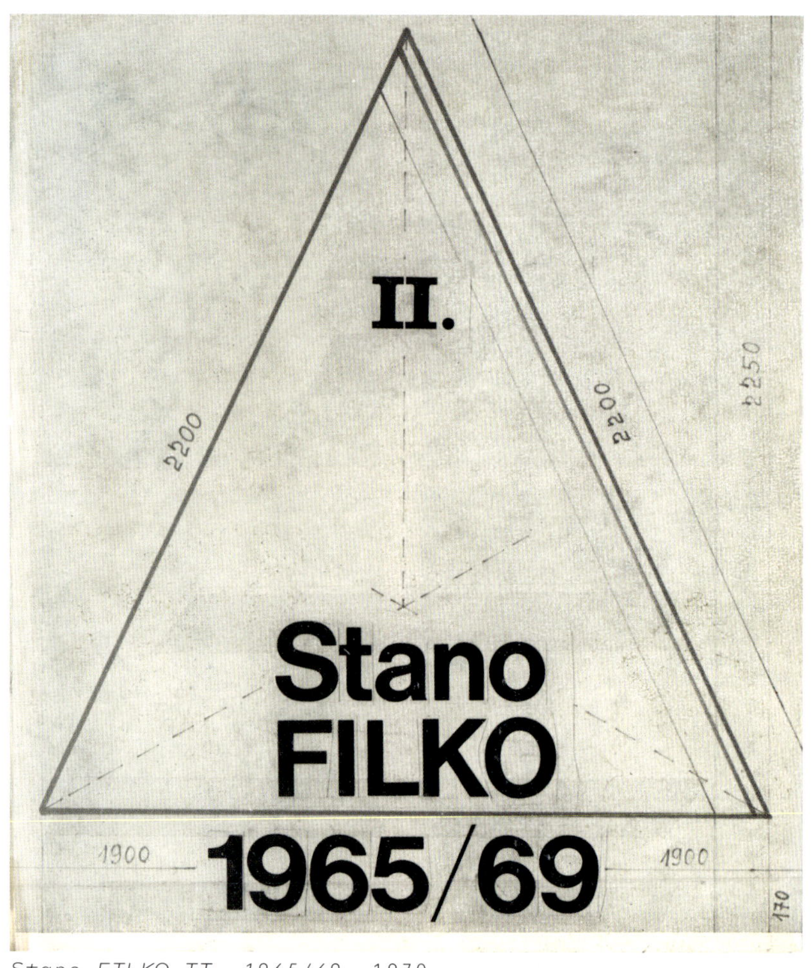

Stano FILKO II. 1965/69, 1970

List of Works / Werkliste
Essays

[03A-B]
Self Installation - Idealism,
1984
  Mixed media; color slide in
  plastic, 5×5cm, *Archive SF* /
  Mixed Media; Farbdia in
  Kunststoff, 5×5cm, *Archív SF*
  Courtesy Slovak National
  Gallery, Bratislava

[04A-B]
Spirit of the Artist, 1983
  Assemblage, mixed media,
  330×178×152cm; color
  slide in plastic, 5×5cm,
  Archive SF / Assemblage,
  Mixed Media, 330×178×152cm;
  Farbdia in Plastik, 5×5cm,
  Archív SF
  Courtesy Slovak National
  Gallery, Bratislava

[05A-B]
White S. Slovak, c. 1987
  Oil, acrylic on canvas;
  color slide in plastic,
  5×5cm, *Archive SF* / Öl,
  Acryl auf Leinwand; Farbdia
  in Kunststoff, 5×5cm,
  Archív SF
  Courtesy Slovak National
  Gallery, Bratislava

[06A-B]
Mobil, 1983
  Oil, acrylic on canvas;
  color slide in plastic,
  5×5cm, *Archive SF* / Öl,
  Acryl auf Leinwand; Farbdia
  in Kunststoff, 5×5cm,
  Archív SF
  Courtesy Slovak National
  Gallery, Bratislava

[07A-B]
Slovak Baby in America, 1983
  Mixed media, 150×330×59cm;
  color slide in plastic,
  5×5cm, *Archive SF* / Mixed
  Media, 150×330×59cm; Farbdia
  in Kunststoff, 5×5cm,
  Archív SF
  Courtesy Slovak National
  Gallery, Bratislava

[08-12]
From the series *CURTAINS* /
Zo série *CURTAINS*, 1985-88
  Acrylic on canvas, mixed
  media, 275×550×510cm;
  colored diapositive,
  Archive SF / Acryl auf
  Leinwand, Mixed Media,
  275×550×510cm; farbiges
  Diapositiv, *Archív SF*
  Courtesy Slovak National
  Gallery, Bratislava

[13A-B]
HAPPSOC 2 Venus Scheherazade /
HAPPSOC 2 Venuša Šeherezáda,
1983
  Collage, montage, color
  photograph, paper,
  perforation, 19×15cm,
  Archive SF / Collage,
  Montage, Farbfotografie,
  Papier, Perforation,
  19×15cm, *Archív SF*
  Courtesy Slovak National
  Gallery, Bratislava

[14A-B]
*Bombs Altar - Foil
Installation*, 1986
  Mixed media; color slide in
  plastic, 5×5cm, *Archive SF* /
  Mixed Media; Farbdia in
  Kunststoff, 5×5cm, *Archív SF*
  Courtesy Slovak National
  Gallery, Bratislava

[15]
7 Pink Bombs / *7 ružových
bômb*, 1987
  Metal on enamel; color slide
  in plastic, *Archive SF* /
  Metall auf Emaille; Farbdia
  in Kunststoff, 5×5cm
  Archív SF
  Courtesy Slovak National
  Gallery, Bratislava

[16A-B]
From the series Cloning USFO /
Zo série *Klonovanie USFO*,
c. 1990
  Archive box, paper, felt-
  tip pen, pen, 30.7×23.7cm,
  Archive SF / Archivbox,
  Papier, Filzstift, Stift,
  30.7×23.7cm, *Archív SF*
  Courtesy Slovak National
  Gallery, Bratislava

[17]
*An Exhibition of Painting by
Stano Filko*, 1987
  Paper, invitation card,
  Donnel Library Center, New
  York, *Archive SF* / Papier,
  Einladungskarte, Donnel
  Library Center, New York,
  Archív SF
  Courtesy Slovak National
  Gallery, Bratislava

[18A-B]
*3.4.5. Dimension FILKO 1960-
1968 to 33. Birthday = EGO* /
*3.4.5. Dimenzia FILKO 1960-
1968 k 33. narodeninám = EGO*,
1970/ c. 1990
  Paper, felt-tip pen,
  21×29.7cm, *Archive SF* /
  Papier, Filzstift,
  21×29.7cm, *Archív SF*
  Courtesy Slovak National
  Gallery, Bratislava

[19A-B]
Cannibal, c. 1985
  Mixed media, 200×762×254cm;
  color slide in plastic,
  5×5cm, *Archive SF* / Mixed
  Media, 200×762×254cm;
  Farbdia in Kunststoff, 5×5cm,
  Archív SF
  Courtesy Slovak National
  Gallery, Bratislava

[20A-B]
ABSOLUTE ONTOLOGIA, 1988
  Mixed media; color slide in
  plastic, 5×5cm, *Archive SF* /
  Mixed Media; Farbdia in
  Kunststoff, 5×5cm, *Archív SF*
  Courtesy Slovak National
  Gallery, Bratislava

[21A–B]
Black Space Installation, 1984
  Oil, acrylic on canvas,
  178×127×508cm; color
  slide in plastic, 5×5cm,
  Archive SF / Öl, Acryl auf
  Leinwand, 178×127×508cm;
  Farbdia in Kunststoff,
  5×5cm, *Archív SF*
  Courtesy Slovak National
  Gallery, Bratislava

[22A–B]
Untitled (*Rebel*), 1984–2015
  Text-art, xerocopy, pen,
  felt-tip pen, paper,
  29.7×21cm, *Archive SF* /
  Text-Kunst, Xerokopie,
  Stift, Filzstift, Papier,
  29.7×21cm, *Archív SF*
  Courtesy Slovak National
  Gallery, Bratislava

  Page / Seite 110–123
  Jan Verwoert

[01]
*Contemplation in the Chakra
Color Spectrum / Kontemplácia
vo farbách čakier-spektier*,
c. 1993–95
  Photo / Foto: *Archive SF /
  Archív SF*

[02]
*Pneumatic Circles I. – XXXX. /
Pneumatické kolesá I. – XXXX.*,
1968
  Orange and red inflatable
  wheels; mirrors / Orange
  und rote aufblasbare Reifen;
  Spiegel
  34 pieces and 12 pieces;
  81 pieces, each 50.5×30cm /
  34 Stück und 12 Stück;
  81 Stück, je 50.5×30cm;
  variable dimensions /
  variable Maße
  Courtesy Linea Collection,
  Bratislava; Layr, Vienna /
  Wien
  Photo / Foto: kunst-
  dokumentation.com

[03]
*Registration of Stano Filko /
Registrace Stana Filka*, 2022
  Fait Gallery, Brno
  Photo / Foto: Martin Polák

[04]
Cathedral of Rockets (model),
1967
  Galvanized sheet metal,
  perforation / Verzinktes
  Blech, Perforation
  Height / Höhe 40cm
  Courtesy Layr, Vienna / Wien
  Photo / Foto: kunst-
  dokumentation.com

[05–08]
From the series *PHYS /
Zo série PHYS*, after 1995
  Mixed media / Mixed Media

[09]
From the series *Clones /
Zo série Klony*, c. 2000
  Paper, felt-tip pen,
  whitening liquid, adhesive
  tape / Papier, Filzstift,
  weißfärbende Flüssigkeit,
  Klebeband
  42×60cm
  Courtesy Linea Collection,
  Bratislava; Layr, Vienna /
  Wien
  Photo / Foto: Daša Barteková

[10]
*SF Railway Customer Card / SF
Železničná preukážka*, 1964
  Collage, paper, B/W
  photograph, latex paint /
  Collage, Papier, S/W-
  Fotografie, Latexfarbe
  21.7×16.6cm
  Courtesy Linea Collection,
  Bratislava; Layr, Wien /
  Vienna
  Photo / Foto: Slovak
  National Gallery, Bratislava

[11A–B]
Boy Angel, 1983
  Assamblage, found materials,
  canvas, oil / Assemblage,
  gefundene Materialien,
  Leinwand, Öl
  122×276×30cm
  Courtesy Layr, Vienna / Wien
  Photos / Fotos: kunst-
  dokumentation.com

[12]
*Models of Observation Towers /
Modely pozorovacích veží*,
1966–67
  Print on cardboard; mirrors;
  5 objects / Druck auf
  Karton; Spiegel; 5 Objekte
  2 pieces, each / 2 Stück, je
  100×100cm; 32 pieces, each /
  32 Stück, je 50.5×30cm;
  variable dimensions /
  variable Maße
  Courtesy Linea Collection,
  Bratislava; Layr, Vienna /
  Wien
  Photo / Foto: kunst-
  dokumentation.com

[13]
*Occupation of the Czechoslovak
Socialist Republic – Pink
Heart / Okupácia ČSSR – Ružové
srdce*, 1968/1978
  Intervention in photographs
  by Ladislav Bielik, montage,
  B/W photograph, tempera,
  paper / Intervention in
  Fotografien von Ladislav
  Bieliks, Montage, S/W-
  Fotografie, Tempera, Papier
  25×17.5cm
  Courtesy Linea Collection,
  Bratislava; Layr, Wien /
  Vienna
  Photo / Foto: Slovak
  National Gallery, Bratislava

[14]
Mobile Germ, 1987
  Oil, acrylic on canvas,
  mixed media, 152×91×5cm;
  color slide in plastic,
  5×5cm, *Archive SF* / Öl,
  Acryl auf Leinwand, Mixed
  Media, 152×91×5cm; Farbdia
  in Kunststoff, 5×5cm,
  Archív SF
  Courtesy Slovak National
  Gallery, Bratislava

[15]
From the series *Altars of
Contemporaneity (Chair) /
Zo série Oltáre súčasnosti
(Stolička)*, 1965
  Assemblage, collage, found
  objects, metal, wood, golden
  pigment / Assemblage,
  Collage, gefundene Objekte,
  Metall, Holz, Goldpigment
  92×45×58cm
  Courtesy Linea Collection,
  Bratislava; Layr, Vienna /
  Wien
  Photo / Foto: kunst-
  dokumentation.com

[16]
From the series *Altars of
Contemporaneity (Chair) /
Zo série Oltáre súčasnosti
(Stolička)*, 1965
  Assemblage, collage,
  mirror, metal, wood, golden
  pigment / Assemblage,
  Collage, Metall, Spiegel,
  Metall, Holz, Goldpigment
  90×60×55cm
  Courtesy Linea Collection,
  Bratislava; Layr, Vienna /
  Wien
  Photo / Foto: kunst-
  dokumentation.com

[17]
*White Bomb in Action. N.Y.C. /
Biela Bomba v akcii. N.Y.C.*,
1989
  Mixed media / Mixed Media
  16.5×15cm
  Photo / Foto: Lubo Stacho

[18]
AIDS Barbecue, 1983
  Assemblage, found objects,
  wood, fabric, mirrors,
  paint / Assemblage,
  gefundene Objekte, Holz,
  Stoff, Spiegel, Farbe
  100×100×100cm
  Courtesy Layr Vienna / Wien
  Photo / Foto: kunst-
  dokumentation.com

[19]
*OLD + NEW TESTAMENT / Dwelling
1966 of Contemporaneity –
Reality / OLD + NEW
TESTAMENT / Obydlie 1966
súčasnosti – skutočnosti*,
1985–95
  Print, drawing paper /
  Druck, Zeichenpapier
  42×29.7cm
  Courtesy Slovak National
  Gallery, Bratislava

[20]
Virtual Old and New Testament,
1992
  Found printed material,
  paper, pen, felt-tip pen /
  Gefundenes bedrucktes
  Material, Papier, Stift,
  Filzstift
  34.5×49cm
  Courtesy Layr Vienna / Wien
  Photo / Foto: kunst-
  dokumentation.com

[21–22]
Stano Filko,
FIYLKONTEMPLACIAKCIEQ, State
Gallery (today's Central
Slovakian Gallery), Banská
Bystrica, 2003
  Courtesy Archive of Central
  Slovakian Gallery, Banská
  Bystrica

[23]
Mobile III. / Mobil III., 1964
Ready-made, wood, wire,
paint / Readymade, Holz,
Draht, Farbe
74×82×48cm
Courtesy Slovak National
Gallery, Bratislava
Photo / Foto: kunst-
dokumentation.com

[24]
Retro SF (Birth and Clinical Deaths) / Retro SF (narodenie a klinické smrte), 2000
Wood, wire, acrylic / Holz,
Draht, Acryl
50×115×2cm
Courtesy Layr Vienna / Wien

[25]
Birth of SF / Narodenie SF,
1960s
Found objects, mixed media /
Gefundene Objekte, Mixed
Media
110×60×60cm
Courtesy Linea Collection,
Bratislava; Layr, Vienna /
Wien
Photo / Foto: kunst-
dokumentation.com

[26]
FILKO CLINICAL DEATHS 1945 and 1952 / FILKO KLINICKÉ SMRTE 1945 a 1952, 1995
Filz, acrylic, pencil,
charcoal / Filz, Acryl,
Bleistift, Holzkohle
350×200cm
Courtesy Layr Vienna / Wien

[27]
SF Clinical Deaths / SF Klinické smrte, 1995
Wood, paint / Holz, Farbe
122×18×4cm
Courtesy Linea Collection,
Bratislava; Layr, Vienna /
Wien
Photo / Foto: kunst-
dokumentation.com

Page / Seite 144–155
Patricia Grzonka

[01]
From the series *Sculptures of the Twentieth century IV. / Zo série Sochy XX. storočia IV.*, 1968–69
Found printed material,
paper, felt-tip pen, pen /
Gefundene Druckerzeugnisse,
Papier, Filzstift, Stift
25.7×18cm
Courtesy Linea Collection,
Bratislava; Layr, Vienna /
Wien
Photo / Foto: Slovak
National Gallery, Bratislava

[02]
From the series *Sculptures of the Twentieth century / Zo série Sochy XX. storočia*, 1968
Found print, paper, felt-tip
pen, pen / Gefundener Druck,
Papier, Filzstift, Stift
29.7×21cm
Courtesy Linea Collection,
Bratislava; Layr, Vienna /
Wien
Photo / Foto: Slovak
National Gallery, Bratislava

[03]
Registration of Stano Filko / Registrace Stana Filka, 2022
Fait Gallery, Brno
Photo / Foto: Martin Polák

[04]
From the series *Monuments of Contemporary Space I. / Zo série Pomníky súčasného priestoru I.*, 1967–68/1995
Paper, pencil, marker /
Papier, Bleistift, Marker
32×44cm
Courtesy Linea Collection,
Bratislava; Layr, Vienna /
Wien
Photo / Foto: Slovak
National Gallery, Bratislava

[05]
UP 300000 KM/S, 2005
tranzit. sk, Bratislava
Photo / Foto: Martin
Marenčin

[06]
Modern Tower of Space / Moderná veža vesmíru, 1966–67
Metal, plywood, synthetic
paint / Metall, Sperrholz,
synthetische Farbe
39.5×75.5×29.8cm
Courtesy Layr, Vienna / Wien
Photo / Foto: kunst-
dokumentation.com

[07]
Breathing - The Celebration of Air / Dýchanie - oslava vzduchu, 1970
Tarpaulin, electric motor,
fan / Plane, elektrischer
Motor, Ventilator
Ø 550cm
Courtesy Slovak National
Gallery, Bratislava
Photo / Foto: Slovak
National Gallery, Bratislava

[08]
Love of Ontology / Láska k ontológii, documenta 7, Neue
Galerie, Kassel, 1982
Courtesy Slovak National
Gallery, Bratislava

[09]
Cosmos - Man / Cosmos - Človek, 1968
Found printed material,
felt-tip pen, pen /
Gefundenes bedrucktes
Material, Filzstift, Stift
14.2×20.2cm
Courtesy Linea Collection,
Bratislava; Layr, Vienna /
Wien
Photo / Foto: Daša Barteková

[10]
Associations III. / Asociácie III., 1968
Print, white plain
cardboard / Druck, weißer
Karton
70×50cm
Courtesy Slovak National
Gallery, Bratislava

[11]
Fedir Tetyanych, Croy Nielsen,
Vienna / Wien, 2022
Photo / Foto: kunst-
dokumentation.com

[12]
Fedir Tetyanych,
Biotechnosphere with Man-Conduits (Biotechnospheres. Cities of Future.), 1980
Paper, watercolor,
gouache, pencil / Papier,
Wasserfarbe, Gouache,
Bleistift
20×28.5cm
Courtesy the artist's family
and Museum of Modern Art,
Warsaw / Warschau

[13]
Ilya und Emilia Kabakov, *The Man Who Flew Into Space From His Apartment*, 1985
© Bildrecht, Wien 2014
Photo / Foto: UMJ/N. Lackner

[14]
Anna Andreeva, *1/2 of the Moon*, 1961
Ink and gouache on special
gosznak paper / Tusche
und Gouache auf speziellem
Gosznak Papier
52×52cm
Courtesy Layr, Vienna / Wien

[15]
Stano Filko RED EXILE, 2022
Layr Seilerstaette, Vienna /
Wien
Courtesy Layr, Vienna / Wien
Photo / Foto: kunst-
dokumentation.com

[16]
12 Chakra Colors Ladder / Rebrík vo farbách 12 čakier,
c. 2005
Found object, wood,
acrylic / Gefundenes Objekt,
Holz, Acryl
400×133×80cm
Courtesy Linea Collection,
Bratislava; Layr, Vienna /
Wien
Photo / Foto: kunst-
dokumentation.com

[17]
7 Chakra Colors Ladder / Rebrík vo farbách 7 čakier,
c. 1995
Found objects, metal,
acrylic / Gefundene Objekte,
Metall, Acryl
188cm×94×41cm
Courtesy Linea Collection,
Bratislava; Layr, Vienna /
Wien
Photo / Foto: kunst-
dokumentation.com

[18]
*Associations XXXI. - I.
Flight - Moon / Asociácie
XXXI. - I. let - mesiac*, 1969
    Print, white plain
    cardboard / Druck, weißer
    Karton
    70×49.5cm
    Courtesy Slovak National
    Gallery, Bratislava

[19]
Print from the album of
*Associations II. / List z
albumu Asociácie II.*, 1968-69
    Print, white cardboard /
    Druck, weißer Karton
    50×70.1cm
    Courtesy Slovak National
    Gallery, Bratislava

[20]
*Associations XXX. - A /
Asociácie XXX. - A*, 1968-69
    Print, white plain
    cardboard / Druck, weißer
    Karton
    50×70.1cm
    Courtesy Slovak National
    Gallery, Bratislava

    Page / Seite 170-195
    Mira Keratova

[01A-B]
Untitled (subtitled *POSTMODERN
HAPPSOC-I. 1965 - DSQ SPIRIT /
POSTMODERNA HAPPSOC-I. 1965 -
DSQ DUCH SPIRIT*), c. 1990s
    Double-sided postcard,
    overpainting, pen and pencil
    on paper / Doppelseitige
    Postkarte, Übermalung, Feder
    und Bleistift auf Papier
    15×10.5cm
    Courtesy Collection of
    Central Slovakian Gallery /
    Stredoslovenská galéria,
    Banská Bystrica

[02]
*Dwelling 1966 of
Contemporaneity - Reality /
Obydlie 1966 súčasnosti -
skutočnosti*, 1967
    B/W photograph / S/W-
    Fotografie
    40×30.3cm
    Courtesy Linea Collection,
    Bratislava; Layr, Vienna /
    Wien
    Photo / Foto: Slovak
    National Gallery, Bratislava

[03]
Stano Filko with model
at *Dwelling 1966 of
Contemporaneity - Reality /
Obydlie 1966 súčasnosti -
skutočnosti*, 1967
    B/W photograph / S/W-
    Fotografie
    39.5×26.7cm
    Courtesy Slovak National
    Gallery, Bratislava

[04]
Clothes from the exhibition
*Dwelling 1966 of
Contemporaneity - Reality /
Obydlie 1966 súčasnosti -
skutočnosti*, 1967
    Print on paper, felt-tip
    pen / Druck auf Papier,
    Filzstift
    30×42cm
    Courtesy Linea Collection,
    Bratislava; Layr, Vienna /
    Wien
    Photo / Foto: kunst-
    dokumentation.com

[05A-B]
*EROTIC - LOVE / EROTIKA -
LÁSKA*, late 1960s
    Color serigraphy, paper,
    marker, paint, wooden
    frame, glass, double-sided /
    Farbserigrafie, Papier,
    Marker, Farbe, Holzrahmen,
    Glas, doppelseitig
    50.5×100.5cm
    Courtesy Collection of
    Central Slovakian Gallery /
    Stredoslovenská galéria,
    Banská Bystrica

[06-09]
Untitled (series subtitled
FEMINISMANSF / FEMINIZMUZSF),
1990s
    Overpainting, redrawing
    with pen and marker of a
    print on paper / Übermalung,
    Neuzeichnung mit Stift und
    Marker eines Drucks auf
    Papier
    21×29.7cm
    Courtesy Collection of
    Central Slovakian Gallery /
    Stredoslovenská galéria,
    Banská Bystrica

[10-14]
Untitled (*Cathedral of
Humanism* with Alexander
Dubček, adapted for
the competition for the
memorial of the anti-
totalitarian demonstration
of 1968 and Dubček's late
80th birthday / *Katedrála
humanizmu* s Alexandrom
Dubčekom prispôsobená pre
súťaž na pamätník proti-
totalitnej demonštrácie v roku
1968 a Dubčekovým nedožitým
osemdesiatym narodeninám),
1968/2001
    B/W analog photograph,
    redrawing, marker;
    B/W analog photograph,
    redrawing, marker, collage,
    paper adhesive tape;
    B/W analog photograph,
    repainting; B/W analog
    photograph, overpainting;
    B/W analog photograph,
    overpainting / S/W-
    Analogfotografie,
    Neuzeichnung, Marker;
    S/W-Analogfotografie,
    Umzeichnung, Marker,
    Collage, Papierklebeband;
    S/W-Analogfotografie,
    Übermalung; S/W-
    Analogfotografie,
    Übermalung; S/W-
    Analogfotografie, Übermalung
    18×13cm; 13×27.6; 16.3×12cm;
    16×13cm; 13×16cm
    Courtesy Collection of
    Central Slovakian Gallery /
    Stredoslovenská galéria,
    Banská Bystrica

[15A-B]
Untitled (subtitled
*HERMAPHRODITSF - MALEFEMALE -
ERECTION - 3.D. - DNA /
HERMAFRODITSF - MUŽENA -
EREKCIEQ - 3.D. - DNA*), 1990s
    Pen, marker, pencil on
    colored xeroxed paper,
    double-sided / Stift,
    Marker, Bleistift auf
    farbigem Kopierpapier,
    doppelseitig
    29.7×42cm
    Courtesy Collection of
    Central Slovakian Gallery /
    Stredoslovenská galéria,
    Banská Bystrica

[16A-B]
Untitled, after 2005
    Double-sided color print
    on paper, handwriting with
    pen, marker, perforation /
    Beidseitiger Farbdruck auf
    Papier, Handschrift mit
    Stift, Marker, Perforation
    42×29.7cm
    Courtesy Collection of
    Central Slovakian Gallery /
    Stredoslovenská galéria,
    Banská Bystrica

[17A-B]
Untitled, 2000s
    Book clippings, pen
    handwriting, overpainting,
    redrawing on paper, mounting
    with paper clips, double-
    sided / Buchausschnitte,
    Federhandschrift,
    Übermalung, Neuzeichnung
    auf Papier, Befestigung mit
    Büroklammern, doppelseitig
    12×15cm
    Courtesy Collection of
    Central Slovakian Gallery /
    Stredoslovenská galéria,
    Banská Bystrica

[18]
Untitled, c. 1997
    Overpainting, squared paper,
    marker, pen / Übermalung,
    kariertes Papier, Marker,
    Stift
    91.5×41.5cm
    Courtesy Private Collection

[19]
Untitled (subtitled
*VENUSSHEHERAZADE -
MORAVANYPIEŠŤANY - SAINT
SEBASTIAN - SHE - SFILKO
1953 / VENUŠAŠEHEREZADA -
MORAVANYPIEŠŤANY - SVÄTÝ
ŠEBASTIAN - KA - SFILKO 1953*),
early 1990s
    Manuscript, pen, marker
    on colored xeroxed paper,
    montage with brown plastic
    adhesive tape / Manuskript,
    Stift, Marker auf farbigem
    Kopierpapier, Montage mit
    braunem Plastikklebeband
    59.5×42cm
    Courtesy Collection of
    Central Slovakian Gallery /
    Stredoslovenská galéria,
    Banská Bystrica

[20A–B]
Untitled (subtitled
*PSYCHOAQ 5.4.D. - PHYSICS
3.D. - FEMALES - FEMALESF -
FEMINISF - VAGINES - PUSSIES /
PSICHOAQ 5.4.D. - FYZIKA
3.D. - SAMIČKY - FEMALESF -
FEMINISF - VAGINKY - PIČKY*),
2000s
    Double-sided color print
    on paper / Beidseitiger
    Farbdruck auf Papier
    42×29.7cm
    Courtesy Collection of
    Central Slovakian Gallery /
    Stredoslovenská galéria,
    Banská Bystrica

[21–22]
Untitled (series subtitled
FEMINISMANSF / FEMINIZMUZSF),
1990s
    Overpainting, redrawing
    with pen and marker of a
    print on paper / Übermalung,
    Umzeichnung mit Stift und
    Marker eines Drucks auf
    Papier
    21×29.7cm; 21×29.7cm
    Courtesy Collection of
    Central Slovakian Gallery /
    Stredoslovenská galéria,
    Banská Bystrica

[23]
Untitled (subtitled *High
School of Art INDUSTRY +
Academy of Fine Arts -
7 CHAKRAS - ENERGIES - FILKO
1950-59 / ŠUP + VŠVU - 7
čakier - energii - filko 1950-
59*), 1992
    Manuscript, drawing, pen,
    marker on cardboard,
    double-sided / Manuskript,
    Zeichnung, Stift, Marker auf
    Karton, doppelseitig
    30×20.4cm
    Courtesy Collection of
    Central Slovakian Gallery /
    Stredoslovenská galéria,
    Banská Bystrica

[24–25]
Untitled (subtitled *SLOVAK
PALEOLITH - VENUS -
SHEHERAZADE = MORAVANY -
PIEŠTANY - 25,000 BC -
DISCOVERED 1937 / SLOVAK
PALEOLIT - VENUŠA - ŠEHEREZADA
= MORAVANY - PIEŠTANY - 25.000
B.C. - OBJ. 1937*), 1990s
    Drawing on paper, painting
    on cardboard, pen, marker,
    collage / Zeichnung auf
    Papier, Malerei auf Karton,
    Stift, Marker, Collage
    35.2×27.6cm; 27.5×35.6cm
    Courtesy Collection of
    Central Slovakian Gallery /
    Stredoslovenská galéria,
    Banská Bystrica

[26]
Untitled (subtitled *FYLKO,
FIRST SEEN LIVE 1982-13.
DECEMBER, SHEHERAZADE - WOMAN
VENUS - MEMORY OF HAPPSOC -
1.-2. 1965-1983, BRATISLAVA -
NYC / Fyilko, prvý-1.krát na
živo videná 1982-13. December,
Šeherezáda - Žena Venuša -
spomienka na Happsoc - 1.-2.
1965-1983, BRATISLAVA - NYC*),
1980s
    Pen on a printed plastic
    bag / Stift auf bedruckter
    Plastiktasche
    49.5×43.5cm
    Courtesy Collection of
    Central Slovakian Gallery /
    Stredoslovenská galéria,
    Banská Bystrica

[27]
Untitled (subtitled *SCOURCE
(company called Zdroj) -
EGOIST - FEMINIST - BEATA -
VENUS - SHEHERAZADE /
Zdroj - Egoista - Feministka -
Beatka - Venuša - Šeherezáda*),
early 1990s
    Pen and marker, handwriting
    on a printed plastic
    bag / Stift und Marker,
    Handschrift auf bedruckter
    Plastiktasche
    50×34cm
    Courtesy Collection of
    Central Slovakian Gallery /
    Stredoslovenská galéria,
    Banská Bystrica

[28–29]
Untitled (series subtitled
FEMINISMANSF / FEMINIZMUZSF),
1990s
    Overpainting, redrawing
    with pen and marker of a
    print on paper / Übermalung,
    Neuzeichnung mit Stift und
    Marker eines Drucks auf
    Papier
    21×29.7cm; 21×29.7cm
    Courtesy Collection of
    Central Slovakian Gallery /
    Stredoslovenská galéria,
    Banská Bystrica

[30A–B]
HERMAPHRODITE (Projectart *The
Real Acidko*) / *HERMAFRODIT*
(Projektart *To pravé
acidkové*), after 2006
    Overpainting, redrawing
    with a pen, marker, book
    and magazine clipping,
    mounting with paper clips /
    Übermalung, Umzeichnung mit
    Stift, Marker, Buch- und
    Zeitschriftenausschnitt,
    Befestigung mit Büroklammern
    17.6×10.5cm
    Courtesy Collection of
    Central Slovakian Gallery /
    Stredoslovenská galéria,
    Banská Bystrica

[31A–B]
From the series *Heart/
Intimacy* / Zo série *Srdce/
Intimita*, 1995
    Found objects, acryl on
    wood / Gefundenes Objekt,
    Acryl auf Holz
    180×118×7cm
    Courtesy Layr Vienna / Wien

[32]
Untitled (*Projectart
Renaissance masters*),
after 2005
    Overpainting, redrawing with
    marker, pen on color book
    reproduction, double-sided /
    Übermalung, Neuzeichnung
    mit Marker, Stift auf
    farbiger Buchreproduktion,
    doppelseitig
    30×48.3cm
    Courtesy Collection of
    Central Slovakian Gallery /
    Stredoslovenská galéria,
    Banská Bystrica

[33–34]
View of Stano Filko's studio
environment in Veľká Hradná,
2011
    Photos / Fotos: Archive /
    Archiv Mira Keratová

Page / Seite 204–217
Christian Höller

[01]
Stano Filko, Miloš Laky, Ján
Zavarský (from left to right /
von links nach rechts), *White
Space in White Space / Biely
priestor v bielom priestore*,
1973
    Academy of Fine Arts
    Bratislava
    Courtesy Slovak National
    Gallery, Bratislava

[02]
Stano Filko, Miloš Laky,
Ján Zavarský, *White Space in
White Space / Biely priestor v
bielom priestore*, 1974
    House of Arts Brno
    Courtesy Slovak National
    Gallery, Bratislava

[03]
Stano Filko, Miloš Laky,
Ján Zavarský, *White Space in
White Space / Biely priestor v
bielom priestore*, 1974
    Photograph, Archive SF /
    Fotografie, Archív SF
    24×13.5cm
    Courtesy Slovak National
    Gallery, Bratislava

[04]
*Stano Filko - Miloš Laky -
Ján Zavarský*, Fiatal Művészek
Klubja / Young Artists' Club
Budapest, exhibition catalog /
Ausstellungskatalog, 1977,
right page / rechte Seite
Sensitivity Manifesto,
1974-1975-1976
    Courtesy Kontakt Collection,
    Vienna / Wien

[05A]
*EMÓCIA. Čistá Emócia. Biely
priestor v bielom priestore -
Text-art / EMOTION. Pure
Emotion. White Space in White
Space - Text-art*, Manifesto /
Manifest, 1977
    Print, pen, felt-tip pen /
    Druck, Stift, Filzstift
    29×40cm
    Courtesy Slovak National
    Gallery, Bratislava

[05B]
*EMOTION. Pure Emotion. White
Space in White Space -
Text-art / EMÓCIA. Čistá
Emócia. Biely priestor v
bielom priestore - Text-art*,
Manifesto / Manifest, 1977
   Print, pen, felt-tip pen /
   Druck, Stift, Filzstift
   29×40cm
   Courtesy Slovak National
   Gallery, Bratislava

[05C]
*EMOTION. Reine Emotion.
Weisser Raum im Weissen
Raum - Text-art / EMÓCIA.
Čistá Emócia. Biely priestor
v bielom priestore - Text-art*,
Manifesto / Manifest, 1977
   Print, pen, felt-tip pen /
   Druck, Stift, Filzstift
   29×40cm
   Photo / Foto: Archive /
   Archiv Hans Ulrich Obrist

[06]
Emotion / Emócia, Anti-
performance, 1977
   Print, pencil, paper /
   Druck, Bleistift, Papier
   19 × 28.7cm
   Courtesy Slovak National
   Gallery, Bratislava

[07]
*5th DIMENSION WHITE ONTOLOGIC
TRANSCENDENCE DEVOURED
EVERYTHING / 5. DIMENZIA BIELA
ONTOLOGICKÁ TRANSCENDENCIA -
ZOŽRALA VŠETKO*, 1980-95
   Print, paper, pen, latex,
   paper / Druck, Stift, Latex
   60.7×42.6cm
   Courtesy Slovak National
   Gallery, Bratislava

[08]
*TRANSCENDENCE I., II. /
TRANSCENDENCJA I., II.*,
1978-79
   Print, paper, pencil, pen,
   felt-tip pen / Druck,
   Papier, Bleistift, Stift,
   Filzstift
   19.1×35.3cm
   Courtesy Slovak National
   Gallery, Bratislava

[09]
From the cycle *Transcendency
III. / Z cyklu Transcendencia
III.*, 1979
   B/W photograph, paper,
   whitening liquid, pen,
   perforation / S/W-
   Fotografie, Papier,
   weißfärbende Flüssigkeit,
   Stift, Perforation
   18×24cm
   Linea Collection,
   Bratislava; Layr, Vienna /
   Wien
   Photo / Foto: Martin
   Marenčin

[10]
From the cycle *Transcendency /
Z cyklu Transcendencia*,
1978-80
   Paper, gold pigment
   photo, whitening liquid,
   perforation / Papier,
   Goldpigment-Foto,
   weißfärbende Flüssigkeit,
   Perforation
   24×18cm
   Linea Collection,
   Bratislava; Layr, Vienna /
   Wien
   Photo / Foto: Martin
   Marenčin

[11]
*Love of Ontology / Láska k
ontológii*, 1982
   documenta 7, Neue Galerie,
   Kassel
   Photo / Foto: Slovak
   National Gallery, Bratislava

[12]
*Cosmos II. - Environment /
Kozmos II. - environment*, 1968
   Photograph, paper /
   Fotografie, Papier
   18×24cm
   Courtesy Slovak National
   Gallery, Bratislava

[13]
*Cosmos II. - Environment /
Kozmos II. - environment*, 1968
   Photograph, paper /
   Fotografie, Papier
   18×24cm
   Photo / Foto: Archive /
   Archiv Hans Ulrich Obrist

[14]
Cosmos I., 1971
   Indian ink on paper,
   tempera / Tusche auf Papier,
   Tempera
   42.5×69cm
   Courtesy Slovak National
   Gallery, Bratislava

[15]
Cosmos II., 1971
   Indian ink on paper,
   tempera / Tusche auf Papier,
   Tempera
   42.5×69cm
   Courtesy Slovak National
   Gallery, Bratislava

[16]
*Concept - Nothing at all /
Koncept - Vôbec nič*, 1967
   Print, white plain
   cardboard / Druck, weißer
   Karton
   50×70cm
   Courtesy Slovak National
   Gallery, Bratislava

[17]
*Transcendence. 5. DIMENSION
ABSOLUT - AQ - Timelessness -
HAPPSOC 5. / Transcendencia.
5. DIMENZIA ABSOLUT - AQ -
Nadčasovosť - HAPPSOC 5.*,
1967/1978/2000
   Paper, pen, marker, white-
   out, xerox, perforation /
   Papier, Stift, Marker,
   White-out, Xerox,
   Perforation
   21×29.7cm
   Courtesy Linea Collection,
   Bratislava; Layr, Vienna /
   Wien
   Photo / Foto: Slovak
   National Gallery, Bratislava

[18]
*White Space on Snow, Open
Installation / Biely priestor
na snehu, otvorená inštalácia*,
1993-95
   Installation, found
   objects / Installation,
   gefundene Objekte
   170×80×50cm

[19]
*Artist's studio Snežienková /
Umelcov ateliér Snežienková*,
2007
   Photo / Foto: Pato Safko

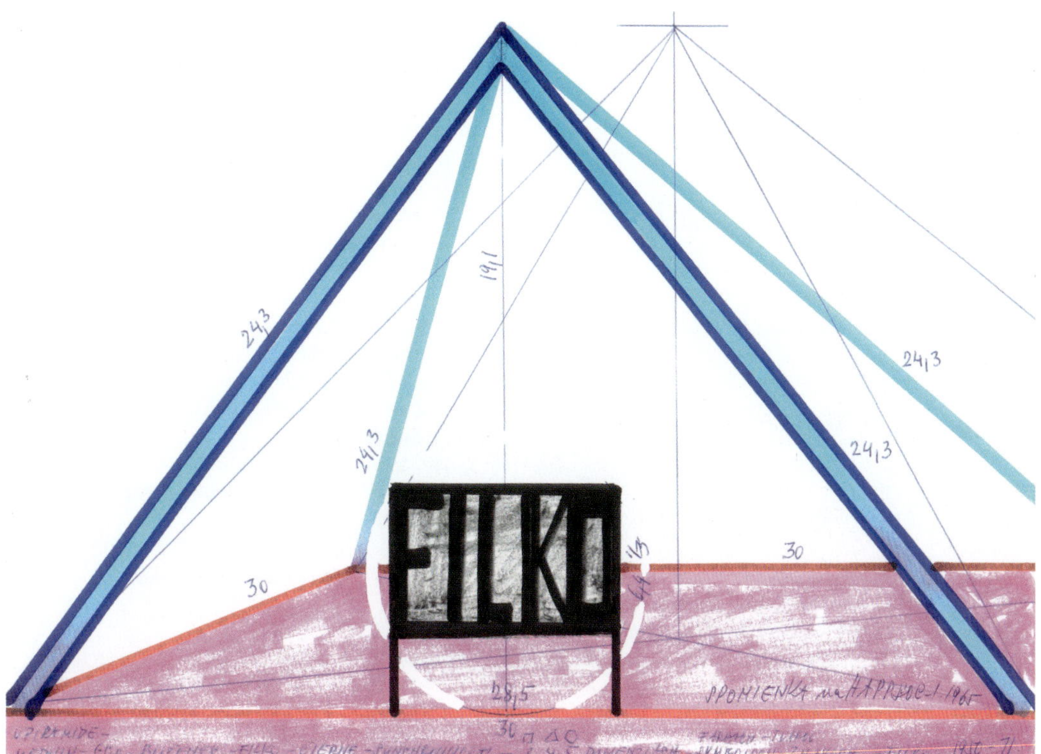

From the series *In the Pyramid (Memories of HAPPSOC I.)* /
Zo série V pyramíde (Spomienky na HAPPSOC I.), c. 1995

Titles and Dating of Works
The titles of the works are taken from the publication *Stano FILKO II. 1965/69* (1970), published by Stano Filko himself. In addition, all work titles mentioned here follow the information provided by the Slovak National Gallery, Bratislava and the Linea Collection, Bratislava as well as the authors of this publication.

The continuous revision, retitling, and redating of the works by the artist himself over a period of forty years does not allow for a clear classification with regard to title and dating of the œuvre, which was presumably intended by the artist. This publication nevertheless attempts, without a final art-historical claim, to locate the works with regard to their genesis and titling in terms of an overall presentation.

Note
In the case that despite intense research any individual copyright holders not cited by name own legal rights, please contact info@halle-fuer-kunst.at.

Betitelung und Datierung der Werke
Die Betitelung der Arbeiten ist aus der von Stano Filko selbst herausgegebenen Publikation *Stano FILKO II. 1965/69* (1970) entnommen. Darüber hinaus folgen alle hier genannten Werktitel den Angaben der Slovak National Gallery, Bratislava und der Linea Collection, Bratislava sowie den Autor*innen der Publikation.

Eine kontinuierliche Überarbeitung, Rebetitelung und Redatierung der Arbeiten durch den Künstler selbst über einen Zeitraum von vierzig Jahren lässt eine eindeutige Einordnung hinsichtlich Titel und Datierung des Œuvres nicht zu, was vermutlich vom Künstler so intendiert war. Diese Publikation unternimmt dennoch den Versuch, ohne einen finalen kunsthistorischen Anspruch, das Werk hinsichtlich seiner Entstehung und Betitelungen in Hinblick auf eine Gesamtdarstellung zu verorten.

Hinweis
Sollten trotz intensiver Recherche einzelne, nicht namentlich angeführte Rechteinhaber*innen Rechte besitzen, ersuchen wir um Kontaktaufnahme unter info@halle-fuer-kunst.at.

Biography / Biografie

Stano Filko

* 1937, Veľká Hradná, Czechoslovak Republic / Tschechoslowakische Republik

† 2015, Bratislava, Slovak Republic / Slowakische Republik

Solo Exhibitions / Einzelausstellungen

2022
Stano Filko. A Retrospective, HALLE FÜR KUNST Steiermark, Graz (AT)
Stano Filko, *RED EXILE*, Layr, Vienna (AT)

2021
Registration of Stano Filko / Registrace Stana Filka, Fait Gallery, Brno (CZ)

2020
Allegra Projects, St. Moritz (CH)

2019
Cosmoscow with Layr, Moscow (RU)
STANO FILKO – STANO FILKO, Layr, Rome (IT)
Multimodal Googlification of Cosmology-Oriented Diagrammatic Experimentations of Stano Filko, Layr, Vienna (AT)

2018
Feature, Art Basel Unlimited, with Layr, Basel (CH)

2017
2037, Kunsthalle Bratislava (SK)

2016
Stano Filko: Poézia o Priestore a Kozme, Slovak National Gallery, Bratislava (SK)
Stano Filko v Žiline. Fragment výstavy, Nová Synagóga, Žilina (SK)

2015
FILKO – FYLKO – PHYLKO, Zacheta – National Gallery of Art, Warsaw (PL)
Focus, Frieze Art Fair, with Layr, London (UK)
5.D., PIATO – platforma, Ostrava, Vitkovice (CZ)
Stano Filko, Kiki Kogelnik, Lira Gallery, Rome (IT)
Kiedy ludzie krążą po mieście (with Janina Kraupe-Świderska), National Museum, Krakov (PL)

2014
WHITE (Essence), 1974 (with Miloš Laky and Ján Zavarský), Layr, Vienna (AT)
Postbigbang – Antebigbangsf, Fondazione Morra Greco, Naples (IT)
ERUPEKCIA-ORGIAMUS-ORGAZMUS-YANG-YING = SLNKOMESIAC-INLIFELOVE-ENTITA-EXIST-BEINGHSF-HERMAFRODIT, KAžDÉMU PODĽA SVOJICH MOžNOSTÍ A SCHOPNOSTÍ 5.4.3.D. – PRE ŽIVOT (with Jiří Kovanda), Donnaregina, Naples (IT)

2012
erupekcia – orgiazmus – orgazmus – yang – jin = slnkomesiac – in life – love – entita – exist – beingsf – hermafrodit kazdemu podla svojich moznosti a schopnosti – v – in – 5.4.3.D. – pre zivot singular truths vsetkych ludi na tejto zemeguli – tranzscendencie – v – in – existencii – len v 3.D., amt _ project, Bratislava (SK)
Stano Filko – White as an ontological space and the beginning of everything, Galeria Nedbalka, Bratislava (SK)
Vernisáz výstavy TRANzSCENDENTEAOQ 5.D. (4.3.), Galéria Cypriána Majernika, Bratislava (SK)
TRANzSCENDENTEAOQ 5.4.3.D. = METODIKA = INTELIGENTEAOQ, Layr, Vienna (AT)

2008
Filkova archa a oltare sucasnosti, City Gallery, Bratislava (SK)

2005
UP 300000 KM/S, tranzit workshops, Bratislava (SK)

2003
Stano Filko. SONDA EGOQ 1937–2037 GEMINIY, Galéria Slovenská sporiteľňa, Bratislava (SK)
FIYLKONTEMPLACIAKCIEQ, SONDA 1950–1969, SONDA 1971–1984, Štátna galéria, Banská Bystrica (SK)

2000
EGOQ, Východoslovenská galéria, Košice (SK)

1999
Starý a Nový testament, Slovenská filharmónia, Bratislava (SK)

1996
Galeria Tatrasoft, Bratislava (SK)

1994
Výber z tvorby (Červená biologická energia, 3. dimenzia, Modrá kozmologická, 4. dimenzia, Biela metafyzická enerhia, 5. dimenzia), Slovak National Gallery, Zvolen (SK)

1993
Stano Filko – Výber z diela. I. Červená energia (cyklus Sondy), Slovak National Gallery, Bratislava (SK)

1987
Stano Fylko, The Donell Library Center, New York (US)

1986
FYLKO. Special Exhibit of Recent Work 1983–1985, P.S. 1 – The Institute for Art and Urban Resources, Long Island City, New York (US)

1984
Stano Filko. Exhibit of Painting, North Arlinghton
  Public Library, North Arlinghton,
  New Jersey (US)

1980
Stanislaw Filko. Transcendencja I. – II. 1978–1979,
  Mala Galeria PSP-ZPAF, Plac zamkowy,
  Warsaw (PL)

1979
Transcendencja. 1978. Stano Filko, Galeria GN
  ZPAF, Gdansk (PL)

1978
Stanislav Filko. Emotion – 1977, Galeria LDK
  Labirynt, Lublin (PL)

1974
*Biely priestor v bielom priestore. Stano Filko –
  Miloš Laky – Ján Zavarský*, Dům umění,
  Brno (CZ)

1969
*Stanislav Filko. Environnement Universel
  1966–1967 und Grafik*, Galerie Ursula
  Wendtorf, Oldenburger Kunstverein,
  Oldenburg (DE)

1967
Grafika, Galeria Václava Špály, Prague (CZ)
Stano Filko. Obydli soucasnosti a skutecnosti,
  Galeria na Karlove namesti, Prague (CZ)
Externé prostredie – komunikácia, Galéria
  Cypriána Majerníka, Bratislava (SK)

1962
Obrazy, Reduta, Bratislava (SK)

1958
Obrazy – Grafiky, Kultúrny dom, Bánovce nad
  Bebravou (SK)

Group Exhibitions /
Gruppenausstellungen
(Selection / Auswahl)

2022
Statements, Art Basel, Basel (CH)
BARBE À PAPA, CAPC, Museum of Contemporary
  Art of Bordeaux, Bordeaux (FR)
*Riding the crest of a high and beautiful wave:
  art as a state of mind*, PLATFORM München,
  Munich (DE)

2021
Enjoy, mumok – Museum moderner Kunst
  Stiftung Ludwig Wien, Vienna (AT)
Lichtenfels Sculpture, Ruine Lichtenfels,
  Lichtenfels (AT)
Stars Down to Earth, Galerie Barbara Weiss,
  Berlin (AT)

2019
Kunstmuseum Basel, Presentation of the
  Collection, Basel (CH)
Going to the Moon, Eres Stiftung, Munich (DE)
*Collective Exhibition for a singel body –
  the private score – Vienna 2019*, Haus
  Wittgenstein, Vienna (AT)
*Signal – The Story of (Post)Conceptual Art
  in Slovakia*, Ludwig Múzeum, Budapest (HU)
Where do we go from here?, Salón Acme,
  Mexico City (MX)

2018
Who was 1968?, Lentos Kunstmuseum, Linz (AT)

2017
MASMEDIÁLNE OBRAZY ŽENY, Bratislava City
  Gallery, Bratislava (SK)

2016
Kunst in Europa 1945–1968, ZKM Zentrum für
  Kunst und Medien, Karlsruhe (DE)

2015
Ludwig Goes Pop + The East Side Story, Ludwig
  Múzeum, Budapest (HU)
Die Schule von Kyiv, Badischer Kunstverein,
  Karlsruhe (DE)
*The Soft Codes, Conceptual Tendencies in Slovak
  Art*, Wroclaw Contemporary Museum,
  Wroclaw (PL)
*Shifters: Signaling in Latin America and Eastern
  Europe*, GB Agency, Paris (FR)
Conceptual art and Communism 1965–1989,
  Gallery BBLA, New York (US)

2014
Personal Hi-Stories, Garage Project Space,
  Moscow (RU)
*Cosmos Calling! Art And Science In The Long
  Sixties*, Zacheta, National Gallery of Art,
  Warsaw (PL)
Strom zivota / Tree of Life, Galéria mesta
  Bratislavy, Bratislava (SK)
*Report on the Construction of a Spaceship
  Module*, New Museum, New York (US)

2013
The Earth Turns And All Things Slip Away,
  Hunt Kastner Artworks, Prague (CZ)
*Collection 1 2 3 / The Tracks of History in
  Acquisitions – Part 3*, GASK, Galerie
  Středoceského kraje, Kutná Hora (CZ)

2012
Blood, Esterházy Palace, Bratislava (SK)
Fremde Überall – Foreigners Everywhere,
  Pomeranz Collection, Jüdisches Museum,
  Vienna (AT)
*zero Years – Slovak Visual Art between 1999 and
  2011 from Four Curatorial Perspectives*,
  MODEM Centre for Modern and Contemporary
  Arts, Debrecen (HU)
Delete – Art and Wiping Out, Esterházy Palace,
  Bratislava (SK)
Strata, Sammlung Lenikus, Bauernmarkt 9,
  Vienna (AT)
*as a poem might celebrate these, Stano Filko,
  Marjorie Keller, Rita Vitorelli*, Pleasantpleasant,
  Copenhagen (DK)
*Mit sofortiger Wirkung: künstlerische Eingriffe
  in den Alltag* (With Immediate Effect: Artistic
  Interventions in the Everyday), Kunsthalle
  project space karlsplatz, Vienna (AT)
*Papier Kole, Czech and Slovak koláz / Collage of
  20th and 21st centuries*, East-Slovakian
  Gallery Košice, Košice (SK)

2011
The Present and Presence, Moderna Galerija,
  Ljubljana (SL)
Eyes Looking for the Head to Inhabit, Muzeum
  Sztuki, Lodz (PL)
A Terrible Beauty Is Born, 11th Biennale de Lyon,
  Lyon (FR)
Ostalgia, New Museum, New York (US)
*East by South West,... sein Dasein verlässt und
  seine Gestalt der Erinnerung übergibt*,
  Layr, Vienna (AT)
Museum of Parallel Narratives, MACBA,
  Barcelona (SP)

2010
Porträt einer Sammlung, Kunstsammlung
  Chemnitz (CH)
Les promesses du passé, Centre Pompidou,
  Paris (FR)
Star City – The Future Under Communism,
  Nottingham Contemporary, Nottingham (UK)

2008
Between Concept and Action, Galleria Sonia
  Rosso, Turin (IT)

2007
Arta Slovaca 1960–2000, National Museum of
  Contemporary Art, Bukarest (RO)
Prague Biennale 3, Prague (CZ)
tranzit, Kunstverein Frankfurt (DE)
OUT OF THE CITY Landart, City Gallery of
  Bratislava, Bratislava (SK)
Stage, Backstage, Auditorium, Kunstverein
  Frankfurt (DE)

2006
*Kontakt… aus der Sammlung der Erste Bank
    Group*, mumok – Museum moderner Kunst
    Stiftung Ludwig Wien, Vienna (AT)
I (ICH), Secession, Vienna (AT)
Living Art – On the Edge of Europe, Kröller-Müller
    Museum, Otterlo (NL)

2005
51st Venice Biennial, Venice (IT)

2004
Collected Views from East to West, Generali
    Foundation, Vienna (AT)

2003
*FIYLKONTEMPLACIAKCIEQ, SONDA 1950–1969,
    SONDA 1971–1984*, státna galéria
    (State Gallery), Banská Bystrica (SK)
Slovak Contemporary Art, Gallery Art Factory,
    Prague (CZ)

2001
Umenie akcie 1965–1980, Slovak National
    Gallery, Bratislava (SK)
Slowakische Träume, Museum Moderner Kunst,
    Passau (DE)

2000
*Samizdat. Alternative Kultur in Zentral- und
    Osteuropa. Die 60er bis 80er Jahre*, Akademie
    der Künste, Berlin (DE)
*Global Conceptualism – Points of Origin,
    1950s–1980s*, MIT/List Visual Art Center,
    Cambridge (US)
*Aspect / Positions. 50 Years of Art in Central
    Europe 1949–1999*, Ludwig Museum,
    Budapest (HU); John Hansard Gallery, City
    Gallery Southampton, Southampton (UK)

1999
*Aspekte / Positionen. 50 Jahre Kunst aus
    Mitteleuropa 1949–1999*, Museum Moderner
    Kunst Stiftung Ludwig Wien, Palais
    Liechtenstein, 20er-Haus, Vienna (AT)
*Global Conceptualism – Points of Origin,
    1950s–1980s*, QMA – Queens Museum of Art,
    New York (US)
Slovak Art for Free, Biennale de Venezia,
    Venice (IT)
*Akce Slovo Pohyb Prostor. Experimenty v umění
    šedesátých let*, Galerie hlavního města Prahy,
    Prague (CZ)

1996
Sculpture in Time / Socha v čase, Centrum Rzeźby
    Polskiej w Orońsku (PL)

1995
Šesťdesiate roky v slovenskom výtvarnom umení,
    Slovenská národná galéria, Bratislava (SK)

1994
Torso – Slovak Photography, Design Works,
    Durham, New Castle (IR)
Enter for Computer, Kunsthaus, Vienna (AT)

1992
*Zwischen Objekt und Installation. Slowakische
    Kunst der Gegenwart*, Museum am Ostwall,
    Dortmund (DE)
Arte Contemporanea ceca e slovacca 1950–1992,
    Palazzo del Broletto, Novara (IT)

1991
Sen o múzeu? Považská galéria umenia,
    Žilina (SK)

1987
Working in Brooklyn, Brooklyn Museum,
    New York (US)

1986
Off the wall, Kamikadze Gallery, New York (US)
Undercurrents in the Visual Arts, Wiesner
    Gallery, New York (US)

1985
Eastern Europeans in New York, La Galerie
    en El Bohio, New York (US)

1984
Mysterious Figurative, Annual Exhibition,
    Staten Island Museum, NYC (US)

1982
documenta 7, Kassel (DE)
Bilder Aus der Slowakei 1965–1980, Galerie
    Pragxis, Essen – Kettwig (DE)

1979
Time, Gallery Kitano Circus, Kobe (JPN)

1975
Biennale de Paris. Manifestation internationale
    des jeunes artistes. Musée d'Art Moderne /
    Musée Galliera, Paris (F)

1971
Arte de sistemas, Centro de Arte y Communicatión
    en al Museu de Arte Moderno de la Ciudad,
    Buenos Aires (ARG)
Junge Tschechoslowakische Künstler,
    Informationszentrale für Ereignisse,
    Bielefeld (DE)

1970
Happening & Fluxus, Kölnischer Kunstverein,
    Cologne (DE)
Contemporary trends (Le dyamisme du présent),
    EXPO Museum of Fine Arts, Osaka (JPN)
International Festival of Contemporary Art,
    Municipal Art Museum, Yokohama (JPN)
Art Concepts from Europe, Binino Gallery,
    New York (US)
*Graveurs tchécoslovaques contemporains.
    Cabinet des Estampes (Cabinet d'Arts
    graphiques)*, Musée d'Art et d'Histoire,
    Geneva (CH)
Polymúzický priestor I., II., III., Kúpeľný ostrov,
    Piešťany (SK)
Slovenské výtvarné umenie 1965–1970,
    Valdštejnská jízdárna, Palác Kinských, Mánes,
    Prague (CZ)
Art Concepts from Europe, Bonino Gallery,
    New York (US), Buenos Aires (ARG)

1969
Biennale de Paris 1969, Musée d'Art Moderne
    de la Ville de Paris, Paris (FR)
*Environnement lumino-cinětique. La Place de
    Chalet*, Centre National d'Art Contemporain,
    Paris (FR)
Pläne und Projekte als Kunst, Kunsthalle Bern,
    Bern (CH), Aktionsraum München,
    Munich (DE)
Vier Aspekte der zeitgenössischen Kunst,
    Kunstverein Oldenburg, Oldenburg (DE)
Arte Contemporanea in Cecoslovacchia, Galleria
    Nazionale d'Arte Moderna e Contemporanea
    GNAM, Rome (IT)
*Ars Popularis. Bilder – Objekte – Grafik von
    18 Künstlern aus Belgien, Deutschland und
    der ČSSR.*, CENTRUM Galerie im Siemers
    Hochhaus, Hamburg (DE)
III. Rassegna Internazionale d'Arte Contemporanea.
    Acirea le Turistico Termale, Catania (IT)

1968
Nová citlivost, Brno, Karlovy Vary, Prague (CZ)
Cinétisme – Spectacle – Environment, Maison
    de la culture, Grenoble (FR)
Danuvius 1968, Dom umenia, Bratislava (SK)
Izložba savremene čehoslovačke grafike. Muzej
    savremene umetnosti, Belgrade (SRB)
Contemporary Prints of Czechoslovakia, National
    Gallery of Canada, Ottawa (CAN)

1967
Tschechoslowakische Graphik, Sonninhalle des
    Kieler Schlosses, Kiel (DE)

1966
Výstava mladých. AICA, Moravská galerie,
    Brno (CZ)
Malarstwo. Rzézba. Grafika Bratislawy, Pawilon
    wystawowy, Krakov (PL)

1965
Celoslovenská výstava, Dom umenia,
    Bratislava (SK)
5 Cecoslovacchi, Galeria Numero, Florence,
    Rome, Milan (IT)

1964
Výstava mladých, Moravská galéria, Dům pánů
    z Kunštátu, Brno (CZ)

1963
S. Filko – L. Gajdoš – A. Mlynárčik – I. Vychlopen,
    foyer of the editorial office of the daily
    paper *Smena*, Bratislava (SK)
Výstava mladých, Moravská galerie, Brno (CZ)

Public Collections / Öffentliche Sammlungen

The Museum of Modern Art, New York (US)
Guggenheim Collection, New York (US)
Tate Modern, London (UK)
Kunstmuseum Basel, Basel (CH)
Slovak National Gallery, Bratislava (SK)
Walker Art Center, Minneapolis (US)
Folkwang Museum, Essen (DE)
Kröller-Muller Museum, Osterloh (NL)
mumok – Museum moderner Kunst Stiftung
    Ludwig Wien, Vienna (AT)
Generali Foundation, Vienna (AT)
Kontakt. Art Collection, Vienna (AT)
Kunstmuseum Liechtenstein, Vaduz (LIE)
National Gallery, Prague (CZ)
V-A-C Foundation, Moscow (RU)

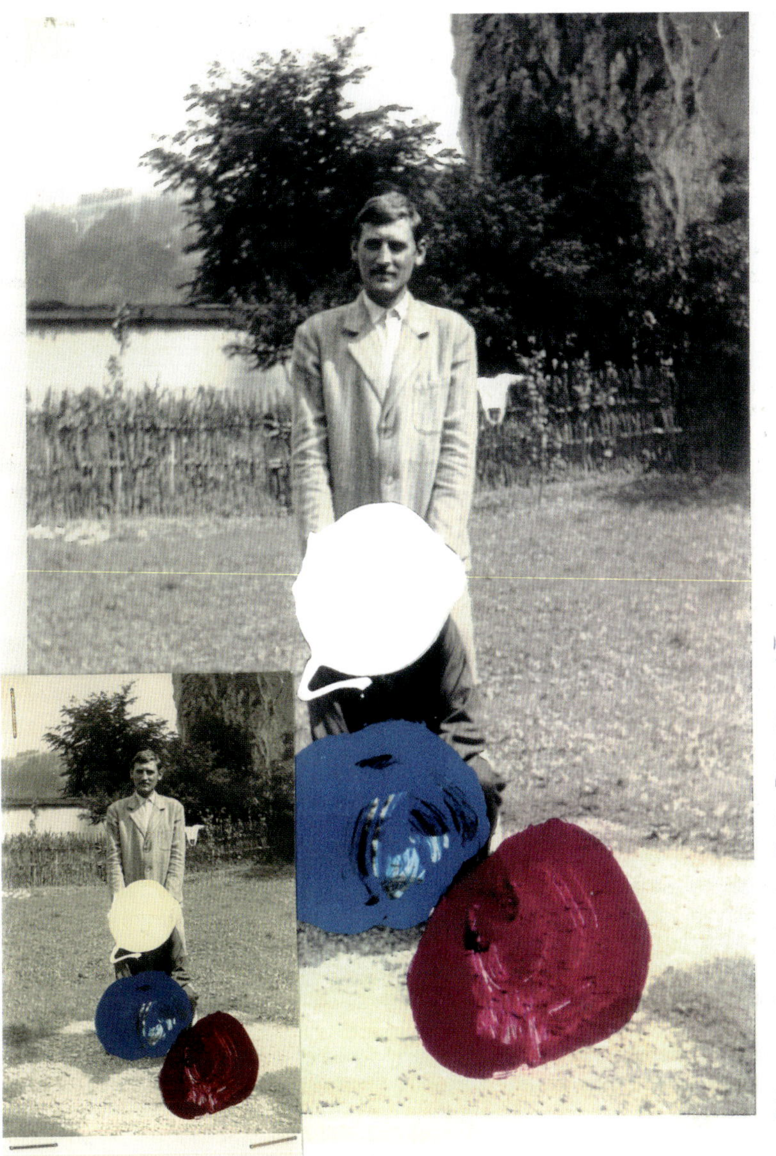

From the series Self-Portrait SF / Zo série
Autoportrét SF, 1970-80

Authors / Autor*innen

Lucia Gregorová Stach

*1975, Slovakia, lives in Bratislava
is an art historian and curator. Since 2013, she has been the Chief Curator
of Modern and Contemporary Art Collections at the Slovak National
Gallery. Gregorová Stach studied art history at the University of Trnava, the
Charles University in Prague, and the Academy of Fine Arts and Design in
Bratislava, where she received her PhD in 2015. In 2015 she curated a
solo exhibition of Stano Filko for Zachęta – National Art Gallery in Warsaw.
With Aurel Hrabušický, she curated Filko's solo exhibition *Poetry on
Space – Cosmos* (2016) at the Slovak National Gallery and published a homony-
mous publication. Gregorová Stach and Hrabušický also published
Stano Filko 1. (2018), which is a first art-historical overview of Filko's
work in Slovak, to be followed in 2023 by the condensed English edition
Stano Filko – Universal Environment published by Scala, London.

*1975, Slowakei, lebt in Bratislava
ist Kunsthistorikerin und Kuratorin. Seit 2013 ist sie Chefkuratorin der Samm-
lungen moderner und zeitgenössischer Kunst an der Slowakischen
Nationalgalerie. Gregorová Stach hat Kunstgeschichte an der Universität
Trnava, an der Karls-Universität in Prag, sowie an der Akademie für
Bildende Kunst und Design in Bratislava studiert, wo sie 2015 promovierte.
Im Jahr 2015 kuratierte sie eine Einzelausstellung von Stano Filko für die
Zachęta – Nationale Kunstgalerie in Warschau. Mit Aurel Hrabušický
kuratierte sie Filkos Einzelausstellung *Poetry on Space – Cosmos* (2016) in
der Slowakischen Nationalgalerie, zu der eine gleichnamige Publikation
erschien. Gregorová Stach und Hrabušický veröffentlichten außerdem die
Publikation *Stano Filko 1.* (2018), die auf Slowakisch einen ersten kunst-
geschichtlichen Überblick über das Werk Filkos gibt, worauf 2023
die komprimierte englische Ausgabe *Stano Filko – Universal Environment*
bei Scala, London folgt.

Patricia Grzonka

*St. Gallen, Switzerland, lives in Vienna
is an art and architecture historian and critic. She is a lecturer at the University of Applied Arts Vienna and teaches at the Institute for Art and Architecture at the Academy of Fine Arts Vienna. Grzonka studied in Zurich and
Rome and received a Ph.D. in architectural theory at Vienna University of
Technology. She has written numerous texts, interviews, and essays
in the fields of modernist art and architectural theory, as well as neo-avant-
gardes. Her texts are regularly published in exhibition publications and
are part of renowned art magazines, including springerin, Texte zur Kunst,
Kunstbulletin, Monopol, and frieze, and newspapers such as Neue
Zürcher Zeitung, profil and Falter. In 2015 she was a laureate of the Art Critics
Award. At the invitation of Dušan Brozman she wrote an extensive text
about Stano Filko for Arbor Vitae, Prague (2005), as well as for the
conference proceedings of the Association of Austrian Art Historians,
Hohenems (2011).

*St. Gallen, Schweiz, lebt in Wien
ist Kunst- und Architekturhistorikerin und Kritikerin. Sie ist Dozentin an der
Universität für angewandte Kunst Wien und unterrichtet an der Universität
Kassel im Fachbereich Architektur, Stadt- und Landschaftsplanung.
Grzonka hat in Zürich und Rom studiert und schrieb ihre Dissertation im Be-
reich Architekturtheorie an der Technischen Universität in Wien. Grzonka
hat zahlreiche Texte, Interviews und Essays in den Bereichen Kunst-
und Architekturtheorie der Moderne, sowie Neo-Avantgarden verfasst. Ihre
Texte werden regelmäßig in Ausstellungspublikationen veröffentlicht
und sind Teil renommierter Kunstmagazine, darunter springerin, Texte zur
Kunst, Kunstbulletin, Monopol und frieze, und Zeitungen wie Neue Zürcher
Zeitung, profil und Falter. Im Jahr 2015 war sie Preisträgerin des Art
Critics Award. Sie schrieb auf Einladung von Dušan Brozman bei Arbor Vitae,
Prag (2005) einen umfangreichen Text über Stano Filko, wie auch für
den Tagungsband der 15. Tagung des Verbands österreichischer Kunst-
historikerinnen und Kunsthistoriker, Hohenems (2011).

Christian Höller

*1966 Weitersfelden, Austria, lives in Vienna
is a freelance author, translator, as well as editor and co-publisher of the magazine springerin – Hefte für Gegenwartskunst, Vienna. Höller teaches
at the University of Applied Arts Vienna and was a visiting professor at the
École supérieure des beaux-arts in Geneva. He has been publishing in
the fields of art and cultural theory since the 1990s, including in the magazines
Texte zur Kunst, Spex, and springerin. He also frequently appears as a curator in the fields of film and music for various institutions and festivals,
including mumok – Museum Moderner Kunst Stiftung Ludwig Wien, Vienna;
Lentos Kunstmuseum, Linz; Kunstverein Medienturm / steirischer
herbst, Graz; and Internationale Kurzfilmtage Oberhausen. Höller is author
and (co-)editor of various publications, such as *Kontakt. The Art Collection
of Erste Group and ERSTE Foundation* (2017); *L'Internationale:
Post-War Avant-Gardes Between 1957 and 1986* (2012); *Time Action Vision:
Conversations in Cultural Studies, Theory, and Activism* (2010); and
Techno-Visionen (2005). Most recently, together with Cathrin Rhomberg
and Daniel Grün, he edited the publication *White Space in White Space.
Stano Filko, Miloš Laky, Ján Zavarský* (2021).

*1966 Weitersfelden, Österreich, lebt in Wien
ist freier Autor, Übersetzer sowie Redakteur und Mitherausgeber der Zeitschrift springerin – Hefte für Gegenwartskunst, Wien. Höller lehrt an der
Universität für Angewandte Kunst Wien und war Gastprofessor an der École
supérieure des beaux-arts in Genf. Er publiziert seit den 1990er-Jahren
in den Bereichen Kunst- und Kulturtheorie, unter anderen in den Magazinen
Texte zur Kunst, Spex und springerin. Er tritt auch immer wieder als Kurator
in den Bereichen Film und Musik für verschiedene Institutionen und
Festivals in Erscheinung, darunter mumok – Museum Moderner Kunst Stiftung
Ludwig Wien; Lentos Kunstmuseum, Linz; Kunstverein Medienturm /
steirischer herbst, Graz; und Internationale Kurzfilmtage Oberhausen. Höller
ist Autor und (Mit)Herausgeber diverser Publikationen, wie *Kontakt. The
Art Collection of Erste Group and ERSTE Foundation* (2017); *L'Internationale:
Post-War Avant-Gardes Between 1957 and 1986* (2012); *Time Action
Vision: Conversations in Cultural Studies, Theory, and Activism* (2010); und
Techno-Visionen (2005). Zuletzt gab er mit Cathrin Rhomberg und
Daniel Grün die Publikation *White Space in White Space. Stano Filko,
Miloš Laky, Ján Zavarskaý* (2021) heraus.

Mira Keratová

*1977 Banská Bystrica, Slovakia, lives in Bratislava
is an art historian and curator in the field of modern and contemporary art
at the Bratislava City Gallery, she also works as a curator for the Central
Slovakian Gallery in Banská Bystrica. Keratová studied art history
at the Comenius University in Bratislava and received her Ph.D. from the
Academy of Fine Arts and Design in Bratislava, where she wrote her
doctoral thesis on performance art of the 1960s and 1970s and its documentation. She works on the neo-avant-gardes of Eastern Europe and is a
specialist in the field of action art and performative art of Czechoslovakia
during the repressive period of "normalization" from 1969–89. Keratová
taught as a lecturer at the Academy of Fine Arts and Design in Bratislava and
at the Faculty of Fine Arts of the Technical University in Brno. She is
the author of various texts on art and editor of publications on Ľubomír
Ďurček (2013) and Peter Bartoš (2014, 2019). Her close collaboration
with Stano Filko led to solo shows at Fondazione Morra Greco, Naples (2014);
Central Slovakian Gallery, Banská Bystrica (2017); also she prepared
his participation at the 11th Lyon Biennale (2011).

*1977 Banská Bystrica, Slowakei, lebt in Bratislava
ist Kunsthistorikerin und Kuratorin im Bereich moderner und zeitgenössicher
Kunst der Bratislava City Gallery, daneben ist sie auch als Kuratorin an
der Central Slovakian Gallery in Banská Bystrica tätig. Keratová hat Kunstgeschichte an der Comenius Universität in Bratislava studiert und erhielt ihren Ph.D. an der Akademie für Bildende Kunst und Design in Bratislava,

 Authors

wo sie über Performancekunst der 1960er- und 1970er-Jahre promovierte.
Sie arbeitet über die Neo-Avantgarden Osteuropas und ist Spezialistin
auf dem Gebiet der Aktionskunst und der performativen Kunst der Tschechoslowakei in der repressiven Periode der „Normalisierung" von 1969–1989.
Keratová war als Dozentin an der Akademie für Bildende Kunst und
Design in Bratislava sowie an der Fakultät der bildenden Künste der Technischen Universität in Brno tätig. Sie ist Autorin von Texten zur Kunst
und Herausgeberin von Publikationen über Ľubomír Ďurček (2013) und Peter
Bartoš (2014, 2019). Ihre enge Zusammenarbeit mit Stano Filko führte
zu Personalen bei Fondazione Morra Greco, Neapel (2014); Central Slovakian
Gallery, Banská Bystrica (2017); auch bereitete sie Filkos Beteiligung
auf der 11. Biennale Lyon (2011) vor.

Hans Ulrich Obrist

*1968 Weinfelden, Switzerland, lives in London and Zurich
is artistic director of the Serpentine Galleries in London, and Senior Advisor
at LUMA in Arles. He is considered one of the most influential curators
in the world and has curated over 300 exhibitions internationally, including
at institutions such as Musée d'Art Moderne de la Ville de Paris; Kunsthalle
Wien; Deichtorhallen Hamburg; and MoMA P.S.1, New York. Obrist
lectures internationally at numerous academic and artistic institutions, writes
for various art magazines, and advises Artforum, Flash Art, AnOther Magazine, and Cahiers D'Art. He has published numerous publications, including *Ways of Curating* (2014); *Lives of the Artists, Lives of the Architects*
(2015); *Mondialité or the Archipelagos of Edouard Glissant* (2017);
and the interview volume *The Athens Dialogues* (2018). He is also known
for his interviews with artists, including an extensive conversation
with Stano Filko.

*1968 Weinfelden, Schweiz, lebt in London und Zürich
ist künstlerischer Leiter der Serpentine Galleries in London und Senior Advisor bei LUMA in Arles. Er gilt als einer der einflussreichsten Kuratoren
der Welt und hat international über 300 Ausstellungen kuratiert, darunter
in Institutionen wie dem Musée d'Art Moderne de la Ville de Paris; der
Kunsthalle Wien; den Deichtorhallen Hamburg; und dem MoMA P.S.1, New York.
Obrist hält international Vorträge an zahlreichen akademischen und künstlerischen Institutionen, schreibt für verschiedene Kunstmagazine und
ist Berater von Artforum, Flash Art, AnOther Magazine und Cahiers D'Art. Er
hat zahlreiche Publikationen veröffentlicht, darunter *Ways of Curating*
(2014), *Lives of the Artists, Lives of the Architects* (2015), *Mondialité or the
Archipelagos of Edouard Glissant* (2017) und den Interviewband *The
Athens Dialogues* (2018). Er ist auch für seine Interviews mit Künstler*innen
bekannt, darunter eine ausführliche Konversation mit Stano Filko.

Boris Ondreička

*1969 Zlate Moravce, Slovakia, lives in Bratislava and Vienna
is an artist, curator and artistic director of the viennacontemporary since
2021. In 1997, Filko and Ondreička established an artistic meta-entity called
FILKONDREICKA. In the following years, they created several projects
together, like *PRAH* at Museum of Vojtech Löffler in Košice, 2000, or
a concept for the Czechoslovak Pavilion at the Biennale di Venezia in 2005
(with Ján Mančuška and Marek Pokorný). In parallel to this, he has been
facilitating Filko's work in the global institutional context of art. Together
with Vít Havránek, he curated Filko's largest project ever in his life—
Up 300000 km/s, at tranzit workshops in Bratislava, 2005. With Fedor Blaščák,
he co-curated the only retrospective of Miloš Laky, 2010. Ondreička and
Havránek then designed an extensive presentation of *White Space in White
Space / Biely priestor v bielom priestore* (1973–82) in Meštrović Pavilion in
Zagreb. In 2019, he curated Filko's solo show *MULTIMODAL GOOGLIFICATION
OF COSMOLOGY–ORIENTED DIAGRAMMATIC EXPERIMENTATIONS
OF STANO FILKO* at Layr, Vienna, and in 2021 the comprehensive exhibition
Registration of Stano Filko at Fait Gallery, Brno.

*1969 Zlate Moravce, Slowakei, lebt in Bratislava und Wien
ist Künstler, Kurator und seit 2021 künstlerischer Leiter der viennacontemporary.
1997 schufen Filko und Ondreička eine künstlerische Meta-Entität namens
FILKONDREICKA. In den darauffolgenden Jahren entwickelten sie zusammen

mehrere Projekte, darunter *PRAH* im Museum von Vojtech Löffler in Košice
(2000) sowie ein Konzept für den tschechoslowakischen Pavillon auf
der Biennale di Venezia 2005 (mit Ján Mančuška und Marek Pokorný). Parallel
dazu förderte er die Arbeit von Filko im globalen institutionellen Kunst-
kontext. Gemeinsam mit Vít Havránek kuratierte er 2005 Filkos größtes
Projekt *Up 300000 km/s* in den Ateliers von tranzit in Bratislava und mit
Fedor Blaščák 2010 die einzige Retrospektive von Miloš Laky. 2017
entwarf er mit Havránek eine umfangreiche Präsentation von *White Space in
White Space / Biely priestor v bielom priestore* (1973–1982) im Meštrović-
Pavillon in Zagreb. 2019 kuratierte Ondreička Filkos Einzelausstel-
lung *MULTIMODAL GOOGLIFICATION OF COSMOLOGY–ORIENTED
DIAGRAMMATIC EXPERIMENTATIONS OF STANO FILKO* bei Layr
(Wien) und 2021 die umfassende Ausstellung *Registration of Stano Filko*
bei Fait Gallery (Brünn).

Jan Verwoert

*1972, lives in Berlin
is a writer, who teaches at the Piet Zwart Institute Rotterdam and at the Oslo
National Academy of Arts. He has also worked at the de Appel curatorial
program, Amsterdam, the Graduate School of the Berlin University of the Arts
and the Royal Academy in London. His texts appear in various art magazines, but also in book form, such as *Bas Jan Ader: In Search of the Miraculous*
(2006); *Tell Me What You Want, What You Really, Really Want* (2010);
Animal Spirits—Fables in the Parlance of Our Time (with Michael Stevenson,
2013) or *Cookie* (2014). His interest in concepts such as emotion, intuition, or action, and conflicting "role models" is also directed against a rampant system of control that supports self-optimization and corresponding
forms of representation. Verwoert has been interested in Filko for quite
some time, and in 2011 he published a remarkable text on eflux, *World as
Medium / On the Work of Stano Filko*. With Søren Grammel, he showed
Stano Filko. RED EXILE at Layr, Vienna (2022).

*1972, lebt in Berlin
ist Autor und lehrt am Piet Zwart Institute, Rotterdam, und an der Nationalen
Kunstakademie, Oslo. Daneben war er auch am de Appel curatorial program,
Amsterdam, der Gradiertenschule der Universität der Künste Berlin
und an der Royal Academy in London tätig. Seine Texte erscheinen in diversen
Kunstmagazinen, aber auch in Buchform, wie in *Die Ich-Ressource –
Zur Kultur der Selbstverwertung* (2003); *Bas Jan Ader: In Search of the
Miraculous* (2006); *Tell Me What You Want, What You Really, Really
Want* (2010); *Animal Spirits—Fables in the Parlance of Our Time* (mit Michael
Stevenson, 2013) oder *Cookie* (2014). Sein Interesse an Begriffen wie
Emotion, Intuition oder Aktion und sich daran reibenden „role models" richtet
sich auch gegen ein grassierendes Kontrollsystem, das Selbstoptimierung
und entsprechende Formen der Darstellung unterstützt. Mit Filko setzt
sich Verwoert schon eine geraume Zeit auseinander, so hat er 2011 einen
bemerkenswerten Text auf eflux veröffentlicht, *World as Medium /
On the Work of Stano Filko*. Mit Søren Grammel zeigte er *Stano Filko.
RED EXILE* bei Layr, Wien (2022).

This catalog is published in conjunction with the exhibition /
Diese Publikation erscheint anlässlich der Ausstellung

Stano Filko. A Retrospective

HALLE FÜR KUNST Steiermark
19. 3. – 5. 6. 2022

Exhibition / Ausstellung

Curator / Kurator
Sandro Droschl

Director / Direktor
Sandro Droschl

Managing Director /
Geschäftsführung
Helga Droschl

Curatorial Assistance /
Kuratorische Assistenz
Tobias Ihl, Jan Tappe

Technical Management /
Technische Leitung
Max Gansberger

Setup / Aufbau
Darek Murawka & Team

Operated by / Trägerschaft
Kunstverein Medienturm „in der
HALLE FÜR KUNST Steiermark"

HALLE FÜR KUNST Steiermark
Burgring 2
8010 Graz, Austria
www.halle-fuer-kunst.at

Publication / Publikation

Editor / Herausgeber
Sandro Droschl;
HALLE FÜR KUNST Steiermark

Editing / Redaktion
Sandro Droschl, Helga Droschl

Coordination /
Verlagskoordination
Sonja Altmeppen

Texts / Autorentexte
Sandro Droschl, Christian Höller,
Patricia Grzonka, Mira Keratová,
Boris Ondreička, Lucia Gregorová
Stach, Jan Verwoert

Interview
Stano Filko, Hans Ulrich Obrist,
Roman Ondák, Koo Jeong A

Texts on Artworks /
Werkbeschreibungen
Tobias Ihl, Sandro Droschl

Copyediting / Lektorat
Helga Droschl; Sandro Droschl
and / und Tobias Ihl (Interview),
Greg Bond (Mira Keratová),
Anja Schulte (Boris Ondreička),
Kevin Slavin (Mira Keratová)

Translations / Übersetzungen
German–English /
Deutsch–Englisch:
Greg Bond (Sandro Droschl,
Christian Höller, Patricia Grzonka,
Jan Verwoert, texts on artworks /
Werkbeschreibungen)
English–German /
Englisch–Deutsch:
Thomas Raab (Mira Keratová),
Anja Schulte (Boris Ondreička,
Lucia Gregorová Stach), Sandro
Droschl, Tobias Ihl (Interview)
Slovakian–English /
Slowakisch–Englisch:
Kevin Slavin (Mira Keratová),
Lucia Gregorová Stach and / und
Štefan Cebo, Miroslava Urbanova
(Interview)

Graphic Design & Typesetting /
Grafische Gestaltung & Satz
FONDAZIONE Europa,
Alexander Nussbaumer with / mit
Leonard Siegwardt

Typefaces / Schriften
ABC Rom (Dinamo), Academica
(Storm Type), NEXT (Optimo)

Production / Verlagsherstellung
Alise Ausmane, Hatje Cantz

Paper / Papier
Condat matt Périgord, 135 g/m²

Printing & Binding /
Druck & Bindung
DZS Grafik

© 2023 Hatje Cantz Verlag, Berlin,
and authors / und Autor*innen

© 2023 for the reproduced works
by / für die abgebildeten Werke
von Stano Filko: Stanislav Filko/
heirs/LITA

Published by / Erschienen im
Hatje Cantz Verlag GmbH
Mommsenstraße 27
10629 Berlin
Germany
www.hatjecantz.com
A Ganske Publishing Group
Company / Ein Unternehmen der
Ganske Verlagsgruppe

ISBN: 978-3-7757-5341-8

Printed in Europe

Cover Illustration /
Umschlagabbildung
Stano Filko, *RETRO VELKAQ
HRADNAQ I.* (Detail), 1995–2005,
Courtesy Slovak National Gallery,
Bratislava

Frontispiece / Frontispiz
Stano Filko, *RETRO VELKAQ
HRADNAQ II*, 1995–2005,
Courtesy Slovak National Gallery,
Bratislava;
Stano Filko, *Concept – Nothing at
all / Koncept – Vôbec nič*, 1967,
Courtesy Slovak National Gallery,
Bratislava

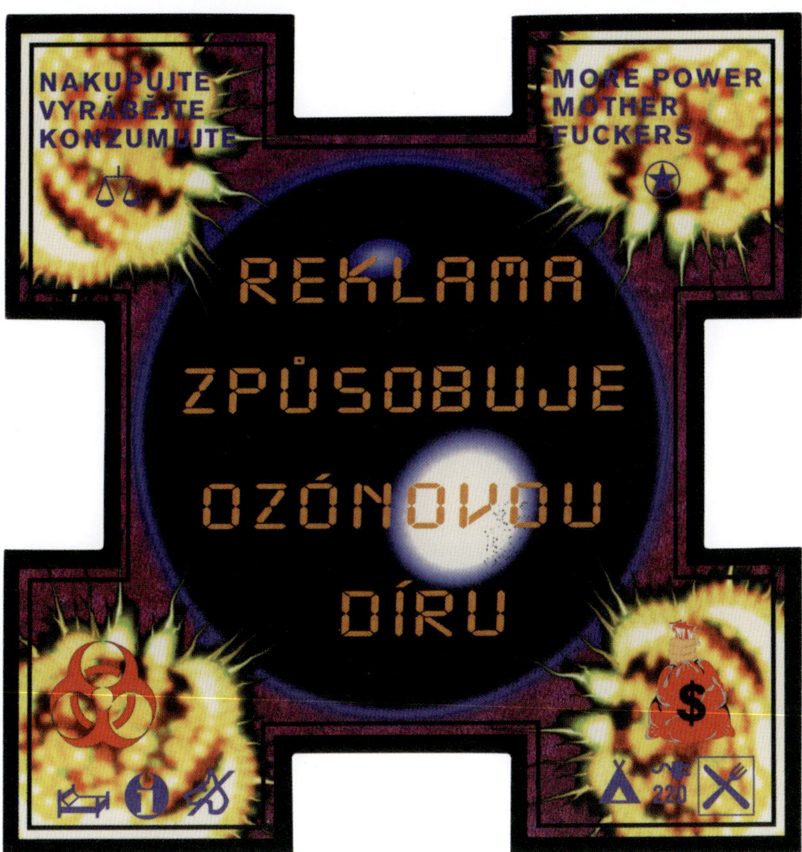

BUY, PRODUCE, CONSUME;
ADVERTISEMENT CAUSES OZON DEPLETION

Special Acknowledgment / Spezieller Dank an
Richard Filko; Alexandra Kusá, Lucia Gregorová Stach, Štefan Cebo
(Slovak National Gallery, Bratislava); Roman Zubaľ, Michal Zubaľ
(Linea Collection, Bratislava); Emanuel Layr; Alexander Nussbaumer &
Leonard Siegwardt; Manuel Carreon Lopez

Acknowlegment / Dank an
all authors, translators and persons involved in the project / alle Autor*innen,
Übersetzer*innen und am Projekt Beteiligten, sowie / and Max Shakelton,
Stredoslovenská galéria, Banská Bystrica, Daša Barteková, Fedor Blaščák,
Museum of Modern Art Warsaw, Fait Gallery

**This publication was realized with the support of / Die Realisierung
dieser Publikation wurde unterstützt von**
Bundesministerium für Kunst, Kultur, öffentlichen Dienst und Sport;
Land Steiermark, Kultur, Europa, Sport; Stadt Graz

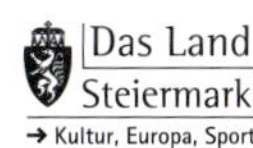

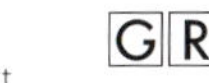

GRAZ

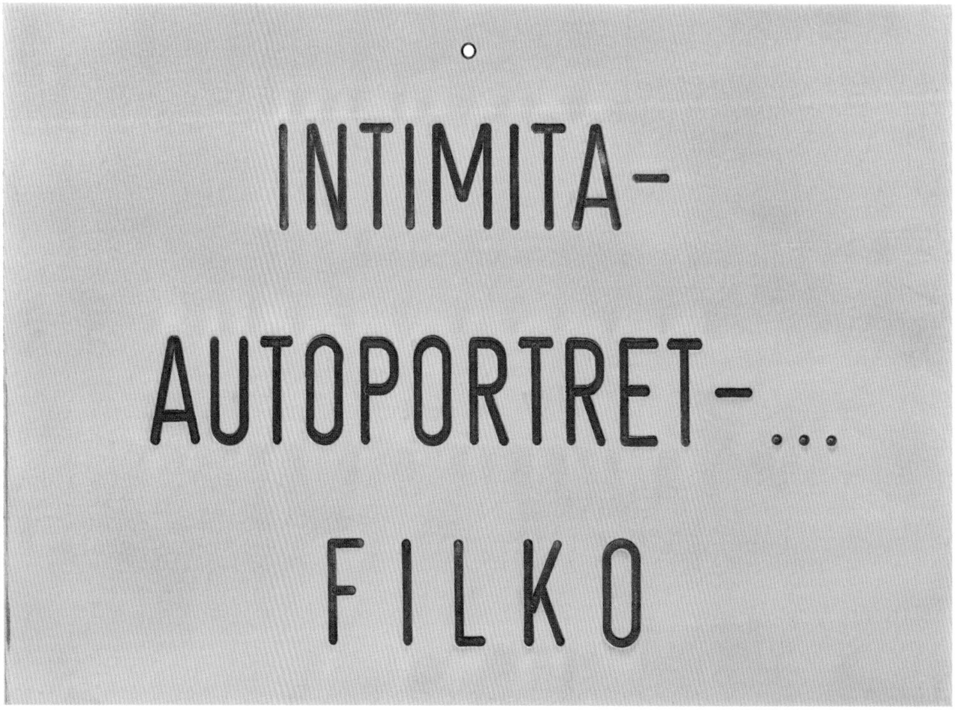

INTIMITA-

AUTOPORTRET-...

FILKO